Character Animation
with LightWave™ [6]

Doug Kelly

CORIOLIS™ # 45023535

2-02

President, CEO
Keith Weiskamp

Publisher
Steve Sayre

Acquisitions Editor
Beth Kohler

Product Marketing Manager
Patricia Davenport

Project Editor
Pat DuMoulin

Technical Reviewer
Phil South

Production Coordinator
Meg E. Turecek

Cover Designer
Jody Winkler

Layout Designer
April Nielsen

CD-ROM Developer
Chris Nusbaum

The Coriolis Group, LLC
14455 N. Hayden Road
Suite 220
Scottsdale, Arizona 85260

(480)483-0192
FAX (480)483-0193
www.coriolis.com

Library of Congress Cataloging-in-Publication Data
Kelly, Doug.
   Character animation with LightWave[6] / by Doug Kelly.
     p. cm.
   ISBN 1-57610-380-3
    1. Computer animation. 2. LightWave 3D. I. Title.
TR897.7.K449 2000
006.6'96--dc21   00-064476
                                             CIP

Printed in the United States of America
10 9 8 7 6 5 4 3 2 1

Other Titles for the Creative Professional

3D Studio MAX® R3 f/x and Design
By Jon Bell

3D Studio MAX® R3 In Depth
By Rob Polevoi

Bryce® 4 f/x and Design
By R. Shamms Mortier

Character Animation In Depth
By Doug Kelly

Digital Compositing In Depth
By Doug Kelly

Canoma™ Visual Insight
By Richard Schrand

To Patty. I promised you wouldn't be bored.
—Doug Kelly

About the Author

Doug Kelly has written books and articles and presented seminars on computer graphics since 1992. His publications include *LightWave 3D 5 Character Animation f/x, Character Animation In Depth, Digital Compositing In Depth*, numerous articles for *Keyframe* and *3D Artist* magazines, contributions to the manuals for several 3D programs, and his LENY '97 Character Animation seminar CD-ROM. He is currently a freelance writer and animation consultant and is editor of *Keyframe* magazine. You can contact him at **dakelly@earthlink.net** or through his Web site at **http://home.earthlink.net/~dakelly/index.htm**.

About the Contributors

Dave Bailey, creator of Mudpuppy
Dave Bailey is a 3D animator and digital illustrator currently working in Southern California. You can email him at **dbailey@pixinc.com** or visit his Web site at **www.pixinc.com**.

Roger Borelli, modeler and texturer of *Starship Trooper* Characters
Roger Borelli is a Supervising Character Artist at Foundation Imaging, currently working on MAX STEEL Season 2. He also develops his own characters and projects. You can email him at **roger-b@foundation-i.com** or **roger-b@socal.rr.com** or visit his Web site at **www.fxstation.com/monsterlab**.

Chris Nibley
Chris Nibley set up, lit, photographed, and digitized the chessboard footage using one of his motion control camera rigs. Visit his Web site at **www.nibley.com**.

Kim Oravecz, creator of Switch A. Roo and Iguana
Kim Oravecz is a freelance artist in Cleveland, Ohio. You can email her at **kimo@en.com** or contact her through her Web site, **www.en.com/users/kimo**.

Shane Ushijima, creator of Minimus
Shane Ushijima is 3D artist presently based in New York City. He is currently working with the Manhattan animation studio Luminetik, as well as doing freelance work. You can contact him via email at **shane@digitaldoo.com** or through his Web site, **www.digitaldoo.com**.

Acknowledgments

Many professional animators and other digital artists contributed case studies, advice, and constructive criticism to this book. Without their contributions, this would be a poorer book by a great deal of real-world experience and fantastic imagery. Thanks to Mike Comet, Steve Pugh, Jeff Scheetz, Jason Goodman, Matt Morgan, Rob Gougher, Phil South, Lee Stranahan, David Hibsher, Chris Nibley, Kim Oravecz, Brian Kelly, Sandra Frame, Steph Greenberg, Ken Cope, Patrick Kelly, Roger Borelli, Eric Kunzendorf, Ed Parenteau, Shane Ushijima, and Dave Bailey.

Those who build the artists' tools are also due a great deal of thanks. It's easy to lock down the code, cash the checks, ship the boxes, and go on to the next project. It's tougher to be there when users need support, reviewers have deadlines that seem to require time travel, and writers like myself ask for much and can promise little or nothing in return. This book is evidence of the faith and support of both official vendor representatives and the helpful, considerate individuals who happen to be employed by those vendors: Steve Roberts, Joanne Dicaire, Isaac Guenard, Stuart MacKinnon, Jose Velasquez, Brick Eksten, Jane Perratt, Michael Kunkes, David Addleman, Sue Addleman, Phil Dench, Gene Sexton, Dan Kraus, Michel Besner, Joe Alter, Miguel Grinberg, and Steve Worley.

The support of the LightWave and CGI character animation communities is crucial to the production of books like this one. Many thanks to the contributors to the LightWave mailing list, the CG-CHAR mailing list, and *Keyframe* magazine.

Finally and most important, Patricia K. Kelly, Ed.D., not only proofreads, edits, and sanity-checks my writing, but keeps me healthy and sane—even when she has to drag me away from my computer to do it. For getting me through the previous books, this book, and all the future books, thank you!

Contents at a Glance

Table of Contents

Introduction

Animation is a special form of that most human of arts, storytelling. It is perhaps the furthest extrapolation of the hand gestures used by the fireside storyteller to draw pictures in the minds of the audience. Just as storytellers use a physical language to emphasize and embellish their tale, animation can use a variety of techniques to accomplish the same goals.

An animator creates the illusion of motion with a series of images. Whether those images are created by the pen of a cartoonist, the knife of a sculptor, the posing of a living body, or the pixel manipulation of the computer artist, the principles of animation are the same. Every branch of animation can learn from every other. Computer-generated imagery, or CGI, is the youngest shoot on the family tree and therefore has the greatest amount to learn from the older forms.

The last 30 years have seen great advances in CGI, from abstract light patterns on vector graphic displays to the photorealism of *Dinosaur* and *Dragonheart* and the character development of *Toy Story* and *Stuart Little*. Those who practiced older forms of animation were restrained by the limits of the physical materials they relied on, whether paper, cel, clay, or even the film itself. Now, with CGI, it is possible to overcome the limits of that materiality, to literally animate anything we can imagine, to make our dreams and fantasies live on the screen.

LightWave animation development has thrived in the area of television and motion picture special effects, animating spacecraft and astronomic phenomena, energy weapons and the explosions they produce. These effects have pushed LightWave to very high levels of cinematic realism, but they cannot tell an engaging story by themselves. People aren't interested in watching special effects unless they advance the story line. Effects are window dressing, not premise.

If LightWave animation is to tell an engaging story, it must be a story about anthropomorphic characters: digital models of humans, creatures, artifacts, or even inanimate objects caricatured into the semblance of life. This is the highest and most difficult form of CGI: Character Animation.

Character animation has always been the apex of any form of animation. Even in the most abstract of line drawings or the most minimalist of stop-motion cinematography, the creative workload of character animation is overwhelming. Each image must first be composed with the obsessively detailed care of any other animation. On top of this, the animator must give the characters that breath of life, the posing, timing, and expressiveness that will convince the audience that the characters are moving of their own volition.

Character animation is a combination of talents so rare that *Fortune*, the *Wall Street Journal*, and the *New York Times* have published profiles of top animators. Salaries for lead animators more than doubled in the late 1990s. Even considering the cyclical nature of the business, the prospects for LightWave character animators are excellent. The viewing public has responded well to the use of LightWave character animation, so advertising agencies, video game developers, and television and motion picture studios are pushing the demand for character animators. How long this market will last is anyone's guess, but the current reality is that demand for competent character animators is larger than the supply.

Training for LightWave character animation has been almost exclusively on-the-job or by way of traditional animation approaches. Until very recently, the hardware and software necessary for CGI character animation have been prohibitively expensive, animation schools have been slow to offer courses incorporating LightWave, and there have been few books or videos on the topic.

LightWave [6] and Character Animation

Recent software development has made character animation tools affordable for even the beginning animator. The necessary hardware can be purchased for a fraction of the price of a good used car, and LightWave [6] and third-party supporting products are priced within reach of the serious hobbyist or student. LightWave will also continue to support you in growing an animation business all the way up to television and feature films.

LightWave has already been used to produce character animation for film, television, and games. The commercial success of these productions has helped build the demand for character animators who can use LightWave. Some studios use a variety of software, while other use only one or two packages. If you have your heart set on working for a particular studio, you'd do well to learn the software they're already using.

Who Needs This Book?

This book is intended to bridge the gap between the LightWave artist and the traditional animator. It is designed to introduce you to the vocabulary and techniques used by both approaches. If you are already an animator, you will learn the LightWave software tools designed to support character animation. If you are a LightWave artist, you will learn the essential techniques of character animation as they apply to LightWave tools.

If you are a beginner in both fields, I suggest that you complete the exercises in the official LightWave [6] manuals before you start to work through this book. At the least, they contain the technical information you'll need regarding system requirements, software installation, and troubleshooting. They also include tutorials that introduce you to the basic functions of LightWave. The creator of LightWave, NewTek, puts a lot of time and effort into these manuals; if you never read them, you're not getting your money's worth. Once you have worked through the materials that came with the software, you will be much better prepared for the projects in this book.

If NewTek has included a particularly helpful tutorial with the LightWave manuals, I'll refer to it at the appropriate point. There's no sense in my repeating what's been written elsewhere; I'd rather provide you with original projects that go beyond the vendor's manuals.

If you're trying to use this book as a "manual" for pirated software, don't. Don't email me for advice about "cracks" or "warez," either; I'll just refer you to **www.spa.org/piracy**.

Throughout this book, each concept is reinforced with projects designed to build your expertise without overwhelming you. Completing all the projects will enable you to produce complete character animation, from storyboard to video or film. This book also shows you how to assemble a demo reel and look for employment as an animator or technical director.

What's Inside?

This Introduction is your guide to using this book to your best advantage. The path you follow through the projects will depend on what you already know and what you want to learn. Whether you are a beginner, an expert LightWave artist, or a traditional animator, you should read this chapter first.

The bulk of this book is organized in pretty much the same order as an animation production. If you are new to animation, you would do well to read through this book in order—from the first chapter to the last. If you are more experienced, you may choose to skim over areas with which you are already familiar and move on to the more challenging new areas. If you are a traditional animator making the transition to CGI, I recommend that you also read through this book in order, noting where the CGI process is similar to traditional processes and where it differs.

The first chapter provides an overview of the production team, something especially useful to freelancers and beginners who have not yet been part of a larger studio. Chapters 2, 3, and 4 provide step-by-step development of the story, script, storyboard, sound track, and timing sheets that are necessary before you can begin to animate the characters. Chapters 5, 6, and 7 cover character design and modeling, proceeding from general guidelines to specific LightWave procedures with advanced tools like 3D scanners and digitizers. Chapters 8, 9, and 10 cover materials and maps, the tools you'll use to control the surface appearance of your characters.

Chapters 11, 12, and 13 introduce the principles of character setup, the critical process of articulating the character so the animator can pose it as intuitively and easily as possible. Chapters 14, 15, and 16 present the principles of character animation, keyed to the corresponding setups in the preceding three chapters. Each project closes with tips on practicing, sometimes recommending that you repeat the project (with interesting changes) and sometimes referring you to other activities that will help hone your skills.

The next part, Chapters 17, 18, 19, and 20, wraps up with projects that teach you how to light your scenes, create titles and credits, composite and move match, and transfer your animations to the final output format.

Along the way, and especially in Chapter 21, you'll find advice from professional animators about the business of animation. You'll learn what to expect from studio, freelance, or independent work, how to get your career started, when not to take a job or project, and other maps through the minefield.

As you might expect, at the back of this book you'll find a glossary, annotated bibliography, and index.

Platform Wars

I've used just about every desktop computing hardware and operating system developed since the mid-1980s, and I have no religious convictions about any of them. The only criteria I use for choosing a platform are current functionality, compatibility with colleagues, longevity, upgrade path, and vendor support:

- Current functionality means the platform has to work right now, and it needs to do what you need it to do to get your work done. Neither promises nor fond memories can cut it in the working world.

- Compatibility with colleagues means you can share files, either across the cubicle or across the world (usually via the Internet). If you can't play well with others, you won't be invited to play as often.

- Longevity means your system will still be productively viable for the three years it takes to depreciate into a boat anchor.

- Upgrade path means you can put a third of the system's purchase price into it each year in the form of new parts and thereby keep it from becoming a boat anchor for another year.

- Vendor support means the system runs software that is commercially available without paying consultants or programmers to tweak it. Personally, I also like being able to run general business software. This enables me to focus my investment in a single machine rather than creating CGI on one and doing bookkeeping and taxes on another.

That said, I've got a few words of advice about choosing hardware for character animation. The general trend in the industry is toward the Microsoft Windows NT platform. For good or ill, that's where the lion's share of the market is headed, and that's where you will continue to find the broadest selection of software, hardware, and vendor support. This trend does not mean you have to immediately abandon whatever investment you have made in another platform; it just means you should seriously reevaluate your hardware purchases any time you upgrade in the future. Vendor support becomes even more important, and you should make sure you buy or lease your system from a dealer who understands your needs.

There is still a large installed base of SGI and Mac machines in studios around the world, and as long as a colleague, client, employer, or software publisher is still using a system that's compatible with yours, you're doing all right. Who knows, by the time the next generation of software is shipping, there may actually be a new operating system that will give Microsoft a run for its money.

About the CD-ROM

Inside the back cover you will find a CD-ROM. This disk contains all the electronic files you will need to complete the projects. You will also find examples of completed work from the projects for you to compare to your own efforts. In addition to scripts, storyboards, sounds, exposure sheets, models, backgrounds, images, and scenes, there are finished animations, artwork, software, and other samples from a number of vendors and artists.

Hardware and Software Requirements

To complete the projects, you'll need whatever hardware is necessary to run LightWave on the platform of your choice. Many of the projects use software written for Windows NT running on the Intel platform, and equivalent tools for other hardware and operating systems may not be available. In each case, sample output from the project is provided on the CD-ROM so you can complete any dependent projects.

So What Are You Waiting For?

By now, I'm certain you're eager to get started. When you've completed all the projects, or when you just have a few nice examples you want to show off, I'd like to hear from you. You can reach me via email at **dakelly@earthlink.net**.

Best of luck, and welcome to the wonderful world of character animation!

Part I

Pre-Production

Chapter 1

Project Management: How Many Hats Can You Wear?

One of the most liberating aspects about character animation with LightWave is that you really can do it all yourself. There are other software tools that, used in conjunction with LightWave, can assist you in doing screenwriting, storyboard and layout art, modeling, texturing, audio digitizing, track reading, animation, rendering, record keeping, financial and scheduling project management, music composition and recording, audio and video mixing and editing, title design, and film or video recording.

The question is, do you want to handle it all?

If you really have a driving, unique artistic vision that you feel only you can realize, then more power to you (just don't try to be your own agent and attorney, as well!). If you prefer to concentrate on one specialty and do it well, then again, more power to you. Whatever your approach, this book shows you how to put all the necessary pieces together to create character animation with LightWave [6]. Even if you have never worked as an animator before, this chapter is a good place to find out what the job is like, either in an animation production house or as a freelance artist.

Along the way, you'll learn a little more about the other professions and trades associated with animated film production. I hope this information will help you become a more effective LightWave animator or technical director (TD), whether you pursue an independent career or join one of the growing number of animation production houses.

Meet the Team

Most production studios have an organizational structure with similar job titles, although the actual responsibilities of the people vary from studio to studio. Generally, the larger the organization, or the bigger the project, the more people will specialize. For smaller shops and shorter projects, each person may handle several different jobs. Whatever the size or scope of the production, there are a few basic job descriptions you can depend on, including director, writer, storyboard artist, art director, supervising animator, animator, technical director (TD), network manager, track reader, sheet timer, layout artist, production assistants, gofers, and peons.

Director

The director is the person responsible for the overall product—for keeping the "big picture" clearly in sight. In smaller shops or on shorter projects, the director will hand you the storyboards and exposure sheets and go over the intent of the shot to make sure you understand the characterization he is looking for. The director will also pass final judgment on your animation.

In effect, the director is a minor deity, answerable only to the executive producer or the client. Some directors will remind you of their status at every opportunity. Others will remind you of their rank only if you do something inadvisable, like continuing to disagree with them after they've made a decision. Voice your opinion once, diplomatically, then go along with whatever the director decides. Making the final decision is what the director gets paid for. Even if you disagree with the director's decision, bear in mind that you often do your best work when being forced to do something you think is a bad idea.

Directors can also be your best mentors. They generally have the most on-the-job experience of anyone on a production team and can be a treasure trove of knowledge and advice. Listen to their critiques carefully, consider their advice, and do your best to learn from their experience.

Writer

The writer develops the script. Unless there are rewrites, the writer has the least influence on the difficulty of your work as an animator. In many cases, once the script has been translated to storyboards, all further development is done visually and the script is obsolete. The writer may still participate in story sessions, but any revisions from that point are collaborative efforts.

Storyboard Artist

The storyboard artist translates the written script to a series of sketches (see Chapter 3) and revises, adds, or deletes sketches during story sessions. Because storyboard artists work in 2D, they can "cheat" or draw character actions that are difficult to animate. If you see a story sketch that is going to be a problem, point it out (diplomatically, of course) at the first opportunity. It's a lot easier to get a story sketch revised than the finished model and exposure sheets!

Art Director

The art director (and in larger organizations, the entire art department) is responsible for developing the overall look—the visual style—of the product. Like the storyboard artist, the art director can create 2D drawings that are nearly impossible to replicate in 3D. Character design is especially difficult to adapt; you will need to work closely with the TD in negotiating with the art director to make sure the proposed characters can be built and animated in LightWave.

Supervising Animator

If the project is a large one, you may be working under a supervising animator. Job titles and authorities vary, but typical examples are directing animator, lead animator, or animation supervisor. Usually, these are senior animators who act as deputies for the director. You will probably receive your shot materials from the supervising animator rather than from the director. If you are new to the profession, the supervising animator may become your mentor, helping you out on problem shots and giving you the benefit of experience. Take advantage of the opportunity to learn from this person! This is another way you move forward as an animator, by doing things you think are a bad idea and by hitting snags in an actual paying job. Solving problems is the best way to learn any software or job, and it can turn a hobby into a career.

Animator

When you strip away the technology, finance, and politics of making an animated film, the animator's work is the heart of it. Whether working solo or as part of a production team, the animator's task is to breathe the illusion of life into a model by creating a sequence of poses that communicate character. You may be able to use LightWave plug-ins to make a model automatically lip sync any line of dialogue, but if the accompanying action is not convincing, the characterization fails. The rest of the production team relies on you to get the animation right.

The materials the animator uses to create a LightWave animation can include storyboards, exposure sheets, model sheets, film footage to be matched, sound tracks, motion capture, objects, and scenes. Who provides these on the job can vary from studio to studio. For this book's exercises, the necessary materials are included on the CD-ROM. The results your director expects you to produce are finished animation files, ready to be lighted and rendered.

Technical Director

The TD can make or break your animation work. In most shops, the TD builds, textures, and lights the LightWave models you will be animating and may develop custom software tools such as plug-ins and shaders as well. In larger shops, lighting, textures, and character setup may be separate job descriptions. In smaller shops, you may be doing all these tasks yourself.

The TD will usually provide you, the animator, with the model sheets and other notes on the modeling and setup of the characters. This information can make your work much easier, so cultivate your TDs and treat them well. TDs tend to have more computer skills and a more analytical and engineering approach than animators, which has led to industry stereotypes about cultural conflicts between the two "tribes."

When you take a problem to a TD, be diplomatic (as with all team members) and make an attempt to understand the TD's side of the problem. One of the goals of this book is to teach you the professional vocabulary of the TD; people are generally more receptive to suggestions if you speak their language. As an animator, you do not need to know absolutely everything about LightWave's programming or the particular computer hardware on which you run it, just as you don't need to know how to make a pencil in order to use it effectively. However, more knowledge can be a good thing; just as in other arts, artists who do not understand how their tools function and are made are at a disadvantage.

Network Manager

In a small studio, the TD may also be responsible for maintaining all the computers, keeping them running smoothly, and handling any upgrades or changes. In larger studios, the maintenance of networks and render farms requires more time and specialized technical knowledge and is usually a full-time job. In the largest studios, network management is an entire department. As with TDs, you need to stay on the good side of network managers, or *sysops* (system operators). Listen when they tell you to do (or not do) something that affects the network or your workstation. If you expect your work to stress the network, let them know in advance. If you ask nicely, they may even clue you in on tweaks that can make your workstation run better, thereby making your work easier.

Track Reader

Track reading has traditionally been performed by specialists, with the director or supervising animator transcribing the completed analysis to exposure sheets, which are then passed on to the animator. In some studios, the track reader may fill in the exposure sheets directly. Software developers have produced several different tools to automate much of the track analysis process, so this specialty may not survive much longer. Many studios already leave track reading up to the animator, and the digitized dialogue or sound track is part of the shot materials.

Sheet Timer

You will usually find sheet timers working in television production, where they take over some of the traditional timing work of directors. After the storyboards are done, the sheet timers mark the musical beats, foley (sound effect) hits, and actions on the exposure sheets. The sheet timers determine the overall timing of the animation; they sometimes have more influence on the final appearance of the action than either the director or the animator.

Layout Artist

Layout artist is a job title that you will only find in larger organizations. In smaller ones, the job is generally split between the director, TD, and animator. The layout artist translates each 2D story sketch to one or more composed LightWave scenes, setting up the camera, characters, set and prop objects, and basic lighting. This is the LightWave equivalent of cinematic or the-atrical *blocking*.

Layout can be a difficult job, especially if the storyboard artist "cheated" shots in ways that can't be staged in 3D. Once the layouts are done, it's possible to substitute rendered frames for the story sketches in the story reel (see Chapter 4). In some studios, layout can also refer to character layout or setup—working with the TD and animator to assemble the model, skel-eton, and controls for each character (see Part IV).

Production Assistants, Gofers, and Peons

Somebody has to pick up and deliver stuff, keep track of schedules and checklists, and make sure nothing falls through the cracks. Animation production is even more detail sensitive than live-action cinematography. Don't underestimate the importance of, or try to complete a major project without, these invaluable assistants. And treat them well—someday you might be working for them!

Working with a Team

Production workflows seem to be one of the most closely guarded secrets in the animation business. As I was researching this book, I found questions about production practices to be the one sure way to get a source to clam up. Whenever you have a job interview, be sure to ask questions about workflow and creative opportunities—it shows that you are interested in doing the work, and the answers will tell you a lot about the organization.

Every shop is different, and even the same shop can vary from project to project. An advertis-ing project may come from a micromanaging client or agency with very specific ideas about everything, or the production team may be asked to come up with the whole concept. A fea-ture or short may start out very nebulous, with the creative team soliciting story ideas from everyone down to the janitor, or the director may have one of those crystalline, burning visions that dictates every detail. As an animator or TD, you need to stay flexible and adapt your working style to your employer or client.

For example, many studios will leave the fine details of character design until later in the pro-cess. Animators often do early tests with rough or low-resolution models of the characters, which are gradually refined as the action shows where changes are needed. This gives the studio a margin of error, so if a character is not working out, it can be revised or discarded at no great loss. In this type of workflow, you need to provide feedback to the TDs responsible for the character modeling, pointing out problems and suggesting solutions so the final model is one you can animate well and easily. Conversely, some studios lock the character designs early so they can do layout, blocking, and storyboard sessions completely in the computer. Studios can get away with this when producing a series because the cast and sets don't change much. Once you've ironed out the characters for the first episode, you can take advantage of stock character setups to speed up the story and layout processes. As an animator, you'll have to make your critiques and suggestions before the director locks the models so you're not stuck with a character that's difficult to animate. Make sure you know how your studio works, and think ahead!

Depending on shop policy (and your seniority), your supervisor may simply hand you exposure and model sheets and tell you to animate them. This kind of creative restriction is intolerable to some animators, but others don't seem to mind. In more flexible shops, you may be allowed or encouraged to contribute ideas in story meetings, storyboard sessions, and other creative collaborations. These are good opportunities to practice your diplomacy and teamwork skills.

> *"If you say anything in meetings, try to confine yourself to this one mission: make sure you understand everything about your end of the job. Conducting yourself professionally in meetings is always more impressive than being the center of attention."*
> —Phil South, animator

You should also keep in mind the ground rules for these meetings, which can vary a great deal among shops, teams, and even directors. One common approach is to separate the creative, brainstorming part of a meeting from the analytical, critical part. If a meeting is being run with this approach, the fastest way to make yourself *persona non grata* is to break the rules, either criticizing during the brainstorming session or throwing in new ideas after the analysis has begun. In any case, don't hare off on topics that aren't on the agenda, don't chime in if you don't have anything constructive to contribute, and never play devil's advocate just for the sake of starting an argument. Try not to think out loud, either; give yourself a moment to phrase an observation or suggestion as concisely as possible, and think about the effect your suggestions may have on the other people in the meeting. If you are not sure of what you have to say, and especially if your remarks may offend someone in another department, consider making discreet suggestions through channels (i.e., your supervisor) after the meeting. You're better off having your supervisor take credit for one of your ideas (yes, that happens) than offending a coworker through ignorance. Diplomacy and tact are essential to all production team members. You want to build a reputation as a person of few words and good ideas, so when you do speak up, your team members will listen.

> *"A lot of creative people, storyboardists, art and set directors, animators, character coordinators, and others are involved, and you have to respect the way the project works. You have to be a team player and get along with others. At times you'll think you have the right idea, and someone else will think he has the right idea. Maybe you both do—or neither of you is close."*
> —Steve Bloom, screenwriter

Pay attention to the person running the meeting, too. Some people run very good meetings, where most participants leave with a positive attitude, good ideas are created, and a lot of work gets done. Try to emulate these people; someday you're going to be the one leading the meeting.

Plan Your Work, Work Your Plan

Character animation, like many other complex endeavors, benefits from thorough planning. For any complicated project involving different talents or groups of people, a successful plan evolves and grows. It never springs full-grown from the mind of even the most Zeus-like director. The plan starts with a basic idea, that idea is fleshed out and detailed, and those details are in turn filled out to the next level of detail. At each level, changes and revisions can be made with a minimum of disturbance to the rest of the plan. If a level were skipped over or not developed completely, revisions to later levels would echo catastrophically back through every part of the project.

In animation, the initial idea is usually a story to be told, and the final level of detail is the individual frame. Getting from one to the other is a series of logical steps—story, script, storyboard, exposure sheets, animation.

Different members of the production team may contribute revisions at each step in the process, depending on the studio and project. Each step produces its own characteristic set of documents, a record of the work completed that also forms the skeleton for the next level to flesh out. Take each of these steps one at a time, with a little thought and practice, and you will be able to master them all.

Organization: Getting There and Staying There

If you are producing your own demo reel or leading a small production team, you are responsible for creating and maintaining the project plan. This may be as simple as keeping track of your own notes or as complex as managing all the working documents and files for your entire team. The larger the project, and the more people involved, the more critical this task becomes.

Small projects can get along with storyboards and a basic schedule showing which shots are at each stage in the production process. That's the low end. The high end goes all the way up through conventional production boards to integrated computer systems like Disney's CAPS, designed to manage projects that employ hundreds of people for years at a time. Most of the time, you'll find yourself somewhere between these extremes. In any case, you can save yourself lots of headaches and redundant effort if you use whatever organizational tools are available. Here are a few general guidelines:

- Keep all the project's working documents stored safely and in an order that enables you to find things quickly.

- Store older versions and backups safely out of the way, at least until the project is finished. You never know what you might need again.

- Don't be cute or cryptic with labels or file names. If several people are creating files, use consistent rules for naming them. You need to be able to tell what a file contains just by reading its name.

- Back up files regularly, and label the storage media when you record it. Few things are more tedious or annoying than having to play "feed the toaster" with a stack of unmarked disks, just to find one file.

- If more than one person is to use a character, setup, or other complex file, document that file. The time you save may be your own.

- If you are using files from a shared network directory, don't change or delete those files without getting the appropriate approvals.

- If you're using a revised version of a file, keep careful track of which version is the most current; back up older versions and remove them from your computer to avoid confusion.

- When in doubt, print it out. Keeping hard copies of critical files is cheap insurance against system failures, and you can always recycle the paper after the project is over.

- If your project has any kind of deadline, put a calendar on your wall that shows the current date, the deadline date, and all the days in between. Mark your milestones, delivery and receipt dates, deadlines, and payment dates. Marking important dates like anniversaries, birthdays, and holidays can save you some grief, too, especially if you're a workaholic.

- Put one person in charge of maintaining the project plan and materials. Choose the most trustworthy, reliable, and detail-oriented person on the production team. If that isn't you, then keep your fingers out of it and let that person do the job!

Goals

The point of all this effort is usually an animated film. Sometimes there are other goals, too: a better job, a distribution deal, a film contract, a political statement, fame, fortune, or just getting credit for a class. Whatever your goal is, make it clear from the start, and keep an eye on it. No project ever goes perfectly, and when you have to choose what to sacrifice, you'll appreciate a clear picture of what's necessary to your goal and what can be discarded. When you're embroiled in all the details of producing an animation, it's very easy to lose sight of your original goal. Once you're no longer focused on the goal, your project can veer off into directions you won't want it to take. At the least, the story and execution may lose focus and not be as powerful as you intended; at worst, the project may come apart completely.

Keep an eye on your goal!

Moving On

I hope this chapter has given you a better idea of what your day-to-day work will be like and that it hasn't scared you away from being an animator. Like most art forms, the thrill of seeing your animations played for an appreciative audience is worth the sacrifices. In the next chapter, you'll learn how to create the story and script that will be the foundation for your animation.

Chapter 2

Story and Script

In this chapter, I'll show you how to build a strong foundation for your character animation. It's possible to create an excellent bit of character animation without a story or script, but the odds are against it. You can bypass these steps if you're doing motion tests or exercises because they aren't necessarily telling a story. For anything more complex, do yourself a favor and work through the story and script process first.

Even the most prominent names in the field of character animation follow this process. The Pixar team had already moved into production on parts of *Toy Story* when they found the story had major problems. They put most of the production team on hiatus while the story team hammered out the problem; only then did production resume. If they had bulled through production with the original, flawed story, the film would most likely have bombed at the theaters.

The Importance of a Story

A good story, even if it is very small, is crucial to a successful animation. Thirty-second television commercials, video game cut scenes, even five-second television station identifications all have stories to tell. If you want clients, employers, or any other audience to pay attention to your animation, make sure you are telling an interesting story. This is especially important for your demo reel. A series of brief, unrelated clips is simply not going to hold the reviewer's attention as well as a good, coherent story built around an engaging character.

Every good story must have a premise, which must suggest character, conflict, and a conclusion. The premise should be simple, as in "Haste makes waste," "Love conquers all," or the premise selected for the example script, "Easy come, easy go." A complex premise generally leads to a muddled and confusing story and should therefore be avoided.

The premise is also crucial to pitching the story if you need to convince investors, producers, talent, or distributors. The premise is your one-line pitch—the hook to interest your audience and get them to listen to the rest of your presentation.

> *"Put your heart into it."*
> —*Harold Harris, TOPIX*

Some film schools put their students through a tough but educational process of making their first film. The student has to choose an event in her own life that was embarrassing, traumatic, or otherwise emotionally very strong, write it up as a script, and produce it as a film. This is an extension of the old writer's dictum, "Write what you know." Harold Harris, creative director at TOPIX, advises beginning animators to "put your heart into it." If you want to make an outstanding film or demo reel, you've got to put something of yourself into it.

This approach has its merits. You will certainly have a personal interest in the production, and you should be able to identify the various emotional states the character goes through. The difficulty lies in extracting the premise of the story. Without that, it's just a disconnected anecdote, a slice of life quickly forgotten by all but the participants.

The essential element of a story for character animation is, appropriately enough, character. Other dramatic forms may emphasize different elements of the storytelling traditions, but this book—and your work—are about character animation.

Character

Character is defined by action. When we first see a character, we have no idea what he will do next. An undefined character can perform any action or speak any line of dialogue without having the least effect on your audience. It is your job as an animator to make that character tell us about himself, to define who he is, so that the actions you animate and the lines your character lip syncs have an effect on the audience and so advance your story. This can be a daunting task. For some television commercials, you may have as little as 2 seconds, a mere 60 frames, to define a character. In longer formats, you may have the luxury of developing your character in terms of physiology, sociology, and psychology. For example, Quasimodo in Disney's remake of *The Hunchback of Notre Dame* is the unique product of all three factors. Had Quasimodo been of a more average appearance (physiology), associated freely with people outside the church (sociology), or been raised under different principles than those imposed by Frollo (psychology), his character would be different and so would the story. In the shorter formats, you usually must resort to caricature and stereotype to establish your character as quickly as possible.

Conflict builds character. Sounds like what they tell you as they cart you off the field, doesn't it? Nevertheless, it's true. Conflict is the friction between the character and his environment (including other characters) that forces the character to change and grow. This change and growth must be in a direction consistent with what we have already seen of the character. A miser shouldn't suddenly empty his wallet into the nearest charity box unless you first tell the whole series of conflicts leading up to his redemption, as in Dickens' *A Christmas Carol*.

Ebenezer Scrooge must incrementally perceive the error of his ways, showing a plausible progression from hard-hearted miser to contrite benefactor, in order for the audience to accept Scrooge's epiphany on Christmas morning.

Conflict also serves to draw the characters more clearly. Even if the change through conflict is very small, with each conflict, your audience will see the character a little more clearly.

So, how do you devise a conflict? No need—the characters create their own plots. If the character was initially a miser, then obviously the strongest conflict would be if the miser's property were threatened. Depict your character strongly, and conflicts will present themselves.

Transition

Another concept I'd like to introduce here is the transition. Although the term means something different in screenwriting and editing, in the dramatic sense, "transition" refers to the dominant emotional state of a character. A transition occurs when a character expressing one emotion progresses through a conflict and changes to expressing a different emotion. Leaving out the transition, or shortening it so the audience does not see it clearly, creates a jump in the character's development that can ruin the story. This is especially important for character animation, because emotions must be displayed more obviously than in live action, and this requires a good deal of planning from the animator. For example, there are several strong, visual emotional transitions for the title character in the animated version of *How the Grinch Stole Christmas*:

- Frustration to evil glee when he gets his "wonderful, awful idea"

- Guilty surprise to smooth craftiness when Cindy Lou Who surprises him and he recovers by telling her lies

- Anger to enlightenment when he discovers the true meaning of Christmas

These transitions are worth studying. How many other pivotal transitions can you remember from your favorite films, both live action and animated?

The end of the story should follow naturally from the growth of the original character through conflict. Don't try to get fancy, outfoxing your audience with surprise endings and bizarre last-act plot twists. Your audience won't thank you for it. Just finish the story with the last transition, in a manner that completes the premise, and leave it at that.

PROJECT 2.1 Developing a Story Line

In this project, you'll develop a story line:

1. First, select a simple premise, and develop a brief story line from it. If you like, choose an incident from your own life that has strong potential for good character animation. Conflicts and transitions should be physically obvious, not internalized philosophical debates. If the story would work as a voiced-over exposition, throw it out. This is character animation, not a radio play.

2. Next, ask yourself the following questions:

- Is your premise 10 words or less?

- Is the premise one you personally can believe in? (Remember, you're going to be spending a lot of quality time with the little monster.)

- Can your character fulfill the premise?

- Is your conflict one that will expose the character more fully or force the character to grow?

- Does the story provide for interesting transitions that will hold your audience's attention?

- Does the end of the story follow naturally from the character's growth or exposition, and does it fulfill the premise?

If all your answers are "Yes," why aren't you a screenwriter? Just kidding! Now you're ready to take your story to the next level.

Drafting the Script

So, now you have an interesting story to tell. The sheer expense of character animation, whether measured in money or work hours, demands that the story be told as succinctly and effectively as possible.

If you want to tell your story effectively, you need to have a plan, a blueprint that lays out all the parts in their proper places. The script is your blueprint. A properly formatted script tells each member of the production team what has to happen in order to tell the story. From this information, each specialist can plan the work she will contribute to the project.

If you can't write up your story as a script, you don't have a clear idea of what you are trying to say. The act of putting words on paper has a great clarifying effect on even the most obscure daydreams. It is also a useful test of the writer's creative vision: If the vision can't survive being translated into a script, it certainly isn't robust enough to survive the rigors of animation production.

Reshooting to correct problems that should have been caught in the script is a good way to blow your budget, your schedule, and your career as a director. A well-formatted script can go a long way toward preventing that kind of disaster. Each conflict and transition is written there in black and white, and if more than one member of the production team can't "see" a particular shot, that's an excellent indication that a rewrite is needed. Paper's cheap, but time and film aren't.

The script is intended as a working tool, not a literary form. Get used to writing in the standard format expected by Hollywood and Madison Avenue. Even as an independent or hobbyist, you may find it useful to consult a working professional or two about some production matter. If you show them an unkempt collection of odd formatting that you call a script, they are not as likely to take you seriously. Writing in the standard format costs you nothing in creativity, helps you stay organized, and makes your eventual transition to professional work that much easier.

It's easy to master the correct format for a shooting script. Get a copy of Blacker's *The Elements of Screenwriting*. This slender but dense volume covers the simple mechanics of punctuation and formatting in less than 10 pages.

I would make one modification to Blacker's advice, specifically for animation scripts: Go ahead and direct the camera. Especially if you are playing Omnipotent Person Wearing All Hats, you probably have some idea of the camera angles and lenses you want for each shot. If not, trust me, you'll get those ideas while you're typing the script. Put them in; it's easier to line them out later than to pencil them in.

Take a look at the sample script at the end of this chapter. Note that the name of each character, the explanation of each sound effect, and the description of each animated prop or live set is typed in all caps. This is an extension of the standard script format. The characters' names are capped so the animators for each character can see their shots, the explanations of sound effects are capped so members of the sound crew can plan their work, and the descriptions of sets and props are capped so the technical director (TD) and animator can plan for the additional modeling and animation. If you are given a more traditional script from which to animate, you may want to amplify it along these lines.

You should be aware that different studios may have slightly different definitions for "shot" and "scene." Generally, and almost always in live-action cinematography, a scene is a collection of shots all in the same set or location, and a shot is the footage between one camera cut and the next. In animation, a scene sometimes refers only to what can be filmed without a change in background. This makes sense if you consider that traditional animation requires the background to be redrawn whenever the camera moves. Throughout this book, I will use the live-action definition of "shot" and "scene."

Screenwriting Software

The sample script reprinted at the end of this chapter was formatted with the Script Maker template for Microsoft Word. This shareware template was distributed by Impact Pictures, but the company seems to have vanished. There are a lot of similar products out there, both shareware and commercial. For links to (and reviews of) demos and shareware, try the following sites:

- http://members.aol.com/swcyberia/scrnsoft.htm
- www.communicator.com/swsoftin.html
- www.execpc.com/~jesser/ScreenForgeInfo.html

For commercial screenwriting and production software, check out The Writers Store:

- http://writerscomputer.com

In the sample script, each shot is described by camera lens, angle, and the subjects contained in the shot. This is over-directing for live action, but it really helps for animation. If you're not familiar with camera directions, jump ahead to Chapter 14's section on camera animation, then come back here.

> *"Some people say your script should be sparse and flow. We detail a lot."*
> —Steve Bloom and Jonathan Roberts, screenwriters

Each emotional transition is clearly written out. You wouldn't want to be this heavy-handed when directing live actors, but for animation, it's a necessity. After months of looking at dozens of shots, often out of order, you will have no idea what emotion was supposed to be portrayed unless it's written down somewhere. You might as well start with the script. Also, if there is to be any dialogue, the written transition instructions will help the voice talent replace the normal interaction between the actors. In many animation productions, the voice talent record their own parts of the dialogue in separate sessions and don't interact with each other during recording. This can be a challenge, and the transition notes can help.

The level of detail in your script can vary according to your production team. For larger teams that are accustomed to a collaborative story process, the script should be less detailed. Other team members—from the director all the way down to assistant animators—may expect to contribute their own ideas to flesh out the script, and if you write in too much detail, they may resent it.

If you are writing a script for a video game cut scene, you should preface each shot with a brief summary of the preceding and following actions. This summary might include what the player has accomplished, which characters are present and any pertinent changes in their appearance, and the situation the player will face after the cut scene concludes. This information makes it easier to write a cut scene script that will enhance the game play. For example, if the following action is a surprise attack by a horde of monsters, you wouldn't want the player's companions to decide that it's safe to take a nap. On the other hand, if the next action is solving an intricate puzzle, the game characters shouldn't end the scene by prepping weapons and hyperventilating.

No scene is complete until it advances character development, story, and premise at the same time. If you develop the character alone, perhaps in a vignette, the story will lag and your audience will lose interest. If you develop the story without showing the character's growth, the character becomes two-dimensional and you lose the audience's empathy. If you ignore the premise in developing either story or character, your film loses focus and wanders away from your goal.

PROJECT 2.2   Drafting a Script

In this project, you'll write a script:

1. Expand the brief story line from Project 2.1 into a properly formatted animation shooting script. When you are writing your shot descriptions, remember the principles of composition and camera motion. If you need to review these principles, refer to the section on camera animation in Chapter 14.

2. If you don't want to script your own story, select and videotape a 30- or 60-second television commercial, then translate it to a script. The purpose of this exercise is to make you familiar with screenwriting conventions. Whether you write your own or work exclusively with other writers' scripts, you need to be able to read these blueprints accurately.

3. Have your script read by at least three other people. Be polite when they suggest plot changes and "improvements" or make other comments; people seem incapable of resisting the urge to muck up somebody else's writing. All you need to do is get answers to these three questions:

   - Could you visualize each shot?

   - Did the characters act consistently?

   - Did you have an emotional reaction to any part of the story?

4. If you get a lot of "No" answers, you probably need to rewrite. If that seems too much for you, set your script aside and try to rewrite it later. You can complete the exercises by using the example script provided; you don't have to create everything from scratch. This book is about animation, after all, not screenwriting.

A Camel is a Horse Designed by a Committee

Here's a tip from animator Phil South: Never give into suggestions from cast members. It's tempting to go with the flow, and especially with an infectious idea. Remind yourself that your script isn't being written by committee, and spur-of-the-moment changes can wreck everything you have worked out so carefully. The best thing to do is spend a little time going over the idea and tell the "suggesters" that you will do it later if you have time. Usually, they just want to be taken seriously or want to appear to be contributing. Treat them with respect of course, smile, but get on with what you already have written down. Troublesome "repeat suggesters" should be dropped from the cast (if you have that power).

Sample Script

The script in Figure 2.1 on the following six pages is included to assist you in completing the projects in the rest of this book, in case you don't want to write your own script. The premise of the story is also the title, "Easy Come, Easy Go."

This script is copyright © 1996 Douglas A. Kelly. Your permission to use the script is subject to the following conditions:

- Permission is granted to purchasers of this book to use this script for educational purposes only.

- Purchasers of this book are specifically granted permission to use this script for completing the exercises in this book in the production of a not-for-resale animated motion picture.

- If you use this script as is or in any revised or derivative form, you are required to display the phrase "Written by Doug Kelly" in the credits.

- If the finished work will be used for any commercial purpose or public display, including any advertisement or solicitation regarding animation services or employment, copyright law requires that you get my permission in advance.

- If you use this script to create a demo reel, you can secure my permission by sending me a letter of request and a copy of the demo reel.

Whether you use it or not, I hope you enjoy the story.

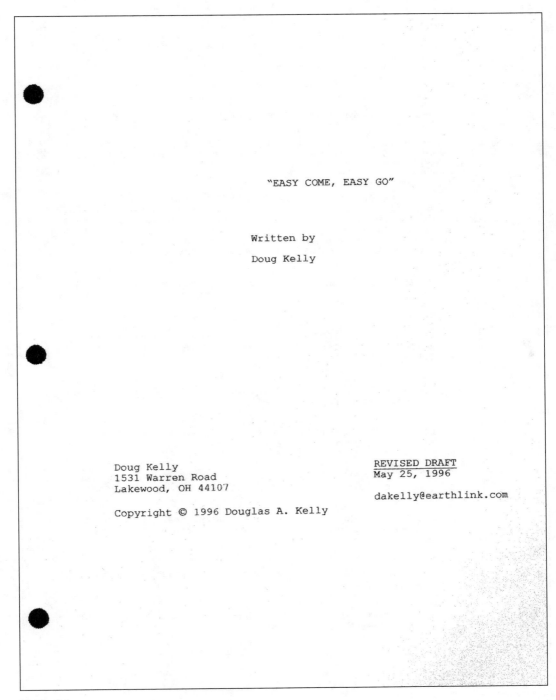

Figure 2.1
Script for "Easy Come, Easy Go."

1

<u>"EASY COME, EASY GO"</u>

FADE IN:

EXT CLOSE SHOT PUDDLE DESERTED CITY STREET LATE AFTERNOON

Heavy rain is falling on a city sidewalk. Puddle reflects
blinking neon in ripples. NEON BUZZES. Rainfall tapers
off, stops.

Truck back, pan up to MEDIUM TRACKING SHOT of FRED.
Storefronts are brick with large plate glass windows. FRED
looks down on his luck. Almost emaciated, holes and tears
in clothing, dirty, unshaven, overlong hair peeking out
under a stoved-in hat, flapping shoe sole, glasses askew.
FRED walks along sidewalk, head down, dragging feet.

THREE-QUARTER MEDIUM SHOT FRED as he glances in darkened
shop window, then pauses. He sees his REFLECTION, stops and
faces window.

CLOSE SHOT REFLECTION over FRED's shoulder. Reflection
morphs to well-fed, well-dressed, happy-looking version of
FRED.

MEDIUM SHOT REVERSE ANGLE THROUGH WINDOW FRED as he perks
up, smiling, tips hat to reflection.

CLOSE SHOT REFLECTION over FRED's shoulder, as reflection
morphs back to Fred's current image.

MEDIUM SHOT REVERSE ANGLE THROUGH WINDOW FRED as he sighs,
slouches again. Fred turns and begins to walk out of frame.

MEDIUM TRACKING SHOT FRED as he shuffles along sidewalk.
Trash blows past. BILL blows into frame, plasters itself
across FRED's glasses. FRED staggers.

CLOSE SHOT FRED as he peels bill off glasses, tries to clear
glasses.

THREE-QUARTER CLOSE SHOT FRED as he looks at bill. FRED
blinks, momentarily baffled.

2

CLOSE SHOT over FRED's shoulder ZOOM to EXTREME CLOSE SHOT
on BILL in FRED's hands. We can read bill as $1000.

THREE-QUARTER MEDIUM SHOT FRED as he looks at bill. Wild
take, as he stretches bill flat between both hands.

THREE-QUARTER CLOSE SHOT FRED recovers, looks up and into
the middle distance, as if at a wonderful vision.

CLOSE SHOT FRED'S FACE. FRED's eyes reflect images of
dollar signs, then a rich dinner, then bubbling champagne,
then the well-dressed image from the storefront.

THREE-QUARTER MEDIUM SHOT FRED clutching bill as he looks
around, reading storefront signs. FRED sees shop he wants,
anticipates and zips out of frame.

REAR MEDIUM SHOT FRED as he brakes to a screeching halt and
performs a 90-degree zip into Restaurant doorway. DOOR
SWINGING. ARGUMENT, ON RISING NOTE. Door opens forcefully
as FRED reappears, arcing out of doorway in midair and
landing on his rump in the middle of the sidewalk, still
clutching bill. FRED protests. BOUNCER'S HAND appears from
doorway, pointing to sign in window.

CLOSE SHOT SIGN with pointing hand. Sign reads, "PROPER
ATTIRE REQUIRED" in elegant script.

MEDIUM SHOT FRED as BOUNCER'S HAND withdraws, SLAMMING DOOR.
FRED gets to feet, dusts himself off, looking disgruntled,
then transitions to determination. FRED looks around at
storefront signs again. He sees the shop he wants across
the street. FRED marches determinedly out of frame, stepping
off the curb.

MEDIUM SHOT TAILOR SHOP as FRED marches up to door and
enters.

HELD SHOT ON TAILOR SHOP. We hear MEASURING TAPE, SCISSORS,
SEWING MACHINE, CASH REGISTER.

3

MATCH DISSOLVE TO:

MEDIUM SHOT BARBER SHOP with spinning barber pole. By the light, it is visibly later in the evening, nearly sunset. We hear SCISSORS, HAIR TONIC, LATHER BRUSH, RAZOR STROP, SHAVING, CASH REGISTER. Door opens. FRED exits with a jaunty strut, clean-shaven and with slicked-down, neatly-parted hair. (Possibly insert humorous cameo from weiner-dog) FRED turns to find restaurant again, and jauntily walks out of frame, back across street.

MEDIUM SHOT RESTAURANT as FRED jauntily walks up and enters.

INT MEDIUM SHOT TABLE RESTAURANT EVENING

WAITRESS'S HANDS hold chair as FRED sits down. WAITRESS'S HANDS present MENU. FRED peruses menu, making a great show of it. FRED smiles broadly, holds menu open toward WAITRESS (OS) and points to several items, nodding rapidly. WAITRESS'S HANDS retrieve menu. WAITRESS'S HANDS serve heaping plates of food, pour champagne.

MONTAGE

fred making pig of self, waistline expanding

drinking more

becoming boisterous

gesturing and calling to other tables (OS)

dishes stacking

champagne magnums accumulating

increasingly tight close shots on Fred, mouth opening wider in eating and talking, actions more broad and out of control

loosening collar, clothing becoming disarrayed

CASH REGISTER RINGING repeatedly

MEDIUM SHOT TABLE FRED as WAITRESS' HANDS gesture Fred to settle down. FRED transitions from gluttonous to irate, then fascinated with WAITRESS(OS), then leering. FRED makes grab for WAITRESS(OS). WAITRESS' HANDS withdraw, fending off FRED, who nearly falls out of chair. FRED, grumbling, resumes guzzling champagne. BOUNCER'S HAND reaches into frame, tap FRED on shoulder. FRED looks up, bleary and obviously in his cups. His reaction time is severely impaired.

4

EXT MEDIUM SHOT RESTAURANT DESERTED CITY STREET NIGHT

CRASHING and THUDS. DOOR OPENS forcefully as FRED reappears, arcing out of doorway in midair. Camera tracks FRED, does zip pan as he COLLIDES headfirst with LAMPPOST. DOOR SLAMS forcefully. FRED defies gravity for a moment, then falls, SPLAT, facefirst onto sidewalk.

CLOSE SHOT MOVING HOLD FRED, left flat on face across sidewalk. Hat is now crumpled, clothing partially soiled from contact with sidewalk and lamppost.(Possibly insert another humorous cameo from weiner-dog) FRED slowly sits up, holds head and weaves a bit. FRED climbs shakily to his feet. He GAGS, but can't hold it in and the camera pans to follow his rush for the alley entrance next to RESTAURANT. FRED drops to knees with head and upper torso out of sight in alley, and GAGS repeatedly.

MEDIUM SHOT ALLEY FRED as he drags himself across the alley on hands and knees to a patch of wall between garbage cans and props himself there.

CLOSE SHOT FRED TRASH CANS His color is slightly better, although still pale. His clothing is now thoroughly soiled and torn. His eyelids flicker a few times, then fall shut as FRED begins to snore.

                              DISSOLVE TO:

MEDIUM SHOT ALLEY FRED as morning light filters into the alley, showing all the damage. FRED's snoring changes, he wakes, blinks repeatedly, winces at the light, shakes his head and immediately clutches it in pain. He is badly hung over.

FULL SHOT ALLEY RESTAURANT SHOP as FRED staggers onto sidewalk in front of store.

CLOSE SHOT FRED as he transitions from bewilderment to total recall, and then to crushing remorse. His shoulders sag.

THREE-QUARTER MEDIUM SHOT FRED as FRED glances in darkened shop window. He sees his reflection again, and turns to face window.

CLOSE SHOT MOVING HOLD REFLECTION over FRED's shoulder. Reflection morphs to well-fed, well-dressed version of FRED. REFLECTION's expression is stern and disapproving, an

5

unflinching glare.

THREE-QUARTER MEDIUM SHOT FRED as REFLECTION morphs back to
real reflection.   FRED SIGHS, slouches further.

MEDIUM TRACKING SHOT FRED as he turns, SIGHS again, and
shuffles down the sidewalk, very much as we first saw him,
holes and tears in clothing, dirty, unshaven, hat stoved in
and glasses askew. TRACKING slows to let FRED pass gradually
out of frame.

FADE OUT

Moving On

You should now have a practical working knowledge of stories and scripts for animation. The next step in the animation process is the storyboard. Chapter 3 will show you the essentials of storyboarding for animation, including a complete sample storyboard for "Easy Come, Easy Go."

Chapter 3

Storyboards

A *storyboard* is a collection of individual story sketches, each illustrating a particular shot from the script as it would appear to the camera. The storyboard itself can be a large piece of board or section of wall with the sketches pinned to it, a portfolio with a few sketches on each page, or even a loose-leaf binder intended to show only one story sketch at a time. If the storyboard is only for yourself, you can draw each sketch on a 4×6 file card and write your ideas and descriptions on the back. You can easily shuffle them into the right order and hold them in place with a rubber band, which is a low-tech, cheap, and portable solution. You can even photocopy and enlarge your sketches onto larger sheets later if you need to give them to a storyboard artist.

Storyboards were developed in the Disney studio in the late 1920s as a way of visualizing the shot flow of the entire story at once. By the mid-1930s, most Hollywood studios were using them as a means of preplanning and managing film production. As you will see, the storyboard is one of the most valuable tools used by an animation director.

The Storyboard as a Tool

A well-done storyboard bridges the gap between the script and the actual animation, providing the next level of detail in visualization. If the script is a film's blueprint, the storyboard is a set of detailed engineering drawings. As with the script, if you have trouble creating the storyboard, you may want to revise or clarify your ideas.

Storyboards are also necessary for dealing with most employers and partners. If you are working in feature films, television, or advertising, the producers and other team members will need to see the storyboards. In advertising, even the client will see the storyboards; ad agencies are notorious for over-approving everything. For an animated ad, expect to produce detailed, finished artwork for storyboards, and be prepared to have it all second-guessed and revised repeatedly. Although it's true that CGI animation can often be laid out and rendered faster than an artist can produce the finished storyboards, speed is not the issue. Client approval and agency c.y.a. are the issues.

If a particular employer requires more storyboarding than you want to do, plan to hire a storyboard artist to do the extra work, and increase your fee accordingly. If there will be several cycles of storyboarding and approval before you can get down to animating, make sure your contract spells out your compensation for the delays and extra work. Pay particular attention to the clause that states that you will get paid for out-of-pocket expenses and work completed, even if the client changes his mind or cancels the project.

If you are working on an independent project like a demo reel, you have a lot more leeway in the production values of your storyboards. Stick figures and rough sketches are adequate if you are doing a solo project, but putting in more information will make your work easier later on. After months of posing and tweaking, it's sometimes difficult to remember exactly what you had in mind for a particular shot. A detailed story sketch is one of the best memory-joggers you can have.

You can also abbreviate storyboards by using a single sketch for several shots (or a traveling shot) of the same backgrounds and characters. Place numbered frame outlines in the sketch, especially if the shots use complex cuts or travel. For example, Shot 14 in the sample storyboards (presented at the end of this chapter) uses a frame outline to show a zoom in rather than using another complete sketch for the zoomed view.

I still recommend using complete storyboards, both to help clarify your vision of the story and as evidence that the work is actually yours. Some animation houses will ask you to prove that you created the work on your demo reel. You should save the script drafts, story sketches, and other production notes and take them to your interviews.

Now that you understand the importance of storyboards, let's move on to practical methods for creating your own.

Script to Storyboard

Exactly how do you expand a script into a storyboard? There are almost as many approaches as there are professional storyboard artists. You can choose the size, medium, and style to suit yourself, and several books listed in the Bibliography can give you ideas. If you have access to a good art supply store, you can buy storyboard panels already printed with television cutoff. These panels are designed for television commercials, but the proper aspect ratio is there.

My personal approach is, I think, simple and effective. Once I have the finished script in a Word document, I save a copy of it and make the following page layout changes to the duplicate:

1. Change the page orientation to landscape.

2. Change the page number in the header to read SHOT #.

3. Immediately after the shot number, insert a carriage return and create an 8x6 frame that is centered in the header, flush against the top margin and spaced 0.2 inches from following text.

4. Change the cover page to read DRAFT STORYBOARD rather than FIRST (or whatever) DRAFT.

To see an example of this formatting, open the EASYSHO2.DOC file in the Chapter 3 directory on this book's CD-ROM.

This starts off every page (except the cover) with a blank 8×6 frame, which is the standard aspect ratio for film work. If you are going to be working in another aspect ratio, change the dimensions of the frame to match. Working with landscape format 8-1/2×11-inch paper also enables you to put the storyboard in a standard three-ring binder. A number of directors prefer working this way because they can flip through the pages rapidly to get an idea of the timing for shot flow.

This format is much larger than most studios work with. I like the extra space, but many storyboard artists are more comfortable with 4x6 or even smaller sketches. There are alternative storyboard layouts that can fit three or more sketches on a single page. Choose the format you like best, but be prepared to work in other formats if a studio or client requests it.

The shots will be numbered automatically. If you need to insert a new shot later, it will probably be easier to hand-letter the shot number on a blank page than to fool around with reformatting the entire document. This was the procedure used for the montage (Shots 49A through M) of Fred's excesses in the restaurant. The composite shot was numbered from the original script breakout. The individual shots used to compose the montage (which was edited together in post-production) were designed later, their descriptions handwritten on blank sheets, and the finished sketches numbered 49A, 49B, and so on. In a more professional production, this whole scene would have been worked out in story sketches first. Independent production lets you cheat in lots of little ways like this.

To create blank story sketch pages in Word, follow these steps:

1. Add a section break and a page break after the last FADE OUT.

2. Turn off the Same As Previous toggle.

3. Change the new section's header to replace the page number with a few underscores.

4. Add the label SHOT DESCRIPTION: under the frame.

5. Print a single copy of this last page and photocopy it or print a lot of copies so that you can keep the blank pages handy in your binder for making changes.

If you don't want to fool around with making your own story sketch blanks, you can print copies of the SKETCH.PDF file located in the Chapter 3 directory on this book's CD-ROM. The Chapter 3 directory also includes a blank three-panel storyboard sheet, 3Panel.tif, of the type commonly used in television cel animation. The sample storyboard sheet is shown in Figure 3.1.

The next step is to go through the script line-by-line and insert a page break after each shot. I carry this a little further for character animation storyboards by breaking after each action or moving hold.

Take a look at an example from an earlier draft of the "Easy Come, Easy Go" script. Originally, the shot in which Fred leaves the barber shop was much longer and involved a visible barber character. Although it was an opportunity to animate some interesting actions, the sequence was cut because it didn't advance the story's premise. This shot broke down into five sketches,

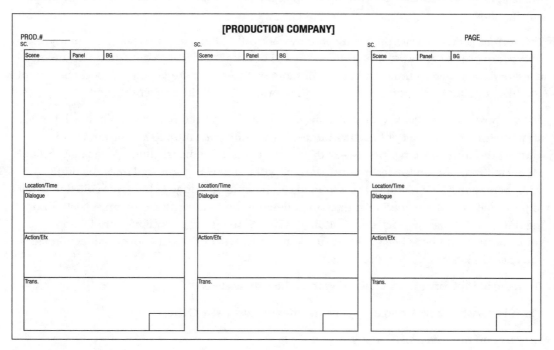

Figure 3.1
Sample board paper (available in the Chapter 3 folder on the CD-ROM).

even though, cinematically, it's a single shot. From a character animator's viewpoint, the actions to be animated are very different and can be handled as a series of separate shots connected by overlapping action:

1. The door opens and Fred exits the barbershop with a particular gait. The main action ends when Fred halts, just before beginning the turn. All the overlapping actions that are part of Fred continue into the next main action.

2. Fred turns and bows to the barber. This should be a single action, flowing and graceful (if a trifle overacted). The action ends when Fred straightens into a moving hold, which overlaps the next action.

3. The barber's hands wave. The action ends when the door closes. The overlapping action is Fred's reaction, which begins just before the door is completely closed.

4. Fred turns again and scans the storefronts. This turn is slightly different from the second action in both timing and emphasis because he now has another purpose in mind. The action ends when he identifies his goal and sets himself to begin walking. Again, the overlapping actions are all associated with Fred.

5. The last action is Fred walking out of the frame. There is no overlapping action because the set is empty of characters.

As you can see, this breakout increases the number of story sketches. I prefer this approach because it helps bridge the transition from storyboard to exposure sheet, giving you more breaking points than a simpler shot breakout. This makes it a little easier to time each action, and you can pencil your timing estimates right on the story sketch margin. This is a big help when you first meet with the music director or composer.

If I'm doing the entire production myself, I prefer working in pencil (and so do most board artists I've asked). I'm not a graphic artist by any stretch of the definition, so most of my storyboards are simple perspective layouts of the sets populated by somewhat-proportional stick figures. For the example production presented in this chapter, I planned to work with a production team and therefore arranged for a professional artist to do the storyboards.

At some point during the script revision process, you will need to do the preliminary character design, as detailed in Chapter 5. The storyboard artist will need a copy of the character model sheets plus whatever concept sketches are available for sets and props. Figure 3.2 shows a design sketch for the Fred character.

If the project is a continuation of a series using existing sets, it's helpful to provide the artist with some appropriate rendered backgrounds from previous projects. There's no need to expend creative effort on a stock interior that has appeared in 12 episodes already—at least, not if you want to stay on good terms with your storyboard artist.

Figure 3.2
Preliminary character designs for Fred.

You should also have sketched plans and elevations (overhead and side views) of the original set elements called for in the script. If you mention a storefront, make sure the storyboard artist has some idea of what kind of storefront you mean. A trendy big-city designer boutique will have a very different look than a small-town barber shop.

At this point, you may find it useful to make some schematic sketches of the objects and their eventual positioning in LightWave. A simple plan sketched on scaled grid paper, as shown in Figure 3.3, will greatly reduce the time you spend setting up the master scene.

It's important that you discuss with the storyboard artist any moods, specific camera angles, or other limitations you want to keep in mind. For example, because everything described in the sample script was to be constructed from scratch, I wanted to limit extraneous backgrounds. One way to do this is to limit camera angles. If the camera is always looking below the horizon line and buildings are in the near foreground, you'll never have to create a sky. Similarly, if the camera is on a slight down angle in a medium shot of a building, nothing above the first floor needs to be modeled. Panning the camera a few degrees one way or the other can mean the difference between modeling an entire street scene and being able to get away with a few false-front shops and a dozen feet of road and sidewalk.

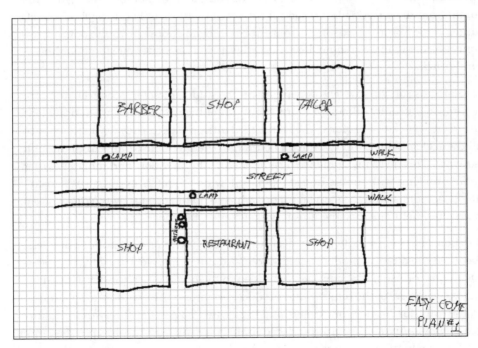

Figure 3.3
A simple preliminary sketch of object placement.

It may help if you think of the camera view as a pyramid, with the point at the focal plane (just behind the lens) of the camera and the base way out at infinity. The frame of the shot is a slice through the pyramid. Anything within the volume of that pyramid is something you are going to have to model, buy, or fake. It's in your best interest to keep that pyramid as empty as possible while still telling an engaging story.

You can't always get away with dodges like these, but for a character animation demo reel, you should concentrate on the animation and avoid having to re-create the whole world.

The flip side of setting limits is that you might damage the story. Before you set limits, carefully consider how they reduce your storytelling options. Sometimes you really need that sweeping panorama or complex cityscape to advance the premise and develop the character.

In most cases, storyboards are prepared before the models, sets, or other LightWave elements are created. Even if you have some or all of those elements on hand, you should resist the temptation to storyboard in Layout. Composing shots by positioning lights, camera, objects, and characters is a time-consuming process that almost always leads to a lot of tweaking. This interrupts the creative flow necessary to create a good storyboard. However, at least one studio, Mainframe Entertainment (*Reboot*, *Beast Wars*), uses the computer for storyboards, layout, and blocking straight from the script. This is a special case because this studio has established sets, characters, and a large library of existing layouts from which to choose. If you're doing a series, you might consider doing the same; for a first project, you are better off storyboarding with paper and pencil.

The storyboard process can vary widely, depending on the studio, director, producer, and format. Feature film work usually allows for many iterations of the storyboards, with many team members participating in story sessions. The storyboard artist makes a *pitch* for a sequence by arranging all the sketches on a wall or bulletin board and then reading (and acting) through the whole sequence. This gives the audience a better idea of the shot flow and makes it easier to spot potential problems with timing and staging. Following the pitch, everyone gets to critique and offer suggestions, and the storyboard artist has to try to keep up by making notes or even drawing replacement or supplemental story sketches on the spot.

Television storyboarding for animated cartoons is usually done with fewer iterations and less interaction between the director, producer, and storyboard artist. A typical storyboard process for an episode might consist of the script being handed to the board artist, the artist creating the boards in two weeks or so, the director and producer critiquing the boards and sending them back to the artist for changes or *cleanup*, and the revised boards being forwarded to the animation team. Obviously, storyboards produced in this way will be much less polished than those produced from a feature-film-type process and will rely heavily on the layout talents of the board artist.

Commercial storyboards are a strange hybrid of television and feature. To keep the client happy, the boards are usually very detailed and a lot of effort is put into the pitch, which is often presented by the ad agency. However, the turnaround time is even shorter than it is for television, and the animation director and board artist are likely to have very little influence over the content of the boards. If you like a lot of creative freedom, storyboarding for commercials is not likely to be your favorite career choice.

Sample Storyboard

The following storyboard is included to assist you in completing the projects in the rest of this book, in case you don't want to draw your own storyboards. These story sketches follow a revised version of the script in Chapter 2, so you will find small differences where shots were cut, added, or changed. This enables you to see how the story changed through the development process. Gaps or additional letters in the shot numbering show where shots were deleted or added in the storyboard sessions; Shots 3, 29 through 34, 36, 37, 46, 47, 49, 63, 71, and 72 were cut, and Shots 18A, 19A, 28A and B, 34A, 49A through M, and 71A were inserted.

I used standard screenwriting abbreviations in the script and storyboard. For complete details on style and abbreviation usage, consult Irwin Blacker's *The Elements of Screenwriting*, listed in this book's Bibliography. In the storyboard captions presented here, the abbreviations EXT, INT, OTS, and OS mean, respectively, Exterior, Interior, Over The Shoulder, and Off Screen. For more information about camera actions, moving holds, and other terms of art used in the shot descriptions, see Chapter 14.

This storyboard is copyright © 1996-1997 Douglas A. Kelly. Your permission to use the storyboard is subject to the following conditions:

- Permission is granted to purchasers of this book to use this storyboard for educational purposes only.

- Purchasers of this book are specifically granted permission to use this storyboard for completing the projects in this book in the production of a not-for-resale animated motion picture.

- If you use this storyboard as is or in any revised or derivative form, you are required to display the phrases "Written by Doug Kelly" and "Storyboard Artist: Brian Kelly" in the credits.

- If the finished work will be used for any commercial purpose or public display, including any advertisement or solicitation regarding animation services or employment, copyright law requires that you get my permission in advance.

- If you use this storyboard to create a demo reel, you can secure my permission by sending me a letter of request and a copy of the demo reel. You can contact me through The Coriolis Group or email me at **dakelly@earthlink.net**.

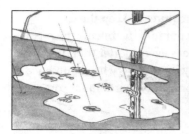

Shot 1: FADE IN: EXT CLOSE SHOT PUDDLE DESERTED CITY STREET NIGHT. Heavy rain is falling on a city sidewalk. Puddle reflects blinking neon in ripples. NEON BUZZES. Rainfall tapers off, stops.

Shot 2: Truck back, pan up to MEDIUM TRACKING SHOT of FRED. Storefronts are brick with large plate glass windows. FRED looks down on his luck. Almost emaciated, holes and tears in clothing, dirty, unshaven, overlong hair peeking out under a stoved-in hat, flapping shoe sole, glasses askew.

Shot 4: THREE-QUARTER MEDIUM SHOT FRED as he glances in darkened shop window, then pauses. He sees his REFLECTION, stops, and faces window.

Shot 5: CLOSE SHOT REFLECTION over FRED's shoulder. Reflection morphs to well-fed, well-dressed, happy-looking version of FRED.

Shot 6: THREE-QUARTER MEDIUM SHOT THROUGH WINDOW FRED as he perks up, smiling, tips hat.

Shot 7: CLOSE SHOT REFLECTION over FRED's shoulder, as reflection morphs back to Fred's current image.

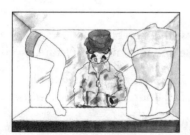

Shot 8: THREE-QUARTER MEDIUM SHOT THROUGH WINDOW FRED as face falls, he sighs, slouches again.

Shot 9: Fred turns and walks out of frame.

Shot 10: MEDIUM TRACKING SHOT FRED as he shuffles along sidewalk. Trash blows past.

Shot 11: BILL blows into frame, plasters itself across FRED's glasses. FRED staggers.

Shot 12: CLOSE SHOT FRED as he peels bill off glasses, tries to clear glasses.

Shot 13: THREE-QUARTER CLOSE SHOT FRED as he looks at bill. FRED blinks, momentarily baffled.

Shot 14: CLOSE SHOT over FRED's shoulder STAGGER ZOOM to EXTREME CLOSE SHOT on BILL in FRED's hands. We can read bill as $1,000.

Shot 15: THREE-QUARTER MEDIUM SHOT FRED as he looks at bill. Wild take, as he stretches bill flat between both hands.

Shot 16: FRED recovers, looks up and into the middle distance, as if at a wonderful vision.

Shot 17: CLOSE SHOT FRED'S FACE. FRED's eyes reflect images of dollar signs, then a rich dinner, then bubbling champagne, then the well-dressed image from the storefront.

Shot 18: THREE-QUARTER MEDIUM SHOT FRED clutching bill as he looks around, reading storefront signs.

Shot 18A: FRED sees shop he wants, anticipates, and zips out of frame.

Shot 19: REAR MEDIUM SHOT FRED as he brakes to a screeching halt and performs a 90-degree zip into restaurant doorway.

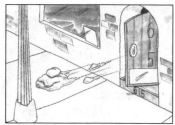

Shot 19A: DOOR SWINGING. ARGUMENT, ON RISING NOTE.

Shot 20: Door opens forcefully as FRED reappears, arcing out of doorway in midair and landing on his rump in the middle of the sidewalk, still clutching bill.

Shot 21: FRED protests.

Shot 22: BOUNCER'S HAND appears from doorway, pointing to sign in window.

Shot 23: CLOSE SHOT SIGN with pointing hand. Sign reads, "PROPER ATTIRE REQUIRED" in elegant script.

Shot 24: MEDIUM SHOT FRED as BOUNCER'S HAND withdraws, SLAMMING DOOR.

Shot 25: FRED gets to feet, dusts himself off, looking disgruntled, then transitions to determination.

Shot 26: FRED looks around at storefront signs again. He sees the shop he wants, across the street.

Shot 27: FRED marches determinedly out of frame, stepping off curb.

Shot 28: MEDIUM SHOT TAILOR SHOP as FRED marches up to door and enters.

Shot 28A: HELD SHOT TAILOR SHOP. We hear MEASURING TAPE, SCISSORS, SEWING MACHINE, CASH REGISTER.

Shot 28B: MATCH DISSOLVE TO MEDIUM SHOT BARBER SHOP, visibly later by lighting, now near dusk. SOUNDS continuous, bridge from TAILOR sounds to BARBER sounds.

Shot 34A: HELD SHOT BARBER SHOP with spinning barber pole. We hear SCISSORS, HAIR TONIC, LATHER BRUSH, RAZOR STROP, SHAVING, CASH REGISTER.

Shot 35: BARBER SHOP DOOR opens. FRED exits with a jaunty strut, clean-shaven and with slicked-down, neatly parted hair.

Shot 38: FRED turns and scans store-fronts, finds restaurant again.

Shot 39: FRED jauntily walks out of frame, back across street.

Shot 40: MEDIUM SHOT RESTAURANT as FRED jauntily walks up and enters.

Shot 41: INT MEDIUM SHOT TABLE RESTAURANT EVENING as WAITRESS'S HANDS hold chair as FRED crosses in front of table, makes slight bow to WAITRESS, sits down as WAITRESS places chair.

Shot 42: CLOSE SHOT TABLE FRED, as WAITRESS'S HANDS present MENU.

Shot 43: CLOSE SHOT MENU FRED as he peruses menu, making a great show of it.

Shot 44: CLOSE SHOT TABLE FRED as he smiles broadly, holds menu open toward WAITRESS (OS, RIGHT), and points to several items, nodding rapidly.

Shot 45: WAITRESS'S HANDS retrieve menu.

Shot 48: MEDIUM SHOT FRED TABLE as WAITRESS'S HANDS serve heaping plates of food, pour champagne.

Shot 49A-49M: MONTAGE: Fred making pig of self, waistline expanding, drinking more, becoming boisterous, gesturing and calling to other tables (OS), dishes stacking, champagne magnums accumulating, increasingly tight close shots on Fred, mouth opening wider, actions more broad and out of control, loosening collar, clothing becoming disarrayed, CASH REGISTER RINGING repeatedly. Evening light dims to night during montage.

Shot 50: MEDIUM SHOT TABLE FRED as WAITRESS'S HANDS (OS, RIGHT) gesture Fred to settle down.

Shot 51: FRED transitions from gluttonous to irate, then fascinated with WAITRESS (OS), then leering.

Shot 52: FRED makes grab for WAIT-RESS (OS). WAITRESS'S HANDS withdraw, fending off FRED, who nearly falls out of chair.

Shot 53: FRED, grumbling, resumes guzzling champagne.

Shot 54: BOUNCER'S HAND reaches into frame from OS RIGHT, taps FRED on shoulder.

Shot 55: FRED looks up, bleary and obviously in his cups. His reaction time is severely impaired.

Shot 56: EXT MEDIUM SHOT RESTAU-RANT DESERTED CITY STREET NIGHT as we hear CRASHING and THUDS.

Shot 57: DOOR OPENS forcefully as FRED reappears, arcing out of doorway in midair.

Shot 58: Camera tracks FRED, does zip pan as he COLLIDES headfirst with LAMPPOST.

Shot 59: DOOR SLAMS forcefully.

Shot 60: FRED defies gravity for a moment, then rear end sags accordion-style down to sidewalk, followed by body, head, and hat.

Shot 61: FRED is left flat across sidewalk. Hat is now crumpled, clothing partially soiled from contact with sidewalk and lamppost. MOVING HOLD.

Shot 62: FRED slowly sits up, holds head, and weaves a bit.

Shot 64: FRED climbs shakily to his feet.

Shot 65: FRED GAGS, but can't hold it in, and the camera pans to follow his rush for the alley entrance next to RESTAURANT.

Shot 66: FRED drops to knees with head and upper torso out of sight in alley and GAGS repeatedly.

Shot 67: MEDIUM SHOT ALLEY FRED as he drags himself across the alley on hands and knees to a patch of wall between garbage cans and props himself there.

Shot 68: CLOSE SHOT FRED TRASH CANS. FRED's color is slightly better, although still pale. His clothing is now thoroughly soiled and torn. His eyelids flicker a few times, then fall shut as FRED begins to snore.

Shot 69: MATCH DISSOLVE to MEDIUM SHOT ALLEY FRED as morning light filters into the alley, showing all the damage.

Shot 70: FRED wakes, blinks repeatedly, winces at the light, shakes his head, and immediately clutches it in pain. He is badly hung over.

Shot 71A: THREE-QUARTER MEDIUM SHOT FRED ALLEY ENTRANCE as he staggers onto sidewalk in front of store.

Shot 73: CLOSE SHOT FRED as he transitions from incomprehension to total recall and then to crushing remorse. His shoulders sag.

Shot 74: THREE-QUARTER MEDIUM SHOT FRED as FRED glances in darkened shop window. He sees his reflection again and turns to face window.

Shot 75: CLOSE SHOT REFLECTION over FRED's shoulder.

Shot 76: REFLECTION morphs to well-fed, well-dressed version of FRED. REFLECTION's expression is stern and disapproving, an unflinching glare. MOVING HOLD.

Shot 77: THREE-QUARTER MEDIUM SHOT FRED as REFLECTION morphs back to real reflection. FRED SIGHS, slouches further.

Shot 78: MEDIUM SHOT SHOPFRONT FRED as he turns, SIGHS again.

Shot 79: FRED shuffles down the sidewalk and out of frame, very much as we first saw him, holes and tears in clothing, dirty, unshaven, hat stoved-in, and glasses askew. FADE OUT.

PROJECT 3.1 Making a Storyboard

Now that you have read theory and seen an example of storyboarding, it's time for you to practice doing your own boards. This project is intended to get you thinking visually, converting the shot descriptions in the script into images that are closer to what you want in the final film.

To make a storyboard, follow these steps:

1. Break out your script from Project 2.2 into a properly formatted storyboard. Stick figures are acceptable, but try to keep them in proportion. If the characters are interacting with part of the set (looking out a window, opening a door), draw that part of the set.

2. If you don't want to storyboard your own script, either use the sample script provided in Chapter 2 or select at least four pages from a motion picture or television script. Break it out as if you will be animating it, even if the script is for a live-action show. If your shot descriptions are longer than two or three short sentences, they are probably too long. Break them down even further.

3. If you use the sample script, make your version of Fred markedly different. How would you compose the shots if Fred were tall and thin? Short and fat? Make all the action work from the opposite side of the street. Do *not* simply copy the storyboard from this chapter!

4. Use a blank sheet of paper to cover the shot description under each sketch. At random, pick a sketch and see if you can tell what the action is and what the character is expressing. Repeat this test for several of the shots.

5. Flip through the storyboard in order, looking only at the sketches. Are you starting to get a sense of the rhythm, the timing for the shot flow? Are there gaps or jumps in the shot flow? If you jump from one camera location to another without a strong common visual reference, you may lose your audience. If you have to make a big jump, make sure you have an object or character that appears in both shots so the audience can immediately orient themselves to the new point of view. For example, the cut from Shot 22 to Shot 23 in the first-draft storyboard does not lose the audience because the "Proper Attire" sign is in the middle of both shots. The cut is a kind of super-fast zoom in. By contrast, the cut between Shot 23 and Shot 24 can lose the audience because there is no common reference point. To correct this, you could widen or shift the frame in Shot 24 to include the "Proper Attire" sign again.

6. If you can, show your storyboard to someone you know who can think visually. Ask her to tell you the story represented by the boards in her own words.

If the responses to the critiques in Steps 4, 5, and 6 are close to what you intended, your storyboard is working. If not, remember that storyboarding, like writing or animating, is a skill that improves with practice. Keep at it! And, as with all the other techniques discussed in this book, be *ruthless* with your editing.

Putting the Storyboard to Work

So you've got a storyboard. Now what? Put it to work, of course, saving you time and effort!

The number one value of a storyboard is that it saves effort for the production team. For example, if there are no shots in the storyboard where the camera is closer than a hundred feet to a particular object, you don't have to build into that object any details that aren't visible at a hundred feet. If every camera angle cuts off at first-floor height, there's no use in modeling and texturing the upper floors and roofs.

This is really where "limitations" are considered and put to use. The first round of storyboards should be fairly free of constraints. It's always easier to scale back than to build up.

Take another look at the revised sample storyboard printed at the end of this chapter. This time, look at the sketches from the point of view of the technical director. Fred is the only character who needs to have a head, feet, or a body—the bouncer and waitress are represented by disembodied hands and arms that appear from off screen. This is an enormous savings in modeling and animation. There is a slight cost in terms of expressive range because you can only communicate so much with hand gestures (we have to assume most of the audience doesn't read American Sign Language).

The sets are almost all false-front shops, with simple (and reusable) sections of sidewalk, street, and alley connecting them. The single interior is also deliberately vague and simple, kept shadowy by lighting so minor details need not be modeled.

Take a look at your own storyboards. Look at each sketch. Is there any object in this sketch that doesn't appear somewhere else? Is there a different way to compose the shot so that object doesn't have to be modeled? Will cropping it out have a negative effect on telling the story? Could a simpler or stock object be substituted? There's no reason to custom-build a 1931 Duesenberg if it's only in one shot for a few seconds and the character could just as easily be stepping out of a stock-model taxi.

Storyboards force you to make these important decisions early on and are therefore an absolute requirement for any sizable animation. Budgets can be broken and deadlines blown by a few overly complex shots. If these shots are necessary to tell the story effectively, the finance people might accept the overrun; if the shots are superfluous, you are likely to hear phrases like "Heaven's Gate" or "Waterworld" as they tell you to clean out your desk.

Moving On

If you've read and completed the project for this chapter, you should have a good idea of the importance and utility of a storyboard for your character animation. The examples shown here should help you avoid making the same mistakes in your own production.

The next level of detail is the timing of each shot—writing up the actions, music, and sound effects on exposure sheets. Chapter 4 will guide you through this step in the production process.

Chapter 4

Sound and Timing

S ilent animations are boring. Even a little generic background music will liven them up, and synchronized sound effects will do wonders. If you are building a demo reel, you can increase your chances of an interview if you pay a little attention to your sound track. The reviewer is more likely to watch your reel, and less likely to cut it off short, if the audio track adds to the flow and continuity of your animations.

Working with sound can also help you develop your timing skills. Timing to synchronize actions with recorded music, dialogue, and sound effects forces you to compromise and collaborate rather than time actions arbitrarily. An audio track's timing provides a framework that is especially useful to beginning animators. If you know that your character's actions have to hit specific poses at specific frames, you will only have to interpolate your own timing in between those hits. The traditional paper tools used to develop animation sound tracks are also useful for both experienced and novice LightWave character animators. Just as the script and storyboard document the story development of your film, the bar sheets and exposure sheets document the development of music, sound, and dialogue.

Making Sound Decisions

You have a variety of options for adding sound to your animation: do without, borrow, buy, or make it yourself. You can always opt for a silent piece—a bad idea in general, but sometimes necessary if your resources are limited.

General background music and sound effects are the next step up. At a minimum, try to dub a song that has a mood and length similar to that of your animation. If your animation has been laid out to a steady beat, you may even be able to find prerecorded music that will match your animation's accents.

If you intend to send your demo reel only to potential employers, you may be able to get away with using commercial recordings; this is a gray area of the fair use doctrine regarding copyright. You definitely cannot use a copyrighted work to make money or in a public performance, and any use on a demo reel must be strictly for "educational or research purposes." That is, you can use a copyrighted work in a student piece, even if you are self-taught. If you are already in the graphics business and the reel is distributed to advertise your services, you can't use the fair use defense. Also, if there is any chance that your reel will be shown in public, you need to comply with all the copyright restrictions or prepare to be sued. To play it safe, if you can afford it you should buy an appropriate piece from a music or sound effects library.

Custom music and sound effects, synchronized to the action, are the most expensive but highest quality sounds for animation. If you don't have the budget to hire professionals, find a friendly musician or composer who is willing to work with you, or even try to do the music yourself. The same is true of sound effects and vocal tracks; locate people willing to help, or do it yourself if you can. *Foley* work (recording sound effects) can still be done effectively by non-professionals. You don't need a license to play the coconut halves, and most theater arts schools will have books on low-end sound effect recording techniques.

Animation and sound are a chicken-and-egg problem. Which should be done first? The answer is an unsatisfying "That depends." There are four basic approaches to coordinating sound and animation, plus combinations of two or more of the basics:

- *Music first*—The music is composed and recorded first, using a strictly regular beat. The director lays out the musical beat in the *bar sheets* so the animators can match the action to it without hearing the score. This approach can force animation into the realm of choreography. It can be challenging for the animator to squeeze a long action into a fast passage or to stretch the action to fill up a slow one. This approach is best used only when there is a strong reason to adhere to a prerecorded piece of music.

- *Music first, but this time with a variable tempo*—The music track is analyzed as if it were dialogue, and the beats are noted on the bar sheets.

- *Simultaneous*—The director and composer negotiate between the director's timing of planned actions and the composer's scoring of individual phrases or passages.

- *Scoring to the action*—The action is laid out in the bar sheets with each accent marked in a dummy score. Then the composer writes a free tempo score to match the actions' emphasis with the music's beat.

Which approach you choose depends on several factors, including the length of the animation, the amount of dialogue or synchronized music, the number of animators and other team members involved, and the production values desired. If you are animating a 10-second motion test by yourself for a personal project and the only sound issues are a couple of foley hits, you can use the most minimal approach. If the animation is a feature film with a full orchestral score and name-actor dialogue tracks, you're going to need every tool in the box just to keep track of everything. If you're just getting started in the business, you should practice using professional tools on your personal and demo reel projects.

Timing Tools

A common tool in coordinating sound and animation for feature film production is the *bar sheet*. A bar sheet (shown in Figure 4.1) is similar to the blank sheets a composer would use, except the three middle staff lines are missing. The measures are marked, and the number of beats to each measure is penciled in. You can use bar sheets with all four of the basic sound timing approaches.

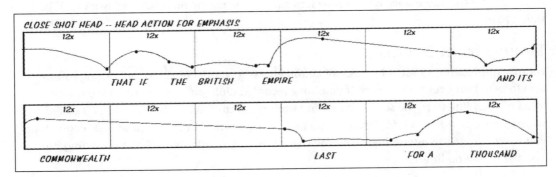

Figure 4.1
Bar sheet.

The director uses the bar sheets to plan the flow of the whole animation, condensing a hundred or more story sketches down to a few pages of cryptically penciled notations. This is where the mood and tempo of the finished film are determined. Prior to this step, there is a great deal of flexibility in how shots are paced and connected and what the mood of each segment can be. Once the director establishes the rhythm and timing of every shot via the bar sheet, the flow of the film is much more definite.

The bar sheets are especially useful because the director, composer, and other members of the production team can easily see if a particular action, sound, or musical passage will fit properly in the time allotted. This helps in negotiating the inevitable trade-offs and compromises necessary to make the sound and animation work together. All these changes are also recorded on the bar sheets. Other people may contribute during the bar sheets' revision, but the final responsibility is the director's.

The bar sheets track most of the information needed to coordinate the entire animation production team. The director, animator, and most of the rest of the crew will live and breathe by these sheets before the project is completed. Keeping track of the sheets is an important job, whether you are being paid to do it as an assistant director or are doing it all yourself on a private project.

Modern television production has diverged from the "classic" mode of bar sheet animation timing. If the relation of the musical score to the animation is not critical, or if the animation is a short one, it's possible to dispense with the bar sheets and either note the timing on the story sketches or go directly to the exposure sheets (more about exposure sheets later). This has become standard practice for television cartoon production, where most of the responsibility for the animation's timing resides with the sheet timer. The timer's influence on the finished animation is similar to that of the film editor in live action: The director may be the front man, but the timer or editor can make or break the finished product. Later in this chapter, you'll learn to use exposure sheets, but for now let's stick to the classic methods and work with bar sheets first.

Timing from Sound

For any approach that includes voice or sound effects, you are going to need timing information to help build your bar sheets. If you have recorded dialogue, you should have several takes of each line from the script. Extracting timing information from these takes is called *sentence measurement*. In addition to extracting the amount of time each line of dialogue takes, you need to note the interval between the line being measured and both the preceding line and the following line.

One way to do sentence measurement is to digitize each usable take from the recording session, then open up the digitized files in a sound editor. It's fairly simple, then, to note the time of each sentence. It's a good idea to do the same for any sound effects you plan to use. If you will be matching action to the sounds, it's essential. Exactly how you organize this information depends on your working style. For a short piece with a small production team, you can get by with hand-written notes. For a longer production with a larger team, you may need to type it all into a spreadsheet with session, take, time, intervals, clip file name, and comments organized in separate columns. This might be overkill on small projects, but it can save you a lot of hassle on big ones by enabling you to sort and search for just the right clip. Again, you should practice using professional-level tools on your personal projects to prepare for using them on a real job.

If you are using your own demo reel materials for the projects in this book, you should complete the sentence measurements for your sound files before you go any further.

Timing from Scratch

If you are animating a sequence with no sound effects, musical, or vocal timing guidelines, you will have to wing it. That is, you'll have to estimate each action's timing to the best of your ability. In the past, veteran animators became masters at this, partly through necessity. Management pressures at some studios dictated the precise length of animated shorts, and directors quickly learned to time an animation exactly to the frame. Similar pressures still exist today in advertising and television, but there is a lot more slack in independent and feature-length productions. You can develop your ability to time actions accurately by working through the projects in Part V of this book.

Professional animators time their work at 24 frames per second (fps), the *frame rate* of standard 35mm motion picture film. NTSC video runs at 29.97 (usually rounded to 30) fps, PAL video at 25fps, and game or multimedia animations at anywhere from 6 to 30fps. Even if you plan to work entirely in video or multimedia formats, you should learn and practice timing at 24fps. All television and film animation is done on film at 24fps. The repertoire of most experienced animators and timers for a given move (for example, snap the arm up in 4 frames, then cushion for 8 frames) is learned for 24fps, and it is difficult and counterproductive to relearn or translate this hard-won experience into 30fps timing. Also, many people who intend to eventually transfer animation to film, or who are using video until the film is ready to be transferred, animate at 24fps.

You can convert 24fps footage to 30fps by using a process called *3:2 pulldown*. This conversion allows the footage to retain the appearance that it was of footage originally shot on film. In the opinion of most television viewers, 3:2 pulldown conversion looks superior to video originally shot at 30fps, although no one seems to have an authoritative explanation. The effect of 3:2 pulldown on animation timing is considered negligible and can't really be detected by viewing animation in realtime. In summary, there are several good reasons to animate at 24fps and no good reason not to.

When you're learning to time action, use any technique that helps. I recommend acting the actions out and using a stopwatch to time them. Repeat each action until you are satisfied with your performance, then take three more timings and average them to get your working time.

You should modify the timing of your characters' actions based on the style of the animation and the character whose role you are acting out. Typically, caricatures or cartoons move much more rapidly than real-world creatures, with a great deal of snap and exaggerated acceleration and deceleration. On the other hand, if you are animating Gulliver among the Brobdingnagians, the hapless adventurer should move at a normal pace while his giant captors move as ponderously as elephants.

Other useful tools for acting out timing include a videotape recorder and camera with a SMPTE timecode display, a laser disk player and a collection of disks with appropriate action sequences, and a metronome (for you traditionalists). There are special stopwatches that measure in frames; if you will be doing this a lot, consider acquiring one. Several animation supply houses carry them, including Cartoon Colour, and as of this writing they cost about $140.

Cartoon Colour
9024 Lindblade St.
Culver City, CA 90232
(800) 523-3665

A much less expensive stopwatch alternative is ToonTimer, a freeware program written by Wesley Grandmont III. This program enables you to use the left mouse button like a stopwatch control, supports most timecodes, simulates a metronome, and performs frame calculations. This is a very handy tool, and I highly recommend it. The zip archive for ToonTimer version 2 is included in the Chapter 4 directory of this book's CD-ROM. You can get updated information, download revised versions, and contact ToonTimer's creator through his Web site at **www.crosswinds.net/~wes3/TOON.html.**

PROJECT 4.1 Timing the Sketches

This project gives you some practice at rough timing story sketches. You will use the complete rough timing to assemble the story reel, the next step in revising and "tightening up" the timing of your film.

To practice timing story sketches, follow these steps:

1. Beg, borrow, download, or otherwise acquire access to a stopwatch or other timing device. Use a 24fps device if at all possible.

2. Act out each shot in the sample storyboards. Repeat each action at least three times. Record the time for each action.

3. Average the performances to give a working time for each action.

4. If necessary, convert the working time to frames at 24fps. This is where timers designed for 24fps can save you a lot of bother.

5. Note the working time, in frames, in the margin of the page next to each story sketch.

Repeat this project with your own storyboards if you have any. Practice your sketch timing at every opportunity. This hones your sense of timing for actions and contributes to your abilities as an animator. As mentioned earlier, sheet timers in television production sometimes have more influence on the final animation than the director.

So, how do you know if your timings are any good? One way to check them is to make a *story reel.*

The Story Reel

A story reel is a motion picture assembled using the story sketches. This is sometimes called a Leica reel, after the camera commonly used to produce it. Each sketch is held on screen for the exact length of time the action depicted is supposed to take. No illusion of motion is created, but the overall timing and shot flow of the animation becomes obvious.

> *"Ideally, you want to complete the storyboards, then have it all on a story reel before you even start production."*
>
> —Kathleen Gavin, coproducer, Nightmare Before Christmas

Fortunately, modern technology has made the task of assembling a story reel almost trivial. The first requirement is to convert the story sketches to electronic image files. You can do this with a scanner, a video camera and digitizer, or my favorite low-tech approach, a fax machine!

If you are strapped for cash and don't have access to a scanner, a cheap used fax machine can be just what the doctor ordered. There are a lot of old fax machines out there designed to print on the slick, expensive thermal paper that everybody hates. These machines are usually retired as quickly as possible, and you may even be able to pick one up for free. The other side of this technique is the fact that most machines capable of running LightWave include a fax modem as standard equipment. The trick that makes this possible is that you can hook a fax machine directly into your fax modem without tying up your phone line. Just drop your sketches in the hopper, tell your fax software to pick up, and press the fax machine's send button. Presto, you've got scanned sketches in your computer! The disadvantages to this technique are that the resolution on fax machines is around 200 dpi, and you still have to translate or export the page images from your fax software to an image format that LightWave can load as a background.

PROJECT 4.2   Checking Your Rough Timing with a Silent Story Reel

This project puts your rough timing into a form that you (and others) can readily critique and revise. The story reel is an important development tool throughout the rest of your film's production, and knowing how to build and edit your reel is a valuable skill. You will find digitized story sketches in TIFF format in the Chapter 3 directory on this book's CD-ROM. Use them for this project.

To complete this project, follow these steps:

1. Make a duplicate of all the story sketch files in their own directory on your hard drive. You'll need about 13MB of free space.

2. Using the timing notations from Project 4.1, calculate the beginning frame number for each story sketch.

   For example, if the first and second sketches are each to be held for 60 frames and the third is held for 120 frames, the fourth would start at 60+60+120, or frame 240. The easiest way to keep track of this is by using a printing calculator that prints the running total as you add in each sketch's timing.

3. Rename each duplicate story sketch to match the appropriate beginning frame number, for example, Shot0090.tif. You should end up with a numbered sequence of images.

4. In LightWave, open a new scene and click on the Settings tab. Open the Image Editor, click on Load, and select the first image in the sequence you just created. In the Source tab, change Image Type to Sequence. Close the Image Editor.

5. Set the number of frames in the scene equal to (or slightly greater than) the total of the story sketch times.

6. Click on the Compositing button to open the Effects panel with the Compositing tab selected. Set Background Image to the image sequence you loaded in Step 4. Close the Effects panel.

7. Choose Render Options from the Render pop-up menu. In the Render Options panel, select the Output Files tab. Choose a directory, file name, and format for the animation you are about to render.

8. In the Rendering tab, set Render Mode to Wireframe. This is the fastest rendering option, but it will still show the background image sequence. Close the Render Options panel.

9. Save the scene file as Story.lws. Render the animation.

Make sure you've got plenty of disk space available. Even though the sketches mostly have very small *deltas* (changes in pixel values between successive frames), most video compression algorithms are not very efficient with this sort of file.

This approach is adequate only for a really quick timing check because it has no provision for music or other sound tracks. However, it's handy, quick, and doesn't require any software besides LightWave.

Re-Timing the Story Reel for Sound

You should now have a rough silent story reel based on your first timing. Before you go any further in production, you need to refine the timing of your story reel to more closely match the sound track. This is another stage where inexpensive changes can be made before proceeding to a level where changes are more expensive and time-consuming.

Bar sheets are the next level of detail, building up from the rough sketch timing toward the finished exposure sheet timing. If your animation is very short or has few sound sync hits, you can skip the bar sheets and go straight to the exposure sheets. If your animation is longer than a few bars of music, or if you need to animate many actions to match the sound track, bar sheets are a useful step between the storyboards and the exposure sheets. It's easier to step back and get an overall look at your film's timing when it's laid out on bar sheets. Exposure sheets only cover a few seconds per sheet, but a bar sheet can cover a minute per sheet or more.

PROJECT 4.3 Writing Up Your Bar Sheets

The purpose of this project is to create bar sheets from your demo reel storyboards:

1. First, get some blank bar sheets or draw up your own. Set the space between bar lines equal to 12 frames.

   This gives you one-half second per measure at standard film speed of 24fps. This is arbitrary, but I like it because it gets an adequate amount of animation onto a single sheet while leaving room for a moderate amount of scribbled notes.

2. Mark the important accents, especially any beats the composer needs to match. Footsteps, strong actions, starts or peaks of sounds, and dialogue accents should all be noted. Refer to Figure 4.1 for an example of a filled-in bar sheet.

3. From each accent, use the sentence measurements you performed earlier to arrange the boundaries of the prerecorded sound effects and dialogue.

   This should immediately show any glaring inconsistencies, like a seven-second speech that is supposed to match an action timed for five seconds or an originally brief interval between sentences that now stretches interminably.

4. Interpolate minor actions and accents in between the major ones.

As you will do later with the actual animation, work from the most important element down to the least significant. The important actions have to be timed to certain frames or musical hits; the less-important actions can slide around the bar sheets more without adversely affecting the story.

Depending on the approach you are taking to coordinating sound and music, you may want your composer or other musical talent to have a hand in developing the bar sheets.

When the bar sheets are complete, you are ready to add sound to the story reel.

Checking Your Plan: The Story Reel with Sound

For a better idea of how your film is progressing and to assist in making various production decisions, you will want to make a more complete story reel. This requires an almost complete set of sound tracks, including voices, music, and sound effects. You will also need the completed bar sheets and digitized story sketches.

Sound track WAV files created to accompany the sample storyboard are included in the Chapter 4 directory on this book's CD-ROM. These include sound effects, voice tracks, and original music and are Copyright © 1996-2000 Patrick Q. Kelly. If you use any part of these files in a production for profit or public display, you must contact him at **PQKelly@aol.com** or at the following address for permission:

509 Division St.
Madison, WI 53704

If you use these files in a nonprofit demo reel, your end credits must include the Musicopy.iff, Music.iff, and Foley.iff images (or equivalent wording) from the Chapter 19 directory on the CD-ROM. You must also send the copyright holder a courtesy copy of the demo reel.

For animations with few critical sound hits, you can add sound to the story reel within LightWave. However, there are limits to the rendering and playback of a sound story reel that make it inefficient for fine-tuning sound sync.

Adding Sound to the Story Reel in LightWave

The goal of this project is to add a single WAV sound track to the silent story reel you created in Project 4.2, using LightWave's built-in audio and Preview features:

1. Using whatever sound editor you prefer, assemble the sound track into a single WAV file. If you want to use your own audio files rather than the sample ones provided, you should assemble your sounds to match the timing of your bar sheets.

   For timing purposes, you don't need stereo or even high-quality sampling. For fastest play-back and fewest sync problems in LightWave, you should create a version of the sound track that is mono, 8-bit, and sampled at 11kHz. As long as you don't change the length of the audio clip, you will be able to substitute the original high-quality audio clip for the final output.

2. In LightWave, load the Story.lws scene file you saved from Project 4.2.

3. Open the Scene Editor.

4. Choose the Audio pop-up menu and select Load Audio.

5. Choose the WAV file you assembled in Step 1.

   The frame slider under the viewports will display a purple waveform, showing a very low-resolution sampling (about 2 samples per frame) of the loaded WAV file.

6. Click on the play button and watch the playback while listening to the sound track.

   Synchronized audio playback in Layout is limited primarily by the screen redraw. If your redraw rate drops below the frame rate, the audio playback will stop until the screen catches up. The slower the redraw, the more stops and starts you will hear in the audio playback. A slow system will produce a stutter instead of clean sound. If you have a good graphics accelerator card and can usually get 24fps or better playback, you shouldn't have much of a problem with synced audio playback.

   If you are having dropouts or sync problems during playback, try reducing the size of the Layout window to lighten the screen redraw load. In general, you should be attempting to sync only a few parameters at a time, so use a single viewport, zoom the viewport in tight on the parameters you're animating, and reduce the size of the Layout window as much as possible. The minimum 800×600 resolution is still plenty of room if you apportion it wisely.

7. Stop the playback.

   One way to get better audio sync is to create a Preview. Because a Preview is rendered, all the background loading and calculation is done and will not interfere during playback. LightWave also enables you to save a rendered Preview as an AVI file. One drawback to this is that the Preview resolution will be the viewport resolution rather than the Camera resolution, so you have to eyeball the viewport size rather than type in exact numbers. If the resolution of a saved Preview AVI is important, you'll need to use trial and error to get precisely the dimensions you want.

8. Make a Preview.

My personal preference for Preview Options is for uncompressed AVIs. These render slightly faster and produce the best image quality. If I need a smaller file size or a particular compression codec, I can always run the uncompressed AVI through another program.

9. Play back the Preview. The sound playback should be noticeably better.

Are all the sounds synchronized correctly? Does the story reel "read" well? Does it give you a better idea of the effect of timing on how the story reads? Is there anything you want to change?

The catch to this process is that the combination of the low sampling resolution of LightWave's waveform display and the choppy audio playback makes it difficult to evaluate and modify the timing of the story sketches. If your system is fast enough, you can tweak the timing by simply renumbering the background image files as you did in Project 4.2 and then creating another Preview. However, retiming the story sketches is still a lot easier than reanimating finished sequences. That's why story reels are an integral part of the work flow for most animators. It's standard procedure because it pays off.

10. Save the Preview as Story.avi.

When you start rendering finished image sequences, you can selectively substitute them for the corresponding story sketches and make an updated story reel. This way, the movie fills out as you make progress, and at any time you can view the whole thing. It's a wonderful feeling to watch your creative efforts grow this way.

If you need a more interactive and accurate way to adjust the timing of your story reel, you may want to use an editing program like Adobe Premiere.

PROJECT 4.5   Adding Sound to the Story Reel in Premiere

This project is written for Adobe Premiere 4.2. Other compositing and editing software may be usable if it has similar functions. You'll be assembling the sound clips, story sketches, and music to match the timing you've written up in your bar sheets. If you are using a different editing software, read through these instructions, then consult your software's user or reference manuals to learn how to duplicate this process.

To complete this project, follow these steps:

1. Start Premiere. Choose the Presentation-160×120 Preset for the new project. Set the timebase to 24fps.

The Project, Info, Preview, Construction, and Transitions windows will appear. You can immediately close the Transitions window because you won't be using any transitions for this project and there's no sense in cluttering your workspace.

2. Choose the File|Import|File option, or press Ctrl+I. The Import dialog box appears.

3. Drag-select all the story sketch TIFF files from the Chapter 3 directory on this book's CD-ROM. Click on Open to import the images.

   The story sketch files appear in the Project window as thumbnails (or smaller versions of images) that are more suitable for on-screen viewing.

4. Repeat Step 3 for the sound effects, voice tracks, and music tracks, as appropriate. The sound files also appear in the Project window, but as audio waveform thumbnails.

   So far, so good. Now you need to set the duration of each story sketch. Premiere has a default setting of one second for still images, which is probably too short for any of the shots from the sample storyboards.

5. Double-click on the first story sketch in the Project window. The Clip window opens. Click on the Duration button at the lower left. The Duration dialog box appears.

6. Enter a duration for the first sketch. This should be equal to the number of frames penciled in the sketch margin from Project 4.1.

7. Click on OK and close the Clip window. Double-click on the next sketch in the Project window.

8. Repeat the process until you have set the duration for each sketch. Save the project with an appropriate name.

9. Drag the first story sketch from the Project window to the top row of the Construction window. Drag the sketch to the left until it is flush with the first frame of the time ruler.

10. Drag the next story sketch from the Project window to the top row of the Construction window. Drag the sketch to the left until it is flush with the right edge of the preceding frame.

    The duration you set for each sketch automatically sets the timing for the whole story reel.

11. Repeat until all the sketches are loaded in the Construction window. Save the project again.

    At this point, you have the same results you had when you rendered a sequence of background images in Project 4.2. The next step adds synchronized sound.

12. Drag the first sound clip from the Project window to the top track of the Audio part of the Construction window. Drag it left or right until it matches the timing laid out in the bar sheets.

13. Repeat Step 12 for the rest of the sound clips. If the timing marked in the bar sheets indicates that two or more sounds will overlap, position one of the overlapping sound clips in a lower track.

    Premiere can handle up to 99 audio tracks at once, so you shouldn't have any problems with overloading.

14. When everything is set up according to the bar sheets, save the project again. Choose Make|Make Movie. The Make Movie dialog box appears. Choose the directory and file name for the movie, then click on the Output Options button.

15. Set the options to create a movie that can play back at full 24fps on your system. Click on OK, then repeat with the Compression options. Click on OK again.

    This may limit you to a 160×120 preview, or you may be using a monster machine that can handle full-screen 24fps playback with stereo sound and lossless compression. Use whatever works—this is just for a working preview!

16. Click on OK in the Make Movie dialog box to begin compiling the story reel. When it's complete, open and play it.

    Are all the sounds synchronized correctly? Does the story reel "read" well? Does it give you a better idea of the effect of timing on how the story reads? Is there anything you want to change? You can adjust the timing of sounds by dragging them left and right in the audio tracks. Adjusting the timing of the individual sketches is a little trickier.

17. In Adobe Premiere, double-click on the thumbnail you want to retime in the Construction window. The Clip window appears.

18. Enter a revised duration for the sketch and click on OK.

19. Select and drag the thumbnails to either side of the retimed clip, if necessary, until they are all flush again.

Retiming the story sketches is a lot easier than reanimating finished sequences, isn't it? That's why story reels are an integral part of the work flow for most animators. It's standard procedure because it pays off.

When you start rendering finished animation, you can selectively substitute image sequences or AVIs for the corresponding story sketches and recompile the movie.

 ## Making Your Own Story Reel

4.6 Repeat Project 4.4 or 4.5, but this time use your own story sketches, bar sheets, and sound files.

Synchronizing Sound

You can add synchronized sound effects to an animation by noting where a sound should start and pasting the appropriate sound file into a sound track at that frame.

PROJECT 4.7   Syncing a Sound Effect to an Animation in Premiere

This project syncs a simple "boing" sound (Boing.wav) to an animation of a vibrating desk lamp (Boing.avi). Both files can be found in the Chapter 4 directory on this book's CD-ROM. Again, most audiovisual editing software can handle a simple edit like this. Consult your software's manuals for specific procedures.

To sync a sound effect to an animation in Premiere, follow these steps:

1. Start Premiere. Choose the Preset and Timebase for the new project.

2. Choose File|Import|File, or press Ctrl+I. The Import dialog box appears.

3. Select the Boing.avi file. Click on OK. The AVI file appears in the Project window as a thumbnail.

4. Choose File|Import|File again. Select the Boing.wav sound clip and click on OK. The sound file appears in the Project window. Note the spike at the beginning of the waveform.

5. Drag Boing.avi from the Project window to the top row of the Construction window. Drag the thumbnail to the left until it is flush with the first frame of the time ruler.

6. Drag the Boing.wav sound clip from the Project window to the top track of the Audio part of the Construction window.

7. Watch the Preview window as you drag the pointer to find the exact frame where the desk lamp is first hit. This is where the sound of the impact should also occur.

8. Slide the WAV file along the Audio track until the boing spike lines up with the frame where the desk lamp is hit.

9. Compile the animation. When it's complete, play it back.

Sometimes it's a good idea to add a 2- or 3-frame delay from a visual cue to the matching sound. For some reason, this "reads" better with most audiences. This is known as slipping the track. It's usually best to wait until the entire track is complete and locked and then slip the whole track rather than slip each sound clip individually.

You can also synchronize a longer sound effect within an animation. Simply note where a significant point (preferably a peak in the waveform) in the sound should appear in the animation and slide the sound file in Premiere's audio track until the chosen point lines up with the correct frame number. For example, a long slide-whistle sound ending in a splat, and immediately followed by clanking and crashing, could quickly be synchronized by the initial spike in the waveform at the beginning of the splat.

If it's necessary to precisely position a sound, use the time unit selector at the bottom of the Construction window to zoom in on the frames in question. This will make it much easier to match the sound to a particular frame.

As you learned earlier in this chapter, LightWave can also load sound files directly, which can help you synchronize animation, but the displayed waveform is very small and does not show details well. If you really need to see the waveform, Project 4.8 shows a trick you can use to fake it.

PROJECT 4.8 Faking the Wave

The goal of this project is to bring a higher-resolution sound track waveform into LightWave so it will be easier for you to sync events to the sound track. One way to do this is to create an object in the shape of the waveform:

1. Take screenshots of the audio file you want to import. In your image processing software, crop the screenshots to just the waveform, plus any significant reference marks. Make a note of the total length of the waveform, in frames at your chosen frame rate.

2. Assemble the screenshots into a continuous horizontal image and save it in Encapsulated Postscript format, EPSF.

3. In Modeler, use the EPSF_Loader plug-in to import the EPSF file and turn it into an object. Save the object and close Modeler.

4. In Layout, add the new object to the scene you want to sync to the sound. Make the object invisible to the Camera, rays, shadows, and fog so it won't appear at all in any rendering.

   It's usually best to parent the waveform object to the Camera so the waveform is always visible in the same place in the camera view window. I like to put the waveform along the bottom edge of the camera view, just high enough to read clearly while leaving most of the scene visible. If you are using the television-safe guides, you can generally fit the waveform object into the lower cutoff area.

   You may find it helpful to add a very small primitive triangle or cone to the scene, centered in the camera view and positioned as a pointer at the top edge of the waveform.

5. Set a keyframe for the waveform object's position so the left edge of the waveform is centered in the camera view (or aligned with the pointer object) in frame 0.

6. Set a keyframe for the waveform's position so the right edge of the waveform is centered in the camera view (or aligned with the pointer object) in the last frame of the scene.

This should move the waveform through the scene in sync with the current frame. Because LightWave is optimized to give the best screen redraw speed rather than the best audio playback speed, this approach can be faster and more reliable than trying to sync to an audio file as in Project 4.4.

Once you've mastered synchronizing your animations to simple sounds, you are ready to tackle the more complex tasks of lip sync.

Exposure Sheets

Syncing a few actions to a well-spaced handful of sound cues is relatively straightforward, and you might be able to get away with only using the bar sheets. Lip sync, however, requires you to animate the appropriate mouth and face shape to match the dialogue track within a single frame of dead-on. This is a lot more complicated, with many more opportunities for error. If you want to make as few mistakes as possible, you should plan your lip sync work using an *exposure sheet*. An exposure sheet is a table that is laid out with a line for each frame and a column for each kind of information needed to plan and track the production of the animation.

The exposure sheet, or *x-sheet*, tracks the frame-by-frame information needed by the animator. For the animator, and to a lesser degree the technical director, the exposure sheets are crucial. These sheets are an order of magnitude more detailed than the bar sheets and are therefore not as useful to most other members of the production team. There's just too much information! Most of the team will be working in units of a complete shot, or of tens of seconds at least. An exposure sheet gets pretty crowded if it contains as much as three seconds' worth of information.

Different production houses use different forms for exposure sheets. I have made up a document that I like to use for character animation with LightWave and included it in the Chapter 4 directory on this book's CD-ROM in Microsoft Word (Xsheet24.doc) and Adobe Acrobat (X_sheet.pdf) formats. Several filled-in examples are printed at the end of this chapter.

To fill in your own exposure sheets, you can print multiple copies from the Word or Acrobat files and pencil in all your notes and changes. This is helpful when you need to make revisions later on because you can easily erase the pencil marks while leaving the printed form intact.

The sheets should be labeled with enough information to keep them in order and to know who is responsible for any changes to their contents. At a minimum, the project name, the animator's name, and the scene number should be written in. Because most scenes will run longer than three seconds, the sheet number is also a requirement. It is advisable to write in the sheet numbers as "1 of 4," "2 of 4," etc., so you know how many sheets should be attached.

The sample exposure sheet is long enough to hold 90 frames, or 3 seconds of NTSC video, on each page. The first column of the sheet contains a waveform of the audio track. A little later, we'll go through the steps needed to capture these waveform images.

The second column is titled *PH* for phoneme. Here, the breakdown editor will write in the phonetic spelling of the sound being pronounced and mark duration and transitions as well. This process is called *track analysis*, and it takes a good deal of practice.

The next column, *DIALOG*, is for the dialogue and sound effects from the script. These words are written with their usual spellings and begin on the frame when the word or sound begins.

The fourth column is labeled *ACTION*. This is where the director or their assistant writes in a description of the action that must take place during the indicated frames. A door slamming, for instance, requires the complete closure of the door to be written at the frame where the sound of the slam begins.

The column labeled *SMPTE* is for the convenience of those who are synchronizing their work to film or video footage. Some foley (sound effects) artists or composers will also work with *SMPTE timecodes*, which usually appear as hours, minutes, seconds, and frames in the format HH:MM:SS:FF.

The next column, *FRAME*, is intended for the frame count of this specific scene or shot. Note that the numbering begins with frame one, and only the last digit is preprinted in the form. You can pencil in your own leading digits; typically, only the tens line is actually filled in.

As with all LightWave animation, it is safest if you establish all your baseline keyframes in frame 0 but do not render it. This prevents a number of problems. The exposure sheet begins with frame 1 so the beginning of the audio track can simply be matched to the first frame of the rendered animation for perfect sync.

The *BACKGROUND* column provides a place for you to note any image sequences or stills that are to be used as backdrops. This is especially useful for compositing with other animations, digitized video sequences, or matched stills.

The last column, *CAMERA*, is a place to put your notes about special camera, post-processing plug-in, or compositing effects. In traditional animation, this information was used by the camera operator. You should list here any changes in lens size or other parameters for camera zooms, tracking, and pans.

Exposure sheets differ from studio to studio, and you may want to make your own.

Making Your Own Exposure Sheets

The next project shows you how to make exposure sheets like those included on the CD-ROM and how to customize x-sheets for your particular needs and preferences.

Before you get started, take a look at the sample exposure sheets at the end of this chapter. Then ask yourself the following questions:

- How much of that information will you want to have in your own sheets?

- What information do you need to track that doesn't appear here?

- How many frames do you need to fit on a single sheet?

- How small can you read and write?

- What size paper can your printer handle?

These are all questions you should have definite answers to before you start building your own exposure sheet.

Making a Custom Exposure Sheet in Microsoft Word

PROJECT 4.9

These instructions are specific to Microsoft Word 6, but the principles can be adapted to any word processor or spreadsheet manager that allows you to embed linked graphics:

1. Open a new document.

2. Choose File|Page Setup. The Page Setup dialog box appears, as shown in Figure 4.2.

   You will want to use as much of each page as possible, and you don't need wide margins because your notes are supposed to fit in the exposure sheet itself.

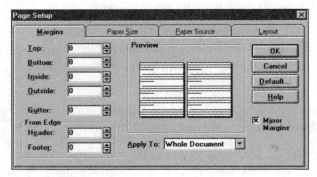

Figure 4.2
Page Setup dialog box with all margins set to 0.

3. Set all the margins to 0 and click on OK. A Warning dialog box gives you the option to use the Fix function. This automatically sets the page margins to the maximum printing area for your printer. Click on the Fix button.

   Because there are many kinds of printers, there is no one set of dimensions guaranteed to work with all systems. This procedure finds the best dimensions for your particular system.

4. The margins will have changed to the minimum. Depending on your printer, the left margin may be less than 1/2 inch. Change the left margin to at least 0.5 if you want to hole-punch your exposure sheets for a loose-leaf binder. When you are done, click on the OK button.

   I tend to design all my working papers with a loose-leaf binder punch in mind. For most purposes, it's one of the better ways of keeping projects organized. The exception is original artwork, which no one in their right mind would punch holes through. I keep those items in binder-punched document envelopes.

5. Choose Edit|Select All. You want the next few steps to affect the entire document.

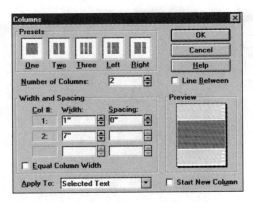

Figure 4.3
Columns dialog box with all settings made.

6. Choose Format|Columns. The Columns dialog box appears, as shown in Figure 4.3.

7. Choose 2 columns and turn off Equal Column Width. Set the first column to 1-inch wide with 0 spacing. The second column defaults to the remainder of the print area. Make a note of the second column's width. Click on OK.

   The first column will be used for the waveform image file. The second column will hold the table that organizes the rest of the exposure sheet's information.

8. Insert 3 carriage returns. After the second carriage return, choose Insert|Frame.

   You'll be positioning a frame to hold the waveform image. It's not absolutely critical, but it makes the printed sheet look a little neater.

9. The cursor changes to the Frame crosshair. This tells you the program is ready for you to draw the frame. Click and hold in the upper-left corner of the first column and drag down and to the right, approximately the width of the first column. Release, and the new frame will be drawn in (see Figure 4.4).

10. Choose Format|Frame. The Frame dialog box appears.

11. In the Horizontal portion of the Frame dialog box, set Position to Left, Relative To to Margin, and Distance From Text to 0". In the Vertical portion, set Position to 0", Relative To to Paragraph, and Distance From Text to 0" and select the Move With Text checkbox. In the Size portion, set Width to Exactly and 0.95 and set Height to Exactly and 9.0" (see Figure 4.5). Click on OK.

   Some of these settings will be changed later, but set them to these values for now. The goal is to have the frame aligned with the table as closely as possible, as if the waveform were actually printed as part of the table.

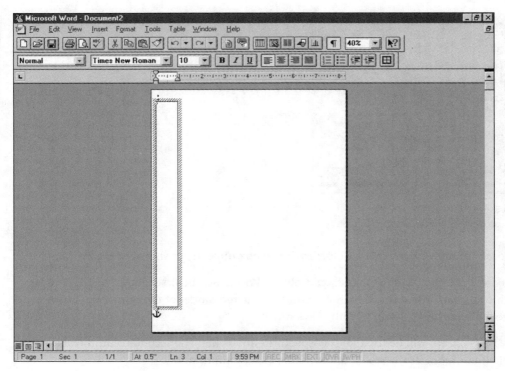

Figure 4.4
A new frame is added.

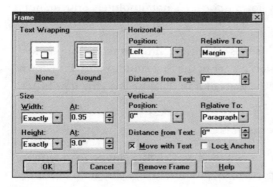

Figure 4.5
Frame format settings.

12. Position the cursor below the frame. Choose Insert|Break, then choose Column Break. Click on OK.

    This leaves the frame in the first column and starts the next column, where you'll be putting the table.

13. At the last paragraph mark, choose Table|Insert Table.

   Did you figure out how many columns you'd need before you started these instructions? If not, stop and get a definite answer now or you'll be wasting your time.

14. Set the number of columns and rows you want, then click on the AutoFormat button. The AutoFormat Table dialog box appears.

   I like to get an even 3 seconds of animation on a single x-sheet, so 72 rows for film or 90 for 30fps video is a good setting.

15. From the Formats list, select Grid1. Click on OK.

   This will draw a simple grid of fine lines around each cell of the table. This is easy to read and doesn't take up much space. You can choose something fancier if you like, but remember that form should follow function.

16. Remember the width of the second column (from Step 7)? Calculate the total width of the second column divided by the number of columns in the table. Set the table column width to this figure. You should have something like the settings shown in Figure 4.6. Click on OK.

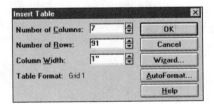

Figure 4.6
Table settings.

17. Just a few more tweaks for the table now. Choose Table|Select Table. Change the table font to Arial 7 point, or larger if you can fit it in; 7 point is the largest that would fit in a 91-row, 7-column table on standard paper for my system.

18. Choose Table|Cell Height & Width. Set Row Height to Exactly 7 point and leave Column Width to the value you set earlier, but set the space between columns to 0.1. Click on OK.

19. Select the top row and click on the Center toolbar button. This centers the labels for the columns. Again, this is a personal preference; I think it's more legible and looks more professional.

20. Select the top cell of the first column. Type the column label. Repeat for the other columns. I prefer making the column labels all caps; with 7-point font, you need all the help you can get!

21. Select the column for the frame numbers, then click on the Align Right toolbar button. This keeps the last digits of the frame numbers aligned. Select the top cell, containing the column label, and reset it to Center.

22. In the second row of the FRAMES column (assuming you have one), type "1". Type "2" in the third row and so on up to "0" in the 11th row. Select the 10 cells you just filled in and copy them. Select the next 10 empty cells and paste the copied values into them. Repeat until all the cells in the FRAMES column are filled in.

    This preprints the last digit of each frame for you. You have only to pencil in the tens and hundreds digits. It is usually acceptable to pencil in the extra digits just at the frames ending in 0, as in the samples provided at the end of this chapter.

23. Drag each of the column markers in the ruler to set the width of the columns. Leave extra space for the columns in which you will have to write words; leave less space if only numbers are needed, as shown in Figure 4.7.

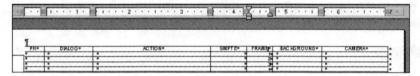

Figure 4.7
Setting the table column margins.

24. Move the cursor to the top of the second column of the page, above the table. Type the sheet information labels and underscored blanks. Select the entire line and change the font to a readable style and size. I prefer Arial 10 point, as shown in the examples. Add a carriage return after the blanks to separate them from the table (see Figure 4.8).

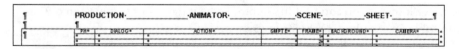

Figure 4.8
Sheet information blanks.

The types of information you use to track your projects will depend on the kind of work you do. If you are an independent or a student, you may need little more than your name, the project, and the scene and shot. On the other hand, if you are one of several animators working on a long and complex animation project, you may need details like lead animator, technical director, and revision numbers. Here are some examples of information that can be useful for headings in an exposure sheet: producer, director, lead animator, animator, technical director, art director, layout artist, camera operator/rendering supervisor, assistants (various), project, client, agency, account or billing number, scene, shot, sheet number, date (start, due, and finish), approvals/checkoffs/initials. And that's the short list!

25. Select the paragraphs above the frame in the first column. Change the font and size to match the changes you just made in the second column.

26. Add another carriage return above the frame. Select the paragraph immediately above the frame, and change the font and size to match the first row of the table. This should bring the top of the frame level with the top of the second row of the table.

27. Type the label "WAVEFORM" in the paragraph above the frame.

    This makes the frame look like an extension of the table because it is now aligned with the other columns and headed in the same style. Now, you're ready to add the waveform image.

28. Click on the inside of the frame to set the cursor. Choose Insert|Picture. The Insert Picture dialog box appears.

    It's a good idea to keep the waveform images in a temporary file directory or a similar location. Generally, the waveform images will be used only once, and there's no need to clutter your system with obsolete images. Because they are so similar, keeping them around can be a definite hazard to your track analysis.

29. Select the waveform image file to paste into the frame. Select the Link To File checkbox. Deselect the Save Picture In Document checkbox (see Figure 4.9). Click on OK.

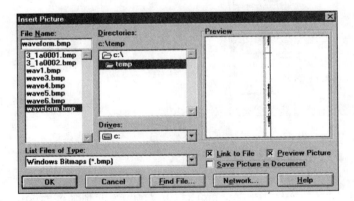

Figure 4.9
Options for inserting the waveform picture.

30. Scroll to the bottom of the page. Select the frame. Drag the bottom of the frame until it is exactly level with the bottom of the table.

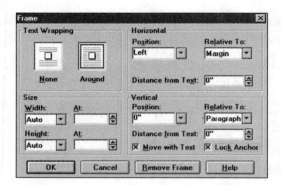

Figure 4.10
Locking the frame anchor.

31. Choose Format|Frame and then select the Lock Anchor checkbox (see Figure 4.10).

    Locking the frame anchor should keep the frame the same size even if the waveform image changes size. This means you should not have to resize the frame or image each time you reload this document.

32. Choose Edit|Links. The Links dialog box appears. Select the Locked checkbox, as shown in Figure 4.11.

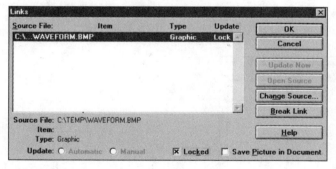

Figure 4.11
Locking the picture link.

    Locking the picture link tells Word to reload the image file every time something happens to either document. This is how the procedures in the next project can produce a stack of exposure sheets—complete with preprinted waveforms—so quickly. It's an example of an appropriate use of computers: automating repetitive work to free up human creative resources.

33. Save the document.

That's it. You are now the proud owner of a brand-new exposure sheet. Go find a track to analyze!

PROJECT 4.10 Track Analysis

This project will show you the basics of track analysis, the craft of breaking out sounds for the animator's exposure sheets.

To begin filling in the exposure sheet, you'll need a clean image of the waveform. It's easy to create one in either the Windows or Mac OS environment. Just open the sound file in an editing program that displays the waveform, take a screenshot, and cut and paste the image of the waveform into an exposure sheet.

Most sound editors can display a waveform. It will be to your advantage if the editor you use can display a timecode or frame count alongside the waveform. My preference is a shareware package called GoldWave. It has a lot of useful tools for sound editing, the waveform ruler is clear and legible, and the screen colors can be customized for the best printing contrast. The only downside is that the ruler is marked in decimal units of time rather than frames. You can find the zip archive for GoldWave version 4.16 in the Chapter 4 directory of this book's CD-ROM. The GoldWave home page (**www.goldwave.com**) contains the latest information and updates for GoldWave. GoldWave and its documentation are copyright © 1993-2000 by Chris S. Craig, all rights reserved. GoldWave is a trademark of Chris S. Craig. Questions, comments, and suggestions are welcome. You can send them via email to **chris3@cs.mun.ca** and regular mail to the following address:

Chris Craig
P.O. Box 51
St. John's, NF
Canada A1C 5H5

This project requires that you keep Word, Photoshop or other graphics software, and your sound editor open at the same time. This requires a significant amount of memory. If you can't keep all the programs open at once, you will have to open and close them in turn for each 3-second waveform image—a tedious business, at best.

For this project, you'll be using a digitized sample from a speech by Sir Winston Churchill, Thishour.wav, which you can find in the Chapter 4 directory on this book's CD-ROM.

1. Copy the sample waveform image file Waveform.bmp from the Chapter 4 directory on this book's CD-ROM to your C:\Temp directory. The exposure sheet document has a built-in link to that file and path. If you do not have a C: drive, you may have to edit the exposure sheet to change the link path.

2. Open Thishour.wav in the sound editor.

3. Adjust the waveform display for full screen-width resolution of a 3-second selection, as in Figure 4.12.

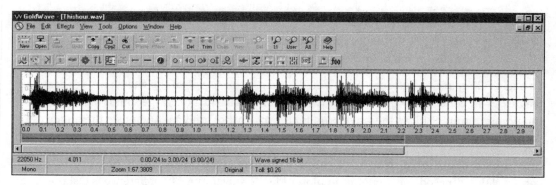

Figure 4.12
GoldWave sound editor showing Thishour.wav.

4. Start Photoshop. (If you use different graphics software, make sure it can paste from the system clipboard.)

5. Open X_sheet.doc in Microsoft Word. Note whether the document found the Waveform.bmp image file in the C:\Temp directory. If not, you will have to change the link to the exposure sheet document before proceeding with the rest of the project. To do so, select Edit|Links to call up the Links dialog box. Click on the Change Source button and choose the directory and file name you want to link to. Press Enter or click on OK to return to the exposure sheet. The image you specified appears in the waveform column. You may have to resize it. If you have further difficulties, review Project 4.9.

6. If everything seems to be in order, press Alt+Esc to switch back to the sound editor.

7. Click on the Print Screen button to take a screenshot of the sound editor display.

8. Press Alt+Esc again to switch back to Photoshop.

9. Press Ctrl+N to open a new document. Accept the default values Photoshop suggests (they match the image currently held in the system clipboard).

10. Press Ctrl+V to paste the clipboard contents into the new blank document. Deselect the pasted area.

11. Zoom in, if necessary, to see details. Drag-select the 3-second waveform section you want to paste into the exposure sheet. Make sure you precisely outline the start and stop points. Include the frame numbers if they are displayed. They will be useful later on.

Steps 11 through 14 can be saved as a macro. This saves a great deal of time when you have minutes of audio track digitized and waiting for analysis. It cuts the cut-copy-paste-print cycle down to less than a minute per sheet once you really get rolling.

If you'd like to try it, I've included my own Photoshop macro on this book's CD-ROM, file Waveform.rec.

12. Choose Edit|Crop. This gets rid of everything outside your selection area and resizes the document.

13. Choose Image|Rotate|90 Degrees Clockwise. This changes the waveform image from horizontal to vertical, which is much easier to use in exposure sheets.

14. Choose Mode|Grayscale. This gets rid of stray pixels of odd colors, which can sometimes cause problems with a black-and-white laser printer.

15. Choose File|Save As and type in the file name and path C:\Temp\Waveform.bmp. The system asks if you want to replace the older file with the new one of the same name. Click on Yes.

16. Press Alt+Esc again to switch back to Word. The X_Sheet document has a locked link to the original Waveform.bmp image, so it will automatically update to the one you just saved.

    I set up this exposure sheet for exactly 3 seconds of animation. Make sure each of your drag-selects clips out precisely 3 seconds worth of audio waveform or the sound and the frames won't match up. Note that it will sometimes be necessary to append a small amount of silence to the end of each audio sample to bring it up to the next 3-second mark. It's easier to deal with exact measures than to readjust the size of the pasted-in waveform for each sheet.

17. Click on the Print icon button to print the exposure sheet. Number it immediately—you'll be printing several, and you don't want to get them mixed up.

18. Return to the sound editor and adjust the waveform display for full screen-width resolution of the next 3-second selection.

19. Repeat Steps 6 through 17 until you have all the sound files laid out in a series of exposure sheets. You might want to make photocopies of these sheets, just in case you ruin one.

    You now have the raw materials for the track analysis. The only other tools you may need are more patience, quiet surroundings, sharp pencils, and a good dictionary.

    Track analysis is not really difficult, just painstaking. There are a relatively small number of *phonemes*, or unique sounds, that are used by all spoken human languages. If you are working in only one language, your task is even simpler.

    You can find a pronunciation guide in the front of any good dictionary. This guide will list all the phonemes for the dictionary's language and explain the letters and diacritical marks used in phonetic spelling. I highly recommend keeping a good dictionary like this handy while analyzing vocal tracks; it can save you a lot of time while you are developing your track-reading skills. Until you can rely on those skills, I recommend that you cheat.

20. Make up a copy of the script for the vocal track, double- or even triple-spaced so you can write legibly under or over each word.

21. Look up each word in the dictionary. Copy the phonetic spelling of each word under the normal spelling in the script. Now you know exactly what phonetic symbols you need to write in the PH column of the exposure sheet; all that's left is figuring out exactly where to put them!

What you will be doing next is looking—and listening—for characteristic shapes in the waveform that correspond to phonemes. Human speech is made up mostly of clicks, buzzes, and hisses. For example, a sharp spike—a click—can represent a plosive sound such as "P" or "B". The word "baby" would therefore have two spikes, and you would mark the frames next to those spikes with the letter "B." Buzzing phonemes like "M" or "N" show up as relatively even zigzags with very similar individual waveforms, sustained over a number of frames. A hissing "S" or "C" looks a lot like static, just a little louder.

Rather than go into a rambling theoretical discussion of all the different phonemes and how they are produced, I'm going to encourage you to experiment and develop your own rules. This all goes back to the principles discussed in Part V of this book. You can take someone else's word for it, or you can observe and draw your own conclusions. Observing speech is a wonderful way to lose your preconceptions about how people communicate.

22. Using the sound editor and the sample WAV file, highlight and play back one word at a time. When you have located the actual beginning of a word (which can be difficult when they are slurred together), write the complete word, spelled normally, on the exposure sheet frame where the word starts. Do *not* simply copy from the filled-in exposure sheets at the end of this chapter. You can check your work with it later, but don't look at it now.

23. Find the plosives and clicks. Look for peaks or other sharp changes within the word. Select and play them back until you can identify their start at a particular frame. Mark the frame.

24. Find the buzzes and hisses. These will appear as relatively even areas, drawn out over several frames. Mark the beginning with the appropriate phonetic symbol and draw a short line through the succeeding frames to the end of the phoneme.

25. Find and write in the phonetic symbols for the remaining sounds, which will probably be mostly vowels. They tend to fill in everywhere but the clicks, buzzes, and hisses. They are also the most visible mouth shapes to animate because they are held longer and generally require more facial distortion.

Congratulations! You've completed your first track analysis.

Compare your exposure sheet for Thishour.wav to the exposure sheet at the end of this chapter. Did you differ by more than a frame or two for the beginning of any word? Did you use any different phonetic symbols?

Don't worry about minor differences; this is largely a matter of opinion. People use a variety of dialects and personal speech idiosyncrasies that make insistence on absolute answers in track analysis a moot point. However, if your reading of the track was significantly different, you might want to recheck your work.

PROJECT 4.11 Analyzing Your Own Voice

Repeat Project 4.10, but analyze a sample of your own voice giving a brief dramatic reading. Compare your pronunciation to the phonetic guidelines in the dictionary. What phonetic symbols might you change in the exposure sheet to represent your own speech patterns?

Power Tools for Sound Sync

There are a number of tools available for use with LightWave that automate part of the sound sync process, especially for lip sync. These tools are explained in Chapter 16 because lip sync is only a part of what you can do with them. If you'd like to use these tools for your initial sound sync, jump ahead to Chapter 16, then come back here to finish your track analysis.

PROJECT 4.12 Using Your Exposure Sheets

Now that you've got the basics of track analysis, you're ready to make up the exposure sheets for your demo reel:

1. If your story depends on synchronized speech, sound effects, or existing music, digitize the sound track and analyze it.

2. Write it all up on the exposure sheets, or use LightWave-compatible sound sync tools as detailed in Chapter 16.

3. Referring only to the exposure sheets, animate a simple action in LightWave to hit the major cues.

4. Load the sound track WAV file into the LightWave scene and create a Preview AVI with sound, as you did in Project 4.4.

5. Play back the Preview.

How close did you get? Was the action convincingly matched to the sound cues? Try slipping the audio track 2 or 3 frames in dubbing it to see if it looks better delayed than with a precise match. Many studios slip the track as a general policy.

If you had trouble, go back over the track analysis projects and see if you can spot what's going wrong. If it's just a matter of a few frames here and there seeming "off," don't worry about it. Your track analysis will improve with practice, as with so many other aspects of animation.

Sample Exposure Sheets

The filled-in exposure sheets document a quote from the "Finest Hour" speech by Sir Winston Churchill (see Figure 4.14; Figure 4.13 shows a blank exposure sheet). A 3-second clip from the speech is digitized in the file Thishour.wav, which you can find in the Chapter 4 directory on this book's CD-ROM. A longer version is in Finesthr.wav. Both are used in lip sync projects in this book.

The shorter quote is "This...was their finest hour."

The full quote is "...so bear ourselves that if the British Empire, and its commonwealth, last for a thousand years, men will still say, 'This...was their finest hour.'"

PRODUCTION ______________ **ANIMATOR** ________ **SCENE** ______ **SHEET** _______

WAVEFORM	PH.	DIALOG	ACTION	SMPTE	FRAME	BACKGROUND	CAMERA
					1		
					2		
					3		
					4		
					5		
					6		
					7		
					8		
					9		
					0		
					1		
					2		
					3		
					4		
					5		
					6		
					7		
					8		
					9		
					0		
					1		
					2		
					3		
					4		
					5		
					6		
					7		
					8		
					9		
					0		
					1		
					2		
					3		
					4		
					5		
					6		
					7		
					8		
					9		
					0		
					1		
					2		
					3		
					4		
					5		
					6		
					7		
					8		
					9		
					0		
					1		
					2		
					3		
					4		
					5		
					6		
					7		
					8		
					9		
					0		
					1		
					2		
					3		
					4		
					5		
					6		
					7		
					8		
					9		
					0		
					1		
					2		
					3		
					4		
					5		
					6		
					7		
					8		
					9		
					0		
					1		
					2		
					3		
					4		
					5		
					6		
					7		
					8		
					9		
					0		

Figure 4.13
Blank exposure sheet.

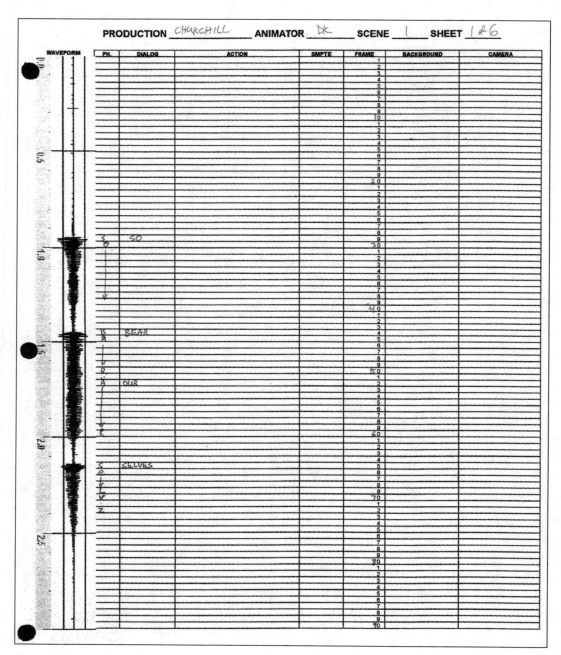

Figure 4.14
Filled exposure sheets.

| PRODUCTION | CHURCHILL | ANIMATOR | DC | SCENE | 1 | SHEET | 2 of 6 |

WAVEFORM	PH.	DIALOG	ACTION	SMPTE	FRAME	BACKGROUND	CAMERA
					91		
					2		
					3		
					4		
					5		
					6		
					7		
					8		
					9		
					100		
					1		
					2		
					3		
					4		
					5		
					6		
	TH	THAT			7		
	A				8		
	T	IT			9		
	I				110		
	T				1		
					2		
					3		
					4		
					5		
	TH	THE			6		
	U				7		
					8		
					9		
					120		
	B	BRITISH			1		
	R				2		
	I				3		
	T				4		
	I				5		
					6		
					7		
	SH				8		
	E	EMPIRE			9		
					130		
					1		
					2		
	M				3		
					4		
					5		
					6		
					7		
	P				8		
	I				9		
	R				140		
					1		
					2		
					3		
					4		
					5		
	R				6		
					7		
					8		
					9		
					150		
					1		
					2		
					3		
					4		
					5		
					6		
					7		
					8		
					9		
					160		
					1		
					2		
					3		
					4		
					5		
					6		
					7		
					8		
					9		
					170		
					1		
	B	AND			2		
	A				3		
	N				4		
	D				5		
	I	IT'S			6		
	T				7		
	S				8		
					9		
					180		

WAVEFORM	PH.	DIALOG	ACTION	SMPTE	FRAME	BACKGROUND	CAMERA
					181		
					2		
					3		
	K	COMMONWEALTH			4		
					5		
	O				6		
					7		
					8		
	M				9		
	S				190		
	N				1		
					2		
					3		
					4		
	W				5		
					6		
	L				7		
					8		
	TH				9		
					200		
					1		
					2		
					3		
					4		
					5		
					6		
					7		
					8		
					9		
					210		
					1		
					2		
					3		
					4		
					5		
					6		
					7		
					8		
					9		
					220		
					1		
					2		
					3		
					4		
					5		
					6		
					7		
					8		
					9		
					230		
	L	LAST			1		
					2		
					3		
	A				4		
					5		
					6		
					7		
					8		
	S				9		
					240		
	T				1		
					2		
					3		
					4		
					5		
					6		
	FR	FOR A			7		
					8		
	A				9		
					250		
					1		
					2		
					3		
					4		
					5		
					6		
					7		
	TH	THOUSAND			8		
					9		
	OU				260		
					1		
					2		
					3		
	Z				4		
					5		
	N				6		
					7		
					8		
	D				9		
					270		

PRODUCTION *Churchill*   ANIMATOR *DK*   SCENE *1*   SHEET *4 of 6*

WAVEFORM	PH.	DIALOG	ACTION	SMPTE	FRAME	BACKGROUND	CAMERA
	Y	YEARS			271		
	E				2		
	A				3		
					4		
					5		
					6		
	R				7		
					8		
	Z				9		
					280		
					1		
					2		
					3		
					4		
					5		
					6		
					7		
					8		
					9		
					290		
					1		
					2		
					3		
					4		
					5		
					6		
					7		
					8		
					9		
					300		
					1		
					2		
					3		
					4		
					5		
					6		
					7		
					8		
					9		
					310		
					1		
					2		
					3		
	M	MEN			4		
	E				5		
					6		
	N				7		
					8		
					9		
	W	WILL			320		
	I				1		
	L				2		
					3		
					4		
					5		
	S				6		
					7		
	T	STILL			8		
	I				9		
					330		
	L				1		
					2		
					3		
	E				4		
					5		
					6		
					7		
					8		
					9		
	S	SAY			340		
					1		
					2		
	A				3		
					4		
					5		
					6		
					7		
					8		
					9		
					350		
					1		
					2		
					3		
					4		
					5		
					6		
					7		
					8		
					9		
					360		

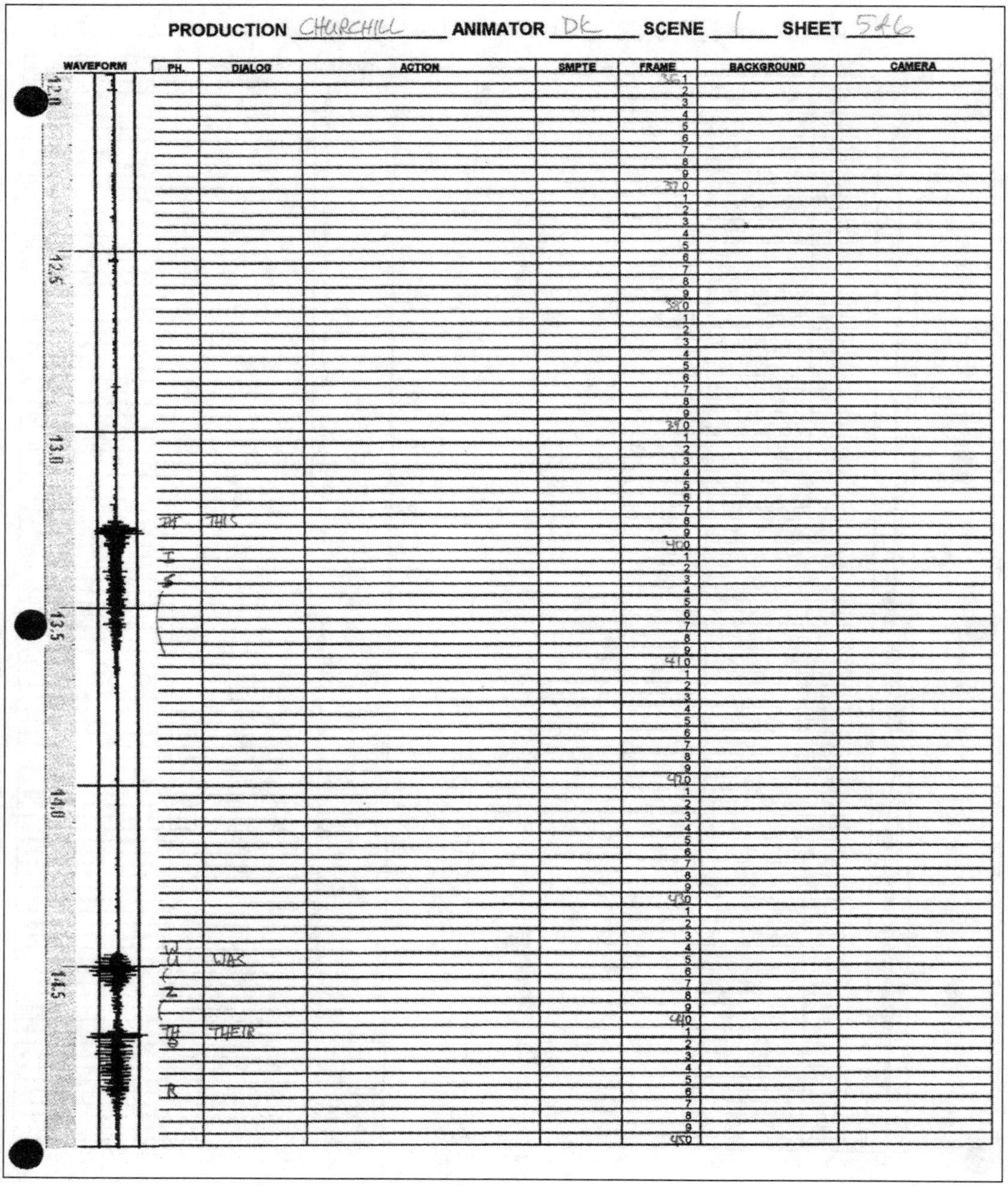
PRODUCTION CHURCHILL ANIMATOR DK SCENE 1 SHEET 5&6
WAVEFORM
PH.
DIALOG
ACTION
SMPTE
FRAME
BACKGROUND
CAMERA
12.0
12.5
13.0
13.5
14.0
14.5
THIS
WAS
THEIR

PRODUCTION _CHURCHILL_ ANIMATOR _DK_ SCENE _1_ SHEET _6 of 6_

WAVEFORM	PH.	DIALOG	ACTION	SMPTE	FRAME	BACKGROUND	CAMERA
	F	FINEST			45 1		
	ƏI				2		
	N				3		
					4		
					5		
					6		
					7		
	E				8		
	S				9		
					46 0		
					1		
					2		
					3		
	Əu	HOUR			4		
					5		
	Ə				6		
	R				7		
					8		
	(				9		
					47 0		
					1		
					2		
					3		
					4		
					5		
					6		
					7		
					8		
					9		
					48 0		
					1		
					2		
					3		
					4		
					5		
					6		
					7		
					8		
					9		
					49 0		
					1		
					2		
					3		
					4		
					5		
					6		
					7		
					8		
					9		
					50 0		
					1		
					2		
					3		
					4		
					5		
					6		
					7		
					8		
					9		
					51 0		
					1		
					2		
					3		
					4		
					5		
					6		
					7		
					8		
					9		
					52 0		
					1		
					2		
					3		
					4		
					5		
					6		
					7		
					8		
					9		
					53 0		
					1		
					2		
					3		
					4		
					5		
					6		
					7		
					8		
					9		
					54 0		

Moving On

If you've worked through the projects in this chapter and all your exposure sheets are filled in, congratulations! Your preproduction work is finished. If production issues force a change in story or sound track, you may have to revise some of this work; otherwise, you should now have a complete script, storyboard, bar sheets, story reel, and exposure sheets. Part II of this book takes you through the next step, building your characters and sets.

Part II

Modeling

Chapter 5

Character Design

In this chapter, you'll learn about the process of designing characters, including the people involved, rules of thumb, mistakes to avoid, and useful tools. To assist you in designing realistic and cartoon characters, I'll explain the underlying muscle and bone structure of the human face and figure, plus dimples, wrinkles, flab, and fat. Examples of each principle are illustrated by the Fred character from "Easy Come, Easy Go" or by case studies of other artists' work.

As you learned in Chapter 1, character animation is almost always a group effort. Good character design, as part of that larger effort, is also a cooperative process that you need to understand.

The Typical Character Design Process

In most studios, you will work with a variety of people to design the characters the animators will use. You will have to cope with suggestions and direction from just about everybody—from the director, the technical director (TD), the layout artist, the animator, and sometimes it seems, even the janitor. Everybody will have a different idea of how the character should look and work.

As a team member, your performance in design meetings is just as important as your performance with LightWave. You can exercise and develop your sense of tact by carefully questioning parts of the proposed script, storyboard, or layout that have a disproportionate effect on your workload.

For example, suppose the storyboard calls for a character to reach into a trouser pocket, extract a key, and open the door with it, and then the camera cuts to the next shot, where the character drops the key on the entryway table. Nowhere else does the character pull anything out of that pocket, nor does the key or lock have any further effect on the story. The action is a throw-away and should be discarded if possible.

You might propose that the character stage the action of reaching into a pocket and then cut on that action to an interior shot of the door, with the sound of the key going into the lock and turning. The rest of the shot is just as before. This approach would save all the expense of modeling and animating the trouser pocket and the complex arm-and-hand movement of fishing for the key.

Always try to have a better idea to suggest before you criticize or complain about something, and if you must complain, state your reasons for doing so in a way that is as productive and team spirited as possible. You're much more likely to get your way if you point out where a change will save money, effort, or time for others as well as for yourself. Keeping a positive tone doesn't cost you a thing, and keeping a production team's morale up through a long project is a lot more important than saving a couple of hours' work on a one-shot model.

Balance is critical to the character design process. The penultimate goal of the entire production team is to put the character animation in front of an audience. Creatively, most members of the team want to contribute their best work, see their own contributions prominently in the final product, and naturally tend to favor their own ideas. Practically, there are a number of constraints, limits, and harsh realities in the production process that will weed out many of these ideas. Part of your job is to help negotiate the delicate balance between creative vision and real-world production. To do this, you need a clear picture of all the checks and balances affecting character design.

Character Design Guidelines

Whenever you discuss character design, you should keep a few critical factors about character construction in mind. These factors will determine the levels of detail, flexibility, and versatility you must build into the character's model, setup, motion, and texture libraries. They may not make a lot of difference to the rest of the production team, but they can make or break the character construction.

Medium

Is this character going to be shown 40 feet tall on motion picture screens or 200 pixels tall on a video game screen? Whether the character will be used in film, television, multimedia, or video games, the medium dictates the level of detail and the constraints on your tools and other resources. Generally, film work is the most demanding, but it also enables you to use whatever tricks and tools get the job done. Television is much lower resolution, so you can cut corners on fine details, but the lower budgets and shorter schedules of television production mean you will have fewer tools and less time to do the work. Multimedia covers a range of resolution, frame rates, and color depths—from close to the specifications you would use for television to lower than those you would use for video games—and your resources can vary just as widely. In several ways, video games can be the most demanding form of character animation: You have to contend with low face count models, few texturing options, restricted timing options (no anticipation or follow-through), and low production budgets.

Distance

How far will this character be from the camera? How much screen space will it actually occupy in the closest shot? If the character is just an extra, seen only in the distance and occupying only a few dozen pixels of screen resolution, you can cut all kinds of corners and save lots of time and effort; the finished product will look just as good. If the character will appear in several extreme close shots, you must plan for more detailed modeling, higher-resolution textures, and more subtle animation controls in the face.

Speed

If the character is to move very fast, you can rely on motion blur to obscure any minor flaws or crudeness in the character design for the faster sequences and focus your resources on more detailed modeling for the slower intervals. A character who always runs at top speed, for example, will require little more for those sequences than a detailed anticipation pose, a follow-through pose for stopping, and a run pose that will look good in motion blur (perhaps with multiple legs in different positions).

Range of Movement

Ideally, every character you build should have at least the range of movement of the equivalent real creature or person. Practically, building such characters would break every deadline and budget you ever come up against. You must find every possible compromise you can make in the construction of the character without affecting the quality of the finished image. If the storyboards never show the character raising its arms above shoulder level, you may not have to build that range of motion into the character.

At the same time, you shouldn't design restrictive motion in from the start. It takes experience to know how to build the model in anticipation of how it will move. It frequently happens that the model can't be said to be fully completed until it has been animated and sent back with a more complete understanding of what it really needs to do. The storyboard is the place to start, but only the animator knows what he needs it to do after the preproduction phase. Build that into your schedule and don't be surprised. Revisions happen!

Range of movement includes emotional or dramatic range, especially if you need to build separate models for the character's facial expressions. If the character is written as surly and nasty, you will probably not have to build its face to express benevolence or compassion. On the other hand, if the character is extraordinarily flexible or mutable (a classic cartoon wise guy, for example), you can plan on creating several times the usual number of models, setups, and textures. A villain can be far more sinister when there is a full range of emotion in his face, which is particularly useful for contrast. A frown is all the more malevolent when it started as a smile. The villain is the hammiest, juiciest role in the picture! It's often the parts that are just a bit off that make a villain creepy—a smile that goes just too far, like the Coachman in Disney's *Pinocchio*.

Style

Is the character to have a very abstract style, or does the director favor photorealism? Can you get by with a simple surface color, or will you have to plan more complex models and layers of textures to get a realistic skin appearance? Can the surfaces remain relatively rigid and look artificial, or must you build them to be fully animated and appear organic?

The style of the character (and the rest of the production) must be compatible with the story you are trying to tell. A bright, primary-colored cartoon is unsuitable for a film noir hardboiled detective, just as a dark, Gothic design is inappropriate for a cheerful comedy. Appropriate character style makes storytelling easier by preparing the audience. A character wearing a tin star and a six-gun is obviously the sheriff. Poor design means the animation has to work harder—a man in a nondescript suit doesn't lead the audience to expect anything and only becomes a character through subsequent actions.

Appeal

Every character you design should have visual appeal. This doesn't mean cutesy, nice, or conventionally attractive; appeal means the character's appearance grabs and holds your audience's attention. Villains, monsters, comics, and even major props and sets must have visual appeal. You want every shot in your film to be able to stand on its own as a piece of art, with the interaction of characters and sets providing the detail and composition that will hold your audience's eyes.

You can give your characters appeal by keeping them strong and simple. Design them for strong poses, with clear lines of action. Keep the details of face and figure as simple as possible so you can animate expressions and actions directly and clearly. Don't clutter your characters with a lot of extraneous detail that muddies their outlines and diverts attention from their expressions. If your character can't communicate, it's worthless.

Line of Action

In a strong key pose, you should be able to draw an arc or broad s-curve from the visual base of the character, up through its center and out to the goal of the action. This is the line of action. If this line is broken, bent too sharply, or veers off in different directions, it's more difficult for your audience to read the pose.

Each part of a character should enhance your ability to pose it with a strong line of action. If part of the character is jutting out at an angle, that part breaks up the visual flow of the pose.

In the early 2D drawing stages of character design, the line of action can be drawn first, and the character sketch built around the line.

As soon as you have a general concept of the character's proportions, you should make a series of pose sketches like those in Figure 5.1, building the figure along characteristic strong lines of action. You can choose these poses from the script, selecting shots that define the character's development or exposition. Once you have a design that will fit the character's most typical or defining actions, you have a better idea of the necessary mesh and joint layout you will have to build in LightWave.

Mike Comet

Figure 5.1
Early character pose sketch for Fred.

Silhouette

It's important to test your designs in silhouette. If a posed character does not read well as an outline, your audience will have to rely on much more subtle clues to understand what the character is trying to do or say. That takes more time, makes your audience work harder, and is generally poor animation practice. On the other hand, a character that reads well in silhouette will only get better and stronger as you add color, depth, and surface details within the silhouette.

You can test a character design sketch in silhouette by laying tracing paper over it and tracing only the outline of the figure. Cover the original sketch and look only at the traced outline. If you can still "read" the pose, the sketch works. If not, go back to the drawing board. How can you make the outline cleaner, less cluttered, and with a strong line of action?

You still need to check your character's silhouette in the 3D modeling phase of character design. Fortunately, LightWave enables you to mimic silhouette tracing automatically by rendering an alpha channel image (see Figure 5.2).

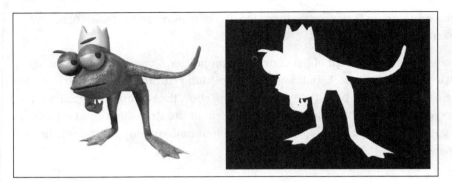

Figure 5.2
Posed character with clear silhouette.

Character Design Tools

If you want to design characters professionally, you need to be familiar with the design tools commonly used in studios. Even if you are doing this for fun, learning to use these tools is good practice and will help you focus more efficiently on the critical factors in designing your characters.

The most commonly used character design tools are sketches, model sheets, maquettes, and photos. Just as you develop a story from premise to script to storyboard, you can develop an original character design from sketch to maquette to LightWave model. If your character has to match an existing real-world actor, photos become a crucial part of the design process.

Sketches

The first tool to mention in a discussion of character design is the sketch. Even if you are a lightning-fast modeler, to deserve the word "artist" in your job title, you should be able to sketch a figure faster than you can model it. Get used to pencils and paper if you aren't already. And don't be shy about not being able to draw if you come from the "propeller-head" side of computer graphics. I rarely attempt anything more character oriented than a stick figure myself, and there are plenty of working LightWave professionals who could say the same.

The obvious advantages of pencil sketching are that it's cheap; you don't need electricity or a computer; everybody in a meeting can have one; it's easy to make revisions; you can start with a fairly light, hesitant line and firm it up or change it as the discussion progresses; and the product is easy to reproduce, fax, or digitize.

The disadvantage to pencil sketching is that it's not a 3D medium, so something that looks good on paper can turn out to be completely worthless in the computer. Caveat emptor.

How does sketching measure up in terms of the five points for an efficient work strategy? Sketches can be revised without starting over from scratch, so they can reduce redundant work. Sketches can progress from very rough to extremely detailed, so they support incremental detailing. Sketches provide rapid feedback because the client and other members of the production team can simply look at the finished sketch or even provide feedback to the artist as the sketch is being drawn. The finished sketch is a document for decision-makers to sign off. Character design sketches can definitely encourage you to stay flexible. A common practice is to work up a variety of sketches representing different looks for a character. The client chooses one sketch, or portions from several sketches, and the artist creates a new set of sketches based on that feedback. At any time during the sketch/revision cycle, you have the flexibility to go back to (or integrate pieces from) an earlier concept. Character design sketches score very well on all five points, making them an efficient part of your character animation work strategy.

Cast in Stone

Once you start putting models into the computer, there is a very strong temptation to leave them alone. The pencil-sketch design process is cheap enough that it enables you to go back and revise or throw out materials without cutting out that "pound of flesh nearest one's heart."

Although you have your design factors firmly in mind, the other members of the design team have their own ideas and concerns. The character usually evolves with a lot of pushing and grinding; everybody pushes their own agendas and grinds their own axes. If things go well, the character develops toward a design that will help tell the story, be economical to model, and be reasonably easy to animate. Sometimes the end design is rather far from the first concept, and sometimes it's pretty close to the original.

You can make your first rough sketches minimalist and dynamic to keep your creative impulses flowing. Use traditional artistic cheats and caricature techniques if you like. As you develop the character, you should firm up your drawings and make them less ambiguous. Figure 5.1 is one of the earliest character sketches for Fred, the lead character in the example script. It was drawn by the film's technical director, Mike Comet, based on some verbal descriptions and a really simple stick figure of my own, which I won't inflict on you. Even a simple figure like this can communicate the actions that define a character.

Figure 5.3 is another step in Fred's evolution, as drawn by storyboard artist Brian Kelly. Again, the drawing captures an action that defines the character. At this point, the drawing also refines the surface appearances and ranges of motion that the TD will be called on to create.

Figure 5.4 is a further refinement of Fred's appearance, as drawn by storyboard artist Sandra Frame. A character may go through many changes at the sketch level before the first 3D model is sculpted.

Model Sheet

When the storyboard is nearly final and the general character design is well along, it's a good idea to sketch a character *model sheet*, a collection of drawings showing representative poses and expressions. For a series using an established character, the model sheet is the standard by which the storyboards and animation are measured. For a completely new production like

Brian Kelly

Figure 5.3
Early storyboard sketch of Fred.

Sandra Frame

Figure 5.4
Revised storyboard sketch of Fred.

"Easy Come, Easy Go," the model sheet is an evolving part of the development process. It's not critical that the model sheet show every facial expression or skeletal pose within the character's range. However, the more complete the model sheet, the fewer unpleasant surprises you'll experience later in the production.

For a general-purpose character that you plan to cast in other productions, you'll want to create a generalized model sheet that covers the full facial and skeletal range reasonable for any character. This approach saves you from having to remodel or rebuild setups every time a character has to express an emotion or perform an action that wasn't designed into the original model and setup. For a one-time production like "Easy Come, Easy Go," you can get away with a more specialized character design. For example, if a character is described as expressing only a few emotions and does not have a speaking part, you can minimize the character's facial designs.

I recommend planning a model sheet by following one character at a time completely through the script and storyboard, making a written list of each extreme pose, facial expression, and spoken dialogue. From this list, you can determine the minimum model and setup design necessary to animate the character. The two supporting cast members of "Easy Come, Easy Go" are the waitress and bouncer. Both of these characters are described and drawn as arms and hands projecting into the frame from off screen. The model sheets for these characters need only show a few key poses of the arms and hands, as described in the script and storyboard. The bouncer's appearances are shots 37, 38, 90, 91, and 93 (shown in Figure 5.5).

Figure 5.5
"Easy Come, Easy Go" revised storyboard shots 37, 38, 90, 91, and 93, showing bouncer's hand and arm.

According to these shots, the bouncer's model sheet list should include pointing index finger with arm straight, index finger arced with wrist flexed upward and arm straight, index finger splayed (on Fred's shoulder) with wrist flexed downward and arm straight, releasing Fred. That's a very simple model sheet, having only four extreme poses. It may be most efficient to simply model targets for these poses and use EndoMorph Mixer to animate them. This bypasses all the complexity of skeletal setups, although it does increase modeling time a bit. The primary danger is that, if any rewrite gives the bouncer character a more complex role, a nearly complete redesign or an inordinate amount of modeling would be required.

The waitress's appearances are shots 50A through 56, 58, 59, 62, and 79 through 85, shown in Figure 5.6. According to these shots, the waitress's hands and arms must be able to manipulate the menu, manipulate check pad and pen, manipulate champagne flute and bottle, serve food plates, make shushing motions, make warding motions, be grabbed and kissed by Fred, and pull out of Fred's grasp. This is a much more complex range of actions than the bouncer's. It might be possible to model each of these extreme poses, but it's almost certainly safer to plan for a full skeletal setup. This will provide the safety of a wide range of actions to accommodate revisions and to coordinate with Fred's animation.

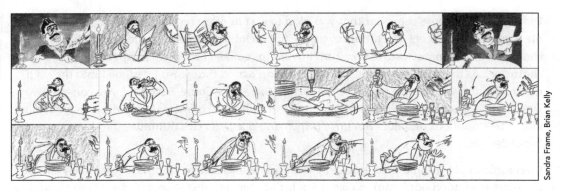

Sandra Frame, Brian Kelly

Figure 5.6
Revised shots 50A through 56, 58, 59, 62, and 79 through 85, showing waitress's hands and arms.

As the main character, Fred has a completely different set of requirements. I deliberately wrote the script to be a character animation exhibition piece. That means Fred needs to show a broad emotional range and have as complete a skeletal setup as possible. Fred is definitely the star of the show and will demand the majority of design, modeling, and setup resources. Here's a partial list of Fred's requirements, excerpted from the complete storyboard:

- *Facial expressions*—Slack (neutral), dejection, pompous pride, surprised dismay, physical shock, wild take, joy, eagerness, shocked dismay, indignation, determination, eureka, condescension, anticipation, pleasure, eating, drinking, bloated, drunk, loudly obnoxious, drunkenly annoyed, lecherous, kissing, fear, impact distortion, concussed, nauseous, panicked, exhausted, unconscious, waking, pained, hung over, sternly disapproving, crestfallen

- *Extreme poses/actions*—Dejected walk, prideful stance, slump, take a slap in the face, manipulate bill, wild take, anticipation to run, zip run, skid stop, bottom-first landing, stand from seated, dust off, purposeful walk, pompous walk, manipulate menu, manipulate champagne flute, manipulate fork, bloat, pop buttons, hunch, grab waitress's hand, get thrown, squash impact street lamp, slump impact sidewalk, clamber erect, stagger run, hands and knees, slide to seat, totter walk

In addition, Fred's overall appearance changes drastically eight times in the course of the story. These "costume changes" will require major model and texture changes and perhaps some setup changes as well. Fred's eight costumes are ragged, well-dressed, overstuffed, drunk, post-fight, post-streetlight impact, post-nausea, and morning after. The model sheet should include at least front and three-quarter views of each costume, with supplementary sketches and notes for important or complex details.

Based on these notes, Fred will require a full humanoid skeletal setup with additional controls for clothing and hair. Fred's face will require a full set of standard emotional poses, plus a number of specialty poses for nonstandard extremes (for example, when he wraps his head around the street lamp). Fred's textures and body models will have to be modified eight times, with changes to the basic setup for half of the body models.

The model sheet should have enough detail to create a set of construction drawings. These final drawings should be as clear and precise as a blueprint, because that is exactly what they are. I strongly recommend that you make a set of orthographic projections, at least the front view and one profile, as shown in Figure 5.7. Make drawings of the underlying skull as part of your final design sketches. In a larger production, these drawings are a sign-off document for the producer, director, and other decision-makers.

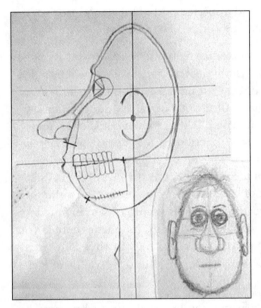

Figure 5.7
Development of Fred's head from rough sketch to construction drawing with skull details.

Flesh lies! Don't overlook the importance of designing a viable skull and skeleton. You should be able to visualize the underlying bone structure of your character. If you cannot clearly see the skull, you cannot clearly see where muscles should attach, where the jaw should hinge, and what should deform the final appearance of the skin. Begin at the beginning, and everything else will follow in logical progression. This is even more important when you are designing fantastic creatures. Attention to zoology and physiology pays off with greater perceived realism and fewer modeling, setup, and animation problems. There are good, practical reasons that art schools teach anatomy along with life drawing.

Maquettes

A maquette is a three-dimensional physical model, usually constructed of clay, plaster, or other easily worked material. The process of creating a maquette allows the design team to visualize, modify, and detail the character in ways that 2D sketches can't support. Modeling in clay requires truth that can be cheated or faked in 2D drawings. Details show up in 3D that are not obvious in 2D, like the complexities of the inner corners of the eyes or the under-cuts in nasolabial furrows (which run from just above the nostrils to the edges of the mouth sphincter near the corners).

Maquettes have been used for many years in animation studios, and computer animation has not changed that. In fact, maquettes have become even more important to LightWave work, because 3D digitizers and scanners now provide a means of bringing the maquette directly into the computer. Maquette sculptors are a traditional and respected part of the design team at many studios, and those that don't have on-staff sculptors often hire freelancers.

As with drawings, maquettes meet the five criteria. Maquettes reduce redundant work by pre-venting miscommunication or misinterpretation. A 3D physical model is about the most effec-tive communication tool you can show to a client, director, or producer. Maquettes support incremental detailing by enabling you to modify them. Until you bake it, a Sculpey maquette remains flexible (more on Sculpey maquettes in a bit). After baking, you can add or remove bits, resculpting problem areas while preserving the remaining work. Maquettes provide (rela-tively) rapid feedback if you are a competent sculptor. If you have a supportive production team, you can even sculpt a rough maquette live in a design meeting. The finished and baked maquette is a document that your client, producer, or director will approve. Getting a sign-off on a maquette is a major step in the production process, and the existence of that maquette can have an anchoring and inspiring effect on the whole team. Finally, maquettes enable you to stay flexible by giving you a safety net. If digitizing and modeling in LightWave fails, you can return to the maquette as the last successful stage in development and repeat the model-ing process from there.

You can build maquettes from a variety of materials, using standard sculpture techniques. Some of the more popular brand-name materials are Sculpey, Fimo, and Cernit synthetic firing clays and Van Aiken and Plastilina oil-based clays. Water-based clays are generally unsuitable for maquettes because they don't fire well and tend to dry out and crack. You can work all of these materials with common sculpting tools of wood, metal, or hard plastic.

Oil-based modeling clays like Van Aiken and Plastilina are suitable for initial model studies that will need lots of revision. These clays stay malleable for a long time and can be reworked repeatedly before they start to lose the proper feel. However, the only way to harden one of these maquettes is to cast a mold of the clay, then make a positive casting in a more rigid and durable material. This is more bother, but it does allow you to make a short production run of identical maquettes so everybody can have a copy.

Sculpey is a family of synthetic clays that can be molded like ordinary clay, then fired at rela-tively low temperatures to harden them. Fired Sculpey maquettes are lightweight and durable and can take paints and other finishes. This material is better for one-off models because it is faster and less expensive, and by using it, you can avoid the restrictions of mold-making.

The original Sculpey is plain white and has a slightly crumbly texture. Sculpey III is not as pliable as the original, so it retains the modeled shape better and doesn't stick to your fingers as much. Super Sculpey is also less sticky and easier to work with. Sculpey III comes in a variety of colors, as does Fimo. Fimo is similar to Sculpey but can be better for fine details because it is harder and less pliable. It's also more difficult to work because it crumbles more easily. Fimo and Cernit have a more waxy appearance than Sculpey, and they tend to scorch or burn more in firing.

You can buy these materials in most art, ceramic, or craft stores. If you can't find a local supplier, you can call Polyform Products (the makers of Sculpey) at (847) 427-0020 or visit the Web site, **www.sculpey.com**, for more information or the address of the nearest distributor.

To fire Super Sculpey, put it in a temperature-controlled oven at 250 to 275 degrees Fahrenheit for 15 to 20 minutes. If you will be firing a lot of maquettes, think about buying an inexpensive toaster oven that you can use exclusively for firing clay. If you overheat Sculpey, it can give off toxic fumes and leave a nasty residue, both on the inside of the oven and on any dishes you use to hold the maquette. Don't use a microwave—the maquette will explode!

Firing time and temperature will depend on the thickness of the Sculpey. Thicker layers take longer and should be fired at lower temperatures to avoid cracking due to uneven heating. On the other hand, if you leave thin spots in the Sculpey, they can scorch and burn.

If parts of your maquette will be very thick, you should consider layering the Sculpey over an armature. The armature can be wads of aluminum foil, a bent coat hanger wire, or anything else that won't melt or distort during firing. A good armature helps hold the maquette together, lowers total weight, and saves clay that would otherwise be wasted on interior volumes.

If any part of your maquette is hollow, you need to leave passages for air to escape during firing. Trapped air will expand when heated, blowing your maquette apart. This is also a good reason to thoroughly knead the clay before modeling the maquette and to make sure you press out all the air bubbles. Also make sure the Sculpey isn't overage. Check the dates on the side of the box. If you get a bad or overage batch by mistake, contact your distributor or Polyform Products for a replacement.

Once you've fired the Sculpey, you need to cool it down carefully. If you cool it too rapidly, your maquette will crack. You can prevent this by leaving the maquette in the oven with the heat turned off and the door open so the maquette cools at the same rate as the oven. You can also remove the maquette from the oven and immediately wrap it in one or more thick towels, which will insulate it and allow it to cool more slowly and evenly. This also has the advantage of getting you and your smelly maquette out of the kitchen sooner, which can be important to domestic peace.

Once the maquette has cooled completely, inspect it for scorches, burns, and cracks. Super Sculpey can be repaired by cutting off the bad part, smoothing on a new layer and refiring. Small burns can be sanded off with a nail file or emery board.

The fired maquettes sometimes don't hold up well over time, cracking in spots and crumbling around the edges. You can make your maquette last longer by coating it with sanding sealer or clear nail polish, which will reduce dusting and crumbling problems.

Sculpting Maquettes

When your construction drawings are ready, I recommend that you actually model the bone structure of your character first, as shown in Figure 5.8 and the SkulGrey.avi clip on the CD-ROM. Later, you can lay sculpting material over the skull to mimic layers of muscle, fat, and skin. This might seem tedious, but it is the surest way for a beginner to avoid major modeling errors. A skull is much easier to model than an animatable human face, but it has subtleties you might overlook if you skip straight to modeling the surface appearance. The most critical features are the orbits of the eyes, the points of the cheekbones, the hinge of the jaw, and the lines of upper and lower teeth. If you model all these correctly, the overlay of muscle, fat, and skin will follow more easily and logically. This approach also gives you a stronger idea of how the finished model should move: Each line of muscle is a line of tension between the attached skin and bone. With practice, you may be able to dispense with modeling the skull, but I still recommend it and do so myself.

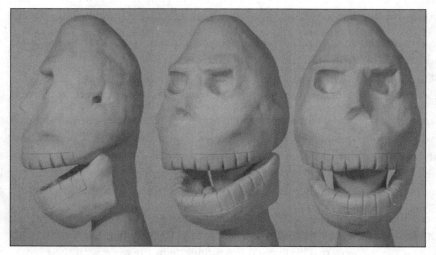

Figure 5.8
Side, three-quarter, and front views of Fred's skull.

Go back to the source! I do not recommend studying art and drawing books except as general background. When you are looking for study models for muscle and bone, study muscle and bone. Buy an inexpensive (but accurate) plastic model human skull. Buy or borrow an anatomy text that is illustrated with photos, not drawings. Find actors or actresses with prominent facial musculature and study clips of their close-ups. I chose Kent Broadhurst because of his facial muscle definition and because I have a laser disk of *Silver Bullet*, in which he has a series of intense emotional close-ups. These clips also provide good material for lip sync tests. With practice, you will be able to choose a model similar to your character. Broadhurst looks nothing like Fred, but I needed to study his muscle definition. Human actors closer to Fred in appearance generally have thicker layers of fat over the muscles of the mouth and jaw, which makes them harder to study.

For example, the medical drawings I referred to for muscle names and attachments were fine as far as they go. However, they leave out surface interactions like the nasolabial folds, which run from just above the nostrils to the edges of the mouth sphincter near the corners. Without close study of a live-action actor, I would not have known where to place this fold and how it changes as the underlying muscles move. Look at the next half-dozen CGI characters you see and note how many of them are missing this feature. Its absence leaves the face looking flat, artificial, and overly simplified.

Speaking of oversimplification, you should resist the urge to model half a character and simply mirror it. Asymmetry is a human characteristic. More asymmetry is generally perceived as uglier, whereas less is conventionally pretty. Perfect symmetry looks inhuman, but only slightly imperfect symmetry makes a fashion model. Fred is definitely not a fashion model. As you may have gathered from the script and storyboard, I have no intention of allowing Fred to become a sympathetic character. To this end, I sculpted Fred to be markedly asymmetric. Although not quite Quasimodo, he will not win any beauty contests.

At this point, you need to select a facial expression or pose for the finished maquette. The expression I selected for Fred is odd, not one you are likely to encounter in real life (see Figure 5.9). However, this pose has the significant advantage of exposing as much unfolded and unwrinkled skin as possible. The lips are drawn wide and down, enabling me to model a default smooth lip surface rather than wrinkles. The lips are also everted, or turned out, which is easier to model smoothly than a compressed pose. The nasolabial fold or furrow is not completely flattened, but it's also not exaggerated to the point of compressing the cheek upward to occlude the skin around the eye. The eyelids are closed but not tightly compressed. The jaw is lowered to stretch the cheeks flat but not gaping so much that the lips and cheeks are overstretched. The eyebrows are relaxed. This is a good compromise for a neutral modeling pose. This is not going to be the neutral animation pose, but that discussion is for later chapters.

I referred to medical illustrations to find the approximate order, attachment points, and layering of the facial muscles. I rolled out thin layers of Sculpey, cut approximate shapes for the facial muscles, then applied them, in order, to the fired skull. After I placed all the muscle layers, I added thin bits of Sculpey and smoothed out all the layers to create the completed head. You can see a 360-degree view of the maquette in file Maquette.avi on this book's CD-ROM. The advantage to doing all this modeling on top of the fired skull is that you can peel off your mistakes without damaging the skull. I did this twice until I was satisfied with the results. If I had modeled the entire head from scratch, it would have taken about three times as long to finish the maquette. It probably would not have turned out as well, either.

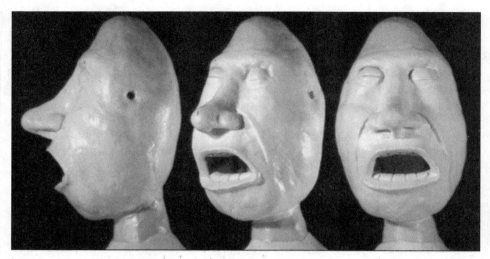

Figure 5.9
Side, three-quarter, and front views of Fred's head.

Once you are satisfied with the complete maquette, fire it to harden the face and head. Because I was using a temporary base of aluminum foil, the head was not perfectly stable. After firing the head, I modeled a thick layer of Sculpey around the base of the maquette's neck to create a rigid base. I fired the maquette a third time and ended up with a solid, durable maquette with a wide, solid, and flat-bottomed base. I am pretty happy with the way it turned out.

Once you have your finished maquette, there are several ways you can use it as a reference for creating a computer model. The simplest (and least accurate) is to simply refer to it while you model freehand in the computer. If you want to be slightly more accurate, you can photograph the maquette from different angles, digitize the photos, then load the digitized images as backdrops in Modeler. Finally, you can be accurate down to machine-shop tolerances by using a digitizer or laser scanner to convert the maquette directly to a LightWave object. The next two chapters go into more detail about each of these techniques.

Reference Photography

If you are working from a live subject or finished maquette, photos can help a great deal during the construction of the character model, setups, and textures. The same digitizing techniques described in Chapter 9 can be used to get these photos into your computer. Getting useful LightWave models from these 2D photos requires a slightly different setup.

One of the goals of reference photography is to enable you to accurately locate any point on the model by referring to two or more photos. The process of loading the photos as background images in Modeler and placing points to create the model is called *photogrammetry*, which is discussed in detail in Chapter 6. The goal of this section is to show you how to get adequate photos for the LightWave process.

You can make your work much simpler by marking your subject with a series of reference points or a grid. If you are working from a maquette, you can mark it with a fine felt-tip pen in a contrasting color. For a live subject, you will need some kind of nontoxic marker that leaves a fine line. An eyeliner pen works well. If you don't have one handy, ask at the nearest makeup counter.

Take two sets of photos, one without and one with reference marks. Try to make the photos as similar in camera setup as possible.

Place reference marks where the curves of the subject change rapidly. You don't need to mark large flat areas—it's the sharp curves and edges where you'll need help in modeling. You'll get better at this with practice. You may want to mark up and photograph several practice subjects before you try a critical maquette or live subject. Halloween masks make inexpensive practice subjects. The more experience you have with LightWave character modeling and setup, the more the markup process will become an unconscious, creative flow. You will develop an intuitive grasp of where points must go to produce the results you need. Don't expect your first maquette markup to be perfect; plan on making lots of corrections.

Don't make more marks than you need. If the reference marks overlap and it's difficult to tell them apart, you'll have a harder time matching the points to the correct marks.

For the initial markup of the Fred maquette, my goal was to cover the maquette with a net of four-sided polygons (using no more than absolutely necessary) to create a MetaForm cage. When building this kind of setup, you have to treat each point as an animation control—whether you want it to be or not. Every extra point can become an albatross around the animator's neck for the rest of the project. The guideline for this markup is not to place a point at each contour change, but to lay out a MetaForm cage that can be tweaked in Modeler and Layout to create a close copy of the maquette. This will not produce a perfect duplicate because MetaForm does not work that way. However, this approach makes it possible to animate a much lighter model with less work and a good level of control.

There are other ways to model and set up LightWave characters for facial animation, and several of them do not demand this level of premeditation and care. However, any markup will produce better results if you know exactly what you want to do with each point, edge, and polygon in advance. Think about this, take your time, and experiment.

Use a fine-point pen or pencil so your marks are as precise as possible. Mark the major contour lines first, as shown in Figure 5.10. These are the lines from which all other polygons will expand. These are also the major lines you will use to animate the face of your character. These lines should mark where the face changes direction, where the influence of one muscle group gives over to another. As a general rule, it is a good idea to bisect the entire head with a contour line. Even with an asymmetric character like Fred, you can save a lot of effort with a Mirror operation. For Fred here, the remaining major lines are the nasolabial fold, the line across

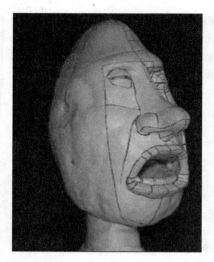

Figure 5.10
Major contour lines marked.

the top of the cheekbone, the line from eyebrow to chin, and most important, the lines follow-ing the sphincters around the eyes and mouth. These last two areas are the most critical for your character's acting ability. You can pull an Oscar-winning performance out of an ani-mated beach ball as long as it has expressive eyes and mouth.

Once you have the major contour lines marked, start filling in between them with four-sided poly-gons. If you are working with a reasonably complex maquette, you will have to solve some inter-esting problems. Look at Figure 5.11 to see some of my solutions to problem areas like the eye corners and how I changed the number of polygons along a contour line. Trapezoids, anyone?

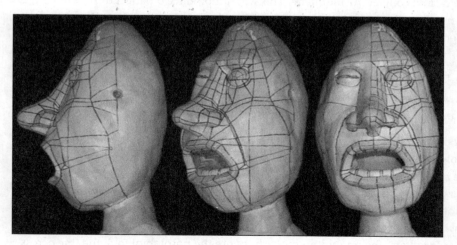

Figure 5.11
Four-sided polygons marked on maquette.

Don't get discouraged if you can't lay out a perfect grid on your first (or tenth!) try. This is the kind of three-dimensional spatial relations puzzle that I love to solve, yet I still ended up with whiteout in half a dozen areas of my maquette. This is a learning process; you will get better at it the more you practice. Also, markup is like drawing or sculpting as part of the production process. If you make mistakes, it is much cheaper to fix them now than during final rendering. Think incremental detailing; do the markup one careful step at a time. Your maquette markup can be another document that the decision-makers can approve. If you get stuck, show your markup around. Other production team members may be able to offer constructive criticism.

When you think your markup is ready, the next step is to capture images to feed into LightWave's Modeler. The basic idea is to line up points in the model with the grid drawn on the maquette in the backdrop images. The more images you use, the more checks you can make to confirm the placement of each point. Unfortunately, every extra image also adds the possibility of error, so you can easily find yourself noodling back and forth between two mutually exclusive errors for the same point. Also, the farther the separation in camera viewpoints, the easier it is to accurately place points. If two photos are shot from only 5 degrees apart, it will be difficult to see a change in the reference marks. If the separation is 45 degrees, the change will be more obvious, and your margin for error will be more generous, too. In general, you should use the minimum number of images you need to cover the subject.

For human faces, I recommend four shots as the minimum: 180-degree face-on, 90- and 270-degree profiles (either side), and 135- and 225-degree three-quarter views. For a full head, you will need 0, 45, and 315 as well. Figure 5.11 shows the 180, 225, and 270 shots for the marked-up Fred maquette. These basic shots should be taken with the camera level at the middle of the subject's height, with as long a lens as possible. Keeping the camera level allows you to ignore the lateral axes, so in modeling, you will only have to rotate the model on the vertical axis to match the angle of the background photo. Using a long lens minimizes the distortion due to perspective. The farther away the camera is from the subject, the flatter and more accurate the photo will be.

If you need to get finicky about details or undercuts, such as the back of the subject's ears or the underside of the nose, chin, or eyebrow ridge, take close-up photos. Try to keep the camera as close to level as you can. If the maquette has hidden undercuts, you will also need to capture tilted poses. Ideally, you want to secure the subject and the camera, then take all the shots without disturbing either. Practically, you will have to move at least one or use a multicamera setup to take all the photos simultaneously. If you are working with a live subject, the multicamera setup is the only reliable way to minimize errors due to the subject's movement.

There are a variety of ways to get images into your computer. A low-cost solution like a Snappy or video capture card is one possibility. For these images, I used an ATI All-In-Wonder video card to capture 1024×768 (oversampled) images from a Hi8 camcorder. For best results, I recommend using a good 35mm camera and having the film developed onto Kodak PhotoCD.

Other methods of image capture or scanning generally have lower resolution, and you want these images to be as sharp as possible. The limit of your modeling accuracy is directly proportional to the quality of the reference images.

To get accurate results, you need to register the maquette's base at 45-degree intervals. If you only capture images at 90-degree intervals, you will inevitably find a few points that are simply not visible. You will have far fewer fugitive points if you have a 45-degree series of images. I found it easiest to print a set of four straight lines intersecting at 45 degrees on a piece of paper (picture an "X" superimposed over a plus sign). I then taped this guide to the surface of my photo stand. I centered the maquette on the paper, then marked on the maquette's base each of the eight points where the lines emerged. With these reference points, I was able to precisely realign the maquette at 45-degree increments for a complete set of reference images. The CD-ROM has a selection of five reference images captured from the Fred maquette: Maq315, Maq270B, Maq225, Maq180B, and Maq135B. You can use these images for the photogrammetry project in the next chapter, or you can take pictures of your own marked-up maquette.

If you will be sharing the maquette among members of a production team, it is a good idea to make a maquette reference video clip that you can distribute. Start with the maquette facing away from the camera. Rotate the maquette counterclockwise through 360 degrees as you grab frames. Assemble the images, in order, into a video clip. With this capture sequence, you can drag the scrub bar in a player to create visual feedback as intuitive as rotating the physical maquette on a turntable. The Maquette.avi and SkulGrey.avi on the CD-ROM are examples of this technique. You can do the same with QuickTime clips.

It's important that you match the horizontal and vertical registration of the entire series of photos before you begin modeling. The easiest way to do this is to load the photos into separate layers in image-processing software such as Photoshop and then move the images around until the reference marks match (see Figure 5.12). A good place to start is the top of the head for both profile and face-on and the tip of the nose and back of the head for profiles. If you cannot match the entire set, you must at least match each 90-degree pair of images (e.g., 180 and 270). These are the image pairs you will load as backdrops in LightWave's Modeler. You should be especially careful to match the images vertically so the tip of the nose, top of the head, and underside of the chin are each at exactly the same height in each image. The outer edges of the maquette's image are the worst places to start. The best reference points are those at a 45-degree angle to both images. For example, the point of the cheekbone is a clear reference point in both profile (Maq270B) and front-face (Maq180B) images.

For the best compatibility with LightWave, and the fewest opportunities for problems, I recommend that you use IFF format for your background images in Modeler. The background image handling in LightWave [6] is much better than in previous versions, but it still seems to like IFF best.

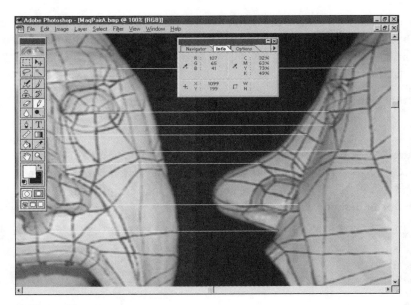

Figure 5.12
Using Photoshop to check the alignment of maquette images.

In addition to the photos used to build the LightWave model, you will need reference photos for texture, color, and specularity. You can use the same procedures outlined in Chapter 9. I recommend using a camcorder with its own spotlight to capture specularity patterns; you can get all the data you need by making a few passes around your subject at different up- and down-angles to record the highlights from the entire face or figure.

Designing the Figure

If you are building characters from scratch, you'll need to study proportion and dimension from life and from caricature. "Winging it" is an excellent recipe for rebuilding models repeatedly. You should at least have a rough pencil sketch before you start modeling.

The best resources on proportion from life are not the artist's books but the industrial designer's and engineer's. When you're planning joints and range of motion, there is no substitute for hard numbers. Dreyfuss's work on ergonomics is still worth consulting, and his *Measure of Man* is usually available from your local public or university library. References on anthropometry can also help you decide just how long to model that arm or how high to place the ankle bone.

On the artistic side, several of the books in the bibliography may be of use: Peck's *Human Anatomy for the Artist* for the realists, and for you game developers, Lee and Buscema's *How to Draw Comics*. If you are leaning toward a cartoon style, the Lemay handbooks give excellent advice on construction and animation of the figure. Blair's *Cartoon Animation* and the various compilations from the Warner and Disney studios have lots of examples.

And don't forget original inspiration! If all you are going to model is a 3D version of the same old caricatures, you might as well stay with ink and paint. LightWave character animation is a new medium. Why not push the boundaries and develop a completely original character design that belongs only to LightWave?

The following sections outline some of the basic design considerations for parts of the character.

Pelvis

The pelvis, shown in Figure 5.13, is the largest single bone in the human body and the nearest to the center of gravity (CG). Because the CG is the first layer of the animation hierarchy (see Part IV in this book), the place where all actions begin, you should consider the pelvis as the starting point for your character design.

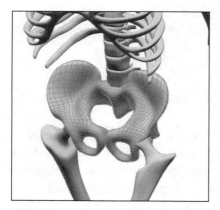

Figure 5.13
The pelvis in the human skeleton.

The pelvis provides attachments for the base of the spine and for the upper ball-and-socket joint of the legs. The pelvis itself normally rotates on all three axes. You can test this yourself. Stand, take a long step forward, and keep both feet planted at full extension—your pelvis will swivel on the vertical axis of your spine. Stand straight again, and bend forward or back at the hips—your pelvis will pitch, bisecting the angle between your thighs and torso. Stand straight again, then bend one knee slightly, taking your full weight on the other leg—your pelvis will tilt down toward the bent leg.

The pelvis doesn't rotate very much on any of the three axes, but a small rotation at the pelvis makes a big difference in the position of a hand, foot, or head. Because the movements are so small and the effects are so large, you should spend extra time studying and animating the movement of the pelvis.

When modeling the pelvis, you should keep gender differences in mind. Although the human race includes wide variations in body type, men generally have a pelvis that is narrower than their rib cage, whereas in women, the opposite is true.

Spine

The spine, or spinal column, connects the pelvis to the head through the rib cage (see Figure 5.14). The spine usually provides at least half the character's line of action. In actual anatomy, the spine is a series of many small bones called vertebrae, which can rotate only slightly in relation to their neighboring bones. This arrangement provides support yet allows a great deal of flexibility. The accumulation of small angles can add up to 180 degrees in a very flexible character.

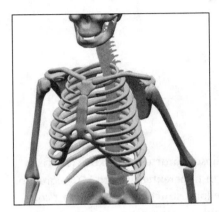

Figure 5.14
The spine in the human skeleton.

In most character designs, the spine is not simulated with an anatomically correct number of vertebral joints. For simple characters, joints at the pelvis, waist, rib cage, and neck can provide most of the flexibility necessary to the character's range of movement. If you are creating a more flexible character, such as a snake or dragon, you will have to build more detail into the spine.

Rib Cage

The rib cage, or upper torso, is attached to the spine between the pelvis and the head (see Figure 5.15). In animation, it's an odd combination of rigid and flexible. It must be expandable enough for your character to breathe deeply yet rigid enough to maintain the character's profile as the rib cage moves with the spine's curvature.

How you model and set up the rib cage depends entirely on your character's intended range. If it needs to breathe deeply, you will have to provide controls to expand and contract the upper torso without displacing other joints. If the character is to swell up in an attempt to bully or impress another character, you need to be able to animate that, too. If none of this is necessary, you may be able to leave the upper torso rigid, with the minimum number of rotational joints at the spine (or waist and neck, depending on how you construct the hierarchy).

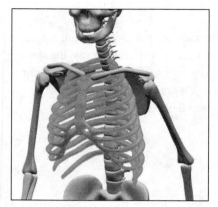

Figure 5.15
The rib cage in the human skeleton.

Legs

The legs (see Figure 5.16) are relatively easy to design for most characters. The knee joint is a simple hinge that can rotate from straight (or a little past, in hyperextension) to 150 degrees or so, limited more by the mass of the calf muscle than by the joint structure. The hip joint connects the leg to the pelvis and is a true ball-and-socket, enabling free rotation in any combination of the three axes.

The two major challenges to modeling and setting up the legs are the appearance of the kneecap, or patella, and the deformation of the mesh around the hip, buttock, and thigh. These difficulties are directly proportional to the realism of the character. For caricatures and primitives, the hip joint is the first place you should cheat.

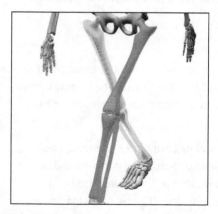

Figure 5.16
Legs in the human skeleton.

Feet

Feet in real-world humans are nearly as complex and flexible as the hands (see Figure 5.17). The toes are articulated just like fingers, and the arch can flex and stretch to change the entire shape of the foot. The ankle can rotate in two axes, and with the torsion of the lower leg, it can appear to rotate in the third axis as well. Modeling and setup for a realistic foot is complex enough that you shouldn't attempt it unless it's essential for the character's performance.

Figure 5.17
Feet in the human skeleton.

If you are designing a caricature or primitive, the first details you want to lose are the toes. Abridge the end of the foot to a shoe or similar uniform lump, with a joint to flex the mesh around the ball of the foot. This will still allow heel-and-toe walks. For an extreme primitive, you can make the foot a single rigid lump, rotating only at the ankle; however, this makes heel-and-toe walks look excessively robotic.

Arms

Arms are similar to the legs (see Figure 5.18). The elbow, like the knee joint, is a simple hinge that can rotate from straight (or a little past, in hyperextension) to 160 degrees or so, limited more by the mass of the biceps muscle than by the joint structure. The shoulder joint is not a true ball-and-socket; it is actually a hinge-and-pivot. The upper arm is not actually connected to the rib cage or collarbone; it's connected to the shoulder blade, which has its own range of movement across the back of the rib cage. The shoulder is a complex setup for characters approaching realism and merits special treatment in Part IV of this book.

You can cheat on the arms for caricature or primitive by using the old cartoon method of *rubber hose* construction. In this style, the limb has no fixed joint—it simply bends in an arc to connect the torso to the hand or foot.

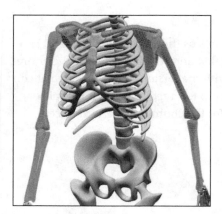

Figure 5.18
The arm and shoulder in the human skeleton.

Hands

Hands (see Figure 5.19) are tough to model and set up, but they are almost always critical to the character's expressive range. People do talk with their hands, and even a primitive character can benefit from a mitt with an opposable thumb.

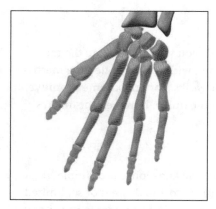

Figure 5.19
Hands in the human skeleton.

The hands connect to the arms at the wrist, which can pitch almost 90 degrees up and down and head about 45 degrees right to left but banks only through the torsion of the forearm. The wrinkles and folds of the wrist are bothersome enough that a cartoon character's rolled-cuff glove is a welcome cheat to hide the wrist joint entirely.

The hands and feet are the tail-end layer of the animation hierarchy, posed last because they don't drive any other part of the hierarchy. They are also the most likely candidates for inverse kinematics (IK) and constraints because they are the parts that interact with surfaces and objects.

Realistic hands are a genuine technical challenge, especially for close-ups. Knuckle protrusion, tendons, skin folds and wrinkles, and the pad of muscle at the base of the thumb are all tricky things to emulate. A common cheat is to use carefully modeled morph targets for the major poses.

Caricature and primitive hands are easier and more fun, such as the traditional three-fingered cartoon glove shown in Figure 5.20.

Figure 5.20
A traditional three-fingered cartoon glove.

Creature Appendages: Tails, Claws, and Extra Limbs

If you're designing a creature with more appendages than a normal human, you'll need to look at the animal kingdom for reference. Tails and snakes are relatively straightforward; they're simply extensions of the spine (see Figure 5.21).

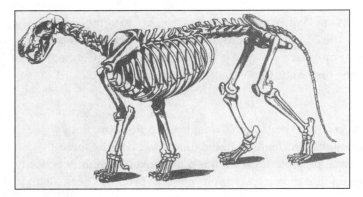

Figure 5.21
Claws and tail in the African lion skeleton.

Claws, exoskeletal plates, and other rigid body parts are easier than the equivalent human appendages because you only have to set up rotation controls at the obvious joints—no deformation controls are necessary.

Invertebrates like slugs, worms, octopi, and sharks are more of a challenge because you don't have definite joints or bones to provide a structure. It's all deformation controls! You have to design the mesh to accept depth-charge controls to drive the meat, as detailed in Part V of this book. This technique is handy for articulating a realistic tongue, too.

Designing Character Faces

You can model the simplest version of an animatable character face after a traditional puppet or ventriloquist's dummy. The eyes should rotate; the upper eyelids are useful for blinks, winks, and a variety of emotional expressions; and you can animate a simple hinged jaw for lip sync. That's a total of five objects in a parented hierarchy. This approach is so simple that I'm not even going to illustrate it with an exercise. If you want to build a Pinocchio, you can refer to the later sections of this chapter on proportion and expression and plan one for yourself.

The problem with a very simple puppet head is that you can't easily animate the full range of human emotion. For real people, more subtle emotion is communicated by the softer tissues of the face than by the simple angle of the eyes or jaw. If you want to mimic emotional expression, you must try to re-create the subtlety of motion of a real human face. If you want your character to lip sync as convincingly as possible, you must be able to deform the lips to match the sibilants and fricatives of the dialog track.

It's possible to assemble a more complex face from separate objects—some traditional puppets have many moving parts in their faces. You would have to accept the seams between objects, however, which rules out parented objects for any animation that hopes to create a higher realism or a smoother style than can be created with traditional marionettes.

The two remaining design approaches to LightWave facial animation are deformation plug-ins and Bones (see Chapters 11, 12, and 13 in the sections about setup for details). Proper modeling, setup, and animation of either approach can give you results from the caricatured to the photorealistic, depending only on the time and effort you put into it.

First Principles

Observing nature is the best way to begin. It's easy to go wrong if you try to work from memory or from your own ideas about how a creature should function. Go to the source! When you are first considering a modeling project, even if it is pure caricature or fantasy, study everything you can lay your hands on that may relate to your project. If you will be modeling animals, study their physiology and visit the zoo to observe how they move. If you will be modeling people, do the same—although for people-watching, just about any street corner will do as well as a zoo.

There are a handful of resources I have found invaluable for modeling and animating faces. On my desk, I keep a mirror and a model human skull, one to study the live play of muscles and skin and the other to study the underlying structures. Both items are cheap, available nearly everywhere, and last a long time. I also keep several books handy when designing characters' heads, the most useful being Faigin's *The Artist's Complete Guide to Facial Expression* (see the bibliography for details). The language is clear, and it's technical only when necessary; the illustrations seem designed especially for 3D construction. A paperback edition of Gray's *Anatomy* gets regular use, too. For caricature and more traditional cartoon design, the materials mentioned in the following section on proportion give plenty of ideas.

All these resources boil down to a relatively small number of guidelines you should keep in mind when designing a character's head and face.

Proportion

The first guideline is proportion—the size and relationship of the head's parts can make or break your character. Audiences expect a certain amount of stereotype in animated films. Characters are expected to act as they look. If the eyes are a bit too close together, the nose hooked, and the forehead too low, the audience will expect a different type of behavior than that of a normally proportioned character. If you choose a realistic style, you must be especially careful to model accurate human proportions.

The baseline for the head is the *orbit*, or socket, of the eye. A line drawn horizontally through the eyes should divide the head in half. One of the most common mistakes is to put the eyes too far up on the forehead, making the character look small-brained. Once the eyes are located, use the rule of thirds to divide the face: the top of the forehead (the hairline) to the eyebrow ridge is the upper third, the eyebrow ridge to the base of the nose is the middle third, and the base of the nose to the bottom of the chin is the lower third. If you get these proportions right, modeling the rest of the head is easier.

Fred's head has several deliberately exaggerated proportions. The top of the skull is very small and comes to a point, the eyes are placed high, but the ears are placed almost normally. The overall effect is to exaggerate the nose, mouth, and jawline and progressively minimize the eyes, brows, and forehead, creating a character who looks as though he thinks with his mouth and doesn't much use any other part of his head. That's exactly the effect I want for Fred's character in "Easy Come, Easy Go."

Bone Structure

The second guideline is to start with the bone structure. Even if you are designing a very flexible fantasy character, you need to understand and borrow from normal human bone structure to create a character your audience can understand. For example, in a normal human, the distances between the eye sockets, base of the nose, and upper teeth are all firmly fixed by bone (see Figure 5.22). If a realistic character's eyes, upper teeth, and nose float around, the effect is quite

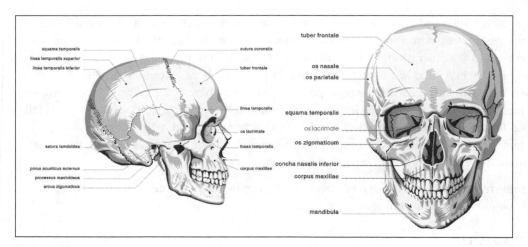

Figure 5.22
The human skull.

disturbing. Even if a cartoony character will squash and stretch to extremes, you should establish the same fixed relationships between facial parts before you create any distortions.

Make a baseline, then play with it any way you like, and the audience will be able to follow along. Jump straight into distorted and variable proportions without that baseline, and your audience will be so busy trying to figure out the character's face they will miss the story completely.

If you refer back to Figure 5.8, you can see that I sculpted all the critical reference points into the skull of the Fred maquette and can refer back to the images and AVI clip whenever I need to see the bone structure again.

Muscles

The third guideline is to follow the muscles. Muscles (and their associated fat and skin attachments) provide most of the surface distortion we use to create facial expressions, so you need to understand the musculature in order to simulate it with your models (see Figure 5.23).

Even if you are building a dragon or other fantastic creature, you must model it with believable muscle action or the character will look like a rubber toy. This is why life drawing and anatomy are so important for artists. If you have a very focused computer graphics background, this may be an area where you can learn from coworkers with more traditional art training.

Feature by Feature

This section examines the proportion, bone, musculature, and range of motion of each part of the face, including tips on designing them for animation and opportunities for caricature and exaggeration.

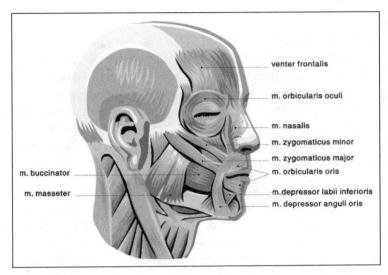

Figure 5.23
Human facial musculature.

Eyebrows

Eyebrows are controlled by two sets of muscles, the frontalis and the corrugator. The *frontalis* runs in two vertical broad bands from the hairline straight down to the brow ridge. The main effect of this muscle is to lift the eyebrows toward the hairline, producing wrinkles in the forehead. Each half of the frontalis can be controlled independently, such as when raising one eyebrow at a time and wrinkling only the half of the forehead above the raised eyebrow. The *corrugator* is a collection of three smaller bands of muscle connecting the bridge of the nose, the lower center of the forehead, and the center of each eyebrow. These muscles pull the eyebrows together and down over the bridge of the nose, forming deep folds.

Realistic eyebrows do not have a very large range of motion. On average, they can move up or down only about half an inch, and the outer ends of the eyebrows hardly move at all. As the eyebrows lower, they tend to compress inward slightly. Caricature eyebrows, however, can be exaggerated to such an extent that you can actually separate them from the face and animate them as individual objects.

The eyebrows can be important for a character's nonverbal communication, as any fan of Groucho Marx or Leonard Nimoy can attest. Eyebrows contribute to many expressions, usually in combination with the eyes and eyelids.

If you look at the eyebrow area of the Fred maquette in Figure 5.9, you can see that any movement is going to require some extra care. Upward movement will either have to follow the backward slope of the forehead or pull away from the skull. Downward movement will quickly shadow the eyes, exaggerating the effect. Fred's eyebrow animation will call for some subtlety.

Nose

The realistic human nose is nearly rigid. The septum, at the base of the nose just above the upper lip, does not move, nor does the entire bridge. The tip can deflect slightly when the nostrils flare or compress or the upper lip moves radically. The root (between the brows) can be wrinkled deeply by the corrugator muscles of the eyebrows. Some people can flare open or partially close their nostrils by flexing the *nasalis* muscle that runs from each wing of the nose across the crest. Because the perimeter of the nose is mostly attached to underlying bone, the nose doesn't affect surrounding tissues very much. On the contrary, the nose is usually moved incidentally by strong motions of the cheeks or upper lip.

The nose has little to do with most realistic character animation. Humans are not generally attuned to flared nostrils as a sign of anger or alertness or constricted nostrils as a reaction to unpleasant smells. The phrase "wrinkling one's nose" is a bit misleading. The wrinkles are formed at the nose's root by the eyebrow's corrugators, and the nose's midsection is compressed by the angular head of the *quadratus labii superiorus* muscle that runs along the *nasolabial furrows* that divide the nose from the cheeks. In other words, the wrinkles are all formed by muscles around the nose, not by part of the nose itself.

Caricature animation can easily employ the nose to humorous effect. Exaggerate the nose to a fleshy mass, make it bob and wobble in overlapping action, and every facial motion becomes laughable.

Fred's nose is going to require more animation controls than the bare minimum, just because it's such a large part of his face. Considering the visual mass, it should probably also be animated with a little extra follow-through.

Eyes: Realistic

Realistic eyeballs are paradoxically the easiest and among the most difficult parts to animate. On one hand, they are slightly modified spheres, easy to model, position, and rotate. On the other hand, they are such a crucial part of nonverbal communication that your audience will be examining your character's eyes more closely than any other part of the scene. On the gripping hand, that means you can often cheat other parts of the scene, as long as you model and animate the eyes well.

If you're going for realism, you can't get away with modeling the eyeball as a simple sphere. You need to model the corneal bulge, and if the eye is going to be seen in extreme close shots, you will probably want to model the *iris* complete with a variable *pupil* opening and set the index of refraction for the *cornea* and the *vitreous humor* (the liquid filling the eyeball, visible through the pupil) to something near the real values. For ordinary concentric pupils, you have two basic choices: a set of image maps with a variety of pupil sizes or a pupil opening that can be animated with mesh controls. If you want to get completely obsessive about realism, consult an ophthalmologist. Then there are all the interesting possibilities for creature eyeballs, from a relatively prosaic cat's-eye slit pupil to weird glowing effects and hypnotically flowing iris textures.

Eyelids: Realistic

Eyelids convey a significant fraction of the eyes' expressiveness. Rotation and pupil dilation are the limits of the eyeball's repertoire, so the eyelids and brows have to do the rest of the work. As with any action involving the eyes, the tiniest changes can make a big difference in the meaning of an expression.

The eyelids are controlled by two muscles, the *levator palpebrae*, which raises the upper lid, and the *orbicularis oculi*, which encircles the eye and squeezes the lids together in a squint. The normal position of the upper lid is between the upper edge of the pupil and the upper edge of the iris. Usually, the upper lid just covers the edge of the iris. If the upper lids cover any part of the pupil, the eyes look sleepy, depressed, intoxicated, or slow. If the upper lids rise high enough to expose the sclera, or the whites of the eyes, the eyes look surprised or alert.

The lower lid has much less influence on expression. Normally, the lower lid simply follows the edge of the iris, within the lid's range of motion. If the eyeball rotates upward, the lower lid cannot follow very far and often leaves part of the sclera exposed. Unlike with the upper lid, exposing the sclera above the lower lid has no particular emotional message. Even when the eyes are squinting, the lower lid rarely covers more than the lower part of the iris and, sometimes, the lowest edge of the pupil. Neither eyelid ever slants beyond its natural angle. This is an effect used sometimes in caricature, but in reality, the illusion of a slant upward in distress or downward in anger is created by an extreme position of the eyebrows that deepens the shadows in the eye socket.

Modeling and setting up the eyelids can be easy or hard, depending on the style of modeling you choose for the character. Exact realism is difficult because of the wrinkling and folding of the lids. Mimicking this precisely would require a plethora of controls and take forever to animate. If you need realistic eyelids, I recommend modeling a series of morph target objects and making good use of bump maps.

A much easier approach is to treat the eyelids as simple hemispheres and allow them to interpenetrate the face. The seam along the penetration will show, but appropriate texture maps can partially disguise it. This makes animation a breeze, and the right setup can automate most of the eyelids' actions.

Eyes: Cartoon

Cartoon eyes behave just like real eyes, only more so. The limits of various expressions are the same, but you have to model the eyeballs, lids, and brows so the animator can distort them to exaggerate and emphasize the central traits of the expression. For example, a very angry scowl for a realistic character would require drawn-down eyebrows, lowered upper eyelids, and the eyes' tracking null positioned on the object of the anger. A caricature of the same expression may require brows pushed farther down the nose, deeper wrinkles across the bridge, swelling and thrusting forward of the brows to make them appear larger and more threatening, and bulging of the eyeballs and lids toward the object of the anger. Obviously, cartoon eyes will require more than a simple rotating-sphere setup.

The need for flexibility means the shape of a cartoon eye depends on the character and the expression. Most cartoon eyeballs are drawn as distorted ovoids, like soft-boiled eggs with the point up, but different characters may require flattened, elongated, or even triangular eyeballs. Because the shape will probably not be suitable for rotating, you don't need to model the eyeball separately from the face. You don't even need to animate the sclera, except for gross distortions like bulging and stretch-and-squash. You can create the illusion of a moving eyeball by simply animating the iris and pupil across the unmoving surface of the sclera. Therefore, you can model a cartoon eyeball as just another bulge in the face, but you need to define it as a separate surface. If there is any way you can use a regular ellipsoid (a stretched-out sphere) for a sclera, it can really make setup and animation easier.

Eyelids: Cartoon

One of the problems with cartoon-style eyes and eyelids is the difficulty of keeping an animated pupil underneath a relatively thin modeled eyelid. Mapping the iris to the sclera is a handy way to solve this problem. If at all possible, design your cartoon characters with very thin eyelids that can be faked with color and bump maps applied directly to the sclera surface.

If your character needs thicker eyelids, you may have to set up deformation controls for modeled eyelids. This gives you the flexibility to match irregular sclera shapes but complicates setup and animation. Either a spherical eyeball or a mapped eyelid will save you effort. An irregular eyeball with thick, modeled eyelids is a tough combination.

Jaw

Most of the expression in a person's face is due to muscles and other soft tissues. Very little unique expression is contributed by the position of the jaw, but it acts as a modifier for many emotions and is important for lip sync. A human jaw is basically a hinge on the local x-axis, with a small amount of play allowing y-axis and z-axis movement. The jaw does not pivot on either the y- or z-axis unless it has been broken or dislocated. The pivot of the jaw is located just under the rear end of the *zygomatic arch*, the ridge of bone that runs from the cheekbone back toward the ear. If you draw a horizontal line from underneath the eye socket to the opening of the ear, the pivot will be on that line and just forward of the ear.

The jaw carries the lower mouth, lower teeth, and the tongue along when it moves or rotates and stretches the cheeks between their upper attachments and the jawline. You can get a better feel for this if you run a finger inside your mouth, along the outside surface of your lower gums, pushing outward on the cheek to note where the flesh is fixed to the jaw and where it stretches to meet the rest of the face. You may be surprised at just how much of your face isn't really attached to anything. From just below the orbits to the jawline, it's all hanging loose. This is one of the times a model skull comes in handy, to correlate what your fingers are telling you with what the bone structure looks like.

The upper palate and teeth are locked to the rest of the skull. You should never try to animate them, unless you're trying to upset your audience with a really unnatural character. The upper front teeth are handy as reference points for facial textures because they are visible in wireframe, do not move, and are near the center of the face.

When you model the lower face, remember that the lower jaw, teeth, lower edge of cheeks, and the base of the tongue are all attached and should share the same parent in the hierarchy, with the x- or lateral axis of rotation at the hinge of the jaw.

As you can see from Figures 5.8 and 5.9, I was careful to sculpt Fred's jaw and the overlying jawline muscles with consideration for the jaw's movement. The markup of the jaw's pivot point visible in Figure 5.11 shows that I designed the polygons defining the middle of the cheek, between the lower and upper jaw, to be able to stretch as much as possible without influencing other polygons.

The tongue itself is extremely fluid and versatile, a mass of muscle with no limiting bone structure. It may be best to limit its use to phonemes that prominently display the tongue, or use deformation controls instead, which enables you to make detailed shapes of different tongue poses.

Mouth

The mouth is one of the most complex areas of a character's face, and it contributes almost as much expression as the eyes. In nature, the mouth is a ring of muscle, the *orbicularis oris*, which forms the lips. There are at least five other major groups of muscles that pull, push, or otherwise affect some part of the mouth. The mouth can be complex enough to justify its own animation hierarchy, depending on how realistic you want your character's face to be.

The mouth is bounded by the rigid septum of the nose above and the equally rigid attachments to the chin and jawline below. Between these extremes, the musculature of the mouth is almost completely free. This shows you where to begin to model and set up the mouth. Parent the upper mouth to the root of the head and the lower mouth to the jaw. This takes care of the grosser movements required for lip sync and extreme emotions. Leaving the larger motions to a parent control also leaves you more flexibility in setting child controls to animate the subsidiary surfaces.

The next level of the animation hierarchy is the lips. Generally, you can get away with leaving the upper surface of the upper lip and the lower surface of the lower lip to fend for themselves. Overlapping influence between the lips' controls and those for the jawline and upper face will stretch the intervening surface enough for most expressions. The lips proper need a fair number of controls, but this setup is important enough to justify the extra effort.

Keep in mind that the corners of the mouth will have to move somewhere between the lower jaw's position and the rest of the face, but not exactly halfway. The lower lip usually stretches more with the jaw opening, and the upper lip stays relatively close to the upper face. The lips also should be able to pucker outwards or suck in, especially for pronouncing "P", "V", and "F."

Cheeks

The cheeks are an interesting challenge after the complexities of the mouth. They can be deceptively simple. The main purpose of the cheeks is to bridge the distance between jaw and eye socket. For a low-resolution character, cheeks can even be single polygons or patches stretched between the jawline, nose, mouth, and lower eyelids. Cheeks bulge up and out near the top when the corners of the lips are pulled up or the eyes squint. They stretch when the jaw is opened and bulge from air pressure just before the character pronounces plosive phonemes or when the character is making a face.

The dual role of the cheeks requires a special solution. The stretching to connect the jaw is pretty easily handled simply by being careful when positioning points in the cheek surfaces. Air pressure bulging, on the other hand, is a bit of a challenge. I recommend tackling it with an additional set of controls designed specifically to puff out the cheeks.

The cheek controls should influence the lips, the upper lip to the base of the nose, the lower lip to the chin, the cheeks up to the lower eyelids and down to the jawline, and the area up to the edges of the nose on both sides. This is the outline of attachment for the loose skin of the cheeks. The cheek controls should not influence the nose, eyeballs, jawline, chin, eyelids, eyebrows, or any part of the top of the head above the eyes or back of the head behind the temples. These are either firmly attached to underlying bone or beyond the cheeks' range of influence.

The preceding sections laid out guidelines for character design based on the character's desired appearance and its relation to the workings of real-world creatures. The next section takes a look at guidelines for designing a character for efficient production.

Nuts and Bolts

When you choose a style for your character, you need to consider what the story requires. If you are creating a digital stuntman to take the fall for a recognizable actor, you've got a lot of work to do just to make the character look acceptable, let alone animate well.

If your story can work with a more abstract or primitive character, you can focus your energy and resources on timing, posing, and actually telling the story. Somewhere between photorealism and stick figures, you'll find the style that suits your story.

Character designs fall into three general levels of complexity and difficulty: primitive, caricature, and realistic.

Primitives

Primitive characters are hierarchies of separate objects, like a skeleton or puppet hinged at the joints. Object hierarchies are very easy to set up and animate in LightWave, because they don't require the use of deformation tools. The challenge for a primitive hierarchical character is that you have to use joint rotation to fake stretch-and-squash. This demands an excellent sense of timing, as exemplified in Pixar's *Luxo, Jr.* Similarly, because it has limited emotional range, even with a fully articulated marionette face, your character will have to act more with posture and gesture than with facial expression. This has the benefit of forcing you to improve your timing and posing skills, which makes primitives excellent practice characters.

Primitive hierarchies are relatively easy to model and are fast and simple to animate as well. The individual objects don't have to be designed to deform. The animator simply moves and rotates the objects as is.

Unfortunately, the joints between objects are difficult to conceal, and they destroy the illusion of life unless the character is supposed to have visible seams. Parented hierarchies are best suited for puppets, robots, machines, and creatures with external skeletons, like insects, arachnids, and silly English kinniggits.

A new style of character construction, unique to computer-generated character animation, is the invisible joint. This approach simply omits the mating parts of the joint, so there is a visible gap between parent and child object. It has been used in a number of computer graphics character animations, including Steph Greenberg's *The Physics of Cartoons, Part I*, as shown in Figure 5.24.

Steph Greenberg

Figure 5.24
Slim and Tubbs from *The Physics of Cartoons, Part I*, showing invisible joints.

The tools for building an object for a primitive hierarchy are so basic that I won't go into a step-by-step tutorial describing them. Essentially, you can create the sliding surface of any rotating joint by using a lathe tool, or you can create a round primitive and modify it as necessary.

There are three basic joint types for character animation: hinge, universal, and ball-and-socket.

The simplest is the hinge, a joint with a single degree of freedom. That is, it can only rotate around one axis. The human knee and elbow are examples of hinge joints; although they can move slightly in other axes, it creates a strain on the joint and is more a matter of slop than design.

You can model a hinge with a simple cylinder. The socket (the hollow part of the joint) must be cut away enough to allow the pin (the cylindrical center) to rotate through the intended range of motion. For example, a hinged knee requires that the thigh and shin objects be cut away at the back so the calf of the lower leg does not overlap the back of the thigh when the knee is bent. Look at the objects in the Puppet character shown in Figure 5.25 for other examples of hinge joint cutaways.

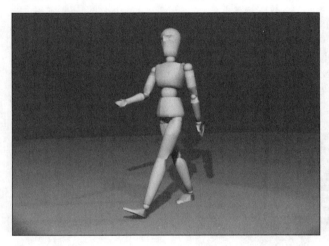

Figure 5.25
Puppet character showing joint cutaways.

The next joint type is the universal joint, or U-joint, which has two degrees of freedom. The wrist and shoulder are universal joints. The wrist can rotate the hand up and down and side to side, but twisting is a job for the forearm. The shoulder can rotate the arm to the side, on the dorsal axis, and forward and back on the lateral axis.

You can model a universal joint with two interdependent hinge joints, but I recommend skipping straight to a spherical socket. It's much simpler. If you really want to do a universal joint, take a look at a marine gimbal or a car's driveshaft U-joint.

Despite the apparent flexibility of the shoulder's combination of motions, it is not a true ball-and-socket joint like the hip. The hip has three degrees of freedom—it can rotate both forward and to the side and also twist around the long axis of the upper leg.

Modeling the ball-and-socket joint is nearly self-explanatory. Create a spherical cap for one object, usually the child. Use the spherical part of the object as a Boolean tool to carve a matching cavity in the parent object. That's it—you have a ball-and-socket joint.

Incidentally, any joint with more degrees of freedom can substitute for lower-order joints. You can animate a ball-and-socket as any of the three types, a universal joint can move as itself and as a hinge, but the hinge construction can only move as a hinge. I prefer to build ball-and-socket joints for everything, just in case the character will be called on to perform an action for which the joints weren't designed.

To help align the objects during setup, I like to mark the center of a joint's rotation with a 3D crosshair. I build one of these into a parent object wherever a child object will be attached. You can build a crosshair by adding six points in three perpendicular pairs, one pair each on the x-, y-, and z-axes. Space the points just far enough apart that you will be able to see them, but try to keep them inside the parent object. This forms a 3D crosshair, like a toy jack, which is much easier to work with during setup than a single reference point.

If you're really eager for some practice at constructing primitive object hierarchies, try building a bug. You can build an insect, lobster, arachnid, whatever—just make sure it's got an external skeleton.

PROJECT 5.1 Is There an Entomologist in the House?

To complete this project, follow these steps:

1. Check out a book on comparative entomology from your local library. I like Fox and Fox, *Introduction to Comparative Entomology*, for its line drawings, but a volume with more photos would probably be more helpful. For range of motion and other constraints, you should refer to the resources on animal studies in the bibliography.

2. Failing that, get down to your nearest seafood restaurant and buy a lobster or crab dinner. Insist that they bring out the whole thing. Hang out by the tank for a while and watch how they move, too. Take your study model apart carefully when you eat, and bring the shell home in a doggy bag for closer study. If you can't finish your model in a couple of days, you'll need to make sure the shell is completely clean.

Welcome to Toon Town: Design for Caricature

The next level of complexity is the caricature. This is usually a more complete character, with full articulation in the hands and face and often built from a single seamless mesh. This requires the use of LightWave's mesh deformation tools like Bones or EndoMorphs. If you aren't ready to handle this level of complexity, you are pretty much stuck with primitive characters.

Cartoons or caricatures are a popular style of character animation. Shading and rendering options enable you to create caricatures for a variety of environments, from the photorealism of *The Mask* to cel shading that mimics traditional 2D drawn animation. Some animators have succeeded in emulating the visual style of classic cartoon animators like Tex Avery, Friz Freleng, and Chuck Jones, whereas others are intent on breaking new ground in ways unique to the computer medium.

The dramatic strengths of the caricature style lie in stereotype, archetypes, and exaggeration. If your character is a villain, he'll have to look like a villain. Don't try to fool with your audience by making a perfectly nice-looking character turn out to be the bad guy. If your story premise is understated or subtle, you may want to consider another style. A notable example is the character of Gaston in Disney's *Beauty and the Beast*. Andreas Deja, the animator, originally wanted a darker, bigger-chinned heavy with a mustache and dark circles under his eyes. Producer Jeffrey Katzenberg wanted to emphasize the "Beauty is only skin deep" moral, by showing how ugly Gaston was with his behavior rather than with his appearance, the perfect complement to the Beast. And yet, many people act surprised when reminded that Gaston was not the hero! "But he was so good looking!" Commercial audiences, especially in the U.S., generally aren't expecting subtlety or irony in an animation, and your more refined dramatic efforts may be lost on them.

Exaggeration means you'll have to design and build the character to exceed the limits of a merely human character. A caricature must be able to pop eyes in surprise, recoil like rubber in a wild take, and generally move as if the laws of physics are as mutable as its anatomy. The key to designing a caricature for exaggeration is finding what defines the character and its actions, then pushing that definition to the breaking point. For example, a primitive or realistic character might reach for a doorknob by straightening out his arm and stepping forward until his hand reaches the knob. The caricatured character would fling out his arm, hyperextending the elbow and stretching his arm until his hand meets the doorknob, at which point the elasticity of his stretched arm snaps him forward, perhaps off his feet. The essence of this action is the extension of the arm with the goal of the doorknob—the exaggeration is in putting all of the character's energy and form into attaining that goal.

Caricatures never do things halfway; it's several hundred percent effort, every time. Even a caricature's casual saunter is an exaggeration of the essential actions of the real-life motion.

Facial design is especially important for the caricature style. You'll almost never see a stone-faced caricature or a neutral caricature face; even at rest, characters must be saying, loudly, exactly who they are and what they are intending. Fortunately, the caricature style can borrow heavily from the existing body of work on 2D cartoon animation. The references in the Bibliography contain many excellent examples of 2D caricature design, and the majority can be adapted (more or less) to LightWave's 3D environment. I especially recommend Brian Lemay's *Designing Cartoon Characters for Animation* and any of Preston Blair's books.

Better than Life?

Realism is the most technically demanding character style, at least for modeling and setup. It is also the style least suited to traditional animation methods and most suited to *mocap*, or motion capture. Before you decide on realism as your character's style, you should be absolutely sure that your story requires this high level of modeling and rendering detail. If so, are there also compelling reasons why you shouldn't simply make it a live-action film rather than animate it?

Modeling and setup for a realistic human is possibly the most complex job in character animation. You must use nearly every modeling, texturing, setup, animation, and rendering tool available in LightWave, plus a number of third-party plug-ins. It's almost impossible to do a realistic human in LightWave alone. It's more common for studios to use a variety of supplemental software and hardware tools, each in its strongest area, to assemble a realistic character.

The design process is mostly a matter of choosing a subject and then doing research and data capture. If you are simulating a particular person, you will have to capture complete geometry, texture, and range-of-motion (if not actual mocap) data. Even if you are building a unique character rather than a digital stuntman, you will find it more efficient to capture as much geometry, texture, and movement data from similar real-life subjects as possible. Trying to model and texture a realistic human from scratch is work for a master, and a gifted one at that.

Finicky attention to detail is the prime requirement for realistic character creation. Subtleties like specularity textures, skin folds, and the translucency of fingernails can make or break an illusion. The same is true for animating the finished character. You must create absolutely perfect timing or the illusion of life is destroyed.

If your realistic character is not human, you will have to do the equivalent research on animals. If the character is fantastic, you'll need to find the most similar bits and pieces in real-life creatures and adapt them with as much wit and talent as you can muster. Concocting a character like *Dragonheart's* Draco from an artist's sketch is the sort of work you'll find at the very top of the field.

If you're just starting out in character animation or you're making the transition to the computer from traditional animation, don't jump straight into realism or even caricature. Go back to the primitives, get your setup and animation skills up to speed, then start adding complexity to your characters.

Set Design

If you're brand-new to LightWave character animation, the most forgiving and least demanding place to start modeling is in building your own sets. Most sets don't have to move or interact very much. In fact, many of them can just as easily be painted backdrops. You won't have to build in many controls, and the ones you do can usually be automated.

Set design also gives you the opportunity to match your story's environment to its characters. If you use the same tools and techniques to create the sets and to later build the characters, it will be easier to maintain the same visual style throughout your production. To judge the consistency of the visual style, you need a way to juxtapose all the pieces at once. The easiest way I've found to do this is to set up rough draft versions of the film's elements in LightWave scenes and replace each element with more refined versions as development proceeds.

It will be a lot easier for you to make scene layout if you combine all the immovable objects in a scene into a single object. Furniture, walls, and architectural details rarely need to be animated. You can also delete unnecessary polygons once you know they won't be seen in a shot, thereby conserving memory and saving redraw and rendering time. And you can add simple looping actions to a set as child objects. You can set fan rotation, clock hands, even dripping water to simple repeating cycles.

If you think ahead about set construction, you can build reusable objects that you can customize with a minimum of effort. Suppose you assigned Bones to lock down all the points defining a window opening. You could drag the Bones to move the window and have a new room layout. With a judicious placement of controls and definition of surfaces, you can make a chameleon room that you can transform into the basis of almost any interior set.

When you're ready to furnish a set, don't neglect 3D clip art. If the animation's style is very quirky and unique, you'll probably have to model everything from scratch. But if the sets are at all "normal," you can probably find some clip art that will save you modeling time. CD-ROM collections are available, including inexpensive compilations from Internet FTP and Web sites. Those sites are also good hunting grounds, if you have the time to browse. I recommend starting at **www.flay.com**, and browsing from the links page you'll find there.

PROJECT 5.2   Building a Simplified Set

To build a simplified set, follow these steps:

1. Assemble a generic office set as a single object in Modeler. Using prebuilt objects, add a floor, a ceiling, walls, a door, windows, a desk, chairs, a credenza, shelves, and a lamp. Cull objects from the Internet, LightWave's CD-ROM, and any other sources you find useful.

2. Define surfaces so you can select the individual parts as necessary.

3. Build child objects for clock hands, a ceiling fan, or other objects that will make cyclical motions. Set up a looping action.

Moving On

You should now be able to make well-informed decisions about how you want your characters to look and move. The next chapter will show you some of the most useful modeling tools appropriate to building animatable characters in LightWave.

Case Study 5.1
Designing Mudpuppy: Character Design

By Dave Bailey, 3D animator and digital illustrator

What follows is a description of the process I used to design a character for my LightWave demo reel. I experienced a lot of false starts (I prefer to call them "learning experiences") along the way, but the final results turned out well.

Finished Mudpuppy character.

The creature, which I named Mudpuppy, was born of a rejected concept sketch I had done for a client who was looking for an alien creature that had "evil, gremlinlike" characteristics. I had done several pages of creature concept sketches, spending only a few minutes on each concept. While the ideas are flowing, it is important to get as many of them down as quickly as possible. This allows for greater creativity by preventing you from becoming too attached to an idea simply because of the amount of time you invest. It also allows the client or art director to redirect you before you waste too much time heading down a wrong path.

In this situation, the client chose a concept that was more insectlike because it would be easier to model, set up, and animate, and therefore, it would be easier on the budget. I really liked the concept for the character that would eventually become Mudpuppy and decided to use it as a project for my demo reel.

The original concept was more of a slimy ogre/gremlin-type character, but as I thought about story lines, the character changed to a creature that was a lot more amiable, agile, and impish. To flesh out the new look of the character, and to get a better feel for its anatomy, I created a maquette with Sculpey polymer clay. I built the armature out of coat hangers and aluminum foil, which ended up being far too flexible and weak to support the weight of the clay. A heavier gauge aluminum wire, which would have been more malleable and less springy, would have been a better choice.

Dave Bailey

Early Mudpuppy concept sketch.

Dave Bailey

Mudpuppy maquette.

I ended up forming a lighter skeleton over the armature with Sculpey, then curing it in the oven. With a firm skeletal base and a human anatomy book in hand, I fleshed out the model muscle-by-muscle. This process of forensic construction helped produce a creature with a believable anatomy. Considering that the last thing I sculpted in clay was an ashtray when I was in elementary school, I was quite pleased with the results.

*Dave Bailey is a 3D animator and digital illustrator currently working in Southern California. You can email him at **dbailey@pixinc.com** or visit his Web site at **www.pixinc.com**.*

Chapter 6

Modeling Tools

The influence of your modeling tools doesn't stop at your character's outward appearance. Modeling tools can limit or expand your options for animation, too. If you model a character correctly, the setup and animation will go more smoothly. If you model without consideration for the necessities of animation and setup, you can create unnecessary work for yourself and others.

Before you work through this chapter and the following one, you should be comfortably familiar with LightWave's modeling tools. You should have at least worked through the Modeler tutorial "The Pecora Love Machine" in the *LightWave [6]* manuals; this tutorial provides a quick introduction to the most-used modeling tools. Once you have mastered the construction of rigid objects, moving up to deformable meshes and complex hierarchies will be much easier. If you need additional introductory-level modeling tutorials, you might consider some of the general LightWave resources. A Web site or book on special effects, flying logos, or zooming spacecraft is a perfectly good resource for learning basic modeling skills. If I attempted to duplicate all that general information in this book, there wouldn't be enough room for the specifics of character modeling.

Evaluating Modeling Tools

LightWave includes a variety of modeling tools. You must determine which tools suit the way you work and enable you to create the characters and other models you need. Whether you are just starting out or you've been involved in 3D animation from its beginnings, you can use a few guidelines to select and judge your modeling tools:

- Look for tools that minimize the number of steps you have to follow to perform a single task. Each step, or *therblig*, costs you time. Going through three or four therbligs to rescale an object will be a less efficient use of your time than using a tool that only requires one therblig to perform the same task. It may not seem like much of a difference, but when it is repeated hundreds, even thousands, of times during an animation production, it will drive you crazy.

- LightWave enables you to use up to 128 levels of Undo. In the General Options panel, set Undo Levels to *at least* 4. Use as many levels of Undo as your system's memory can support. It's both a safety net and an encouragement to your creativity.

- Slow feedback is sometimes worse than no feedback at all. If the redraw rates on your machine are lousy, find the bottleneck and fix it. Both RAM and fast OpenGL video cards represent only a fraction of your investment in LightWave, and the additional outlay will pay for itself very quickly in boosted productivity and reduced frustration.

- If you are working from photos, drawings, or maquettes, the ability to accurately register and position background template images in Modeler's viewports is crucial.

- The user-definable Magnet and other soft deformation tools are highly valuable for modeling characters, especially when you are modifying morph targets.

- Tools for subdividing polygons and merging or welding points are useful for optimizing models.

- Remember that modeling and setup are closely related, iterative processes. LightWave's Hub enables you to easily port your models between Modeler and Layout.

Fitting the Tools to the Job

The tools and procedures you choose or develop will depend on the type of character animation you do and the resources you have available to do it. A work strategy that succeeds for a sizable commercial shop like Foundation Imaging is not necessarily a good one for a one-person shop doing local television ads. The opposite is also true; a work strategy that you have been using successfully as a solo animator may fail when you try to apply it to a larger production team.

Again, consider my short list of criteria for an efficient work strategy:

- Reduce redundant work.

- Support incremental detailing.

- Provide rapid feedback.

- Create documents for decision-makers.

- Stay flexible.

Before you make changes to the way you model, check the new procedures against these criteria. If your proposed changes don't measure up, you should fix the problem before you go any further.

By reducing redundant work, I mean that you shouldn't have to repeat any work that isn't creative. Bringing a revised low-resolution model up to hi-res is the kind of work you should automate, if possible. Doing it once is a learning experience, doing it twice is annoying, and doing it a couple times a week can be a sentence in Purgatory. Work smart. Find ways to create macros, batch files, programs, or other tools that can do most of the repetitive work for you. This is the type of work at which computers excel—repetitive, complex tasks with no artistic judgment required. If you don't use the computer for these tasks, you're not using LightWave character animation's primary advantage over traditional methods. You might as well be using pencils or clay.

Supporting incremental detailing means your work strategy should enable you to rough out the entire model before making revisions and changes. Odds are good that you, your production team, or the client are going to make some major changes to the character design. It's almost unheard of for a first draft design to be identical to the final character in a film. Because you can be certain of changes, you should make as many of them as you can at the lowest, cheapest level of detail. If your work strategy requires you to complete a detailed character model before the design is approved, you will almost certainly be wasting a lot of that effort. A mistake in design that goes uncorrected until final animation can waste many, many hours and sink your budget.

Providing rapid feedback means you should be able to make go/no-go decisions as soon as a task is completed. This is one of the problems with traditional cel or clay animation that LightWave animation can eliminate almost entirely. If you design your character setups properly, you can rapidly test new character models in existing animations. These tests can tell you if the object is going to work properly or if it will have to be remodeled to eliminate creases, intersections, or other unwanted artifacts.

Creating documents for decision-makers has two purposes for your work strategy: to make your work more efficient and to limit your risks. The first purpose is reason enough for you to habitually document your work. When you have a concrete document to refer to, you can concentrate better and waste less misdirected effort than if you were winging it from memory alone. When you get bogged down in the details of character modeling, it's almost impossible to keep everything straight in your head.

When you're building a character for a client, the second purpose becomes more important. Nothing can guarantee that you won't have to make major changes once you're in the later stages of production. You can expect decision-makers to waffle and change their minds right up to the last minute and sometimes beyond. The important criteria for your modeling work strategy is to have firm, contractually binding approvals at each level of detail, based on the documents you produce. When the client signs off on the maquette, you need to be confident that you can go ahead with building and setting up the model. A good contract will spell out how you are paid for each deliverable, including the rough model. If the client wants to make changes after they've already approved the work, they should pay you to do the work over. If it's not in your contract, you'll end up either eating the costs or having an irate client. When the client makes an expensive decision, you don't want to be the one paying the bill.

Staying flexible means just that. If your work strategy is too rigid, it's likely to snap on you someday. You shouldn't get too attached to any part of the project plan. You have to be prepared to deal with the setbacks and roadblocks that happen in every project. You should get in the habit of trying out alternatives, experimenting with different approaches to typical character design and modeling problems. When your usual approach doesn't work, you'll have a spare, and you'll sometimes find an application for a procedure you never expected to use.

Taking Advantage of Polygons

Anybody who has played a realtime 3D game is very familiar with the look of polygonal surfaces. As geometry engines become more powerful, they'll be capable of slinging even more polygons, until even games lose that trademark polygonal look. However, polygons aren't yet history. Even if polygons can't be detected in your final product, they have much utility in the production pipeline.

An appropriately sized polygonal cube can be a stand-in for a more highly detailed prop or character until you drop in the finished model. Using only a few simple commands and some talent, you can turn that cube into a finished model. Even if you need to deliver a NURBS (Non-Uniform Rational B-Spline) model, you can model in low-polygonal detail to block out basic shapes and proportions, round up to higher detail, and use the resultant smoothed shape as a virtual maquette template for a NURBS surface.

With a low-detailed polygonal surface, you can focus entirely on shape and proportion and easily refine it, putting detail only where you want it. At low enough detail, proportions are even easier to change with polygons than with clay. When you need to define a surface with the least amount of detail, polygons are the way to go as long as you don't care about harsh edges in your silhouette. Even if you're never, ever going to make game art and all your finished models are going to be made of NURBS, there is still much utility in polygonal modeling. Polygons allow for flexibility of resolution in the planning stages, letting you design with the least amount of detail to manage.

Low-detail NURBS grids don't map readily onto complex surfaces like the folds and openings of a human face. If you design with polygons to begin with, you can increase or decrease detail as you go and then later apply a patch surface. Sometimes you have to deliver NURBS, but polygons can be the best choice, particularly for something as highly detailed as a face.

Working with Polygons

With polygonal modeling, you must be able to visualize and manage your model in terms of points, edges, and faces to build up complex organic curves from collections of flat faces. This is generally not difficult for people with a technical illustration, drafting, or engineering education, where orthographic projection is a basic technique. It can be more difficult for people from art or design backgrounds, where the tools have traditionally been better suited to managing 3D curves as single entities rather than by segments.

When modeling a character, it's up to you to determine where to put the detail. There should be detail sufficient to both reveal the shape and allow for proper deformation when the character moves. There are a number of issues to consider before you even get that far. First, what are you building the model for? A limited-detail, realtime 3D game? A low-resolution prerendered image? A high-resolution film? Will your model need to function in more than one of those environments? Can you or do you need to plan for resolution independence? How much geometric detail can be provided by textures and shaders and volume, bump, or displacement maps? How much do you like to punish your machine? How long are you willing to wait for a screen refresh? How much time do you have available? What have you already got in a morgue file that you can kit-bash? Will anybody ever see that part you were just obsessing about? What does the model need to be able to do that can be built in from the start rather than later, when it would be much more difficult to change?

Polygon points are always part of the surface. However, NURBS or SubPatch models use control points that modify but are not directly part of the surface they define. This can be annoying when you're trying to locate the points that will make the surface go where you want it to be.

Even animators would like modeling if it weren't for the problem of connecting the dots. As if point placement alone weren't a big enough problem, where should the resultant surface be in relation to the points, through them or near them? How will the surface deform when points are moved? How can adjacent surfaces be adjoined? How will it light? Why does everything have to be an infinitely subdivisible grid? Shouldn't I be able to place detail where I need it without all that adjacent baggage? What is the balance between too little detail and too much? What's the proper balance between detail sufficient to define the surface yet simple enough to be controlled by an animator? Why don't you model and set it up and call me when it's ready for an animator? Modeling can be tedious, often frustrating work. If you understand common problems and the solutions provided by LightWave, your modeling will go much more smoothly.

For the simple reason that you can add or subtract detail where you want it, polygons are the simplest way to work. Of course, polygonal models will be quite faceted. But polygonal surfaces can be rounded up with a button push in LightWave, and your low-detail polygonal model can drive the high-detailed model used for final render, as shown in Figure 6.1.

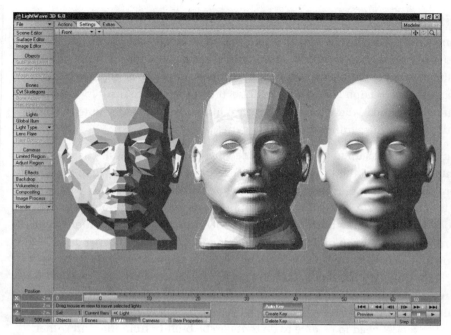

Figure 6.1
A low-resolution polygonal model (left) subdivided using LightWave's SubPatch (middle) to create a high-resolution model (right).

Connecting the Dots

The first modeling approach I am going to explain is brute-force, spare-no-effort that some might consider overkill for many characters. I agree, when the character in question carries a minor role or is designed for realtime game or multimedia resolution or a simplified style. However, Fred is the lead character in an emotionally and physically demanding role that may someday (hey, I can dream, can't I?) end up on the big screen. Ergo, Fred gets the full treatment.

Not coincidentally, this approach also turns out to save the most effort in the long run. Remember those five criteria I keep harping on: Reduce redundant work, support incremental detailing, provide rapid feedback, create documents for decision-makers, and stay flexible. The following character modeling process meets all five criteria.

You'll generally achieve best results with a single mesh for a face. Facial expressions affect much of the face at the same time. If you're raising the corners of the mouth, you're also raising the cheeks, nostrils, eyelids, and associated wrinkles. Multiple surfaces can be done, but at the cost of isolating parts of the face that don't really behave by themselves.

What we really want is something that matches most of the muscular structure of the face, with lines radial from the mouth, the nose, and each eye. The advantage is that natural folds can be defined with lines that are already where you need them.

PROJECT 6.1 Modeling Fred's Head

The following project will show you how to build a character's head in Modeler by adding individual points and connecting them into polygons. This demonstrates the highest level of detailed control you can exercise to build a model. In addition, this project shows you how to use the matched pairs of maquette images from Chapter 5 to create an accurate LightWave duplicate of the physical maquette, a process called *photogrammetry*.

1. Launch Modeler. Press "d" to open the Display Options window. In the Layout tab, choose the Double Vertical layout and make sure Enable Backdrop is checked.

2. In the Viewports tab, set the View Type option for the Left viewport to Back(XY) and for the Right viewport to Right(ZY). Set Rendering Style to Wireframe for both viewports.

3. In the Backdrop tab, load the backdrop images in 90-degree pairs. I recommend Maq270B.iff (left profile) and Maq180B.iff (full face) as a good starting pair (see Figure 6.2). Set Image Resolution to 1024 and adjust the Brightness and Contrast values if necessary.

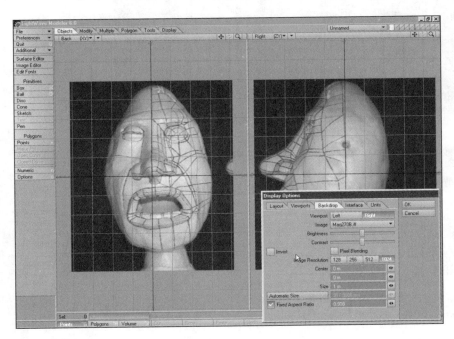

Figure 6.2
Display options set to load matched profile and front maquette images as backdrops.

4. In the Back view, add a point to cover each intersection visible in the backdrop image. Connect the points along the backdrop image's lines to form quad polygons. You can choose whatever tool you prefer to create polygons. My personal preference is the Pen.

5. Select and Merge or Weld any redundant points. If necessary, tweak the points' positions after the Weld operations. The new points should all originate in the zero Z plane, as shown in Figure 6.3.

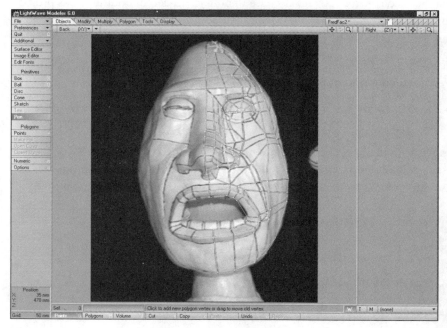

Figure 6.3
New four-sided polygons Penned, Merged, and Welded to match Maq180B.iff backdrop.

6. When you have covered as many intersections as you can see clearly, switch to the side view.

7. Drag each point in the negative z-axis until it matches the side view backdrop.

8. In the side view, add new polygons that were not visible in the front view. Your results should look like Figure 6.4.

   This might not seem to be the most efficient way to work, but I can really get cranking without making mistakes. My overall productivity with this method is pretty good.

9. When you have created all the necessary polygons, check the stats for nonfour-sided polygons. Even while being careful, I usually manage to create two or three of these.

10. Make whatever changes are necessary to change the nonquad polygons to quad polygons.

11. When the face and side views are done to the best of your ability, clear the backdrop images and load the Maq315B.iff and Maq225.iff images. Again, you need to work in 90-degree pairs to match the side and face views.

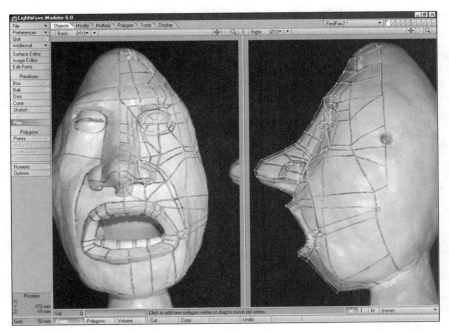

Figure 6.4
Points moved along z-axis, and new polygons added to match the Maq270B.iff backdrop image.

12. Move and rotate the model to align it with the new backdrop images. You should be able to set the Rotation value by using the numeric panel and typing in exactly "45.0" around the y-axis. Your results should look like Figure 6.5.

13. Repeat the polygon creation process to match all the lines and intersections visible in the new backdrop images.

    Even with backdrops captured at 45-degree increments, you will probably run into under-cuts and involute surfaces that you just can't see clearly. This is why you kept the maquette. For the final touches, you just have to eyeball the maquette and try to make the model in LightWave match it. Hey, this is still an art, not a science.

14. Once you have completed the right side of the head, use the Mirror function to duplicate it as the left half.

    Because Fred is far from symmetrical, the Mirror operation does not really give you a use-ful mesh. What it does give you is an identical number and distribution of points and polygons.

15. Move each mirrored point on the left side to match the left-side backdrop images. That's significantly easier than creating all those polygons from scratch, isn't it?

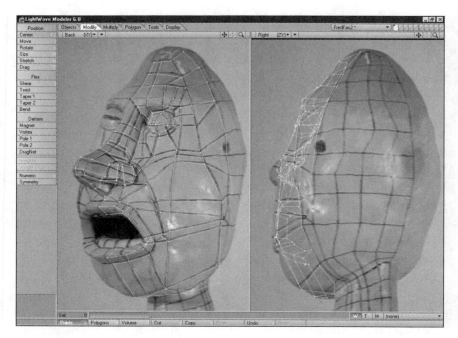

Figure 6.5
Maq315B.iff and Maq225.iff images loaded as backdrops, and model rotated and moved to match.

16. Repeat the process for the rest of the images, working your way around the whole maquette.

17. When you have added every point you can see in every backdrop image, test the model by executing Metaform.

You should get something like Figure 6.6. You will notice that it is not an exact match for the maquette. The original object is simply a cage for the Metaform process, not the final geometry itself. To get an exact shape, you have to tweak and distort the cage to allow for Metaform's idiosyncrasies. You need to go through a similar process if you use the cage as a SubPatch object. You can either do that fine-tuning in Modeler or in a Layout Boned setup for creating morph targets.

Creating Symmetry

There are several ways in LightWave to model one side of an object and see what it looks like in symmetry. You can duplicate one side of the face and scale it -1 in the x-axis, or you can use the Mirror tool. With the Symmetry option enabled, the new side will update while you work on the original, though you should finish adding or subtracting all points, edges, or polygons before you try this. This is useful primarily so that you can see the proportions properly. Of course, when it's time to finish the face, you'll have to remove the symmetry by working on the other side of the final mesh.

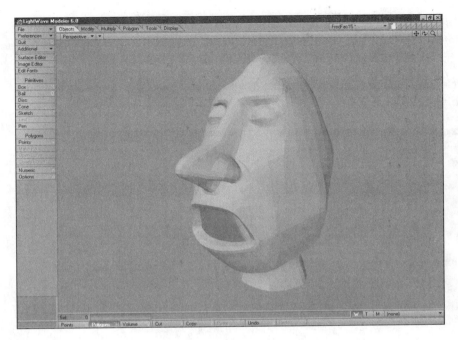

Figure 6.6
Metaformed Fred head.

Point and Polygon Density and Placement

No matter how powerful your computer, you will always be negotiating a balance between rendering speed, level of detail, hard drive space, and memory requirements. As the old joke goes, if you're not running out of memory, your scene isn't complicated enough.

Part of that balancing act is determining how many polygons you need and how many you can afford. More polygons will generally respond to mesh-deforming animation tools with better interpolation and will also render curves more smoothly. Fewer polygons will redraw faster, use less memory, and be easier to edit when necessary.

One way to control the complexity of a character's objects is to place the polygons exactly where you need them. Some parts of a character need very few polygons and other areas need more. Shoes, mid-sleeves, or mid-legs with little or no motion or deformation can get by with fewer polygons, whereas joints and flexible masses of soft tissue will require more subdivisions. You can use a few simple tools to turn a cube into any shape you need.

Roughing Out a Reference Figure

PROJECT 6.2

The goal of this project is to demonstrate how quickly and easily you can turn a primitive box into a humanoid body, using only the Smooth Shift, Knife, Move, Rotate, Size, and Subdivide tools. As I've stated before, unless you are already an experienced

LightWave modeler, creating accurately proportioned models is much easier if you work with a backdrop template. For this project, you'll need front and side images of a character. Use anything you have handy or the Back.iff and Left.iff images from the CD-ROM.

1. Set up Modeler and load the backdrop images as you did in Project 6.1. Your screen should look something like Figure 6.7.

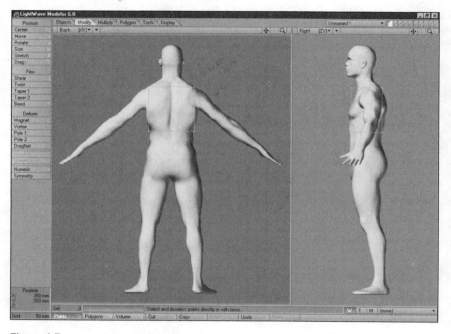

Figure 6.7
Modeler with side and back images of a human model loaded as backdrop templates and box fitted over rib cage.

2. Create a box then move and scale it to fit over the backdrop's rib cage, as shown in Figure 6.7. If you have problems with this or any other steps in this Project, you should repeat the basic modeling tutorial in the *LightWave [6] Introduction and Tutorials* manual.

3. Use the Knife tool to cut the box in half horizontally, as shown in Figure 6.8. This creates polygons at the sides of the box that can be smooth shifted and moved to create the arms.

4. Select the polygon at the root of the arm and smooth shift it. Resize, rotate, and move the new polygon to conform to the upper arm in the backdrop images. Repeat to form the elbow, as shown in Figure 6.9.

   Always use a smooth shift value of zero to avoid creating nonplanar polygons. After smooth shifting polygons, you can move, scale, and rotate them.

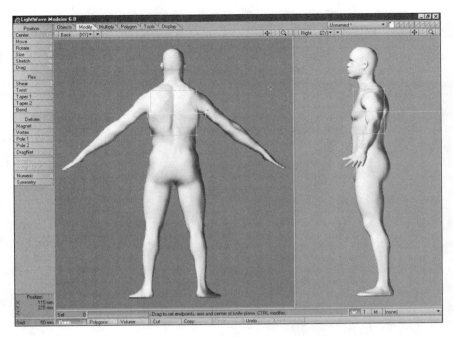

Figure 6.8
Box cut in half with the Knife tool.

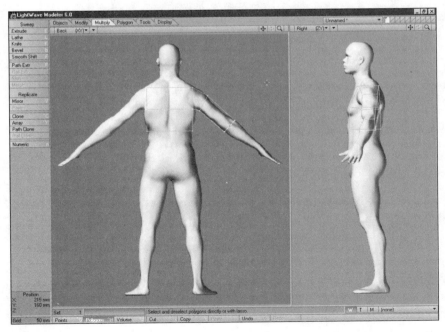

Figure 6.9
Upper arm formed with Smooth Shift, Move, Rotate, and Size tools.

5. Use the Knife tool to cut the upper arm polygons and then move the new points to conform the mesh more closely to the backdrop images. Repeat the smooth shift and move points operations to extend the arm as far as the wrist, as shown in Figure 6.10.

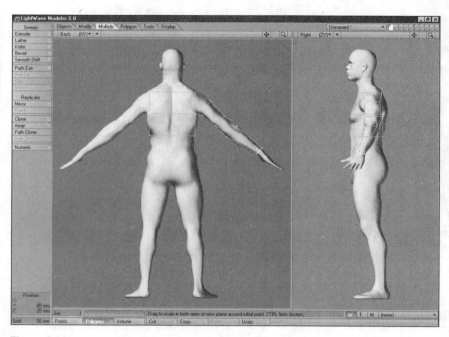

Figure 6.10
Arm formed with Knife, Smooth Shift, Move, Rotate, and Size tools.

6. When the arm is roughed out to the wrist, select the polygons of the arm and perform a Subdivide|Metaform operation. Your results should look like Figure 6.11.

7. Move the new points to more closely conform the polygons to the backdrop images.

8. Repeat the knife, smooth shift, and point adjustment operations for the lower torso and the leg. Your results should look like Figure 6.12.

You can continue this process to build the rest of the body in a very short time. If you build only one side of the body, you can mirror it, then weld any duplicate points along the center line.

With practice, you should be able to accurately perform the preceding steps in a few minutes. If you want to improve your modeling efficiency, you should practice using the hotkey shortcuts until you have them memorized. You can create complex features (such as hands, feet, and head) separately, then manually weld them into the body mesh. You should avoid using Boolean operations because they are likely to create multiple irregular polygons that are hard

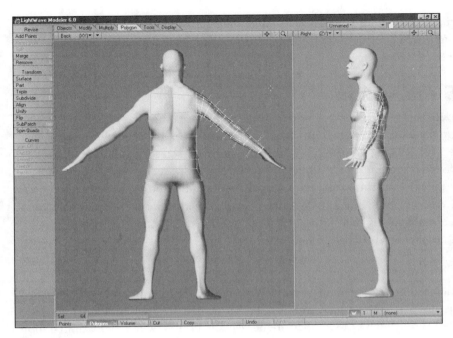

Figure 6.11
Arm after Subdivide|Metaform operation.

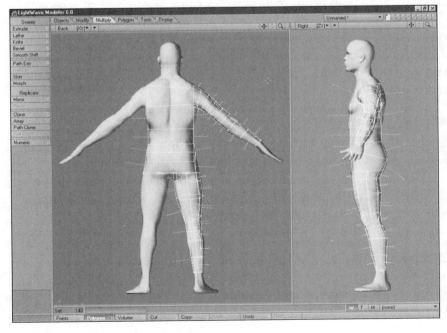

Figure 6.12
Roughed-out torso and Metaformed leg.

to clean up. It's more efficient for you to decide where the points and polygons should go. This will preserve the four-sided polygons, preventing pinching problems and enabling you to properly Metaform or SubPatch the object.

Surface Subdivision

On its way to picking up an Oscar, Pixar's *Geri's Game* generated some buzz about how it was made (as if it were the tools that gave it its edge). You could drive yourself crazy trying to model Geri's face in NURBS, let alone manage that amount of detail for animation. Pixar's trick was to subdivide a comparatively simple polygonal surface at render, using proprietary code that let them predict the shape and mapping attributes of the surface without having to do iterative subdivision beforehand. LightWave also lets you work with a low-detail polygonal mesh that drives a multi-subdivided surface for use at lighting and render time, freeing you from dealing with higher levels of detail until critical.

SubPatch

I usually recommend using SubPatch for characters, especially facial animation. Whichever techniques you use to model, set up, and animate, SubPatch lightens the workload. A low-polygon cage object is much easier to remodel, Bone, section, or otherwise modify than a high-polygon object suitable for final rendering. For example, Fred's head as a SubPatch cage has 532 points; at SubPatch Level 3, it has 4,518. When you consider that some facial animation techniques require you to manage every one of these points, the choice for SubPatch becomes a no-brainer. Also, screen redraw times are markedly faster, and there is much less confusing clutter to sort through in Layout when you animate using simple cage objects. The only time I would not use SubPatch is when a facial feature has details (skin folds, for example) that the SubPatch process smoothes out too much. Even then, I would try to add more detail (and therefore more control) to the cage object before giving up the advantages.

Subdivide Metaform

Animation can certainly be easier with SubPatch, but this may not be the best way to initially model your characters in LightWave. One drawback to using SubPatch is the exaggeration you have to apply to create features. The Metaform option of the Subdivide tool enables you to work with a low-polygon-count model and periodically Metaform it to a higher complexity to check your results. In addition, a low-resolution polygonal model more closely resembles the final Metaform output.

When using Metaform, you can build a low-resolution version of the model, then apply Metaform to add a controlled amount of detail and smooth the mesh. You can create features by dragging points out of a primitive cube until they resemble the outline of the feature, then smooth shift the polygons to add detail. Although it can also work with triangles, you should try to use only quad polygons with Metaform. Executing a Metaform operation also converts any remaining triangles to quads, setting up the model for SubPatch.

Modeling for Morphing

Modeling for morph animation is possibly the most restrictive task a modeler or technical director (TD) has to perform. The rigid requirements of identical point and polygon count and distribution automatically exclude most of your modeling tools. If you make a mistake and add or delete a point, the difficulty of rematching the point order pretty much guarantees that you've ruined the object. You should therefore limit your modeling operations to tools that move points without adding or deleting them.

In LightWave, you can safely use all the Modify tab functions in Modeler: Move, Rotate, Size, Stretch, Drag, Shear, Twist, Taper 1 and 2, Bend, Magnet, Vortex, Pole 1 and 2, DragNet, and Symmetry. If you are careful and consistent in setting them up, you can get away with using Skin, Morph, and other functions in the Multiply panel. Be warned—any change in the settings will produce an object with incompatible point and polygon counts and ordering. You can also use SubPatch if the cage object and the Freeze detail settings remain the same.

One advantage morph modeling has over other forms is that you can use setup and animation tools too. In LightWave, the Save|Save Transformed Object function will save a copy of the currently selected object from the current frame, including all position, attitude, size, EndoMorph Mixer, Bones deformation, and displacement map changes to the object's geometry. This means that you can use nearly any Layout function to modify an object, then save those changes in a permanent snapshot that will morph perfectly with the original object. This opens up a lot of opportunities that would be difficult or nearly impossible in Modeler.

Before you get too excited, there is a drawback to using Layout for creating model libraries. The UV mapping coordinates are not saved with the same deformations. If you apply a map to an object, deform that object with Bones or other Layout tools, and save it in its deformed state, the map will not match the original. The only available workaround is to always use the original object as the base of the endomorph and only incorporate the transformed object as a morph map.

Problems like this make it doubly important to keep a clean copy of the original object somewhere safe. You will be using working copies all the time to create new objects, and it's entirely too easy to inadvertently save over the original. There's nothing like trying to reconstruct an original from a lot of transformed copies to remind you to be more careful.

Options for Facial Morphs

There are several approaches for morphing a seamless head with a broad range of emotional expression, but they all boil down to moving points around. Let's see which approaches meet my five criteria for efficient work flow.

One of the best approaches for facial animation in LightWave is to use morph maps for everything but the eyeballs. The shape weighting that is possible with morph maps in Layout's

EndoMorph Mixer, shown in Figure 6.13, enables the animator to create very subtle facial expressions and emotional transitions. For a full range of realistic facial expressions, you can create one or more morph maps for each muscle or muscle group, then blend them in the Mixer to get highly realistic results with a maximum of flexibility. You can make changes to the base object or any morph maps without affecting the rest of the project. This gives you a remarkable amount of resilience, both for correcting mistakes and for accommodating the changes common to long, complex projects. In all, endomorph facial animation passes all five criteria with flying colors.

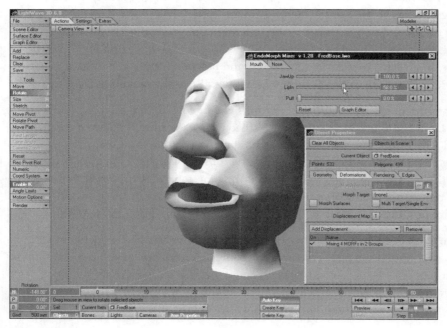

Figure 6.13
Fred's morph maps blended in EndoMorph Mixer.

Point by Point

The most basic seamless animation technique is to select and move individual points in Modeler, then save the modifications as a morph map. Feedback is quick, and your ability to salvage mistakes is limited only by Modeler's levels of Undo. This approach fails the first criteria, but it passes the other four.

Bones

A slightly more complex approach is to use the minimum Bones (and other Layout deformation tools) to create specific poses, then use the Save Transformed operation to create morph targets. For example, Figure 6.14 shows a simple two-Bone setup designed to puff out Fred's left cheek. This approach is relatively quick and simple to set up and much more resilient than straight modeling. You can save the scene, set up several poses in one scene, and use keyframe tools to copy and paste elements of one pose into another. If you have to replace the original object, you only have to reset the Bones that are affected. For a very simple character, you might be able to get by with a handful of Bones for the eyes and mouth. However, this approach does not enable sufficient control to animate a realistically expressive human face.

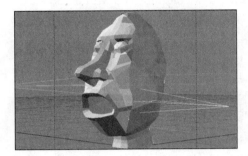

Figure 6.14
Puffer Bone moves to bulge Fred's left cheek.

More Bones

Bone-per-point is a more extensive version of the minimum Bones approach. You set a Limited Range Bone over each movable point in the object, then move the Bones to create a new pose. This meets all five criteria, but just barely. It forces animators to rely on their own knowledge and judgment of facial musculature for the movement of every single point. It's hard to animate consistently and easy to make mistakes, especially by pulling the skin away from the underlying musculoskeletal structures. For example, in Fred's head, there are over 60 points that should move with any rotation of the lower jaw. With the simplest Bone-per-point approach, that means manually repositioning each point. With a properly set-up skeleton, it means rotating a single Bone. A Bone-per-point setup also makes it more tedious to reuse part of a pose; you have to copy and paste keyframes for each Bone rather than for an entire branch of the skeleton hierarchy. These disadvantages are even more apparent if you decide to animate the setup in Layout directly rather than by creating morph maps.

Realistic Facial Skeleton Setup

If you want to animate a face through a broad expressive range and need maximum flexibility for your production process, here is the approach I recommend. In Layout, set up a skeleton of Bones to mimic the underlying structure of real facial bones, muscle, and connective tissue. This is parallel to the maquette modeling techniques I described in Chapter 5, and the study aids I recommended will be a help here too. The idea is to control the movement of points in the cage object just as real skin is moved by real muscle and bone. Although it sounds like overkill, it's often the simplest and most reliable way of getting acceptable results. A properly designed skeleton will require fewer Bones than the Bone-per-point technique while enabling much finer and more accurate control than a minimum-Bones approach. If you have to modify the cage object, you only have to reset the Bones that affect the new or repositioned points. In addition, building a complete facial control skeleton enables you to quickly and easily reconstruct any new expression in a matter of minutes. If you cut corners with a limited setup, you may find yourself needing an expression you did not plan for and with no time to build the setup you should have had. This realistic skeleton approach passes all five criteria.

The first step is to lay out the parents of the skeleton. The root of everything is the skull. From there, control divides between points attached to the skull and those attached to the lower jaw. For example, the root points of the upper lip should be direct children of the Skull Bone, but points in the lower lip should be children of the Jaw Bone. When the jaw rotates for gross motion, the lower lip should follow along while the upper lip stays put.

When I am laying out a complex facial skeleton, I like to turn Display SubPatch Level down to 1 so I can easily see the position of Bones relative to the surface (Figure 6.15). You will want most of these Bones to be embedded exactly halfway into the surface, on a point or along an edge.

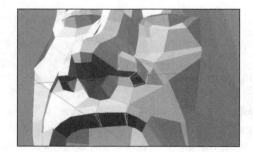

Figure 6.15
Fred's head cage object showing Bones for left nostril and part of upper lip.

I set up Bones to rotate, move, or scale to move points in a cage object. Move Bones are the most common facial animation Bone. However, you should use them with caution because it's very easy to move points away from the underlying skull in an unrealistic way. Generally, I limit Move Bones to the z-axis and align the Bone so its local z-axis lies along the edge the moving point will follow. This setup demonstrates why it's so important to mark and digitize the maquette with animation in mind. If you can simply animate the Move Bones to follow the lines, it's a no-brainer. If you have to remember the location and direction of the line of tension for a muscle, animation is much harder.

Using Scale Bones is a good way to control the length of an edge. Position the root of the Bone over the first point, align the Bone along the edge, and set the Rest Length to just touch the second point. Animating the scale of the Bone will move the second point in the direction of the Bone's long axis. This is a good way of confining the movement of a point to the contours of the underlying skull.

Generally, I do not often use Rotate Bones because muscles do not usually contract with a circular motion. Notable exceptions are the Bones used to evert or extrude the lips, as shown in Figure 6.15. If you set up the Heading and Bank angles for these Bones properly, you can make the same angle of Pitch produce identical eversion for all the lip Bones. This enables you to animate the lips' pucker with a single control, either by setting up an expression to make the Bones all point toward a null or by applying a mimic expression so all the Bones do what you animate a single Bone to do. Fred's head has 16 lip sections, so I get 16 times the labor savings from this setup. This makes animating the lips as close to effortless as I think you can get.

Once you have the skull and jaw hierarchy figured out, expand the skeleton from each set of flesh-to-skull attachment points. I was surprised to find out how much of the human face is not really attached to anything directly. Bones that control free-floating points like the middle of the cheek and the lips should be the last children in a chain. Make sure your setup keeps skin over bones; that is, do not allow the points to penetrate the underlying skull. Remember that all morphing techniques move points on straight lines. If a point has to turn a corner, you have to build that into the skeleton—and make sure you build it into your morph maps.

Let's take a look at a simple part of the facial skeleton. One of the easiest setups is to flare the nostrils. The muscle that does this in reality has no effect beyond the wings of the nose, so it is easy to isolate (muscle interactions can get very tricky). It's also easy to study this muscle action in a mirror. Very few people can isolate the action of one nostril, so you can safely make a single morph target with both nostrils flared. Note that this muscle's action is omitted from Faigin's *Artist's Complete Guide to Facial Expression*, an otherwise excellent reference book. Flared nostrils are especially important for the character to express rage or take a deep breath. This muscle can also be used to comic effect when a character smells something.

The head object on the CD-ROM has 10 points in the left wing of the nose, as shown in Figure 6.16. Nostril flare expands these points outward and forward, enlarging the nostril and smoothing out any creases between the tip and wings of the nose.

Figure 6.16
Left wing of Fred's nose; 10 points to move, defining 11 polygons.

The nose is part of the skull, so add a child Bone to the Skull Bone. Hold down the "r" key and drag the new Bone to one of the points defining the outer curve of the nostril opening. When the Bone is in position, release the "r" key to make the Bone active again. Switch to Rotate mode, hold down the "r" key, and rotate the Bone until it lines up with the edge to the next point. Switch to Rest Length mode, hold down the "r" key again, and drag the Bone size down until the tip is just covering the next point, as shown in Figure 6.17. Set Limited Range to values that cover just these two points; I used 10 mm.

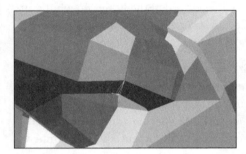

Figure 6.17
First nostril Bone moved, rotated, and sized.

Add a child Bone and use the same procedure to move, rotate, size, and limit range to affect the next point in line. Repeat this one more time, so the vertical line of four points is controlled by three Bones, as shown in Figure 6.18. Repeat the process for the other sectors, starting with a child Bone from the Skull. The most forward sector only requires two Bones because the center of the nose does not move with the nostril flaring. This setup will enable you to animate one sector line at a time without disturbing the other points (or any other part of the face).

Figure 6.18
Eight Bones set up to control nostril flare.

Once you have all the Bones set up, set a keyframe for everything at frame 0. Go to frame 10 and move and rotate the Bones to create a flared nostril pose. You can do more than half the pose simply by moving the first Bones outward from the center of the nostril opening. Once you have the nostril opening the diameter and shape you want, tweak the rotation of the second and third Bones to refine the shape of the nose wing, as shown in Figure 6.19. When you are satisfied with the pose, set a keyframe for the Bones.

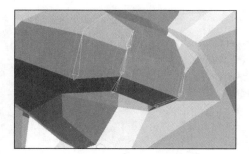

Figure 6.19
Nostril flare pose.

This might seem like a lot of work for something you could do in a few minutes in Modeler by moving points. However, it demonstrates the principles and gives you practice. Here is one advantage: Click the Play button. You can watch the nostril flare and return to normal. You can't do that in Modeler! When you get into more complex areas, it is invaluable to be able to preview movement like this. A glitch detected at this stage can warn you to add an intermediate morph target, redesign the skeleton, or revise the cage object. If you were working in Modeler, you might not get the necessary feedback before you had wasted a lot of other work.

Keyframed Bones Animation

A realistic facial setup also enables you to choose between morph animation and keyframed Bones animation. I do not recommend keyframed Bones for most facial animation because it is more time-consuming, but it does provide more fine control. If you just can't get the nuances of performance through EndoMorph Mixer, this may be what you need.

For keyframed Bones animation, you may need to stabilize immobile portions of the skull with more Bones. You should not need many; most facial Bones should have extremely small Limited Range values. It is generally more important to stabilize the skull against the influence of neck Bones. Incidentally, I highly recommend setting up neck Bones and inverse kinematics (IK) for head tracking, just as you might for eyeball tracking. Remember to use a different Null for a target, and make sure the head's target Null lags behind the one tracked by the eyes.

If you want some advanced practice, you can set up the remaining skeleton for Fred's head. Get a good medical or artist's reference on facial musculature (such as Faigin, noted earlier) and match the major muscle groups to the corresponding edges in the Metaform cage. In most cases, I have laid out edges along the tension lines for muscles. If you set up Bones along these edges, you should be able to accurately animate most of the face. For more complex muscle interactions that move points in more than one direction, there is no shortcut. It simply takes lots of study and experimentation.

Moving On

If you've read this chapter and worked through the projects, you've acquired a good familiarity with the basic character modeling tools available in LightWave. If you expect to do high-end work or are just curious about what the professionals use, go on to Chapter 7 for a look at digitizers, scanners, and the software that goes with them.

Case Study 6.1
Modeling Mudpuppy: A Case Study in Character Building

By Dave Bailey, 3D animator and digital illustrator

This continues the description, begun in Chapter 5, of the design process for my Mudpuppy character. After finishing the maquette, my next step was to create the 3D model in LightWave. I needed to use only the basic Smooth Shift, Bevel, Metaform, and point manipulation tools to get the results I wanted.

I made sure the polygons were placed in a way that allowed the joints to flex properly. I started with a rough silhouette of the body made of quadrangles, making sure the polygons could be smooth-shifted where the model needed appendages. I extruded and Metaformed this silhouette to create the base for the torso. I created arms, legs, and neck with the smooth-shift command and point manipulation. I placed points at the beginning and end of ridged sections of the body and (as much as possible) kept out of areas that needed to be flexible. I modeled the head separately so I could use a slightly denser mesh, then hand-stitched it to the neck with triangles and polygons.

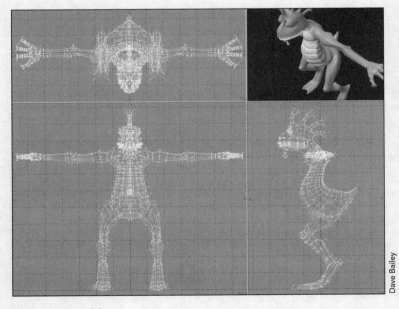

Dave Bailey

Mudpuppy model.

I removed the polygons between sections where flexibility was needed before I segmented the model for setup. This ensured that the saved object points would not overlap.

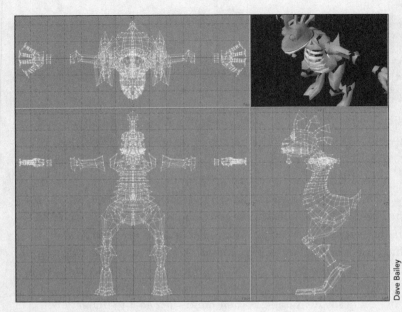

Dave Bailey

Model segmented for setup.

Because of the level of detail in the abdomen, the points were too close to get the flexibility in the torso I wanted. For example, there was pinching and shearing when the segments were rotated past the point where they began to intersect one another. To solve this problem, I used a single object for the torso and set up Bones for the deformation in Layout.

*Dave Bailey is a 3D animator and digital illustrator currently working in Southern California. You can email him at **dbailey@pixinc.com** or visit his Web site at **www.pixinc.com**.*

Dave Bailey

Finished model set up, posed, and rendered in LightWave.

Chapter 7

Advanced Modeling Tools

Recent years have seen a dramatic growth in the number of games, television, and film projects using humanoid characters at photorealistic (or near-photorealistic) levels of modeling and texturing. The demand for this level of work will be consistent in the future, because once the public (and clients) know it can be done, they will continue to require it. That means you had better learn to model and texture photorealistic human characters. If you already know how, you had better learn more ways to make the process as streamlined and efficient as possible.

Accurately reproducing highly detailed maquettes or live actors for animation requires functions that are not part of LightWave's standard modeling tools. For this kind of modeling work, you need to know how to digitize a maquette or life cast, work with laser-scan data, and make a heavy mesh more efficient to set up and animate.

Chapter 5 showed one method for sculpting a character maquette, and Chapter 6 showed a photogrammetric method for converting images of that maquette into a LightWave model using standard Modeler tools. However, it would be difficult or impossible to use manual photogrammetry to bring more complex maquettes into LightWave. If a complex maquette is a sign-off item for clients, you need the ability to make a very accurate duplicate of that maquette in LightWave. A digitizer or laser scanner is an appropriate tool for this task.

Sculpting maquettes is appropriate for caricature or creature modeling, but not for digital stuntmen. The talents of a gifted sculptor are required to build a LightWave model that is accurate enough to substitute for a recognizable actor in a feature film. If you need to make a photorealistic LightWave model from a live subject, you'll be better off using either life casting or laser-scanning techniques.

Laser Scanners

A laser scanner is a device that bounces a low-power laser beam off the subject to precisely measure the subject's surface contours. The general process of laser-scanning a complex maquette or live actor is to perform several raw scans, combine the scans, clean up artifacts in the data, optimize the mesh to reduce density without losing necessary contours, convert the geometry to LightWave format, and adapt the LightWave model for setup and animation.

Laser scanners are the most accurate means of capturing 3D data. Most laser scanners are built for industrial use, where they are used in reverse-engineering, prototyping, and biomedical engineering. Sales of laser scanners to entertainment production houses are a small fraction of the total market. Entertainment sales do have a higher public-relations profile, however. Laser scanners have contributed to films and television shows such as *Jurassic Park*, *The Abyss*, *Terminator 2*, *Dragonheart*, *The Mask*, *Deep Space 9*, and *Apocalypse*. The laser scanners most often used in the entertainment industry are manufactured by Cyberware, Inc. This company's product line includes tabletop models suitable for scanning small maquettes, head scanners (pictured in Figure 7.1), and full-body scanners (shown in Figure 7.2), which can capture life-size sculptures or actors.

Figure 7.1
Cyberware 3030 with PS motion platform.

Figure 7.2
Cyberware full-body laser scanner.

Cyberware scanners use a 780nm infrared (IR) laser, so the beam is not visible. The power of the laser is well within safety standards, so it's safe to scan live subjects with their eyes open. At the same time the laser is scanning the subject's surface (a 17-second process), a second sensor is capturing the color map. In the 3030 HRC scanner, a 2,000-element linear CCD (charge-coupled device) is paired with a cold light source (no infrared is emitted, to avoid interfering with the laser) to capture a 2K-by-2K color image that is perfectly matched to the captured geometry. Previous models used a lower-resolution CCD to capture less-detailed color maps. If you're working in television or multimedia, the older maps are fine. If you're working in feature film, you should definitely consider the higher-resolution HRC model. Cyberware laser scanners are far more accurate than necessary for character models—the 3030 is accurate to 700μm vertically and 200μm radially. Technically, there is no question that a Cyberware scanner can capture adequate geometry and color data from your maquette or live subject.

At this time, all software for driving the scanners and processing the raw data is available for the WinNT and Silicon Graphics platforms. Cyberware scanners require a workstation with a moderate amount of RAM and a decent processor. Raw scanner files are pretty large, so a bottom-end machine won't cut it. Most individuals and organizations that have occasional need for laser scanning choose to deal with a service bureau. If you need only a few scans a year or only for special projects, it doesn't make economic sense to invest $22,000 to $410,000 in a scanner that will be idle much of the time. On the other hand, some firms that have acquired Cyberware scanners have created another source of revenue by providing scanning and processing services to others. You can get more up-to-date technical, financial, and service bureau information by contacting Cyberware through its Web site or directly:

Cyberware, Inc.
2110 Del Monte Avenue
Monterey, CA 93940
Tel: (831) 657-1450
Fax: (831) 657-1494
www.cyberware.com

I've found the folks at Cyberware to be unfailingly polite, helpful, knowledgeable, and enthusiastic about anything pertaining to 3D scanning. It's especially nice that the company has a strong corporate interest in the arts—its employees are not just a bunch of techies. They are always looking for creative new ways to use the technology. The company's Web site contains sample copyright-free models, documentation for most of its software, and lots of helpful tips and advice. The Cyberware vendor directory on this book's CD-ROM contains selected models and documentation from the Cyberware site. Two especially nice full-body human models are shown in Figures 7.3 and 7.4.

Figure 7.3
Female whole-body scan.

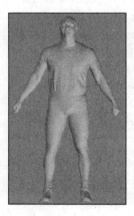

Figure 7.4
Male whole-body scan.

One problem with laser scanners is accurate capture of areas shadowed from the laser. These areas appear as holes in the mesh. Cyberware software includes several utilities for closing up these holes with various interpolation algorithms. Both these sample models have been edited with linear interpolation to remove shadow holes. A typical raw scan contains about 400K points. This is an enormous amount of data, much of which is redundant. Both samples have been decimated (surplus points removed) with automatic decimation software. This combination of processes may take half a day to a day and a half, depending on the skill of the operator and the speed of the processing workstation. I was fortunate in having Phil Dench, the author of the CySurf program, process my head scan at the Cyberware facility in Monterey. Although I can't match his expertise, the following section detailing my own novice efforts offers a useful comparison.

Getting My Head Examined

The first step in getting a usable scan is centering the subject. Depending on the scanner setup, the scanner head may circle around the subject, or the scanner head may be fixed, with a turntable rotating the subject. In either case, it's important that the axis of rotation pass through the center of the subject's head. If the subject is off-center, you won't get as good a data set, and many of the cleanup, modeling, and mapping tools will not work as effectively. For my scan, the scan head rotated around me. A guide like a small knitting needle just above my head marked the axis of rotation. The scanning operator (David Addleman, Cyberware's president) had me shift position until the guide was centered over the crown of my head.

The scan takes approximately 17 seconds. The subject has to hold perfectly still or the scan data will have errors. It's like moving the original while you're making a photocopy—the information gets smeared. It's possible to correct some of these errors with the Cyberware software, but it's better to get a good scan at the beginning. It's not absolutely necessary for the subject to hold his breath during the scan, but it can't hurt. Likewise, the subject should be as calm and relaxed as possible to reduce his heart rate because the scanner is sensitive enough to pick up the pulse in the throat. A strong, rapid pulse will appear in the raw scan as a series of vertical ridges spaced across the base of the throat.

The biggest problem for me was keeping my eyes still. At the same time the invisible laser is scanning for geometry, a bright white light is illuminating the subject for the color scan. This is distracting, and I found my eyes trying to track the scan head. To avoid this, the subject should pick a distant reference point (preferably at eye level and straight ahead) and stare at it throughout the scan. I found that it was easier to keep my eyes open and still if I closed them for the first part of the scan (the back of the head), then held them open for the second part. It's the old paradox: If someone tells you not to blink (or yawn, or look behind you), you can't help but do it. It's easier to keep your eyes open and unmoving for 8 seconds than it is for 17.

Once the scan is complete, it takes a few minutes for the workstation to process the range (geometry) and map data and display it. You can view the raw data as either an unwrapped view (shown in Figure 7.5) or a wrapped, or radial, view (shown in Figure 7.6).

The wrapped view is better for evaluating the overall shape, whereas the unwrapped view is more useful for selecting and editing the data.

Figure 7.7 shows my first scan's color map. This scan is only 512x512 resolution, but the latest Cyberware 3030 HRC scanner can produce maps up to 2048x2048, which is good enough for close-ups in feature films.

You can also choose to display the color map applied to the range data as a grayscale, as in Figure 7.8.

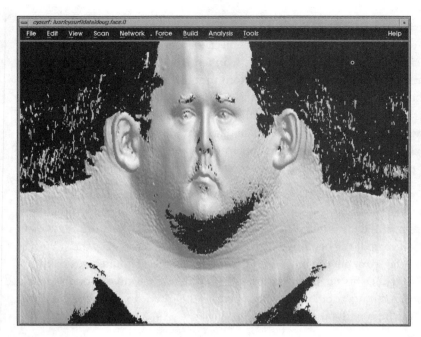

Figure 7.5
My first scan—unwrapped view.

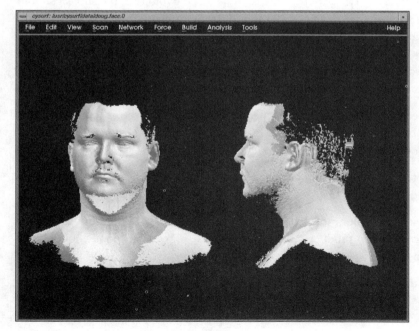

Figure 7.6
Same scan—wrapped view.

Figure 7.7
Color map.

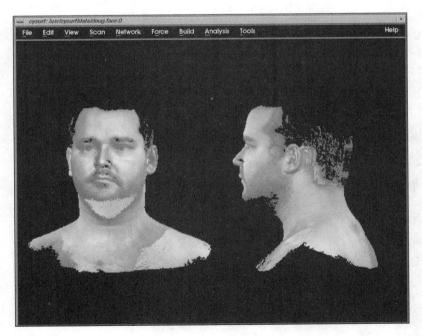

Figure 7.8
Wrapped view with color map applied.

Viewing the wrapped view with the color map applied makes it easier to evaluate the scan and to make corrections for the next scan. For example, if you look closely at Figure 7.8, you will see that almost all the dark areas of my hair, beard, eyebrows, and even my irises have gaps. This happens because the IR laser used to gather range data doesn't reflect strongly enough from dark surfaces to give a clear measurement. The result is a hole in the data wherever the subject is too dark. In addition, any undercut—the underside of the chin, back of the ears, inside of the nostrils—may not be visible to the laser or CCD and also results in a hole in the data. The crown of the head is almost impossible to capture accurately because the crown's surface is parallel to the laser beam and therefore doesn't reflect in the right direction.

There are several ways to solve these problems. My first solution was to shave off my beard, removing the compound problem of dark hair and undercut surface that caused most of my throat and chin to disappear. The next step was to spray my hair with a fine white powder recommended by David Addleman. It's not damaging to hair and most other surfaces, but you should test it on a small area first. Spraying a patch on my forearm didn't cause an allergic reaction, so we liberally dusted my hair and eyebrows with it.

If your subject has long hair, you can either tuck the hair up into a bald cap or slick it down and tie it back in a tight ponytail. This minimizes the roughness of the hair and prevents it from obscuring the contours of the back of the head and neck. As you can tell from these figures, my hair is cut bristly short, so this step wasn't necessary for me. The last solution is to tilt the subject's head to minimize undercuts. If your subject has a hook nose or prominent eyebrow ridges, you may have to scan the head with several degrees of backward tilt. In my case, a very slight backward tilt was enough to eliminate most of the undercut problems. My second scan came out much better, as shown in Figure 7.9.

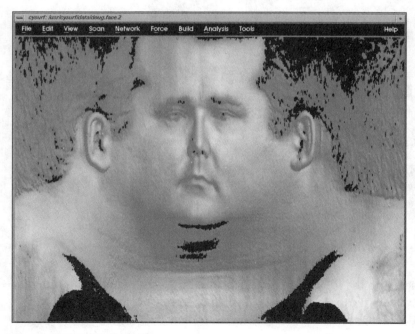

Figure 7.9
Second scan, with beard shaved, hair powdered, and head tilted back slightly.

Once you solve the major problems, you can take additional scans at no less than five-minute intervals. This time is necessary for the workstation to process and save each scan's data and for the operator to set up for the next scan. This limits how quickly you can capture different poses for morph targets. For example, in *Terminator 2: Judgement Day*, actor Robert Patrick plays a "mimetic poly-alloy" android, apparently made of liquid metal. In one scene, the liquid form of the android flows through a hole in a helicopter window, resumes human form in the left seat, then lip syncs the words "Get out" to the chopper's pilot. Separate Cyberware scans of actor Robert Patrick were used as morph targets to animate this lip sync sequence. The five-minute delay in setting up a new scan made it impossible to simply capture Patrick speaking the line all at once, so he had to hold each pose through a separate scan. If you watch carefully, you may be able to detect differences between Patrick's normally fluid lip movements elsewhere in the film and the discrete poses captured by the Cyberware scanner.

I hope I'm making it clear that laser scanning is an experimental process for each subject. It almost always takes some experimenting to get the desired results. If you think you can walk into a service bureau, put your subject in front of the machine, and walk out again in 10 minutes with a complete scan, you're overly optimistic. You should plan to take several scans of each subject and to spend some time with the scanner operator to tweak settings between scans. In my case, a total of seven full-head scans with varying levels of editing took just over three hours to produce with the most skilled operators in the business. You need to keep this in mind when you negotiate pricing with a scanning service bureau. Either allow for extra time to tweak scans or insist on a flat rate for each acceptable scan. Otherwise, you can end up with excessive per-hour fees, unusable raw data, or both. A good service bureau will be aware of these problems and should be willing to compromise on a fee structure that compensates them adequately while guaranteeing you the quality data that you need.

Cleaning Up After Yourself

A successful scanning session produces one or more sets of raw range and map files. These files almost always need a little cleanup to close holes in the range data caused by undercuts, dark surfaces, or a surface that's parallel to the scan. Cyberware's CySurf software provides a set of tools designed to make this cleanup as quick and easy as possible. The first step is to start CySurf. You'll see a splash screen like Figure 7.10, with the version and build information and the author's name and email address.

Load the range data, also known as an Echo file, for the scan you wish to clean up. Your screen should look something like Figure 7.11.

Note the black areas, the holes in the scan data. You will need to use several different tools to close them up. No one tool can do a good job on all the different types of scan errors and omissions. The first tool, Fill, is the easiest and most intuitive to use. Choose an area you want to fill in and pan and zoom the display until you can clearly see the individual pixels of the scan data, shown in Figure 7.12.

Figure 7.10
Starting CySurf.

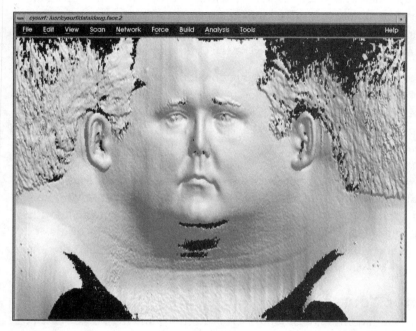

Figure 7.11
Loaded raw scan.

Open the Edit dialog box. In the Functions window, click on Fill. Left-click and drag the cursor over the hole to paint it red. Make sure you cover all the missing areas. You can paint over the edges of the hole without doing any damage because the Fill function won't delete or change any of the original scan data. When you execute the Fill function, the software will close up all the red-shaded areas using a straight-line interpolation, like covering the top of a container with plastic wrap. You can paint more than one hole before executing the Fill function, but it's safer to fill one hole at a time so you can Undo it if you make a mistake (see Figure 7.13).

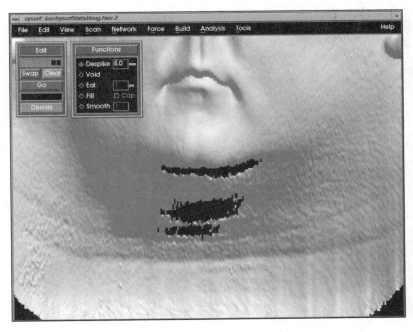

Figure 7.12
Display zoomed in on hole in surface.

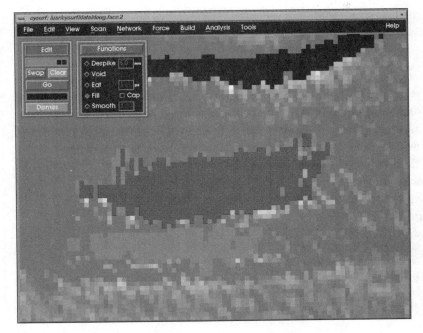

Figure 7.13
Choose Edit|Fill and paint over the hole in the surface.

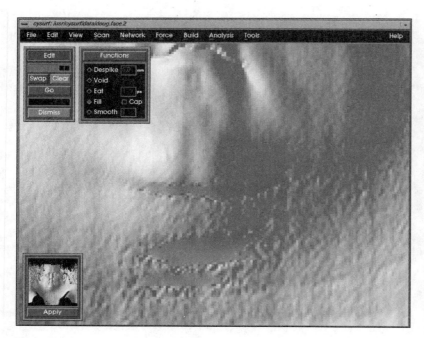

Figure 7.14
Hole in the surface after the Fill function is executed.

When you've painted the hole, click on Go to execute the Fill function. It shouldn't take long. Your results should look something like Figure 7.14.

Note that the original scan data has a lot of small surface detail, but the Fill area doesn't. Skin texture, surface imperfections, wrinkles, and similar artifacts can't be created by the Fill function, so the filled area is perfectly flat from one edge of the hole to another. CySurf includes embossing, sculpting, and bump-mapping tools you can use to disguise the Fill areas. You can repeat the Fill process as necessary to close gaps at the front of the shoulders and small holes in the nose, ears, and elsewhere. After you've finished with Fill, the next cleanup function is Smooth. This function flattens out dimples or bumps in the surface by comparing the selected area (just like Fill) to the surrounding surface and pushing the selected area in or out to match (see Figure 7.15). The variable next to the Smooth button sets how far Smooth looks to determine the adjoining surface level: 1 equals one pixel. The larger the number, the smoother the surface, but the processing takes longer and more surface detail is lost. If you are simply trying to smooth out scanning errors, the default setting of 1 will suffice.

The last basic cleanup function is Fill Cap. This is a special form of the Fill function that closes up the top of the head. If you simply selected the top edge of the scan and executed Fill, the straight-line interpolation of the Fill function would form a sort of cylinder coming out the top of the subject's head. The Fill Cap function gives you some extra controls to shape the fill, so it looks like a normal skull rather than one of Dr. Frankenstein's creations.

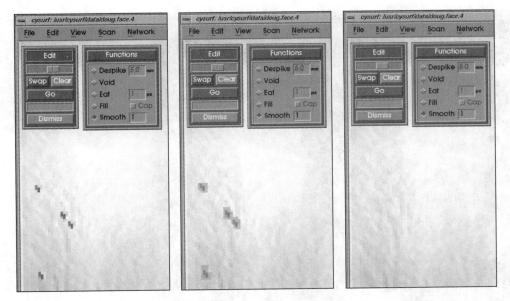

Figure 7.15
Using the Edit|Smooth function to blend bump or dimple error with surrounding surface (left, visible bumps; center, selecting bumps; and right, the results of executing the Smooth function).

Fill Cap uses both the wrapped and unwrapped views. For the first part of the process, switch to the wrapped view. You will see a set of control nodes defining a hemispherical spline patch. The Fill Cap function will fill the hemisphere, connecting the hemisphere's surface along radial lines to the existing surface. You need to position the control nodes to create the appropriate hemispherical shape for your subject's head. To do this, you will need to be able to visualize what the subject's head would have looked like if the scan data were complete. A set of front and side reference photos comes in handy for this.

The best place to start moving the control nodes is in the front view, using the bottom nodes. Drag these nodes until they are just touching the sides of the existing surface and well below the highest remaining gaps, as shown in Figure 7.16.

Next, drag the top center nodes to the point where you want the peak of the subject's crown. Adjust the upper corner nodes to change the curvature of the hemisphere. You don't have to worry about the curves matching existing areas of the surface because Fill Cap only fills in the missing areas. It's OK to overshoot the curve in existing areas as long as you get the curve you need in the missing areas. There are lots of possibilities. Refer to photos of the subject if you have them, look in the mirror if you're the subject (it worked for me), or use trial and error.

The next step is to select the area to be affected by the Fill Cap function. Just as with the original Fill function, use the unwrapped view and select the area (see Figure 7.17). You can select

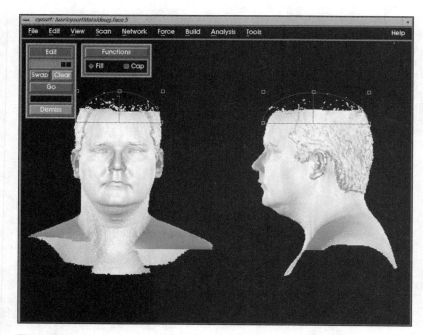

Figure 7.16
Setup of the Cap spline to match the missing part of the head.

the area more quickly if you use the cursor to trace the lower boundary of the area and then double-click above it. The entire area above the selection line will fill in. You should be cautious when using the double-click fill, though—a single pixel gap will allow it to select the entire surface.

Change back to the wrapped view. Click on Go to execute the Fill Cap function. You should get results that look like Figure 7.18.

You can check the accuracy of your Fill Cap shape by applying the color map and looking for overshoot at the peak of the crown. If you refer back to Figure 7.7, you can see that the top of the color map shows the background of the scanner room, as seen over the top of the subject's head. This usually gives a contrasting color that will appear at the top of the Fill Cap surface if it goes too far (see Figure 7.19). If you are adjusting the Fill Cap hemisphere by trial and error, you should make the peak high at first, then reduce it incrementally until the background color just barely disappears. Your results should end up looking something like Figure 7.18, with a crown curvature closely approximating the original subject's, and just a trace of background color along the top of the crown where it shows through the hair.

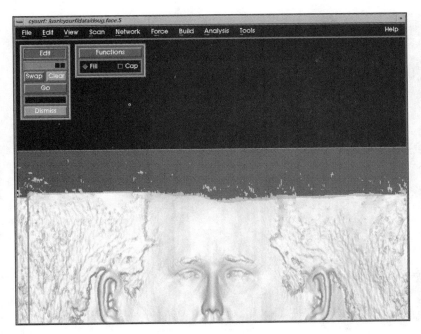

Figure 7.17
Select the Fill Cap area in unwrapped view.

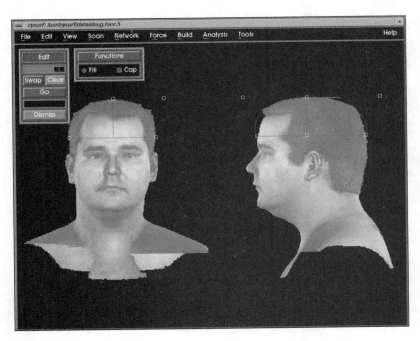

Figure 7.18
Results of using the Fill Cap function to close the missing crown of the head.

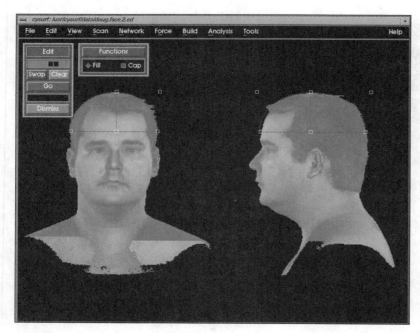

Figure 7.19
Fill Cap hemisphere set too high, showing background color at peak.

The last step in a head scan cleanup is to simplify the raw data, smoothing out irrelevant details and random spikes. In the case of my head scan, most of the irrelevant detail was in the hair (see Figure 7.20).

You can use either the Smooth or Despike functions to reduce this complexity. Smooth tends to blend out all the details at once, averaging them into the surrounding surface. Despike is similar to Smooth but acts only on certain points. If one point has a certain range value and all its neighbors have another, it's likely that the odd point is a spike. The Despike threshold is the maximum range a point can differ from its neighbors before Despike will void it out (make it a hole). If you use Despike, you'll have to go back and Fill the new holes again. The advantage of Despike is that you can decrease the threshold, execute Despike, see how much detail is left, and decide whether to continue Despiking or leave the rest of the details. This gives you a little more control than Smooth, especially if you have a very complex subject. With either function, you should be able to create something like Figure 7.21, a finely detailed face with completely smoothed hair. This makes the mesh much simpler without losing any real detail, because most of the apparent detail in a character's hair is provided by color and texture maps.

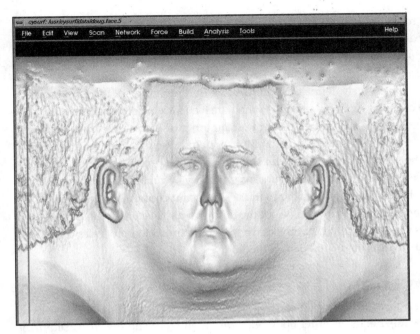

Figure 7.20
Unwrapped view of Filled, Smoothed, and Capped head, showing remaining irrelevant detail in hair.

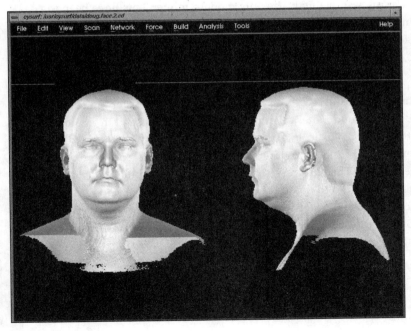

Figure 7.21
Smoothed hair on a cleaned-up mesh.

The Cyberscan process measures up fairly well to my five criteria. Redundant work is minimal because much of the scanning and cleanup process is automated, and you can save incremental versions of the scan data so you don't have to start completely from scratch if something does go wrong or requires revision. Incremental detailing is supported in the ability to progressively clean up the scan data and to interactively define the optimization and resolution of the final model. Both the scanning and cleanup processes provide immediate feedback on the quality of the model; decision-makers can actually participate in the scanning process if necessary and say yea or nay to a scan, just as they would for a live-action film shot. Both the scan data and the final model are documents that the decision-makers can sign off. The scan process is flexible during data capture; you can re-pose and re-scan your subjects until they or your budget give out. However, once the scanning is finished, the only way to make significant changes to the data is to run another scan. You need to make sure you've got the data you need before you halt the scanning session. As long as you've got that data, the cleanup and optimization processes can always be repeated or modified, giving you a good deal of flexibility.

Casting from Life

If you choose not to use a laser scanner, you can still get accurate 3D data from live subjects by making casts of faces, whole heads, or other body parts and then digitizing the casts. Digitizing from casts (or sculpted maquettes) allows you to use a variety of techniques that are not suitable for directly capturing live subjects. Making casts from life is a craft with a centuries-long history, and the procedures are well defined. The only modern refinements have been the development of new casting materials that make the process faster, easier, and more reliable for the artist and less stressful on the subject. You can still make an acceptable cast from plaster of paris applied directly to the subject's face, but much better options are available.

This section is a quick, practical overview of the basic life-casting process for a face. However, if you are planning to make a life cast, I recommend that you contact Monster Makers. This company carries just about any tool, material, or guide you may find useful in making life casts or life-size maquettes in clay, plastic, latex, or plaster. The primary business of the folks at Monster Makers is making latex masks for motion picture special effects, so their expertise in full-head life casting is extensive. They are very knowledgeable and helpful and can guide you through the myriad of choices to find the procedures and materials that are right for your project. Even if you choose to make a traditional plaster cast with materials from your local hardware store, you should consider buying one of the Monster Maker books or videos as a guide. You can contact them at the following address:

Monster Makers
7305 Detroit Ave.
Cleveland, OH 44102
Tel: (216) 651-SPFX (7739)
www.monstermakers.com

One of the best modern materials for life casting is alginate, a two-part liquid mixture that rapidly hardens into a tough, rubbery coating. There are several trade names for alginate, and each product has different hardening and mixing qualities that are suitable for its specific jobs. Alginates are kinder to the subject's skin than plaster, set more rapidly, are less prone to air bubbles, and retain finer details. Alginate is also much nicer to facial hair; plaster tends to just pull it all out, including eyebrows, unless you thickly coat the hair with Vaseline. I deliberately trimmed my beard and hair very short before these casts were taken, and the alginate gave a faithful reproduction without pulling out much hair. In fact, several areas around the chin and hairline were so completely penetrated by the alginate that the skin was reproduced perfectly while the hair wasn't reproduced at all. More commonly, you will have to cast subjects with longer hair. For these situations, you should carefully fit a bald cap over the subject's hair and tape it down without deforming or stretching the subject's skin.

Even though alginate comes off most surfaces cleanly, I recommend that you do all the molding and casting over a concrete floor or that you put down a large tarp. These processes get messy, and a slip or spill can be disastrous in the wrong environment. A basement, garage, or industrial space is best. Office and computer environments are definitely off limits because dust and liquids can damage or destroy equipment, furniture, and carpeting.

There are several ways to apply alginate. My personal preference (based on previous mistakes) is to use several layers. The first is a thin, slower-setting mix, painted on in a thin layer to avoid distorting the subject's face with the weight of the alginate. It's surprising how much the human face can distort under just a little pressure. For example, you should never take a life cast of a reclining subject if you can possibly avoid it. Gravity pulls down any loose mass of flesh, with an effect similar to a face-lift. The change will be obvious to your audience, so you should always take a life cast in the same attitude you will use for the final model. Similar problems result if you load a single, heavy layer of alginate onto a subject. The alginate itself can pull the cheeks down, stretch the eyebrows down over the eyelids, and generally make your subject look half-melted. Look at Figure 7.22 for an example of the distortion in a plaster positive cast from a mold made with a single heavy layer of alginate.

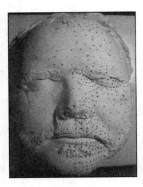

Figure 7.22
Casting Mistake 1: Plaster life cast showing the distortion of a too-heavy alginate application.

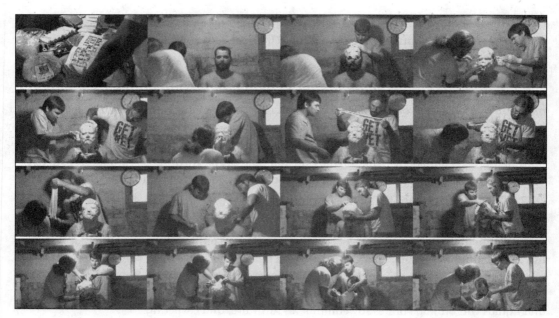

Figure 7.23
Making a life cast for a full head.

Figure 7.23 is a montage of the process for making a life cast for a full head: assembling the materials, applying alginate, applying plaster bandages, slitting back the mold, and peeling the mold off the subject. Keep in mind that slitting the back of the mold to remove it makes it more difficult to get an accurate reproduction of the head's shape.

A thin first alginate layer also enables you to test the placement and securing of breathing tubes. You want to use tubes that are large enough for the subject to breathe easily but not so thick that they distend the nostrils or markedly deform the lips. I recommend using plastic soda straws if possible, because they separate easily from both alginate and plaster. Aside from the practical aspect of keeping your subject breathing, there is an important factor of trust and comfort too. If your subject gets panicky or claustrophobic because he imagines that he can't breathe, he will tear off the mold, and you will have to start all over.

From the subject's point of view, you can't blame them. I had my breathing tubes inadvertently blocked for about half a minute during the second mold for this chapter, and I was seconds away from ripping off the alginate when they finally cleared the tubes. Never joke around about the procedure, don't let anyone else do so, and keep up a cheerful, steady, loud chatter with your subject. Even with earplugs and a thick layer of alginate and plaster, the subject can hear you. Also, you might consider keeping a pad of paper and a pencil handy for him to write messages for anything more complex than "Yes" (thumbs up) or "No" (thumbs down).

Once the first layer of alginate is setting up, you can add a second, thicker layer. Reinforce the thinnest areas, especially around the nose, eyelids, lips, and breathing tubes, where the subject's movement may have disturbed the first layer. While the alginate layers are setting up, add layers of plaster bandages (see Figure 7.24). The alginate remains rubbery and flexible, but the plaster bandages will set up hard and rigid, supporting the alginate in the general shape of the subject's head. Layer the plaster bandages thickly enough to reinforce the alginate layers, making the whole assembly rigid. Too little plastering will allow the mold to spread out under the weight of the casting material, deforming the final cast (see Figure 7.25). Cast the face alone to make it easier to reinforce for a more accurate mold.

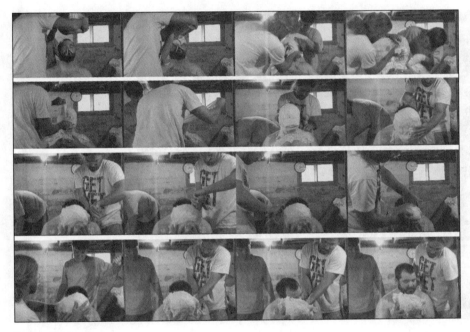

Figure 7.24
Making a life cast for a face.

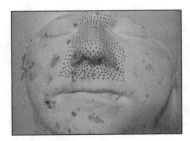

Figure 7.25
Casting Mistake 2: Results of alginate mold spread out under weight of plaster. No, my face isn't really that wide.

If I had this to do over again, I would invest (imbed) the alginate mold in a box full of freshly mixed plaster and let the plaster set up to support the mold. Mold rigidity is less critical if you will be making a lightweight plastic positive, but plaster is very heavy and will spread any mold that isn't solidly reinforced. The procedures and materials recommended in the Monster Makers guides describe how to make a lightweight plastic full-head cast. For Figures 7.22 through 7.26, and the casts shown in the rest of this chapter, I made two face casts plus separate ear casts (see Figure 7.26), using alginate for the negative molds and ordinary plaster of paris for the positives. Separate casts produce more accurate results with less tearing and distortion than casting the ears in the same piece as the face.

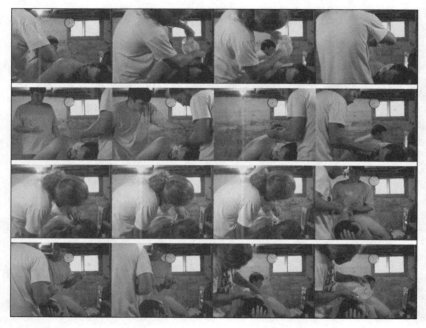

Figure 7.26
Making separate ear casts: applying alginate to right ear, removing mold, applying alginate to left ear, removing mold.

If you will be storing your casts for any length of time before digitizing them, be careful. Plaster is very porous and sensitive to many kinds of contamination. The packing material I used to ship the casts absorbed moisture from the air, encouraging mildew to grow in the plaster wherever the packing touched it. Fortunately, it caused discoloration only by the time I caught it, but if the surface had become pitted, the casts would have been a total loss.

The casting process does not measure up well to my five criteria. The process is very sensitive to errors, and being a physical process, there is no Undo button. If anything goes wrong anywhere along the line, you pretty much have to start from scratch. It's an all-or-nothing process that does not allow you to incrementally detail the results. Feedback is very slow; it can be hours, even a day or more, from beginning to end, and you can't really judge the intermediate results at any level more detailed than a go/no-go decision. The final positive casting is a deliverable document for decision-makers to sign off, but if they don't like it, you are back to square one.

Digitizing with the MicroScribe-3D

There are a variety of contact-based digitizers available, but the most common tool for digitizing maquettes or casts is Immersion Corporation's MicroScribe-3D digitizing arm (see Figure 7.27). You will find at least one of these devices in most creature and effects shops, animation studios, and game developers' studios worldwide. It's a simple, robust machine that works with a variety of software on most computer operating systems, including Macintosh, SGI, and Windows. If you get a chance to work with one, take advantage of it. Experience with any digitizing tool is a valuable addition to your resume. If you are running your own shop, you should consider how much modeling you do and whether investing approximately $3,000 in a digitizer can save you time and labor costs over freehand modeling. If you're already using maquettes as a design and client-approval tool, you're more than halfway to an animatable computer model via the MicroScribe.

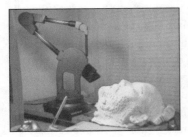

Figure 7.27
Immersion's MicroScribe-3D with a plaster face cast ready to digitize.

The MicroScribe-3D works by reporting the exact x-, y-, z-coordinates of its stylus tip to the computer via the serial port. You simply hold the stylus tip against the surface of the object to be digitized and trip a foot pedal or press a key to capture each data point, as shown in Figure 7.28.

Figure 7.28
MicroScribe-3D stylus positioned to capture a data point.

Depending on the software you use, this can produce a point cloud, a series of contour lines or splines, a polygonal mesh, or a NURBS surface. For more information about the MicroScribe-3D, you can contact Immersion at the following address:

Immersion Corporation
2158 Paragon Drive
San Jose, CA 95131
Tel: (408) 467-1900
Fax: (408) 467-1901
www.microscribe.com

Before you start digitizing, you need to fix the digitizer and the cast or maquette firmly to your work surface. If either the MicroScribe-3D or the cast moves during digitizing, you'll have to reorient the cast and digitizer by already-captured reference points or start over and piece the model together in the computer. Neither option is very efficient, so nail everything down before you start. The MicroScribe has a standard threaded hole in the base, just like a camera, so you can use tripods and other mounting hardware. My personal preference is for a Craftsman Workmate portable folding workbench. It has a lot of predrilled holes in the top, plus you can adjust the height of the working surface. To stick the cast or maquette in place, I like to use Power Putty. This is the same type of silicone putty as Silly Putty, but it comes in different levels of color-coded hardness. The green Power Putty is the stiffest and will keep even a heavy full-head plaster cast in place. You just pull off a bit and mash it into the corner of the work surface and cast, as shown in the lower right corner of Figure 7.27. When you're done, the putty comes off without staining the plaster or carrying off fragments of the cast. It's clean and reusable. You can find Power Putty in martial arts or fitness stores, where it's sold as a hand-grip exerciser.

The first step in preparing a cast for digitizing is to think carefully about what you'll be doing with the finished model, just as you did for marking up the maquette in Chapter 5. If all you need is a low-polygon model for a realtime game, you won't need to capture many points. If you'll be animating a digital stuntman in close-up for a feature film, you'll have to capture much more detail. Most digitizing applications fall somewhere between these two extremes. The critical measure is the profile of the model. You can simulate face-on surface details with shaders or maps (see Chapters 8 through 10), but you don't want straight lines and sharp angles to be clearly visible in your character's profile. You need to digitize enough points from the cast that the model's profile will appear smooth and rounded in the final rendering. This takes a certain amount of experience to judge accurately. It's difficult to redigitize without starting completely over, so you should get as much practice as possible on noncritical test objects before you have to digitize a challenging maquette under a tight deadline.

For practice, you should digitize a series of simple tests before you try to digitize an entire cast. I recommend starting with the subject's nose, because it usually provides a set of short and long curves as a good representative sample and it is unobstructed in profile. Start with one point each at the outer corners of the nostrils, the tip of the nose, the base of the nose at the top of the philtrum (those two lines on your upper lip), and the top of the bridge. This will form a rough pyramid. This is the simplest level of digitizing. Import the model into your rendering software and render it in profile at several different resolutions. Compare it to the cast or reference photos. How high a resolution can you render before the polygons of the model become obvious? Digitize the nose again, adding points along the wings, bridge, and nostrils. Render the new model and see how much higher resolution you can use before the model starts to show its flaws. Repeat this process until you've found a level of detail that produces smooth profiles at your project's finished resolution. That's the level of detail you will need to use for digitizing the entire cast.

You can save a lot of time and effort—and make a lighter, more efficient model—if you plan ahead and place each point carefully. For example, you may need to space points less than a millimeter apart near the corner of the nostril or eyelid to capture the tight curves there. The forehead, temple, and cheek may have broad, flat areas where you can space points a centimeter or more without losing detail (see Figure 7.29).

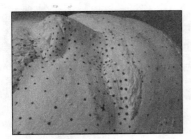

Figure 7.29
Vary the spacing of data points to suit the curvature of the surface. Flat areas need few points, whereas curved areas need more.

You need to examine the cast, visualizing each point connected to each adjacent point. If you are making a polygonal model, you should visualize each point connected to its neighbors with straight lines. Start with a single point, perhaps in the center of the forehead. How far away can you make a second point, connected to the first point by a straight line, without missing any important details in the cast? Once you've placed the second point, repeat the process for a third point, and so on until you've covered the entire cast with a mesh of points.

The most significant advantage of the MicroScribe and other manual digitizers over laser scanners is that manual digitizing enables a skilled operator to get efficient, complete surfaces where a scanner can't. For example, most scanners have serious problems with involute surfaces or overhangs. The back of the ears and the underside of the chin, nose, and eyebrows are typical problem areas of the human head. Take a look at Figure 7.30 for a laser scan of my left ear, showing the inaccuracy of data capture for the back of the ear.

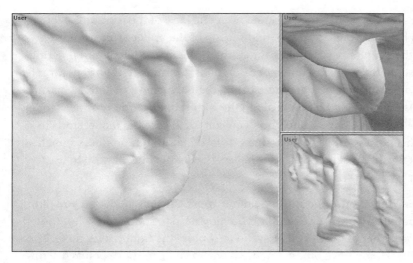

Figure 7.30
Laser scan inaccuracy for back of ear.

In contrast, the MicroScribe stylus is easy to maneuver to capture accurate data from the back of the ear and most other undercuts or involute surfaces (see Figure 7.31).

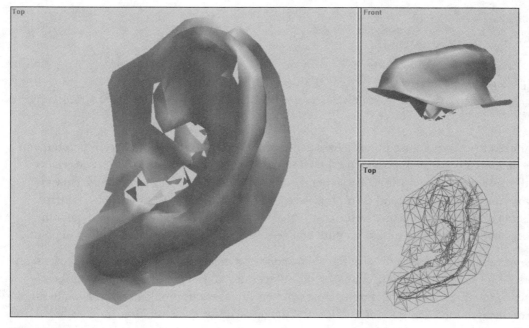

Figure 7.31
MicroScribe-3D accuracy for back of ear featured in Figure 7.30.

The only problem areas for the stylus are those that are difficult to reach, such as the inner recesses of the ear and the underside of the inner cartilage, where there just isn't room to maneuver the stylus. Neither laser scanner nor digitizer can accurately capture all surfaces. You will always have to do some patching and cleanup to finish the model.

Digitizing Software Choices

The details of the digitizing process depend on your software. When you choose a digitizing tool, you need to keep the entire modeling, setup, and animation process in mind. A tool may be efficient for one part of the process but generate lots of unnecessary work in another part. You need to find an approach and a set of tools that is most efficient for the process you are following. There is no one solution, no magic bullet, suitable for all digitizing. Whichever software you choose to drive your digitizer, the basic processes and skills remain the same. These are assets you need to develop through practice.

Immersion's (**www.immersion.com**) own VertiSketch for LightWave is a Modeler plug-in that enables you to digitize in a familiar environment and maintain access to the complete suite of LightWave modeling tools. It supports the MicroScribe in LightWave 3D versions 4 through 5.6. As of this writing, there was no information available regarding compatibility with LightWave Modeler 6. VertiSketch features include audio feedback and four digitizing modes: point, select, snap, and continuous.

Rhinoceros (Rhino) is a very powerful and flexible modeling program developed by Robert McNeel & Associates. You can download a demo version from its Web site at **www.rhino3d.com**. Rhino is definitely intended for the power user. In addition to offering the standard menu and icon interface, Rhino enables you to directly enter command-line instructions. This is not the most intuitive approach, but I can see its value for the experienced power user. One very nice feature is that Rhino allows you to completely customize the keyboard equivalents, so you can automate your most often-used functions with a handful of keys. This is especially important to the digitizing process. If you try to rely on the standard menu options and icon buttons, you'll be putting down the stylus and using the mouse and keyboard every few minutes. With the appropriate keyboard equivalents, you can manage the digitizing process with one hand, keeping the stylus moving with the other. I suggest that you keep track of the functions you use most often, then draft a list of keyboard equivalents that make sense for your personal working style. At first, you may only have a few keyboard equivalents, but over time, your preferences will change. Within a week of starting to use Rhino, I had built a full complement of keyboard equivalents and was using a complex series of operations without having to slow down or think about them. With practice, using Rhino with the MicroScribe is very fast.

Starting the digitizing process with Rhino takes a bit of effort. Rhino requires you to go through a 13-action calibration and orientation process each time you begin using the MicroScribe. I can understand that this is useful to a power user with an odd digitizing setup, but the software really should have a default setup that enables most users to get right to digitizing.

Rhino is designed to work with NURBS and has a slight edge in creating splines and NURBS surfaces directly from the MicroScribe data. As you can see in Figure 7.32, Rhino makes it possible to generate complex surfaces, like the human ear, from a relatively small number of splines. Making these splines is simply a matter of choosing the Sketch Curve function, then dragging the stylus tip along the curved surface.

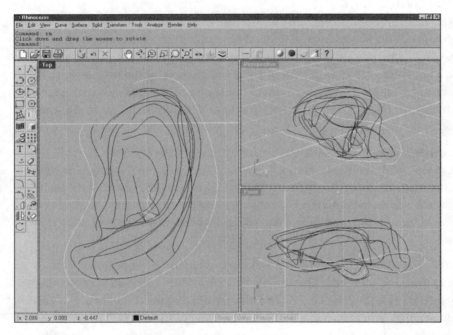

Figure 7.32
Ear digitized with Rhino as a set of Sketch Curves.

You need to be very careful when using any of the Sketch functions because any slip or skip of the stylus will generate data points out in the air, making an inaccurate model. I found it best to practice following the new path with the stylus at least once before enabling the Sketch Curves function. Tracing the path in soft plaster forms a slight groove, making it easier to follow the second time. It also enables you to anticipate any odd bumps or irregularities in the cast, so you can slow down and prevent errors. The drawback of plaster's softness is that you have to Sketch by dragging the stylus tip. If you push the stylus, the steel tip will dig into the plaster, damaging the cast and halting the Sketch operation. On the other hand, if you are working from a maquette or plastic cast with a harder surface, you will need to be that much more careful not to let the stylus slip during a Sketch operation. Despite these drawbacks, the Sketch functions make digitizing much faster than the point-by-point process.

Once you have digitized either the points or curves to define the entire model, you can use Rhino's surfacing tools to create NURBS surfaces or polygonal meshes. For most parts of a face cast, the standard lofting operations will give good results. For tricky areas like the involute curves of the ear, you will need to select and loft curves one at a time. Even with careful digitizing and lofting, a human ear will end up with errors that you will have to correct by hand (see Figure 7.33).

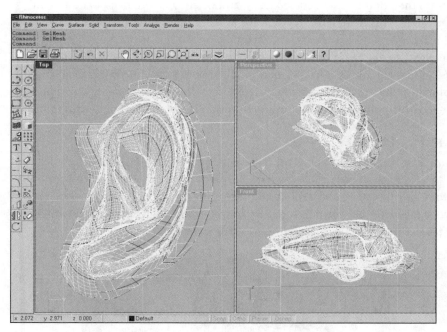

Figure 7.33
NURBS surface and polygonal mesh of a digitized ear.

Rhino has a number of modeling tools that can make it easier to create complex organic shapes for characters. Even if you are comfortable with LightWave's Modeler, you should consider adding Rhino to your toolbox. It can export to a variety of file formats, including IGES, Wavefront OBJ, AutoCAD DXF, 3D Studio, LightWave, Raw Triangles, POV-Ray mesh, Moray UDO, STL, VRML, Adobe Illustrator, Windows Metafile, Renderman, and Applied Geometry (.ag). Rhino is almost guaranteed to work with any other 3D application.

Digitizing Practice

Capturing enough detail to render an accurate profile is only the first step in producing a usable model. You also need enough extra detail to provide enough flexibility in the model to set up and animate it. This means you have to add details based on your experience in setup and animation, which is a completely different set of criteria from the static rendered profile test. For example, most life casts are made with a closed mouth. Few subjects would let you coat their teeth and tongue with alginate. This means the corners of the mouth will be compressed. You need very few points to accurately reproduce this area if it were to always stay compressed. However, you generally need to model the mouth so it can open wide, express emotion, and form words. This means you have to understand how that area of the model will need to expand and distort from the original digitized geometry and where you will need to add extra points to make it possible. This is something you have to learn by trial and error. To make it as easy as possible, I recommend that you concentrate on one facial feature at a time. Again, start with the nose. Practice digitizing, setting up, and animating the nose by itself until you can accurately and efficiently mimic the deformation of wrinkling and furrowing the bridge and flaring and pinching the nostrils. After you've learned to do this with one model, you can apply that experience, with minor modifications, to almost all other humanoid facial models.

Mesh Layout Practice

Your first few attempts at laying out an efficient mesh will probably not be satisfactory. I recommend using a soft lead pencil because it won't permanently mark the plaster. You can rub off most of the markings and start over or make changes as necessary. Once you feel more confident about your mesh layout, you can move up to water-based felt-tip markers, which will soak into the plaster and make permanent marks (see Figure 7.34).

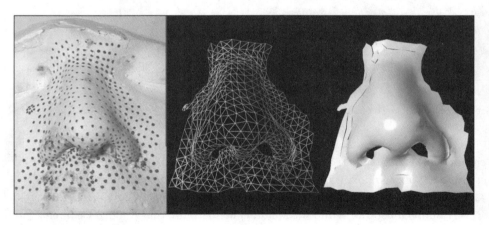

Figure 7.34
Nose marked with felt-tip pen and corresponding digitized model in wireframe and smooth shading.

If you have the opportunity to choose your own first practice subject, I highly recommend that you start off with a hard plastic toy or bust. Most plastics are durable, will take grease pencil or other markings easily, and can be scrubbed clean without pitting or gouging the surface. This gives you the opportunity to experiment with different patterns and complexities of dots, grids, and contour lines in order to find the approach that best suits your tools and working style.

Once you have succeeded in digitizing a plastic subject, you can graduate to fired Sculpey maquettes. These are not quite as forgiving and durable as plastic, but they are not as fragile as uncoated plaster. When you believe you're ready for the nasty stuff, try digitizing a plaster cast with lots of undercuts and involute surfaces. Face casts like those in Figure 7.28 are some of the most challenging and unforgiving subjects you'll ever have to deal with. Plaster face casts are fragile, heavy, and hard to re-mark, and they take etch lines from the stylus and flake, crack, and powder at the least excuse. If you can digitize plaster quickly and well, everything else will seem like child's play.

Digitizing plaster casts or sculpted maquettes is a process that measures up pretty well to my five criteria. Even when you make mistakes, you can usually salvage previous data and thereby reduce redundant work. You can make a first low-resolution rough pass and later redigitize at higher detail, integrating the new points with the old to support incremental detailing. The feedback during the process is nearly realtime. The finished 3D model is a document for decision-makers to sign off. Because the process is digital and each software program has an Undo feature, it's very flexible and forgiving of errors.

Lightening the Load

The results of a Cyberscan cleanup session or a sketch-based MicroScribe digitization are very dense models. These aren't of much use in character animation because they are much too heavy to set up and animate. For a full-body example, you can load the file FemaleWB.lwo from the Cyberware directory on this book's CD-ROM. This scan has nearly 250,000 polygons and takes a long time simply to load. It would take a very long time and be overwhelmingly frustrating to set up and animate this mesh. Similarly, the cleaned-up model of my head is much too heavy to set up and animate (see Figure 7.35).

The solution to the problems of a heavy mesh is to simplify and optimize it. The goal of this process is to create a polygonal mesh or SubPatch surface that preserves the appearance of the original scan but is much lighter and easier to set up and animate.

You can also use these tools to build morph targets across different scans. Simply adapt the same base model to several raw scans, and the resulting adapted models will have compatible point counts and distribution. You can even morph one person into another, like the water-tentacle effects in *The Abyss*.

You can also boost your character-modeling productivity by using this process to recycle models. I don't mean using the same generic head and body for every character and only modifying the textures. Although that approach is still viable for very limited game work, it won't pass muster with higher-end game, television, or film audiences. Instead, you can employ several techniques to transform a stock character into a markedly different, apparently unique one. Used properly, these techniques can be much more time and cost effective than the process of creating a new character from scratch.

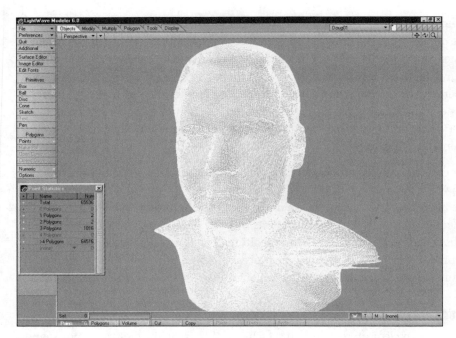

Figure 7.35
Cleaned-up head scan, showing prohibitively heavy mesh.

The increased efficiency of adapting an existing model over creating one from scratch is especially true for humanoid heads, which usually have similar features and require only some repositioning of existing points rather than a completely new mesh. Once you have created a head model that is useful for emotional expressions and lip sync, there is no reason you should not recycle that model in order to create other characters. This approach can also enable you to recycle morph libraries and other animation tools from one character to another, changing only what is necessary rather than starting from scratch.

BGConform

One of the built-in LightWave tools you can use for the reshaping process is the BGConform plug-in. This Modeler plug-in performs an operation with results something like shrink-wrap. You load the form model as a background object, load the model to be recycled in the foreground (Figure 7.36), then execute BGConform to snap all the visible foreground points to the nearest background points (Figure 7.37).

The catch is that BGConform isn't terribly bright and simply moves each foreground point to the nearest background point, whether that placement makes sense for the 3D surface or not. For character modeling, you will almost never be able to get a usable model from a single BGConform operation executed on an entire foreground model. Instead, you need to use the

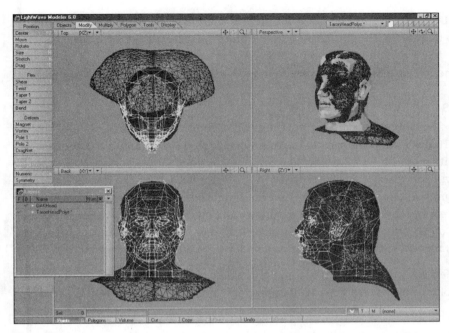

Figure 7.36
Cyberscan head loaded as background model, and a light polygonal model loaded as foreground and aligned with background.

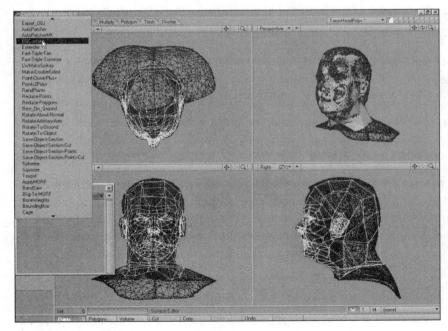

Figure 7.37
Polygonal model BGConformed to background model.

Select, Hide, and Unhide functions to limit BGConform's effect to a few points at a time and be prepared to Undo frequently. This is a trial-and-error process. Once you get the hang of it, you can hide all but a few individual points, reposition them near the desired corresponding background points, and reiterate BGConform very rapidly.

Impressions

If you want more flexibility and better control than BGConform can provide, you should consider using Dave Hudek's Impressions plug-in. This Modeler plug-in is also something like shrink-wrap, but it's more controllable. Just like BGConform, you load the form model as a background object, load the model to be recycled in the foreground, then use Impressions to conform the foreground to the background. However, Impressions gives you a number of handy options to control the direction of the shrink-wrap, and only operates on selected points. In addition, you can reiterate Impressions operations with a few key presses, so you can select individual points, reposition them, and reconform them to the background very rapidly.

There are only a few steps to the process of using Impressions to reshape a model to fit a form. It's just a matter of repeating these steps, with appropriate artistic judgment to get the results you want:

1. Load the recycle object and send the layer to the background. This is the generic head model that you have used to model and animate a character successfully in the past. LightWave [6] includes a variety of head models you can use for practice.

2. Load the form object. This is the Cyberscan, digitizer, or other new model that you want to make compatible with an old model that is efficient to set up and animate.

3. Move, rotate, and scale the form object to fit the orientation and size of the recycle object as closely as possible. The distance between the eyes, and between each eye and the base of the nose, are good reference points for most humanoid heads.

4. Send the form object layer to the background and bring the recycle object layer to the foreground. The form object should appear as a black wireframe. Your form and recycle objects are now set up for Impressions.

   The next pair of steps describes how to apply the Impressions plug-in to conform the recycle object to the form object. You will need to repeat these steps many times to complete the process, so you should learn how to use hotkeys to make each iteration as quick and easy as possible. Also, you should start with points that are easiest to locate in all three orthographic views. I suggest starting with the points that define the profile of the nose.

5. Select a point, move it well clear of the form's surface, and align it in the Front view with the final location you want for that point.

6. Apply the Impressions plug-in with an Arbitrary Direction opposite to your movement of the point away from the form's surface.

If your heads are facing forward, you can make most of these changes by pulling the point −Z, positioning the point in the Front view, and applying Impressions in an Arbitrary Direction move +Z. Think of it as pulling an elastic skin off the form and letting Impressions snap it back for a close fit. Figure 7.38 shows the results of Impressions moving the selected polygons to fit the background form. With practice and care, you can move groups of points with a single operation. Don't get greedy; it takes far more time to fix an error than to do it right with fewer points.

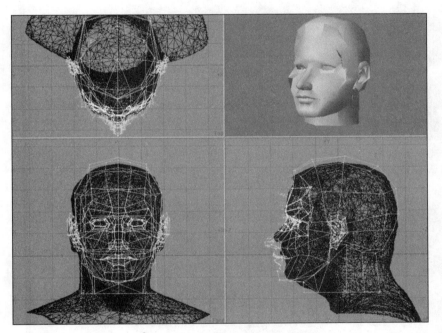

Figure 7.38
Cyberscan of my head used as a form to recycle the Caucasian_Male model.

7. Repeat Steps 5 and 6 until you have reformed the entire recycle object to fit the form object, Figure 7.39. When you are done, save the foreground layer with a new name.

Because the original recycled object and the reshaped one have identical point counts and distribution, all the morphing tools available in LightWave will be able to morph them. Figure 7.40 shows an example of using this morphing capability to apply a color map accurately to a very different head shape. Create your own evil twin!

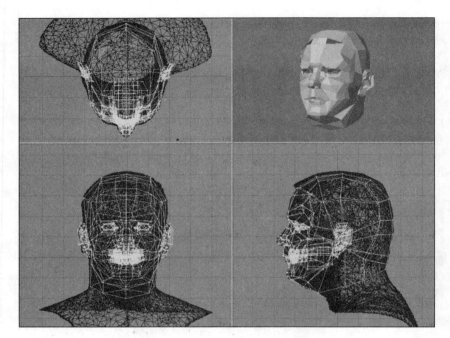

Figure 7.39
Completed recycle of the Caucasian_Male model.

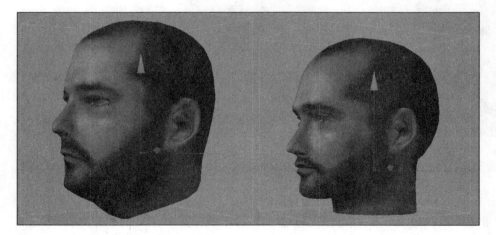

Figure 7.40
Morph between the Caucasian_Male model (right) and the recycled version of my head (left), with Cyberscan color map applied.

Impressions tested very well with LightWave [6]. To install the plug-in, I simply copied the Impressions2_1NoNag.p file from my version 5.6 C:\NewTek\LightWave3D\Plugins\Modeler directory to my version 6 C:\LightWave\Programs\Plugins\Model directory, then added

Impressions via the Add Plug-ins option of Modeler's Preferences menu. The plug-in worked flawlessly, just as it does in version 5.6. For more information about Impressions and other plug-ins by Dave Hudek, visit his Web site at **www.ultranet.com/~dhudek/graphics/lw/** or email him at **Hudeks@aol.com**.

SubPatch Remodeling

LightWave's SubPatch model format presents some interesting new modeling and animation tools that can make polygonal models a less-attractive option. In these cases, you will want a way to adapt a SubPatch model to a form. Impressions won't be much help because shrink-wrapping the SubPatch controls to the form surface will create a SubPatch surface that is markedly different from the form surface. Instead, you will need to manually position the SubPatch controls to match the SubPatch surface to the form surface. Fortunately, a simple setup in Modeler 6 makes this a relatively easy and intuitive process:

1. Load a SubPatch model. For this example, I'll use the Taronhead object in the L6 Projects\Character\Heads directory of the standard version 6 installation. Send this model layer to the background.

2. Load a form object, in this case the Cyberscan of my head, to the foreground layer.

3. Make sure the Perspective view is set to Smooth Shade. This is important because the background layer will be shown as a black wireframe and the difference between the wireframe and the smooth shaded foreground will be an important guide for your fitting operations.

4. Move, rotate, and scale the form object to fit as closely as possible the orientation and size of the SubPatch surface, *not* the control cage. Again, use the interpupillary distance and the distance from each eye to the base of the nose as reference points.

5. Change the form object layer to the background and the SubPatch object layer to the foreground. You should now see the SubPatch object as smooth-shaded in the Perspective view and the form object as a black wireframe. The wireframe should show through the SubPatch object in some places, as shown in Figure 7.41.

6. Modify the SubPatch control cage until the wireframe barely shows through, all over the SubPatch object surface.

   Figure 7.42 shows six control points adjusted over the upper surface of the nose. Note that the underlying wireframe barely shows through the smooth-shaded surface, indicating that the surfaces are closely matched. If you can see all points and edges of the polygons, the SubPatch surface is too deep; if you can't see any of the black wireframe, the SubPatch surface is too high. If you can see most of the black points and parts of the edges, the SubPatch surface is just right.

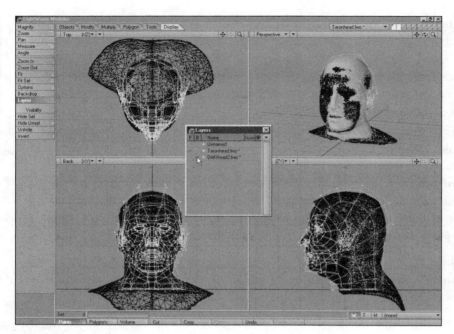

Figure 7.41
Taronhead SubPatch model loaded over the background form of my Cyberscan head, ready for recycling.

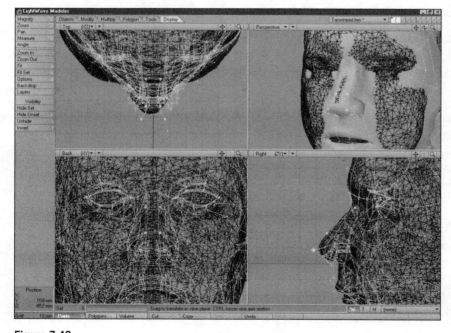

Figure 7.42
Six SubPatch controls moved to match the SubPatch surface of the nose closely to the underlying wireframe of the Cyberscan head.

This particular model has a total of 586 control points to modify, but the control positions for much of the head surface are no-brainers and go very quickly. The finer details around the eyes, nose, and mouth require more time and care. These are very small adjustments, so you will probably find it easier to use the numeric requester. If you select a group of control points that should all move in the same direction, you can repeatedly apply a very small increment (a quarter millimeter or less) to get very fine control.

7. When you are satisfied with your work, save the SubPatch model.

If you have a head model of your own lying around, I highly recommend using one of these methods to either adapt another model to your model's shape or adapt your model's mesh to another model's shape. Either way, you will develop a useful (and potentially lucrative) skill for recycling models.

Moving On

You should now have a solid working knowledge of the tools and techniques available for digitizing maquettes and live subjects. Along with the character design and modeling basics from Chapters 5 and 6, this knowledge prepares you to design and build almost any character model. In the next three chapters, I'll show you how to add to your models' visual appeal and realism with texture maps and shaders.

Case Study 7.1
Cyberscanning the Fred Maquette

The manual photogrammetry process I described in Chapter 6 is a reliable and cost-effective one, and it will produce a reasonably accurate low-polygon mesh that is efficient to set up and animate. However, this process does take more time than you may have in a commercial production with client-imposed deadlines. This is an example of the truism, "When you have more money, you have less time." The solution, appropriately, is to throw a little money at the problem. Build a maquette and send it out to a service bureau that uses one of Cyberware's laser scanners. Because you only need the raw surface data, you can negotiate for the service bureau's minimum setup and scan charges. You don't need to pay them a fortune for some operator's idea of an efficient NURBS surface.

What you'll get back is a very heavy and *very* accurate polygonal model like the one shown in the image here. This is a Cyberscan of my Fred maquette, scanned and cleaned up by Sue Addleman at Cyberware. Sue is probably one of the most experienced and capable Cyberscanner operators in the world, and she did a very thorough job of integrating several partial scans and closing any gaps. You would pay higher for a scan of this quality, but because the rest of this process is tolerant of gaps and partial scans, you can still work with the cheaper raw scan data.

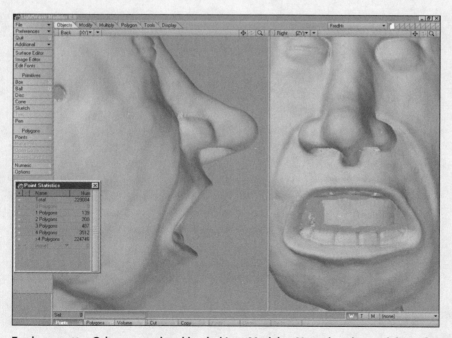

Fred maquette, Cyberscanned and loaded into Modeler. Note that the model's surface in the smooth shaded view (right) is almost indistinguishable from that in the flat shaded view (left) due to the very high polygon count.

The scanning and minor post-production editing took just two hours. Sue scanned Fred in 4 different orientations using a Model Shop Color 3D Scanner (3030RGB/MS) and CyDir software—on his side (a set of 18 linear scans), upright (a set of 18 linear scans), side view under chin right (a set of 3 scans), and side view under chin left (a set of 3 scans). Scans from the different orientations can be found on this book's CD-ROM in subdirectories labeled a, b, c and d. The files labeled hires.ply and fred.ply are the final merged raw 3D model (no editing); the freded.ply file is an edited version with all holes automatically filled and minor smoothing of hole areas and 2mm into the surrounding surfaces.

Part III

Texturing

Chapter 8

Surface Basics

This chapter is like a quick tour through the makeup department of a motion picture studio. Just as actors need makeup before going in front of the cameras, your models need appropriate colors and other surface attributes before you render them. When you have finished modeling a character, your next step is to assign surfaces to the model: the coloring, textures, and shaders that add realism—or that extra touch of fantasy—for the finishing touch. This chapter offers a brief introduction to the types of surfaces available and a few guidelines on how you can apply them to make your characters more effective.

In LightWave, a combination of polygon attributes, procedural textures, image maps, and plug-in shaders is referred to as *surface attributes*, or simply *surfaces*. This is a convenient catchall label for a large number of variables. LightWave groups all the surface settings and controls into a single Surface Editor (Figure 8.1) that makes it as easy as possible for you to experiment, so you can create exactly the surface you need with a minimum of bother. Each LightWave model can have several different surfaces, and you can layer multiple surfaces over one another. This is critical to simulating materials with translucency or depth, such as human skin. LightWave also enables you to save complex sets of surface attributes in surface files that you can load, modify, and save again; you can then reuse as many of them as possible and thereby speed up your work. In the *LightWave [6] Shape* manual, Chapter 9 covers the Surface Editor; you should at least read through it before continuing in this book.

Surface appearances are critical for any style of LightWave character animation. The appearance of the character should agree with its actions. If a character moves as if made of flesh and bone but you texture it to look like hard plastic, you will confuse the audience. Your texturing should help tell the story without intruding. Ideally, no one should specifically notice the sur-

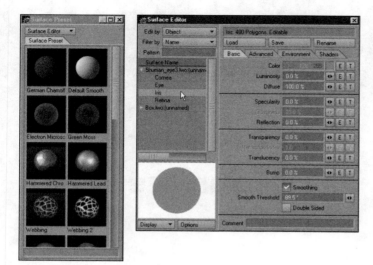

Figure 8.1
LightWave [6] Surface Editor and Surface Preset shelf.

faces you apply. The audience should simply accept them as a natural part of the character. A great job of surfacing may not redeem a lousy piece of animation, but lousy surfaces can distract the audience from an otherwise excellent animation.

Base Attributes

Base attributes are settings that control the model's rendered appearance without any maps or shaders. These attributes in LightWave include color, luminosity, diffuse, specularity, glossiness, reflection, transparency, and translucency.

Base color refers to the red, green, and blue (RGB) values of a surface as it would appear under ambient white light, without shadows or highlights. Generally, color used alone is useful for cartoons and other primitive characters, but it does not provide enough variation in detail for more realistic characters. Figure 8.2 shows color attributes applied to an eyeball model: one color for the iris, another for the sclera, and a third for the pupil.

Base luminosity controls the amount of self-illumination of a surface. A high value makes the surface appear to glow, with no shadows affecting it, as shown in Figure 8.3. This surface attribute is rarely used in characters. You may occasionally have a fantasy character with glowing eyes, but a more common use is in light-emitting props like flashlights, torches, and headlamps. If you need to simulate the highly reflective eyes of an animal in the dark, it's usually easier to set their irises or retinas to high luminosity than to position lights and camera to catch the true reflection.

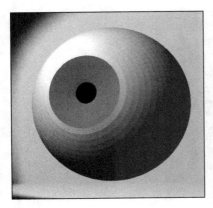

Figure 8.2
Base colors for an eyeball.

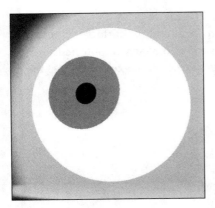

Figure 8.3
Base luminosity set to 100% for the eyeball. Note that the shadows on the eyeball have disappeared but that the eyeball's glow has no effect on the lighting of the background.

The base diffuse setting limits the brightest color of the surface. A value of 100% diffuse means the surface will be as bright as the lighting allows; 0% pretty much blacks out the material, preventing lights from illuminating it at all. Most natural materials have a diffuse value between 80% and 40%.

Base specularity describes the intensity and extent of the *hot spot*, the area of a surface that reflects the light directly into the camera lens. A tighter, brighter specularity is appropriate for shiny materials, like chitin (arthropod shells), fingernails, eyeballs, and hair. A broader, dimmer specularity is appropriate for skin, most fabrics, and matte-finished or oxidized metal. In LightWave, specularity and glossiness work together. Specularity determines the intensity of the hot spot, and glossiness determines the extent or spread. With both settings near 100%, you get a pinpoint hot spot; with high spec and lower gloss, you get a bright but spread-out spot, as shown in Figure 8.4.

Figure 8.4
Base specularity for the eyeball. Left, 100% glossiness; right, 50% glossiness. Note the relative size and shape of the hot spot.

Base reflection determines how much of the surrounding environment the surface will mirror, as shown in Figure 8.5. A high reflection mimics a surface such as mercury or polished silver. Generally, few character surfaces will require high reflection settings. The exceptions include eyeballs, fingernails, and similar wet or polished surfaces.

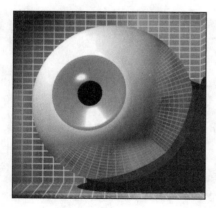

Figure 8.5
Eyeball surfaces with high reflection show the model's surroundings.

Base transparency controls the amount of light that passes through a surface. The Index Of Refraction setting is a modifier of transparency and determines how much light will bend as it passes through the surface. Most characters will have very few transparent surfaces, but fingernails, corneas, sheer fabrics, and accessories such as eyeglasses make very good use of transparency for realistic characters. Some transparency effects may require you to model several closely spaced layers of the same objects, with outer layers having different transparency values, as in Figure 8.6.

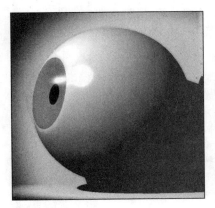

Figure 8.6
Base transparency for eyeball, showing as a thin overall layer plus the corneal bulge.

Base translucency is similar to transparency, but with a more diffused effect. This is similar to the difference between ordinary window glass and frosted glass: You can still see light and color through it, but the details are blurred. For characters, the translucency setting can be of most use for clothing and other fabrics that are backlit, enabling shadows to be cast on the fabric. This can be highly effective for sheer fabrics in multilayered costumes. However, creating realistic draped fabrics can be a resource-intensive process, as later chapters will show. For most characters, you can ignore the translucency setting for most of their surfaces.

Texture Maps

Realistic characters need complex surfaces for facial features, skin, and clothing. If you are working in a more abstract style that lets you get away with solid colors and uniformly smooth surfaces, you can ignore this. But the closer you work to realism, especially when you're matching to live action, the more complex surfaces you will have to create for your characters. Skin must look like it has a subtle roughness, that it grew, aged, and wrinkled from use; clothing has to look like it's really made of thousands of separate fibers with a definite weave, drape, and nap; sheet materials, like polished leather and vinyl, must have the right shine. Texture maps enable you to create these highly detailed surfaces while retaining the most efficient simplicity of the underlying model.

A map is an image file applied to a character or scene to override or modify the base surface settings. LightWave enables you to apply a map to modify nearly every surface attribute. Theoretically, you could create a character that would use at least one map of each type, but most of the time, you'll only need to use a few map types.

Color and Shading Maps

Color maps modify or override the base color of the model without affecting any of the other base attributes. The left side of Figure 8.7 shows a Cyberware model of my head with a gray

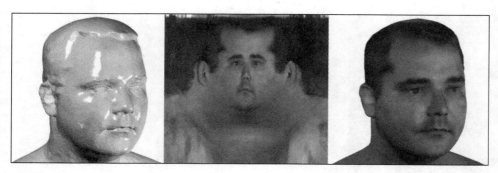

Figure 8.7
A Cyberware head scan object, color map, and object with color map applied.

glossy surface applied. The center shows the matching Cyberware color map. The right side shows the model with the color map applied and no other changes to the surface or lighting.

Color maps are the most obvious choice for dressing up a character, but don't neglect the more subtle effects you can create with the other map types. A good technical director (TD) can make an object look like almost any material without using any color map at all. Conversely, even a photographic-quality color map is going to look wrong if it isn't complemented by other map types. For that reason, I recommend using color maps only as references early in the mapping process and not actually applying them to the model for rendering until last. You should use a light gray base color instead, with straight 192,192,192 RGB values. Color is so overwhelming that it can distract you from getting the other settings just right. However, if a solid gray character looks good with the other maps in place, it will look great with the final colors added.

Color is also the easiest type of map to create. All consumer video, photography, and digitizing equipment is designed to capture the visible wavelengths that define surface colors, so you have a variety of tools at your disposal to gather color maps from the real world. Once that data is in your computer, even the most primitive image editing software can modify a color map. The next chapter covers these tools and techniques in more detail, including how to create the maps shown in this chapter's figures.

Specularity maps vary or override the model's base specularity according to the map's grayscale values. These maps are necessary for mucous membranes, fingernails, claws, eyeballs, oily skin, and any other surface that should appear wet, polished, shiny, or oily in some places and dry, roughened, or matte in surrounding areas of the same surface. Human faces almost always require a specularity map. A color map alone will not reflect light properly from oily patches or taut skin while retaining the thoroughly matte areas under the cheekbones and jaw (see Figure 8.8). A uniform specularity setting is a dead giveaway that the character is computer generated.

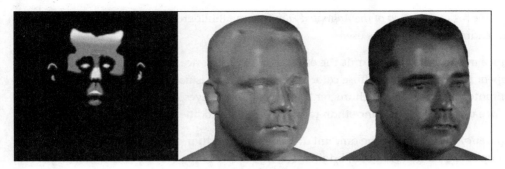

Figure 8.8
A specularity map, head with specularity map, and head with both specularity and color maps.

If you'd like to take a more detailed look at the effect of this specularity map, open animation file 08_05.avi from this book's CD-ROM. You can use the scrub bar in your animation viewer to rotate the mapped model through a 180-degree arc while you observe the specular reflections. Note the difference in specularity between the forehead, nose, and jawline. You can compare this example with the specularity of your own face. Set up a mirror so you can see your face under a single strong light, then turn and tilt your head to reflect the light from different parts of your face. Observe the difference in strength and spread of the highlights. In Project 9.3, in the next chapter, you will create your own specularity maps using this technique.

Specularity mapping is also excellent for simulating the variations in woven fabric, brightening the highlights from the top of the threads and absorbing light in between the weave. The specularity map should be darker where it will absorb the light and lighter where it will reflect it. The effect of the mapped specular highlights will make the flat surface appear three-dimensional. The deepest parts of the weave will be subdued, while the highest parts reflect the brightest light.

Diffuse maps darken the color of the model without affecting the other attributes. This type of mapping is useful for simulating dirt and other surface contaminants. The usual giveaway for LightWave-rendered elements composited into live action is not enough dirt. In the real world, anything outside a sterile clean room is going to collect crud. Corrosion, contaminants, precipitated smog—you name it, dirt is everywhere. Add some rust, some dust, and some smudges and smears to your map collection. Spread some of it on your models if you have to get realistic or just want to add visual appeal. Look at how your characters will move and come into contact with their environments. Any place they make habitual contact should get smudged and dirty: soles of shoes, elbows, cuffs, and knees will all collect crud over time. Keep your eyes open out in the real world, and observe and remember how surfaces change as they age and are abused. Take a look at an old, scuffed shoe, for instance. How would you texture a pristine LightWave model of the same shoe? What color, diffuse, and specularity maps would you use? An excellent example of mapping for wear and dirt is the Sid's Room set for *Toy Story*. The book

Toy Story: The Art and Making of the Animated Film (see the Bibliography) has a detailed explanation with examples of the maps used.

Luminance maps control or override the effect of base luminance, making light areas of the map appear to glow with the diffuse color of the model. This is useful mostly for special effects on inanimate objects. Even if a character has eerily glowing eyes, it's usually easier to create that surface using base luminance than to bother with an additional map.

A transparency map controls the amount and color of light that passes through a model based on the map's RGB values. A higher, brighter setting for one of the colors permits more light of that color to shine through, making the surface transparent in that range (see Figure 8.9). High values for all three colors enable light to pass uniformly so the color of the penetrating light appears white. Transparency maps are especially useful for wing membranes, toe webbing, leaves, and other thin organic tissues that vary from fully opaque to semi- or fully transparent based on the fine details of a map rather than modeled faces or patches.

Figure 8.9
An image of a leaf applied as a color map and as combination color and transparency maps. Note the leaf colors in the shadow cast on the horizontal surface.

Reflection maps should be used primarily for high-specularity surfaces (like eyeballs, fingernails, and mucous membranes) or polished accessories (like metal and glass). Even if a surface is supposed to be highly polished, you should use some noise or dirt to simulate real-world imperfections. Nothing gives away a LightWave rendering more quickly than perfectly reflective chrome or glass. Reflection maps are applied only to the surface and can be any map. This is especially useful when you need to cheat a scene, showing reflections of objects and sets that aren't actually there, as in Figure 8.10.

Figure 8.10
An environment reflection map applied to a reflective sphere, creating the illusion of objects that are not actually in the scene.

Environmental reflection maps in LightWave are assigned, reasonably enough, in the Environment tab. There are several methods of environmental reflection mapping in LightWave, including Backdrop Only, Raytracing+Backdrop, Spherical Reflection Map, and Raytracing+Spherical. Figure 8.10 shows the results of Spherical Reflection Map. This requires a special type of image map to produce realistic results. Raytraced reflection maps will give you the most accurate realism. The map is created by rendering an image of the scene from the mapped object's point of view, as if it were a camera with a fish-eye wide-angle lens. The drawback is that it's very difficult to cheat a scene with these reflection maps because you have to either actually build the entire scene to be reflected (see Figure 8.11) or paint a really good faked image.

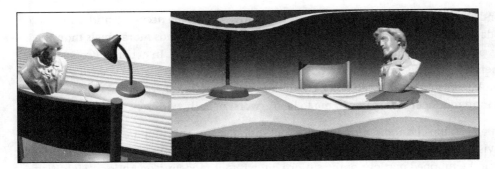

Figure 8.11
The original scene (left) and the spherical reflection map rendered from the scene (right).

The preceding attributes control the color and shading of the object's surfaces. The remaining attributes change the appearance of the underlying geometry, enabling you to use maps to modify the shape of your characters.

Shape-Changing Maps

You can use bump maps to provide an illusion of fine surface details and imperfections that can markedly increase the realism or visual appeal of a character. These maps can make a model appear much more dimensionally complex or detailed than the model's geometry alone could achieve, without making it more difficult to set up or animate. The major disadvantage of bump maps is that the illusion of depth is only apparent face-on; the actual three-dimensional profiles of the model are unchanged. Nevertheless, there are many good applications of bump maps for both realistic and abstract characters.

Bump maps create the illusion of changes in surface depth or height based on the map's grayscale value. Bump maps generally have 8 bits (256 levels) of gray, which is plenty for most applications. You may find it useful to think of the bump map's effect as one pixel equals one vertex, as if the underlying geometry is actually made more complex by the map.

Avoiding Bump Map Jaggies

When you are creating bump maps, remember that sharp gray-value changes equal sharp 3D *jaggies*. The difference between one map pixel and the next creates a slope. If the difference is only a few gray values, the slope is very gentle. If the difference is between black and white, the slope is nearly vertical, and you get a 3D jagged edge in the rendered image. To avoid sharp slopes in your bump maps, you can increase the map's resolution, then apply blur or edge dither effects to smooth out any abrupt differences in gray values (see Figure 8.12).

Displacement maps are similar to bump maps but actually shift the model's geometry so the illusion of depth variations is also preserved in profile (see Figure 8.13). Note how the upper and left edges in Figure 8.12 differ from those in Figure 8.13. The bump map leaves the profile unchanged, whereas the displacement map alters it.

The major drawback to displacement maps in LightWave is that the accuracy and continuity of the rendering relies on a sufficient number of points. If the map has more pixels than the model has points, the displacement becomes blocky and inaccurate. In general, I consider displacement maps to be more trouble that they are worth. Except in certain special situations where their benefits outweigh their costs, combining an unnecessarily complex object with the hassles of map management seems to me to be the worst of both worlds.

A third type of shape-changing map is the clip, or alpha, map. This map makes parts of the surface invisible to shadows, specular highlights, colors, and reflections. The effect is that of clipping out the mapped portions of the surface but without modeling operations. LightWave can also accomplish this effect with a combination of transparency and specularity maps. If

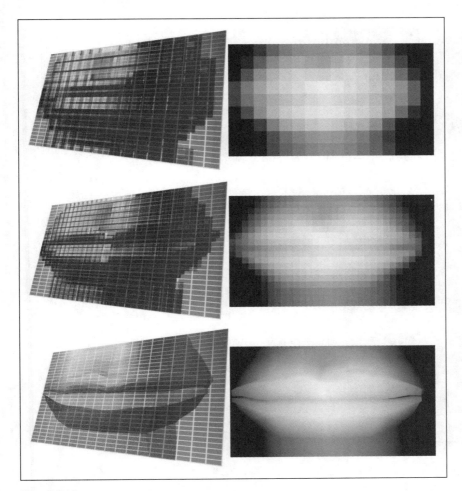

Figure 8.12
A plane object with 16x9, 32x18, and 640x360 resolution bump maps applied.

you need to animate an opening or break in a model's surface, using a sequential or animated clip map can be a more efficient solution than modeling the effect. For example, if you are using bump or displacement map sequences to animate a character's mouth for lip sync, you also need to cut out the mouth opening to match the inner edge of the lips (see Figure 8.14). A matched clip map sequence will do the job perfectly and can be derived easily from the bump or displacement map sequence.

Where and how you place surfaces is almost as important as designing the surfaces themselves. A well-painted color map that's applied to the wrong part of a character doesn't do much good.

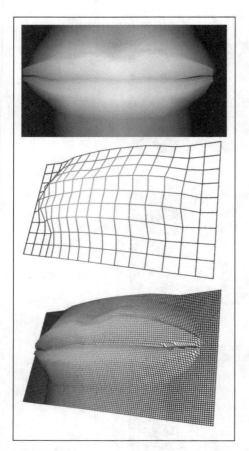

Figure 8.13
A displacement map applied to simple and tessellated plane objects.

Figure 8.14
Matched color, bump, and clip maps applied to an object.

Texture and Map Placement

Ideally, the textures you apply should conform to the character's surface geometry so the texture appears to be an integral part of the model. Textures that don't follow the appropriate surface contours can make your character look like it was worked over by a wallpapering machine instead of a professional makeup artist.

Assigned textures should also move and deform along with the surface geometry when the character is animated. If you don't choose the right method of mapping a surface, the map may stay in one place while the character slides out from under it. The best way to avoid these disasters is to know in advance exactly how each surface must behave and what you have to do to create the effects you need. To do this, you need to understand and be able to work with LightWave's texture placement and coordinate system.

UV Mapping

By now you should be familiar with the XYZ coordinate system used to build and animate models. LightWave [6] uses a second, parallel set of coordinates to control mapping. The mapping coordinates are labeled U and V. U corresponds to the x-, or horizontal, axis and V to the y-, or vertical, axis. Technically, this system is called UVW mapping, but because the third axis is rarely used, this system is more generally called UV mapping.

This separate map coordinate system enables you to change the application of textures without having to remodel the underlying geometry. It's like pinning material onto a dressmaker's dummy. You don't have to rebuild the dummy when you make an alteration; you just move the pins to reposition the material. UV coordinates are your dressmaker's pins. In most cases, UV mapping will give you the best control for assigning materials to your characters. LightWave enables you to control material placement down to the individual points of your models. This is especially important if you are working with realistic characters. For example, look at Figure 8.15. This model of my head was created by a Cyberware scanner that also recorded the surface colors. The Cyberware software assembled the model from the XYZ point data and also assigned the appropriate UV mapping coordinates.

Figure 8.15
A color map applied to a head model with UV mapping coordinates.

If you can import the embedded UV mapping into LightWave, all you have to do is load the model and assign the color map using the built-in UV coordinates. You will get perfect material alignment every time. This is especially important when you have complex geometry and maps that have to match precisely. UV coordinates can wrap a material all around an irregular object, getting into the undercuts and smoothly covering compound curves without inaccurate distortions. UV mapping isn't just for scanned images, either. Most of the available 3D paint software also uses UV mapping. In the next two chapters, several exercises will show you how to use UV tools to paint accurate, detailed 3D materials for your characters (see Project 9.5 in the next chapter).

If you choose not to use UV mapping, you have a few options that can work almost as well with a little more effort: planar, cylindrical, spherical, and repeating pattern mapping. The most basic mapping is planar.

Planar Mapping

A planar map is like the image from a slide or motion picture projector—it passes all the way through the model, as shown in Figure 8.16.

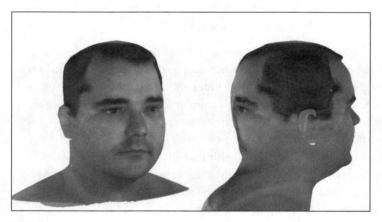

Figure 8.16
A color map applied to a head model with planar mapping coordinates.

The obvious problem with planar mapping is that it can't get into undercuts and that it smears the map along any surface that nearly parallels the line of projection. Planar mapping is therefore limited to applications in which you can ensure that the projected distortions won't be visible or are not important. You can do this by assigning separate planar materials according to surface normals, the orientation of each polygon. If your model is at all complex, it's very time-consuming to find all the polygons that share a common direction, assign a planar material to them, and repeat the process for all the polygons. It can be done, but there are better uses for your time. There are applications in which planar projections are useful—transparency-mapped lighting and front projection, for instance. However, those fall under the heading of special effects rather than character animation.

Cylindrical Mapping

Cylindrical mapping is more useful for character textures. With a little care, it can be almost as versatile as UV mapping. In principle, it's like rolling the applied material into a cylinder inside the model and projecting the material outward until it hits the surface. This takes care of the planar smearing problem in one direction because the cylindrical projection looks accurate from every side (see Figure 8.17). The only visible distortions are at the end caps of the cylinder. In this example, the lower end cap is invisible, and the upper one is matched by flaws in the model itself. Some minor alignment problems still remain. The rear edge of the ear catches a bit of misplaced shadow that true UV mapping would place precisely.

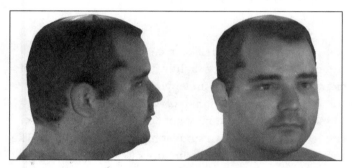

Figure 8.17
A color map applied to a head model with cylindrical mapping coordinates.

If you can construct your characters so the ends of their cylindrical forms are concealed by other materials, you can hide the discrepancies of cylindrical mapping. For those situations where the end of the cylinder must be exposed, you'll need to be a bit more careful designing the map to blend inconspicuously at the end cap.

Spherical Mapping

Spherical mapping takes the principle of cylindrical mapping one axis further, wrapping the material in two directions at once. This can be handy if you have a material specifically designed to be spherically mapped. However, if you are trying to adapt a planar or cylindrical material for spherical mapping, it's about as much work as tweaking two cylindrical maps. If you don't spend enough time tweaking LightWave's texture axes and center, you'll end up with something like Figure 8.18. These results are close enough in one direction, but the second axis just causes too much distortion to be usable. Generally, spherical mapping requires spherical material design from scratch.

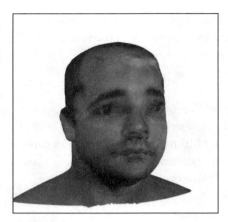

Figure 8.18
A color map applied to a head model with spherical mapping coordinates.

Repeating Patterns

Many natural materials have repeating but variable patterns. Skin creases, scales, denticles (sharkskin), and cloth all have consistent patterns that vary slightly depending on the part of the creature covered and the movement or distortion of the underlying surface. One way to deal with this challenge is to paint a huge map, large enough to cover the entire model and high resolution enough to show all these fine details. That may not be the most efficient way, however. You may do just as well, with less work, by using a smaller map and repeating it. The most common way to repeat materials is called tiling, after its similarity to laying floor tiles. This method repeats the material at regular intervals, producing results like a checkerboard or quilt. You can tile a map in LightWave by enabling the Width Repeat and Height Repeat options in the Texture Editor. However, the results of tiling are often too uniform for characters.

There is another way to repeat maps, but it's in another dimension entirely—the fourth dimension—time! LightWave enables you to apply a video clip or a sequence of images as a map or to animate the surface attributes by using envelopes. These techniques can be very useful if used deliberately and when appropriate, but they can be really annoying if overused or abused. Color cycling, for example, has been beaten to death and is rarely a good addition to a character animation. On the other hand, one of the easiest and most educational uses is to create mapped lip sync sequences. This makes lip sync easier to practice and modify for the beginner and can even be used in production if map sequences can suit the character's design. The next chapter will show you a few more examples of animated materials and how to make them.

Moving On

I hope this chapter gives you a solid foundation for designing appropriate surfaces for your characters. The next chapter is about the tools and techniques you can use to create and modify your own texture maps and apply them to your models.

Chapter 9

Making and Applying Maps

The importance of two-dimensional maps to LightWave character animation is in direct proportion to the realism of the characters. Learn to make and use cartoon and realistic maps and your characters will be more effective storytellers. This chapter covers the creation and application of 2D maps. Projects in this chapter show you how to capture textures from real-world materials, process them into maps to fit your characters, and create fantastic or caricature maps that don't yet exist outside your imagination. This is the nuts-and-bolts practice for the theories described in the preceding chapter and a prerequisite for the next chapter on 3D painting tools and shaders.

If you are compositing LightWave elements into live footage, you simply can't create a believable character without using maps or shaders. Simulating the natural materials that are necessary for characters (such as skin, mucous membranes, nails, claws, chitin, eyeballs, wrinkles, scales, feathers, fabric, leather, rubber, armor, keloids, or denticles) would be difficult or impossible without maps. Good maps also make your characters more appealing to your audience's eyes. Humans are built to appreciate visually complex textures and patterns, and if your characters are interesting to look at (in addition to moving well), your audience will appreciate them that much more.

Real-World Texture Capture

The most efficient way to get complex, naturalistic maps is to start with nature. Most natural materials reveal their origins in growth layers, wrinkles, wear patterns, and other traces that are difficult or time-consuming to mimic by hand. If you are an accomplished 2D artist, by all means use your talents to create your own maps from scratch. If you are less experienced, you can largely make up for it by starting with the natural world and simply working minor changes on the best raw materials.

There are at least four major ways of getting real-world images into your computer: scanners, video cameras with digitizer boards, PhotoCD, and digital cameras. Each approach is viable for creating character animation maps, but for each one there are some trade-offs that may make a difference for your specific application.

Scanners

Scanners have been around for a relatively long time, and there are many models, prices, and feature sets to choose from. Many print shops and service bureaus also provide access to scanners, so it's not even necessary for you to own one. You can pick up a good color flatbed scanner for under $200, and almost all the current models can be controlled directly by graphics programs like Photoshop. Most scanners use either SCSI, USB, or parallel-port interfaces. If you are considering a scanner that requires a proprietary interface card, I don't recommend buying it. The advantages of flatbed scanners for mapmaking are that you can scan anything you can flatten on the glass platen—such as photos, cloth, leather, even raw meat—and bad scans don't cost you anything. The disadvantages are that you can't readily scan materials that are rigidly 3D, that you can't get to the scanner (or get the scanner to them), or that require special lighting that the scan head can't match.

Video

A video-digitizing board and a video camera or camcorder are good additions to a character animator's workstation. These systems can be add-ons to your computer's main video card or replacements for it. Generally, they have a selection of input jacks for RCA, cable, S-Video, BNC, or IEEE-1394 video connectors, a duplicate set of output jacks and an SVGA connector for your monitor, and they can record images or video directly to your computer's hard drive. In addition to digitizing still frames for maps, many boards can also digitize video sequences for match footage and motion studies. If you choose a board that also has video output, you can record your animations to videotape without any additional investment (see Chapter 20 for details). The advantages for digitizing maps are that anything the camera can see, you can digitize; you can work from VCR or camcorder tapes as well as from a live camera; you can set up whatever kind of lighting you need with a standard camera stand; and bad shots don't cost you anything. The disadvantages are that you usually can't get as high a resolution or color depth as you can with film or scanning, you have to pay closer attention to lighting, and if you want to do on-location capture, you need a camcorder.

PhotoCD and Pro PhotoCD

PhotoCD is an especially versatile means of capturing raw materials for character maps. This process requires you to shoot color film in a standard camera (usually 35mm), then have the film processed by one of Kodak's licensees onto a PhotoCD that you can put in your computer's CD-ROM drive. The PhotoCD format is supported by Photoshop and most other paint software. The advantages are that you have access to the full range of photographic lenses, filters, camera stands, lights, and setup techniques; the resolution (2048×3072) and color depth of the PhotoCD images can match feature film requirements; you don't have to invest in any special equipment; and you "pay as you go" for the images you need. The disadvantages are that you have to wait for processing and the per-image costs can add up quickly, so it's awkward and expensive to experiment. You really need to know what you're doing before you drop off a roll of film for PhotoCD processing. If you need maximum resolution, you can also opt for Pro PhotoCD service, which increases resolution to 4096×6144 but costs more. When you're shooting tests, you can use slide film and have only selected slides scanned or post-processed. That usually costs more per image, but it can save you money over processing whole rolls just to get a few good shots. Ask your local film shop for details. I've generally found photo professionals to be very helpful about the PhotoCD and Pro PhotoCD formats.

Digital Camera

The most recent entry to the field of electronic imaging is the digital camera. These devices are like self-contained cameras and digitizing cards, enabling you to capture and store images for later download to your computer. The advantages are that you can see your results immediately, so you can discard and reshoot bad images; you can use lights and camera stands; you can shoot on location without carrying awkward amounts of gear; and bad shots don't cost you anything. The disadvantages are the maximum number of images the camera can hold, the generally lower resolution (compared to PhotoCD or scanners), and the high cost of a good camera. At the bottom end, you can get a digital camera that will produce snapshots suitable for your Web page. But if you need high-resolution images for television or feature film work, a 3-megapixel camera that captures 2K film-resolution images can set you back up to $800.

Matching Reality

When you are called on to match live action, especially to insert a LightWave character into live footage, you have to use all the realism tricks at your disposal. Materials have to be an exact match, their appearance under the matched lighting has to be identical, and in general, you have to do your best to duplicate reality.

If at all possible, you should photograph and digitize materials on-site at the time of the live-action shoot. This gives you the opportunity to get extreme close-ups of textures and materials that may not show up clearly in the match footage. If a character is going to extrude itself from the tile floor, it's a good idea to have an exact full-color scan of that tile floor to use as a map. If you can't get shots on-site at the time, talk to the set and prop crews afterward to see if you can get shots of the materials later.

You should also shoot general coverage of the scene for use in reflection maps. Even a clean plate shot for the compositing effects may not be what you need for reflection mapping, but if you've got some nice clear 35mm prints, you can usually piece together a decent environment map. Make sure you make the map large enough. If a reflective object has some broad convex curves, a tiny fraction of the reflection map can stretch across quite a bit of the object.

If you have to work exclusively from the match footage, use image processing software with an eyedropper tool to sample the footage for material colors. You will also need to sample hotspots or a white card to pick up the original light colors, because they will affect the material's appearance as well.

Clothing

Fabric is second only to skin as an important part of your mapping palette. With the obvious variety of fabrics available, you might think that you'll have to build a huge library of fabric maps. Not so! I'm never one to discourage map collecting, but you can fake a surprising number of fabrics with a handful of basic elements. Fabrics are either woven or sheet. If it's a sheet material, like leather or vinyl, the texture is easy enough to figure out just by looking at it. If it's a woven material, simulating the texture gets a little more complex. Here are some hints:

- *Identify the weave.* Fabrics are manufactured in a wide variety of weaves, but half a dozen good bump maps will enable you to fake most of the materials you'll run across. I like digitizing shots of coarse-woven cloth, like canvas and burlap, and then applying them at a very small size to simulate finer materials.

- *Identify the finish.* Fabrics can be rough and slubby or smooth and satiny. The finish will determine what type of specularity and diffusion maps you apply. These can generally be modified versions of the bump map.

- *Identify the color.* This is where you may have to collect a lot of swatches, especially for patterned materials. On the positive side, you can create original tileable patterns and overlay them on the standard weave and finish maps to create your own fabrics.

Making Cloth Maps from Digitized Images

The three map types that most identify a fabric are transparency, bump, and specularity. If you are using a video digitizer, PhotoCD, or a digital camera, it's easy to get all three. If you are using a scanner, it's a little more difficult because you have very little control over the lighting.

The first step is to set up your capture gear to get a close-up of the samples with very strong backlighting and no front lighting. My own setup is a transparent Lexan clipboard mounted in front of a flood lamp, which is secured in front of my camcorder. You may be able to get away with stretching a fabric sample directly in front of a light source, but that's a fire hazard, and I strongly encourage you to find another way. Figure 9.1 shows some examples of raw captures made with a Hi8 camcorder and an ATI video capture card.

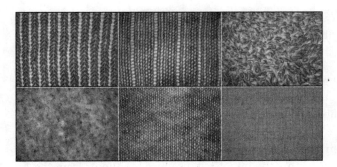

Figure 9.1
Video-captured backlit fabrics.

These captures can be used as is for transparency and translucency maps; the lighter areas will be more transparent. If you want to simulate dyed fabrics, you can convert the raw captures to grayscale, then filter them with the fabric color to get a more accurate transparency appearance.

You can also use the raw capture as is for bump maps if the sample does not have any areas that are completely opaque and if it's uniformly colored. I recommend digitizing only white fabrics for transparency values. Any color in the weave throws off the transparency values and also distorts bump values. If any area of the sample is completely opaque, you may lose necessary surface details in the blacked-out areas. You can try using brighter light sources to punch through the darker areas, but be careful not to overlight the thinnest, most transparent areas.

If transparency lighting can't give you an adequate bump map, you can try side-lighting. This works best with a camera stand with two or more positionable lights. The idea is to place the light sources so the light is cast nearly parallel to the surface to be captured. If you do it right, the highest bumps catch the brightest light, and the deeper parts of the fabric are cast in shadow, as shown in Figure 9.2.

Figure 9.2
Video-captured side-lit fabrics for bump maps.

You need to carefully balance the light so the sample is evenly lit from both sides. Any strong gradation from one side to the other will make it much more difficult to match the image's edges for a tileable map.

A little modification of the bump map will give you a good specularity map. Generally, you catch highlights from woven fabrics at the high points in the weave; a few stray highlights come from loose or protruding single fibers in the deeper parts. You can simulate this with a moderate amount of effort. Convert the bump map to grayscale, increase the contrast, and lower the brightness until the high points are in sharp relief. Then apply a noise filter to the entire map. When applied as a specularity map, the image will produce highlights from the highest "threads" plus random highlights throughout the surface, mimicking stray fibers catching the light. It's seemingly minuscule details like this that make the difference between "a nice simulation" and "is that really computer generated?"

Capturing color maps is easy by comparison. Just light your sample evenly, and if color accuracy is important, scan a color reference chart; then follow your paint software's procedures for color calibration.

Once you have the raw images, you'll generally want to make them tile seamlessly. This is a straightforward process—it just requires patience and attention to detail. There are a number of software tools that can automate most of the process in Project 9.1, but you can often get better results by doing it manually.

PROJECT 9.1 Making Tileable Maps

This project will show you the basic process of using Adobe Photoshop to turn a captured image into a tileable map. If your preferred paint software enables you to cut, copy, and paste, and to smudge or feather edges, you can use it instead of Photoshop to complete the project.

To turn a captured image into a tileable map, follow these steps:

1. Open the Cloth060.bmp image from the Chapter 9 directory on this book's CD-ROM.

2. Convert the image mode to grayscale. Turn on the Info palette. From the File menu, select Preferences|Units & Rulers and set the units preference to Pixels. This will make it easier for you to precisely select, copy, and paste specific ranges of pixels.

3. Examine the image for vertical and horizontal match-lines.

   Match-lines are rows or columns of pixels that have similar patterns on both sides. If you cut and paste an image along a match-line, the seam is much harder to see, and the pasted image looks like a single image rather than a patchwork. Spotting match-lines takes practice, so I've included a lot of raw fabric scans in the Chapter 9 directory on this book's CD-ROM. After you complete this project, you should go back and repeat the process with some of the other patterns, just for practice.

For this project, I've selected an image with relatively clean and obvious match-lines. Most real-world materials won't have clean match-lines, which means more work in cleanup and edge smudging. This example is an easy one for you to practice on. The most prominent vertical match-line is at 202 pixels from the left, and the most prominent horizontal match-line is at 215 pixels from the top.

4. Select from 202,215 up and to the left until the selected area is 128W by 216H, according to the Info palette.

Take a close look at the borders of the selected area (see Figure 9.3). Compare the left and right edges and the top and bottom. Note how similar they are and where they have prominent differences.

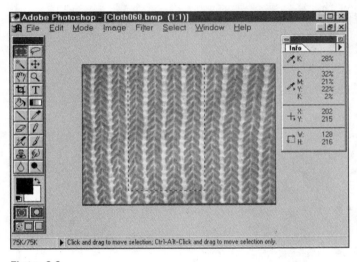

Figure 9.3
Selected area with match-lines.

5. Copy the selection. Choose Image|Canvas Size and increase the dimensions to double the selection's resolution, 256X and 432Y. This is to give you the necessary space to paste four copies of the selection.

6. Paste four copies of the selection into the enlarged canvas, aligning the edges and precisely filling the canvas, as shown in Figure 9.4.

7. Zoom in on the seam areas running through the vertical and horizontal centers of the image.

You need to obliterate the obvious dividing line between the pasted sections without destroying the overall pattern. In Photoshop, the tools I use most for doing this are the Smudge tool and the Blur filter. Smudge, blur, or otherwise camouflage the seams between the pasted sections. Your results should look like the right side of Figure 9.5.

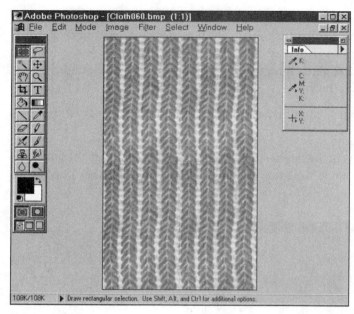

Figure 9.4
Four copies of the selection pasted together.

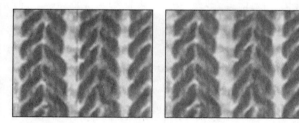

Figure 9.5
Before (left) and after (right) smudged portions of a pasted seam.

When you've finished hiding the seams, you should have an image that looks like a continuous piece of cloth. This is still not a tileable map—the top/bottom and right/left edges are still imperfect matches. However, the pasting and smudging has created an area that you can select with perfectly matching edges. Any selection equal to the original pasted image—that is, 128W by 216H—will automatically have matching edges.

8. Using the Crop tool, select a 128W-by-216H area, not including the outer borders of the image or within smudging distance of the outer borders or the vertical or horizontal seams. If you are still using Photoshop 3, use the Select tool followed by the Crop menu option. You want the selection's edges to run through previously uncut parts of the image. This selection will tile seamlessly.

9. Save the cropped image with a new file name. Because you'll probably be using it as a transparency map, KnitTran.bmp would be appropriate. Your results should look like Figure 9.6. If you like, you can test the tiling ability of this image by repeating Steps 5 and 6 with it.

Figure 9.6
Finished tileable map.

Now that you have a basic tileable map, you can use it as a building block for tileable maps with finer detail. For ordinary tiling, you can use the map as is and reduce its applied scale in LightWave's Texture Editor to get the necessary level of detail. You can get acceptably realistic results simply by applying this tileable map as a transparency and bump map over an object with a base color, as in Figure 9.7.

Figure 9.7
Tileable map applied as transparency and bump.

Planar Mapping

The simplest form of mapping for characters is a combination of orthographic projection and multiple planar maps. Orthographic projection simply means that there is no perspective or parallax—no foreshortening or distortion of the image due to the convergence of light rays passing through the camera lens. Blueprints and engineering drawings are examples of ortho-graphic projections. In LightWave, you can fake an orthographic projection by setting the camera as far away as possible with a very long zoom lens setting. This combination makes the objects look just as close but minimizes the distortion of perspective (see Figure 9.8).

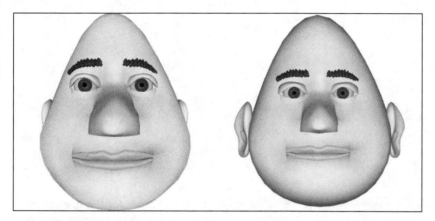

Figure 9.8
Face rendered with close-up focal length (left) showing perspective distortion and with long focal length (right) simulating orthographic projection.

If you render a series of wireframe images in this way, you can use them as guides for painting a series of planar maps. If you apply six separate planar maps in the form of a cube surround-ing the model, you will minimize the smearing that planar projection usually causes because no face or patch will be more than 45 degrees off the plane of the applied map.

Creating maps for flat surfaces is relatively easy, but most characters' surfaces are curved. In the next section, I'll show you the tools and techniques that can help you map curved surfaces.

Spherical Mapping

One of the best tools for creating spherical maps is a Photoshop filter named Polar Coordi-nates. This filter changes the normal xy coordinates of a 2D image to polar coordinates, like a Mercator projection. The center of the image is stretched out along the top edge, and the four sides of the image are spread out to form the bottom edge of the polar image. Project 9.2 will show you how this filter can be used to assemble a spherical eyeball map from a collection of digitized images. The same principles can be applied to create an accurate spherical map for any suitable object.

PROJECT 9.2 Making a Realistic Eyeball Color Map from Digitized Images

The first step is to capture a series of close-up images of your subject's eyeball. I did this by setting up a video camera with a spotlight next to it and grabbing a series of stills as I rotated my eye as far as possible in every direction. This gave me a variety of images to choose from, but you need only enough to provide overlapping coverage of the front surface of the eyeball. The images I selected are in the Chapter 9 directory on this book's CD-ROM, files eyeba008.bmp, eyeba010.bmp, eyeba012.bmp, eyeba013.bmp, eyeba015.bmp, eyeba018.bmp, eyeba020.bmp, and eyeba040.bmp, as shown in Figure 9.9.

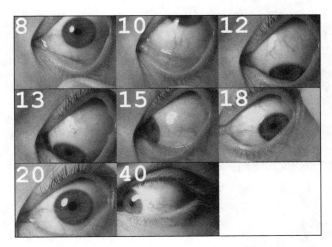

Figure 9.9
Digitized frames of an eyeball to be assembled for a spherical map.

The Polar Coordinates filter requires a consistent center for an image to be converted. You need to make sure all the images are centered around the pupil.

To make an eyeball color map, follow these steps:

1. Load eyeba008.bmp. Erase all of the image except the sclera (white), iris, and pupil. Choose Image|Canvas Size and change it to 320-by-320 pixels.

2. Open the Info palette. Select the color portion of the image contents, as shown in Figure 9.10.

3. Zoom in on the pupil. Grab the exact center of the pupil and drag the selection so the coordinates readout in the Info palette reads 160,160 (the exact center of the canvas), as shown in Figure 9.11.

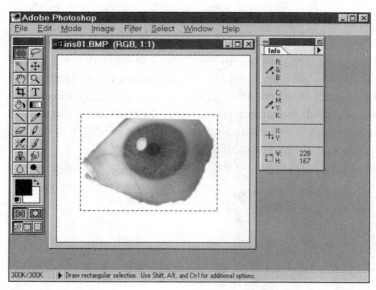

Figure 9.10
Eyeball image area selected.

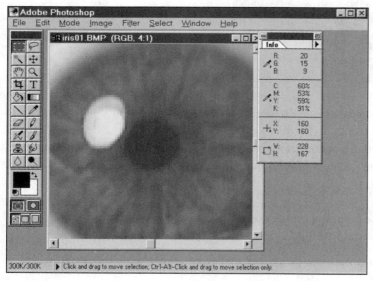

Figure 9.11
Pupil centered precisely at 160,160.

4. Choose Select|None, or click anywhere to drop the selection. Save the file with a new
name. Repeat these four steps for the other eyeball images, being careful to center the
pupil as precisely as possible. For some of the images, the pupil will appear to be an

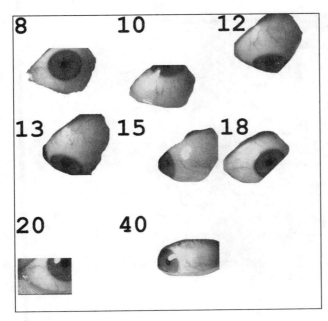

Figure 9.12
Centered eyeball images.

ellipse. Estimate the top-to-bottom and left-to-right centerlines of the ellipse and select the point where they cross as the pupil's center. Your results should look like Figure 9.12.

You may have noticed that the first image has a strong highlight in the upper-left iris. This would look odd in the final rendering because there would be correct highlights from the scene's lights plus this incorrect one, which would move around with the eye's motion. You need to get rid of the highlight while preserving the rest of the iris.

5. Reopen the first image. Zoom in on the highlight. Select (I would use the Lasso tool) a similar area on the opposite side of the pupil, as in Figure 9.13.

6. Copy and paste the selection. Choose Layer|Transform|Flip Horizontal to reverse the selection left to right. Use the left arrow key to slide the selection over the highlight, being careful to match the selection's edges as closely as possible to the surrounding area. Choose Image|Adjust|Brightness/Contrast, and with Preview turned on, adjust the brightness and contrast of the selection to match the surrounding area as closely as possible. When the selection is matched, deselect it (see Figure 9.14). Save the corrected image.

Now that you've got all the eyeball segments cut out and the iris highlight corrected, you're ready for the polar coordinate conversion.

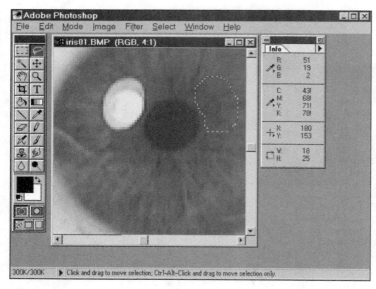

Figure 9.13
Selected mirror area for covering highlight.

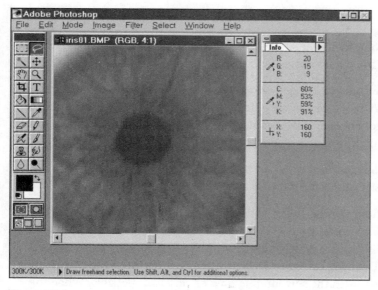

Figure 9.14
Highlight covered and selection blended in.

7. Choose Filter|Distort|Polar Coordinates. Choose the Polar To Rectangular option (see Figure 9.15). Save the filtered file under a new name. Load each of the other eyeball segment images and filter them to polar coordinates, as in Figure 9.16.

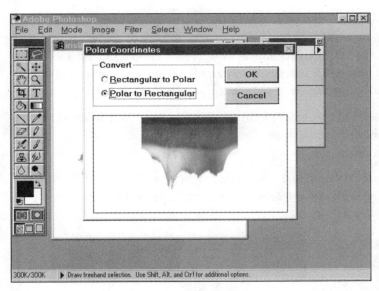

Figure 9.15
Polar Coordinates filter dialog box.

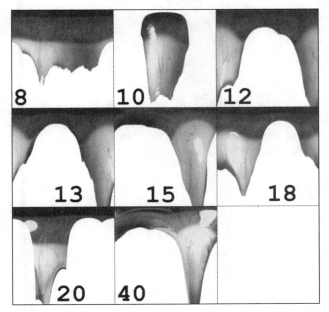

Figure 9.16
All eight eyeball segments converted to polar coordinates.

Polar coordinates enable you to select, paste, and modify spherical sections with the same tools and techniques you use with conventional 2D images without worrying about spherical distortions. If you tried to assemble the images in Figure 9.12 into a spherical map, you would have a really hard time. With polar coordinates, it's a relatively simple matter of piecing together rectangular selections in a definite, easy-to-see relationship.

With all the eyeball segments in convenient rectangular packages, you're ready to copy and paste them into a complete eyeball map. There are a couple of tricks you can use to make the map a little smoother.

8. Open the first image (frame 8), and open the second one (frame 10) beside it, as in Figure 9.17. Use the Magic Wand tool to select the color area from 10 and paste into 8, as in Figure 9.18.

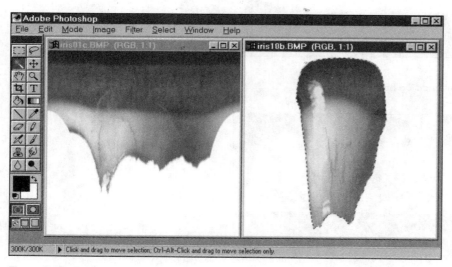

Figure 9.17
Color section of frame 10 selected using the Magic Wand tool.

Here's the fun part. There's an option for the Erase tool called Erase To Saved that erases through the current changes to an image to reveal the version of the image as it was last saved. This enables you to selectively erase parts of the pasted segment, leaving the original image intact.

9. Double-click on the Erase tool to select it and open the Options palette. Set the Erase To Saved option, as shown in Figure 9.19.

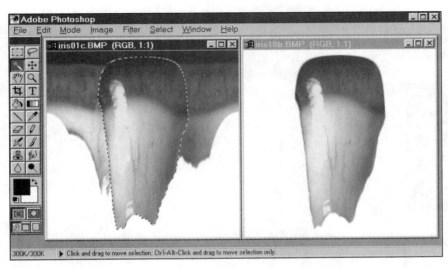

Figure 9.18
Selection from frame 10 pasted into frame 8.

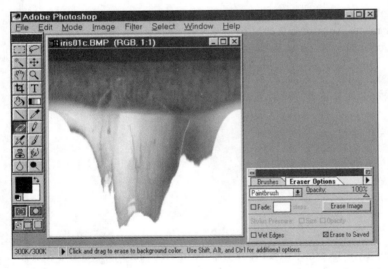

Figure 9.19
The Erase To Saved option selected and portions of the pasted image erased to reveal original image beneath.

10. You can use any of the brushes or other settings to modify the Erase tool's effects. I recommend starting with a very small dithered brush until you are familiar with the tool's effects. Carefully erase hotspots, dark areas, and other flaws from the pasted segment, allowing better areas of the first image to show through. When you're satisfied that you've combined the best of both images, save the file with a new name.

11. Repeat Steps 8, 9, and 10 to add the best parts of images 12, 13, 15, 18, 20, and 40. Fill in any blank areas with patterns sampled from nearby areas. You should end up with something like Figure 9.20.

Figure 9.20
Assembled eyeball polar coordinate map.

With the eyeball segments all assembled and blended together, you're ready to convert the eyeball map from polar coordinates back to normal coordinates.

12. Choose Image|Distort|Polar Coordinates. Choose the Rectangular To Polar option. Save the filtered file under a new name. Your results should look something like Figure 9.21.

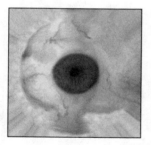

Figure 9.21
Completed eyeball map.

Ugly sucker, isn't it? Trust me, my eyes really don't look that bad. The overall effect is a combination of too yellow a light source for the video capture, shadows on parts of the sclera that were not revealed brightly in other segments, and no color correction. You can make a much nicer looking eyeball map if you want to, but I figure this one is good for a monster or two.

For planar projection, this map will work as is. For cylindrical or spherical projection, you will have to increase the size of the image canvas to provide additional map space needed to cover the back of the object without stretching the front out of proportion (see Figure 9.22).

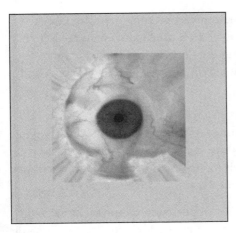

Figure 9.22
Spherical projection eyeball map.

UV Mapping

Spherical and cylindrical mapping can be useful, but most characters aren't perfectly round. They tend to have more irregular curves and surfaces, and there's no simple geometric projection that will make those surfaces easier to paint or map. That's where UV mapping comes in. This is a new feature in LightWave [6] that enables you to unwrap the complex geometry of a character, roll it out flat in a wireframe view, and pin down an image map to precisely match each polygon. With this feature, you can accurately apply maps to the most difficult areas of your characters, including undercuts like the underside of the chin and the back of the ears. Previously, these areas almost always had problems with smearing or through-projection. UV mapping solves those problems.

There are two basic approaches to using LightWave's UV mapping features: Use the UV Texture viewport to modify the model's UV map, or use the flattened UV wireframe as a painting guide to modify the image map. Both techniques are explained in sufficient detail in Chapter 9 of LightWave's *Shape* manual. Rather than duplicate that documentation here, I'm simply going to point out a few pertinent facts about LightWave's implementation of UV mapping.

The UV mapping uses the same point selection and moving tools that you would use in modifying an ordinary model. If you can select, move, and deselect a point, you can tweak a UV map. It's that simple. The most difficult part of the process is getting your head around the concept that moving a point in the UV Texture viewport does not move the selected point in the other views but instead distorts the UV image map.

Here's a typical application of a modified UV map. Suppose you need to create a quick-and-dirty human for a background character in a game. You're on a tight budget and deadline (as usual), so to save time and effort, you want to reuse as much of the necessary material as possible. You rummage through your model and image libraries and come up with a stock head model and a wraparound head image that you haven't yet used together. In the following example, I'll use my own Cyberscan head image and the Caucasian_Male head that comes with LightWave [6]. If you like, you can follow along, using your own head model and the head scan image located on this book's CD-ROM.

Following the basic process, I load the head model in Modeler, click on the T-for-Texture button, and choose and name a new UV texture map. I change a viewport to the UV Texture type and change the Perspective viewport style setting to Texture so I can monitor my progress in tweaking the UV map. I choose Make UVs from the Tools menu and accept the default settings. The UV Texture viewport now displays a flattened, spread-out view of the head model.

Next I open the Surface Editor, select the Face surface of the model, and set the surface's color projection to UV. I select the UV texture map I created previously and load the Cyberscan head image. At this point, the image is mapped to the head model in both the Perspective and UV Texture viewports. I click on Use Texture and close the Surface Editor. My screen now looks like Figure 9.23.

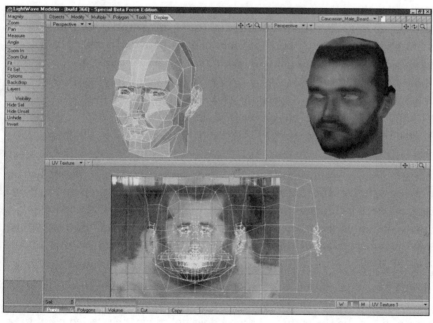

Figure 9.23
Default UV mapping setup for Caucasian_Male head and Cyberscan head image.

Of course, the initial raw UV map for the Caucasion_Male head is not a very close fit for the Cyberscan image of my head. The geometry of the two subjects is very different, and the Cyberscan image includes quite a bit of open space above my head and about halfway down the shoulders below it. Even with this gross disparity, however, it's a pretty easy and simple task to modify the UV map for a closer fit.

The worst areas are the top and bottom of the image, where the UV map overlaps empty space and shoulders that aren't present in the head model. There is also some obvious misalignment around the mouth and both ears. In the UV Texture viewport, I select the points making up the upper edge of the model and drag them down to the top of the hair in the image map so it looks like Figure 9.24.

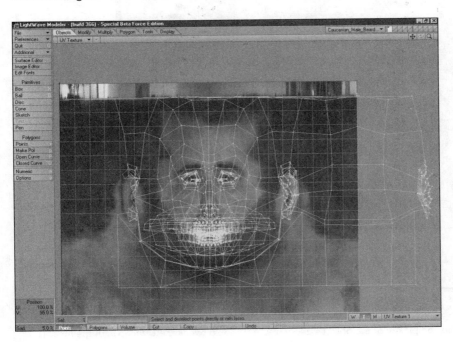

Figure 9.24
The uppermost UV map points have been moved to align with the top hairline of the image map.

This select-drag-deselect process is exactly the same one I would use to change the shape of a model, but this time only the UV map coordinates are affected. None of the point movements are reflected in the other viewports. However, I can still use the other viewports to select points. This is a big help in areas where a lot of points overlap. Because the UV Texture view is a flattened version of the model, many points are compressed into a smaller space, making clear selections difficult. It's a lot easier, for example, to select the upper lip in a Side viewport than to try to differentiate between the lip and teeth in the UV Texture view.

Continuing with the select-drag-deselect tweaking, I move the eyebrows, the lower face, the lips, and the nose to more closely match the image map. I also scale, rotate, and move the ears. Figure 9.25 shows what about 15 minutes' tweaking can do. The more time you have, the more precise you can be. If you are mapping a digital stuntman for a feature film, there's no reason you shouldn't be able to tweak every point into exactly the right place.

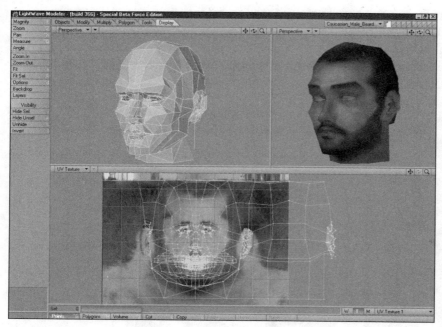

Figure 9.25
Fifteen minutes' tweaking of the UV map produces a much closer match of the image map to the stock model.

Work Simpler, Not Harder

Whatever changes you make to a UV map will hold true through subdivisions and other operations that increase the complexity of the object's geometry. You should tweak the UV map with the model at the simplest level possible so you have the fewest points to move.

The second approach to UV mapping is to take a screenshot of the UV Texture viewport and use it as a template layer in Photoshop or other paint software. This makes creating an accurate map almost as easy as painting by numbers. When you paint colors in a polygon of the wireframe template, you know that those colors will map precisely to that polygon on the original model.

To create a wireframe template that you can use to paint a face map, you need an image large enough to match or exceed the resolution of the final map. When you plan to take a UV map screenshot, you should maximize your display's resolution, maximize Modeler to occupy your entire desktop, and make the UV Texture viewport the only viewport. Taking a screenshot of a smaller viewport won't do for any but the smallest maps; you need the largest wireframe you can get. If you still need a larger template, you can always resample the screenshot to a higher resolution in Photoshop. If you know you will be painting a small image map, you may want to make the screen capture at a smaller size. If you downsample a wireframe image, you will lose a lot of the fine wireframe lines.

Open the screenshot in an image editor and crop it down to exactly the edges of the wireframe to create the template image. This enables you to use the automatic sizing in LightWave's Texture Editor and practically guarantees an exact fit when you apply maps derived from the template.

Once you have an accurate template, you can paint an image map over it any way you like. Load the template as a background layer in Photoshop and paint on another layer. Save the painted layer as a separate image. If you are working with someone else's models, it's often helpful to apply the original template to the model as a color map, then render a few images like Figure 9.26.

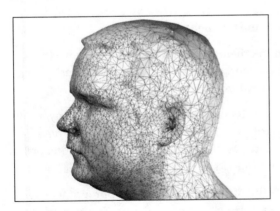

Figure 9.26
Head object surfaced with modified UV screenshot template.

This gives you a handy reference for the object geometry, and the rendered shading is much easier to interpret than a standard wireframe render. The shading provides depth cues that make it easier for you to discriminate between faces that are nearer and farther.

Matched Maps

You can add a lot of visual appeal or realism to a character if you apply a set of matched maps for at least color, bump, and specularity. Sometimes you can use the same image for several different types of mapping, but more often you will need to create modified versions. When you are using more than one image, it's important that the images line up properly. It's sloppy and obvious when the bumpy texture of an eyebrow sticks out from under its coloring!

PROJECT 9.3 Making a Head Specularity Map

This project demonstrates how the layers feature of Photoshop can be very useful in creating matched maps.

Your first requirement is a mirror and strong directional light. It will be best if you can move them around to get the necessary angles to reflect light brightly from every part of the subject's face. I recommend that you practice on yourself—you'll have much more patience for this process than some hapless friend or relative. A clamp-on work lamp with a small spotlight bulb works well, or a fully equipped makeup table.

To make a head specularity map, follow these steps:

1. Print a copy of the color face map and select a highlighter felt-tip pen that gives good contrast on the print.

2. Use the mirror and light to locate the shiniest spot on the subject's skin. This is usually near the hairline or across the bridge of the nose. You are looking for smooth, taut, oily skin. This area is the reference for the white end of the map gradient. Mark it with the highlighter. Mark the perimeter of the shiny area with spots. When you've completely outlined the shiniest area, fill it in solidly with the highlighter.

3. Locate the areas of medium shininess and mark them with a pattern of dots. Leave the least shiny, matte areas blank. When you have marked the entire face appropriately, keep the marked print by your computer for reference during the next step.

4. Load the color face map in Photoshop. Choose Window|Show Layers to open the Layers palette. Add a new layer and name it Specularity. Use the Paint Bucket tool to fill the Specularity layer with black. In the Layers palette, set the Specularity layer to around 50% opacity so you can see the face map through it (see Figure 9.27).

5. Refer to the print you highlighted earlier. Use the Airbrush tool with an appropriate brush size to make the shiniest areas white. I suggest starting with a smaller brush and working your way up to larger brushes as you feel comfortable with them.

6. Change the airbrush color to the next level of gray and apply it to the areas marked on the print as half shiny. Leave the blank, matte areas black.

7. Go over the entire image, blending edges between levels of gray so there are no sharp dividing lines. You should end up with an image like Figure 9.28. When you're finished, delete the color image layer and save the grayscale Specularity layer as an image file with a new name.

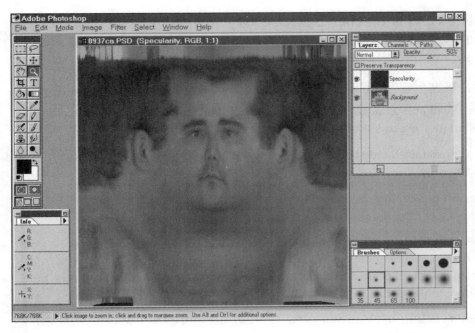

Figure 9.27
Layers for creating a matched specularity map.

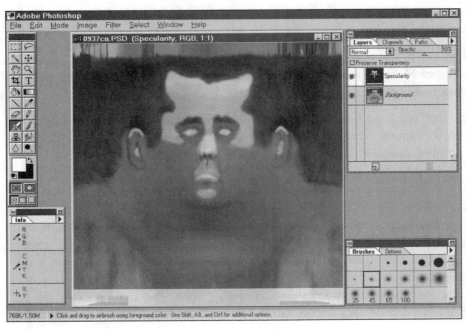

Figure 9.28
Completed specularity map.

PROJECT 9.4 Making a Better Specularity Map

If you want more realistic detail and have the equipment, you can make a more accurate specularity map by assembling digitized images of the subject's skin:

1. Capture close-ups with strong side lighting to show the skin's texture.

2. Assemble the digitized images with blended seams to match the color map, using the same techniques you used for the eyeball map in Project 9.2.

3. Change the assembled map to grayscale, then equalize and compress it to average 128,128,128 gray.

4. Copy this grayscale image as a new layer over the color map in place of the solid black Specularity layer from the preceding project.

5. For the shiniest areas, use the Airbrush tool with a white color, the Lighten option, a small diffuse brush, and very light pressure, around 5%. This will enable you to "fade out" the highlighted areas of the Specularity layer while leaving the finer details of wrinkles and other surface imperfections.

6. For the matte or least shiny areas, use the Airbrush tool with a black color, the Lighten option, a small diffuse brush, and very light pressure again, around 5%. This will darken the brushed areas without obliterating details.

7. You can leave the remaining areas—the moderately shiny ones—at the original equalized gray. When you're finished, delete the color image layer and save the grayscale layer as an image file with a new name.

The final results should show a realistic variation in specularity due to follicles, pores, and other skin details from the original digitized images.

So what do you do if you don't have photos or a Cyberscan map to use as a reference? At some point (especially with fantasy characters), you'll have to create a skin map from scratch. In the next section, I'll show you how.

Skin 'Em

Unless you're animating the Invisible Man, you're going to have to texture your character's skin. A variety of skin maps is the core of your image collection. You can start off with high-resolution images of leather, which seem to be popular in clip-art and background collections. Converted to grayscale and applied at smaller sizes, well-grained leather does quite nicely as human skin. For more bizarre characters, keep an eye out for images of snakeskin and reptile hides, and for the truly disgusting characters that populate some role-playing games, you might skim through a dermatology textbook or two for the "worst case" photos.

In addition to more general skin maps, you may want to add bump maps to specific locations like the hands and eyes. Knuckles, palms, and eye corners tend to wrinkle deeply when flexed. If the character's style leans toward realism, you need to simulate this too. LightWave enables you to animate a bump map's depth with an Envelope, so you can use advanced setup techniques (Chapter 12) to link the depth of wrinkles to the angle of a joint or the bulge of a muscle.

If you want to paint your own knuckle wrinkle bump map, you should first look at your own knuckles for a model. Make the background white and the folds grade down to black in the middle. Design it for planar mapping, applied from the top of the hand. As an alternative, you can digitize close-ups of your own knuckles in flexed and relaxed positions and use these images as templates.

Because the exact placement and depth of wrinkles is highly sensitive to the model's design, setting up animated wrinkle maps should be one of your finishing touches, after most of the action has been finalized. If you create wrinkle maps and set up complex automated linkages too early, you may waste more time revising them than you originally spent creating them.

Mapping Cartoon Faces

Simple character head objects can use animated maps instead of modeled features to provide facial details. This approach works best for cartoon-style caricatures and is best for features that do not protrude very much in profile. You can generally get away with mapping eyes and mouths, but you are better off modeling noses. This technique is especially handy for lip sync; if you are a good 2D artist, you can probably paint a set of lip sync mouth maps faster than you can model and set up a single mouth object. You may want to consider doing tests for a new character with drawn maps for experimental features and model them when your ideas have firmed up a bit.

PROJECT 9.5   Painting a Mouth

The simplest approach to facial feature mapping is to paint just the color image maps to be applied to the character's lower face. You can use any paint software that enables you to use foreground and background layers to paint over rendered images. Make sure you keep backup copies of any drawing templates you create. Just as with objects, there will always be additional demands on a character's dramatic and spoken range as the project progresses. If you can reuse the original mouth templates, it will be much easier for you to create more maps or to revise the existing libraries.

To paint a mouth, follow these steps:

1. Set up a scene to render a close-up wireframe of the character's face, centered on the mouth. Render a wireframe that you can use as a painting template.

2. Crop the image to include only the area below the nose and above the chin. Save the cropped image.

   When you paint mouths for lip sync, you should consider keeping them compatible with the Magpie Pro lip sync software described in Chapter 16. Try to keep the proportions of the cropped image close to square; Magpie Pro requires 128-by-128 BMP images. Even if you use higher-resolution maps for the finished animation, creating a duplicate set of thumbnail images for Magpie Pro does not take very long and can be a great time-saver for the person doing the lip sync exposure sheets.

3. Use the cropped map template as one layer and paint your maps in another layer. You can use the lines of the original modeled mouth (if any) as guides, or you can paint something completely original.

4. Paint an image of the mouth closed and at rest, a default image with no strong emotional message. Save the new layer as a separate image.

5. Repeat Step 4 to create image maps of the mouth for the basic emotional and lip sync mouth shapes: smile, grin, frown, fear, disgust, stern, crying, sad, disdain and AI, CDGK, closed, D, E, FV, LTH, MBP, O, U, and WQ.

   You can refer to the default mouths supplied with Magpie Pro for examples of the lip sync shapes. Figure 9.29 shows a complete model sheet. You might also look in either Levitan's or Blair's books from the bibliography. Both contain good mouth model sheets.

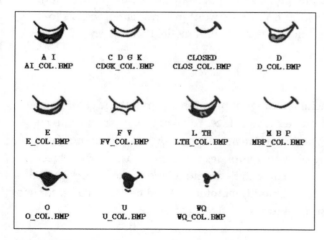

Figure 9.29
Magpie Pro default mouth maps.

6. If you like, make 128-by-128 resolution BMP format thumbnails for each lip sync image to use with Magpie Pro.

7. Paste together a model sheet of all the thumbnails and write the file names of the full-size maps under each image, as in Figure 9.29. This is another item for the character model sheets you'll need when you're ready to animate.

PROJECT 9.6 Creating Bump Maps

The goal of this project is to create bump maps that match the color maps you painted in the preceding project. A properly executed bump map gives a sense of depth to the object and smoothes out some of the disparity between the drawn maps and the modeled object.

To create bump maps using any paint program, follow these steps:

1. Load the first color map into one layer of your paint software. Add a new layer and name it Bump. You can either save and load a duplicate of the color map into the Bump layer or start off with a clean slate.

2. Paint over the mouth opening (if any) in the Bump layer with solid black. Cover the teeth or tongue with very dark gray.

3. Draw pure white lines down the middle of the lips, tracing the highest points of the mouth.

4. Trace the perimeter of each lip in medium gray, defining where the slope of the lips drops back toward the level of the face.

5. Create gradient fills or airbrush smooth transitions between the white "high" lines and the medium gray perimeter lines.

6. Paint a white line around the perimeter of the map. Create a gradient or airbrushed fill between the outermost perimeter line and the borders of the map.

    This is done to smooth the mapped area back to the normal height of the unmapped area. The smoother your gradients, the better your bump maps will look. As shown in Chapter 8, if the jump between adjacent gray levels is too large, the bump map will create a jagged, stepped appearance.

7. Save the new layer as a separate image. You don't have to create Magpie Pro-compatible thumbnails for the bump maps.

8. Repeat for the remaining color maps.

You can test your bump map by applying it and the matching color map to a modified head object with no modeled lips, just a flat area suitable for mapping. If you are feeling ambitious, you might try painting displacement maps that bulge the character's cheeks or wrinkle the corners of the mouth. You may be surprised to see just how much of the face you can successfully animate using only painted maps.

PROJECT 9.7 Clipping and Saving

The ultimate mapping for a cartoon mouth is a matched set of color, bump or displacement, and clip maps. Color and bump maps provide the surface appearance, and the clip map cuts away the mouth opening to create an unmistakably 3D effect. Of course, if you apply a clip map, you will also have to model and animate a set of teeth and a tongue.

Clipping occurs precisely where the luma (brightness) value for the map drops below 50%. Because the edge of a clip map can't be dithered, if you use a low-resolution clip map, any curved or diagonal edge will show jaggies. If the bump map you are matching has a dithered edge, you can make the clipped edge smoother by duplicating the bump map, doubling or quadrupling its resolution, and converting it to a black-and-white bitmap. Because it has a lower bit depth, this image will save space even though it's several times the resolution of the color and bump maps. The clip map will also make the clipped edge jaggies much smaller and will still precisely match the bump and color maps in proportion.

To complete this project using any paint program, follow these steps:

1. Open a copy of one of the bump maps you created. Quadruple its resolution. Save it under a new name.

2. Change the mouth opening to pure black. Change the remaining areas to pure white. In Photoshop, one way to do this is to lighten the entire image about 60%, then use the Magic Wand tool to select the mouth opening, varying the range of the wand to get exactly the selection you want. With black as the foreground color, use Fill. The mouth opening should be solid black. Use the Brightness and Contrast settings to keep the mouth opening dark, and lighten the rest of the image below 50% gray.

3. Change Mode to Bitmap, using 50% threshold, to turn the image into a black-and-white clip map. Save the modified image as a bitmap.

When you apply the clip map, be careful to position it to match the surface of the mouth area as closely as possible, and limit the mapping depth so the clipping doesn't go clear through the object. If a modeled tongue or teeth are part of the mapped object, you will have to be especially precise with the mapping dimensions or you'll clip them too.

Hold It

If you choose to animate any part of a character by using image sequences, you must pay careful attention to transitions. Because there is no automatic interpolation between images as there is for morphing objects, maps are inherently more jerky and difficult to smooth. Smooth interpolation is especially important for emotional transitions, which can take several seconds. Held vowels are also prime candidates because there is usually a slow transition from the first extreme pose to the more relaxed hold. Either of these situations will be unacceptably jerky with only the basic extreme pose maps. If you need a smoother transition, your only option is to create interpolated image maps. It's more work, but the difference in your lip sync and other transitions will be well worth it.

Environment Maps

If your character has any reflective surfaces—like eyeglasses, eyeballs, or highly polished accessories—using environment reflection maps instead of raytracing can save you a lot of rendering time. It's possible to make a reasonably accurate environment reflection map with a few quick renderings and a little cut-and-paste image editing, and the results will be difficult to distinguish from true raytracing.

PROJECT 9.8 Making an Environment Reflection Map

If possible, render an image of the scene with raytraced reflections. This image will be useful as a reference for aligning the finished reflection map and as a comparison to judge the effectiveness of mapping versus raytracing. If you can't raytrace the image first, you'll have to be more knowledgeable and aware of the factors you're dealing with. It's easy to make a time-wasting mistake, so take the time now to render a good reference image.

To make an environment reflection map, follow these steps:

1. Place the camera at the center of the reflective object in the scene to be reflected. Hide, make invisible, or delete the reflective object itself (otherwise, the camera will give you a nice view of its interior). If possible, set the object to cast shadows but remain otherwise invisible.

2. Set the camera field of view (FOV) to 60 degrees.

3. Rotate the camera horizontally at 60-degree increments in six sequential frames, giving full 360-degree coverage like a cylinder surrounding the object.

4. In the seventh and eighth frames, point the camera straight up and straight down, with the camera FOV set to 120 degrees. These renderings will cap the ends of the cylinder made by the previous six frames.

   You can save out the motion and focal length files for the camera and quickly reapply it to other scenes. This can partially automate the setup for making environment maps.

5. Render all eight frames.

6. In your paint software, load the first rendered image. Change the canvas size to six times the width of the image to provide room to paste in the other five horizontal images (see Figure 9.30).

Figure 9.30
Canvas size increased to hold horizontal images.

7. Load each of the horizontal images in order and position them carefully to match the vertical seams, as shown in Figure 9.31. Save the assembled image.

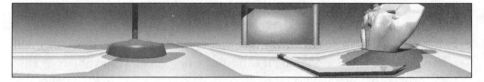

Figure 9.31
Horizontal images assembled.

8. Open the top image. Apply the Polar Coordinates filter (Filter|Distort|Polar Coordinates), with Polar To Rectangular selected (see Figure 9.32). If you are not using Photoshop, check your program's documentation to find a similar feature.

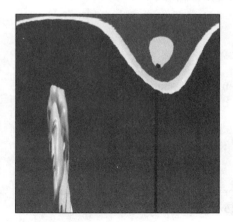

Figure 9.32
Top image filtered to polar coordinates.

As described earlier in Project 9.2, this filter changes an image from flat XY coordinates to a sort of Mercator projection, spreading out the periphery of the image as the lower border and stretching the center of the image to cover the top border. This enables you to paste the bottom of the filtered image to match the top of the assembled horizontal images.

Figure 9.33
Top image scaled to match width of horizontal images.

9. Change the top image size to six times its original width, to match the width of the assembled horizontal images, as shown in Figure 9.33.

10. Activate the assembled horizontal image. Change its canvas size to provide room to paste the top image above it, with the existing image in the bottom of the canvas.

11. Copy the entire top image and place it in the blank canvas area, but do not deselect it. You will probably have to slide the top image back and forth to match its lower border with the top of the lower images. When the borders match as closely as possible, deselect the top image. This will most likely leave a gap at one side or the other, as shown in Figure 9.34.

Figure 9.34
Top image pasted to match horizontal images.

It may help you to think of these images as continuous cylinders. The sides are just arbitrary seams; you can cut and reassemble them anywhere, and the overall image will have the same effect.

12. Paste in a second copy of the top image. Position it to fill the gap, as shown in Figure 9.35.

13. Repeat the preceding five steps for the bottom image, but flip the filtered image vertically before you copy and paste it. The center of the original image must form the bottom border rather than the top.

The next part of the process is centering the map so the seam in the cylinder is in the direction LightWave expects it. This is where the reference image you raytraced comes in

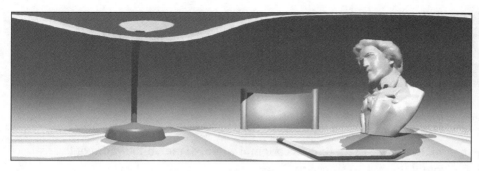

Figure 9.35
Second copy of top image pasted to fill in gap.

handy; if you didn't make one, try to estimate what object or reference point is at 180 degrees behind the Camera. That's your centerline for the finished reflection map. In the example scene, the center of the reflection should be pretty much in line with the center of the chair back, so that's your centerline.

14. Select the entire image and copy it. Move the selection to the side until the centerline is centered in the canvas.

15. Paste in another copy of the image and move it to fill the remaining space. Your results should look like Figure 9.36.

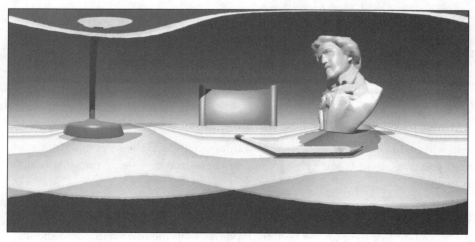

Figure 9.36
Centered environment reflection map.

When you apply this environment reflection map, the results can be very close to a true raytraced image. Figure 9.37 shows a mapped reflection and a raytraced one. Can you spot the difference?

Figure 9.37
Results of a raytraced reflection and an environment reflection map in the same scene. Which is which?

Keep in mind that this cheat only works if the object is not moving too much within the scene. Reflective object rotations are OK, but translations would change the rendered perspective of the surroundings so the reflections would have to be raytraced.

Moving On

You should now have a good idea of how to make the 2D maps you'll need for your LightWave characters. In the next chapter, I'll show you how to use surface power tools: LightWave's procedural textures and shaders and 3D paint software.

Case Study 9.1
Texturing Switch A. Roo

by Kim Oravecz

Switch A. Roo is a character I created as a demo reel project. He's the little guy who lives in your refrigerator and turns the light on and off for you when you open and close the refrigerator door. You don't normally see him because, when the light comes on, he becomes invisible. In this case study, I describe the planar mapping techniques I used to create this character's skin textures.

Kim Oravecz

Switch A. Roo at home in the refrigerator.

Basic Skin Texture

The first thing I did was to go in search of a good skin texture. I knew I wanted the skin to look tough and leathery because he does live in a cold environment. I have Sherry London's book, *Photoshop Textures Magic*, and it has many rock textures that were well-suited for Switch's skin.

The skin texture is basically a four-part texture: two color maps and two bump maps. The first color map, skin-color-1, is a variation of the rocks texture in the book with some variations that I made; I just wanted to use the color portion of the texture. I made the second color texture, skin-color-2, with a Clouds filter in Photoshop, using orange for the foreground color and a very light beige for the background color.

I created the first bump map, skin-bump-1, by following the first few steps of the cobblestone texture from *Photoshop Textures Magic*. I created the second bump map, skin-bump-2, by following the first couple of steps for the stucco texture in the same book.

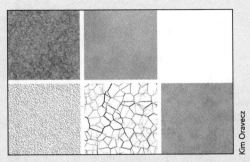

Top row: Skin-color-1, Skin-color-2. Bottom row: Skin-bump-1, Skin-bump-2, and combined skin texture.

I applied all image maps in each texture channel with cubic mapping. This mapping is like planar mapping from all six directions; it enables you to apply a patterned texture to the surfaces without seams showing where the surfaces meet.

In the Color channel, the underlying surface color is a Caucasian flesh tone color with RGB values 220,194,180. I applied skin-color-2 with 40% opacity in layer 1, and skin-color-1 with 30% opacity in layer 2.

In the Diffuse channel, I applied skin-color-2 with 10% opacity in layer 1, skin-bump-1 with 20% opacity in layer 2, and skin-bump-2 with 7% opacity in layer 3.

In the Bump Map channel, I applied skin-bump-1 with 40% opacity and 50% texture amplitude in layer 1, and skin-bump-2 with 40% opacity and 50% texture amplitude in layer 2.

In the Specular channel, I applied skin-bump-1 with 12% opacity and low glossiness in layer 1, and skin-bump-2 with 7% opacity and Low glossiness in layer 2.

I decided to use all planar mapping to prevent image smearing. I split up my character's surfacing based on the direction the polygons were facing. For example, instead of having one surface for the torso and wrapping the texture maps cylindrically, I split up the surfacing into front, left side, right side, and back. I did the same for the arms, legs, and head. For the feet and hands, I created only a top and bottom surface. Because the ears are translucent, they have only one surface that projects completely through.

Creating Map Templates

For the rest of this case study, I'll use the image map for the face as an example. To create a template of each texture surface, I rendered a very high-resolution image of my character in its neutral pose from the front, back, sides, top, and bottom.

Kim Oravecz

High-resolution front rendering of Switch A. Roo in a neutral pose.

I then broke the rendered images down into the individual surface areas to be used as templates in Photoshop. I brought each image into Photoshop, then cropped the image to the exact edges of each surface area. Creating individual surface maps this way enables you to use Automatic Sizing in Layout for the texture size. I saved the image files as PSD files, using the surface name as the file name to make it easy on myself. I then used Undo to get the full uncropped image back, cropped the next surface area, saved, and so on until I had saved out all the surface templates.

In Modeler, I loaded the Switch object. I isolated each surface by selecting the desired polygons and hiding the rest of the polygons. I expanded the view of the selected surface to take up the whole screen in Modeler and then hit the Print Screen key. This copies the current screen image into the Clipboard buffer.

Kim Oravecz

Screenshot of the Switch face surface zoomed to fill the Modeler screen.

Next, I went back to Photoshop. At the bottom of the screen on Photoshop's status bar, the message "Importing Clipboard" was displayed. Photoshop knows when there is something on the clipboard that you may want to bring into Photoshop. I selected the File|New menu option. In the image size boxes, Photoshop has automatically filled in the size of your screen. Photoshop assumes you will be pasting the contents of the clipboard into a file, so it assumes the size of the image of the clipboard; that's pretty handy.

My next step was to crop the wireframe image to the edges of the surface. Then I held down the Shift key, clicked on the wireframe layer in the Layers palette, and dragged that layer over to the cropped shaded image file. When I let go of the mouse button and the Shift key, the image was perfectly centered in the layer. Then I used the Edit|Transform|Scale menu option to bring the wireframe up to the same size as the shaded surface layer. At this point, I had a Photoshop layered image with two layers: the flat shaded rendering from Layout and the wireframe screenshot from Modeler.

Kim Oravecz

Shaded and wireframe face surface layers in Photoshop.

I then created a couple of blank layers on top of those two, one layer for the color texture and one for the wrinkles (to be used as a bump map). One of the nice things about using Photoshop layers is that you can create all of the maps for a surface in one file, then just save each layer separately as an IFF file for use in Layout.

Painting Maps

I painted details for each surface on transparent Photoshop layers so I could see the wireframe and shaded layers underneath to use as a guide. First, I had to take into consideration that Switch lives in a refrigerator, a cold environment. I determined which parts of his face would have a reddish color because of the cold: his chin, his nose, the eyebrow area above his eyes, the flaps of skin in front of his ears, and his cheeks. Because his skin has an overall orange tint to it, I made those areas a red-orange color. I also thought Switch probably doesn't get much deep sleep, having to be alert at all times in case someone opens the refrigerator door. I

Kim Oravecz

Retouched areas of Switch's face surface.

thought he should have some dark circles under his eyes, so I made that area a gray-purple color. Then I made the eyelids a yellowish tinted color; looking at my own eyelids, I noticed that the skin coloring was lighter in that area.

I saved the results as a PSD file to maintain the layers. I then made only the color layer visible, flattened the image, and saved that as an IFF file (I'm used to working with IFF files from my Amiga days—they are more memory efficient than TIFFs). When you flatten a multilayer Photoshop image, what was once transparent turns white. If I used this image file as is in Layout, the white areas would obscure the nice skin texturing I applied earlier; Switch's face would be all white and he would look like a mime. I needed an alpha image so all that would show through on the object would be the areas that I just painted.

I undid the Flatten Image command in Photoshop to get my layers back. I duplicated the color texture I had just painted by choosing the Duplicate Layer option from the Layers menu. I named the new layer Alpha. (By the way, I recommend that you name your layers in Photoshop, just to make your life easier when you go back to edit a texture. Trust me; I learned the hard way!) Now I needed to make all the colored areas black. I desaturated the Alpha layer to make it strictly grayscale by choosing Image|Adjust|Desaturate. Then I selected the surrounding transparent area with a Color Range fuzziness setting between 100 and 150. Then I chose Select|Inverse to select the gray/black areas. Executing an Edit|Fill and selecting black finished the alpha map.

I added a new layer to the file and created a layer of wrinkles. This was very easy to do. Using the shaded view of my surface in the background layer again, I painted wrinkles on his forehead and under his eyes, a crease running from the bottom edges of his nose down to the corners of his mouth, a set of wrinkles near the corners of his mouth (laugh lines, I believe they are called), and the wrinkle lines on his bottom lip. Again, I saved the file in layers, flattened it with only the wrinkle layer showing, and saved that as an IFF file.

The alpha map for retouched areas of Switch's face surface.

Kim Oravecz

Wrinkle map for Switch's face surface.

Kim Oravecz

Applying Maps

My next step was to apply the maps in Layout. I had already applied the basic skin texture to all of the character's surfaces. Now I needed to add the color detail layers on top of that. In the Surfaces panel for the face texture, I clicked on the T button next to the surface color, and in the Texture Editor, I loaded the face color texture image as a planar image map, clicking on Automatic Sizing and applying it on the z-axis.

I then added a Texture Alpha layer and loaded up the face alpha map (the black-and-white image map) that I created. With an alpha map in LightWave, whatever is white is allowed to show through and whatever areas are black are blocked out from showing. Because I made my alpha map black on white instead of white on black (I work better that way for some reason), I checked the Invert button. I used a texture opacity of 40%. My Texture Editor panel looked like the figure shown here.

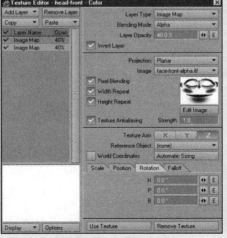

Kim Oravecz

Texture Editor showing color and alpha image map layers for Switch's face surface.

The final stage was to apply the wrinkles. In the Surfaces panel, I clicked on the T button next to Bumpmap and added a third layer of bump mapping. This was for the wrinkle texture that I created. I experimented with the opacity and texture amplitude settings and finally settled on a texture opacity of 100% and a texture amplitude of 120%.

That did it for the face. I went through the same steps for each surface on my character. The ears, hands, and feet also had some extra bump maps for the veins and tendons.

The ears also had a transparency map to make them slightly translucent. I really enjoyed working on this project; the modeling and texture mapping was challenging and a great learning experience!

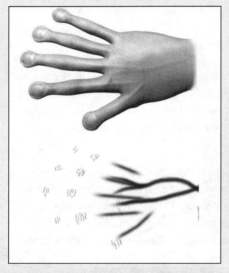

Bump maps for veins and tendons in hands and feet.

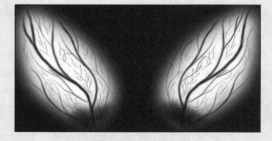

Transparency map for ears.

Kim Oravecz is a freelance artist in Cleveland, Ohio. You can contact her through her Web site, **www.en.com/users/kimo** *or email her directly at* **kimo@en.com***.*

Chapter 10

Advanced Material Tools

This chapter will give you an overview of 3D paint software and LightWave procedural shaders. These tools can make your texturing work easier and can produce results that would be difficult or impossible to achieve with more basic material tools. If you are creating characters to appear in high-resolution media, you have tight deadlines, or you are a perfectionist, you'll want to use these tools.

3D Paint Tools

3D paint software is a valuable tool for character animation for several reasons. A minor consideration is that few 3D modeling packages have incorporated the advanced painting tools you can find in 2D software, such as Photoshop or Painter. A good financial reason is that production teams with a limited budget can have an artist painting character maps on a computer without LightWave installed. It's slightly more important that 3D paint tools can sometimes compensate for absent or awkward mapping functions in LightWave. The most significant reason, however, is that 3D paint software can provide a more intuitive and efficient interface, especially for traditional artists making the transition to the computer.

For the 3D artist, there is an inherent drawback to working with a computer. The nature of 3D applications in the essentially 2D interface of most desktop computers creates a cognitive gap between how your mind works and how the computer requires you to act. Lifelong experience has conditioned you to reach for, grasp, and manipulate 3D objects. You can unconsciously manipulate tools to meet the surface of these objects, either alone or in coordination between your object-grasping and tool-wielding hands. You don't have to think about it—you just do it.

A standard desktop computer provides only visual feedback, and only through a 2D window. It does not provide feedback to your sense of touch, true 3D stereoscopic vision, or kinesthetic sense. Whenever you work with a computer, you willingly cut off five and a half of your six senses, at least three of which a sculptor or painter would regard as indispensable. One empirical measure of this is the fact that you can use every feature of most software with only one eye and two fingers. Considering the handicaps, it's amazing we have any decent 3D art at all!

2D software used for painting 3D model maps has generally made these handicaps worse. When you attempt to paint on a flattened wireframe template, instead of a moderately clear and intuitive 2D image, you see a warped and distorted projection. An untrained eye has difficulty associating this map with the original model. This difficulty makes the already steep learning curve for 3D character creation just a little more vertical.

Publishers have developed 3D paint software in an attempt to restore some of the intuitive ease of use of conventional painting and sculpting tools. The general concept is that you should be able to select a tool that has an effect that is identical (or at least reasonably similar) to its real-world counterpart, use it with the same strokes (both motion and pressure), and get the results you intuitively expect. Several software publishers made the attempt, and a few have succeeded to a remarkable extent.

Hardware

Hardware vendors are also making valuable contributions to artist-friendly computer interfaces. One of the most cost-effective investments you can make is a pen-and-tablet like those manufactured by Wacom, shown in Figure 10.1.

Figure 10.1
Wacom Intuos pen-and-tablet.

These devices replace (or supplement) your mouse with a powered tablet and a stylus shaped like a pen, with a blunt plastic tip and a push button in place of an eraser. When you move the tip of the stylus over the tablet, just as you would an ordinary pen, the computer's cursor follows along. Advanced versions also sense the angle of the stylus, which end you're using, and how hard you're pressing. If the paint software supports these features, the feel and results are as close as you're going to get to a real-life artist's media. An added bonus is that you're less likely to suffer repetitive stress injuries because the angle of your wrist and fingers is much more relaxed and natural. As of this writing, you can find good tablets like the Wacom 6x8 Intuos through mail-order houses for under $300. I've found that they also make work easier in 3D modeling and animation, as long as the mouse-emulation drivers work properly. As with any purchase, try to evaluate it before you buy, and make sure it will pay for itself in boosted productivity, higher quality, or reduced aggravation. Wacom's contact information is as follows:

WACOM Technology Corporation
1311 SE Cardinal Court
Vancouver, WA 98683
Tel: (360) 750-8882; (800) 922-9348 (U.S. only)
Fax: (360) 750-8924
sales@wacom.com
www.wacom.com

A relatively new entry to interface hardware is the 6D trackball. This device takes a variety of forms, depending on the manufacturer. Labtec produces several models in the Spaceball line. The Spaceball 3003FLX (shown in Figure 10.2) includes drivers for Windows 95/98/NT and Unix and uses two buttons and a pop-up function menu. Its street price is currently around $450. The 3003FLX is also more sensitive than earlier models, which required a pretty healthy push; the newer machine responds to a lighter touch.

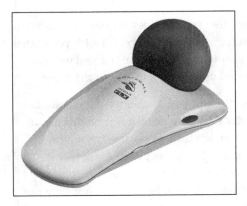

Figure 10.2
Labtec Spaceball 3003FLX.

The Spaceball consists of a sphere the size of a tennis ball mounted on an ergonomically designed platform. You use it by resting your wrist on the platform and gently grasping the ball around its equator. The ball itself does not move but responds to slight fingertip pressure. As you apply gentle pushing, pulling, or twisting motions to the ball, the 3D model moves in those same directions on screen. The greater pressure you apply, the faster the model moves or rotates. The Spaceball provides six degrees of motion—translation in the x-, y-, and z-axes, plus rotation in the pitch, bank, and heading axes, as shown in Figure 10.3.

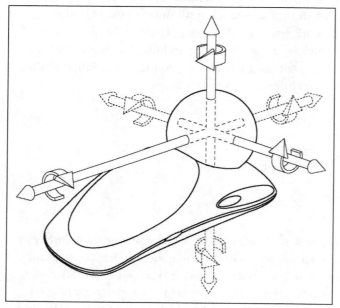

Figure 10.3
The Spaceball's six degrees of motion.

The Spaceball is not intended to replace your mouse or other pointing device, but to work with it. You control the mouse or stylus with your dominant hand and the Spaceball with your other hand. Using both devices closely mimics the way you manipulate objects in the real world—you hold, move, and turn a workpiece with one hand and apply a tool to it with the other.

You can learn to operate a Spaceball very quickly. Nonetheless, you should try out a Spaceball before you hand over the money, or buy it from a vendor that provides a no-questions return policy for a reasonable trial period. You should spend as much time as possible using the Spaceball on real work, the kind of stuff you do on a regular basis, then decide whether it makes your work sufficiently easier or faster to justify the investment. I haven't heard of anyone who hates the Spaceball, but I have heard from artists who bought it, like it, but only use it once in a blue moon. As with any investment, make sure you'll get a good return on it. Labtec's contact information is as follows:

Labtec 3D Motion Control Technology Group, USA
100 Foot of John Street
Lowell, MA 01852
Tel: (978) 970-0330
Fax: (978) 970-0099
info@labtec.com
www.labtec.com

Deep Paint 1

Deep Paint is a standalone 3D paint program designed to work independently or as a plug-in with a variety of 3D modeling and animation software and Photoshop. Deep Paint is the successor to 4D Paint, one of the better 3D paint programs available in the past few years, so this program is more highly evolved than the version number might lead you to believe.

If all you need to do is create a single map to fit an object in LightWave, you can probably do an adequate job with the techniques described in the section "UV Mapping" of Chapter 9. However, if you need to match up two or more maps such as color, bump, specularity, opacity, or luminosity, Deep Paint can save you a great deal of time and bother and produce much better results. This program enables you to paint any or all map types simultaneously on a 3D model, making it much easier and faster to create accurate, complex maps of up to 6,000×6,000 resolution.

If you have ever used Painter, Designer, or another program designed for traditional painting techniques (rather than Photoshop's darkroom metaphor), Deep Paint will seem familiar. There is a broad selection of traditional tool styles, including chalk, charcoal, acrylic, pencil, crayon, and so on, plus canvas choices that mimic textures ranging from cloth to water drops on glass to skin. Deep Paint is also designed to work best with Wacom's Intuos or other pressure-sensitive tablets, the digital artist's input tool of choice. If the feel of the interface is important to your mapping, you should definitely choose Deep Paint over other software that does not support these input devices. After working with Deep Paint with my Wacom tablet, I won't go back to anything that requires a mouse or doesn't handle the tilt and pressure data. By comparison, painting with the mouse is like painting with a bar of soap with an oversized brush stuck through it. You simply don't have the fine control and precise sense of where each pixel is going.

The Deep Paint documentation is better than average, and it's certainly adequate to explain how to use the software. The printed manual is just under 200 pages, and a PDF version of the manual is included on the CD-ROM. The seven tutorials in the manual cover the features you are most likely to use, and you should be able to work through them in a few hours. The program includes context-sensitive Windows help, and there is a link to a FAQ on the Right Hemisphere Web site.

The default installation occupies 132MB on your hard drive, but 103MB of that is filled by the Examples folder, which you can delete after working through the tutorials. Memory usage on startup is between 5 and 10MB. However, opening a project drastically increases RAM usage based on the resolution and number of maps. For example, loading the 28,000-vertex Fred model with three 1,608×512 maps (color, bump, and specularity) consumed an additional 40MB. Considering the unlimited levels of Undo and the very fast screen refresh, this memory hit is reasonable. The manual's Introduction is very explicit about this need for memory, including recommended minimum RAM levels for the most common map resolutions. Basically, any machine capable of running LightWave at the resolution of the maps should be capable of running Deep Paint without any problems.

Feedback while painting is very fast, and it's adjustable based on your preferences and your system resources. With only 128MB in my system, pushing the feedback to highest speed didn't seem to have a negative effect on anything else. Deep Paint is stable and runs well with both LightWave and Photoshop open simultaneously. My only quibble is that the default format for saving maps is TIFF, and the current version won't recall that you prefer a different format. Because I prefer TGA, I had to deal with the annoyance of changing the default TIFF to TGA every time I saved the project or exported the maps. I hope Right Hemisphere can fix this minor oversight in the next revision.

Deep Paint works in 3D mode by default. You can call up the 2D maps and paint in those if you like. However, you'll get faster response time and a more intuitive work flow if you stick with the 3D view as much as possible. Deep Paint's layers give you a great deal of flexibility to create detailed organic maps that you can edit with a minimum of fuss or wasted effort. You can use a base layer for the character's basic color, then add layers for wrinkles, skin defects, folds, scars, and whatever else makes the character interesting and unique. Combined and exported as a single image per map type, the result is easy to manage in LightWave. Preserved as layers in Deep Paint's native project format, it's easy to modify and edit. The only disadvantage is that Deep Paint's native project format is not terribly efficient. If you want to preserve all the layers and other information (which I strongly recommend!), you have to save a DP3 project file. This is actually a file folder containing a proprietary project file plus copies of all the contributing maps. These project folders can get very large very quickly, but if you want to be able to edit your character's maps, it's the only way to go.

Getting up to speed in Deep Paint is not a problem. Without reading the tutorials, I went straight to the one-page guide to working with LightWave and followed the instructions. I loaded a low-resolution copy of the Fred Cyberscan model, and in about 15 minutes of playing around I had the color, bump, and specularity (or shininess) maps you see in Figure 10.4. One of the nicer features of Deep Paint is the realtime update of both bump and specular maps; getting the scar to look right took only a few strokes. Getting an acceptable skin texture was simply a matter of flood-filling the base skin color, then brushing a charcoal tool containing the top color over a veined canvas. The beard stubble was charcoal over a more literal canvas;

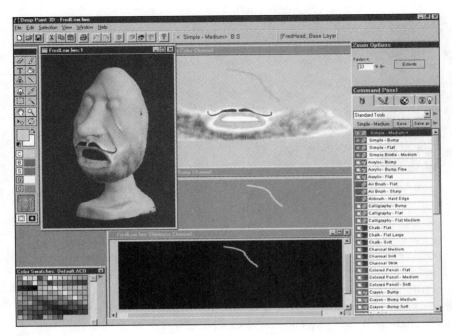

Figure 10.4
Fred maquette loaded and painted in Deep Paint 1.

as I said, this was the result of goofing around for a few minutes, but the results are surprisingly good for a first (and less than serious) effort. I'm looking forward to creating more detailed and complex texture map sets with Deep Paint. It's fun to work with, and it helps you avoid many of the frustrations inherent in 2D approaches to texture painting. If you'd like to try before you buy, you can download a demo version of Deep Paint from the Right Hemisphere Web site. Here is Right Hemisphere's contact information:

Right Hemisphere (U.S. office)
215 West Holly, Suite H-22
Bellingham, WA 98225
Tel: (360) 738-7940
Fax: (360) 738-2091
support@righthemisphere.com
www.righthemisphere.com

Cyberware Color Scans

The Cyberware scanning process, as described in Chapter 7, is fast and painless as a means of acquiring 3D surface data. The current hardware can also capture 24-bit color map data as it measures the surface geometry. The Cyberware software also creates UV mapping coordinates automatically. That's what produced Figure 10.5, the UV color map of my head.

Figure 10.5
Unretouched Cyberscan of the author's head.

There's only one real drawback to this technique: The older scan hardware has limited resolution, precisely one pixel per data point. This produces maps with only 512x512 resolution, whereas a film or television shot may require a much higher resolution map for close-ups. However, the Cyberscan map is especially useful as a template for creating more detailed maps. If you unwrap a model as discussed in the UV mapping section of Chapter 9, you can take a screenshot of that mesh to load into Photoshop as a painting template. You can then apply a Cyberscan map as a layer underneath the flattened mesh and paint in yet a third layer with both color and mesh available as templates. If you're trying to match a live subject, you can't beat a Cyberware map as a template. If you really need an original high-resolution map, you should use Cyberware's newer HRC scanner, which captures color maps at 2,048×2,048 resolution.

Shaders

A shader is a program or set of instructions used with LightWave's renderer to modify the rendered image. Shaders are often used to color or transform the surface of models, including animated characters. Shaders and maps can produce similar results, but they do it in very different ways. A map changes a surface one pixel at a time. The renderer "sees" the map's value for a particular area, calculates the effects of light and shadow, and adds the resulting value to the appropriate place in the rendered image. A shader changes the surface by calculation. The renderer "sees" that the shader controls a particular area, asks the shader for the surface's value, and the shader calculates it.

This points out the two deciding factors between maps and shaders: speed of rendering and resolution of finished image. A map can be preloaded into RAM for fast access, and because all its values are present at all times, the renderer can calculate the surface values very quickly. The limitation of maps is that the quality of the final rendering depends on the resolution of the map. If the map is too small, the pixels stretch across the screen and become obvious. Too large a map and you need a more expensive computer to render the image. Shaders have a complementary set of strengths and limitations. Shaders must calculate the appearance of each pixel in the final image. There is no shortcut, preloading, or cheating that can bypass the rendering calculations. However, shaders take up very little memory, and they can render to any resolution you choose without increasing demands on anything but CPU cycles. For example, a map of a character's face might look acceptable for long shots, but in close-ups, the map's pixels would appear blocky and obvious. A shader designed to duplicate the map's effects would maintain a smooth, accurate appearance, even if the camera zoomed in until the character's nose filled the frame.

Shaders have the same advantage over hand-painted maps that desktop publishing has over hand-setting type. Shaders, being programs, can use the computer's calculating power to rapidly repeat a simple set of actions to create an arbitrarily complex result. If you have ever seen a Mandelbrot or Julia set, you've seen a simple example of what a shader can produce. Just a few lines of code can sometimes produce naturalistic, complex textures that can draw and hold your audience's eye.

Shaders are especially useful for surfaces that are too complex to model or paint efficiently and that repeat a pattern based on factors that you can derive or define. For example, the pattern of veins in a leaf is complex in the end result, but a small number of rules determine the direction of growth, the frequency and angle of each fork, and the decreasing width of each vein. If you program these rules into a shader, you could apply it to a leaf-shaped flat surface and produce a highly detailed, photorealistic veined leaf. Animated characters' skin, clothing, hair, fur, scales, and other complex, rule-based surfaces are excellent subjects for shaders.

Because shaders are so useful, LightWave includes a library of shaders as part of the package. For example, the Imp's skin in Figure 17.1 is an application of LightWave's Vein shader. With a smaller interval and different color and bump settings, it makes a good human skin too. Third-party software publishers also market plug-in shader libraries for LightWave. One of the most popular new shader types as of this writing is designed to simulate fur and hair, both of which are notoriously difficult to either map or model.

Joe Alter's Shave And A Haircut

Joe Alter's Shave And A Haircut (Shave for short) plug-in for LightWave is a good example of a hair/fur shader. It provides a set of controls suitable for producing realistic or fantastic effects and is powerful once you figure out how to use it. Joe Alter wrote Industrial Light + Magic's (ILM's) first hair renderer six years ago. The Shave package consists of a software download from **www.joealter.com**, a hardware dongle, and an online HTML manual. The plug-in's installation is easy. You can work through the manual's examples in a few hours, including time for playing with settings and admiring your results. Shave is one of those visually fascinating programs that makes interesting images straight from the default settings. You really have to make an effort to create an ugly, boring image.

Shave includes a variety of hair modeling tools. In addition to automatic grooming, the guide hairs are fast bidirectional IK chains that you can control one at a time, or you can grab thousands and just comb away. There is collision detection built into the sculpting process as well, so hair goes around the skull, not through it. Other features include the following:

- Self-shadowing

- Cast shadows

- Soft shadows

- Motion blur

- Transparency

- Breakthrough fractal algorithm

- Interactive IK modeling

- Collision detection

- Dynamics

- Gravity

- Wind

- Deforms perfectly with skin

- Very light on RAM usage

- Seamless integration

- Multiple characters

Shave And A Haircut is a standalone application (SHAVE.EXE) plus a series of LightWave plug-ins that communicate via standard LightWave object (LWO) and special-purpose Shave And A Haircut (HAIR) files. Most of the controls are located in the standalone interface, as shown in Figure 10.6. In LightWave Layout, you set the name of the HAIR file in the displacement plug-in (HAIRdisp), and the activation of the render plug-in (HAIRrender) in a pixel filter.

Shave's hair placement and motion is based on the geometry of the *rest position model*, usually the head of a character. Shave uses spheres as proxy surfaces to detect hair collisions with the model. You need to add these *collision spheres* to match any surfaces that the hairs may contact. It takes a little up-front effort in Modeler to add these spheres to your rest position model, but this approach makes the calculation of hair collisions much faster.

You can add up to 255 collision spheres to your model. The total collection of collision spheres must be assigned one surface, named skull. The collision detection function will make all the

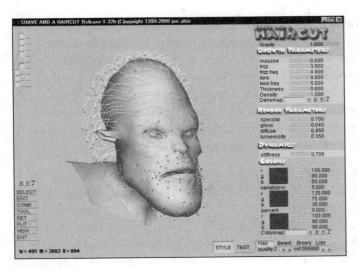

Figure 10.6
Shave And A Haircut standalone application interface.

hairs bounce off this skull surface rather than passing through it. However, for many cases like fur or grass, you won't need collision surfaces at all. Just dialing up the Stiffness setting is all that's required.

Growth surfaces are the polygons you choose to use as bases from which the hair will grow. You may find it helpful to visualize a growth surface as the lining of a wig. Shave is designed primarily for human hair patterns, so the four built-in growth surface names are *hair*, *beard*, *eyebrow*, and *eyelash* (note that these names are case sensitive). From Modeler, you load the rest position model, assign the growth surfaces to the polygons you choose, and save a copy of the surfaced model as the growth model.

You control the appearance of the rendered hairs by *grooming*, or setting growth, density, dynamics, and color parameters for the guide hairs. These guide hairs are 15-segment IK chains, which are MetaFormed to 60-segment chains at render time. *Autogroom* is a first-pass automatic setup of hair surface parameters based on the most commonly desired results for each of the built-in named hair surfaces. When you finish grooming all the guide hairs and hair surfaces in the standalone interface, you save a HAIR file that LightWave can use to render the hair effects.

In LightWave's Objects panel, you apply the HAIRdisp displacement plug-in and the saved HAIR file to the rest position model. In the Effects panel, you'll apply the HAIRrender pixel filter. Once you have your ScreamerNet set up to run tests, opening your HAIR file from the standalone application takes less than a second. Opening up your scene for modification in LightWave takes a lot longer.

Shave enables you to add highly realistic hair, fur, grass, and similar effects to LightWave objects. Shave does especially well at dynamics, making hair that moves realistically under the influence of gravity, wind, parent object motion, and collision detection. Shave is a very powerful program, and as such it requires some work to learn. However, once you've mastered the basic steps of applying Shave hair to your objects, you'll quickly be able to produce good-looking hair and fur. In fact, you would have to work pretty hard in the wrong direction to produce bad-looking hair. The default settings generate a tolerable first pass, and unless you ignore the evidence of your eyes, any changes you make should be for the better.

Shave was originally written for (and continues to work well with) LightWave 5 and 5.6. It is completely compatible with LightWave [6]. The only significant sticking point for some users seems to be how to apply Shave to LightWave [6] SubPatch objects, especially those with EndoMorph shape sets. Performing this operation successfully is not inherently difficult, but it does require a slightly deeper understanding of the whole modeling/Shave/layout process. In Object Properties|Geometry, the Subdivision Order setting of Last should allow you to use a HAIR file created with the low-polygon version of a SubPatch object. However, this LightWave feature has a bug: Subdivision always happens first, no matter what the setting says. It is supposed to be fixed in the 6.1 release, but until that time you have to work around the bug. Project 10.1 spells out the details of one workaround process, and along the way it introduces you to the major features and capabilities of Shave And A Haircut.

Shave consists of a standalone application, a deformation plug-in, and a pixel filter plug-in. The application processes a LightWave model to create a HAIR file; the deformation plug-in applies the HAIR file to the rendered model; and the pixel filter plug-in renders the hairs, including the resulting shadows and other effects.

Because the actual rendering is a post-process effect, it is generally best to leave the Shave process to near the end of your animation work flow. Although Shave is a relatively fast renderer, as HAIR plug-ins go, it can still multiply your rendering times. You will do better to apply Shave after you have finished tweaking your models, lighting, and animation. A change to any of these three factors will require you to repeat some (but usually not all) of the steps in the Shave process.

PROJECT 10.1 Growing Hair on an EndoMorph Character

To grow hair on an EndoMorph character, follow these steps:

1. For this project, I simply loaded the EndoMorph head that is included with LightWave [6], object file StuHead_WithEndoMorphs. I then animated the EndoMorph Mixer sliders to run through the basic shape set in 60 frames and set all the graphs to loop. This provides an arbitrarily long animation that I can use to experiment with hair dynamics (motion and collision detection) without having to create additional keyframes. Figure 10.7 shows Layout with the object loaded, EndoMorph Mixer active, and the Graph Editor displaying the looped actions.

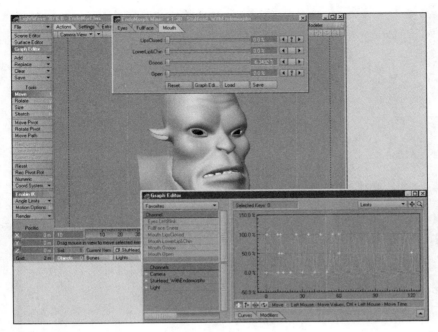

Figure 10.7
Layout with EndoMorph object loaded, EndoMorph Mixer active, and Graph Editor displaying looped actions.

2. Once you have a completed EndoMorph animation, save the scene and clear Layout. Make a copy of the EndoMorph object. Load the copy into Modeler.

The next steps add collision surfaces to the copied object. Shave uses these surfaces to prevent rendered hairs from intersecting the object's skin. Collision surfaces are only necessary for areas that are likely to be contacted by long hairs. If you are applying Shave to a short-furred animal, simulating grass, or your character has a medium to short haircut, you can skip the collision surfaces.

As of this writing, Shave uses spheres for collision surfaces. This makes the calculation of collisions much faster, and is easy to set up for most character objects. The calculations are based on the sphere's average radius, not the actual points and polygons, so you can use very simple spheres; the point/polygon count does not matter at all.

3. The simplest approach is to add a single collision sphere inside the character's head, as shown in Figure 10.8.

Note that the sphere is actually a little smaller than the character's head, so none of the sphere will be visible in the final rendering. Shave automatically increases the size of the collision sphere 7 percent during calculations, so you can safely hide the sphere inside the

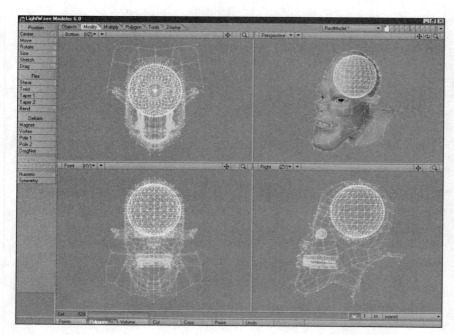

Figure 10.8
Single collision sphere added to object.

object without worrying about stray hairs glancing through your character's skin. There are more complex approaches to add and conceal more collision spheres, which I will mention later in this project.

4. Change the surface of all the collision spheres to one named "skull" as shown in Figure 10.9. Only the skull surfaces will be used by Shave to calculate collisions.

5. Deselect the collision spheres, and save the whole object as RestModel.lwo. This object should be identical to the original EndoMorph object in your animation, except for the additional collision sphere(s). All other surfaces should be intact. The next step will change that, so make sure you have RestModel saved in a safe location and be careful not to save over it during the next stage.

6. Now you need to define the patches where you want hair to grow. Shave uses four pre-defined surface names to control hair growth: hair, eyebrow, eyelid, and beard. Note that these names must be all lowercase; if you misspell one, it won't work in Shave. If you're animating a creature with short, dense fur, the surface name "beard" is probably closest to the effect you want.

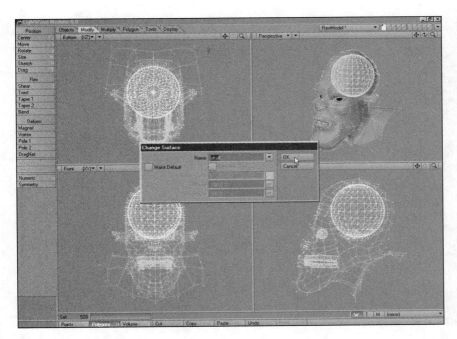

Figure 10.9
Changing collision sphere surfaces to "skull".

7. When you have assigned hair surfaces to all the appropriate patches (as shown in Figure 10.10), save the whole object as SurfModel.lwo. Next, load SurfModel in Layout. Choose the Settings tab, and set SubPatch Level to 3 (or other, final-rendering level), as shown in Figure 10.11.

8. From the Save menu, choose Save Transformed Object, and save the transformed object file as 3Growth.lwo. This object will have exactly the number of points and polygons as the final rendered SubPatch object; this match, like most morphing operations, is crucial to applying Shave to SubPatch objects.

   One problem with using objects subdivided at the same level as the final rendering is that they have a lot of points and polygons, many more than you need for grooming hair in the Shave application. Having too much data can slow down screen redraw and suck up more RAM than necessary. You can avoid these problems by creating and working with a lower-polygon model in Shave, then transplanting the HAIR file onto the high-polygon model before rendering.

9. Set SubPatch Level to 0 or 1 (they both do the same thing). From the Save menu, choose Save Transformed Object and save the transformed object file as 0Growth.lwo.

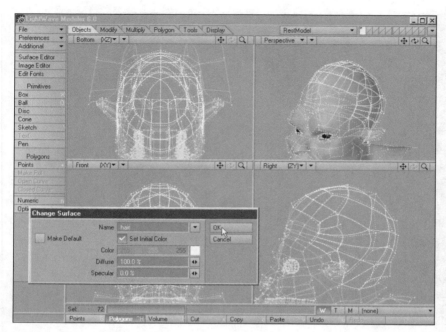

Figure 10.10
Changing selected SubPatches to surface "hair."

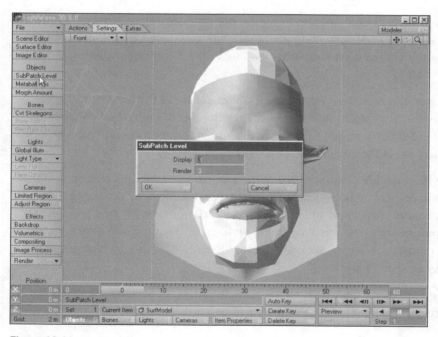

Figure 10.11
SurfModel loaded in Layout, and setting SubPatch Level to 3.

Now you have a high-polygon model and a low-polygon model. The only remaining catch is that the LightWave [6] object format includes some data structures that are incompatible with Shave And A Haircut's standalone application. This is an easy fix: Simply import both objects into Modeler, and export them in LightWave 5 object format.

10. Load 0Growth.lwo in Modeler. From the Additional menu, choose the Export_LW5 option. Save the object as 0GrowthL5.lwo. Close all objects.

11. Repeat the preceding step for 3Growth.lwo, the high-polygon model, saving it as 3GrowthL5.lwo.

12. You're done with Modeler now, so you can close it.

At this point, you should have your original animation and EndoMorph object, the RestModel object, the SurfModel object, and the high-polygon and low-polygon LightWave [6] and LightWave 5 format objects. Don't worry about all this stuff you're creating; most of these files are intermediate materials, and you'll be able to delete them later. For now, keep them handy in case you want or need to repeat part of this process.

13. Fire up Shave And A Haircut. If you haven't used this program before, don't be intimidated. It has a lot of tools, but you only need to use a few at a time, and the default settings work very well for most characters. By the time you want to try something really exotic, you'll understand the more advanced tools you'll want to use.

14. First, load the low-polygon LightWave 5 format model, 0GrowthL5.lwo. In Shave, this is referred to as a growth model, because it is only used for growing hair. When you first load a model, Shave automatically performs a first-pass autogroom, applying the default settings for color, length, and other parameters to the named hair surfaces as shown in Figure 10.12. Note that this relatively small number of hairs are only guide hairs; the actual rendering in Layout will be much denser. Fewer guide hairs make it easier for you to select hairs and groom the model, and dramatically speed up screen refresh.

You can modify this grooming with a variety of tools. You can use the left-side menu options to change the hair length, comb or translate hair in various directions, or stand the hair on end, among other things. The right-hand sliders and controls change the rendered appearance of the hair and its dynamic behavior in LightWave Layout.

You should experiment with all the tools and controls in Shave, but you can significantly shorten your learning curve by reading the online manual and tutorials available through Joe Alter's website, listed previously.

Clicking on the Test Mode button enables you to try out dynamics. This mode is a good reason to use a low-polygon model, because your screen redraw will be much faster with fewer polygons and hairs. Click the Style button to return to Style mode without saving changes. Press the Esc key to save the current state of the hair. This can save you a longer dynamics run-up in Layout, especially with longer hair. If you use Test Mode to let the hair

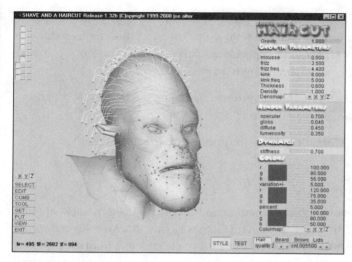

Figure 10.12
Autogroomed 0GrowthL5 low-polygon growth model.

settle over the collision spheres according to gravity, the differences between the HAIR file you export and the hair's rest state in Layout will be much smaller.

Adjust Stiffness, and try Test Mode again to see how this parameter affects the dynamic movement of the hair.

You can choose the View|Draw Preview menu option to see a rendered preview of the hair, as shown in Figure 10.13. Press Esc to close the preview.

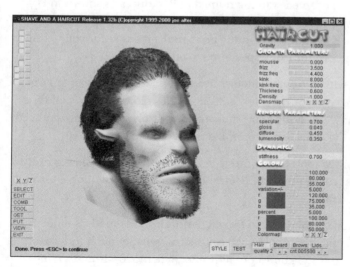

Figure 10.13
Rendered preview of autogroomed model.

15. When you are done experimenting (either you're happy with your results or you want to move on), choose the Put|Hair menu option and save the HAIR file as 0GrowthDefault.hair. This is just a backup file, in case something goes wrong with the next step. You can delete it later if you don't need it.

So far, you've applied and modified the hair of the low-polygon model. But you need a HAIR file that is compatible with the high-polygon count of the original SubPatch model. This is exactly what the Xplant feature was designed for. This enables you to import a model of a different resolution, but of similar distribution and shape, and Shave automatically reassigns the existing hair.

16. Choose the Get|Xplant Model menu option, and select the high-polygon 3GrowthL5.lwo object. Shave automatically reapplies the low-polygon model's hair grooming to the new, high-polygon model, as shown in Figure 10.14. Cool, huh?

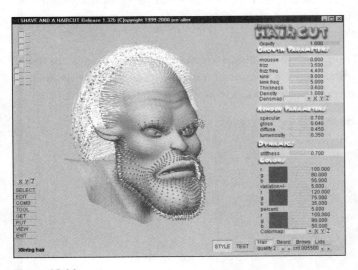

Figure 10.14
The Xplant operation transfers low-polygon model's hair to the selected high-polygon object.

This can be a huge time-saver, especially if you are working with models and hair densities that are close to your system's RAM and screen redraw limits. This approach enables you to get the most performance out of your computer.

17. If you like, make another preview to see the difference between the low- and high-polygon versions of the same grooming. When you're done, choose the Put|Hair menu option again, and this time save the HAIR file with the name 3GrowthL5.hair.

At this point, you have the minimum two files you need to render hair in Layout: the RestModel object and the 3GrowthDefault.hair file. The other objects and HAIR files are intermediate files that you can discard once you finalize all settings for the rendering.

However, I recommend that you archive them, just in case. In particular, backing up the SurfModel object can save you a lot of wasted time, because you can re-create growth models from it very quickly.

18. Open Layout. If you have enough RAM available, you can keep Shave and Layout open at the same time. You can make grooming changes to the HAIR file, and save it out again, without making any changes to the scene in Layout. At rendering time, the plug-ins will automatically reload the updated HAIR file.

19. Load the scene containing your original animated EndoMorph character. Replace the EndoMorph object with RestModel.lwo. The only differences between these two objects are the collision sphere(s) you added to RestModel.

20. With RestModel selected, open the Object Properties panel. In the Geometry tab, set both Display SubPatch Level and Render SubPatch Level to 3 (or whatever you used for the high-polygon version of Save Transformed Object earlier—they must be the same or an unpleasantness called *hair explosion* will result).

21. Go to the Deformations panel and load the HAIRdisp1 plug-in. Open the plug-in. In the Hair File field, select the 3GrowthL5.hair file you saved from Shave. In the Stat File field, name a new stat file, "stat." Turn on Pregen. Your screen should look like Figure 10.15.

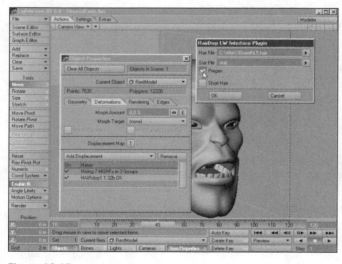

Figure 10.15
Settings for the HAIRdisp1 deformation plug-in.

Dynamics in Shave are saved in stat files, one file per frame, that record which hairs are doing what. You create stat files by making a wireframe preview in Layout. This calculates the stat files without a big rendering overhead, enabling you to conserve system resources and thereby complete projects that would otherwise be too big or complex for your machine.

However, stat files for complex, high-count hair movements can be several megabytes per frame, so make sure your hard drive has the space available before you create the preview.

Once the deformation plug-in has calculated stat files for an animation, you don't have to calculate them again unless you change the animation. This is another reason I recommend that Shave (like any other post-process) be added at the end of your animation workflow.

22. Close the plug-in and Object Properties panels.

If the dynamic motion of the hair is important, you should design your animations to include a *run-up*, a sequence of frames which will not be rendered but which are necessary to get everything moving. If you render a sequence without run-up, everything will start to move on the first frame from a standing start, as if it just snapped out of a time warp. That's not usually the effect you want, so make sure you have at least 10 frames run-up before the beginning of your animation sequence. If necessary, use the Graph Editor to shift all your keyframes ten frames later, then render starting from frame 10 rather than frame 0. You'll need to run the preview from frame 0, however, when you generate the stat files for dynamics.

23. In Preview Options, enable Virtual Memory, and choose Wireframe compression. Make a preview of the entire animation, from frame 0 to the last frame you want to render. This will create a stat file for each frame. The stat files also enable you to use F9, or otherwise render any subset of images, and have accurate dynamics for the rendering.

24. When the preview is complete, end the preview and then choose Free Preview to clear the wireframe preview from memory. Your content directory will now contain the stat files, one for each frame of the preview.

25. Open the RestModel properties panel again. Open the HAIRdisp1 plug-in, turn off Pregen, and close the plug-in and Object Properties panels.

26. In the Effects panel, add Pixel Filter hairRENDER plug-in. This plug-in has no options to adjust or select, so you can close the Effects panel.

27. Aim all the scene's lights (even the Distant and Area lights) as if they were all shadow-mapped spots to illuminate the hair to best effect. Shadow maps are most effective if they closely fit the illuminated subject. The shadow map has a finite size, and if most of it misses the subject that part of the map is wasted. If you are lighting with spotlights (which Joe Alter highly recommends), you should aim and size their cones to look like Figure 10.16.

28. Set the Camera to render in one memory segment, and for best results, use at least Medium AntiAliasing, no Adaptive Sampling, with Motion Blur at least Normal. For faster rendering, you can choose no AntiAliasing or Motion Blur, but your animations will have a lot of chatter.

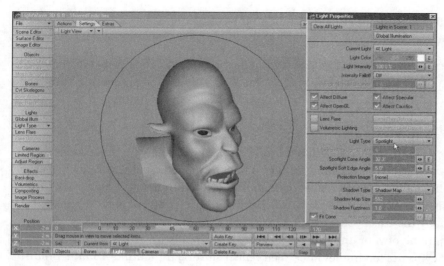

Figure 10.16
Spotlight configured for best hair-lighting results.

29. Change Render Options to display rendered images in the Image Viewer. Select a frame and press F9 to render the current frame. Your results should look like one of the images in Figure 10.17. Try another frame where the EndoMorph settings are markedly different. Note that the hair, especially the beard, precisely follows the deformation of the EndoMorph shape weighting. This demonstrates how well Shave works with LightWave [6].

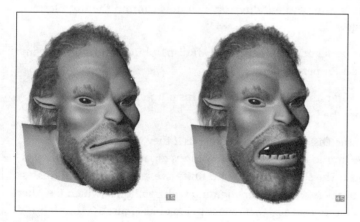

Figure 10.17
Frames 15 and 45 from a test animation, using autogroomed hair.

Rendering with the hairRENDER pixel filter plug-in active can multiply your rendering time. You should make sure that all your other animation, lighting, and camera settings are complete before you start experimenting with the hairRENDER plug-in. If you do need to change any other settings, I suggest you temporarily disable the hairRENDER plug-in to speed up your test renders. The rest of your scene will render normally, only the hair will be missing. Once you have all the other parameters nailed down, you can enable the hairRENDER plug-in again.

PROJECT 10.2   Clip Mapping to Hide Collision Spheres

If you have a character with very long hair, you may want to add more collision spheres to prevent hair from passing through the object. If the object deforms a great deal, you may also have trouble keeping the collision spheres hidden inside the object. Here are a few extra steps you can take that will give you full, animated control over your collision spheres, and keep them invisible from the camera:

1. While RestModel is still loaded in Modeler, add more collision spheres. Surface them as "skull," as before. Add them wherever you anticipate problems. For example, in Figure 10.17 you may have noticed a few stray hairs penetrating the character's right ear. I decided to eliminate that problem, and any unseen problems at the back of the head, neck, and shoulders, by adding collision spheres as shown in Figure 10.18.

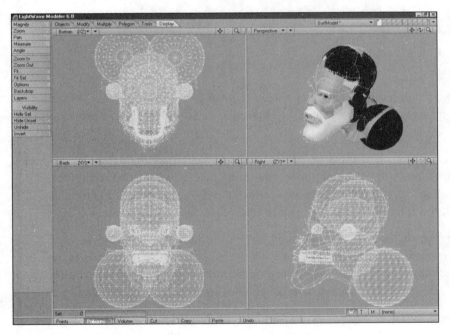

Figure 10.18
Plenty of collision spheres here!

2. Once you're done adding spheres, select them all. Use the numeric requester to move the collision spheres a precise number of units in one direction, well clear of the rest of the object. Make a note of how far you move the spheres; you'll need that number later. You

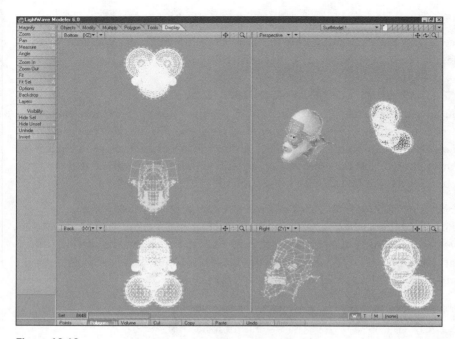

Figure 10.19
Collision spheres moved 5.0 units clear of the rest of the object, providing room for bones to be applied.

need to have enough room to apply bones with Limited Range, so the bones only affect the collision spheres and not the rest of the object. Figure 10.19 shows my approach; yours may vary.

3. Follow the rest of the process as before. After you replace the original EndoMorph object with RestModel, you'll have all those collision spheres hanging off the back. Add bones to the RestModel, and set the Limited Range, Rest Position, Rest Length, and Rest Rotation to nail down the collision spheres, as shown in Figure 10.20. Set a key for the bones at frame 0.

4. Now let's hide the collision spheres. We can't just make the skull surface 100 percent transparent, because there's a quirk (some say a bug) in LightWave [6]'s renderer that makes perfectly transparent objects still show up in post-processing filters and buffers. Instead, you can apply a clip map to completely hide the spheres from the camera.

5. Select RestModel and open the Properties panel. In the Rendering tab, click on the T-for-Texture button labeled Clip Map. Apply the black-and-white clip.jpg map that's included with the Shave download, or make your own. It doesn't need to be fancy, it just needs to hide the spheres while leaving the rest of the object visible. Your panel settings should look like Figure 10.21. Close the panels.

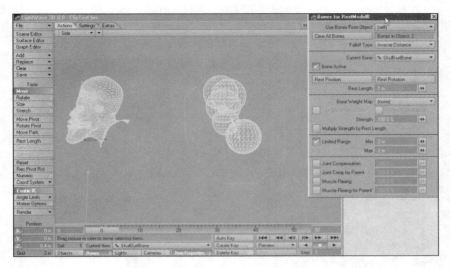

Figure 10.20
Bones in RestModel set to fix the shape of the collision spheres and insulate the rest of the object from the bones' influence.

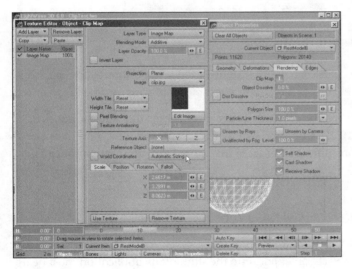

Figure 10.21
Clip map settings for hiding the collision spheres.

6. Go to frame 1. Move the bones in precisely the reverse direction and distance you moved the collision spheres in Modeler. Set a key for the bones at frame 1. Your results should look like Figure 10.22.

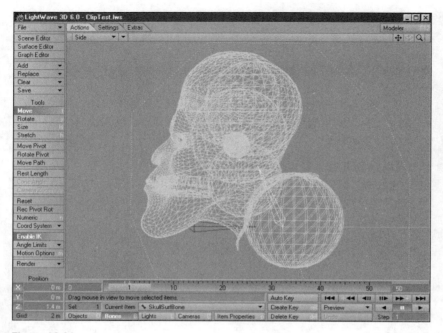

Figure 10.22
Collision spheres repositioned inside object.

You now have completely invisible collision spheres that are sized and positioned to repel hair from most of the character's surfaces. You can repeat the rest of the process as described earlier.

The difference is visible between Figure 10.17, with relatively short hair that still manages to interpenetrate the ear, and Figure 10.23, with long, wildly flying hair that does not interpenetrate anywhere. Setting up collision spheres may seem like more work up front, but it sure saves lots of mistakes later.

Product Restrictions

There are some restrictions to using Shave And A Haircut:

- As of the 1.33 release, Shave And A Haircut works with LightWave versions 5, 5.5, 5.6, and 6. The only limit is that the growth object you export into the standalone application must be a standard LightWave object (LWO) and is limited (by that format) to 65,000 vertices or less. However, you can attach the HAIR file you make with the growth object to the original LightWave 6 native object in Layout (see Project 10.1 for details).

- All texture maps must be 24-bit-per-pixel (no alpha channel) color TGA image files. This is not likely to change, but a future release will add mapping options to more parameters and will also allow you to use image sequences.

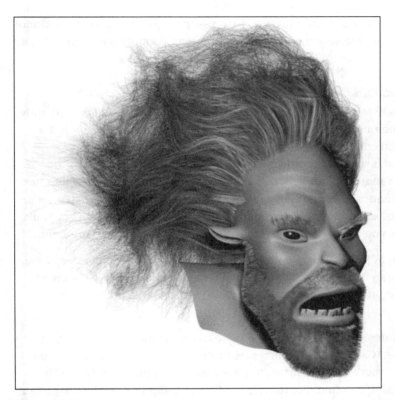

Figure 10.23
Final image showing effects of dynamics with clip-mapped collision spheres.

- As of release 1.33, you can make only one rest state for the hair. However, multiple states will be available with LipService if you want to keyframe the hair chains.

- The software is single threaded, but you can run ScreamerNet on multiple processors to take advantage of all your CPUs.

All Things Considered

So how does Shave And A Haircut stack up against my five criteria for production tools? It provides many opportunities for incremental backups, many levels of undo, and a reasonable ability to recover work at any stage of the process. It allows you to adapt existing work to changed models, and to modify hair files right up to the final rendering, so it supports incremental detailing. The feedback is very rapid, as long as you work with reasonably-sized models and HAIR files, or have a decent OpenGL accelerator card. The Preview renderings work well as documents for decision-makers to sign off. Finally, the process has a great deal of flexibility (as long as you pay attention to details), enabling you to mix-and-match hair files and models.

All things considered, Shave And A Haircut makes a clean sweep of my criteria for professional product tools. Novices may find it slow going at first, but experienced LightWave users can get up to speed in no time.

Programming Shaders

Creating new shaders is a very technical subject, well beyond the scope of this book. Generally, shader development is the domain of the technical director and other programming staff. If you're not that technical, you can simply use built-in or plug-in shaders or stick to maps. To write good shaders, you need a working knowledge of at least one programming language, a fairly deep understanding of mathematics, and the creative and problem-solving abilities to implement a purely mathematical function into a working, robust shader program. It's not an overly common set of talents, so good shader programmers can always find work. If you'd like to try programming shaders yourself, there are several resources that can get you started.

Brenden Mecleary writes a regular column, "Programmer's Hideaway," for *Keyframe Magazine*. This column is worth collecting from back issues because Brenden explains in detail how to program LightWave plug-ins, including shaders. You can also email Brenden directly at **bman2@ix.netcom.com**.

If you develop an ongoing interest in shaders and the more technical end of computer graphics, I suggest you consult the ACM SIGGRAPH references in the last chapter of this book. You may find *Transactions on Graphics* especially interesting because it's the place many shader algorithms are first published. If you find a particular renderer or programming language that interests you, try searching for a Usenet newsgroup devoted to it. You can usually find a plethora of free advice, worth every bit of what you pay for it. Aside from the technical assistance and directions to pertinent books and Web sites, the platform and software flame wars can do wonders for your vocabulary of invective, which, in turn, is handy for the next time you try to write a shader under a tight deadline.

Moving On

If you've worked through all the chapters up to this point, you should be able to produce working storyboards, soundtracks, exposure sheets, and textured character and set models. The next chapter introduces you to the last step before the animation begins—character setup.

Character Animation with
LightWave [6] Studio

*On the following pages, you'll see color
examples of the character animation projects
using LightWave [6] presented in this book. You'll
also see the work created in LightWave by several
noted animators, modelers, and artists.*

An early Mudpuppy sketch. **The Mudpuppy maquette.**

Ultimately rendered in LightWave, this character, named Mudpuppy, is shown in an early concept sketch. Dave Bailey then created a maquette with Sculpey polymer clay and formed a skeleton over the armature, also with Sculpey. With a firm skeletal base and a human anatomy book in hand, Dave fleshed out the model muscle-by-muscle. To learn more about the process of designing Mudpuppy (and his creator), see Case Study 5.1.

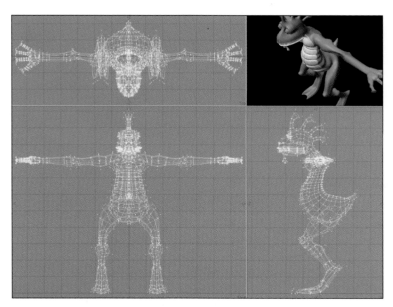

The next step was to create Mudpuppy as a 3D model in LightWave. Only the basic Smooth Shift, Bevel, Metaform, and point manipulation tools were used. The finished model set up, posed, and rendered in LightWave. To learn more about the process of modeling Mudpuppy (and his creator), see Case Study 6.1.

These images represent individual frames from a Mudpuppy QuickTime movie that can be found on this book's CD-ROM (Mp-cd1.mov).

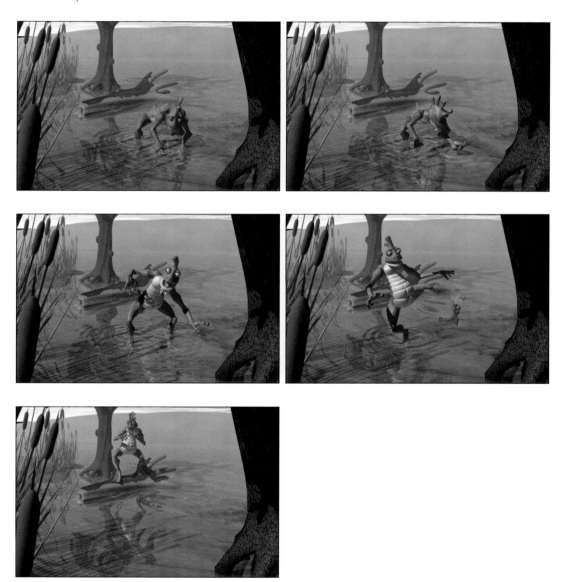

Here's a character progressing from a hand-sculpted maquette to a character animated in LightWave. Try Project 6.1 and see if you end up with the Metaformed Fred head.

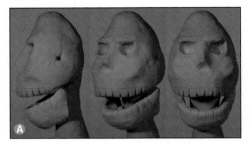

The bone structure of the skull is modeled by hand.

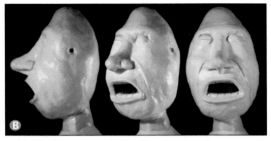

Muscles, fat, and skin are added.

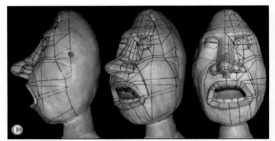

A fine-point pen or pencil is used to mark four-sided polygons on the maquette.

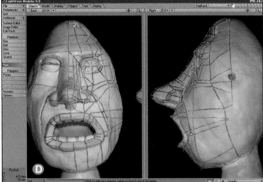

LightWave Modeler is used to build Fred's head.

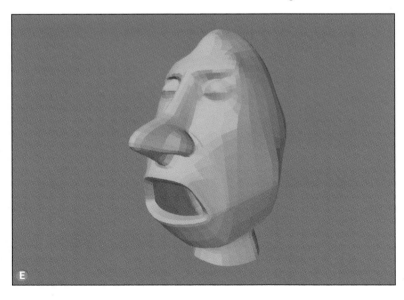

The Metaformed Fred head.

LightWave [6] groups all surface settings and controls into a single Surface Editor with a Surface Preset shelf. Chapter 8 explains how to apply them to make your characters more effective. Shown below are examples of basic attributes.

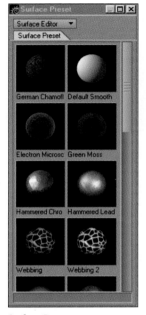

Surface Preset.

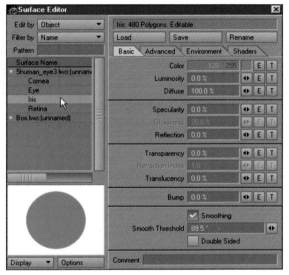

Surface Editor.

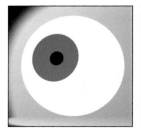

Original image.

Specularity, 100% glossiness.

Specularity, 50% glossiness.

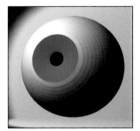

Luminosity set to 100%.

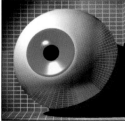

High reflection.

Transparency.

Bump maps create the illusion of changes in surface depth or height based on the map's grayscale value. To avoid sharp slopes in your bump maps, you can increase the map's resolution, then apply blur or edge dither effects to smooth out any abrupt differences in gray values. To learn more about bump maps, see Chapter 8.

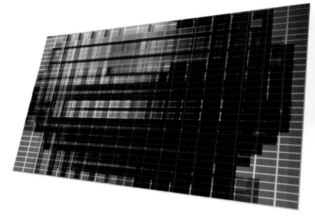

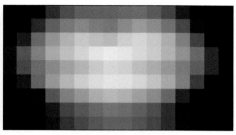

Plane object (left) with 16×9 bump map applied (above).

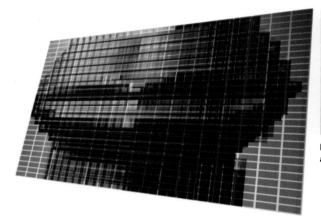

Plane object (left) with 32×18 bump map applied (above).

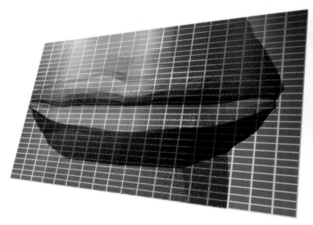

Plane object (left) with 640×360 bump map applied (above).

In LightWave [6], combinations of polygons, textures, and maps are referred to as *surfaces*. Surface appearances are critical in character animation. Basic surface attributes are settings that control the model's rendered appearance. Basic reflection determines how much of the surrounding environment the surface will mirror. The following are examples of different kinds of reflection maps. To learn more about various types of maps, see Chapters 8 and 9.

Environment reflection map applied to a reflective sphere, creating the illusion of objects that are not actually in the scene.

The original scene.

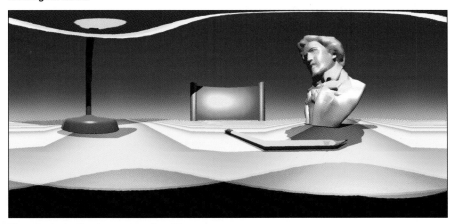

The spherical reflection map rendered from the scene.

The nearly identical results of a raytraced reflection and an environment reflection map rendered from the same scene. Which is which?

Creator Kim Oravecz conceived, designed, modeled, and textured the character of Switch A. Roo in LightWave—specifically to make the skin tough and leathery because the character lives in a cold environment. To learn more about the process of texturing Switch A. Roo (and his creator), see Case Study 9.1.

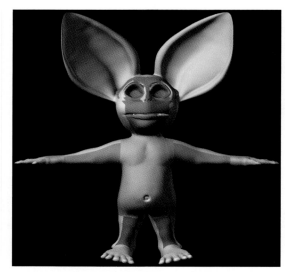

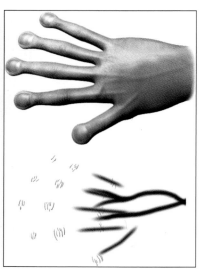

In order to make a template of each texture surface, a high-resolution front rendering of the character in a neutral pose was done.

Kim used planar mapping techniques to create this character's skin textures, such as bump maps for veins and tendons in hands and feet.

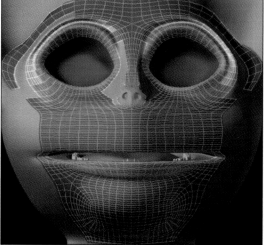

Details were painted for each surface on transparent Photoshop layers (left) so the LightWave Modeler wireframe screenshot layer and LightWave Layout flat shaded rendering layer underneath could be used as guides (right).

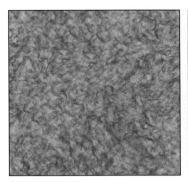

Skin-color-1. **Combined skin texture.** **Skin-color-2.**

The skin texture is basically a multipart texture of color maps and bump maps.

Switch A. Roo at home in the refrigerator.

The overall effect of LightWave lighting and rendering makes the difference between a seamless composite and one that does not ring true. After completing Project 17.5, you will be able to add LightWave elements that composite seamlessly with the background. Chris Nibley created the raw chessboard footage; see the Color Section Contributors page for details.

A frame from the motion control shot (ChesP276.iff on the CD-ROM) showing reflections, highlights, and shadows on the chessboard.

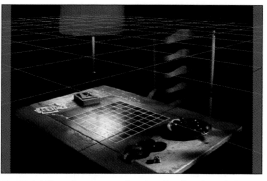

The LightWave chess scene showing the chessboard object matched to the background image.

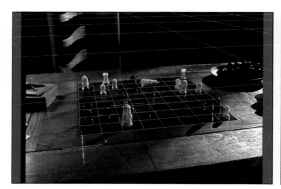

Nulls placed to mark the peak of the chess piece and shadow.

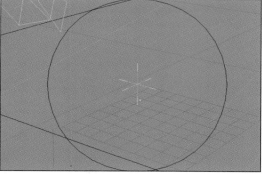

The Light View aligned with nulls.

The Walker robot crossing a chessboard, with matching shadows and reflection, is an example of the effects you can create.

LightWave [6] enables you to project a map with a light. In cinematography, a cutout or filter used this way is called a cookie. Iguana images courtesy of Kim Oravecz.

Iguana with basic lighting.

A cookie is applied to mimic shadows of leaves on the iguana's back.

This is a sequence of modeling and texturing for a *Starship Troopers* character named Clone E, who is an alien bug disguised as a human. This character was modeled and textured by Roger Borelli; see the Color Section Contributors page to learn more about Roger.

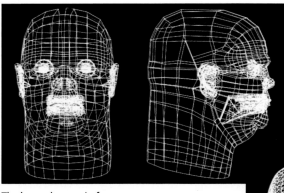

The low-polygon wireframe cage.

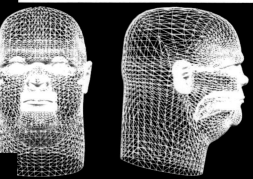

The wireframe base.

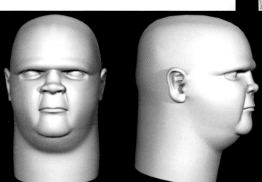

The smooth-shaded model before texturing.

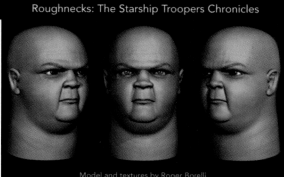

Roughnecks: The Starship Troopers Chronicles

Model and textures by Roger Borelli

The fully textured model.

Additional characters modeled and textured by Roger Borelli; see the Color Section Contributors page to learn more about Roger.

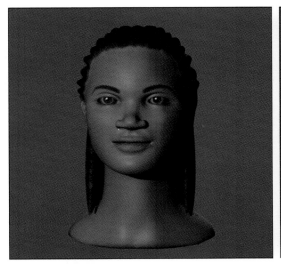

This is a *Starship Troopers* character called Young Trooper.

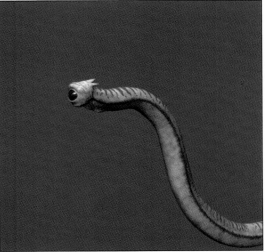

Here's another character from *Starship Troopers* named One-Eyed Bug.

This character, an alien with an exoskeleton, is based on a design done for a film (that was not made)—the film was going to be called *IronClad* and the alien was known as a Nyette.

A challenge of character animation in LightWave is compositing a character into live-action footage. This requires a seamless match of LightWave lighting and rendering. Take a look at Chapter 17, especially Projects 17.3 and 17.4, for more information.

Start off with a clean plate.

A close-up of a lighting reference object with gnomon and white ball.

A lighting reference object with gnomon and white ball.

LightWave lighting reference objects and character composited into a clean plate.

A sunlight setup rendered in LightWave.

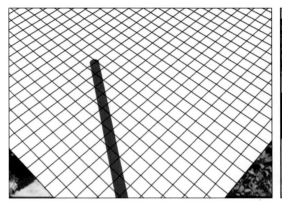

LITEREF/LITEGRID (named lighting reference objects) as rendered by the LightWave camera.

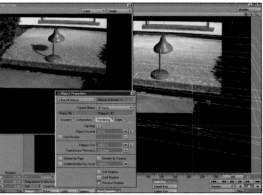

Desk lamp and shadow rendered over the image-mapped porch object and backdrop.

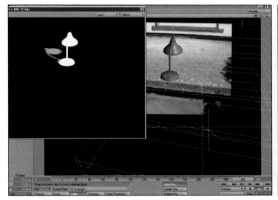

An alpha channel created in LightWave for the desk lamp and shadow render to retain more control over the shadow density and color.

The rendered foreground and alpha channel rendered over a clean plate background to create a composite.

Slight blur and grain filters added to LightWave elements to match blur and noise in the original footage—work through Projects 17.3 and 17.4 and see if your LightWave lighting and rendering match mine.

Minimus, an original character designed by Shane Ushijima, was first developed using LightWave 5.6 and has been converted to LightWave [6]. See the Color Section Contributors page for more information about Shane.

©2000 Shane Ushijima

©2000 Shane Ushijima

©2000 Shane Ushijima

An early version of Minimus with fewer textures and some differences in modeling.

Minimus converted to LightWave [6].

Minimus rendered using the Radiosity features of LightWave [6].

©2000 Shane Ushijima

Minimus composited over a live-action background and rendered to simulate old black-and-white film.

Part III

Texturing

Chapter 11

Essential Setups

Setups are the flesh and bone of animated characters. You need to understand how animation works before you can set up a character, and you need to understand how a character is set up before you can animate it.

A *setup* is a scene file containing everything necessary for an animator to bring a character to life. This can include objects, hierarchies, constraints, expressions, lights, cameras, and just about any other item or function used in LightWave. A setup can be as simple as a few objects arranged in a hierarchy or as complex as several photorealistic humanoid characters with full musculoskeletal structures and a plethora of constraints and expressions.

Before you can build a setup, you need to understand how an animator will use it. This chapter shows you the basic principles behind character animation, with projects that guide you through the process of setting up simple characters. The next two chapters show you setups that are progressively more complex, from primitive caricatures up to realistic emulation of muscle, skin, cloth, and hair. Each setup chapter has a companion animation chapter. Chapter 14 shows how to use this chapter's setups to practice basic animation techniques.

Animator-Friendly Setups

Character animation is hard. You should try to use your setups to make it as easy as possible. Ideally, the animator should be able to open up the setup and immediately start posing the character, with a minimum of confusion, bother, or wasted effort. A good setup can make a character intuitive and efficient to animate. A bad setup, or one the animator doesn't understand, can ruin a project—maybe even a career. You will either be animating the little monster yourself (in which case, you will have no one else to blame for a frustrating setup) or setting it up for another animator (in which case, he can focus all his frustration on you). Either way, it's in your best interest to make your setups as animator friendly as possible.

Character setup can also be a way into the animation profession. If your animation skills are not yet up to professional standards, you may still be able to find work doing setups. Most professional animators I've interviewed prefer not to do setups. There is a constant migration, from setup person to junior animator, that leaves entry-level setup positions open. Make sure your demo reel, résumé, and other materials show off your setup skills!

Learn from Others' Mistakes— It's Much Cheaper!

There are many similarities between LightWave character animation and the more traditional forms used in the past century. I've always believed in the wisdom of learning from other people's experience and mistakes, because it is much cheaper and less painful. That said, let's take a look at what we can learn from the masters of character animation.

Setting up for LightWave character animation has more in common with clay or puppet animation than with 2D-drawn animation, for a number of reasons. In three-dimensional animation, you must set before the camera models of everything the audience will see, whether you use LightWave, clay, or puppets. You have, in compensation for this extra effort, a great deal of freedom in moving your camera to compose your shots. The correctness of perspective and depth, so difficult to attain with drawn animation, is also integral to 3D, whether physical or virtual. Last, 2D animation generally relies on the laborious redrawing of anything that must appear to move. This is a huge burden. Enormous resources have been poured into developing production shortcuts to reuse as much hand-drawn artwork as possible. In 3D formats, you have the comparative luxury of reusing almost everything in nearly every frame; changes between frames are incremental or piecemeal rather than substantial or total.

This is only to say that puppet or clay traditions have more bearing on setup techniques for LightWave character animation. After the setup is complete, the efficient LightWave animator's workflow more closely resembles that of a traditional 2D animator. For staging, timing, general workflow, and other animation principles discussed in Part V, we will rely heavily on the much larger (and somewhat more relevant) body of work supporting 2D character animation. Where the traditional animator would draw a handful of key poses, the LightWave animator sets a handful of keyframes. Where the traditional animator would flip his sketchpad to judge the action, the LightWave animator renders a preview. Where the traditional animator would add, delete, or reshuffle drawings to vary the timing of an action, the LightWave animator shifts, scales, cuts, copies, and pastes keyframes along the timeline. Neither traditional 3D nor 2D character animation techniques are wholly or exclusively applicable to LightWave character animation, but both have much to contribute.

So, what does puppet animation have to offer for LightWave character setup?

First, let's get the terminology straight. There really isn't an official name encompassing puppet, clay, and related forms of animation. The phrase "stop motion" ("stopmo" for short) is used by a lot of people in the industry. However, this term was originally used for a larger body of special effects that were performed in the camera, including optical dissolves, split screens, and other effects that have nothing to do with animation. The alternatives of "dimensional animation" and "puppet animation" have their drawbacks. More recently, market forces have bred neologisms such as Claymation and Go-Motion in an effort to differentiate one studio's or animator's techniques from the others. For the sake of consistency, I will use the term "puppet animation" to refer to puppet, clay, and all other forms of physical 3D animation. If the term offends you, feel free to scratch it out and insert your own favorite term—but only after you've purchased this book!

There are two major divisions in puppet animation techniques: *replacement* and *displacement*. Each has advantages and disadvantages, depending on the needs of a particular animation sequence. They are often combined in hybrid replacement/displacement animation, which can use the strengths of one technique to shore up the weaknesses of the other.

Replacement Animation

Replacement puppet animation uses a complete model for each pose, swapping out the model for each change, sometimes for each frame. The models are generally cast or similarly mass-produced in batches of one pose, then deformed, sculpted, or otherwise modified to create the individual poses. As you can imagine, this method requires a large number of models for even simple actions. The advantage is that the actual staging and shooting of the animation proceeds very quickly, because the entire sequence of models has been determined in advance and they can be rapidly swapped out during photography.

For a noncharacter example of this technique, you can look at the peach glop in *James and the Giant Peach* (1996). One of the few examples of this technique being used for a complete character in a feature film is the *Tyrannosaurus rex* in *The Beast of Hollow Mountain* (1956). The replacement models of *T. rex* were used for walking and running sequences—the cyclical actions were a good match for the strengths and limitations of replacement puppet animation.

Simple replacement animation depends on having one complete model for each frame of motion. For example, suppose you created a replacement animation using 30 model replacements and each model was only slightly different from the next. If the animation takes only 30 frames, you would have enough replacements for a smooth animation. If you tried to stretch this same animation out but still changed models only 30 times, you would see jerks, or *strobing*, each time the pose changed. Because the models are not really connected from frame to frame (the way morph or deformation models are), there are no in-between poses for LightWave to render. Even motion blur won't help, because the model is not actually moving during the in-between frames. This is one reason other techniques are generally more useful than single-frame replacement animation.

LightWave has a number of tools that can be used for replacement animation. Each has strengths and weaknesses. It's possible to create character animation this way, but I have to ask, "Why?" Manual replacement combines the worst of traditional puppet animation and CGI. As with puppet animation, you can't tweak or edit the timing. It's all done straight ahead, frame by frame. If you need to modify an action, you have to animate the sequence all over again. As with all CGI, you have to build everything you'll set before the camera and in a much less intuitive medium than clay and wire.

Replacement Animation Using Poser

Here's a tip from animator Phil South: One of the best reasons for using replacement animation is if you are using Metacreations Poser to design walk cycles. It's the only way to get the objects in, and it works. Poser creates all the replacement objects—all you have to do is put them in using a replacement object plug-in.

I'm not providing any detailed projects for simple replacement techniques; the odds are good that you will never have to use them in LightWave. However, understanding these techniques and their good and bad points may give you a better perspective to judge other LightWave character animation tools. In case you really want to experiment with simple replacement animation, I've included 30 replacement objects for an animated desk lamp in the Chapter 11 directory of this book's CD-ROM. You should be able to figure out the basic process from the section on ObjList and ObjectSequence plug-ins, on pages 2.16 and 2.17 of the *LightWave [6] Motion: Animate & Render* manual. There are a couple of common problems with simple replacement:

- The requirement of an extensive and varied library of models

- Visible strobing in the animation if a model is replaced on twos or higher

Morphing solves the second problem and goes a long way toward reducing the first one. LightWave's morph replacement tools come in three types: *simple morph*, *morph sequence*, and *EndoMorph*.

Simple Morph

Just as for other replacement techniques, when you use morph replacement, you specify a beginning model and the model that is to replace it. But instead of popping directly from one model file to the next, the morph function calculates an in-between position for each vertex or control point for every frame. This makes the changes very smooth, even when the model and target are hundreds or thousands of frames apart. It also means that models designed to be used with LightWave's morphing must share the exact same number of points and polygons, arranged in the same order. This makes creating complex morph models more of a challenge.

Unfortunately, morph doesn't know that models sometimes move in arcs. When you provide the two models to morph, all LightWave can do is calculate a straight-line change, or *interpolation*, in the position of each point relative to that point's counterpart in the target model. This can cause problems, as the following project demonstrates.

Before you begin any of the projects in this chapter, you should copy the files from the Chapter 11 directory of this book's CD-ROM to your default LightWave content directory.

Project 11.1 shows you how to create a very basic morph setup, one that will produce a smooth, gradual interpolation of a model's shape from one morph target to another. It also demonstrates some of the problems and restrictions that are part of the morphing process. Simple morphs can be very useful for changing the shape of complex organic models. As the later *hybrid setup* Project 11.9 shows, you can also combine a simple morph of some character parts with other setup techniques for the rest of the character. Faces and hands are especially good candidates for morph techniques, so this is a project you should study carefully. When you understand how morphing works, you can better judge when to use it and when to choose another approach for your character setups.

PROJECT 11.1 Setting Up Desk Lamp Animation with Simple Morph

To create a basic morph setup, follow these steps:

1. Load the L6CA1101.LWS scene file into Layout. The scene contains only the REPLAC00 object, the default pose model of the desk lamp.

2. Load object file REPLAC05, and open the Objects panel. With REPLAC05 selected, set the Object Dissolve value (in the Rendering tab) at 100%, and press Enter to accept the change. This keeps the object invisible during renderings. We don't want to see it, we just want to use it to change the original object.

3. Repeat Step 2 for object files REPLAC10, REPLAC15, REPLAC20, REPLAC25, and REPLAC30. These are the different morph target objects you'll be using.

4. In the Objects panel, select REPLAC00 from the Current Object drop-down list. This is the object the morph will start with.

5. Choose the Deformations tab. In the Morph Target drop-down list, select REPLAC30 as the target object (see Figure 11.1). This is the object the morph will go toward.

6. Click on the E (for Envelope) button to the right of the Morph Amount data field to open the Graph Editor panel, as shown in Figure 11.2.

   The Graph Editor controls how quickly and to what extent the morph will take place. This is a very important and powerful animation tool, and we really can't do it justice in this

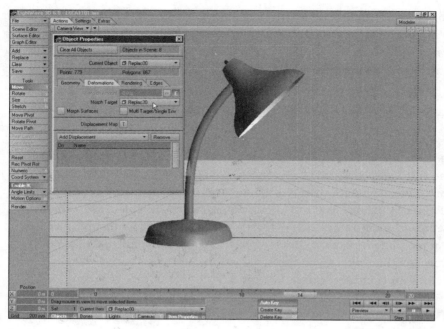

Figure 11.1
Objects panel with REPLAC00 object selected and REPLAC30 as morph target.

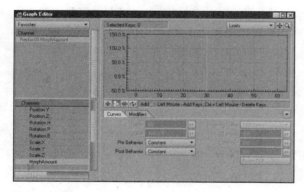

Figure 11.2
Graph Editor panel for REPLAC00.

chapter. If you haven't already, you should read through pages 3.6 to 3.10 of the *LightWave [6] Motion: Animate & Render* manual so you understand the basic operations of the Graph Editor. The more complex operations you can perform with the graph controls will be described later in the book. For now, we'll just make the transformation happen smoothly over 60 frames.

7. Add two keyframes to the Envelope, one at frame 0 and the other at frame 60.

8. While the keyframe at frame 60 is selected, type "100" in the Value field and press Enter. This will put the keyframe dot at the top-right corner of the Envelope, as shown in Figure 11.3. Set the keyframe at frame 0 to a value of 0. Your Envelope should look like Figure 11.3.

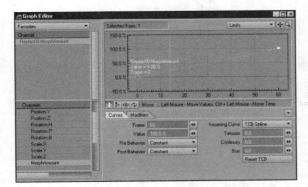

Figure 11.3
Envelope for REPLAC00, after editing.

This straight-line envelope means that the morph will go smoothly from 100-percent REPLAC00 to 100-percent REPLAC30 over the course of 60 frames.

9. Close the Graph Editor and return to the Objects panel. Close the Objects panel and return to the Layout window.

10. Make a wireframe preview of frames 1 through 60. Play the preview. Your results should look like Figure 11.4.

What in the world is going on here? The shade, in fact the entire upper part of the lamp, seems to be shrinking in the middle of the animation!

Remember what I mentioned earlier about morph handling only straight-line changes? If you draw a line connecting the frame 0, frame 30, and frame 60 positions of any point in the lamp, you will draw a perfectly straight line. Even though the lamp's neck is bending, moving the shade in an arc, morph is taking each point on the shortest path between two points—a straight line. As you can see, this distorts the shape of the object and produces unrealistic actions. The lamp looks like it is melting from one position to the next.

To avoid this problem, you need to use morph targets that are fairly close in shape to the preceding object. The difference between REPLAC00 and REPLAC30 is pretty extreme, but REPLAC00 and REPLAC05 are much closer in shape.

11. Open the Objects panel again and select REPLAC05 for the morph target object. Close the Objects panel and make another preview. Your results should look like Figure 11.5.

Figure 11.4
Frames 0, 30, and 60 from morph straight-line interpolation between very different targets.

Figure 11.5
Morph straight-line interpolation between more similar targets.

This one turned out much better. There is not much arc between the original object and the REPLAC05 target object, so Metamorph's straight-line interpolation is almost undetectable.

12. Repeat Step 11, using objects REPLAC10, REPLAC15, REPLAC20, and REPLAC25, to see how much distortion you can get away with. When you're done, save the scene for use in the next project.

Later in this chapter, Project 11.2 shows you an alternative solution to morph interpolation problems, the *morph sequence*, or in LightWave terminology, *Multiple Target Single Envelope (MTSE)*.

Morphing Problems

The morph technique eliminates the strobing problems of LightWave's manual replacement, ObjectSequence, and ObjList techniques. Unfortunately, morph can't read your mind. You know that a bending lamp should move in an arc, but morph doesn't know that. When you provide the two models to morph, all it can do is calculate a straight-line change, or interpolation, in the position of each point relative to its counterpart in the other model.

One way to compensate for this problem is to use enough targets, closely spaced, that the straight-line interpolation is not noticeable to your audience. This is most important with actions like a character's curling fingers or bending arms, where the points describe relatively large arcs between their start and end positions. You generally won't have this problem when morphing for facial animation because the arcs are much shorter and straight-line interpolation works just fine. For this and other reasons, facial animation is one of the most common uses for morph and its big brother, morph sequence. In LightWave, you can use morph settings to precisely control the transition between models. This gives you the power, for example, to animate a face precisely 65 percent of the distance from an "anger" model to a "rage" model to get the exact emotional nuance you want for your animated transitions.

Even if you have to use more targets to disguise straight-line interpolations, you will still use fewer targets for morphing than you would have for an equivalent ObjList, ObjectSequence, or manual replacement animation. Morph requires four or five targets for a smooth desk lamp bend. The simple replacement techniques need 30.

One obvious limitation is that morph is designed to transform from one model to another. What do you do if you want a whole string of different targets within a single animation, as in lip sync? That's what the next function, morph sequence, is all about.

Multiple Target Single Envelope

Multiple Target Single Envelope (MTSE), LightWave's implementation of morph sequence, was one of the most versatile and powerful replacement tools available in LightWave 5.6 and earlier. It still provides a useful combination of control, ease of use, power, and flexibility. There are a few replacement animation tricks you can't perform with a morph sequence, but not many.

Morph sequence enables you to chain together a number of morph target models, then control the morph between the default model and any of the targets. This is incredibly powerful because you can manipulate the morph sequence controls to interactively insert the exact percentages of each morph target exactly when you want them.

For example, if you have a model library of heads for the basic phonemes and emotions (anywhere from 15 to several dozen models), you can load them all in a morph sequence chain, then make the head lip sync and run through any full-face emotional transition within the library's range.

Morph Sequences in the Movies

Two prominent examples of morph sequence animation are the face-mimicking water tentacle in *The Abyss* and the T-1000 in *Terminator 2: Judgment Day*. In the latter, actor Robert Patrick plays a "mimetic poly-alloy" android, apparently made of liquid metal. In one scene, the liquid form of the android flows through a hole in a helicopter window, resumes human form in the left seat, then lip syncs the words "Get out" to the chopper's pilot. Separate Cyberware scans (see Chapter 7) of Patrick's head were used as morph targets to animate this lip sync sequence.

Needless to say, morph sequence can be very useful for advanced topics such as lip sync and facial animation. For now, you can concentrate on the basics.

Project 11.2 shows you how to set up a basic morph sequence between seven desk lamp morph targets. This demonstrates one method of working around the problem of morph distortion in broad angular actions. You can apply the principles of morph sequence animation to lip sync, hand gestures, or any other repeated change to the shape of a complex model.

MTSE enables you to control the morph between the default model and any of the targets by using a single envelope. This is incredibly powerful because you can manipulate the spline controls of the envelope to interactively insert the exact percentages of each morph target exactly when you want them.

For example, if you have a model library of heads for the basic phonemes and emotions (anywhere from 15 to several dozen models), you can load them all in an MTSE chain, then use the Envelope spline to make the head lip sync and run through any emotional transition within your model library's range. That's a little complex for a first setup, so this project concentrates on the simpler task of animating the desk lamp without the distortions of the simple morph.

PROJECT 11.2   Setting Up a Desk Lamp Animation with Morph Sequence

To set up a desk lamp animation with morph sequence, follow these steps:

1. Load the L6CA1101.LWS scene file you saved at the end of Project 11.1. It should contain object files REPLAC00, REPLAC05, REPLAC10, REPLAC15, REPLAC20, REPLAC25, and

REPLAC30. These are the morph sequence target objects you'll be using. All but REPLAC00 should be set to 100% Dissolve so they are invisible when not selected.

2. Select REPLAC00 from the Current Object drop-down list. This is the beginning object for the morph sequence.

3. In the Morph Target drop-down list, in the middle of the Deformations tab, select REPLAC05 as the target object. This is the object the first morph in the chain will go toward.

4. Select REPLAC05 from the Current Object drop-down list. This is the second object in the morph sequence chain.

5. In the Morph Target drop-down list, select REPLAC10 as the target object. This is the object the second morph in the chain will go toward. Do you see the pattern you are following?

6. Repeat Steps 4 and 5 for morph sequence object pairs 10 and 15, 15 and 20, 20 and 25, and 25 and 30.

7. Select REPLAC00 from the Current Object drop-down list. Check the Multi Target/Single Env button, located just below the Morph Target drop-down list, to enable the MTSE feature. Click on the E (for Envelope) button next to the Morph Amount data field to open the Graph Editor panel (see Figure 11.6).

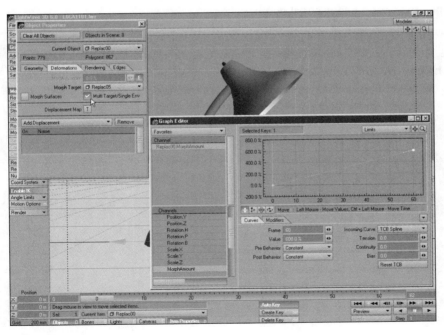

Figure 11.6
Graph Editor panel for REPLAC00.

The morph values for morph sequence target objects are increased by 100 for each object in the chain. If there were only two targets, the top of the scale would be 200 percent. With six targets, the top end is 600 percent; 0 through 100 percent controls morphing to the REPLAC05 object, 101 through 200 percent controls morphing to the REPLAC10 object, and so on.

8. Change the value at frame 60 from 100 (which you set in Project 11.1) to 600 and press Enter. Choose Auto Limits from the Limits pull-down to resize the graph window. Your Graph Editor should look like Figure 11.6. This straight-line graph means that the morph will go smoothly from REPLAC00 to REPLAC30 over the course of 60 frames.

9. Close the Graph Editor and return to the Objects panel. Close the Objects panel and return to the Layout window.

10. Make a wireframe preview of frames 1 through 60. Play the preview.

    Pretty smooth, huh? That's using only seven objects, and the motion over 60 frames is just as smooth as it would be if you were using 30 objects with ObjectSequence or ObjList over 30 frames. Now, let's have a little fun before we wrap this up and move on to displacement animation.

11. End the preview. Open the Objects panel again. Click on the E button next to Morph Amount to open the Graph Editor panel again.

12. In the Channel list, right-click on the REPLAC00_MorphAmount item to open the pop-up menu (Figure 11.7). Choose Replace. From the Chapter 11 directory on this book's CD-ROM, select the file STAGGER.mot. This is a quick little envelope I made just for fun. Press Enter to close the file dialog and return to the Graph Editor panel, shown in Figure 11.7.

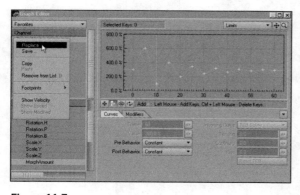

Figure 11.7
Graph Editor panel with STAGGER.mot envelope loaded.

13. Close the Graph Editor and return to the Objects panel. Close the Objects panel and return to Layout.

14. Make a new preview. Play the preview. If you like, render an AVI. Your results should look something like L6CA1102.AVI, frames from which are shown in Figure 11.8.

Figure 11.8
Frames from L6CA1102.AVI, of desk lamp animated using MTSE with Envelope STAGGER.ENV.

Boing! Isn't that fun? Fiddle with the envelope; create your own—this is a good way to learn something while amusing yourself. This particular envelope was based on something I remembered about a pendulum's period being constant but the amplitude decreasing over time due to friction. This desk lamp is a flexible pendulum with a lot of friction and a short period.

As you can see, MTSE is powerful and at the same time relatively easy to use. The control it provides is pretty fine, and it can be accurately tweaked by direct numerical entry but is still malleable enough for freehand animation work. A very nice combination. The downside is that MTSE is a bit of a RAM hog if your models are at all complex. All your target models are loaded at all times, so extensive target libraries can really tax your system.

Although morph sequence and morph animation require fewer models than simple replacement techniques, you still need a good-sized model library to have a decent dramatic range for character animation. Add the fact that compatible models pretty much have to be modified from the same base model, thereby limiting the modeling tools you can use, and it's pretty much a bed of roses—you have to take the thorns with the blooms.

EndoMorph

EndoMorph is a new feature in LightWave [6]; it was designed to overcome some of the problems inherent in the simple morph, MTSE, and Morph Gizmo functions of earlier versions. Before you proceed with the next project, you should have read the section on EndoMorphs in the *LightWave [6] Motion: Animate & Render* manual, pages 4.33 through 4.39.

EndoMorph is more flexible than simple morphing because it can include many targets, organized into groups for efficiency and convenience. EndoMorph bypasses the organizational problems of morph libraries by incorporating all target objects into one file with the base object. EndoMorph avoids the excessive RAM usage of MTSE by storing only the *deltas*, or changes, between base and target objects rather than all the point data for every model. This makes it much easier to manage the many targets and high level of detail necessary for complex facial animation. EndoMorph is overkill for our simple desk lamp animation, but working through the following project does illustrate the basic concepts of setting up a character with EndoMorphs.

PROJECT 11.3 Setting Up a Desk Lamp Animation with EndoMorph

The goal of this project is to animate the desk lamp through the same bending action as in the preceding projects, but you'll use EndoMorphs and the MorphMixer plug-in:

1. Load the same seven objects you used in Project 11.2 into separate layers in Modeler.

2. Set REPLAC00 as the foreground. Set REPLAC05 as the background.

3. Execute the Bkg-to-MORF operation from the Additional menu (Figure 11.9). This adds the background model to the foreground model as an EndoMorph target shape. Name the EndoMorph REPLAC05 so you can easily remember which target is which.

4. Repeat the Bkg-to-MORF process for the remaining target models. Give each EndoMorph the same name as the background object.

5. When you have added all six EndoMorphs, save the model as LampMorf. Close Modeler.

6. In Layout, reopen scene file L6CA1101.lws. Replace the REPLAC00 model with the LampMorf model.

7. In the Objects panel, choose the Deformations tab. From the Add Displacement pull-down list, choose the MorphMixer plug-in. The plug-in line should read, "Mixing 6 MORFs in 1 Group," as shown in Figure 11.10.

8. Click on the MorphMixer plug-in line to open MorphMixer.

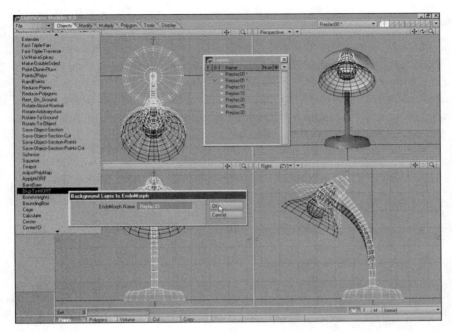

Figure 11.9
Bkg-to-MORF operation, with REPLAC05 background object being added to foreground REPLAC00 object.

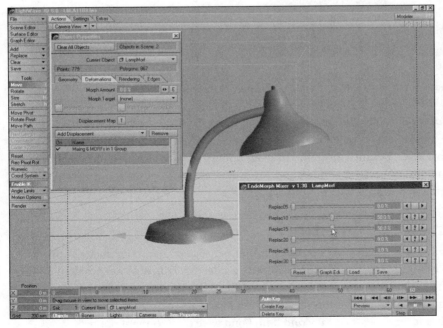

Figure 11.10
MorphMixer plug-in applied to LampMorf, showing the six EndoMorph targets you added in Modeler.

9. Experiment with the slider settings.

   Moving the top slider, Replac05, from 0 to 100 is the same as the simple morph from Project 11.1. Moving more than one slider at a time can cause distortions in the lamp's shape; for best results for this character, you should apply no more than two sliders at a time, work only with adjacent pairs of sliders, and keep the combined value of those sliders at or below 100. For example, if you want the lamp to bend halfway between the positions of REPLAC10 and REPLAC15, you should set each of those sliders to 50, as shown in Figure 11.10.

10. If you want to make the lamp bend from the default REPLAC00 pose all the way down to REPLAC30, you will need to set up a complex sequence of slider motions, each slider "handing off" to the next one at the 50-percent mark. Your envelopes for the six sliders should look something like Figure 11.11. If you vary too much from this graph, you'll get distortions in the lamp's shape.

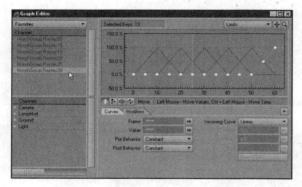

Figure 11.11
Graph of six envelopes, for the six EndoMorph sliders, necessary to make a simple lamp bend.

A linear, sequential motion like the lamp's bending is a waste of the power inherent in EndoMorphs. The most effective use of EndoMorphs is the complex animation of a character's face, where you can layer, balance, and fine-tune emotional expressions and mouth shapes to create a convincing and appealing performance. However, this project demonstrates that you can use EndoMorphs to animate even simple actions.

Displacement Animation

Displacement animation is the process of posing joints or bones to change a character's appearance. This approach usually requires only one complete model (in contrast to replacement animation) and is much better suited to animation of major skeletal actions, like arm and leg motion. Displacement animation is probably more familiar than replacement animation to most people because popular characters such as Gumby and King Kong were displacement puppets.

Traditional displacement animation requires a model that is jointed or flexible enough to be posed but rigid enough to hold the pose while it is being photographed. Clay, rubber, urethane foam, and similar materials are often used for the external appearance of the displacement puppet, but these materials don't hold a pose very well under hot studio lights. That's why almost all displacement puppets have a metal skeleton, called an *armature*, that provides more rigid support. The design and construction of the armature is critical to the puppet's successful use, and there are many rules, guidelines, and trade secrets to building a good armature.

Displacement animation using LightWave is similar in many respects. The exterior appearance of many models, especially the organic shapes favored in character animation, is not readily animated. The geometric structure needed to form the surface details doesn't lend itself well to the deformations—bending, stretching, and swelling—necessary to character animation. Accordingly, LightWave includes a number of functions designed to replicate the effects of an armature.

The simplest form of armature is to string together separate objects, placing them in a linked, or *parented*, hierarchy. This is a lot like assembling a marionette or a bare armature because all the joints are exposed and very mechanical in action. If joints must have a realistic appearance, the objects must be modeled with mating surfaces, just like an armature's. Ball-and-socket, lap hinge, and other joint constructions are typical.

If a more organic armature is required, the most common approach is a *bones* setup. A LightWave bone is a method of distorting the shape of a model in a controlled fashion within a defined area. During setup, a series of bones is added to a model to form a skeleton. Some bones may actually be placed outside the model's surface, but in most cases, they are placed approximately where you would put a physical armature, through the middle of the body and limbs.

Each bone in a model's skeleton influences the points in its immediate area and can also be used to influence the rest of the model, kind of like a configurable magnet. Bones can also be used to control purely muscular distortion, such as tongues, tentacles, worms, and other invertebrate structures. This is a difficult job with even the best traditional armatures, and it's nearly impossible with other types of CGI hierarchy tools.

As you might have guessed, bone setups are powerful character animation tools, but it does take some extra effort to master their full range. Let's take a look at the more basic parent functions first.

Transformation

The most basic form of displacement animation is a collection of rigid models, joined together like the pieces of a traditional armature or puppet so they can rotate at the joints. LightWave has a Parent function that can duplicate this effect, enabling you to assemble complex puppetlike characters. You can animate these hierarchies of objects by posing or *transforming* them, rotating, moving, and scaling each object to change the character's appearance.

There are several advantages to transformation animation using parented hierarchies. You have very accurate control of the positioning and posing of each child object because there is no approximation or distortion as with replacement or bones. You can animate as much or as little as you need; each object's motions can be interactively tweaked at each frame or simply bracketed with a single keyframe at each end of the animation. Finally, there is no need to create extensive libraries of morph models.

The disadvantages are that parent hierarchies are limited by a rather mechanical joint appearance that needs to be disguised if used to animate organic models and that transformation animation takes longer than some other approaches. For example, using a parented hierarchy, the animator must pose the character for each key frame. Using replacement animation, the animator could much more quickly select from a sequence of prebuilt poses, which might have been constructed by a modeler or technical director (TD). When you choose a setup method, you are also choosing who does how much of the work.

A pure transformation hierarchy is an excellent setup for practicing animation. It is fast and simple to set up, the screen redraw is usually the fastest of any setup LightWave can handle, and it doesn't require model libraries or any other complicating elements. What you see in the scene is what you have to work with. To animate it, you simply select an object, transform it to the desired appearance, set a keyframe, and go on to the next object. This simplicity enables you to use the most basic (and easy-to-understand) LightWave features. Once you choose to animate with deformation or replacement techniques, you need to use more powerful (and therefore difficult-to-master) LightWave features.

Project 11.4 shows you how to set up a parented hierarchy based on the replacement animation desk lamp used in the preceding projects. This demonstrates the basics of parented hierarchy setup, with a relatively small number of objects, and it provides you with a setup you can animate in some of Chapter 14's timing projects. Parenting objects in LightWave is relatively simple. Parented hierarchies are the basis of all skeletal animation, so no matter how complex your setups eventually become, the basic techniques you'll learn in this project will still apply.

The desk lamp is a useful setup for a number of reasons. First, it's traditional, in a field that has few traditions because it's so young. *Luxo Jr.*, a short film directed by John Lasseter and produced at Pixar Animation Studios, stars a pair of animated swing-arm desk lamps. It was nominated for the 1986 Best Animated Short Film Oscar. Everybody in the industry is familiar with it, and it's one of the earliest examples of CGI animation with real character. It seems like everybody animates a desk lamp at some point, and it's a good training exercise. Second, Pixar chose the eponymous little lamp as a subject for very good technical reasons: The lamp model's geometry can remain rigid, so you don't have to use deformation tools to animate it. The hinge points are obvious from the lamp's structure, and your audience will expect it to move mechanically around those joints, so it's much easier to model and set up than a more organic character would be. Third, the visual simplicity of a desk lamp forces you to animate it well because there are no fancy textures or deformations to hide behind. If you can successfully complete the timing projects in Chapter 14 using this desk lamp setup, you will have thoroughly learned the essentials of timing. If you tried those same projects with a fully articulated humanoid character, you'd get so distracted by extraneous trivia that you'd miss the basic principles. Finally, the four simple objects that make up the desk lamp can be loaded and manipulated by even the slowest and most limited computers capable of running LightWave.

PROJECT 11.4 Setting Up the Desk Lamp with Parented Objects

To set up a parented hierarchy, follow these steps:

1. Load the four lamp objects—LampBase, LowStrut, HiStrut, and Shade—from this book's CD-ROM. The loaded objects should look something like Figure 11.12. Each object has a pivot point plus a marked center for attaching child objects:

   - *LampBase*—Bottom center of base, center of pivot cylinder

   - *LowStrut*—Center of space between bottom of struts, center of pivot cylinder

   - *HiStrut*—Same as LowStrut

   - *Shade*—Center of neck stub

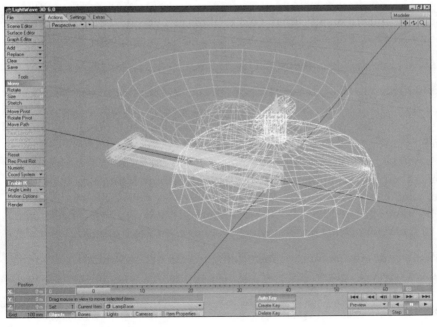

Figure 11.12
Desk lamp objects loaded and ready for parenting.

2. Select the first child object, LowStrut.

3. Open the Motion Options panel. Choose LampBase from the Parent Item drop-down list. Close the panel to accept LampBase as LowStrut's parent.

   Generally, you should parent an object from its default loading position and rotation before you move or rotate it. If you parent it afterward, LightWave will recalculate position and rotation changes from the new parent's origin, and the results will probably not be what you intended.

4. Move LowStrut up to align its pivot point with the center of the pivot cylinder part of LampBase. Set a keyframe at frame 0.

   This sets up LowStrut to follow LampBase's motions and to rotate around the center of the pivot cylinder. Try rotating LowStrut on the pitch axis, just to test. While you're at it, you might want to turn off Heading and Bank axes, just to avoid inadvertent changes.

5. Select HiStrut and parent it to LowStrut.

6. Move HiStrut so its pivot point aligns with the center of the pivot cylinder part of LowStrut. Set a keyframe for HiStrut at frame 0.

7. Select Shade and parent it to HiStrut.

8. Move Shade so its pivot point aligns with the center of the pivot cylinder part of HiStrut. Set a keyframe for Shade at frame 0. You should end up with something like Figure 11.13.

9. Pose the assembled lamp in a default position like Figure 11.14.

   The default position for any character setup should be the pose that is most common or natural for that character. The idea of a default pose is to save the animator time. Ideally, the animator should be able to load a scene, select the character, and immediately proceed to creating the first pose. For most characters, the pose in which you initially set up the hierarchy is not the best default pose. For example, if you left the desk lamp stretched out flat (as you parented it), an animator would have to transform it into a more natural pose before she could begin animating it. This wastes time every time she opens the original setup file. It's more efficient for you to take a few minutes now and create a default pose that will be useful (or at least not annoying) every time the file is opened.

10. Test the lamp's range of movement by transforming (rotating) LowStrut, HiStrut, and Shade in the pitch axis. In Chapter 14, you'll be animating this setup to create actions like those shown in Figure 11.15. Can your lamp setup be transformed to create each of these poses?

11. Save the scene file with a new name. You'll be using it in Chapter 14.

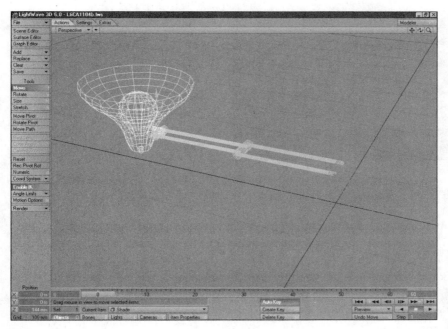

Figure 11.13
Desk lamp objects parented into hierarchy.

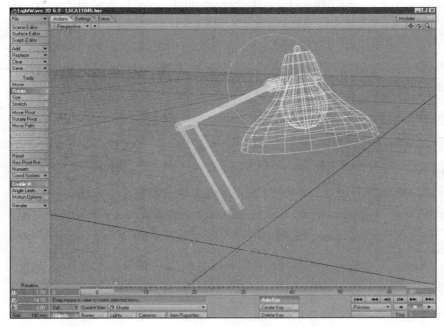

Figure 11.14
Desk lamp posed in default position.

Figure 11.15
Test poses for desk lamp.

Once you've set up a hierarchy, LightWave allows you to load the whole setup into any scene with the File|Load Items From Scene menu option. Being able to save and reload entire parent object hierarchies makes it much easier to reuse complex setups and actions. Once they're loaded, you can edit them just as when you first created them. Just as with replacement models, the longer you work with a setup, the more actions you will have available for reuse. Keep this in mind while you are working, and save as a separate scene any actions that you think you might be able to use again.

Using the Load Items From Scene function brings in the whole enchilada whether you wanted it or not (you can choose not to load lights). If you think you might want to load just part of an action, save a duplicate of the original setup and delete all the extraneous stuff. It'll save you time later on when you might really need it.

Project 11.5 shows you how to add eyeballs and eyelids to a head model using the parent functions you learned in the preceding project. In addition, this project introduces inverse kinematics (IK) and tracking functions that can help you automate eye movement. You'll be using the same procedures as you did for the lamp, with just a couple of new wrinkles. If you haven't already completed Project 11.4, I suggest you go back and do it now. The abbreviated directions in this (and following) projects may seem cryptic if you aren't completely familiar with the preceding projects.

Giving your character eyes opens up a whole new range of acting capabilities. Aside from emotional expressions and other intentional communication, the eyes can convey an extraordinary amount of unintentional or unconscious information. Any parent, teacher, or police officer can tell you how a miscreant's eyes move when they are lying. A loud noise, bright light, or rapid motion also produces an involuntary or unconscious reaction, which is usually readable in eye movement.

If you animate your character to mimic these natural motions, you'll be taking a big step toward convincing your audience. You'll also be able to use those motions to tell the audience what is going on, in a subtle and natural way, and so advance your story. This technique is especially important with animals or creatures that have little facial expression, so eye movement and body posture are about all you have to work with.

PROJECT 11.5 Setting Up the Head and Eyes with Parented Objects

To set up this character's head, you'll be loading four objects: the head, one eyeball (duplicated for left and right), and two eyelids:

1. Load objects Face, LEyelid, and REyelid from this book's CD-ROM. Load object Eyeball twice. Each object, as with the desk lamp, has an obvious or marked pivot point.

2. Following the same procedures you followed in Project 11.4, position and parent the eyeballs and eyelids within the Face object. Both the eyelids and eyeballs should be set up as direct children of the Face object. You may find it helpful to position the eyeballs first, in relation to the lower eyelids that are part of the Face object. The lower edge of each iris should just touch the eyelid, and the Eyeball objects should closely fit the inner curve of the lower eyelids. The upper eyelids should, in rest position, just touch the upper edge of the irises. Your results should look like Figure 11.16.

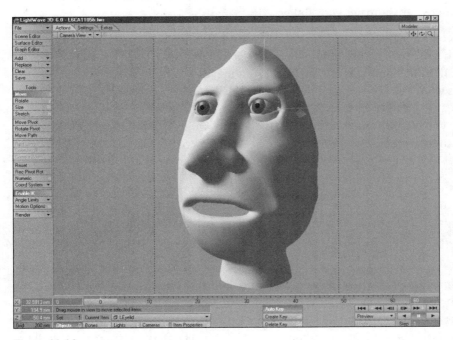

Figure 11.16
Scene with Face, Eyeball, LEyelid, and REyelid hierarchy set up.

3. Because the eyeballs and eyelids will be following the head, which is the parent, they don't need to move on their own. Turn off all three movement axes to lock down the position of the eyeballs and eyelids relative to the Face parent object.

4. The eyeballs need to pivot on both pitch and heading axes, but the eyelids need to pivot only on the pitch axis. Lock off rotation on the bank axis for both eyelids and eyeballs and also lock off heading rotation for the eyelids.

5. Save the scene.

6. Play with the eyeballs and eyelids, creating expressions and making the eyes track imaginary objects. Pay special attention to trying to synchronize the eyeballs so they appear to be looking at the same object.

If you do this for a while, you will quickly tire of repeatedly posing one eyeball, then matching the rotation for the other eye. Imagine trying to do this for a long shot, in which your character intently watches the erratic and convoluted flight of a mosquito!

The sensitivity of your audience to *sight lines*, the apparent direction of the eyeball, makes your job harder. We learn almost from birth to deduce exactly what someone is looking at by observing tiny variations in the angle of their eyes. Your least mistake in aligning the eyes can shatter your character's credibility.

Of course there is a better way to do this. LightWave has a function called *inverse kinematics (IK)*, which can make an object in a hierarchy point consistently and precisely at another object. IK is, in simplest terms, a tool for posing a hierarchy in reverse. Normal kinematics is what you do with a parented or boned hierarchy, for example an arm and hand: Rotate the shoulder, then rotate the elbow, then rotate the wrist, then rotate the fingers, until you get the fingertips to point at or touch what you want them to. This is tedious and counterproductive for most character animation.

Inverse kinematics, as the name implies, inverts this process. You drag the fingertip to point to or touch what you want it to, and the IK software figures out the appropriate angles for all the joints. "Magic!" you say, but of course there's a catch. For the arm, or any hierarchy with two or more joints, there are several possible poses that will put the fingertip in the same position. Think about it, and try this experiment: Touch your finger to the end of your nose, and see how much your arm can move while keeping your finger in place.

What sometimes happens when you're trying to use IK is that the hierarchy flops all over the place and you spend a lot of time confining it to a reasonable set of poses. LightWave [6] has a number of features that handle IK problems very well. IK is really useful in certain situations, and we'll be spending more time with it in other chapters. In this project, we'll be working with a very simple hierarchy having only one joint, so there will be only one IK solution for any pose and IK flail won't happen at all. The following steps show you how to use IK to keep both eyeball objects pointed at a single target.

There are some problems in LightWave with setting an object to track a target directly. The usual approach is to add a null object to the end of the hierarchy and set the null to track the target. This also gives you better control over how the rest of the hierarchy reacts to the target's movement:

7. Add a null and change its name to EyeNullLeft.

8. Parent EyeNullLeft to the left eyeball object.

9. Make sure the null is still selected. Position the null (represented by a three-axis crosshair) directly in front of the pupil of the left eyeball, as in Figure 11.17.

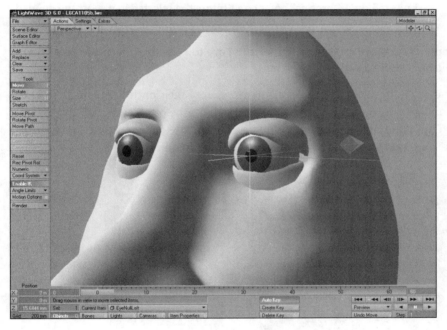

Figure 11.17
EyeNullLeft null positioned in front of left eyeball.

10. Create a keyframe for the null at frame 0. Save your work.

11. Repeat Steps 7 through 10 to add, parent, and position a null named EyeNullRight to the right eyeball.

12. Add a null named EyeTarget and position the null in front of the character's nose.

The next step will be to limit the IK effects on the head hierarchy. You want the eyes, not the entire head, to track the target.

13. Select the Face object. Click on the Motion Options button at the lower left of the Layout window. The Motion Options panel appears.

14. Click on the Unaffected By IK Descendants checkbox. This tells the head to ignore any IK effects from the parented nulls, eyelids, or eyeballs. It will only move according to its own key frame settings.

15. Select EyeNullLeft. In the Motion Options panel, click on the Full-time IK checkbox. This tells the IK routine to run constantly, updating the position of the affected objects whenever you make a change. In general, it's a good idea to use full-time IK whenever possible. You may eventually run into some complex situations when you won't want full-time IK, but for now, make it a habit to enable it.

    You also have the option to set rotation limits for the selected item for the Heading, Pitch, and Bank axes. These limits tell the IK process that it can't rotate the selected item past the defined angles and it will have to pass along any further rotation to another item in the IK hierarchy.

    Just for practice, let's set some rotation limits for the eye to keep this character from trying to look out the back of his head.

16. Select the left eyeball. In the Motion Options panel, choose the Controllers And Limits tab. Set the rotation limits as shown in Figure 11.18. Repeat for the other eyeball. These limits are just rough approximations. The limits you use will change depending on the shape of the character's face and the range of expression you need to animate.

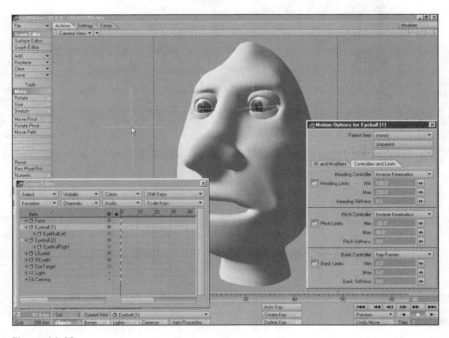

Figure 11.18
Eyeballs' rotation limited and targeted to follow null.

17. Both eyeballs are set to follow the EyeTarget null. To test the IK, select the EyeTarget null and move it around in all three axes. The eyeballs should rotate to look at the null, as in Figure 11.18.

18. Save the scene with a new name.

If all went well, you now have a head with eyes that are much easier to animate.

Alternate Eye Setups

Parented eyeballs and IK goals are my personal preference for animating eye movements, but there are other methods that are appropriate for different circumstances. For realistic animation, you should mimic the actual physiological structure of the creature's eyes as closely as possible. You can adapt the projects you just completed for most of these situations, and the projects in Chapter 9 show how you can apply maps to create photorealistic eyes from very simple models.

For cartoon or caricature animation, all bets are off. Extreme caricature animation will call for squashing, stretching, and generally distorting the eyes—demands that pretty much rule out the nice, neat Parent-and-IK approach. If you can get away with an iris and pupil that don't distort much, you can use a fixed *sclera*, or white, that is part of the head object, then simply animate the pupil and iris as a separate or parented object. You may even be able to use IK goals if the eyeball won't change its curvature much. If the eye will be distorting a lot, this approach can be more trouble than it's worth because precisely matching the iris to the surface of a distorted eyeball can be tedious and time-consuming.

One way to overcome the problems of a grossly distorted eyeball is to use an image or image sequence to map the iris and pupil. This is definitely not interactive, requiring about the same level of preplanning as lip sync.

If the eyes need a lot more flexibility—especially if you are trying to imitate the style of Tex Avery—I recommend that you treat them as you would any other object to be animated using replacement or displacement methods.

Replacement animation of eyes is very straightforward when you use the techniques you learned earlier in this chapter. For most normal actions, you can probably get along with a morph target library of a dozen or so eyes. If you build them properly, you should be able to use one set for both left and right eyes. Simply model the baseline eye with the iris and pupil in the middle of the sclera. Make sure the edges of the iris and pupil have enough vertices to avoid showing straight edges, even in close shots.

Save a duplicate of the eye. Select and move the vertices defining the iris and pupil so the iris's rim is tangent to one edge of the sclera. Save this as one of your morph targets. Repeat this for each target object, moving the iris and pupil to another point along the edge of the sclera. I recommend building the up, down, left, and right models first, then continuing to split the angles between targets until you are satisfied that you can animate a morph to any required eye position. Alternatively, you can set up an eye animation in advance using an object or morph sequence.

Project 11.6 builds on the experience you have accumulated in the preceding projects and provides a preview of the complexity of a full humanoid character. This character setup will require 15 separate objects, plus a few null or dummy placeholders, to build a complete Puppet. With this setup, you should be able to animate most human actions well enough for practice. Later setups will build on this one, adding details to the head and hands to increase this character's dramatic range.

The Puppet used in the following projects, and pictured in Figure 11.19, was originally modeled by Jim Pomeroy of Arlington, Texas, in December 1991 and released by him into the public domain. Thanks, Jim!

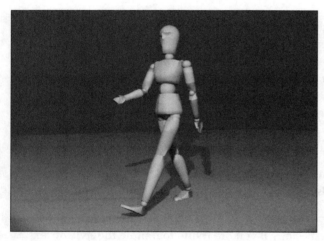

Figure 11.19
Puppet character.

I've made just a few modifications, mostly scaling the Puppet up to more average human dimensions and tweaking a few pivot placements. This Puppet is about as simple as you can get within the limits of human proportions and joint structure. It uses only 15 small objects and two nulls in a parented hierarchy and no bones or other deformation setups at all.

There are several reasons to use such a simple model:

- Screen redraw is a lot faster than if you had the same objects animated by bones. Redraw times with hierarchical characters can quickly get out of hand, especially when you are down to trial-and-error tweaking of fine detail. You will be more productive and learn more easily if you can minimize your waiting time.

- This Puppet can be loaded by just about any system that can run LightWave. The polygon count is very low, and the memory requirements are minimal. This also translates into faster redraws, less waiting, and more effective learning.

- There are fewer distractions in a simple character. If the Puppet had bandoleers, fighting knives, and Uzis dangling off a combat harness, you could spend all your time just animating the overlapping action of the bells and whistles. Keep it simple, and concentrate on the lesson at hand. When you've mastered the animation of a simple character, you can apply the same principles to a complex one—then spend extra time on the frills and gewgaws.

- This Puppet is also easier to keep track of than a more complex or boned object. The parented joints clearly show the physical limits of their rotations. The shin should obviously pitch no more than 110 degrees relative to the thigh, and so on. The necessary notes a TD might deliver with this character are relatively brief.

There are a few disadvantages to this Puppet. It has no fingers or toes, so subtler gestures or a more refined heel-and-toe stride aren't possible. The low polygon count and minimal structure mean that there is no provision for object-level squash-and-stretch deformation. Any squash or stretch must be animated by posing the joints. The Puppet also lacks some crucial joints for expressive characters because it has no independent shoulder joints and therefore can't even shrug without literally coming apart at the seams.

This project is good practice for another reason. This Puppet is a grossly simplified form of a humanoid character but still requires extended attention to detail to set up and animate. You should think of this as practice in stretching your attention span. One of the most important assets for an animator is an extremely long attention span and the willingness to follow through a long sequence of painstakingly detailed work. This Puppet isn't all that hard to set up, but it will prepare you for more advanced setups ahead in Chapters 12 and 13.

PROJECT 11.6 Setting Up the Puppet with Parented Objects

To set up the Puppet with parented objects, follow these steps:

1. Load objects Chest, Head, Hips, Lfoot, Lhand, Llowarm, Lshin, Lthigh, Luparm, Rfoot, Rhand, Rlowarm, Rshin, Rthigh, and Ruparm from this book's CD-ROM. Most of the objects have obvious centers of rotation and child attachment.

2. Using the techniques you learned in Project 11.5, arrange the objects in a parented hierarchy. If you have trouble, refer to Figure 11.19 for an example of how the Puppet should be assembled. In the Motion Options panel, set rotational limits for all objects according to the following notes.

   These character notes are intended to help you pose the Puppet in simple walk and run cycles. The recommendations for joint constraints and usage may not be appropriate for animating other actions. All surfaces are set to a default material. This is a simple parented hierarchy of objects. There are no bones, morph, or other deformation setups. The letters preceding each note refer to the object's place in the animation hierarchy. You may also want to consider using these letters as a load order to make it easier to locate objects in LightWave's drop-down object selection menus.

a *Puppet_Ground_Null*—This null controls the position of the character in the x,z plane. This null and the Puppet_CG_Null are the root level of the animation hierarchy and should be roughed out first for almost any action. You should always position the Puppet_Ground_Null at ground level, and on uneven terrain, you should position it at the height of the grounded foot or other grounded body part. This null is separate from the Puppet_CG_Null, so you can animate the vertical and horizontal components of the character's movement on different keyframes. You should not rotate or scale this object. You may find it helpful to think of the Puppet_Ground_Null as a support rod for the Puppet and the Puppet_CG_Null as a clamp that can only travel up and down the rod.

a *Puppet_CG_Null*—This null controls the y-position and 3-axis rotation of the character as a whole. It is located at the approximate center of gravity (CG) of an equivalent real-life human. This null and the Puppet_Ground_Null are the root, or first, level of the anima-tion hierarchy. You can animate this null in the y-axis to keep the contact foot (or other contact body part) on the ground and rotate it on the appropriate axes for free-fall tum-bling. If you need to rotate the character while it is in contact with the ground, rotate the Hips object.

b *Hips*—This object includes the lower abdomen, the ball joint that forms the pivot for the Chest object, and the ball joints of the two Thigh pivots. This is the parent object of the character's body. It is the second level of the animation hierarchy, and you should ani-mate it immediately after the CG and Ground nulls for almost any action. The pivot point is located at the center of gravity. You can rotate this object a few degrees on the bank and heading axes to enhance leg motions, but anything more than that will look really strange unless accompanied by a balancing movement of the rest of the character.

c *Chest*—This object includes the rib cage, the ball joint for the Head object, and the two ball joints for the UpArm objects. This is the third level of the animation hierarchy and the parent for the upper half of the body. You should animate the Chest's action completely and to your satisfaction before beginning on the head or arms. You can animate the Chest to pitch nearly 60 degrees, as for a deep bow, and bank 40 or so. You should not animate heading more than 30 degrees without some complementary action of the Hips.

d *Head*—This object is part of the fourth level of the animation hierarchy. Generally, you can animate the rotation of the Head with the inverse values (-3.4=3.4 and so on) of the same axes of rotation of the Chest, simply to keep the Head level and pointed in the original direction. Because the Head tends to follow the eyes, in more complex actions, the Head is a good candidate for IK and tracking setups, as explained earlier in this chapter and in Chapter 12.

d *LUpArm, RUpArm*—The upper arms are also parts of the fourth level. You can animate these objects' headings with the inverse heading value of the Chest to keep the arms pointing in the right direction. You should keep pitch values between -160 and 70 and bank values between -30 and 135 degrees.

d *LThigh, RThigh*—The thighs are also parts of the fourth level. You can animate these objects' headings with the inverse heading and bank values of the Hips to keep the legs pointing in the right direction. You should keep pitch values between -120 and 45 and bank values between -20 and 45 degrees, unless you are animating a gymnast.

e *LLowArm, RLowArm*—The fifth level of the animation hierarchy includes the lower arms and lower legs. These joints are simple hinges, and you should animate them only in the pitch axis. You should animate other rotations using the hand or upper-arm objects. The lower-arm objects can pitch between 0 and -120 degrees relative to the upper-arm objects.

e *LShin, RShin*—You should animate the shins between 0 and 110 on the pitch axis, relative to the thigh objects. Animate the feet or thigh objects for other rotations.

f *LHand, RHand*—For these projects, you only need to animate the hands through small angles on the pitch axis as overlapping action to the swing of the arms. The hands are set to 15 degrees bank rotation to give them a more natural line with the rest of the body. The pitch limits are -60 to 60, but 5 to 10 degrees are enough for the overlapping action. The fingers and toes for this character are not articulated, so the hands and feet represent the sixth and last level of the animation hierarchy.

f *LFoot, RFoot*—You can reasonably animate the feet from -45 to 70 degrees on the pitch axis, but much shallower angles are sufficient for these projects. You should not use the other two axes of rotation unless they are necessary to match the feet to odd terrain angles. Keyframing the foot rotations should be your next-to-last step in posing the hierarchy; any change in higher layers will change the alignment to the ground. Generally, you should align the feet by eye with the ground surface and keyframe them as often as necessary to keep them from penetrating or floating over the ground. Keyframes for a foot that is not in contact with the ground can be spaced as for overlapping action, similar to the pitch animation of the hands.

When you've finished parenting, limiting, and testing the Puppet setup, you should write up any additional notes pertinent to your final LightWave scene. You'll be using the Puppet extensively in Chapters 14 and 15, and your notes will come in handy.

Deformation

Deformation is a subset of displacement animation; it is based on displacement-style skeletal joints but associated with the deformable geometry of a model. This combination can enable you to animate a seamless mesh using setups similar to those you built for the swing-arm desk lamp and the Puppet. This gives you the smooth characters of replacement animation with the fine interactive control of displacement.

Most CGI character animation today is done with some form of displacement deformation setup. You need to understand how to set up deformations, if only to remain competitive in the industry. You will also find that deformations broaden the range of styles you can use and stories you can tell, enabling you to set up and animate anything from extremely abstract caricatures to photorealistic digital stuntmen.

There are as many approaches to deformation as there are software packages that support it. Each program handles deformation setup in a slightly different way. However, there are two general approaches that can serve to categorize the available tools: parametric and bones.

Parametric deformation is usually based on placing a cage of control points around the model to be deformed, then animating the cage's controls. The software interpolates the cage's deformation in applying it to the model. This approach is only loosely connected to the original model and can be quickly revised without damaging the rest of the setup. However, parametric deformation does not provide as detailed a level of control as bones. Parametric deformation is generally most useful for squash-and-stretch and similar overall distortions, when a character (or part of one) appears to deform under outside influences. Parametric deformation can be used to create muscular or skeletal deformation, but it's not well suited to the task.

Bones deformation is based on inserting and binding a skeleton of control handles to the character's geometry. Bones deformation can be easy or extremely difficult to set up, depending on what you want the bones to do. The end result, when it works, is that you can animate the deformation of the model by animating the bones as if they were a traditional puppet armature and the mesh an overlay of foam rubber. Bones enable you to create a more precise setup, which the animator can use to interactively tweak even the lift of an eyebrow or angle of a fingertip. The disadvantage is that the closer binding and control of a bones setup makes it that much more difficult to revise or adapt to changes in the model. In some setups, reconnecting a bones skeleton to a revised mesh is so complex that it's more efficient to start over. More about this issue is discussed in Chapter 12. For now, the next few projects in this chapter will show you the basics of deformation setups.

A traditional puppet can have visible rotating joints like those you emulated in the Puppet setup. It can also have a flexible outer covering over a jointed *armature*, or inner skeleton, allowing the puppet's skin to deform without visible seams. LightWave's bones functions can duplicate this effect, enabling you to assemble complex characters that simulate the appearance of bone, flesh, and skin.

Bones can be placed individually or in hierarchies and can be used to deform a single joint or provide a flexible armature for an entire creature. Bones are a very powerful tool and especially useful for the major skeletal joints. Also, the complete model, bones, and motions can be loaded from a previously saved scene, just as with a parented object hierarchy.

Probably the most popular use of bones is in the animation of skeletal joints, but bones can also be used to animate loose flesh or slack muscle, which is especially useful for overlapping action (see Chapter 14). You can adjust the handling of geometry shared between two or more bones to emulate the flabbier behavior of less muscular tissues. For especially loose masses, you can borrow motion files from the character's CG, delay it a few frames, and apply it to the "flabby" bones to create a first approximation of overlapping action.

Designing for boned animation is one of the easier modeling tasks. Bones are relatively tolerant of your modeling procedures, and they don't care much in what order you created the points they will be pushing around. Your biggest challenge in modeling for bones will be planning a model that the bones won't warp into garbage and that can reach the range of motions the animator needs without using umpteen-zillion bones to do it. As mentioned in Chapters 5 and 6, the more polygons around a boned joint, the smoother the deformation will appear. If you don't have enough polygons in the area, you may end up with sharp corners where you don't want them.

Designing for a joint's range of motion is a matter of balancing the overlapping influence of the adjoining bones so the result looks plausible. Note that I did not say "realistic," just "plausible." Bones are useful and powerful tools, but I don't know anybody patient enough to animate the number of controls you'd need to realistically emulate each and every perceptible muscle in the human body. If you want photorealism, you are going to have to master the most complex constraint and expression setups described in the next two chapters.

Your primary concerns for bone setup are to make sure the model has enough points in the affected areas and to make sure the bones have the optimum position and settings for the deformation required. You also need to run a few basic tests and document the results to hand over to the animator.

Project 11.7 will show you how to set up bones to distort muscular masses that in reality wouldn't have a skeleton. This technique can be applied to facial animation, squash-and-stretch, and almost any situation where a character must deform in a precisely controllable manner. This project is deliberately set up to be the simplest possible example of bones deformation, but the principles shown here apply just as well to a fully articulated humanoid setup. It's just more of the same, like setting up the Puppet after setting up the desk lamp.

Setting Up the Ball for "Shmoo" Deformation

The goal of this project is to deform a sphere into an animatable approximation of one of Al Capp's Shmoos. If you're not a *Li'l Abner* fan, think of Flubber.

The idea is to have a sphere that can deform enough to show a little self-motivation, if not personality.

To set up a ball for deformation, follow these steps:

1. Open a new scene. Create a sphere.

2. Add a single bone to the sphere, starting at the sphere's center and extending upward about two-thirds of the way to the sphere's top. If you don't know how to add a bone, you need to review pages 4.15 through 4.19 of the *LightWave [6] Motion: Animate & Render* manual.

3. Add a second bone as child of the first bone, extending upward just past the top of the sphere. You should end up with something like Figure 11.20.

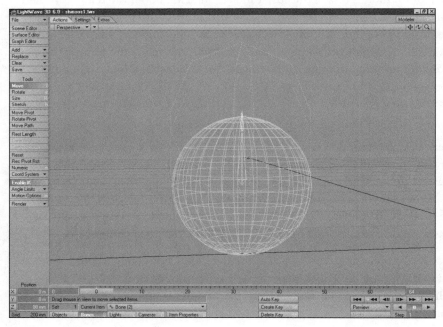

Figure 11.20
Sphere with two bones as set up.

4. Modify the influence of the bones to affect only the upper hemisphere. You want a combination of influences that produces results like Figure 11.21.

You should experiment with the bone settings, pushing the limits and finding out how LightWave handles bone interactions. This is probably the simplest bone setup you'll ever work with, so make your mistakes now!

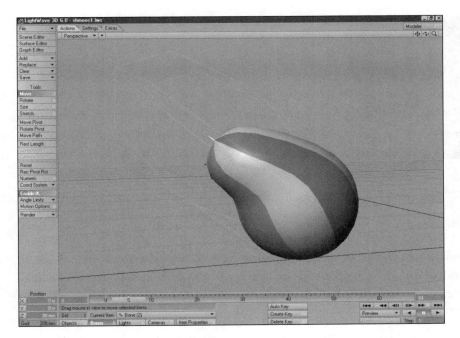

Figure 11.21
Sphere with two bones in action.

![Project 11.8] Give 'Em a Hand!

Here's a more challenging project in applying bones to a model. It's the classic cartoon character glove, with three fingers for easier animating and the high style of three stitched lines on the back and a rolled cuff. You're pretty much on your own with this one. If you worked through the Shmoo project, I think you can handle it:

1. Open a new scene. Load the LGlove model from the Chapter 11 directory on this book's CD-ROM.

2. Add, position, and set the parameters for the bones required to pose the hand. Give it three knuckles for each finger. You might refer to Figure 11.22 for an idea or two about bone placement.

    One special concern is the opposable thumb's transverse bulge. This is a real pain to animate properly. If you want to experiment with any kind of "muscle bulge" feature, this is a good place to try it out.

3. When you are satisfied with the setup of the boned hand, save the setup for use later in this chapter. In the following section on hybrid animation, you'll be adding the articulated hand to the Puppet setup.

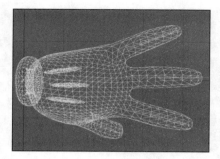

Figure 11.22
Cartoon glove with bone setup.

In LightWave, you can save a posed deformation as a new model by choosing the Save Trans-formed function from the Save menu. You can use this function to start building a library of hand poses for morph and morph sequence animation. Most of Preston Blair's books have a wonderful page full of cartoon hand poses. Brian Lemay's textbooks go into even more detail. You can make right hand duplicates of all the left hand models by making a copy, then scaling it by -1 on the x-axis.

If you get an idea for a more efficient or powerful setup, by all means try it. It's good experi-ence to solve problems in as many different ways as you can. Each solution has its advantages and disadvantages. One of your strongest assets as an animator or setup person is your ability to solve problems quickly, efficiently, and reliably. The more practice you have, the more valu-able you'll be and the better position you'll be in for negotiating a raise, promotion, or the next creative opportunity.

Hybrid Animation

Hybrid puppet animation is, as you might expect, a combination of displacement and replace-ment techniques. Most puppet animation now being done in professional studios is a mixture of techniques. As in any business with deadlines and budgets, it's whatever gets the job done.

Generally, the gross skeletal animation is best handled with a displacement armature. In ani-mation software terms, that means either parent (if joints can show) or bones (if it has to look seamless). There are a few special circumstances—long repetitive sequences, perhaps—where replacement techniques can be used for the whole-body motions, but generally this is done with displacement.

Replacement pieces really shine when there is fussy, detailed yet repetitive animation to be done. Lip sync is a prime candidate—if a character needs to speak, it's a lot easier to swap head or face parts from a library of phonemes than it is to pose the 20 or more deformation controls necessary to shape a decent-looking mouth. Sometimes, hands are also animated with replacement model parts, because they are smaller than the rest of the armature and the fine wire of their skeleton tends to break more often.

The usual technique, then, is to build displacement armatures with pegs or keys at the extremities, the neck, the wrists, and so on, to which the replacement bits are readily attached and removed. A wonderful example of this technique is *The Nightmare Before Christmas*. The protagonist, Jack Skellington, had approximately 180 replacement heads, covering every permutation of lip sync and emotional expression. His displacement armature, by comparison, had about 18 joints (not including the hands, which used flexible wire rather than machined joints).

Hybrid replacement/displacement animation has its advantages. As with straight replacement, it gives faster layout of fine detail in sequences. As with bones and parent hierarchies, you can reuse poses and action sequences. Consistent use over time will build a growing range of retrievable poses. Because only part of the character must be modeled for replacement animation, there can be far fewer total models to make and track, plus more flexibility in whole-figure posability using bones and parenting.

Of course, hybrid replacement/displacement animation has its disadvantages. Changes in replacement head and hand poses must be created and managed as separate models or morph targets. This requires tracking and storage of a larger number of models than would a pure displacement method.

PROJECT 11.9 Setting Up the Puppet with Deformation Hands

The goal of this project is to set up a hybrid animation figure with a displacement body and deformation hands. Basically, you'll be using the Puppet you set up in Project 11.6 and substituting posable hands for the rigid mittens of the original setup:

1. Reload the Puppet setup, and save it under a new file name.

2. Use the File|Load Items From Scene function to merge the Cartoon Glove setup from Project 11.8 into the Puppet scene.

3. Replace Lhand (and Rhand, if you created a matching glove setup) in the Puppet hierarchy with the root of the Cartoon Glove setup.

4. Save the new setup; you'll be using it in Chapter 15.

You can also substitute other hand setups, or even a morph sequence. As I said before, it's good experience to solve problems in as many different ways as you can.

Default Setups

Whether you are making an entire animated film yourself or just doing setup work for a team of animators, you should try to make the animator's job as easy as possible. One of the ways you can save the animator a lot of time and effort is to set up default scenes for each character. This is especially important on long projects with lots of shots and group projects with more than one animator handling the same characters. It's a good way of keeping to standards and preventing conflicts. This section shows you how to set up a basic default scene for a complete character.

A default scene contains a character with all its associated textures, bones, hierarchies, plugins, morph libraries, and view lights set up and ready to animate. A good rule of thumb for including items in a default scene is: If the animator has to set it up before she can start animating the character, then include it. If not, you can let it slide unless the animator specifically asks for it.

Unless the animator tells you otherwise, pose the character in a typical default posture. Although there are technical advantages for setting up using the jesus, leonardo, or spread-eagled-on-the-ground positions, the animator shouldn't have to stand the character up every time they reload the scene. Also, for dramatic reasons, a character's hands are usually carried at or above waist level, so it saves time for the animator if you pose your characters' arms this way by default (see Figure 11.23). You should do all this in the default scene.

Figure 11.23
Default pose, minimizing startup work for the animator.

Animators can work faster and more efficiently if they can get a clear picture of the part of the character they are posing without having to tweak a view every time. LightWave enables you to set up extra cameras or inactive lights to enable the animator to quickly switch between close-up views of parts of the character. Because LightWave enables you to use each light as a view, you can simply add a set of inactive lights, assigned to the various bones or models that require close-up views, so the animator can change views by changing lights. You can add as many lights as you need, and once they are set, you never have to tweak them. Also, anytime you use Load Items From Scene to import the character, you can import all the View Lights at the same time.

Setting up these View Lights for a parented or boned hierarchy is no problem, you just parent the View Lights to the appropriate models or bones. You should have at least one View Light covering each area the animator will need to see in detail. Generally, anywhere there are a lot of active bones or an especially tricky piece of a hierarchy, you'll want to set a View Light. A typical character might need face front, right face, left face, left hand, right hand, left foot, right foot, and perhaps full-body front and full-body side View Lights.

Set View Lights for black and 0%Light Intensity, and turn off the following checkboxes: Lens Flare, Volumetric Lighting, Affect Diffuse, Affect Specular, Affect OpenGL, Affect Caustics, Shadow Type. Remember to give them appropriate names that you can recognize quickly in the Lights selection list.

Keep in mind that lights are displayed in selection lists in the order they are added to the scene. Unless you want to spend a lot of time manually rearranging the scene list, you should use Load Items From Scene to add the character before any other lights are added so the View Lights are at the top of the selection menu and are easiest to find. If you work with OpenGL, you should leave the most important active lights at the top of the list. OpenGL uses the top lights in the scene's list, so you don't want all the eligible slots filled by inactive View Lights. Once you start setting active lights for the character (see Chapter 17), you should put the first key light at the top of the list. All these considerations mean you should carefully plan your View Lights before you start building the scene.

If It Slows You Down, Throw It Out

Another important rule for setups is: Exclude anything that slows down the animator. If images, shaders, complex lighting setups, and highly detailed objects are included, they'll slow the animator down. If they're not important to creating the animation, hold them out until after the animation is complete and add them just before the final rendering. Try to minimize bones or other deformation setups that slow down screen refresh. Fast feedback for the animator is more important than making pretty pictures, especially during the first rough-out of an action.

The simplest object hierarchy character setups are the LightWave equivalent of drawing stick figures. They may not look like much compared to a finished rendering of a boned and deformed model, but they're a quick-and-dirty way of testing poses and actions, and they're easy enough to make that you can afford to throw them out and experiment more.

Chapter 12 describes setups that enable the animator to work with a bare-bones skeleton to animate, and then link a complex model to the skeleton after the animation is complete. You should definitely try out this approach. It can make an enormous difference in the quality of the finished animation because it provides more practice and experimenting time during the entire length of the project.

Creating a Default Scene

To create a default scene, follow these steps:

1. Load the last Puppet setup you created, complete with deformation hands.

2. Add preset views for detailed areas of the setup, as shown in Figure 11.24. Use lights, cameras, or viewport presets.

Figure 11.24
Character sheet showing default preset views.

3. Pose the character in the default pose shown earlier in Figure 11.23.

4. Save the setup with a new file name.

This default scene will make it much easier to use this character in the projects in Chapters 14 and 15. You just have one thing left to do—document the setup.

Write It Up

If you're working with other animators or it's a long project, you should document the character's default scene, including the view and name of each light. At minimum, you can make a model sheet by assembling a screenshot from each preset view, as in Figure 11.24, and handwrite your notes around the images. Include this with the modeler's notes and any other documentation for the character. This documentation makes it faster and easier for other animators to understand your setup, and it's a good memory-jogger for you, too. If there are any special quirks in the setup, like extra controls or odd hierarchies, write that up, too. The career you save may be your own!

PROJECT 11.11 Documenting the Default Scene

Write up the lights, positions, and views for the default scene you just set up. Include notes on joint ranges, bones, deformation controls, and morph target libraries or EndoMorphs. You should write down anything that isn't obvious from just looking at the setup. When in doubt, write it up. Others may not think something is obvious, whereas you've been staring at it so long it's engraved on your retina.

You should now be able to set up and document a default character scene that is faster and easier for an animator to use. Many of these setup tips apply to sets as well, especially complex ones with moving parts or lots of materials.

Moving On

If you've completed each project in this chapter, you have set up the necessary default scenes for the animation projects in Chapter 14. You can either jump ahead to Chapter 14 for some animation practice or continue learning about setups by going to Chapter 12.

Advanced Setups with Constraints

A humanoid character is too complex to efficiently animate by manually keyframing every control. This chapter shows how to link controls to one another using constraints. A constraint setup enables the animator to use a small fraction of the total controls to pose the character faster, more intuitively, and with more consistent results.

In the early days of computer graphics, objects could be moved or rotated only by themselves, without any reference to other objects. If, for example, you wanted to lift a character's hand, you would have to move the hand to where you wanted it to go, translate and rotate the forearm until the wrist connected with the hand, rotate the upper arm until the elbow connected with the forearm, somehow try to keep the torso attached to the shoulder, and so on.

Then, hierarchies were developed. When an object is in a hierarchy, it picks up the sum of all transformations (rotation, scale, and translation) that have occurred to its parent, the parent of its parent, and so on. This was a great improvement. But then you'd rotate and translate the hips (and maybe scale them) and do the same up the line to rotate the shoulder, the upper arm, the elbow, and then the hand. If you wanted the hand to be in a particular place, you would have to keep in mind that all the other transformations came before it. This is called forward kinematics, or FK.

Inverse kinematics changed that to a certain extent. Like nearly everything in computer graphics, inverse kinematics was developed for another purpose, and that purpose was almost always related to engineering. Whenever possible, NASA preferred to simulate things on a computer before actually trying to do something in space. If NASA had a crane arm on the Space Shuttle and wanted to pluck a satellite out of its orbit and put it in the cargo bay, imagine trying to rotate the joints on that crane arm this way and that until finally it connected with the satellite. What was needed was a way to tell the crane arm to go precisely to the point in space where the satellite was, and backward-calculate the joint rotations to get the end of the crane to the satellite. This backward calculation was called inverse kinematics (often abbreviated to IK), a catchy name that has stuck ever since. Of course, IK has other implications as well, for engineering in all fields. It isn't a big stretch to actually use IK for measuring torque or simulating how the suspension of a car works.

In many ways, our human musculoskeletal system resembles a very complex machine. IK is a pretty handy way of representing some of the goal-based movements that humans and other creatures (including those only in our imagination) might be inclined to perform. But for both forward and inverse kinematics, it's obvious that—where apparent solid objects are concerned—particularly those that are going to be manifested in physical objects in the real world—limits on movement must be placed on joints to reflect the realistic movements of real-world objects and their limitations. These limits on rotation and translation were the first and simplest type of constraints.

Constraints

Constraints are pretty easy to demonstrate on one's own body. Bend an arm at the elbow, and at some point, it simply can't rotate anymore. The skin stops it, or the muscle, or an actual limitation on the design of the joint itself. In the Space Shuttle example discussed earlier, the crane arm is moving relative to the Shuttle itself. Presumably, the travel of the Shuttle would be precisely matched to that of the satellite, so it's just a matter of reaching out and grabbing the satellite. But this example is simply too limited to represent the movement of everything. You can demonstrate how inadequate this representation is by placing your hand firmly on a desk or table and moving your body toward the desk or away from it. Your hand stays on the desk and, for the most part, doesn't rotate, and the chain of your arm from your wrist to your shoulder rotates to accommodate it. We'll start with the hands instead of the feet because it's easier for a person to look at an arm on his own body and analyze the movement than the legs.

If you've been following along, your hand is now in a space related to the desk, and it's relatively unaffected by the overall contortions of the rest of the body. Moreover, as the body is moved, watch your elbow. The bends at the elbow and shoulder are constantly being evaluated and recalculated. In this case, the position of the hand is constrained to the desk, as is the orientation of the hand. (Although it could be said that the rotation of the hand is being constrained, and in a world that always yielded to dictionary definitions it would be true, the term "orientation" is used because "rotation" was already co-opted to define the local rotational limits of objects.) A way was needed to represent this relationship of the desk to the hand. Various schemes that would act like nailing the hand to the desk were initially devised to handle the problem. But this specific solution doesn't address the problem of sliding the hand across the desk or any of the more general problems encountered by extremities.

But suppose the hand could be fastened to an object outside the body's hierarchy and that object could be placed on the unmoving desk. The hand would stay attached to the object, yet it could be moved along the desk without interpenetrating, and the body could contort in all sorts of ways, yet it would still appear that the hand was on the desk. The object that the hand is attached to would be positionally and orientationally constraining the movement of the hand. It would be, in effect, a remote control for the hand. This object, which is usually a null object or a bone, is referred to as a constraint (regardless of the other definitions and uses of the term "constraint"). A constraint object can be placed in its own hierarchy and can itself be constrained to other objects, including other constraints. When I refer to "a constraint" or "the constraint" in this chapter, it will be a reference to a constraint object unless further described as a positional constraint or orientation constraint.

What You Should Already Know

The official LightWave [6] manuals contain a lot of information and several tutorials on basic character setups, including IK and constraints. Before proceeding through this chapter, you should already have read and worked through the tutorials in pages 4.51 to 4.75 and 4.78 to 4.81 of the *Introduction and Tutorials* manual and pages 2.9, 3.27 to 3.41, 4.15 to 4.30, and 5.1 to 5.12 of the *Motion: Animate & Render* manual.

No Floating

One of the signatures of the motion of marionettes is the way they float. Everything overshoots a little bit or a lot, with nothing changing its rate of acceleration or deceleration abruptly unless it hits an obstacle. This look might be fine if you're animating Diver Dan, but it identifies the work of a beginner in computer graphics. Avoiding the floaty, underwater ballet look requires experience and understanding of timing for animation. The long learning curve will be painfully steep if your character setups do not allow you both to apply your timing and to readily revise it.

You could see this in so many early computer graphics films. Struggling with tools made for anybody but an animator, the aspiring filmmaker would pose the character and drop keys on every joint at once. Then he'd drop a key on the next pose 8, 12, 16, 24 frames later, and then the computer would "do all the poses between for free!" Characters that were supposed to be walking would be peddling invisible bicycles instead, while their feet rotated through the ground with even unbroken timing, every part of the body moving to the next pose at the same unvarying tempo.

Characters were hard to pose in the first place, particularly if the animator used only the least common denominator of FK. Sure, starting with the hips and working out to extremities was fine for the first pose, but what about the next one? Think of all the poses you could have generated if you hadn't spent most of your time doing back flips just to make sure nothing moved when you altered the position of the parent of a foot or a hand. Even when an animator stuck to a careful plan and structured the animation from the torso on out (getting a sign-off at every step), it would be costly to incorporate new inspiration in the middle of a scene. If the animation needed revision, it needed redoing. Too often, a director, grateful that the feet touched the ground at all, approved scenes in which the torso just floated through weightlessly.

At least it moved, so animation it must be!

Some who noticed it wasn't looking very good tried the motion capture end-run around animation. Worse yet, it became conventional wisdom that you couldn't learn how to animate using a computer, so big studios started giving shots only to animators who had proven chops with pencils or stop motion. In some shops, animators worked out the entire scene in pencil, reducing the job of computer animator nearly to one of data entry. Pencil animation is costly, especially when reduced to preproduction for computer animation.

Some of the higher-end packages allowed for the efficient incorporation of constraints to drive IK skeletons. IK had been an improvement over FK, but it still required one to drop a key on every joint in the skeleton at the same time. IK by itself did not make it much easier to avoid floatiness for the simple reason that it still required special effort to layer events with uneven timing. I might be moving my head at one rate, my hand at another, and be doing something entirely different with the rest of my body, such as pushing away from the desk on a rolling chair. To suggest something as simple as weight involves moving the center of mass of the body faster on the way down than on the way up, and at the right time. Delay that up and down motion of the hips a frame or two in a simple revision that leaves the rest of the action untouched. You'll have given your character more weight, and you'll have used constraints to solve your float problem.

Constraints allow you to position something when and where you want it, in isolation from what the rest of the body is doing. If feet are constrained to a position on the floor, it is far easier to animate the appearance of weight shifting from one leg to the other merely by moving the hips. If I move my hand to my chin, I think only about what my hand is doing and where my chin is. I shouldn't have to work much harder in an animation package. I'll check on what my elbow is doing later, in a refinement pass, especially when I only need to deal with a small set of handles that allow me to finesse that hand motion clearly and intuitively.

You will never learn why and when to do this for LightWave character animation if it is prohibitively difficult to animate and revise your work to competitive standards. Wouldn't you rather learn from your mistakes in time to apply that hard-won knowledge to your scene? If you can't afford to change something that looks wrong, you'll have to pay the price of signing your name to it anyway. If the work you've done so far has kept you from working in places where properly crafted setups are created for you, then you'll have to learn how to do it for yourself. It's among the best investments you can make in yourself, and in your craft.

Setup Pathologies

by Steph Greenberg (**stephg@pobox.com**)

These are the top 15 pathologies that I find in character setups. If you can diagnose and repair these pathologies as early as possible in the animation process, you'll save a lot of time and effort (not to mention frustration) for everyone:

1. Feet sliding when at least one foot should be planted firmly on the floor.

2. Inability to point knees in a particular direction and keep them pointed in that direction, regardless of what the lower torso or feet are doing. The direction of the knee is part of the physical motion that not only defines a character but can also indicate the physical load being borne by that character.

3. Constantly having to correct the rotation of the feet to keep them pointed in a chosen direction. This is an indication of improperly isolating the foot at the ankle joint from the rest of the leg hierarchy.

4. Inability to point elbows in a particular direction and keep them pointed in that direction without frequent correction and additional keyframes. Correcting this pathology accommodates arm snap and successive breaking of joints.

5. Inability to isolate the position of hands for a chosen animated arc, independent of the rotation or movement of the torso.

6. Inability to isolate the rotation of the hands for a chosen gesture from the rotation of the torso, forearm, and elbow.

7. The necessity of reposing the entire torso hierarchy to change the tilt of the pelvis between poses and during secondary animation. All that should be needed is the adjustment of a bone/joint's channels.

8. Lack of head isolation, creating the necessity of altering the head rotation to compensate for additional or secondary animation (particularly rotation of the upper torso) between main poses just to keep the head rotation arcs the way they were intended.

9. Failure to create a collarbone for use when the arm is raised beyond the point where the humerus (the bone that goes from the shoulder to the elbow) is parallel to the ground plane.

10. Failure to create a skin/bone relationship that allows the shoulders to appear natural when a character does the following:

    - Scratches its own back without aid of optional tools or instruments
    - Reaches across its chest to hold the other arm's shoulder in pain and massage it
    - Reaches up for the top shelf in the pantry
    - Reaches down to tie its shoes
    - Reaches behind to scratch its own butt

11. Failure to build in a character's ability to place a hand on a desk and keep the hand planted or slide it across simply even when the body is involved in other contortions.

(continued)

(continued)

12. Failure to account for the meat inside of the skin and plan some way for it to move independently of the torso.

13. Failure to provide a way for a character to stand on its toes and keep the ball of the foot planted without constant re-keyframing of the in-betweens on the foot.

14. Failure to create a mechanism to lift the toe and keep the heel and ball of the foot planted.

15. Failure of a way to animate the upper torso completely independently of the leg mechanisms other than reaching the stretch limits of the bones.

Diagnosing setup pathologies, along with prescribed remedies, is something gained through logical deduction, gut instinct, and experience. The setups described in this chapter can be deployed to solve many of these problems in different situations and can be combined with solutions described in other chapters, even adapted across different software platforms within the allowances of the software features.

It is often helpful to write down the problem, describing it in as much detail as is possible, because in defining a problem the solution can often be found. Sometimes it helps to have some Erector Set pieces to screw together and make a primitive physical model to analyze. Popsicle sticks, Legos, cardboard, and those thick straws from fast food restaurants can help too.

People who can create complex setups and solve their pathologies are in demand, and it's worth the investment in time to learn how to look at setups as a challenge both to your creativity and to your problem-solving skills.

Positional Constraints

A positional constraint constrains the position in space of another object. This is an important building block for the more complex setups later in this chapter.

LightWave has several options for positional constraints. In the Motion Options panel, you can apply the LW_Follower modifier (Figure 12.1). This modifier enables you to make any item follow any other item in position, rotation, or scale and within or outside the constrained object's hierarchy.

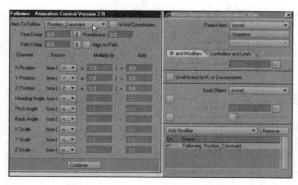

Figure 12.1
LW_Follower modifier applied in the Motion Options panel.

A second option is to apply the LW_ChannelFollower modifier in the Graph Editor (Figure 12.2). One problem with either of these constraints is that the modifiers are not currently updated until you set a keyframe and then step forward or back a frame to refresh the scene. This can be very counterintuitive, especially when your character distorts all over the screen. Until NewTek fixes this problem (if they see it as a problem!), you'll just have to deal with it.

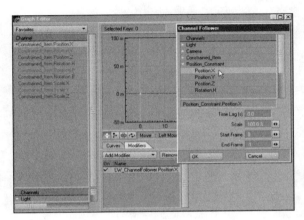

Figure 12.2
LW_ChannelFollower modifier applied in the Graph Editor panel.

This positional constraint enables you to move an item by moving the constraint, without affecting any other parameters of the item. You can play with this by selecting the constraint and moving it around. The constrained item follows along automatically.

Locking Items

When you have items that you want to see but don't want to select, lock them in the Scene Editor. This will keep the items visible but prevent you from selecting them by accident. This is especially useful in a complex setup where it's difficult to choose between bones and nulls that are close to one another.

Orientation Constraints

Orientation constraints make one object assume the orientation of another. As with positional constraints, this basic orientation constraint setup described in Project 12.1 is very simple, but it is a building block for more complex setups.

PROJECT 12.1 Orientation Constraints to Animate Fingers

To complete this project, follow these steps:

1. Load the hand you set up with bones in Chapter 11. If you did not build that setup, you can load the scene and object files from this book's CD-ROM. If you open the Scene Editor, your screen should look something like Figure 12.3.

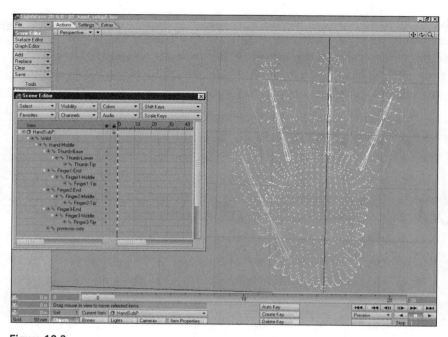

Figure 12.3
Hand setup showing finger bones and the points of the hand object; the hierarchy is visible in the Scene Editor panel.

2. Add a null to the scene and name it Index. This will be the orientation constraint for the finger bones.

3. Parent the Index null to the hand object. Position the null over the middle of the palm. If you like, you can add an inactive light and parent and position it to provide a Light View of the hand.

4. Select the Finger1-End bone. This is the base bone of the index finger.

5. Open the Graph Editor. In the Channel list, select the Finger1-End.Rotation.P channel. This is the rotation channel that controls the bone's pitch toward the palm of the hand.

6. In the Modifiers tab, click on the Add Modifier button and choose LW_ChannelFollower from the drop-down list.

7. In the Channel Follower dialog box, expand the Index item. Choose Rotation.P from the expanded channel list. Your screen should look like Figure 12.4.

8. Close the Channel Follower dialog box and the Graph Editor.

9. Test the new orientation constraint by setting several keyframes to pitch the Index null. The Finger1-End bone should follow the Index null's orientation.

10. Repeat Steps 4 through 8 for the remaining eight finger bones.

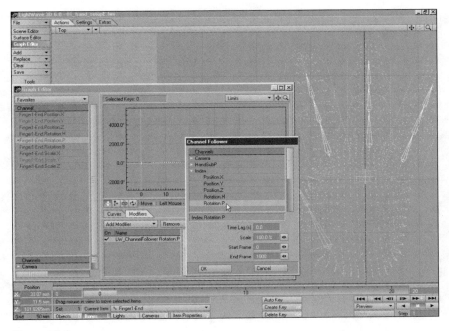

Figure 12.4
Finger1-End bone selected in the Graph Editor, with LW_ChannelFollower modifier applied using the pitch rotation channel of the Index null.

When the setup is complete, you should be able to animate the closing of all three fingers into the palm simply by rotating the Index null, as shown in Figure 12.5. This setup can reduce the animator's workload for the hand by almost an order of magnitude.

It's even more intuitive for the animator if you can build a slider control into the Light View for the hand. Unfortunately, as of this writing, the GuideObject custom null type is missing from LightWave, although it is documented on pages 2.15 and 2.16 of the *Motion: Animate & Render* manual. This null type is very useful for constraint setups because it enables you to set up simple, consistent, easy-to-use slider controls that are invisible to the renderer. This is a much more efficient and powerful option than using ordinary nulls. I hope that by the time you read this, the GuideObject custom null will be enabled again. Until that time, you can find comparable slider controls in the Project: messiah plug-in interface.

Aim Constraints

Aim constraints do exactly what it sounds like they do—they aim one object (or bone, null, camera, or other item) at another object (or whatever). This enables you to precisely match the rotation of one item to the motion of another. The aim constraint is a very useful and powerful function, and you will probably find yourself using it several times within even the simplest character setup. As with rotational and positional constraints, the aim constraint is a standard building block for the more complex setups later in this chapter.

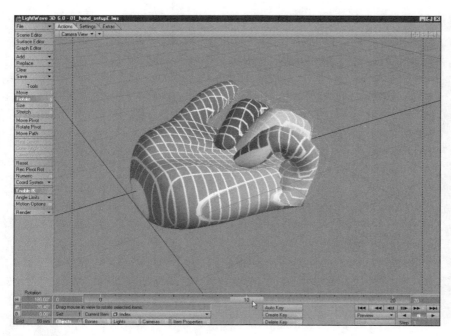

Figure 12.5
All nine finger bones constrained by the LW_ChannelFollower modifier to the pitch rotation channel of the Index null.

Unfortunately, LightWave [6] does not have an all-around native aim constraint. As of this writing, the official documentation on LightWave's Target function is not accurate. The manual states that items can target other items, but as of version 6.0b, only cameras and lights can target. Objects and bones cannot. Also, the rotation information for lights and cameras that are targeting is not available to other items through LW_Follower, LW_ChannelFollower, LW_ChannelExpression, or other motion modifiers. In short, if you want an object or bone to look at another item, you must use either an IK setup (as described in the head and eye project in Chapter 11) or a third-party solution such as Worley Labs' Track plug-in.

Roll Constraints

The roll constraint type controls the rotation of a bone around the long axis, or the axis that lines up from the pivot to the end effector of the bone. The roll constraint is most often applied to keep parts of a character from twisting or rolling uncontrollably as they track an aim constraint. The roll constraint is not usually an animation control by itself. It is more like a safety limit on other constraints. As with preceding constraints, the roll constraint is another standard building block you will use in the more complex setups later in this chapter.

The most common type of roll constraint in LightWave is a goal object positioned somewhere near the middle of an IK chain and allocated just enough Goal Strength to bias the IK chain in the constraint's direction.

(Don't) Do the Twist

Gimbal lock is a common problem for 3D animation software. If the target of an aim constraint passes directly over the axis of the constrained object, that object will abruptly roll 180 degrees. In many cases, this is a bad thing. Imagine if that box is a bone controlling how part of a mesh deforms. When it rolls, the mesh will suddenly twist and contort at that point. LightWave can produce gimbal lock, so you need to find a reliable technique to avoid or prevent it.

One of the easiest ways to prevent gimbal lock is to insert a null object or a very small inactive bone into the hierarchy and align it so that its children will be at zero rotation for the rest or default pose. You can also omit the extra element and rotate the pivot point of each child object to produce the same result. This provides the children with the maximum range of rotation before gimbal lock becomes a problem. For most joints, the built-in rotation limits prevent the bone from reaching the 90-degree pitch value that triggers gimbal lock.

Rotation Constraints

Rotation constraints in LightWave are called Heading, Pitch, and Bank Limits. These limits are useful when using FK bone/joint hierarchies, but they become even more useful when using IK methods because the joint angles are calculated for you.

You can set joint limits in the Controllers And Limits tab of the Motion Options panel. These limits are expressed as absolute values, in degrees. Refer back to Project 11.5, the head-and-eye IK setup, for an example of setting rotational limits.

LightWave also enables you to set the stiffness of a joint so joints in an IK chain can respond to the IK influence at different rates. This feature can be very helpful in getting IK to respond intuitively. A stiffened joint can be set up to behave very much like a real one, as if muscles, ligaments, and bones are interacting to constrain its rotation. Joint stiffness is also one way to build successive breaking of joints into an IK chain. Stiffness is always available for each axis, whether the corresponding Limits box is checked or not. Positive values make the joint stiffer, or more resistant to rotating by IK; lower values loosen the joint and make it rotate more freely under the influence of IK.

Expressions as Constraints

Expressions horrify artists once they learn that the full phrase is "mathematical expressions." Fear not, you can put down that voodoo crucifix. Even the irrationally mathphobic can readily learn to take advantage of expressions to make the process of animation less painful and far more efficient. You'll use expressions for everything from setting the way a bicep should bulge whenever its elbow bends to creating elegant widgets for controlling multiple events with one mouse click. Proper use of expressions will simplify and maximize your control of the figure to be animated.

There will always be a trade-off between macro and micro control of a character. Expressions are handy for getting your character close to where you want it in a rough first pass so that a few choices put the things you care about into place. You can iteratively refine your poses and timing with secondary modifiers. It's easy to go overboard, with so many actions triggered by your input that you have no way to prevent the occurrence of automatic events. Setting up a character so that its hips will always remain at the center point of the two feet is fine until you need the hips to be somewhere else. When it's finger twiddling time, I'll do it expressively rather than crack one explicitly named knuckle at a time, and get on with my life.

For example, say you need to create a lashing cat's tail. Supposing there are more segments than you want to keep track of individually, you can use expressions in a variety of ways that each simplify and magnify your control over that tail while you're animating.

Typically, you'll use some or all of a null object's Scale, Rotation, and Translation channels to "remotely control" the affected element, in this case, the segments of the cat's tail. One approach is to take the (animator's) input value of one of the null's channels, such as its x rotation value, and use that to drive the x rotation of the root segment of the cat's tail. As you rotate the null in x, the cat's tail will simultaneously rotate in x, although the tail will be stiff as a board. Copy and apply that expression to each subsequent tail segment. When you rotate the null, every segment of the cat's tail will rotate simultaneously on its x-axis, curling up rapidly. Use the null's other y and z rotation channels the same way, and you'll have quite a thrashable tail.

There are many ways to modify this basic setup for maximum simplicity and versatility. Add a modifier to each expression using your null's x scale value to multiply the null's x rotation value. While the x scale value is 1.0, the rotation value will not change. When it's less than 1.0, each segment will rotate.

Expression-Safe Naming

In LightWave, expressions will cause errors if any of the item names contain spaces. When you name items, use underscores (_) instead of spaces. You need to be especially careful when cloning objects or adding child bones because LightWave will automatically add a space and a number to both the duplicate and the original item. In effect, LightWave automatically booby-traps its own expressions! You should check the Scene Editor periodically during the setup process, and always before you add expressions, to make sure that no items have spaces in their names.

An Elementary Overview

In the computer environment, we generally structure a skeleton hierarchically from the hips to the extremities. The feet and hands inherit any motion of the hips, unless we use some method of constraining their position, outside of the skeleton structure, so that they stay where placed no matter where we move other parts of the body.

A stop-motion animator can secure feet or hands where they need to stay while adjusting the spine for that perfect line of action. It's as simple and elegant a solution as pushing the hips down while the floor prevents the feet from moving. You could say the feet were constrained by the floor. With pencils, an animator can retrace the position of the feet until choosing to move them. When altering the placement of the hips to improve a given pose, the pencil animator never has the computer animator's problem of the rest of the character spinning whichever way the hips do. What we need is a way of working that will allow us to capitalize on the freedom from real-world physics, and from the necessity of redrawing the entire character for each new frame, without giving ourselves even thornier problems. If we're busy worrying about how to plant a character's feet on the ground, it will be impossible to focus sufficiently on a performance.

You've seen the kinds of motion that initially led many of the earlier generations of animators to dismiss the computer as a serious medium for quality work. Stiff, mechanical movement was the norm. Characters floated, lacking the semblance of weight. The torso would glide in a straight line while the feet pedaled an imaginary unicycle through the ground plane. Hips, heads, hands, and feet bobbed about in strange little multiply dependent epicycles, inheriting the motion of their parents rather than fluidly tracing out the intentional arc of any actual hand or foot. If, through some miracle of patience and perseverance, the feet successfully maintained contact with the ground without skating, you could forget about readjusting the hips without having to discard hours of work. Naturally, you'd moved the hips up and down, but the notion of experimentation with when and how was out of the question. When that was the best that a good animator was expected to be able to do, no wonder motion capture seemed like a good idea.

Animating without using constraints typically yields such unsatisfactory results that there is little chance of achieving a good walk without doing nearly all the work in pencil beforehand and essentially rotoscoping. That approach begs the question of animating in the computer at all; it reduces the task to a dry keyboard exercise after the pencil work is complete. Dropping a keyframe on every bone at every frame makes the subsequent task of revising the animation nontrivial, to say the least. By then, the opportunity to effectively exploit iterative refinement in the computer environment is lost.

Some animators, after tiring of covering the monitor with grease pencils and holding their heads just so while adjusting a pose to match a maze of smudges on the screen, try animating simple boxes as position holders for feet. After reposing the hips, they struggle to match the foot placement to its shoebox for each frame. This approach yields moonwalking, jittery feet, the tendency to avoid challenging animation problems by framing the feet out of the shot entirely, even designing floating characters with no feet. Although one can move a character without having set it up with constraints, it's nearly impossible to effectively animate that way.

Time spent chasing undesirable artifacts is time better spent animating.

It's easy to animate the foot's desired position independently of the foot's hierarchical relationship to the skeleton—by explicitly translating a positional constraint rather than the foot itself. It is a far more effective use of resources to let the computer map the constraint's position onto that of the foot so that it stays where you want it to, while you adjust other parts of the pose.

Once you achieve fluency with constraint-based character setups, the problems that stifled your creativity before will no longer be an issue at all. Animating a walk will be easy to experiment with and push further, even on tight deadlines. When you can work out a quick first pass on the feet and hips, the torso, the head and hands, you can play back your rough approximation while your original plan is still fresh in your mind. You can see to what extent moving the hips from side to side was a good idea and readily change it if it wasn't.

Setting up a constraint structure allows you to move parts of the body without altering the rest of the pose. A dancer routinely uses what's called isolation to move a shoulder or hips without affecting the position of other parts of the body. Without constraints, you wouldn't dare to try such a thing after you'd already posed the feet.

Without modifying any other part of your animation, you can change the personality of a character by selecting the part of the body with which your character leads when he walks. Does he puff out his chest like a manly man or does he lead with his pelvis canted forward like some deviant hipster? What if he rounds his shoulders forward, dragging his arms with his chest caved in? If he's a heavy character, you can see the effect of moving his torso down for a few more frames although his legs have already begun to push his mass back up.

Subtle revisions can completely change a character from being a weightless floater to one whose mass is apparent entirely from the way he moves. When your director suggests that you change just one thing, you can readily and cheerily incorporate the suggestion without painfully introducing new artifacts. Even better, you won't need to offer some explanation about how prohibitively hard it would be to change it, so you'll have to try that the next time, if there is a next time. The process will be one of iterative discovery and refinement rather than the desperate effort to complete something that you can even use at all.

These days, there is no compelling reason to do it the hard way. The little additional time it takes to properly organize a constraint structure as a routine part of the procedure of setting up a character for animation is nothing compared to the time you'll save while animating.

Constraint Switching

Among computer character animation professionals, character setups provoke religious fervor rivaling that of platform or program preferences. This situation has largely persisted because, once you pick a setup technique, that's the way it has to be done for the duration of a project. Changing setups means scrapping everything—animation, blocking, maybe even models—and starting over.

Constraint switching can alleviate this. However, it can be a complex process to set up, and it would be a good idea to practice on simple examples first.

Simply put, constraint switching allows you to do two things: You can turn constraints on or off during the course of an animation, and you can switch to another constraint in the process.

Suppose that for some reason we want the hand to orient like the forearm. There are many reasons we might want it to do so, in particular to save time if the arm is doing many wild swings or if the character is repetitively swinging its arms. This would be a no-brainer if we knew that we were going to want the arm to orient to the forearm for the whole animation. But in this case, suppose we want to start off with the hand oriented to its own constraint, but at frame 10, we want to have the hand orient to the forearm constraint? What then? We don't have to delete the previous orientation constraint to the hand and start a new animation.

PROJECT 12.2 Setting Up a Constraint Switch

The easiest way to switch constraints is to use a control to change the test state of a conditional expression; that is, animate a null to act as a switch. It's pretty straightforward to set up an expression to test the value of the control and choose between constraints based on that value. This project shows you how to switch an object between two rotational constraints:

1. Clear Layout. Add three nulls and name them right, left, and switch.

2. Rotate the right null to -45 on the heading axis and set a key at frame 0.

3. Rotate the left null to +45 on the heading axis and set a key at frame 0.

4. Add an object. Anything will do, as long as you can easily tell what direction it's pointing.

5. Select the object and open the Graph Editor.

6. From the Channels list, choose the object's Rotation.h channel. In the Modifiers tab, click on Add Modifier and choose LW_Expressions from the pull-down list.

7. Add the expression for the left null's heading rotation to the A field of the Channel Expression panel, as shown in Figure 12.6.

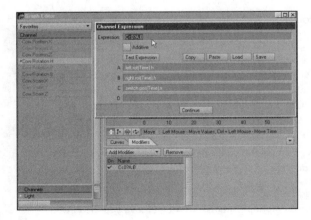

Figure 12.6
The Graph Editor modifier LW_Expression set up to switch between left and right rotation constraints for the cow's heading, based on the switch null's x position.

8. Add the expression for the right null's heading rotation to the B field of the Channel Expression panel.

9. Add the expression for the switch null's x position to the C field of the Channel Expression panel.

10. Add the *conditional expression* C<0?A:B to the Expression field of the Channel Expression panel.

    A conditional expression asks a question such as "Is the value of field C less than zero?" and chooses from the available options based on the answer to that question. In this case, a value of less than zero means choosing field A, and a value of zero or more means choosing field B.

11. Click on the Test Expression button. A message will pop up confirming that the expressions are OK. If not, recheck your work to make sure it is accurate and complete, and try again.

12. When the expressions are OK, close the Channel Expression panel and the Graph Editor panel.

13. Animate the switch null from -1 to 1 on the x-axis.

    As the switch null passes zero, the constrained object will switch abruptly from one rotation constraint null to the other. This is a simple two-state constraint switch. There are more graceful ways to ease into the transition, such as animating both constraints so that, as the object switches orientation, it doesn't jump. Covering up little flaws like this is easy compared to the tweaking you'd have to do without constraint switching.

    This type of constraint switching can be very useful for picking up objects or having objects control the movement and orientation of a character's hand. This would also include a character leaning his hands on a desk or wall, holding the bars of a jail or fence, holding onto a steering wheel, or picking up a cup of coffee and putting it down again.

14. Save your results for use in the next project.

Dry Erase Markers

You will sometimes need a dry erase marker, china marker, or grease pencil to mark positions of the items on your screen, especially when animating constraint switching. Dry erase marker comes off your computer screen the easiest and won't cause you to rub off the antireflective coating on your computer screen. Expo's fine-point dry erase marker yields the best results, and having multiple colors doesn't hurt, although you won't need them for simple projects. Whatever you do, *don't* use an ordinary felt tip marker because it can leave permanent marks on your screen and be very costly to clean up. If it does not say *dry erase* on it, *don't use it under any circumstances*.

This is a pretty low-tech but effective way to add a placeholder on the screen between different modes of a program, different keyframes, even different programs. Just don't move your head when you're using this technique because the glass on your computer screen is thick enough to create a difference in the position of your marks due to the effects of parallax.

Constraint Mixing and Blending

You can constrain an object with more than one constraint target, and you will get an average constraint value between the two.

You can also adjust the weight of influence of one constraint over another. Mixed or blended constraints are used to solve a variety of setup problems. They can be used to average orientations between two bones to smooth out an elbow or shoulder; they can float a bone between two other bones or nulls so that, as the bones approach or recede from each other, the bone in the middle will always stay the same distance between them (unless weights or percentages of influence of the constraints are animated). And of course, the influence percentages or weights can be animated.

 Setting Up a Constraint Blend

To set up a constraint blend, follow these steps:

1. Using the scene you created in Project 12.2, select the constrained object and open the Graph Editor.

2. From the Channels list, choose the object's Rotation.h channel. In the Modifiers tab, double-click on the LW_Expressions modifier to open the Channel Expression panel.

3. Add the expression for the *average* of the left and right null's heading rotations to the D field of the Channel Expression panel, as shown in Figure 12.7.

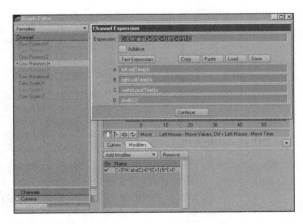

Figure 12.7
The Graph Editor modifier LW_Expression set up to smoothly transition between left and right rotation constraints for the cow's heading, based on the switch null's x position.

4. Change the conditional expression in the Expression field of the Channel Expression panel to C<0?A*abs(C)+D*(C+1):B*C+D*(1-C), as shown in Figure 12.7.

The new conditional expression makes the same two-valued choice, C<0?, as it did in Project 12.2, but now the choices are between variables that smooth out the switch between constraints. The first choice, A*abs(C)+D*(C+1), is selected when the switch's x value is less than zero. In English, the value of this choice is (deep breath!) the left heading multiplied by the absolute value of the switch's x position plus the average of the left and right null's heading value multiplied by the sum of the switch's x position plus one. If the switch's x position is -0.5, the left null is at 45, and the right null is at -45, the equation is

```
45*abs(-0.5)+0*(-0.5+1)=22.5
```

Now suppose the switch's x position is 0.5, and the left and right nulls remain at their headings. The conditional expression will now choose the other variable, so the equation is

```
-45*0.5+0*(1-0.5)=-22.5
```

Don't worry if it takes you a bit of thinking to figure out what an expression will do. Most of us haven't calculated anything more difficult than a checking account balance since we left high school, so it's natural to have a little rust in the mathematical gears. Most LightWave expressions are not very difficult once you break them down into small, manageable chunks.

5. Click on the Test Expression button. A message will pop up confirming that the expressions are OK. If not, recheck your work to make sure it is accurate and complete and try again.

6. When the expressions are OK, close the Channel Expression panel and the Graph Editor panel.

7. Animate the switch null from -1 to 1 on the x-axis.

   As the switch null moves toward zero, the constrained object will transition smoothly from one rotation constraint null to the other. This is a constraint blend based on the simple averaging expression in field D of the Channel Expression panel. If you want to apply a weighting other than a simple average, all you have to change is field D; the rest of the expressions will still work.

8. Experiment with variations to the two expressions and three variables in the Channel Expression panel. Is it easier to animate the constraint switch by using some channel other than x position? What effect does it have if you change field D to (A+B)*2? When you find an interesting effect, save a copy of the scene so you can reuse it later.

This technique can be used, for example, for bouncing fat or keeping control points separated but spaced in a completely controlled manner. You might then animate the enforce percentages to give the fat some secondary motion or jiggle. You are not limited to the influence of only two bones, but mixing the influence of more bones can slow down your computer's performance.

As with mixing position constraints, mixing orientation constraints allows a bone to assume an equilibrium between the rotational values of two (or more) other bones. The most basic use of this technique is to smooth out rotational values at the joints (such as the elbow) so that the skin of the character appears more elastic. This also gives the appearance that the joint underneath the skin has a larger "ball" to which the skin molds itself.

You can animate the values that maintain the tension between the bones, particularly where it solves a problem that occurs during the course of the animation. It's a good idea to experiment with this concept and practice setting up characters using it. When a nasty character setup problem lands on your desk, you want to have as many tools as possible (and as much experience with them) to help you find a solution.

Constraint Hierarchies Can Save Your Sanity

Constraints enable you to do several different tasks. They can enable you to isolate various body parts; you can isolate the feet from the movement of the pelvis or the arms from the movement of the torso. They can also allow objects to move along with other objects without inheriting their hierarchical rotation. But these are merely the mechanical manifestations of the power of constraints.

There is also a strategic purpose that constraints can serve. Often, when starting a project (particularly one that involves other people and perhaps clients), you find yourself in a position where you have to begin animating right away yet the final model isn't completed and the skeleton can't be finalized. The complexity of a setup develops as an approach to its particular set of problems. For example, the setup may need to make the biceps rotate as the forearm points up or down, make the biceps bulge, and make the deltoid lift with the collar bone. Those demands on the skeletal structure, including methods for solving them, could not have been fully anticipated until a more complete skeleton was available. The character setup will go through a lot of revisions.

It is common for animators to animate with a simple skeleton and character to get a general idea across, either to themselves or their clients, and then abandon any animation done at that stage. There is simply too much of a difference between the setup for those early tests and the final setup for the initial animation keyframes to be efficiently adapted. But by developing a hierarchy that can drive a more sophisticated skeleton and animating that hierarchy in the earliest tests, it is possible to salvage the animation. You can even transfer it from character to character when that is a useful animation strategy.

This salvaging of animation is an enormous advantage if applied properly. If you have to wait until the models and setups are perfectly finalized before you can even begin to animate, the animation will always be under the worst time and resource crunches. If you can experiment with animation tests throughout the modeling and setup development, you will have a stock of animation that you can immediately apply to the final character. Essentially, you will be able to develop your character's movements, mannerisms, and acting throughout the project instead of tacking them onto the end of the project like an afterthought.

This strategy of using constraints in a hierarchy of their own, to drive bones in a separate hierarchy, works for LightWave [6]. There is a caveat to this approach. If the bones in your initial simple hierarchy have different names than the ones in your final skeleton, you will have to reconstrain the bones. It's not a big deal (probably around an hour of work for a typical setup), but with some planning, it can be avoided altogether.

Advanced Character Setup Analysis

LightWave [6] includes an as-yet-undocumented scene, AdvancedCharacter, that uses a variety of constraints in a lower-body setup. This setup avoids or solves a number of the pathologies listed earlier (in the sidebar "Setup Pathologies") and is worth studying. If you load the scene, your screen should look like Figure 12.8.

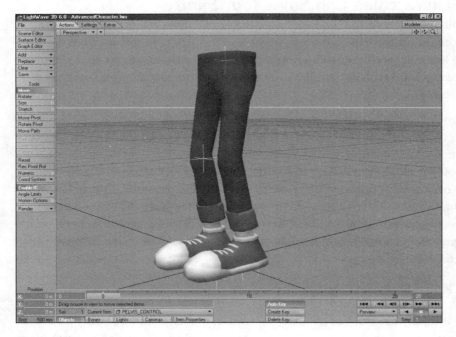

Figure 12.8
The AdvancedCharacter scene.

Figure 12.9 shows a composite screenshot of the Scene Editor displaying the full hierarchy of model, bones, nulls, light, and camera contained in this scene.

Open the Graph Editor, and starting from the first item in the Channels list, open up all the channels and examine their contents one at a time.

The Camera has one set of position, rotation, and scale keys at frame 0 to lock it in place.

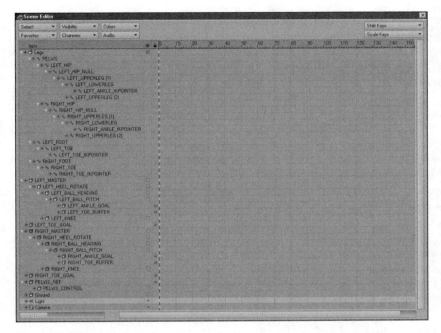

Figure 12.9
Composite screenshot of the Scene Editor displaying the full hierarchy of model, bones, nulls, light, and camera contained in the AdvancedCharacter scene.

The Legs object has no position, rotation, or scale keyframes other than frame 0 and no modifiers or expressions. The Unaffected By IK Of Descendants option is enabled in the Motion Options panel. All the motion and deformation of the Legs object will come from the bones and nulls in the rest of the setup.

Bones

There are 19 bones in the Legs object. Refer to Figure 12.9 for a complete list of the bone names and their positions in the skeleton hierarchy.

None of the Legs object's bones have modifiers applied to them in the Motion Options panel. However, several have controllers, limits, and IK applied. Several bones also have modifiers applied in the Graph Editor panel.

In the Motion Options panel, the PELVIS bone has the Unaffected By IK Of Descendants option enabled, thereby isolating it from the IK influence of all the other bones. All three rotation axes are controlled by keyframes.

In the Graph Editor, the PELVIS bone has modifiers (including one or both Channel Follower and Channel Expressions) on all three position and rotation channels, but no controls or keyframes on the scale channels. All three position channels for the PELVIS bone have both a Channel Follower modifier (which is first in order) and a Channel Expression modifier:

```
LW_ChannelFollower PELVIS_REF.Position.X
PELVIS_CONTROL.pos(Time).x
LW_ChannelFollower PELVIS_REF.Position.Y
PELVIS_CONTROL.pos(Time).y
LW_ChannelFollower PELVIS_REF.Position.Z
PELVIS_CONTROL.pos(Time).z
```

The PELVIS bone rotation channels have different modifiers. The heading channel has, like the position channels, both a Channel Follower modifier (which is, again, first in order) and a Channel Expression modifier. However, the pitch and bank channels have only the Channel Expression modifier:

```
LW_ChannelFollower PELVIS_REF.Rotation.H
PELVIS_CONTROL.rot(Time).h
PELVIS_CONTROL.rot(Time).p
PELVIS_CONTROL.rot(Time).b
```

The LEFT_HIP bone has Heading limits of minimum 80 and maximum 97.5, stiffness of 40, and Pitch stiffness of 20. Both Heading and Pitch are controlled by IK.

The RIGHT_HIP bone has Heading limits of minimum -102.5 and maximum -76.5, stiffness of 20, and Pitch stiffness of 20. Both Heading and Pitch are controlled by IK.

Note that the pelvis and left and right hip bones are arranged in the correct anatomical relationship. The pelvis pivot point is located at the base of the spine, and the hip pivot points are located at the sockets of the pelvis. If these pivot points were arranged in a straight line (a common mistake for beginners), the character's hip movement would look wrong for both realistic and caricatured actions.

The LEFT_HIP_NULL and RIGHT_HIP_NULL bones are very small, with a rest length of 0.010. They have no modifiers or limits and are set to keyframe control on all three axes.

The LEFT_UPPERLEG (1) and RIGHT_UPPERLEG (1) bones have no limits or modifiers and are both set to IK for the Pitch axis and keyframe control for the Heading and Bank axes.

The LEFT_UPPERLEG (2) and RIGHT_UPPERLEG (2) bones have no limits or modifiers and are both set to keyframe control for all three rotation axes. The purpose of these bones is to adjust the deformation of the buttocks to correct any problems resulting from the bone influence of the LEFT_UPPERLEG (1) and RIGHT_UPPERLEG (1) bones.

The LEFT_LOWERLEG bone has the Goal Object LEFT_KNEE and Goal Strength of 1.0, is set to full-time IK, and has pitch limits of minimum 0 to maximum 140. The other two rotation axes are controlled by keyframes. The RIGHT_LOWERLEG bone has identical settings, except that the Goal Object is the RIGHT_KNEE null.

The LEFT_ANKLE_IKPOINTER bone has the Goal Object LEFT_ANKLE_GOAL and Goal Strength of 10.0, is set to full-time IK, and has all three rotation axes controlled by keyframes. The RIGHT_ANKLE_IKPOINTER bone has the same settings, but its Goal Object is RIGHT_ANKLE_GOAL.

The LEFT_FOOT and RIGHT_FOOT bones both have IK controlling their Heading and Pitch axes but keyframes controlling the Bank axes. Neither bone has modifiers or limits. Note that these bones are parented directly to the Legs object, at the same hierarchy level as the PELVIS bone.

In the Graph Editor, the RIGHT_FOOT and LEFT_FOOT bones have Channel Follower modifiers on all three position channels, with the following expressions:

```
RIGHT_ANKLE_GOAL.wpos(Time).x
RIGHT_ANKLE_GOAL.wpos(Time).y
RIGHT_ANKLE_GOAL.wpos(Time).z
LEFT_ANKLE_GOAL.wpos(Time).x
LEFT_ANKLE_GOAL.wpos(Time).y
LEFT_ANKLE_GOAL.wpos(Time).z
```

The LEFT_TOE bone has the Goal Object LEFT_BALL_HEADING and Goal Strength of 1.0, is set to full-time IK, and has the Heading and Bank axes controlled by keyframes with no rotation limits. The RIGHT_TOE bone has the same settings, but its Goal Object is RIGHT_BALL_HEADING.

The LEFT_TOE_IKPOINTER bone has the Goal Object LEFT_TOE_GOAL and Goal Strength of 10.0, is set to full-time IK, and has all three rotation axes controlled by keyframes with no rotation limits. The RIGHT_TOE_IKPOINTER bone has the same settings, but its Goal Object is RIGHT_TOE_GOAL.

Nulls

This scene contains 18 nulls outside the Legs object hierarchy. Only three of them have any Graph Editor modifiers: LEFT_TOE_GOAL, RIGHT_TOE_GOAL, and PELVIS_REF.

The Graph Editor modifiers for the LEFT_TOE_GOAL null's position x-, y-, and z-axes are as follows:

```
LEFT_TOE_BUFFER.wpos(Time).x
max ( 0.05 , LEFT_TOE_BUFFER.wpos(Time).y )
LEFT_TOE_BUFFER.wpos(Time).z
```

The Graph Editor modifiers for the RIGHT_TOE_GOAL null's position x-, y-, and z-axes are as follows:

```
RIGHT_TOE_BUFFER.wpos(Time).x
max ( 0.05 , RIGHT_TOE_BUFFER.wpos(Time).y )
RIGHT_TOE_BUFFER.wpos(Time).z
```

The Graph Editor modifiers for the PELVIS_REF null's position x-, y-, and z-axes and rotation heading axis are as follows:

```
center( LEFT_MASTER.pos(Time) , RIGHT_MASTER.pos(Time)).x
1.165 - (0.15 * (abs(LEFT_MASTER.pos(Time).x - RIGHT_MASTER.pos(Time).x)
    + abs(LEFT_MASTER.pos(Time).z - RIGHT_MASTER.pos(Time).z)))
center( LEFT_MASTER.pos(Time) , RIGHT_MASTER.pos(Time)).z
center( LEFT_MASTER.rot(Time) , RIGHT_MASTER.rot(Time)).h
```

The LEFT_BALL_PITCH null is the only one that has Pitch limits in the Motion Options panel. The minimum is -36.5 and the maximum is 0. However, I believe this is an oversight, and I recommend that you add comparable pitch limits to the RIGHT_BALL_PITCH null.

All the other nulls are controlled by keyframes and have no rotational limits or modifiers. The position of each null in the hierarchy is shown in Figure 12.9.

Setup Control Summary

There are 12 potential animation controls in this scene, but the majority of character animation can be performed with only 3 to 5 of the controls. The remainder can be hidden most of the time and only made visible or selected for special poses that require their intervention.

The Legs object can be animated directly, but not very much. Moving this object a small amount along its y-axis, up off the ground plane, straightens the legs and points the toes as in a jump. However, moving even a little in the x- or z-axes deforms the object, so I recommend locking off the x and z move axes. Any change in rotation, size, or stretch will also deform the object, so lock off those controls as well.

The PELVIS_CONTROL null is a crucial animation control for nearly every conceivable action. Moving or rotating this null controls, as its name states, the pelvis of the character setup. The default or rest position value for each of the six axes is zero, making a reset easy to do. Movement on the y-axis is generally best kept on the negative side; positive values stretch the character's ankles like taffy. Negative values bring this null closer to the LEFT_MASTER and RIGHT_MASTER controls, making the IK chains bend the knees. You can make this character squat simply by reducing the y-axis value for this null to something like -500mm, as shown in Figure 12.10. Cycling the x- and z-axis values between 100mm and -100mm to move the null in a circle will make the pelvis bank and pitch and the legs bend and swivel automatically, all without affecting the feet, as shown in the Pelvis.avi animation on this book's CD-ROM.

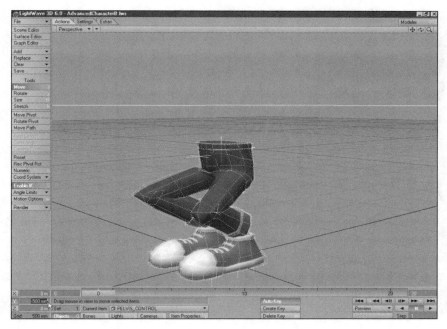

Figure 12.10
Character squats with a PELVIS_CONTROL y value of -500mm.

The rotation channels for the PELVIS_CONTROL null can make the character's hips perform just about any action, including the hip isolation moves of a hula dancer, without affecting the feet or the rest of the character. This setup is a very nice solution to Setup Pathology 7.

The LEFT_MASTER null has an initial rest position of 137.5mm on the x-axis, with all other position and rotation rest values at zero. The RIGHT_MASTER null is approximately the same distance on the negative side of the x-axis, so the feet are positioned to center the pelvis. One of the nice features of this setup is that the pelvis will automatically reposition and rotate to suit the animation of the feet, keeping the character balanced.

Rotating the LEFT_MASTER null on its Heading axis automatically points the knee, but don't rotate the null past 141.5 degrees (as shown in Figure 12.11) in either direction or the setup will deform badly at the ankle. This range of motion is more than you'll ever need, even for caricatured ballet. On the Pitch axis, don't rotate this null more than 30 degrees up unless you want to deform the ankle and lock the knee. Also, the ball and toe constraints in this setup are designed to bend the foot if it intersects the ground plane, so if you pitch the LEFT_MASTER null down when the left foot is on the ground, the foot will fold. Raise the null on the y-axis and the fold will straighten out again. In general, you'll do best to keep this null's pitch between +24 and -45 degrees.

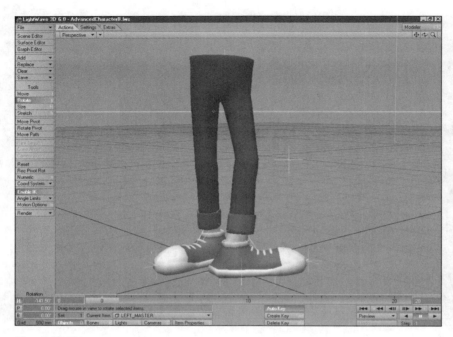

Figure 12.11
Maximum nondeforming heading rotation for LEFT_MASTER null.

Rotating this null on its Bank axis moves the geometry in ways I don't see as particularly useful, but you may find some skateboarding moves that could use these distortions. Unless you have a use for this, I recommend locking the Bank axis for this null. Also, don't animate the Size or Stretch values at all or you'll cause severe damage to the setup.

The RIGHT_MASTER null is essentially a mirror-image duplicate of the LEFT_MASTER null. Its rest position is -130mm x position; all other position and rotation rest values are zero.

The LEFT_HEEL_ROTATE null, as its name implies, is strictly for rotation. Don't try to move, stretch, or scale it. As with the LEFT_MASTER null, any Pitch rotation beyond 24 degrees up or 45 degrees down (assuming the left foot is clear of the ground) will deform the mesh in undesirable ways. The useful Heading range is about 140 degrees plus or minus. The major difference between this null and LEFT_MASTER is that the pivot point is at the heel rather than closer to the middle of the foot, so this control is more useful when animating a heel strike or similar pose. Most of the time, you can leave this control hidden and get the poses you need with the LEFT_MASTER null.

The RIGHT_HEEL_ROTATE null is essentially a mirror-image duplicate of the LEFT_HEEL_ROTATE null.

The LEFT_BALL_HEADING null, and its mirror-image counterpart RIGHT_BALL_HEADING, enable you to animate the character pivoting on the ball of each foot instead of on the heel.

You should leave all three position axes and both the bank and pitch axes locked off for these nulls. Animate the heading between 90 or so degrees, plus and minus, and you should be safe.

 Doing the Twist

Using only the controls described thus far, you can do a fair imitation of Chubby Checker:

1. Lift the MASTER nulls 100mm on y.

2. Pitch the MASTER or HEEL_ROTATE nulls down 30 degrees.

3. Animate the BALL_HEADING nulls in a cycle from -30 to 30 and back again to do the Twist.

Your results should look like Figure 12.12 or the animation Twist.avi on this book's CD-ROM.

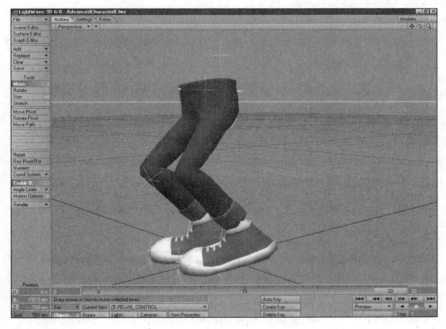

Figure 12.12
Do the Twist.

Animating the LEFT_BALL_PITCH null's single valid channel, pitch, makes the character lift its heel. With the pitch limit, you can't drop the heel below ground level or distort the foot with too much bending. You should add the pitch limit (Minimum -36.5, Maximum 0) to the RIGHT_BALL_PITCH null too.

If you repeat the preceding Twist project, substituting BALL_PITCH for MASTER pitch and lift, you'll get the same apparent key leg poses. However, because the BALL_PITCH nulls are isolated from driving the knees and pelvis, you won't get the same motion. Do you see how an apparently identical local constraint can have very different effects elsewhere in the hierarchy?

The LEFT_KNEE null is the goal that keeps the knee bent and oriented in the correct direction. Most of the time, you want the knee to point in the same direction as the foot, so this null is parented to the LEFT_HEEL_ROTATE null. Rotating LEFT_HEEL_ROTATE rotates the foot around the heel and also points the knee. If you want the knee to point in a different direction (as for a bowlegged or knock-kneed character), simply offset the LEFT_KNEE null on the x-axis. In most cases, you can simply leave this null invisible and locked.

The RIGHT_KNEE null is essentially a mirror-image duplicate of the LEFT_KNEE null, with the same capabilities.

Humanoid Setup Guidelines

The following sections discuss the most crucial constraint design and setup issues for humanoid characters.

Torso

The basis for the torso is, of course, the pelvis. It seems fairly obvious—the backbone is attached to the pelvis, and the thorax, or upper body, is attached to the backbone. Well, not so fast there, Sparky! Turn on the television and look at dancers and ice-skaters. They often rotate or swing their hips while there appears to be no change of rotation or orientation of their upper torso. This is simply an elegant and obvious occurrence of upper torso isolation. It occurs because the body of most vertebrates is under the control of their mind and is not determined by mere mechanical linkages.

In computer animation, we all too often allow these virtual mechanical linkages to determine the fate of our animation. Besides our own human hands and eyes, the brains of our characters can be found in their animation channels. If an animator noodles with the animation channel curves, more lively animation can often result. But the results of such noodling can be unpredictable unless you build isolation into your character.

So, what do you do? One approach is to set up the entire upper torso to be driven by one null or bone with the pivot at the pelvis, and a second level of bones or nulls that can be animated independently. This may seem obvious. However, there are several different ways that these constraints can be strung together on the torso, and they in turn can be constrained to one another. You can choose setup options to either save time or just make better-looking animation.

To start, think of the upper torso and lower torso as two separate, rigid structures. The area in between is a bit mushier and facilitates distension (like slouching) or extension (like standing at attention). The upper and lower torso are not connected with a rigid linkage, as is the common practice in LightWave character animation.

On the other hand, when you're roughing out animation or moving characters around for blocking, having to move the upper torso separately from the lower torso seems like more work than is absolutely necessary. The question you should be asking is, "Is there a way to do this so you can operate a character both ways?" Now really, would this question even be presented to you if the answer weren't "Yes"?

The two Thorax and Pelvis hierarchies represent the basic animation structures for the upper torso. For practical reasons, they must be tied together in a way that will allow them to function independently when needed yet also move together during animation roughing or blocking stages.

As we've seen with the constraint switching project, it is possible to have a constraint setup work one way in one part of an animation but change functions in a later stage of the animation. So, create a linkage that will hold both the Pelvis and Thorax and allow them to be moved as a single unit yet will allow them to be moved independently as well.

One dead giveaway that screams "Computer Animation!" is when a character stands with its hips motionless. This is particularly noticeable when animating realistic humans or characters that interface with the real world. Your setup should enable you to prevent or fix the motionless hip problem. By making small, slow random alterations to the x-translation curve, you can make it appear that the character is constantly shifting the distribution of weight on its hips. This is something we humans do constantly. Exaggerate those translation curves and your character can be doing the hula.

With this setup, you really can't get too far lost. Because the Pelvis, Midsection, and Thorax are in a hierarchy with the Backbone, you can type zero values in their Translation and Rotation to realign them with their respective parent backbone. No matter what the Backbone is doing, you still have the freedom to animate these structures any way you like. But the biggest advantages to this setup are being able to adjust the structures directly through the animation curves and having the confidence that poses won't unpredictably whack out.

Normally, when you create a constraint hierarchy, you do so with the model and first skeleton in place. But the beauty of a constraint hierarchy is that it can be moved to accommodate not only the present character being worked on but any character. Individual elements can be moved around as needed.

The structure of the constraint torso in many ways replicates or appears to obviate the need for a separate bone hierarchy. However, the constraint hierarchy is only a simplified way of driving the main hierarchy. The main hierarchy may be a much more complex skeletal system, designed to replicate the effects of muscle and fat as well as the mechanical effects of bones in a body.

Legs

There are several problems with most leg setups. Because the foot bone is connected to the leg bone, and because in most IK systems the root bone takes precedence over the child bones, the leg forces the ball of the foot down when the leg is in certain positions and pulls on the ball of the foot when the leg is stretched completely to its limits. Of course, it pulls the heel up first, and sometimes that is the arrangement you want.

But when slight unplanned movements appear in the feet in animation, it ruins the appearance that the character is rooted to the ground. What you need is a solution that leaves the foot rock steady. Like nearly everything in animation, increased control requires increased diligence. When the foot is rooted to the ground but you pull the hip up beyond the leg's full extension, something has to give, extend, or stretch or the bone structure will break.

As an animator, this is a small price to pay, and in the case of cartoon-style characters, this is actually a desirable outcome that you can use to your advantage.

If you are setting up a dancer or other character that spends a lot of time standing on its toes but is otherwise human, you can modify the setup by simply moving the foot's positional constraint to the location of the ball of the foot. This way, when the character pivots on its toes, the ball of the foot remains the center of rotation and you don't have to do a lot of compensating. However, if the character does a lot of conventional running or walking, you will have to work harder by moving the heel's constraint just to keep the heel from going through the floor all the time.

There are other examples of characters that pivot on the balls of their feet. For example, the hind leg of nearly every quadruped, any kind of bird, all bipedal dinosaurs, and goat-legged mythical creatures. In these cases, what appears to be a backward facing knee is actually the ankle, and you can include that ankle in the pivot from the ball of the foot, or you can exclude it from that rotation.

This setup is fine as far as it goes, and it could be used for many types of animation with this type of leg. But sometimes, you want the ball of the foot to act as the heel would on a normal leg, and this requires a rearrangement of the constraint hierarchy in the model. Note that the former heel should now remain stationary as you move the ball of the foot.

With a free-floating, cartoon knee, there is no fixed length to the bones that make up the leg. The bones are used for orientation of the control points assigned to them or of the bones parented or otherwise subordinate to them, to which control point assignments are made. This makes it easy to distort the apparent proportions of the leg. Distortions require care, because something that doesn't conserve the character's apparent volume just looks wrong, unless it's deliberate and controlled. It's a good start, however, if you're doing something wild in the vein of the Fleischer Bros., Warner Bros., or Spumco animation styles.

As mentioned earlier, part of the goal of constraint hierarchies is to maintain isolation between body parts while allowing coherent manipulation of those parts. There is no relationship in the body where this is more obviously necessary than that between the torso and the legs. The torso must remain able to move freely while the feet remain planted (or moving independently).

This becomes increasingly important when you manipulate animation curves directly. With an independent foot hierarchy, you don't have to worry about the feet shifting when you adjust the up-and-down movement of the torso.

The angle of the bones should be designed primarily for easy selection. The ankle and heel bones should be aligned along one axis, preferably the z-axis. This way, when animating, you will always be able to tell if the foot is above or below ground by its movement on the y-axis.

Arms

Like the basic leg assembly, there is a basic arm assembly, which features the humerus (the bone the biceps is attached to, between the shoulder and elbow), the forearm, and a single bone representing the hand.

Although the methods for handling the elbow are identical to the methods you can use for the knee, there are different options for the way the hand works relative to the arm.

The strategies for dealing with elbows vary. The simplest method has the humerus constrained at the shoulder and the forearm constrained at the wrist. With a good setup, you can simply move the hand to where you want it to go, then move the elbow by simply moving the elbow constraint.

This is a fine solution at a really basic level, but it generates rotational channels, and if you look at the Graph Editor, you won't easily be able to tell if the elbow is pointed up or down. Because channel editing is an important part of refining a character performance, the very slightly more complicated setup of using an aim constraint at the elbow is much easier to edit later by looking at simple-to-understand translation channels. You can tell where the elbow will be pointing at a glance. This is a good example of a little more work during the setup phase saving a lot of work during the animation phase. If you are setting up characters for someone else to animate, or you will be under a tight deadline (and who isn't?), you should always take the time during setup to make the character's animation as easy as possible.

Elbows that are set up to be targeted at a constraint also aid in giving the arm (and its constituent joints and apparent muscles) the illusion of mass.

Although connecting the hand to the end of the arm would seem to be a no-brainer, other options exist. Animation allows opportunities to create movement that doesn't exist in the real world. Traditional animation techniques, such as overlap and secondary motion, can also be assisted by the setup choice that you make. Finally, your setup choice can make interaction with props or the character's environment less problematic.

The basic arm's main kinematic chain consists of two bones driven through IK and a third bone (to which fingers can later be attached) that stands independently, bound to the kinematic chain of the arm only through constraints.

We intuitively know that our hands are bound to the rotational whims of the parent bones in our arms, but our minds know the position and orientation of our hands at all times. Close your eyes and lift your hand. You can form a mental picture of the position that your hand assumes in space. In fact, when you are moving your hands in space, the actual positioning of your arm bones is usually an afterthought, determined only by the limits and torque of your bones and muscles.

So, as you lift your hand to the position requested by your brain, you twist your forearm to best adapt the orientation of your hand to that prescribed by your brain. There are times (when reaching for that cereal box on the top shelf, for example) we wish that the reach of our hands could exceed the boundaries placed on them by their connections to the bones and ligaments of our arms. This is why the hand in these projects is disconnected from the arm. Animation is not bound by the conventions of the physical universe (though the animator can choose it to be so). Setups should allow characters to perform as if they inhabit our universe yet alternately perform as our imaginations let them.

The arms in many setups are drawn straight out from the shoulder, parallel to the ground, as if the character is trying to form the letter "T." This is sometimes referred to as the jesus pose by people in the entertainment industry. The rationale behind this pose is simple, and your own arm will serve as the example. Stand up and stick your arm straight out from your side, parallel to the ground. Now, put it against your side. You have just rotated your arm 90 degrees downward. Raise your arm to stick straight out from your side again. Now, attempt to reach straight up, but don't hurt yourself. Your arm has rotated 90 degrees upward (though not exactly, because your collarbone and shoulder blade also rotated when your shoulder reached its rotational limit). In general, your arm can rotate approximately 90 degrees in any direction from the T position.

The geometry in three-dimensional characters is much less forgiving than the flesh and bone of our human arms, even when you use SubPatches in LightWave. Yet this advice to create characters in a T pose often competes with some people's preference for the hands-at-the-sides pose for setup purposes. If you set up a character with the hands at the sides, the shoulder geometry would have to be constructed to allow 180 degrees of movement just for the arm to reach up above the head. This pose also complicates other setups that can accommodate movement of the clavicle (collarbone) and scapula (shoulder blade) and simulate the deltoid (shoulder muscle).

The bend in the arm should be exaggerated (as in the legs) for most setups. A very slight bend can be employed, but it is better to always create bones with an obvious bend in the preferred direction.

A basic arm setup should establish a constraint relationship with one constraint anchoring the shoulder, another steering the elbow, and another determining the position of the hand. When you move the hand constraint, the hand maintains the orientation of the forearm but can be rotated as an addition to that orientation. This is essentially the same effect you would have gotten if you had just continued drawing the hand as a child of the forearm in a continuous chain.

So, why take this convoluted route? Because there are times when you don't want the hand to automatically assume the orientation of the forearm. For example, when a hand is on a desk and you are pushing on the desk to rise up, you don't want the hand sliding around or rotating through the desk. When you're animating an overlapping action, the elbow might change direction while the hand is still moving in its previous direction for a frame or two. Yet without the ability to override the mechanical orientation of the forearm, the hand would suddenly jerk out of its intended movement, and you (as the animator) would have to manually counterrotate it. At times like that, it is valuable to have other options. Character animation is difficult enough to do well without adding the arcane task of compensating for parent rotation. The hand of your character need not become a rotational slave to its parent bone, but adding these features will increase the up-front work for your first pass of animation.

It has probably occurred to you that it would be really convenient if you could just switch between different setups whenever you want. Well, you can, as discussed in "Constraint Switching" earlier. That is another reason for having the hand separate from the forearm; that relationship can be changed in the middle of an action.

A setup that enables the hand to detach from the arm can be useful. If the skin were attached to the bone, the hand would stretch the length of the forearm. This is handy when binding the hand to another surface, providing a little "give" for it. This setup will result in the hand being rock steady when, for example, a character is holding on to bars in a prison, violently shaking his body back and forth, screaming, "Let me outta here! I'm innocent, I tell ya!" You don't want those fingers going through the bars just because on a frame or two the arms were pulled to their kinematic limits.

There are many reasons to choose a particular setup. Sometimes it's mechanical or the only way to do something. Sometimes it's an arbitrary choice based on a stylistic preference, either the style of the character or the way an animator feels more comfortable working.

In many setups, the hand is the primary factor determining the fate of the arm's motion. The hand had full priority, with the aim constraint at the elbow suggesting the direction the elbow would point. But no matter how far away from the arm that aim constraint was moved, it had no pull, no force, to draw the elbow to it unless the hand allowed the arm to slacken.

Well, sometimes you want that elbow to be more steady, with the hand orbiting around it like a moon orbits around a planet. Or, sometimes you want a character to be leaning on a table with his elbows. Some animators just want to place that elbow exactly where they want it, and the hand is a second priority.

The arms are one of those multifunction areas; sometimes it is best for the arms to follow the translation and rotation hierarchies of the upper torso, sometimes the translation only, sometimes the rotation only, and sometimes neither.

Head and Neck

Conventional, orthodox methodology always has the head operated using forward kinematics. As far as the neck is concerned, that is the best approach under most circumstances. But we can leave our options open by using constraints.

But what of the head? When the body rotates, does the head not rotate? When the shoulders rotate, does the head not rotate along with them?

The answer is, *"No way!"* On all of our bodies, the head tends to hold itself independently right up to the physical limits of the neck. If you're looking at something and you adjust your posture, your head stays pointed at where it was looking. If your head looks away, it's because you're thinking about something, being evasive, or are just bored and trying to find something interesting to place your gaze upon. If you bend over, you'll probably look at the floor first and continue looking in the same place. The head is arguably one of the best automated tracking devices ever.

One thing is constant—your head stays attached to your neck. Even if you (or the character that you're animating) are drunk, although the head motion might lag behind the body, the base of the head stays attached to the neck.

You now have the guidelines for a complete constraint hierarchy, which by adjustment of the location of the constraining bones can work for any bipedal character, offering optimal animation flexibility. It can also work for quadruped characters, but the wrist and elbow constraints would have to be bumped up to the same level as the feet and knees.

There are a few things that can be added to this hierarchy, like eye bones that point to an aim constraint at a distance and other facial subhierarchies like ponytails, jawbones, and maybe eyebrows, but those methodologies truly change so much from character to character that they are best handled on the character skeleton level.

And Now for Something Completely Different

If you can't create the character setup you want in LightWave [6] alone, you may want to try out *project:messiah* (**www.projectmessiah.com**). This program began as a plug-in for LightWave 5.6, with the goal of providing all the character animation tools that were missing from LightWave at the time. The initial release of project:messiah contained enough tools that users could effectively disregard LightWave 5.6's animation features and use it simply as a rendering engine for animations they created solely in project:messiah. The release of LightWave [6] contains a number of features that duplicates or otherwise makes redundant some features of project:messiah. However, there are many professional LightWave animators and studios who are continuing to use project:messiah in production with LightWave [6].

project:messiah retains several advantages over LightWave [6], including functioning versions of not-quite-working-yet LightWave [6] features. For example, the audio waveform display in project:messiah's motion graph editor actually synchronizes the audio track accurately to the frame, unlike LightWave's uselessly choppy plug-in sampling and Layout frame slider playback. project:messiah's slider object actually works, unlike LightWave's documented-but-not-really-there slider null.

The documentation for project:messiah is in HTML format, and much of it is available for download from the company website. Fred Tepper has done a pretty good job on the reference, introduction, and tutorial documentation. However, you should be familiar with LightWave and with general principles of animation (particularly character animation) before you attempt the more advanced tutorials. One of the better tutorials for project:messiah is a leg setup similar to the AdvancedCharacter setup I analyzed earlier in this chapter, in "Advanced Character Setup Analysis."

If you have read through the preceding parts of this chapter, the tutorials and other documentation for project:messiah should be easier for you to understand. One of the primary strengths of project:messiah is the variety and extent of its constraints. This is a very powerful program for the experienced technical director (TD) or character setup specialist, and the best setups that are possible with project:messiah are an animator's dream.

In my opinion, the biggest disadvantage to using project:messiah, either for individual projects or in a studio production, is the uncertainty and risk inherent in dealing with such a small group of high-powered creative minds. The software began as an internal tool for Station X Studios, then the development team spun off to form its own company. At the time of this writing, project:messiah version 1.5.5 is shipping, and the next product from this company is supposed to be a standalone program that no longer needs LightWave for rendering. The principals (Fori Owurowa, Lyle Milton, and Dan Milling) are brilliant at software and have an impressive track record of developing tools for LightWave users, but they also have a track record of less-than-stellar product support for individual users. The new documentation is a healthy step in the right direction, but that's a very recent change. If you need a lot of hand-holding, you may want to think twice about committing a major production to project:messiah. Then again, if you need a lot of hand-holding, you're going to have a tough time with any character animation software.

Pulling It All Together

You should use the techniques in this chapter to build a character setup that goes beyond the simplified human model that most LightWave animators seem to use. Your setup will have a superstructure of constraints driving the torso, legs, shoulders, and head. The implication of this is that, if you animate the constraint hierarchy only and later upgrade the model and skeleton, the animation should still work just fine. This bears repeating: If you set the character up right the first time, you can make all the model and skeletal changes you want, anywhere along the line, without a bit of wasted effort.

In creating a structure of constraints, outside and apart from the IK chain hierarchy, you have added a meta-level to the degree of control you can have over your character. You can use FK, or IK, or neither, as you choose. You need never drop a key on the bones, using them more as a way to distribute the weighting of vertices and other aspects of skin deformations. You can more easily control the position and rotation of the joints with constraints alone. Unshackled by the physical proximity of bones that typically dictate parenting, you can arrange the relative position of these constraints in a hierarchy in any way convenient to you. A character's shoulder position constraints can be parented to a null that lets you shrug them both at the same time, no matter what you told the head, hips, and hands to do with their constraints. All of those are siblings too. Make those constraints follow a path if you'd like to make your character's fingers spell out a word in midair without spending weeks on the project.

Hierarchiphobia

It's easy to be intimidated by complex hierarchies, but they are always methodically constructed one step at a time and constrained one step at a time. Take it systematically and it's not nearly as intimidating.

It's good to keep in mind that there are two ways bones are being employed on any character. The first is as a driver for the skin. Skin-driving functions are simple. You assign points, via weight maps, to a bone. (For details, see pages 4.25 through 4.28 of the *LightWave [6] Motion: Animate & Render* manual, and pages 4.37 through 4.42 of the *Shape: Model, Surface & Light* manual.) But the needs of driving the skin are often different from simple mechanical relationships. The mechanisms that can drive muscles and fat, however, can be subordinate and additive to the standard skeletal movements. Thus, the biceps mechanism can be subordinate first to the standard bicep=>forearm mechanism (anatomically, the humerus, the bone running from shoulder to elbow) and the twin forearm bones (the radius and ulna). The mechanism within the biceps can be designed to rotate the biceps muscle when the elbow is bent, aiming the biceps muscle at the hand. Another mechanism can be subordinate to the biceps rotating mechanism, designed to bulge the muscle as the elbow bends at a steeper angle.

Limiting the rotation of joints to a single axis makes the biceps rotating mechanism unnecessary. The movement of the elbow forces rotation of the bone on which the biceps rest. Then the problem becomes isolating the rotation of the deltoid and collarbone mechanisms from the rotation of the biceps.

Among the more conventional meat mechanisms is some way of making muscles like the biceps look like they are flexing. Most methodologies for doing this can certainly make the muscle look like it's bulging, but few work in such a way as to make the bulge move along the length of the bone, nor do they usually allow a muscle to show strain under an animator's control. This is true whether the muscle bulge is based on expressions that convert joint or bone rotation to bulging via morphs or shape animation or whether such joint deformation is a built-in characteristic of the skinning process with the exaggeration a programmable feature. In the case of expressions, similar control can be exerted on the muscle, but it takes mathematical sophistication.

Another arm mechanism that needs to be addressed is the twisting mechanism in the forearm. If you have any detail at all in your model, you will need a mechanism that allows different parts of the forearm to rotate proportionally to the hand, which would include the wrist. In this way, control points closer to the wrist will almost rotate along with the wrist, while points closer to the elbow will rotate less or not at all when the wrist rotates. This avoids the shearing or tearing that often results from wrist rotation on a LightWave character.

The shoulder has generally been problematic for LightWave since people started trying to do characters. There are numerous software-specific solutions for dealing with shoulders, many involving expressions, morphs, and IK. The truly ambitious person doing IK setups might refer to George B. Bridgman's *The Human Machine* (ISBN: 0486227073). This book gives excellent mechanical descriptions of how the human muscular and structural mechanisms function, in a way that translates readily into LightWave.

What should be visible for animation? The answer is that for the first pass, the major constraints should be exposed. This makes the first pass of animation easier. And, of course, any element of the character can be selected and animated from the Scene Editor.

Put your setups to the test. Choose different setups for each side of a character, then compare the way the left and right sides animate. Try to think of other uses for the constraining techniques described. Try to find other ways to drive the biceps, collar, and shoulder.

Most of all, try to do things no one has ever done before.

Moving On

If you've worked through this chapter's projects, you have a better understanding of the use of constraints. Now you're ready to use your best character setup in the animation projects in Chapter 15. The projects dealing with full-body acting and caricature actions will put your setup to the test and make very clear how much time and effort a good setup can save you.

If you want to continue exploring setup issues, go on to Chapter 13, which shows you how to handle challenging technical setups such as facial animation, lip sync, cloth, and soft-object physics.

Power Tool Setups

Power tools and procedural setups, like any animation tools, are worse than useless if they get in the animator's way. As a setup person, you need to know when a power tool can save the animator work and when it's a counterproductive geek toy.

Building setups for complex characters is a catch-22. On one hand, you are expected to be up-to-date on the latest technological fixes, a wizard on the order of Ian Fleming's Q. On the other hand, the animator is more of an artist than an engineer and wants a setup as intuitive as a stop-motion puppet. To balance these competing demands, you need to both keep your techno-lust in check and protect the animator from power tool overload. Give him the most elegant, efficient setup he needs to animate the character and save the bells and whistles for your own amusement.

The preceding chapters show you the essential tools and processes you need to create good character setups. This chapter introduces a class of optional tools: power tools that can (sometimes) produce more efficient setups by giving more animation control to the computer. Sometimes that trade-off in control isn't worth it. If you are a setup person, you need to work with the animator to make sure the setup is what she needs, not what you'd like to set up.

How much should you automate? It's perfectly natural for setup people to rely too heavily on the computer. It's the old hammer-and-nail dilemma: When the only tool you have is a hammer, every problem starts to look like a nail. As long as your setups are relieving the animator of the mindless drudgery associated with traditional animation production, well and good. If the setup becomes so automated or difficult to use that it begins to cramp or fight the animator's creative style, it's time to back up and take another look at who's really running the show. Computers are simply complex tools—don't ever let them dictate the animator's creative options. Your job as setup person is to provide the animator with a setup that is as transparent and intuitive as possible.

Some of the most useful character animation power tools have applications for facial animation, lip sync, physical simulation, and cloth simulation. This chapter shows you how to set up these power tools to make the animator's job a little easier.

Facial Animation

For most characters, you will want to set up facial animation using morphing or displacement techniques. In some cases, you may be able to simplify animation of part or all of the face by using maps rather than animating changes in the character's geometry. Both morphing and displacement techniques create in-betweens automatically and with finer control, so they give you a significant advantage over maps when you animate emotional transitions.

The human face is made up of many layers of muscle and other tissues, overlapping in different directions and bridging attachment points from the shoulders to the top of the skull. The goal of character facial animation is not to realistically simulate every one of these muscles, but to mimic the surface appearance produced by their combined actions well enough to tell the story. This means you can cheat a lot in creating facial morph targets and nearly as much in setting up displacement controls.

Because LightWave supports several forms of morphing—simple morphing, Multiple Target Single Envelope (MTSE), and shape weighting via EndoMorph Mixer—you will generally be setting up facial animation by creating libraries of morph targets. It's still possible to set up and animate a complex or realistic face in LightWave by using displacement controls such as bones, but these approaches are usually prohibitively difficult to animate. Morph targets are significantly faster, more reliable, and easier to animate. They are also more compatible with lip sync software such as LipService, as detailed later in the section "Fourth Level: Lip Sync Setup for LipService."

Building Morph Target Libraries

Once you've decided on a morphing approach, the next decision is how to produce the necessary library of morph targets. LightWave's Modeler includes a selection of point and surface sculpting tools, so you could choose to simply reshape the basic face into the new targets. As an alternative, you could set up Bones to deform the face, then use the Save Transformed function to create a new morph target from each new Bones pose.

Most characters will need a basic repertoire of facial expressions and the ability to lip sync the language of the vocal track. This gives you a baseline library of morph targets that you should build for each new character. Once you have the baseline library, you can add to it, when necessary, to expand the dramatic or linguistic range of the character. Depending on the flexibility of your facial animation setups, you may be able to get by with a very small library. If your setups are not as versatile in weighting or mixing morph targets, you may have to build a larger library.

You have several options for defining a baseline library. One is to simply copy an existing library, either from an existing character, a commercial data set, or the sample set (if any) provided with your lip sync software, such as LipService. Another is to consult reference sources on traditional animation, human facial expression, or acting and create a library to cover the range of expressions illustrated. If you choose the latter approach, either the Faigin books or the Lemay books listed in the Bibliography are excellent resources.

EndoMorph Mixer and Shape Weighting

Although simple morphing may be the most straightforward approach, it loads a lot of work onto the modeler and the animator. Morphing from one shape to the next requires you to craft every shape you'll use. In reality, people tend to hold expressions such as smiling or frowning while they're talking. Do you want to create all your target shapes smiling and then create them all over again for a frown and again for any other transitory expression? It took 180 distinct heads to give Jack Skellington that range of emotional and spoken expression in *The Nightmare Before Christmas*. If you can blend or weight more than two shapes at the same time, you need only create a few targets for mouth shapes and for eyelids and brows and a few others for overall expressions. Weighting shapes is a powerful approach so long as you understand what to expect from it, and why.

LightWave includes a plug-in, EndoMorph Mixer, that provides shape-weighting functions. The *Motion: Animate & Render* manual describes how to set up and use this plug-in on pages 4.33 to 4.39, so I'll just present a quick overview here.

EndoMorph Mixer (Figure 13.1) enables you to load a base, or *anchor*, object with layers of targets built in. A slider for each target determines the weight of that target's effect on the anchor. The requirements for target objects are the same as for simple morphing or MTSE—each target must have the same point count and distribution as the anchor object. Surface attributes don't matter because only the point movements are used to deform the anchor object. Any surfaces applied to the anchor are the only ones that will appear in the final rendering.

You animate the shape weighting by setting slider values, then creating a keyframe. You also have the option of saving new morph targets from any keyframe. Layout shows the changes to the anchor object in realtime. You can drag the scrub bar to view the animation, but depending on the speed of your system, the playback might not be at full speed.

As with other setup methods, you should document the EndoMorph setup of each anchor object for the animator so she can tell which page or group to look in for a particular target.

Simple and weighted shape interpolations differ greatly from each other. Suppose you start with a neutral face A, with lips slightly parted and eyes open, then modify duplicates to create two more shapes—B, with the eyes closed, and C, with an open mouth. Simple morphing to the closed-eye shape B would not change the mouth shape; the mouth would remain closed.

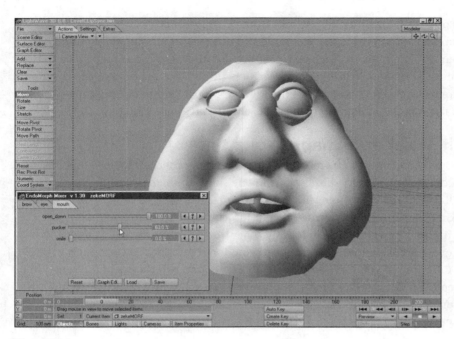

Figure 13.1
EndoMorph Mixer plug-in showing brow, eye, and mouth groups for zekeMORF object.

Simple morphing to the open-mouth shape C would open the eyes again. When you interpolate back to the eyes-closed shape B, the mouth shuts. The result of 50 percent of B and C is a half-lidded drooler. Using only those three shapes, you would not be able to close the eyes while keeping the mouth open—unless you used weighted shapes.

Weighted shape interpolation starts with a neutral shape and considers each target relative only to the neutral shape, not to the other target shapes. Only the differences from the original neutral shape matter for each new target. You modify the neutral by layering more interpolations from other targets. Each interpolation remains separate: The open-mouth target does not modify the position of the eyes in the neutral pose, so the eyes don't change. The eye-blink pose does not change the mouth points; only the mouth targets modify the mouth points. With weighted shape interpolation, your character can babble and blink incessantly without costing nearly so much of your modeling, setup, and animation time.

Take a look at Figure 13.2. All targets define deltas from this original neutral starting shape. Relative to their original location in the neutral shape, points move on a vector (straight line) toward a new target shape, weighted or blended by a percentage with any other specified target shapes. That percentage includes negative values and values past 100%. (The sliders only go from 0 to 100; you have to type other values in the numeric entry fields.)

Figure 13.2
Weighted shape setup for mouth, in neutral position.

If a target shape's point is one unit in positive Z from its original on the neutral shape, morphing 100% to that target moves the point one unit forward. Morphing 200% would move it forward two units. A negative value will move it in the opposite direction on the same vector. When you blend in an additional target that raises the same point one unit in positive Y (relative to the original shape), the point moves up from its new position without changing its Z value. The points of each target shape move relative to their position in the starting shape, even if you used other targets to animate those points to a new shape.

Although you can still simply blend from one target shape to the next, that does not take full advantage of the power of this approach. While modeling, don't forget that for every shape you create, you're also creating its opposite. Create a raised smile by taking a copy of the original shape, translating the mouth points only in Y, and raising the corners of the mouth slightly higher (Figure 13.3). Using a negative value yields a frown (Figure 13.4).

Pursing the lips widens the mouth when using its opposite. Note that this is the product of a very small change. Use a light touch or the weighted interpolations can perform unpleasant exaggerations on your shapes.

Keep track of the direction you send your shapes while you model so that you don't encounter any areas flying off in directions you don't want. Modeling a raised smile so that it also pushes

Figure 13.3
Full weighting for smile target.

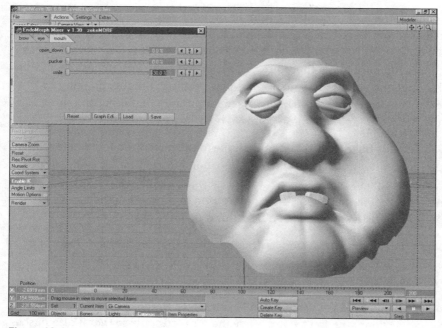

Figure 13.4
Negative weighting for smile creates a frown.

back into the face will pout it out away from the face when sent on its opposite vector from neutral. Perhaps that's what you want, but this method magnifies the bad as much as the good. Surprises abound, some serendipitous, others not so.

If you use this method, it helps to use an entire face at once. If you raise a smile, you may also want to raise the cheeks, the corners of the nose, and the bottom eyelids slightly. These fleeting changes to the overall look of the face help to keep things alive, if that's the sort of thing you're looking for. It wouldn't be easy to implement that kind of subtlety with an individual muscle setup. One rapidly loses track of which muscle to use to change an expression. Because a lot of little changes can add up fairly quickly, you'll spend time tweaking to determine just how much of it suits your taste.

Use of multiple target shapes is not limited to facial animation. You can use them for bulging biceps, flesh folds, jiggling bellies, and other fun ways of faking soft tissue dynamics. You can confuse your programmer friends by telling them you did it by running a realtime simulation that you wrote on your coffee break. Naturally, you will want to trigger those shapes by rotations or other events using expressions, because the arm will look funny the first time it bends and you forget to make the biceps bulge.

Generating Target Shapes

Start with a good face that you and/or your client like. Nobody will think any less of you if you sculpted it out of clay or band-sawed sections of a mannequin head, then traced them onto grid paper and typed in each point coordinate. (I don't recommend the latter method unless you're being paid by the hour on client-provided tools.) You may have already modeled a face entirely in the computer yourself. If you have, the next section will give you no trouble at all.

The most important thing to remember is, don't alter the geometry of your neutral face or that of any of the targets once you've started generating them. If you decide you need to add just one more point here or delete an edge there, unless you can execute exactly the same procedure on all the other targets you have generated, just don't do it. The point list in each target must refer to the same points in each of the models. Unless you're looking for unique ways for the face to crumple on the monitor, only their x-, y-, and z-coordinates can differ, not the number or order of the points in your original, hero face. The simplest way to do this is to duplicate the original and move the points on the copy until you have the shape you want.

One simple reason for starting with a partially open mouth is for the convenience of the modeler. It's easier to add a target that closes it the rest of the way later, and a slack mouth is as good a definition of a neutral face as any. If your character is supposed to be smiling a lot according to yours or the client's specifications, the smile is a target, not the central, neutral, anchor object. You want all of your expressions to be relative to neutral, not to a smile. If you really want to use something other than a neutral mouth shape for your central shape, such as an open mouth (it has been successfully done), remember that all of your targets will move relative to that one. Any variance from my recommended procedures that works better than what I tell you is encouraged, but don't say I didn't warn you.

Asymmetry is a valuable and desirable thing, though not mandatory in the neutral target unless we're talking Quasimodo. You can create plenty of target variations on the neutral shape that have exactly the kinds of asymmetry you'll want to be able to choose from when you need it. Asymmetry does not mean making a lopsided neutral base model and forgetting about it. The idea in all cases is to provide maximum control of the character as an animator, not to lock some pose into the base model.

Although those pressed for time on a rush job may opt for only a neutral mouth and an open one, you can do so much more with the neutral, open mouth and a raised smile. Don't complain that you won't have time to animate it. A good puppeteer can get quite close in realtime. As a keyframer, your control is even more precise. Pursing the lips into a big, exaggerated "ooh" mouthed pout puts you ahead of the game. Everything else is asymmetrical gravy. You only translate selected points along the y-axis when creating an open mouth or raised smile target. A pursed lips target involves a lot of scaling in X and more exaggeration than you think is appropriate when you push it forward in Z.

It's easier than you might think to move the mouth over to one side of the face or the other, as you might in a whispered aside. Think of it as creating a new neutral mouth, just with one corner near the middle and a nasolabial crease formed on the other side, but still a neutral mouth. This is an important idea to grasp. The raised smile target translates in Y from wherever the neutral mouth points happen to be, based on where other targets have placed them. Create a target by grabbing all the points of a copy of the neutral mouth and translating them down an inch. Layering in that target will simply slide all of the dialogue you've previously animated down to the chin as that target reaches 100 percent. The lips will purse from wherever you place the mouth.

You should also bear in mind that there are no rotations with shape deformation. All movements are linear unless modified by another target, as shown in the bending desk lamp projects in earlier chapters. Points defining the open eyelid, and its position when closed, interpolate at 50 percent along a straight-line vector somewhere inside the eyeball. You can create an additional half-lidded target and adjust your motion graphs to slide those lid points forward as the lid moves from either extreme. You may still need to add a target at each third.

Although you may find it easy to create a target by selecting all the points of the mouth and rotating them on Z, the interpolation from neutral when you animate will not be a rotation. Worse, its negative value won't be a rotation in the opposite direction. You must remember that each vector is a straight line through the neutral and the target, and an interpolation goes only along that vector. Wishful thinking won't make it turn left at Albuquerque.

For moving a neutral mouth target around on a face, you don't have considerations as critical as matching a lid to the surface of an eyeball. If you do want to slide one corner of the mouth back and over for some sort of smirk, check out how that neutral smirk looks blended at 50 percent from only the neutral. If teeth are poking out, copy that shape, fix it, and blend it in as a new target on your way to the extreme. Few targets require what is in essence a breakdown pose to get to them, but they are easy to add if you need them.

Eyebrows are fun. Raise one, the other, or both. Furrow them, arch them, and make them dance around like the love child of Spock coupled with Shields and Yarnell. They won't rotate around the brow unless you add a target to do so, if you really think anybody will see it. Just be sure to apply any brow targets to a copy of the neutral, not to copies of previously modeled targets.

Any stunt shapes, like puffing the cheeks like Dizzy Gillespie, should be modifications to the central, neutral mouth shape. Have I hammered that one home enough yet? Give yourself a few extra degrees of control, such as raising only one corner of the mouth, then the other on a separate target. You can move that corner up and down, wherever you need it to be, from wherever it happens to have moved.

While moving the points to make additional targets, you may want to leave the target model overlaid on the neutral so you can see just how far you've moved it relative to the neutral. If you prefer, you can always pop it down and overlay it to check your work. On a raised smile, first raise the corners and then select the rest of the points of the mouth, raising them all at once. Then select more of the surrounding points and raise them along, and add or lose a few as you go to make sure the skin does what it ought in such a move. Don't just move it all up in a solid mass without considering what the skin around the mouth would do. The lips should maintain their basic shape, especially if you're not going to change the corners of the mouth but are creating the target primarily to move the mouth around the face.

When you create a new target, either for simple morph, MTSE, or EndoMorph Mixer, you should take a screenshot or render an image of it, then add that image to the character's model sheet, labeled with the name of the target. This not only tells the animator where to find a particular target, it helps the setup person locate the nearest matching target when it is necessary to sculpt a new one.

Lip Sync

Lip sync is a subset of facial animation, so you can use the same tools and techniques described in the preceding section. Setting up a character for lip sync is essentially a process of making sure the animator has enough morph targets, maps, or displacement poses to choose from. The last thing an animator should have to do while he's rolling hot on a long lip sync sequence is stop and ask the setup person for another morph target or map. Anticipate the animator's needs, and you'll get a lot fewer Nerf missiles bouncing off your forehead.

LightWave character animators now have the luxury of choosing between several approaches to lip sync. This is a very good thing, because even a good technique can drive you crazy or broke if you try to apply it to the wrong project. Making the right choice is especially important when you have tight deadlines and limited resources. Following are my evaluations of the fastest and cheapest available lip sync options and my recommendations on when to use each of them.

As I have stated in previous chapters, I evaluate and recommend techniques based on my five criteria for efficient animation: reduce redundant work, support incremental detailing, provide rapid feedback, create documents for decision-makers, and stay flexible. Lip sync carries some special challenges to these criteria, mostly pertinent to paying clients. If you are animating lip sync on a purely personal or fine art project, much of what I have to say will not be as crucial for you. If you are making a living doing lip synced animation for paying clients, especially in advertising, listen up!

The criterion of staying flexible is the paramount virtue for paid lip sync animation. This is mostly due to the simple fact that a client who knows nothing about animation can still spot a bad piece of lip sync, so it is harder to fake or to cut corners. You simply have to do it right or the client will not buy it. Another stressing factor for staying flexible with lip sync is that many clients will change the copy on you at the last minute. My guess is that they are used to playing this dirty little trick on live talent and do not understand that you cannot deliver a cold reading with an animated character.

So how should you deal with this? First, make sure your contract for any job includes a firm series of sign-offs, with clear surcharges for redoing work on any changes requested after the pertinent sign-off. This will not protect you from a client who really likes to change his mind, but it will ensure that you are paid for your wasted work. Sign-offs do not give you the right to slam the door on a client either. Simply saying "No" can lose future business for you, while a more diplomatic "Yes, but it will cost you X amount" may dissuade them without driving them away.

Second, keep lip sync where it belongs, at the very end of the animation process. This relates to the "incremental detailing" criteria; lip sync is the fussiest, most timing-critical level of detail, so it should be last. Early on, put your efforts into creating well-composed shots, strong poses, readable transitions, and good timing. If you animate a strong performance in mime, the client is much more likely to overlook flaws in the lip sync. Contrariwise, even the best lip sync will not save an otherwise poor performance. Moreover, the strength of a character's grosser body movements can fall farther out of sync than lip movements without seriously hurting the performance. Sweeping arm gestures or the rhythm of a walk cycle generally do not have to precisely match every syllable of the character's dialogue. This means you can use the first dialogue track to block out the key poses, refine the in-betweens, and fine-tune the performance's timing without worrying about wasting too much work. If the client comes in at that point with some rewrites to the copy, odds are excellent that the changes will not materially affect the arc of the performance.

The shorter the piece, the more true this tends to be; there is simply not much space for fiddling in a :30 commercial. For longer formats, the client tends to be either better informed about (or more thoroughly insulated from) the animation process and therefore less likely to rewrite copy at the 11th hour. At the highest level, feature film production, you will almost always work from a completely locked sound track.

Third, choose a lip sync process that suits the client, your resources, and the character, in that order. Suiting the client means both being acceptable to the client (so you get paid) and accommodating the client's behavior. You can choose almost any method for a reasonable and well-informed client. For a vacillating or ignorant client, you should choose a process that supports rapid last-minute revisions. Your resources are only slightly less important than the client is; if the client is willing to pay enough, you can always acquire more resources. Once the contract is signed and you have a fixed budget to meet, staying within your resources can make or break your profit on the job. If you miscalculate, the only workable solution may be expensive plug-ins or additional animators. Make sure you have a very clear picture of the software, hardware, and animator's time your chosen lip sync process will consume. Finally, design the character to suit the process. If your client and resources leave you with any choice, you can select the process that best suits the design and animation of the character.

I like to classify lip sync into four levels of sophistication. The most basic level is what you can do with a ventriloquist's dummy: opening and closing the mouth, usually to match the volume of the dialogue track. The next level includes some hand-keyframed changes to the width of the mouth so you can make a distinction between loud AH and loud O phonemes. The third level of sophistication is fully formed phoneme targets. Finally, the fourth level of sophistication blends facial expressions over a third-level lip sync.

PROJECT 13.1 Setting Up the Simplest, Fastest, and Worst Lip Sync

Let's look at the worst case first. The client, a local used car dealer, has a very short time before his air time deadline. (He has wasted most of the available time shopping for the lowest price on the animation.) The client's business already has a mascot, and the poor slob who has had to wear the mascot costume at grand openings has been hired to record the dialogue. The client signs off on some very simple storyboards and provides you with the audiotape and some promotional stills of his dealership to use as background plates. Now all you have to do is model, set up, and animate the mascot (including lip sync) in two weeks.

If you are a competent LightWave user with the requisite amount of talent, you could pull this off with time to spare. The joke arrives in a series of phone calls and faxes, as the client sends copy changes almost daily. At this rate, the client is going to try changing copy while you are dumping the animation to tape. What do you do? Design the character to use the method of lip sync that is simplest and easiest to automate. You want loading the digitized WAV file to be one of the last steps before your final rendering, and you do not want to have to tweak the lip sync at all.

One way to do this is to use the AudioChannel plug-in (Figure 13.5). This Graph Editor Modifier enables you to load a WAV file and convert it to an envelope that you can apply to any channel for any LightWave item. Before you load it into LightWave, you may want to process the WAV file in GoldWave or other software to downsample the "noisy" dialogue into a simpler, low-frequency amplitude envelope.

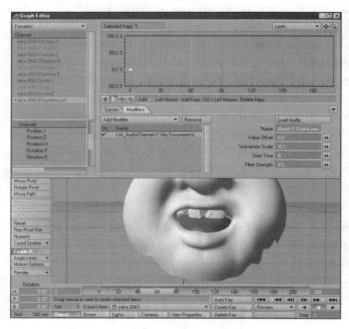

Figure 13.5
AudioChannel interface.

You can apply the results in Layout to a single bone or null that moves the character's lower jaw. The results will look something like a novice puppeteer's performance, with the mouth opening wider according to the loudness of the dialogue. However, the timing of the movement will be an exact match, so the inappropriateness of any particular mouth position is easier to overlook.

To complete this project, follow these steps:

1. Run the WAV file through an audio-processing program that will turn it into a downsampled, low-frequency waveform.

2. Create an anchor object with a closed mouth and a target object with an open mouth.

3. Load the two objects into Layout, with the open mouth set as a morph target of the closed mouth. Set the open mouth object to 100% Dissolve so you don't see it.

4. Open the Graph Editor and select the MorphAmount channel for the closed mouth.

5. Click on Add Modifier and choose LW_AudioChannel.

6. Open the LW_AudioChannel panel. Load the WAV file you prepared in Step 1 and adjust the Offset, Scale, Start Time, and Filter Strength settings to produce the graph you want.

   Once the setup is complete, it's a very quick and simple matter to swap out the WAV file. This enables you to cope with literally last-minute changes to the dialogue.

If you plan to animate lip sync using this method, you should design the character's head like a ventriloquist dummy's or a Muppet's. Because the lip sync will be somewhat less expressive than a sock puppet's, it is critical that you get as much of the performance as possible from the character's attitude and movement. An excellent case in point is Miss Piggy, as performed by Frank Oz. The Muppet's face is almost entirely fixed, especially while speaking; the lips cannot pucker or widen, the corners of the mouth cannot be drawn up or down. Almost the entire emotional performance is driven by the attitude of the head; a few degrees of tilt creates a completely different impression. This is your gold standard when designing a character for single-control lip sync: All expression comes from the rest of the character, and the lip sync control is used only to hinge the lower jaw.

You have three modeling choices for a character's head to be animated using AudioChannel: a single mesh to be deformed by bones, an anchor-and-target pair to be animated using a morph envelope (as shown in Figure 13.5), or a separate piece for the lower jaw to be rotated like that of a traditional puppet or ventriloquist's dummy.

So, you model and set up your character's head to lip sync from a single envelope. You animate the entire shot according to the storyboards and spend the remaining time before your rendering deadline tweaking the character's skeletal performance. At the last possible minute, the client sends the voice talent over to your studio to record the final dialogue. You digitize each take straight into your computer as a WAV file, choose the best one, and convert it to an envelope. You spend about 10 minutes tweaking the envelope to close each "M," "B," and "P" and do a quick test rendering. You fix a couple of minor problems, everything checks out, and you render the final animation and dump it to tape. The client makes his air time, you get paid, and you have another story to tell (but probably not another piece for your demo reel).

Setting Up the Second-Level Lip Sync

You can create the next level of sophistication in lip sync with a modification of the preceding project:

1. Instead of just two morph targets, open and closed, you need to create four targets: open, closed, puckered (or "Ooo") and stretched horizontally (or "Eee").

2. You won't be able to use a simple morph for this; you'll have to assemble an EndoMorph. Load the four objects into Modeler.

3. Choose the closed model as the foreground layer and choose the open model as the background layer.

4. Apply the Bkg-To-MORF plug-in and name the new EndoMorph "Open."

5. Select the next model as the background layer and repeat Step 4 with an appropriate name. After adding all three objects, you should end up with a model named Closed that has three EndoMorphs: Open, Eee, and Ooo.

6. Load the Closed object into Layout and open the EndoMorph Mixer. You should see something like Figure 13.6. From the Mixer, click on the Graph Editor button.

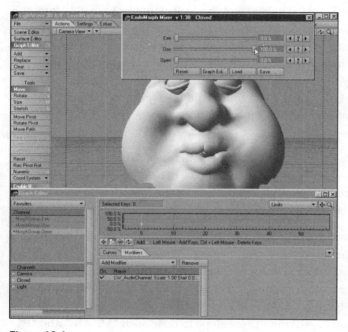

Figure 13.6
AudioChannel modifier applied to MorphGroup.Open channel, leaving the remaining two sliders available for manual keyframing.

7. In the Graph Editor, select the MorphGroup.Open channel and add the AudioChannel modifier to it, just as you did in the preceding project.

You will now be able to manually keyframe the Ooo and Eee sliders in the EndoMorph Mixer to make the width of the character's mouth more closely match the phonemes being pronounced. You should be able to get a much better quality lip sync sequence than the preceding project, in much less time than a third- or fourth-level lip sync process.

PROJECT 13.3 Setting Up the Third-Level Lip Sync

If you want to produce the next better level of lip sync and are working on a shoe-string and cannot afford any plug-ins at all, you are pretty much stuck with an EndoMorph Mixer setup and manual analysis. This is the most time-consuming form of lip sync in LightWave, and you should attempt it only when you have a final dialogue track and plenty of time. If you can get the Audio loader to work in Layout, you can do your analysis and animation at the same time. Be warned: This is a demanding process, and it takes a lot of practice to become proficient. If you botch the analysis or your client wants to make last-minute changes, most of your work will be wasted.

To complete this project, follow these steps:

1. Sculpt models and compile them into EndoMorph targets for the major phonemes.

2. Load the anchor object into Layout and open the EndoMorph Mixer.

3. In the Scene Editor, load the audio file. Close the Scene Editor.

This setup will enable you to scrub through the audio track listening for the peaks and transitions of each phoneme. Adjusting the EndoMorph Mixer sliders to emphasize each phoneme, and setting keyframes, is the labor-intensive part of this process. If you are also blending in emotional expressions, the workload is even heavier. A more user-friendly process is to use Miguel Grinberg's Magpie Pro software. The latest version can automatically export animation files that are compatible with EndoMorph Mixer in LightWave [6]. For details, see the Magpie Pro sections later in this chapter.

The three preceding approaches are for those times you need quick-and-dirty lip sync. If you have the time and other resources to do a more professional job, you should definitely consider Joe Alter's LipService plug-in.

Fourth Level: Lip Sync Setup for LipService

Joe Alter's LipService plug-in for LightWave includes some very powerful tools, and the interface for some of them is very intuitive and a significant improvement over other lip sync tools I've used. If you are an experienced animator and are familiar with any other lip sync software (or even the manual dope sheet approach), you should be able to use LipService effectively. The LipService documentation is rather sparse for a combined reference and tutorial manual, so if you're a beginner, you may find LipService difficult to use at first. Stick with it; the results are worth the effort.

In evaluating any production tool, the most important factor is the quality of the final product. LipService has produced (in expert hands) some of the most entertaining lip sync performances I've seen in computer-generated animation. If you are considering LipService, I highly recommend that you view the animations on Joe Alter's Web site, **www.joealter.com**.

LipService is a fairly successful attempt to reconcile the dichotomy that is part of the lip sync process. On the one hand, lip sync key poses are dictated by the voice track, with very little room for the animator to interpret how long or how strongly to emphasize a phoneme. This requires a rather technical, analytical approach. On the other hand, the facial animation to express emotions is highly subjective, and the animator has a great deal of freedom (and responsibility) to create a strong performance. This requires a fluid, improvisational approach. The problem is how to successfully support both these approaches in the same software.

LipService is a standalone application (Figure 13.7) plus a LightWave displacement map plug-in (Figure 13.8). You perform the lip sync operations in the application, then import objects and deformation files into LightWave for rendering. LipService requires a set of morph targets with identical point count and order, the same rules as for simple morph, MTSE, or EndoMorph. The tutorial files include the base Zeke character face, 18 phoneme targets, 32 facial expression targets, some scene files, and a WAV voice track. The models are very well done, and it really helps the new user to start using the program with such a nice data set.

The LipService work area (the large window) can show the loaded object as wireframe or shaded solid and allows you to make surfaces appear white, green, or invisible. White means you can manipulate the surface; green or invisible means the surface is frozen.

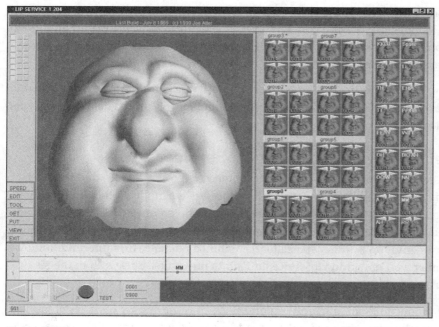

Figure 13.7
LipService interface.

Figure 13.8
LipService deformation plug-in loaded in Layout.

If you need to create a set of morph targets, LipService includes some unique and powerful tools to help. You can load the base object into the work area using the Get|Model menu option, make changes to it with a variety of sculpting tools, then save the modified object to one of the Pose slots. When you have completed sculpting your morph targets, the Put|Poses function saves all 50 objects in a numbered sequence for easy reloading.

One function that I especially appreciate is Edit|Deform Poses. It measures the changes you have made to the work area (presumably the base or neutral object) and applies those changes to all 50 target objects. This can be a lifesaver if you have a lot of finished facial animation and the client wants to make changes to the character's face. This function enables you to make changes to the character right up to the last render. If you make a living with facial animation, the Deform Poses function alone may justify the price of LipService.

You can rotate the object in the work area by holding down the left mouse button and dragging. The sculpt tool is activated by holding down the right mouse button. You can vary the range of the sculpting tools by holding down both mouse buttons and dragging out a circle to cover the area you want to affect. The sculpting tools include *translate*, *inflate*, and *to neutral*. Translate moves points in the x,y plane, parallel to the screen. Inflate moves points in or out along their own normal axes, which is very useful for organic swelling or sucking-in changes. To neutral is like a controlled Undo; it changes the current object back toward the shape of the base or neutral object. This is especially handy if you have overexaggerated a change and simply want to reduce it a little.

If you'd like to play with LipService, there is a demo version of it in the Alter directory on this book's CD-ROM. Once you have a LipService setup you like, you can skip ahead to the section in Chapter 16 on facial animation and lip sync using LipService.

The old rule applies to lip sync: "Time, Cost, Quality; pick any two." If you are fortunate enough to have a client with deep pockets and lots of time, you can produce the best lip sync you have the talent for. Unfortunately, most lip sync projects are more limited in time and resources, so you have to compromise on quality. I hope this section has given you the information to choose the lip sync approach that will give you the best results for your time and money.

As with most animation processes, the more time you spend at lip sync, the better and faster you will become.

Mapped Lip Sync Using Magpie Pro

The simplest setup for lip sync is a set of maps to be applied to a flat surface instead of a modeled mouth. This approach makes it very easy to use software like Magpie Pro to automate most of the lip sync process. Several projects in Chapter 9 covered the process of creating matched color, bump/displacement, and clip maps for lip sync. The only remaining setup work is adding the new maps to Magpie Pro's library.

You can customize Magpie Pro to better suit your own track analysis style and needs. All you need to do is create a set of thumbnail images from your library of morph targets or maps and add those images to a Magpie Pro expression set. An expression set is a list of every phoneme, emotion, or action that is represented by an image file. Each image file can be used for more than one expression. For example, a single image file can be used for many of the consonant phoneme expressions. The MGE (MaGpie Expression) file controls image and channel assignments. You can edit this file directly with a word processor or interactively from within Magpie Pro.

You can find more information about Magpie Pro in the Magpie directory on this book's CD-ROM. This directory also contains a demo version of Magpie Pro, which includes a default expression set named SEGISMUNDO.MGE with 18 rendered images of a character's face (Figure 13.9).

Here's the text of the SEGISMUNDO.MGE file:

```
[Pictures]
A=a1.bmp
B=b2.bmp
C=c3.bmp
D=d4.bmp
E=e5.bmp
F=f6.bmp
G=g7.bmp
H=h8.bmp
```

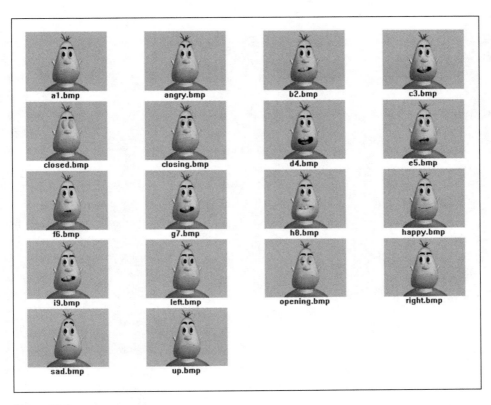

Figure 13.9
Segismundo sample expressions.

```
I=i9.bmp
Closed=closed.BMP
Closing=closing.BMP
Left=left.BMP
Down=A1.bmp
Right=right.BMP
Opened=A1.bmp
Up=up.BMP
Opening=opening.BMP
Smile=happy.BMP
Angry=Angry.BMP
Sad=Sad.BMP

[Channels]
Eyes=1,138,73,189,114
Eyebrows=1,134,57,190,73
Mouth=2,72,100,154,212
```

```
[Eyes]
Closed=1
Closing=1
Left=1
Right=1
Opened=1
Opening=1

[Eyebrows]
Down=1
Up=1
Angry=1
Sad=1

[Mouth]
A=1
B=1
C=1
D=1
E=1
F=1
G=1
H=1
I=1
Smile=1
```

As you can see, the expression set is a simple, readable file that you can customize in any text editor. Be careful to not corrupt the file. If you're not completely sure of what you are doing, you should follow the directions in Magpie Pro's online help files to create an expression set by drag-and-drop. This approach is easier but more time-consuming. Direct editing of the MGE file is a quick way to add a new expression set to your existing libraries, such as when you create a new character.

The images supplied with Magpie and Magpie Pro are good samples, but if you want to animate more accurate lip sync, you'll want to customize your own expression sets. For example, the provided sets have no transition pose for the character's mouth other than Closed. If you are animating lip sync with maps, you should also have mouths shaped for the in-betweens, or transitions, between each of the key phonemes. These in-betweens can make the difference between a jerky, distracting lip sync and one that appears fluid and natural. You can also make some of the key phonemes more specific. F and V, for instance, should have a slightly different placement of the upper front teeth against the lower lip.

Projects 9.5, 9.6, and 9.7 show how to paint matching color, bump, and clip maps for mapped lip sync. Project 13.4 shows you how to add your own maps to Magpie Pro's expression sets.

Creating Your Own Magpie Pro Expression Sets

13.4 If you are animating lip sync with mapped images or image sequences, creating Magpie Pro expression sets is very simple:

1. Create a new directory inside the Magpie directory and name it for the new expression set you are creating.

2. Copy all the map images to the new directory, with appropriate file names.

3. Resize all the images to 320x240 pixels and change the format (if necessary) to BMP.

4. Using Notepad or another text editor, open an existing MGE file. Save it under the name of your new expression set. This makes it easy for you to use the old MGE file as a template for the new one.

5. Edit the MGE file to add the new image file names to the appropriate expression labels.

6. Save the new MGE file to the same directory as the expression images.

7. Launch Magpie Pro, and in the Options dialog box (see Figure 13.10), add the new expression set.

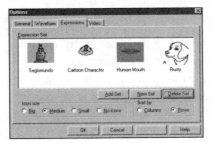

Figure 13.10
Expressions tab of the Options dialog box.

You may have some difficulty selecting names that accurately describe the expression represented. Unfortunately, accurate diacritical marks are not available in the standard screen fonts. To make up for this deficiency, use more letters or even complete words to describe the expressions. For example, either e_macron or eee clearly represents the long-e phoneme.

The most important consideration is that the animator is able to quickly identify and choose among the available expressions. You should print out the MGE file and a thumbnail sheet of the expression images and add them to the documentation for the character setup.

EndoMorph Lip Sync Using Magpie Pro 1.1

The latest version of Magpie Pro supports LightWave [6]'s EndoMorph objects for both the 3D Preview and animation export. To add EndoMorphs to the 3D Preview, proceed as usual by opening the expression properties dialog box for each expression, then selecting the EndoMorph object file. If Magpie Pro detects EndoMorphs inside the object file, it will pop up a menu of the available shapes. Select the shape you want for the current expression. Repeat until each EndoMorph has a corresponding Magpie Pro expression.

To use the LightWave [6] export function, you must first have a scene file containing your EndoMorph character. The character must have the MorphMixer plug-in already applied. It doesn't matter if there are keyframes defined for MorphMixer or not. In the Export dialog box, you choose your base scene and the EndoMorph object you are exporting to. Magpie Pro will read your scene, find the object and add (or update) the MorphMixer keyframes for it. You can then choose whether Magpie Pro will output a new scene file or overwrite the old base scene.

Physical Simulation

One of the most tempting classes of power tools for LightWave character animation is physical simulation. When an animator has to manage dozens of controls, it's hard to deny the opportunity to foist some of that management off on the computer. Unfortunately, physical simulation is also one of the best ways of killing the illusion of life. Most forms of simulation end up making the character look driven by outside forces rather than motivated from within. With the exception of a few narrow applications, physical simulation is not a good idea for character animation.

On the other hand, if your characters are to interact with a complex environment, you can save enormous amounts of time and effort by automating the behavior of that environment. Any prop, set, or other animatable element is a candidate for physical simulation. Furthermore, you have total control over the environment's parameters, so you can animate gravity, wind, mass, inertia, and other physical forces in ways that mimic the caricatured environments of classic cartoons. Suppose, for instance, a falling piano is supposed to squash flat when it lands on a character. Physical simulation software can create that effect with a standard model and a simpler setup that is also easier to animate than conventional keyframing. The lack of apparent motivation is not a problem with the falling object. In fact, motivation would spoil the effect. Thus, physical simulation is a definite asset when manipulating the character's environment but should be used only with extreme caution when animating the character itself.

There are a number of basic concepts collected under the heading of physical simulation. The most obvious is ballistics—the process of moving objects in paths and with velocities based on mass, inertia, and applied energy. Any falling object or missile is a good candidate for ballistics. In addition to being the most obvious, it's also one of the simplest forms of simulation. The parameters are few, well defined, and generally intuitive, and the calculations are not terrible system hogs.

The next class of simulation is collision detection. This, as you might guess, is the process of calculating when one object in the scene comes into contact with another. This type of simulation has definite advantages for characters if the software enables collision detection to perform tasks such as automatically constraining the character's feet to the floor rather than allowing them to pass through it. Collision detection plus ballistics can be used for bouncing balls and other ricochets and for establishing the areas affected by friction and other material attributes. Collision detection can be simple, based on the crudest bounding-box approximations, or it can be refined enough to rely on the finest details in the objects' surfaces. Due to the high number of calculations necessary, the more complex the objects and the more accurate the desired results, the more computation intensive (that is, dead slow) the simulation will be.

Material attributes are a crucial part of any physical simulation. If you want a model to look as if it's made of rubber, you need to set attributes—such as elasticity, friction, density, compressibility, and damping—to simulate rubber. Otherwise, the simulation might just as easily make the model move like porcelain. In the best simulation software, you can also animate material attributes. This enables you to change the parameters of characters or their environment during an action. This capability is invaluable for caricature because objects must sometimes appear to be realistically solid at one moment, then turn to jelly the next.

The most advanced form of physical simulation that is of use in character animation is soft-object deformation. This is a process that enables you to animate an internal skeleton with the keyframe tools you're accustomed to, then turn the simulation software on to animate the meat of the character. This essentially automates squash-and-stretch and other overlapping action within the aforesaid limits of character motivation.

Whether you are a setup person or an animator, there are several warning signs that indicate when you are applying too much physical simulation at the expense of the character's performance:

- *Lack of control*—The simulation insists on making things move the way it has been programmed rather than the way the animator wants it to.

- *Too much animator time spent tweaking the simulation parameters rather than creating a performance*—This means there are too many controls and the simulation is not actually saving any effort for the animator.

- *Mushy, off, or staggered timing*—Strong character performances are based on timing; that is, hitting a pose precisely at a particular keyframe. Most simulations simply run their course, and the timing is not controllable to the frame. This tends to smear the action across a number of frames, making the action unclear and ineffective.

- *Interminable waits for screen updates or test renders*—Simulation software requires many more calculations than keyframing requires, even for rough previews. Most simulations also cannot be scrubbed in realtime to evaluate their results. This slows down the animator's work, often to the point where an experienced animator could keyframe the shot faster than the software could simulate it.

- *Homogenized characters*—For effective caricature using soft-object simulations, the animator must be able to animate the character's modulus of elasticity to get differential effects. Differential effects make the objects appear to change elasticity, just as a muscle reacts differently depending on whether it's taut or relaxed. Different parts of the character must have different reactions to the same forces or the character looks like it's all made of the same stuff, like a balloon filled with meat.

LightWave now includes basic physical simulation as part of the package. Motion Designer, the Motion Options Modifiers, and a little imaginative use of expressions can go a long way toward automating physical simulation in LightWave.

Cloth Setup Using MotionDesigner

If you've worked through the animation projects in parallel with the setup projects, you have had a fair amount of practice animating overlapping action and follow-through by now. Those are the most important principles of animation if you are trying to do realistic clothing. Fabrics are tedious to animate, and it is nearly impossible to hand-animate a surface to precisely mimic the behavior of cloth. This is one of the areas where a simulation or procedural setup can make the difference between the impossible and the merely challenging.

Q: How do you pick the computer-generated character out of the crowd?
A: It's the one wearing a leotard and body armor.

Traditionally, computer-generated characters have dodged the problems of cloth simulation by wearing clothing that's very close to the skin (leotards and such) or rigid (armor). Related problems with skin deformation were covered over with carefully designed joints or oddly heavy accessories and jewelry. For the past several years, a number of studios and software developers have been working on the myriad of problems associated with cloth simulation, and their results have been very encouraging. Pixar's Oscar-nominated short *Geri's Game* demonstrated the high end of this effort, showcasing the cloth simulator developed by Michael Kass. Where Kass's approach addresses fine points such as warp and weft, cutting cloth on the bias, and virtual starch, the cloth simulation available to LightWave users takes a more lenient approach. You can expect a certain amount of rubberiness or lack of apparent weight in cloth animated with MotionDesigner, but double knits and silk still beat spandex and Kevlar for visual appeal.

The online documentation for MotionDesigner is included on the LightWave Content CD in HTML format, and copying it to your hard drive is one of the installation options. Look for it in your LightWave installation directory, in the path /online_docs/motiondesigner2/indexe.htm. This documentation is perfectly adequate to show you how to clothe your characters. There are 12 tutorials with sample files, including making a flag, a T-shirt, a skirt, draped cloth, and similar projects. In addition, there is extensive reference material on setting up and optimizing MotionDesigner. You should read the entire file; it's very dense, no spare words. Getting your head around the concepts and tutorials before you attempt your own projects will save you an enormous amount of trial and error.

Pay special attention to the weight parameter, and try the Randomize option. Real fabrics vary in weight and will not fall or drape as a perfectly smooth surface. Viscosity, resistance, and spring parameters also interact to create the appearance of different materials. If you want to mimic a particular thickness and type of fabric, you need to adjust these parameters carefully. Another common error is to keep Compress Stress too low; true natural fabrics, even fine silks, have a Compress Stress value higher than zero. A value that is too low makes a fabric that appears unrealistically thin and flexible, a dead giveaway that the material is computer-generated.

If you're going for that windblown look, you need to pay close attention to the turbulence settings. Setting incompatible axis, wavelength, or wind values will make your fabrics look subtly wrong. Your audience may have trouble precisely verbalizing what looks odd, but they'll certainly spot that the results aren't realistic.

If you like, you can try creating a basic setup by adding a cape, kilt, skirt, apron, or other simple mesh to one of the characters you animate in Chapter 15. If you do, document the setup, and try animating it in Chapter 16. If you're up to a challenge, try adapting the T-shirt tutorial to one of your own characters.

Moving On

By this time, you should have a good grasp of the issues in power tool setup and be better able to make decisions about which tools are useful and which are counterproductive.

There are several things you can do to make power tools better:

- Experiment with new tools as they become available.

- Try new ways of using old tools.

- Pay attention to feedback from animators.

- Reuse what works, and solve problems in (or discard) what doesn't.

- Give feedback to software developers and publishers, and demand better tools. Be specific about how a feature should work, how it can make a difference in your work, and why more people will buy their product if the new feature works properly.

- Most of all, practice animating, even if your primary job is setup.

With that in mind, jump ahead to Chapter 16 and try your hand at a few character animations using these setups.

Part V

Animating

Chapter 14

Essential Character Animation

To create the illusion of life, you need to animate characters with the basic principles of timing: anticipation, snap, ease, cushion, squash, stretch, follow-through, overlapping action, secondary action, and holds. To animate efficiently, you need to understand spline and keyframe controls. To communicate effectively, you need to compose your shots. Finally, you need to animate your characters with uniquely characteristic actions to keep your audience entertained and interested.

This chapter is about the very basics of character animation. If you complete these projects and practice the skills you learn through them, you will have an adequate working knowledge of character animation. The remaining animation chapters of this book build on these basics, so you should take your time, practice, and master this chapter's contents before you move on.

What Is Animation?

Character animation is the creation of the illusion of life. This is a deliberate, systematic application of poses and timing to an inert object (whether drawing, puppet, clay, or pixels) to create the appearance of self-motivation.

Character animation can imitate reality, but more often it is used for caricature. An animator transcends realistic motion by abstractly representing the ideal of movement, in a manner sufficiently skillful to read as *true* if not necessarily *real*. With animation, life can be amplified in ways that aren't possible with live-action filmmaking. Audiences can look at themselves reflected in a world that would be filtered by their vanity were they to simply look in the mirror. By learning and applying the tricks of the animation trade, not only can you make characters that move, you can make characters with which people can identify, sympathize, and empathize. The best animation persuades an audience to suspend its disbelief and communicates on an emotional level that transcends linguistic and cultural barriers. Animation is a universal language.

The only limit to an animator's ability is the capacity to visualize. The various methodologies that accumulated in the traditional animation industry were attempts to break up the enormous organizational workload into a few simple steps. These tricks and techniques are relatively simple to learn and will eventually help you improve your visualization skills.

Norman McLaren, the great Canadian animator, said, "Animation is not the art of drawings-that-move, but rather the art of movements-that-are-drawn."

In response to this, Chuck Jones says, "Animation is not drawings that move. It's drawings that move as they already exist in the director's mind."

Layout

Your first step in committing an animation to the computer is *layout*, sometimes called *blocking*. This is the equivalent of a stage production's blocking, where marks are taped on the floor to show where the characters will stand at critical points in the story. This is the logical next step in roughing out the animation, following directly from the storyboards. Ideally, layout consists of adding each character in its default setup to a position within the set to match that shot's storyboard sketch. At this point, you won't be doing any detailed tweaking of the character's pose, just setting its basic position and attitude.

Layout is a critical step, just as important as the storyboards. It's possible (even likely) that the storyboard artist has cheated a few sketches in ways that you can't readily lay out with the modeled sets and characters. The layout process is intended to red-flag those problems before the production makes any expensive, time-consuming mistakes.

One of the mistakes that consistently gets beginning animators (and sometimes experienced animators too) into trouble is not doing proper layout, or not getting approvals on the layout from the client or director. Layouts, and especially camera setups, must be locked down before the characters can be animated.

Locking Down the Camera

If you don't get a lock-down on the layouts, you will have to reanimate entire sequences if the client or director decides to move the camera. In film and television work, it's important that the actors be able to play to the camera. It's possible to get a much stronger performance, and therefore tell a story better, if the actors' full talents are focused in one direction. You can cheat poses, facial expressions, actions, even costumes if you can rely absolutely on what the camera can and can't see. (Can you tell if that television anchor is wearing anything under the desk?)

Locking down the camera is even more important in LightWave character animation. The techniques and requirements of actors playing to the camera are just as necessary for

LightWave characters as for live action. In addition, if you thoroughly examine any LightWave character, you are going to find flaws and inconsistencies—it's just the nature of the current state of the art. It's very difficult to thoroughly mimic reality in a character setup, even if realism is appropriate to the style of the animation. More often, the characters will be cartoony or fantastic and have little use for an anthropometrically correct skeletal structure. The result is that character animators have to develop a bag of tricks, cheats, and workarounds to create poses and actions that hide these flaws so the results look good to the camera. Most of these cheats fall apart if the camera angle changes even a few degrees.

If you try to animate a character to look good from all possible camera angles, you will spend a lot more time tweaking and still get the most boring, lifeless poses you can imagine. Lock down the camera during layout so you can turn your creative efforts to maximizing the dramatic or comedic effects of every pose.

One extremely difficult venue to animate for is realtime 3D games where the end user has control over the camera point of view. In this type of animation, you can't cheat the camera; you just have realistic balance, and movement that cannot trick the eye. What makes animation difficult in these realtime 3D environments is that the animation must not look pathological from any angle. It must look convincing from all possible viewing angles and therefore takes longer to animate.

This isn't a problem for a character that is running and jumping, doing your basic locomotion and action moves. For a character that is acting and performing, it's a different story. Even a live-action stage actor rarely performs theatre in the round. When an actor performs on a traditional theatrical stage, the audience begins at the proscenium, and the projection of gestures and poses directed at the audience in general still has limitations on the viewing angle.

But in realtime animation that can be viewed from arbitrary angles, it is difficult to animate a character's eyes so that they can meet the viewer's eyes when the animator so desires. Poses can't employ graphic design techniques to lead the viewer's eye. Poses get mushed out. Bones can no longer be bent the wrong way. Eyes pointed to the side in evasive mock conversation can mistakenly look a viewer in the eye with solid confidence when viewed from the wrong angle. You can't depend on close-ups, specific camera heights, or cutting—absolutely none of the conventions of filmmaking. All of these things are pathologies inherent to realtime animation and the interactive environment in which they reside. You simply have to expect this from a medium in which the user controls the point of view (POV).

Camera Animation: Composing Shots for Effect

One of a director's jobs is to compose each shot, using the camera to control what the audience sees, to set the mood, and to advance the story. If, as an animator, you are simply handed sequences to animate, you may not have any choice in composing the shots. If you have directing authority, and especially if you are wearing all the hats, you need to know how to compose effective shots for character animation. This chapter shows you the basics.

An animator or director who thinks clearly sees the shot he needs in his mind. Clear thinking and planning can not only save you an enormous amount of time and trial-and-error heart-aches, it can mean the difference between animation that is met with a yawn and animation that wins awards.

Shot composition shows off one of LightWave animation's major advantages over other cin-ematic forms—you have absolute control over your camera. You are not limited by the physi-cal size and weight of a camera, nor by the tracks, dollies, and cranes required to move one. You can choose any lens you like, move the camera in any fashion and at any speed you de-sire, and generally indulge your creative whims without paying the exorbitant costs of more traditional cinematography.

This is not to say that you should do all those things, at least not if your purpose is to tell a story using character animation. For each camera move, ask yourself some questions: Does it advance the story? Does it help develop the character? Does it distract the audience from the focus of this shot? Your audience is used to a more limited range of cinematography, so going to extremes with the camera may distract them from the story and characters. Keep it simple.

The first choice in composing a shot is the distance from the camera to the subject, or central character, of the shot.

Keeping Your Distance

Distance affects how much information falls within the frame, how much of the frame the character occupies, and the emotional impact of any actions on your audience. Let's take a look at some of the stock distances used in traditional cinematography and note how they affect these three variables.

The Long Shot

A *long shot* contains a great deal of information. It includes the complete central character of the shot; it also includes a good bit of the environment surrounding the character. This is espe-cially useful for an *establishing shot*, one that shows the audience the general environment in which the action will take place. Framing references for the long shot are generally not to hu-man scale. Frame composition usually derives from a building or other large object, with the character (if any) being a minor focal point.

The long shot has the greatest emotional detachment from the audience. Any action composed at this distance will generally have much less impact than a closer shot. Also, minor actions will be so small a part of the screen that your audience will probably overlook them. A long shot is not a good choice for showing subtle emotional transitions or actions.

PROJECT 14.1 Composing a Long Shot

To compose a long shot, follow these steps:

1. Load the Street01 scene included in the Chapter 14 directory on this book's CD-ROM. The scene contains the restaurant building, sidewalk, lamp, and street models called for by the "Easy Come, Easy Go" storyboards.

2. Use the File|Load Items From Scene function to load the Puppet character from the default scene you set up in Chapter 11, or load any other humanoid character you prefer.

3. Position the character just to one side of the restaurant door.

4. Align the camera so it is centered on the character's chest, and position the camera at least 10 meters away from the character. Set a keyframe.

5. Render an image at whatever resolution and anti-aliasing you prefer. You should get something like Figure 14.1.

Figure 14.1
Long shot.

The Full Shot

The *full shot* is an emotional step closer than the long shot. Any action shot at this distance will have a greater impact because the audience will feel closer to it. The audience can also see more clearly the posture and the grosser expressions of the character, so you have a greater practical dramatic range for character animation.

As shown in Figure 14.2, the full shot conveys less information about the character's surroundings but can add details that are lost at the greater distance. The full shot is a good choice for establishing the character's general appearance, including props and clothing that have a bearing on the story. A long shot might show only the profile of a character in front of a building, whereas a full shot will reveal the six-gun on his hip, the silver star pinned to his vest, and the lettering over the building's doorway reading "Sheriff."

Figure 14.2
Full shot, including feet.

You can compose a full shot of the character by trucking the camera in (moving forward along the axis of the lens) toward the character. A full shot must always include the character's feet. If you frame the character as cut off at the ankles, you will not get a pleasing composition.

This brings us to the concept of *cutting heights*. Because most films are about people, you can usefully describe most shot compositions in relation to the human body. Over the years, directors and cinematographers have developed a set of empirical rules for composing shots relative to the actor. The standard cutting heights are under the armpits, under the rib cage, under the waist, across the upper thigh, and under the knees. If a script or director uses a term like "waist shot," she means a composition that ends just below the feature described.

The Medium Shot

The *medium shot* brings the audience another emotional step closer to the action. From a character's POV, this is only a couple of steps away, just beyond arm's reach. All but the most subtle facial expressions can be read by the audience, but any body language expressed using the legs is, of course, lost off screen.

The audience can still pick up information about the character's immediate surroundings, but most of the screen is now occupied by the character and the audience's attention will generally be focused there.

You can compose a medium shot of the character by trucking in closer to cut the character off at the upper thigh, as shown in Figure 14.3.

Figure 14.3
Medium shot, upper thigh.

The Close Shot

The *close shot* focuses the audience's attention on the head and upper body of the character, which occupy most of the screen. This composition shows just enough of the character's body for the audience to readily perceive shrugs and general body posture. The emotional distance is arm's length, a conversational distance, so any action will have a fairly strong impact on your audience.

It will be difficult for audiences to absorb any information from the background because most of their attention will be drawn to and held by the foreground character. Conversely, any information conveyed by the character will be that much easier for audiences to read.

You can compose a close shot of the character by trucking the camera in again, this time cutting the character off at the lower ribs, as shown in Figure 14.4.

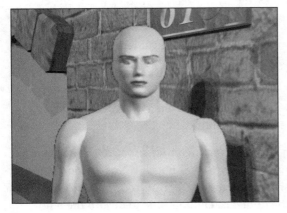

Figure 14.4
Close shot, through rib cage.

The Specific Close Shot

The next closer distance is the *specific close shot*. The example in Figure 14.5 shows a Close Shot Head, but descriptions such as Close Shot Hand, Close Shot Window, and so on are also used. The composition is generally interpreted as including the specified object and a visual border around the object. Again referring to Figure 14.5, the head is shown with a visual border beginning well above the head and extending below the chin. The specified object occupies the entire action area of the screen.

Figure 14.5
Close Shot Head.

This composition is very strong emotionally. The nuances of facial expressions are easy for the audience to read, and there is almost no chance of a distraction from the background. The only information the audience can observe is that expressed by the character. From a character's POV, this is a very intimate distance, used only between friends or when one character is violating the other's personal space.

You can compose a Close Shot Head of the character by trucking the camera in close enough to fill the frame vertically with the character's head.

The Extreme Close Shot

This composition is literally in your face. Audiences are being force-fed the information, whether they want it or not. Audiences can't see anything but the object of the shot.

Emotionally, this composition can be so strong as to be overwhelming, especially on a large screen. You should be careful not to overuse it and keep extreme shots like this as short as possible. The emotional intensity is difficult to sustain, and you risk boring your audience with an overly close, overly simple composition. Give the audience enough time to absorb the emotional impact, then move back to a more distant shot.

You can compose an extreme close shot of the character's eyes by trucking the camera in close enough that the character's face fills the frame horizontally (see Figure 14.6).

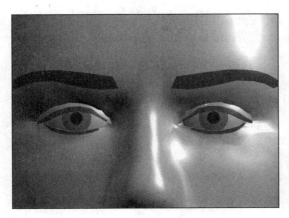

Figure 14.6
Extreme close shot eyes.

Pick a Lens, Any Lens

The exact position coordinates you use for the camera will depend on the lens equivalent you select. LightWave's default Zoom Factor of 3.2 was used for each of the preceding examples. A higher zoom value would require more distance between the character and the camera to achieve the same composition, and vice versa.

Depth of field (DOF) is one more variable you need to keep in mind when setting the distance for a shot. Unlike real-world cameras, LightWave, by default, has infinite depth of field, so all objects are in perfect focus. If you want to simulate the focal behavior of a real-world camera, you need to use LightWave's DOF feature. When activated, DOF determines what is in focus at different distances from the camera. Objects at the exact focal distance from the camera are in sharpest focus, whereas those closer or farther are progressively out of focus.

You can use DOF to minimize distractions for your audience. You can make backgrounds (or foregrounds) so blurry and out of focus that the audience ignores them. You can even set the controls so everything but the central character is out of focus. In LightWave, you can animate these settings to shift the audience's attention without moving the camera. For more details about LightWave's DOF feature, you should read pages 7.11 through 7.14 of the *Motion: Animate & Render* manual.

 ## Blurry, Blurry Night

This project shows you how to set up an extreme depth of field for a medium shot of the character using LightWave:

1. Load the scene PROJ1402.LWS from this book's CD-ROM. Open the Camera panel.

2. Set Antialiasing to Medium or higher. The Depth Of Field option will not work with Low or Off anti-aliasing settings.

3. Choose the Stereo And DOF tab. Click on the Depth Of Field button at the lower left of the panel. Set Focal Distance to 4.0. This is the distance between the camera and the character you want to be in sharpest focus.

4. Set Lens F-Stop to 0.5. This setting specifies a very shallow depth of field, producing a large amount of blurring in the foreground and background. Close the Camera panel.

5. Render frame 0. You should get an image like Figure 14.7.

Figure 14.7
Shallow depth of field.

You can see how the character in Figure 14.7 is still in sharp focus, but both the street lamp in the foreground and the brick wall in the background are blurred and, therefore, much less of a distraction. In a close shot like this, you can even use a fixed background image to save yourself render time: Simply blur the image in Photoshop, and then animate your character over it.

Note: If you need to match the DOF of a shot to live action, the Aperture Height pull-down list in LightWave's Camera panel includes presets to automatically emulate the settings for many real-world film and video formats. Combined with the Lens Focal Length setting (in the Zoom Factor pull-down list), you can match nearly any real-world camera and lens combination.

What's Your Angle?

The second part of composing a shot is selecting the camera angle. The basic criteria for selecting camera angles are the same as for setting the distance. You want the angle to help control what the audience sees, set the mood, and advance the story.

The most common camera setup is probably the *omniscient observer*, a camera positioned and angled as if it were another character in the scene. The POV is usually near or below the other character's eye levels, so the *pitch* (or elevation) angle of the camera is nearly zero.

The *heading* (or azimuth) angle varies but is rarely close to the cardinal points (0, 90, 180, 270). These angles would give head-on, perfect profile, and rear views that would read as flat and artificial because you rarely get a view like that in real life. It is usually better to keep the heading at a more natural angle, at least five degrees away from any cardinal point.

If you consistently use omniscient observer camera angles, your shot compositions will quickly become boring. If you want to keep your audience's attention, you need to spice up the mix a little with more dramatic camera angles.

Try using higher and lower camera positions, with corresponding pitch angles. There are no absolute rules governing the emotional impact of camera angles, but here are some useful rules of thumb:

- *High angles*, where the camera is above the character and looking down, tend to give the audience a literally lower view of the character. The character is perceived as smaller, weaker, less important, or threatened. Subtlety counts for this type of composition. An extreme high angle loses the audience simply by being extreme. A relatively small high angle has the desired emotional effect without tipping off the audience.

- *Low angles*, reasonably enough, tend to give the audience a higher view of the character. The character is perceived as larger, stronger, and more important and, in closer shots, can readily be perceived as threatening. Again, subtlety counts; a worm's-eye view will lose the audience, but a more subtle angle will have the desired effect.

You may have noticed I didn't mention camera angles using the third axis *bank* (or roll). That's because it's generally a bad idea to bank the camera at all, unless you are going for a very specific type of effect. Bank angles have the effect of tilting the horizontal edges of the screen frame relative to the sets and characters. This off-kilter view can be very disturbing to the audience and is rarely used apart from action sequences or psychological thrillers.

The action shot can justify banking the camera if the character's POV is actually going through a bank angle, as in a car turning over or an aircraft doing a barrel roll. This is consistent with the action expected by the audience and will not have a strong effect—other than making the audience unconsciously lean into the angle!

The psycho thriller uses of the bank angle are more disturbing. The basic technique is to compose a more normal shot, then slightly bank the camera to skew the composition. If it's done subtly enough, audiences may never notice the angle. They will, however, become emotionally tense, sensing that something is not right. A variation on this technique is used to underscore a progressively more unbalanced character or setting. If you gradually increase the bank angle of any shot from the character's POV (or a shot that includes the character), audiences will sense that the psychosis is becoming worse.

The best rule for camera angles in character animation is to keep it simple. Barraging audiences with lots of odd camera angles is confusing and can get in the way of telling your story. The audience will spend too much time adjusting to the new POV and miss whatever you are trying to communicate through the character. Using the same angle in several shots gives audiences a POV that they can identify quickly, so they can concentrate on the character's actions. Try to find a balance between standard shots and more unconventional compositions. Choose your camera angles to emphasize and work with, not against, the current action.

Continuity

You also need to keep continuity in mind. Look at the shot compositions you have planned to precede and follow the current one. You need to match screen position, on-screen movement, and sight lines between successive shots or you will lose continuity.

Screen position means keeping the character in the same approximate relation to the screen frame. If the character appears on the left of the screen in one shot, he should not appear on the right in the next shot.

Matching movement means you should keep the character moving in the same direction in successive shots. If the character is walking left to right in one shot, he should also be walking left to right in the next. If the character is to change direction (Oops! Forgot something. I'll be right back!), you need to show that change of direction within a single shot.

Matching sight lines means the character should be looking in the same direction. If a character is looking out a window in one shot, the following shot should not show her staring at the tabletop. As with direction of movement, if a change is necessary, you need to show that change within a single shot. In this case, an insert shot of the character's head swiveling from the window sight line to the tabletop sight line would bridge the change nicely.

Finally, it is best to keep the camera on the same side of the action throughout a sequence. The main action should be following a *slalom*, as discussed in detail in the section "Throw 'Em a Curve" later in this chapter. You can use this slalom as a spatial dividing line for the sequence, sometimes referred to as the *line of action*. Keep the camera positioned on one side of this divider. If you jump from one side to the other, your audience will become disoriented. If you shift the camera from one side to the other at the end of a sequence, you should hold the first shot a little longer to give the audience time to adjust.

Another way to cross the line of action or to easily change continuity is to use what is known as a Clean Exit. Basically, the character leaves the scene and the camera pauses for a short moment with the character totally off screen. The next shot can be composed with more freedom without breaking continuity.

Animating the Camera

You can animate the camera in a number of ways to connect shots in a sequence. There are two major divisions of camera animation in LightWave: the *move* and the *cut*. Moves are continuous transitions from one position, attitude, and lens setting to another, whereas cuts are abrupt changes between one frame and the next. In traditional cinematography, cuts are accomplished by editing. In LightWave, you are free of the constraints of a physical camera, so you can make a cut within the animation.

Camera animation should be treated as any other animation technique, used only to tell the story. Inappropriate use will distract the audience and detract from your story and is the mark of an amateur still infatuated with technological toys.

It's Your Move

A camera move is generally one of several stock types or a combination of more than one. The stock moves are *pan*, *tilt*, *dolly* (or *truck*), *tracking*, and *zoom*. The following projects will show you how to set up each of these stock moves.

PROJECT 14.3 Setting Up a Pan Camera Move

To set up a pan move, follow these steps:

1. Reload the scene you used for Project 14.1.

2. Rotate the Camera 15 degrees to the left on the Heading axis. Leave the other two axes alone.

3. Set a keyframe at frame 1. Go to frame 30.

4. Rotate the Camera 15 degrees to the right of its original position, for a total of 30 degrees on the Heading axis. Again, leave the remaining two axes unchanged.

5. Set a keyframe at frame 30.

6. Render and play back the animation.

The pan, shown in Figure 14.8, is one of the simplest and most often used moves, both in traditional cinematography and LightWave. All you have to do is rotate the camera.

Figure 14.8
Beginning, middle, and end frames of a camera pan.

PROJECT 14.4 Setting Up a Tilt Camera Move

The tilt move is essentially identical to the pan, but on the pitch rather than heading axis:

1. Delete the changes you made in the preceding project.

2. Change the camera pitch to -5. Leave the other two axes as they are.

3. Set a keyframe at frame 1. Go to frame 30.

4. Pitch the camera up 15 degrees. Again, leave the other two axes unchanged.

5. Set a keyframe at frame 30.

6. Render and play back the animation. You should end up with something like Figure 14.9.

Figure 14.9
Beginning, middle, and end frames of a camera tilt.

PROJECT 14.5 Setting Up a Dolly Camera Move

To set up a dolly camera move, follow these steps:

1. Delete the changes you made in the preceding project.

2. Move the camera well back from the character. Set a keyframe for the camera position at frame 1. Go to frame 30.

3. Move the camera forward along the lens axis until the character fills the frame in a close shot. Leave the other two position axes as they are.

4. Set a keyframe at frame 30.

5. Render and play back the animation.

The dolly move, shown in Figure 14.10, mimics a traditional camera mounted on a wheeled dolly and moving down a track. You can combine the dolly move with a pan or tilt to produce a compound motion. The dolly move is also a part of the tracking and dolly-and-zoom moves.

Figure 14.10
Beginning, middle, and end frames of a camera dolly.

PROJECT 14.6 Setting Up a Tracking Camera Move

The other camera moves are pretty much independent, although you should always animate them with an eye to framing the action. The tracking move, however, is intended to follow a particular object, character, or action exclusively. There are several ways to do this. The easiest is to simply parent the camera to the object or hierarchy to be tracked, then position and rotate the camera in relation to that object, as appropriate:

1. Reload the scene you've been using for the camera animations.

2. Parent the camera to the root of the character's hierarchy.

3. Offset and rotate the camera so it has a clear full shot of the character.

4. Create a keyframe for the camera at frame 1.

5. Animate the character moving along the sidewalk. Because the camera is parented to the character, it will go along for the ride. The simplest approach is to set a keyframe for the character's beginning and ending positions and just let the character float.

6. Render and play back the animation.

The tracking move, displayed in Figure 14.11, is especially useful for following transportation animations like walking, running, or moving vehicles.

Figure 14.11
Beginning, middle, and end frames of a tracking shot.

PROJECT 14.7 Setting Up a Zoom Camera Move

The zoom depends on LightWave's ability to animate the camera lens parameters:

1. Reload the scene again.

2. Change the Camera Zoom setting to a minimal value that will make the character look like it's far away.

3. Make a keyframe for the Camera Zoom at frame 1. Go to frame 30.

4. Change Camera Zoom to a higher value that will make the character look very close.

5. Create another Camera Zoom keyframe at frame 30.

6. Render and play back the animation.

The zoom move, as shown in Figure 14.12, is another simple camera move that has been grossly overused. Avoid it wherever possible, and use dolly moves or cuts instead. If you must use a zoom, keep it to a minimum, and make sure it is essential to telling your story. You should also apply ease-in and ease-out to Camera Zoom envelopes; your audience is used to physical cameras that accelerate and decelerate, and a camera move with too much snap can disorient them.

Figure 14.12
Beginning, middle, and end frames of a zoom.

PROJECT 14.8 Setting Up a Dolly-and-Zoom Camera Move

The dolly-and-zoom is, obviously, a combination of zoom and dolly camera moves. The interesting and useful part of this move is that the dolly and zoom are registered to each other to maintain the position and focus of the central object while the rest of the frame changes.

To set up this move, follow these steps:

1. Reload the scene again.

2. Move the camera well back from the character. Set a keyframe for the camera position at frame 1.

3. Change Camera Zoom to a high enough value that it will frame a full shot of the character.

4. Make a keyframe for Camera Zoom at frame 1. Go to frame 30.

5. Change Camera Zoom to a lower value that will make the character look like it's very far away. Set a keyframe for Camera Zoom.

6. Move the camera forward along the lens axis until the character fills the frame in a full shot again, as close as possible to its proportions at frame 1.

7. Set a camera position keyframe at frame 30.

8. Render and play back the animation.

The distance between the camera's first position and the second is equivalent to the distance covered by the Camera Zoom you set in Step 3. This matches the distance the camera travels to the distance the camera lens zooms.

This camera move (see Figure 14.13) produces a unique effect. The central object, located at the camera's focal distance, appears to remain in place and in focus. The background and foreground both appear to shift, producing a very strong disorienting effect.

Figure 14.13
First, middle, and last frames of dolly-and-zoom.

This is another camera move that is prone to abuse, especially by amateurs fascinated with new toys. Use it only when it serves a valid dramatic purpose for your story. Otherwise, leave it in your bag of tricks.

Go Ahead and Cut

You may find it useful to think of a cut between shots as simply a move with zero frames between keys. The same guidelines for continuity still apply, you just have to pay a little more attention to some additional timing issues.

A cut that changes the volume of the shot or its contents creates a *visual jar* or disorientation for your audience. The *volume of the shot* is the space contained in the pyramid formed by the lens (the apex) and the four corners of the frame. The apparent volume of the shot ends at the central object or character.

A close shot of a character's head would enclose only a few cubic feet, whereas a long shot of the Empire State Building might contain millions. A cut between these two shots would cause an extreme visual jar due to the difference between volumes. A series of intermediate cuts, bridging from close to medium to full to long shots, would soften that shock; the difference in volume between each cut would be much smaller.

Sometimes, you will want to use the visual jar of a cut for dramatic reasons. Probably the most famous example of this is the shower scene in Alfred Hitchcock's *Psycho*, a series of such fast cuts between different contents (but nearly identical volumes) that the audience "sees" what is not actually there.

More often, you need to make the cut to a shot that is simply a better composition for the following action, and your goal is just to get there as quickly as possible.

Cutting on the action is the technique of changing from one camera position to the next during the character's action. This timing of the cut relieves the visual jar because the audience focuses its attention on the action, not the shot composition.

You can also animate a character to presage a cut—warning audiences so they expect it—to reduce the visual jar. Animate the character to reach for or look intently at something out of frame, in the direction of the cut. Audiences will follow the look or the action with their eyes, and the subsequent cut will be expected and, therefore, less jarring. You can also presage an action by slightly moving or zooming the camera toward the object of the action.

Cutting between angles is another way of changing the shot composition without jarring your audience. Simply keep the distance between camera and object constant and move the camera to a new angle. The audience will have to reorient itself only to the new angle because the volume and content of the shot will be essentially unchanged.

You can also minimize visual jar for an entire sequence of shots by creating a *master shot*. The master shot establishes the entire environment of a sequence, laying out a visual map for the audience. When you *inter-cut* a tighter *insert shot* of some part of this environment, the audience can quickly orient itself from the master shot. This is also known as an *establishing shot*. Often a master shot comes at the start of a sequence. However, directors sometimes will place the establishing shot later in the sequence to build suspense.

Cheats

Here's a tip from director Steph Greenberg: Getting the best shot and action often means breaking the rules. The key to an appropriate cheat is to see the finished shot in your mind, before you lay out the scene, and to create the scene in your storyboard, complete with props, exactly the way you would like to see it when it is completed. Don't leave details until later! Improvisation in 3D is much harder than it is with a pencil, even if you can't draw well.

Updating the Story Reel—Making an Animatic

As you may recall from Chapter 4, the story reel is the first genuine test of your animation's timing and flow. The limitation of story reels is that they are made of drawings, not renderings, so you don't really have an accurate representation of the LightWave animation's final appearance. It's important that you keep an accurate record of each step in your film's progress so you can catch problems early. When a shot's layout is complete, you can render single images, selectively substitute them for the corresponding story sketches, and recompile the movie. This way, the movie fills out as you make progress, and at any time, you can view the whole thing.

PROJECT 14.9 Replacing Sketches in the Story Reel

This project is an extrapolation of Project 4.5 and is written for Adobe Premiere 4.2. If you are using a different editing software, read through these instructions, then consult your software's user or reference manuals to learn how to duplicate this process:

1. Start Adobe Premiere. Open the project (PPJ) file you saved when you built the story reel.

2. Choose the File|Import|File option, or press Ctrl+I. The Import dialog box appears.

3. Drag-select all your test-rendered images. Click on Open to import the images.

   You shouldn't change the duration of any of the story sketches until you have added all the new rendered images. The cut-and-paste approach to editing a story reel is a very different cognitive process from the evaluation and execution of animation timing. To avoid mistakes, replace the images in one session, render the new story reel, then critique the reel's timing as a whole.

4. Arrange the new rendered images in the second video track, exactly underneath their corresponding story sketches.

5. You have two ways to make the rendered stills fit their appointed slots in the story reel. You can click and drag to stretch each rendering across the (approximate) number of frames. More accurately, you can double-click on the original sketch, note the time allocated, then double-click on the new image and assign it the same duration.

6. Delete the old sketches from the upper video track. As you remove each one, immediately replace it with the new rendered image from the lower video track. Repeat until all the new images are in place.

7. Render a new story reel. As mentioned earlier, you need to set the options to create a movie that can play back at full 24fps on your system. This may limit you to a 160x120 preview, or you may be using a fast machine that can handle full-screen 24fps playback with stereo sound and lossless compression. Use whatever works—this is just for a working preview!

8. When it's complete, open the story reel, and play it. Are all the sounds still synchronized correctly? Does the story reel read well? How have the test renders changed your impression of the story compared to the original story sketches? Does the updated reel give you a better idea of the effect of timing on how the story reads? Is there anything you want to change?

9. If the layout of a shot isn't working, you need to go back into LightWave, tweak the scene, rerender the image, and import it into the story reel again. If there's something in the timing you want to change, you can adjust the duration of the individual images.

10. Double-click on the thumbnail you want to retime in the Construction window. The Clip window appears.

11. Enter a revised duration for the image and click on OK.

12. Select and drag the thumbnails to either side of the retimed clip, if necessary, until they are all flush again.

At this point, you should ideally have all your shots blocked out, with at least one rough layout for each shot and a single rendering replacing every original story sketch. In reality, there are always shots that finished early, balanced by shots that won't be done until the last minute. For most of the production cycle, the story reel is a hash of pencil sketches, rendered stills, and the occasional full-motion clip.

Once you have a signed-off and locked layout for a shot, you can proceed to refine the timing of actions within that shot. This is the core of what a character animator does—everything else is prep work or window dressing.

Timing Is Everything

Timing makes or breaks character animation. A single frame is often the difference between an action that works and one that doesn't. To paraphrase Mark Twain, the difference between the right timing and the almost right timing is the difference between lightning and a lightning bug.

In Part IV, you learned to create basic setups to move and deform characters. The following section shows you how to set the timing of those movements to get exactly the effect you want.

LightWave Timing—The Basics

The basic unit of timing is the frame. The *frame rate* is measured in frames per second, or fps. Feature films are projected at 24fps and NTSC video at 29.97fps, usually rounded up to 30fps for convenience. The high cost of transferring animation to film means that you will most likely be working in video formats for your first few projects. However, it is easy to use a process called *3:2 pull-up* to convert 24fps footage to 30fps, but it's more difficult to convert 30fps to 24fps.

With experience, you will be able to pick out a single frame's difference in an animation. You may start off being able to judge only a quarter-second or more, but with practice, you will learn to estimate and work with a 24th of a second. Even if your final output will be on video, you should use 24fps as your baseline for timing. Most professional animators work to the 24fps standard and will expect you to do so if you work with them. Developing your sense of timing is a long learning process, and it's very difficult to translate that skill to a different frame rate. Even if you never work in film, you should almost always animate to 24fps. You may work on a game or multimedia project that has a completely different playback rate, but for those occasional exceptions, you will be better off converting your timing estimates from 24fps to whatever rather than trying to relearn the right timing at some arbitrary new frame rate.

The smoothest, most realistic animation is shot *on ones*. That is, each image is shown for only one frame. This is sometimes referred to as *full animation*. Shooting on ones is also the most expensive form of animation. More often, animation is shot on twos, where a single image is held for two frames. This cuts the cost of animation in half because only 12 images are required for 24 frames' worth of projection time.

To save money, *limited animation* is often shot on fours. Even shooting on sixes is not unheard of when a budget is tight. Other cheap tricks include animating only part of a character while leaving the rest of the scene untouched, animating camera moves over still images, and reusing image sequences of standard actions such as walks and gestures.

Why is it so simple to think in terms of 24fps? An average pedestrian beat is 2 beats, 2 steps per second, or 1 foot contact on each 12th frame. Some walks are slower, at 16fps, or faster, on 8s. That walk on 12s (1 step; you should be able to infer everything else from half the cycle) can be conveniently divided into thirds and fourths and sixths and halves. A walk on 16s is more evenly divisible into quarters. It's no coincidence that many of the best animators are also musical in some way. Even if you have no skill in performance, your skill in appreciation will translate into timing for animation.

Think in terms of whole notes at 24 frames per second, half notes at 12, quarters at 6, 8ths at 3, even 6ths (4), and 12ths (2). So, many traditional animators use their standard exposure sheet, divided at 8 frames for half of a foot of film and 16 for a foot. One more half foot of film and you have a second, or one and a half feet of film per second, 90 feet of film per minute. Eight frames is one third of a second; if you're only drawing, rendering, or exposing every other frame, four images get you one third of the way through a second.

If you're animating *on twos* and you've posed an extreme on frames 1, 9, 17, and 25, there are halfway (or *breakdown*) frames on 5, 13, and 21. This is not to say that the action represented at the breakdown frame should be an exact halfway interpolation between the two extremes. How that pose, or elements within that pose, favors one extreme or another defines a universe of nuance, interpretation, and acting. Frame 5 will be displayed halfway between frames 1 and 9, yet your subject's position in space may be closer to one third of the distance between 1 and 9. This breakdown pose can be said to favor 1, or to be a cushion out of frame 1. If it favors frame 9, it cushions into, or eases into, frame 9.

A clearly readable short scene often has only two basic poses, a transition from one emotional state to another. Even if the shot lasts just a few seconds, you will use such fractions of a second to time and space those transitions. You will internalize them so deeply you'll forget that you know them. How well you accentuate or gloss over little subevents in that transition, and whether you've used sufficient frames to ensure that the idea you need to convey will register with an audience, is a measure of your skill at timing. Timing *is* animation.

Game display rates, video, HDTV, e-cinema, and specialized film formats like Showscan all pose a challenge to that convenient 24-frame structure. However, there are ways to think in terms of 24fps regardless of the frame rate. Although 24 into 30 doesn't factor well, 12 and 60 frames, or fields per second, do. The fact that your timeline is infinitely subdivisible makes conversion a readily surmountable task. One twelfth of a second is 5 video fields, or 5 frames at 60 frames per second. The critical notion is to make sure that the poses you want to be seen are rendered, not lost in some discarded subdivision.

In 3D animation, you can't use most of the shortcuts employed in limited animation. Audiences seem more tolerant of such tricks when the animation is drawn, but when the images are three-dimensional, the audience becomes very critical of anything not animated on ones. This is true for both puppet animation and LightWave—animating on twos produces a jerky, strobing effect that destroys much of the illusion of life. Fortunately, LightWave animation has a few advantages of its own.

There are two major approaches to animation. The simplest, most improvisational approach is *straight ahead*. This means just what it sounds like: The animator starts with the first frame of the animation, poses the character, then moves on to the next frame. Straight-ahead animation is most used in 2D, drawn animation, but it has a lot in common with puppet animation too. You can improvise, exercise an intuitive grasp of timing and posing, work with a minimum of paperwork and planning, and lose lots of work with a single mistake. It's definitely not a technique for beginners.

The drawback to straight-ahead animation for LightWave character work is that you create so many keyframes—one per animated variable per frame—that it is almost impossible to go back and correct errors. It is easier to simply junk an entire sequence and start over from the last good frame.

The other major approach is *pose-to-pose*. This is the approach used in most 2D animation productions. It is also much more forgiving for the beginner, although it does require more planning.

An animated character's acting and timing is defined by its extreme poses. An extreme pose is where an action changes speed or direction. Filling in from one extreme pose to the next are *breakdowns* and *in-betweens*. Breakdowns, and to a lesser extent, in-betweens, are frames that show how poses are at variance with those that would be yielded by smooth interpolation between the extremes.

The important thing to remember is the notion of extremes, breakdowns, and in-betweens. You will be dropping keys on any part of, or all of, all three types of poses. In full animation, it can be said that there is no such thing as an in-between. Some parts of the same pose may be extreme, others a breakdown, and other parts delegated to rote in-betweening. You make as much of an animation decision when you allow the computer to interpolate evenly as you do when you decide to break it down "out of in-between."

The great advantage of computer-generated animation is, supposedly, that the computer generates every in-between. The animator keys extreme poses, ranging anywhere from every frame (for fast, complex action) to fewer than one in 24 (for slow or repetitive actions). The rest of the frames, or parts of poses where no keys were dropped, are interpolated and rendered automatically. This is a huge savings in the most expensive production commodity, the animator's time. If the computer system is powerful enough, the animator can tweak a key pose and generate a new *pencil test* sequence faster than a skilled traditional animator could draw one. Unfortunately, computers are not that good at performing the in-betweener's job, and in general, the fewer keyframes you set, the more "floaty" or obviously computer animated your results will appear.

Another advantage is that LightWave pose-to-pose animations can also be revised piecemeal, without starting over and losing everything as in traditional cel or clay animation. A skeleton of bones or parented objects can be animated one layer at a time, perfecting hip action, for instance, before investing any time in animating the rest of the legs. Also, you can save each revision of an animation as you work and reload it if something goes wrong with a later version. This safety net encourages animators to experiment and try different compositions, actions, and timing. This is one reason LightWave animation is more forgiving of, and easier for, the beginning animator.

A number of elements contribute to good timing. To be a competent character animator, you need to learn them all. You also need to learn how to apply them to each animation so they work in harmony. The upcoming projects introduce one element at a time, building up to a project that ties them all together.

Mass and Energy

LightWave objects have no mass or energy of their own. They are simply illusions displayed on your computer screen. To appear real in an animation, LightWave objects must move in ways that simulate the mass and energy of the real-world materials they represent.

The mass of an object limits how fast it can be moved by a given amount of energy. An inflatable beach ball, for example, has very little mass, so a small amount of energy—a finger snap—can move it rapidly. The same amount of energy applied to a bowling ball would produce a much slower movement. Energy can be expended to change an object's speed, direction, or shape. This energy can come from outside (another character's action, the wind, an Acme falling anvil) or inside, from the character's own muscles.

Gravity, for all practical purposes related to character animation, is a form of energy that constantly tries to force objects toward the largest mass in the neighborhood, typically the ground. (This definition is not scientifically correct, but this is not a physics textbook.)

The behavior of an object is also governed by *inertia*, the tendency of objects to keep doing what they've been doing. If a large rock is just sitting there, it will continue to sit there until some other object acts to change it, perhaps by levering it over, dragging it away, or even shattering it into smaller rocks.

You can mimic all of this behavior simply by controlling the timing of the action. For example, let's look at one of the simplest actions, an inanimate object—a rock, let's say—falling to the ground. The rock is initially at rest, with no velocity relative to the ground. You can imagine a character holding it up, if you like. When the character releases the rock, it stays in midair for a tiny fraction of a second. This is due to inertia—the rock was motionless; inertia says it will remain motionless until something else acts on it.

That something else is gravity. Immediately, gravity overcomes inertia by pushing the rock toward the ground at an *acceleration* of 9.8 meters per second, per second. This doesn't mean the rock is falling at 9.8 meters per second—this means 9.8 mps is added to the rock's downward speed for every second that it falls. Given the constant acceleration due to gravity and leaving out any other influences, such as updrafts or a character's intervention, you can figure the exact position of the rock for each fraction of a second. The equation is

```
Y=Ys-(1/2gt2)
```

where "Y" is the y-axis height in meters, "Ys" is the original y-axis height in meters at the start of the drop, "g" is the constant of acceleration for gravity of 9.8, and "t" is the time in seconds since the start of the drop. In simpler form, it reads

```
Y=Ys-(4.9t2)
```

If you calculate the distance for each 24th of a second, you have the positions of the rock for each frame of a second of animation.

If you now create an animation of a rock object starting it at frame 0 with no velocity in any direction, you can set the rock's position in each frame to mimic the fall of the real rock, as shown in Figure 14.14. The rendered animation will show the rock object falling with a realistic acceleration.

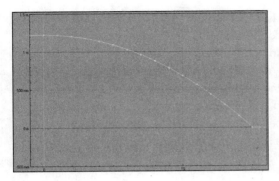

Figure 14.14
The simple timing of a falling rock.

Table 14.1   Fall distance per frame at 1.0 g.

Frame	Distance	Frame	Distance
:00	0.000	:07	0.417
:01	0.009	:08	0.544
:02	0.034	:09	0.689
:03	0.077	:10	0.851
:04	0.136	:11	1.029
:05	0.213	:12	1.225
:06	0.306		

Table 14.1 shows the distances for the first half second, or 12 frames, of a standard fall.

Table 14.1 is provided as a guide to get you started. You should not habitually type in a calculated value for every keyframe of an animation, especially for a simple action like this. There's no art or human judgment involved in that approach, and you could easily be replaced by a piece of software. Your animations will look like it, too. If you plan to animate simulations of real-world physics, I recommend relying on software to do the calculations. No sense reinventing the wheel, right? For example, one of LightWave's Motion Options Modifier plug-ins is LW_Gravity, which does a fine job of animating a simple falling object or bouncing ball. In addition, a variety of built-in and third-party software is available to simulate a lot of other useful behaviors that are tedious or difficult to set up by hand.

Why Bother?
The point of the following projects is to get you to do this work manually just once, so you understand the principles behind the plug-ins. You can't convincingly caricature action until you thoroughly understand realistic actions. Once you've hand-keyframed a falling object, you should be able to exaggerate and caricature the same action.

A slightly more complicated motion you should be able to animate is the *parabola*, the arc followed by a projectile. Parabolas define the movement of a character in midleap, as well as the flight paths of cannonballs and hurled anvils. A parabola is just like the acceleration curve of a falling rock, except there are two of them, connected at the top and spread apart at the base. The horizontal distance between the starting and ending points of the parabola depends on how much energy the projectile has and the angle at which it is launched. A thrown rock moves up at the reverse of the rate it falls, starting off fast and slowing down until it reaches zero vertical velocity at the peak of the parabola. Then it falls, following the same acceleration path it would follow if it had simply been dropped from that peak's height (see Figure 14.15). The horizontal velocity of the projectile remains the same throughout the parabola—only the vertical velocity changes.

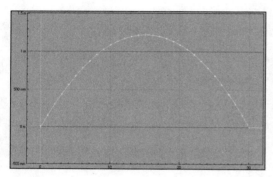

Figure 14.15
A parabola defining the path of a thrown rock.

It's relatively simple to use keyframes to set up a parabola. It requires only attention to detail and a little basic arithmetic. If you haven't already, you should read through Chapter 3, "Keyframing," in the *LightWave [6] Motion: Animate & Render* manual before you proceed to the next project.

Keyframing a Parabola

This project shows you how to keyframe a standard parabola for Earth's gravity:

1. Calculate the y (vertical) positions for the keyframes of a straight fall beginning at the height of the parabola's peak. If the parabola is the exact height of one of the distances in Table 14.1, you can simply copy the values from the table. (Hint, hint.)

2. Open the Ball scene you set up in Chapter 11.

3. Make keyframes on frames 13 through 24. In LightWave, open the Graph Editor, select the Y Position graph, and create keys.

4. Type in the calculated values for the appropriate y-axis keyframes. Start at the peak of the parabola and proceed down the right-hand leg, as shown in Figure 14.16.

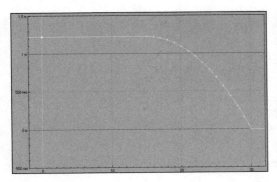

Figure 14.16
First leg of parabola defined by calculated keyframes.

5. Copy the values from each calculated keyframe to the corresponding keyframe on the left-hand side of the parabola, as shown in Figure 14.17.

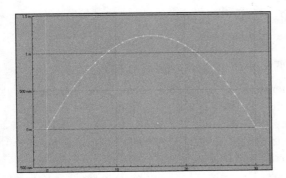

Figure 14.17
Second leg of parabola defined by duplicated keyframes.

6. Presto! You have created a parabolic spline! Save the scene file under a new name. You'll be using it in the next project.

The constraints of mass, inertia, and gravity apply to animated characters as well as to inanimate objects. Once a character leaves the ground (also known as *going ballistic*), the path it follows is a parabola. The character's limbs may thrash or make gestures, but the *center of gravity* (CG) must remain on the parabola (see Figure 14.18).

You can create this type of action most easily by adding a null object to the scene and animating the null along a parabola. Parent the character to the null object, and position the character so its CG is centered on the null. This enables you to rotate either the null or the character for a tumbling motion. If you animate the null for both position and rotation, you have the advantage of not disturbing the keyframes used to pose the character.

Figure 14.18
Character tumbling along a parabola.

PROJECT 14.11 Beach or Bowling Alley?

This project shows you how to create a series of diminishing parabolas, first for a very bouncy object, a ball, then for a heavier object, a bowling ball:

1. Open the scene file you just saved from Project 14.10.

   Each bounce of the ball will be a little shorter than the one before, so you need to accurately model the shrinking parabolas. Fortunately, there is a quick-and-dirty way to do this without recalculating and typing a bunch of y-coordinates. The y-coordinates of every gravity-based parabola are identical near the peak. The only differences are in the length of the legs. Therefore, you can cut and paste the top of a parabola to create shorter ones. This creates an automatic diminishing bounce. The only choice you have to make is how many keyframes you cut off the bottom of the preceding bounce. If you cut off more frames, you create the appearance of a heavier, less bouncy object. This is like setting the *modulus of elasticity* for the object's material in the LW_Gravity plug-in. It should not vary within the same action (except for comic effect), so keep track of the number of frames you delete and be sure to use the same number for each bounce.

   Depending on how LightWave handles cut-and-paste operations on keyframes, you may need to be careful to cut off one more frame on the trailing (lower frame number) side of the parabola than on the leading side. The last frame of the preceding parabola should become the first frame of the new one.

2. Drag-select the middle keyframes of the parabola, leaving out the two beginning and two ending keyframes. This will make the ball rather bouncy, so it will appear light and resilient in the finished animation.

3. Choose the Add mode. Hold down the Ctrl key and right-drag the selected keyframes (this quick-copies them, leaving the original keyframes in place), then paste the copied keyframes one frame after the end of the parabola.

4. The copied frames are pasted in place at their original y-axis values. You need to drag them vertically so the first copied keyframe is level with the last original keyframe. Deselect the original keyframes. Drag-select the copied keyframes. Choose the Move mode and left-drag the copied keyframes until the first key is level with the last key of the original parabola.

5. Hold down the Ctrl key and left-drag the copied keyframes until the first key is over the last key of the original parabola. Deselect the copied keyframes, then delete one of the overlapping keyframes (it doesn't matter which one). Your results should look like Figure 14.19. If you like, you can make a preview to see how the bounce looks.

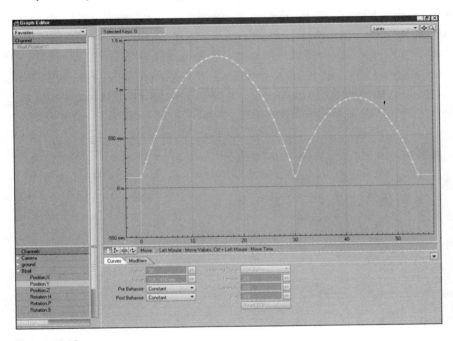

Figure 14.19
First derived smaller parabola, copied and dragged.

6. Repeat Steps 3, 4, and 5 until the progressively smaller bounces fill the graph to frame 90. Edit the graph as necessary to make sure the last keyframe y-coordinate matches the value of the first keyframe. Save the scene under a new name. You'll be using this scene in the next project. You should end up with a graph like the one displayed in Figure 14.20.

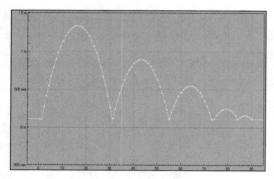

Figure 14.20
Beach ball spline.

7. Load another copy of the ball model. In frame 0, position it a couple of diameters along the x-axis to one side of the other ball so you can see it clearly. Create a keyframe for the new ball.

8. Repeat Steps 2 through 6 for the duplicate ball. This time, chop off more keyframes to make the bounces even shorter. Try to make a graph like Figure 14.21. This is more like a bowling ball than a beach ball, wouldn't you say?

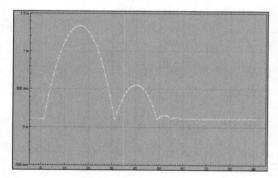

Figure 14.21
Bowling ball spline.

9. Render and play back the animation.

Photographers sometimes capture a complex motion by leaving the camera shutter open and using a high-speed flash to illuminate the action many times per second, a technique called *stroboscopic* photography. This is useful for showing a series of actions within a single image. I used a simple rendering trick (loading each rendered frame as the background image for the next frame) to simulate this effect for several figures in this book. If you tracked the camera during a stroboscopic rendering of this animation, you might get a final image like Figure 14.22.

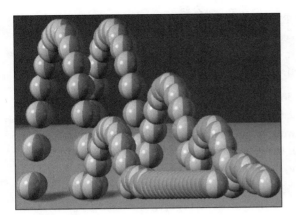

Figure 14.22
Stroboscopic image of bouncing different masses.

Caveat Animator

LightWave animators have the tremendous advantage of being able to analyze motion graphs in a variety of ways. With just a little experience, you'll be able to pick out significant details and predict just how an action will look, even before you play it back. With practice, you should be able to identify and correct any aberration from the accurate, realistic representation of the physical world and do it with the minimum number of keyframes. *However*, that which is real is not entertaining enough, or is insufficiently communicative, to be of any value to the filmmaker. If the audience doesn't get the idea intended by the shot, it doesn't matter if it was real. *Your job is to tell a compelling lie.* If it looks right, it is right. It's *all* cheating.

Timing with Splines

Traditional puppet animators making the transition to LightWave have a tendency to drop a key on every frame, nailing down the character before moving to the next frame. This works, but it's a real mess to revise or edit. There's just too much data, so you end up throwing it all out and starting over, which isn't very efficient and doesn't take advantage of the computer's assets as an artist's tool.

A curve defined by lots of keyframes, as you saw in the preceding projects, resembles a connect-the-dots picture. Just as with modeling, you can also create a curve by using fewer points and connecting them with splines. If you learn to use LightWave's spline editing tools, you can animate faster, with fewer keyframes and better control. You will also be able to revise and edit your animations much more easily, which makes it possible for you to experiment more to find just the right timing and poses.

The best spline controls are a matter of personal preference and the demands of the current job. The paramount requirement is proper control handles. It doesn't matter if you're using

Bezier, Hermite, Tension, Bias, Continuity (TCB), or whatever variety of splines, as long as you have adequate control. You should be able to completely and interactively control the in-and-out slope and curve of the spline at every control node. You should also be able to flatten out a segment or nail down a value without restricting what you can do with the rest of the spline.

If your software puts limits on what you can do, it's not up to the job. If your software requires data entry or other technical actions, it will distract you from the essentially creative act of timing. The goal of character animation software should be to make timing as intuitive as posing a traditional armature, combined with the jog/shuttle wheel of a good VCR. That's the essence of what you're doing, after all—setting poses, then playing with their timing. Good spline tools can come close to this ideal, but bad ones can make you feel like you're beating your head against a wall.

The shape of an animation channel is of paramount importance to the way it in-betweens. An entry and exit to a keyframe on an animation curve, on the spline of the curve, must be independently adjustable on both entrance and exit. You must be able to break the slope of that curve. Even where you can't break the slope of the curve, it must be adjustable under the animator's control to determine its contour.

An experienced LightWave animator can select a handful of curves on a piece of animation for hand editing. Keyframes for individual actions like y-rotation, or x-translation can be moved around to break synchronous timing. A section of a curve that starts up on a steep slope and then slowly levels off, for example, will give a snap and cushion to the animation. A section of a curve that appears not to change values between keyframes will *hold*. If an animator changes the value of the keyframes so that there is a small change in value during what was a hold, the animator will get a moving hold.

LightWave provides a variety of tools to adjust the tangents of the curves on the animation channel splines. That adjustment alters the slope of those curves. You can even change the magnitude of those curves, to expand them out, make the curves wider, or contract them in, to make the curve more peaked. LightWave includes the conventional Bezier spline control handles used throughout the rest of the industry and familiar to many artists from 2D graphic software, such as Illustrator. These tools enable you to create versatile, efficient character animation timing.

TCB is the oldest LightWave spline control. Tension controls the apparent speed or rate of change of an object in the vicinity of the keyframe. Higher tension bunches up the adjoining frames, bringing their values closer to the keyframe. There is less change between these frames, so the motion appears slower. A lower tension has the opposite effect—objects appear to move more rapidly near the keyframe. The Bias control (Curves|Incoming Curve) pushes the bulge of the spline to one side of the selected keyframe. A negative value pushes the curve back, and a positive value pushes it forward. Continuity controls the curvature of the spline as it passes through the selected keyframe. A negative value takes away all curvature, making the spline cut a sharp corner. A zero value pushes the curvature of the spline outward, so it is nearly flat as it passes through the keyframe. A positive value pushes the spline into inverted entry and exit curves around the keyframe. Figure 14.23 shows how a TCB spline can closely match a manually keyframed parabola.

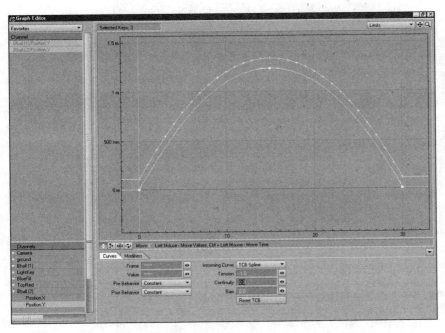

Figure 14.23
TCB spline matched to manually keyframed parabola.

TCB spline controls generally limit you to more realistic, true-to-life physics. For character animation, you need to be able to push the splines into shapes that create exaggerated actions. For that extra level of control, you will usually want to use either the Hermite or Bezier spline controls. Figures 14.24 and 14.25 show how Hermite and Bezier splines, respectively, can closely match a manually keyframed parabola and also provide more flexible options for reshaping splines into extreme shapes.

PROJECT 14.12 Curves Ahead

Thi project shows you how to duplicate the realistic bouncing motion from Project 14.11 by using fewer keyframes combined with the spline tools:

1. Open the finished scene file you saved from Project 14.11.

2. Load a second copy of the ball. In frame 0, position it a couple of diameters on the x-axis to one side of the other ball so you can see it clearly. Create a keyframe for the new ball.

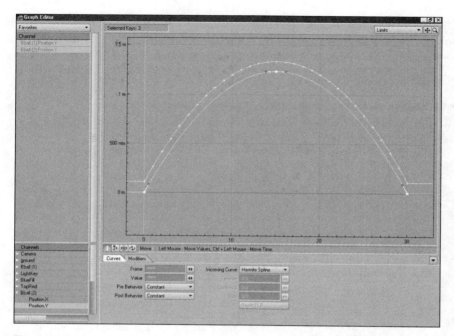

Figure 14.24
Hermite spline matched to manually keyframed parabola.

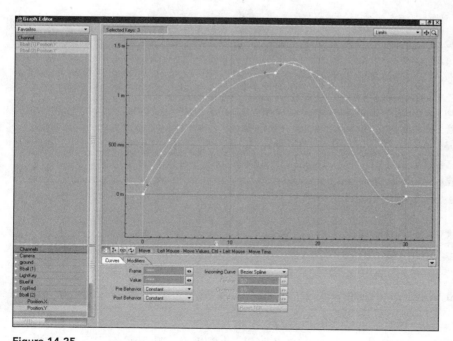

Figure 14.25
Bezier spline matched to a manually keyframed parabola on the left side. The right side shows a more typical character animation spline with anticipation, snap, and follow-through.

3. Add keyframes at the peak and end of the parabola for the new ball.

4. Use LightWave's Bezier spline tools to smooth the parabola into a close approximation of the original keyframed parabola. The Graph Editor enables you to display as many splines as you need, so you can use the manually keyframed parabola as a guide to quickly and easily move the spline handles for the new parabola.

The beginning and ending keyframes should be as sharp as possible; you can *break* (make discontinuous) the spline handles by holding down the Alt key while moving one of the two handles. LightWave's support of these *breaking splines* is another feature that makes it easier to create snappy character actions.

5. Make a preview. Compare the first bounce from Project 14.11 and the one you just created. If they are not an exact match, go back to Step 4 and try again.

6. You should end up with a parabola like the one in Figure 14.26. When you are satisfied with the ball's bounce, save the motion. You may find a use for it later.

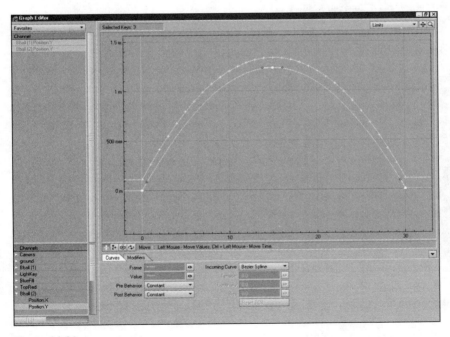

Figure 14.26
A Bezier spline parabola.

Placing Spline Handles
Keyframes for splines work best when placed where there is the most change in direction.

Squash, Stretch, and Motion Blur

Squash is used to show the effects of rapid deceleration and of energy expended to compress the shape of an object (see Figure 14.27). Stretch is used to show rapid acceleration and energy expended to lengthen the shape of an object (see Figure 14.28).

Figure 14.27
Squash frame from a bounce cycle.

Figure 14.28
Stretch frame from a bounce cycle.

To maintain the visual volume of an object, squash and stretch are usually synchronized on tangent axes. That is, if an object stretches in one axis, it must also squash in the other axes to maintain its original volume. This particular rule can be broken for extreme cartoon-style effects, but it's usually more effective when simply exaggerated. If you intend to break this rule for comic effect, you should establish the rule very firmly before you break it. The sudden, unexpected change in the rules is the source of the humor.

The easiest way to create squash in LightWave is to simply scale the object, as shown in Figure 14.27. However, this makes the animation look subtly wrong to most viewers, and to an experienced animator, the problem is obvious. The part of the character that impacts the surface should deform more strongly, squashing out flat, whereas the opposite surface should hardly deform at all. You can produce much more accurate and pleasing results by deforming the character proportionately, as if it were actually impacting a surface and deforming to suit. There are several ways to deform all or part of a character, as you learned in Chapter 11. They take a little more work in setup and animation than a simple scaling, but the results are definitely worth it. The same is true of stretch, although the problem is not as obvious. Stretch is usually applied to show the effects of acceleration rather than physical contact, so there isn't any opposing surface to show where the stretch isn't accurate. 2D traditions use stretch to prevent *strobing,* changes between frames that are too extreme, catch the audience's eye, and destroy the illusion of smooth movement. The LightWave artist can use *motion blur* instead of stretch to maintain visual continuity and prevent strobing.

Motion blur occurs when an action is faster than a camera's shutter speed—the action appears blurred between the beginning and ending positions of the moving objects. LightWave simulates motion blur by interpolating and rendering extra frames in between the actual numbered frames. The rendering engine then composites these extra images together, using a slight transparency. Anything that moves has a number of ghost images that combine to create a blur.

 ## One Standard Bounce, Please

The first part of this project shows you how to add stretch to an animation of a bouncing ball to prevent strobing:

1. Reload the last bouncing-ball scene file you created in the preceding project.

2. Select the ball. Go to frame 1. Rotate the ball to align its vertical centerline with the parabola. Set a keyframe.

3. Repeat Step 2 for the keyframe at the peak and end of each parabola. You should end up with an animation of a ball that rotates perfectly in sync with its bouncing.

4. Add stretch to the ball for the up and down legs of the parabola. Increase the ball's y-axis size by 150 percent, and reduce the size proportionally for the z- and x-axes. I used 75 percent. Leave the ball's proportions normal at the peak frame.

5. Add squash to the hit frames, the beginning and end of the parabola. Decrease the y-axis size and increase the size proportionally for the z- and x-axes.

6. Save the file under a new name. Render and play back the animation. You should get an animation like Figure 14.29.

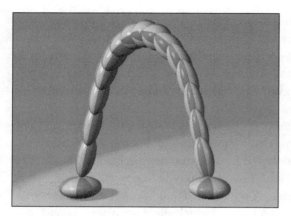

Figure 14.29
Bouncing ball with stretch-and-squash. Note the overlap of the stretched ball images, which prevents strobing.

7. Now try the same effect, using motion blur instead of stretch. Reload the scene file you just saved.

8. Remove the stretch from the ball along the up and down legs of the parabola, leaving the ball's proportions normal at the peak frame and along each leg. Only the squash at the beginning and ending frames should remain.

9. In the Camera panel, set Antialiasing to Low or better, set Motion Blur to Normal, and set Blur Length to 100.

10. Render and play back the animation. You should get an animation like Figure 14.30.

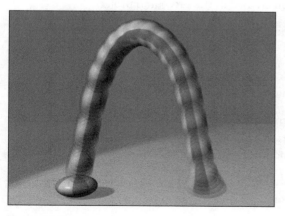

Figure 14.30
Bouncing ball with motion blur. Stretch is not necessary. Squash is used to show deformation of the ball against the floor.

Compare the effect of motion blur to the effect of stretch. Which animation would you prefer to watch? Which looks more realistic? Motion blur is almost always better than stretch for smoothing rapid motion. It is more realistic, and LightWave renders it automatically, so it is easier for the animator. Stretch is still useful, but mostly for exaggerated action.

Finally, add an accurate deformation instead of the cheesy-looking scale to the squash positions.

11. Reload the scene file from the preceding steps in this project.

12. Remove the squash from the ball's keyframes.

13. Load the Boned beach ball deformation setup you created in Chapter 11.

14. Rotate the ball to point the bones at the floor in frame 0, and set a keyframe. Size the first bone to 0.5 to flatten the bottom of the ball, and set a keyframe.

15. Lower the ball in frame 0 to keep the flattened part of the ball level with the floor. Resize the bone to unsquash the ball as it leaves the floor; when it stops touching the floor, it should be perfectly round again.

16. Squash and lower the ball again at frame 30 and set keyframes for the ball and bone.

17. Make a preview, or render and play back the animation. You should get an animation as shown in Figure 14.31.

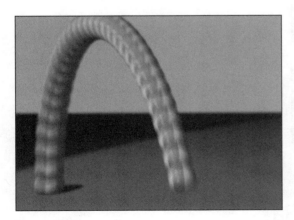

Figure 14.31
Bouncing ball with accurate squash.

Squash and stretch tell the audience a lot about the material of an object. Different parts of a character should have different amounts of squash and stretch. A hard wingtip shoe, for instance, should not stretch or squash nearly as much as a flabby potbelly.

Stretch and squash can also be very effective in showing a character's internal energy, as shown in the next two projects.

Ease-in, Ease-out

Objects in the real world can't abruptly change from standing still to moving very fast. Any object that has mass needs a little time to get up to speed. The more mass, the longer the acceleration (that is, more energy is required). The same is true for slowing down, changing direction, or distorting the object's shape.

In animation, a gradual change that leads into an action is called an *ease-in*. Coming out of an action gradually is called an *ease-out*. The precise timing of an ease tells the audience just how massive the object is and how much energy it is using to perform the action. The quickest way to understand ease and how to apply it is to study and experiment with LightWave's spline motion tools.

Figure 14.32 shows two motion splines, superimposed. One shows a constant speed between the start and end positions, and the other shows an acceleration curve, or ease-in, at the beginning and an ease-out, or deceleration, at the end. Note that the object still moves from the first position to the second in the same amount of time—it just moves faster in the middle and slower on each end.

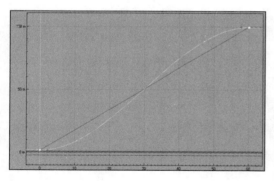

Figure 14.32
Splines for linear (straight) and ease-in/ease-out (curved) motion.

PROJECT 14.14 Getting the Ball Rolling

To use the motion spline, follow these steps:

1. Reload the original ball setup scene. Remove any keyframes you may have set during the bouncing-ball projects.

2. Select the ball and activate your spline controls.

3. Create keyframes for the ball's pitch rotation at frames 0, 1, 20, and 40.

4. Set x-position values for the new keyframes. The ball is to start from a standstill at frame 1, then ease in to its maximum speed at frame 20 and roll off screen in three complete rotations to frame 60. In LightWave, the ball is 0.111 units in radius, which means that it can travel 0.6974 units ($2\pi r = 2 \times 3.1416 \times 0.111$) for each complete rotation. That's a total of 2.092 units to travel. Let's start the ball off at -0.5 on the x-axis for both frames 0 and 1, pass through 0 at frame 20, and roll right to 1.592 in frame 60. Your settings may vary.

5. Adjust the spline controls for each keyframe. You want the last section, between frames 20 and 60, to be at the maximum speed, a constant. LightWave's Graph Editor enables you to choose a Linear interpolation option to make the spline a straight line between frames 20 and 60. Adjust the spline controls for frames 1 and 20 so the end of the curve nearest frame 20 closely matches the slope of the line from 20 to 60. If the slope changes abruptly at frame 20, the ball will jerk noticeably at that frame. See Figure 14.33 for one possible solution.

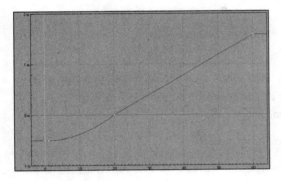

Figure 14.33
The x-position spline for rolling ball's ease-in.

6. Set the ball's rotation keyframes. You want the ball to start off at 0 degrees and make three full rotations by frame 60, for a total of 1080 degrees. Frame 60 should therefore be set to -1080 degrees (or 1080, depending on the orientation of LightWave and the direction you are rolling the ball) and frame 0 and 1 left at 0 degrees.

7. Determining a value for frame 20 is a little more of a challenge. The distance from 1 to 20 is 0.5 units, the total distance from 1 to 60 is 2.092, a ratio of 0.239. Multiply that by the total of degrees rotated, and you get 258.12, the number of bank rotation degrees to set for frame 20. Don't forget to make it a negative rotation. Again, the sign and value of these settings may vary according to your setup.

8. Save the scene under a new name. Render and play back the animation.

Your results should look something like Figure 14.34. If the rolling contact with the floor does not exactly match the lateral travel of the ball, go back and tweak a few keyframes until you have an acceptable match.

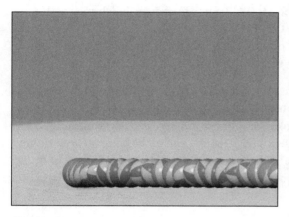

Figure 14.34
Stroboscopic rendering of ease-in for a rolling ball.

 Easy Does It

This project is an example of how a difference in timing of a frame or two can have a great effect on the animation:

1. Reload the scene file you saved from the preceding project.

2. Move the key at frame 1 to frame 10. This compresses the ease-in into half the time, making the acceleration much more sudden.

3. Adjust the spline controls for frames 1 and 20 so the end of the spline nearest frame 20 closely matches the slope of the line from 20 to 60. As noted in the preceding project, if the slope changes abruptly at frame 20, the ball will jerk noticeably at that frame.

4. Save the scene under a new name. Render and play back the animation.

Your results should look something like Figure 14.35.

Notice how the different rates of ease made the ball seem to roll itself forward with greater energy. See what a difference a few frames make? Character animation timing is very sensitive to small differences, and you need to practice enough to understand and use them.

Snap

Don't overdo ease-in and ease-out. It is tempting to use spline interpolation to make the whole action a smooth curve, like a lazy integral sign as shown in Figure 14.36. Spline interpolation is a wonderful tool. It's unique to computer animation and can save you a lot of effort if you use it

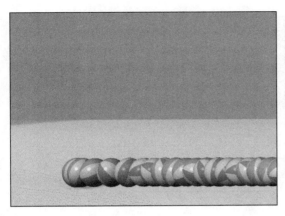

Figure 14.35
Stroboscopic rendering of faster ease-in for a rolling ball.

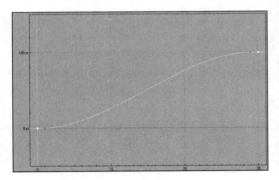

Figure 14.36
Spline for lazy, mushy movement.

properly. But if you overuse it, your animations will look just like all the other beginners' out there. Splines like this will give you soft, mushy actions, as if the characters are moving underwater.

Almost always, you'll want your animations to have more *snap*. "Snap" is the animator's term for action that is quick, lively, and full of energy. To create an action with more snap, use splines more like the one shown in Figure 14.37. Remember that it takes more energy to accelerate and decelerate an object more quickly. To have more snap, the ease-in and -out curves of a spline should be shorter and sharper, and the middle section of the spline, where most of the action takes place, occupies as few frames as possible.

Take a look at animation file SNAP.AVI, located in the Chapter 14 directory on this book's CD-ROM. The upper ball has a spline like Figure 14.36, and the lower ball has a spline like Figure 14.37. Compare the motions of the lower ball and the upper ball (see Figure 14.38). Which looks more lively? Which looks more sluggish? Which one has more personality, and which one looks like a computer animated it?

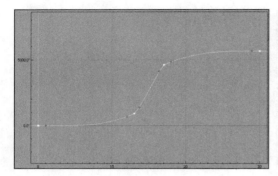

Figure 14.37
Spline for snappy movement.

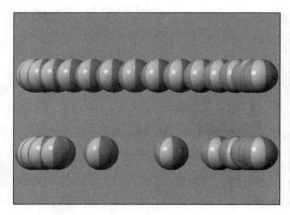

Figure 14.38
Stroboscopic image from SNAP.AVI, showing snap (bottom) and mush (top).

Judging the balance between ease and snap takes practice. Take advantage of every opportunity you can to play with the splines, testing trade-offs and noting what values work for specific situations and moods. There are no hard-and-fast rules for this aspect of timing—you have to develop your own judgment.

Anticipation

Anticipation is an action in one direction intended to prepare the audience for a much larger action in the opposite direction. A baseball pitcher's windup is an example of anticipation.

You anticipate every time you prepare to take a step. Try this: Stand with your weight balanced evenly on both feet. While concentrating on your posture and balance, take one slow step forward. If you pay attention, you'll notice that you lean back and to one side as you raise your foot, then lean forward and to the other side as you put your foot down. That is an antici-pation and action. You moved backward a little in order to move forward even more.

PROJECT 14.16 Rolling 'Em Again

This project shows you how to apply anticipation to the rolling ball:

1. Reload the scene file you saved from the preceding project.

2. Shift keyframes 1 through 60 by 10 frames, leaving frame 0 intact. This adds 10 frames of no action onto the front of the animation because frame 0 is still nailing down the initial position and rotation of the ball.

3. Create a new key for the ball at frame 5. Move it to -0.557 on the x-axis. This is an appropri-ate distance for an anticipation movement. You could push it farther for an exaggerated move or make it more subtle for a realistic move. This setting is somewhere in between.

   You can find appropriate values for an anticipation by moving to the symmetrical frame on the other side of the motion's origin. For example, this motion begins at -0.5 x at frame 0. The ball is located at -0.5 x again as it passes frame 11, after the anticipation. The an-ticipation is centered on frame 5. Frame 11 is six frames after frame 5, so move six frames further along after frame 11, to frame 17. Make a note of the rotation and position values at frame 17, in this case, 29.4 degrees and -0.443. Note that these values will not be accu-rate if you have the spline controls set to anything but zero for any of these frames. You can change the spline handle settings later, but at this time, you need the spline segments to be evenly balanced between the keyframes. As noted earlier, these settings will vary depending on your setup, but the basic principles apply.

4. The x-axis position is (0.500-0.443), or 0.057. Subtract this from the resting x-axis position of -0.5 to get -0.557. The ball's rotation at frame 17 is -29.4. All this requires is a change of sign because the ball is rolling in the opposite direction. Set the rotation for the ball for keyframe 5 to 29.4 degrees.

   Frame 5 should now have the correct position and rotation values. The only remaining tweak is to smooth out the acceleration curves to create the proper ease-in.

5. Revise the spline controls for frames 0, 5, 11, and 30 so the anticipation is smooth. The end of the curve nearest frame 30 must closely match the slope of the line from 30 to 70. As noted earlier, if the slope of the spline changes abruptly at any keyframe, the ball will jerk noticeably at that frame. You should end up with a spline like Figure 14.39.

6. Save the scene under a new name. Render and play back the animation. Your results should look something like Figure 14.40.

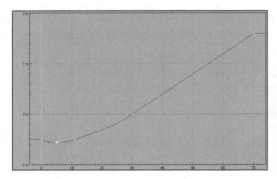

Figure 14.39
Spline showing anticipation at frame 5.

Figure 14.40
Ball anticipates, then rolls.

It Lives!

PROJECT 14.17 So far, all the animations have given the impression that some invisible hand, or maybe the wind, moved the ball. The ball itself seemed inert, as if it was being acted upon by outside forces but not taking any action of its own. Now let's try combining anticipation with stretch and squash to make the ball seem alive and capable of moving itself:

1. Load scene file Proj1417 from the Chapter 14 directory of this book's CD-ROM. This is the same as the file you saved from the preceding project, except the ball now has a bone deformation setup to stretch it into a shape like one of Al Capp's Shmoos (see Figure 14.41).

2. Set the deformation keyframes to stretch the ball upward during anticipation, then squash down and stretch forward during the start of the forward roll, then back to normal as the top of the ball reaches the ground. See Figure 14.42 for examples.

Your deformation splines for the ball should look something like Figure 14.43.

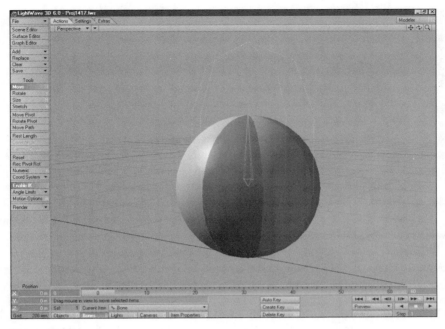

Figure 14.41
Example deformation setup in ball, using a bone.

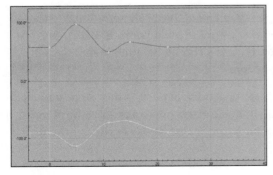

Figure 14.42
Ball deformation during anticipation and start of roll.

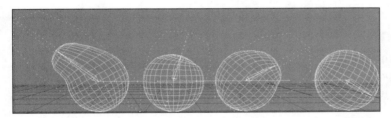

Figure 14.43
Bone Z Scale and pitch rotation splines for ball.

Figure 14.44
Ball appears to motivate its own anticipation and roll.

3. Save the scene under a new name. Render and play back the animation. Your results should look something like Figure 14.44.

This shows how a very minor change in an animation can make the difference between an object that is animated (passive) and one that has the illusion of life (active). Your characters should always appear to be motivating themselves, to be acting from internal forces. Your characters should never look like someone is pulling their strings.

Follow-through

Follow-through is almost exactly like anticipation, but on the other end of the action. You already acted out an anticipation. Let's do it again, but instead of starting a walk, let's stop one. Take a couple of steps, just enough to get up some momentum. Stop suddenly.

Did you notice how your body swayed forward a bit until your muscles could bring you to a complete stop? Did you rise up on your toes a little or have to brace one foot ahead of the other? Either of these actions would be a shock absorber, dissipating some of your forward motion.

You can watch another example of follow-through if you repeat that walk-and-stop exercise while carrying a cup of liquid. Not hot coffee, you don't want to scald yourself! Watch the liquid when you stop suddenly. That slop-up-and-fall-back is a contest between inertia, gravity, and the extra energy you put into your stopping action.

Your animated characters will have to perform the same kind of actions. If they simply stopped dead, they would look weightless and artificial. If your characters are to appear to have mass, they must overshoot the goal a little, then bounce back to it. These types of actions are called *follow-through*.

PROJECT 14.18 Whoa, Nellie!

By this time, you should have had enough practice modifying splines that you don't need step-by-step directions. The goal of this project is to create a complete set of splines for anticipation, stretch, ease-in, snap, ease-out, squash, and follow-through.

1. Load the scene file you saved at the end of the preceding project.

   The goal for this shot is to make the ball roll backwards and stretch in anticipation, then squash and ease in to a forward roll with plenty of snap, ease out to a stretch in follow-through, then squash back to a hold position.

   As a guide, Figure 14.45 contains the splines used to make one version of this animation. You don't need to duplicate these graphs exactly. It will be a better project if you create a different timing that still achieves the goal of the shot.

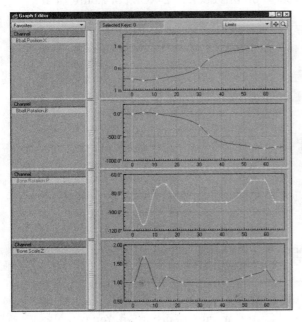

Figure 14.45
Splines for one version of this animation.

2. Set position keyframes to move the ball across the camera's view, making at least two full revolutions. Start at frame 0 with the ball at rest position, then move it back in anticipation, then forward again. Make sure you put some snap in the middle of the motion. Finish it by easing out past the final hold position in a follow-through, then sliding back to the hold.

You might end up with something like the X Position graph in Figure 14.45, but then again, feel free to make up your own interpretation.

3. Set rotation keyframes so the ball rolls in contact with the ground, not sliding or spinning. Don't forget the reverse rotations for the anticipation at the beginning and the follow-through at the end. Again, you can refer to Figure 14.45 for one possible solution.

4. Save the scene with a new name. Render and play back the animation to check the motion so far.

5. Set the deformation keyframes as appropriate to accentuate the anticipation and follow-through motions. See Figure 14.45 for an example.

6. Save the scene again. Render and play back the animation.

Your results may look something like SHMOO.AVI on this book's CD-ROM, or Figure 14.46.

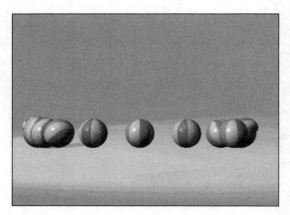

Figure 14.46
Ball rolls, then follows through with ease-in, ease-out, stretch, and squash.

In LightWave, you can also tweak the deformation keyframes in the camera view if you find it easier to work this way rather than using a spline editor. I personally prefer to tweak squash-and-stretch in close-up views to get the best feel for the amount of distortion. You can also tweak the keyframes in the Graph Editor while the scene is playing; this is a really nice feature for fine-tuning a character's performance.

Moving Holds

A 3D character cannot hold still for more than one or two frames before it loses the illusion of life. If the character must stay in one place or position for a number of frames, you should create a *moving hold* to keep the character alive.

A moving hold is a series of tiny, subtle motions that mimic the behavior of a real living creature. Your audience perceives these clues unconsciously and automatically accepts the illusion that the animated character is alive.

For example, most creatures breathe. You can imitate this subtle movement for a moving hold by stretching and squashing the character's torso (or whatever it uses for a lung casing) in the appropriate rhythm. Eyelid blinks, shifting of weight from one foot to the other, and small twitches of the hands are other useful actions you can add to a moving hold. If the scene setup permits, you can even create a slightly modified copy of the entire character and create a moving hold by performing repeated morph changes between the original and the copy.

Moving That Hold

This project shows you how to add subtle motions to an object to create a moving hold:

1. Reload the scene file you saved from the preceding project.

2. Add four new deformation keyframes at 65, 80, 95, and 110.

3. Animate a slight swell-and-shrink of the ball, peaking at frames 80 and 100 and dropping at 65 and 95, as if the ball is breathing.

4. Save the scene with a new name. Render and play back the animation.

5. Critique the action, and make revisions to the breathing action until you are satisfied with it. You may want to render the animation at a higher-than-usual resolution so you can evaluate the subtlety of the breathing motion more easily.

6. Animate a very slight forward-and-back wobble for frames 65 through 100, rotating the ball about 5 degrees, as if the ball is preparing to roll again.

7. Save the scene again. Render and play back the animation. Critique the action, then make revisions to the timing and amplitude of the wobble until you are satisfied with it.

You can generally add moving holds to a sequence after the main action is complete. If a moving hold requires special setups or models, you need to lay out the moving holds in your storyboards and all the ensuing design processes just as you would any other action. In this example, you could just as easily have used the ball's scale and rotation keyframes to achieve a very similar effect.

Showing a Little Character

This project shows you how to combine all the preceding timing principles to animate a desk lamp hopping. This project is patterned after John Lasseter's exposition (in the 1987 SIGGRAPH paper referenced in the bibliography) of Luxo Jr.'s hop.

To animate a desk lamp hopping, follow these steps:

1. Load the desk lamp scene file you set up in Chapter 11, or use file Proj1420 from the Chapter 14 directory on this book's CD-ROM.

   The lamp's base is very heavy. The lamp can only lift it with a strong, quick jerk, so the base will leave the ground with no ease-in at all. For the same reason, the base falls back to the ground very quickly and does not rebound at all. It behaves like a solid, heavy, rigid piece of metal.

2. Add and drag keyframes to create a spline like the one in Figure 14.47 for the lamp, to make it move in a parabola on the y-axis. Turn linear interpolation on for the motion keyframes at the takeoff (frame 20) and ending (frame 60) keys for the y-axis so the lamp base leaps up and slams down abruptly. Adjust the spline for the x-axis so it is straight throughout.

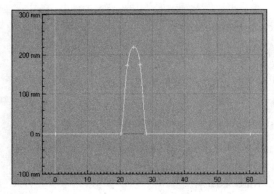

Figure 14.47
Y-position spline for hopping lamp.

   Note that the lamp is only airborne for eight frames, just over a quarter second. If you keep the core of the action short and fast, the overall action will have more snap.

3. Create pitch (elevation) axis keyframes to rotate the base during the lamp's hop. Use ease-in and ease-out so the hop starts toe-last and ends heel-first. Make the lamp base flush to the ground, with zero pitch, at both the takeoff and landing keyframes. The maximum pitch angles should be just before and just after the peak of the hop, as in Figure 14.48.

4. Refer to your notes on the lamp's bending setup you created in Chapter 11. The following procedure will differ depending on the setup technique you chose for the bend.

   If you chose a morph sequence setup, such as LightWave's Multiple Target Single Envelope, a 0 MTSE percentage will stretch out the lamp neck, and a 600 percent setting will bend the neck so the shade nearly touches the base. Reasonably enough, 300 percent is the middle or resting position for the lamp.

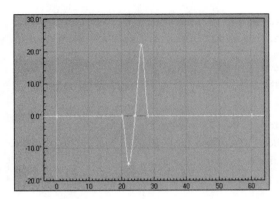

Figure 14.48
Spline for lamp's rotation on the pitch axis.

If you chose the object hierarchy setup, you will have to set rotation keyframes for the individual parts of the hierarchy to create the bend poses. You can also copy keys from one frame to another, which makes it much easier to repeat a pose later in an animation.

You already set the movement and rotation values, so the lamp's base should be going where you want it to. The challenging part of this project is to use the bend setup to give the lamp the illusion of life.

5. Create and modify bend keyframes so the lamp bends (squashes) in anticipation, stretches out just before the takeoff keyframe, returns to rest position in midhop, compresses immediately after landing in follow-through, and vibrates slightly in a moving hold to the end of the animation. If your bend setup enables you to use a single spline to control the depth of the bend, you should end up with something like Figure 14.49.

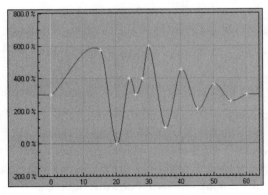

Figure 14.49
MTSE envelope for lamp hop.

6. Create keyframes for a *tracking shot* for the camera to make it line up with the lamp at the beginning and end frames of the animation. This makes the animation *hook up* for a seamless repeating cycle.

7. Save the scene with a new name. You'll be using it in the next project. Render and play back the animation.

You can modify the timing of the bend and motion splines to change the character of the lamp. Drag out the number of frames between hops to make a more tired or melancholy lamp, or scale down the interval and the hop itself for a more energetic lamp.

Overlapping Action

When a character has loose parts or appendages that are not held rigidly to the main body, these parts must demonstrate to the audience that they also have mass and energy of their own. A hound's floppy ears, for example, will continue to drag behind after the dog begins to run, and after the dog stops, the ears will flop forward under their own inertia. The ears' motion is an *overlapping action*.

The usual guidelines for stretch-and-squash and follow-through apply to overlapping action just as to the main action. Anticipation, snap, and ease don't apply because they mimic motivated action and the overlapping action is completely passive.

Up to this point, you've been animating objects with only one part or with parts firmly fixed. Now, let's try something just a little more loosely constructed.

 Adding Overlapping Action to the Lamp

This project shows you how to add a loosely attached object to your main object and animate the additional part using overlapping action:

1. Open the scene you saved from the preceding project.

2. Load the TAGRING and PRICETAG models from the Chapter 14 directory on this book's CD-ROM.

   The TAGRING model is modeled after the flexible plastic O-rings sometimes used to attach price or ID tags, and the tag is modeled after a very common retail sales tag profile. I could have modeled a loop of string instead of the O-ring, but the string's flexibility would have required a much more complex setup, and the extra complexity might have distracted you from the point of this project. If you want to try that approach on your own, please do so—it's an excellent practical exercise in modeling, setup, and animation.

3. Parent TAGRING to the desk lamp and position it on the lamp's neck, as shown in Figure 14.50. Create a key for it at frame 0. You won't be moving or rotating the O-ring again, so lock off all its motion channels.

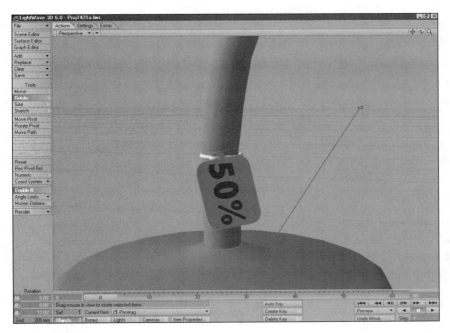

Figure 14.50
TAGRING and PRICETAG models loaded, parented, and positioned.

You want the price tag and O-ring to remain visibly attached to the lamp, but you also need as much space as possible for the price tag to move. If you used a morph sequence setup to bend the lamp, you should position the O-ring near the base of the lamp's neck, where any gaps caused by the neck's bending will be small and less noticeable.

4. Parent PRICETAG to TAGRING and position and rotate PRICETAG, as shown in Figure 14.50. Create a key for it at frame 0. You should have a scene like Figure 14.50, with the price tag hanging naturally off the loop in the plastic O-ring.

This arrangement of the tag and O-ring enables you to animate the price tag using only rotation keyframes. The pivot point of the tag is inside the loop of the O-ring, so pivoting the tag simulates the constraints of a real tag. If you want to push the simulation further, you can reposition the tag anywhere along the O-ring's loop, as long as you keep the tag's pivot point within the loop and keep the tag from penetrating the lamp or O-ring.

Note the angle of the tag in Figure 14.50. The thickness of the O-ring loop and the profile of the paper tag prevent the tag from hanging straight down. The tag can never be rotated to less than 13 degrees of bank angle without penetrating the O-ring. The allowable range of motion for the tag is 13 to 165 degrees bank, 45 to -4 degrees pitch, and 30 to -30 degrees heading. Any angle exceeding these limits will probably push the tag into the O-ring, the lamp itself, or both.

5. Make a series of keyframes for the PRICETAG model. Rotate the tag around its heading, pitch, and bank axes to create overlapping actions.

The tag has no motivation or life of its own. Any movement of the tag must be initiated by the lamp or an outside force, such as wind or gravity. You need to keep four factors in mind when animating the price tag's overlapping action—lamp motion, inertia, gravity, and air resistance:

- *Lamp motion* is the prime mover for the tag. The tag goes along, willy-nilly, following the lamp's position changes. This helps you choose where to set keyframes for the tag. One at each of the lamp's Position keyframes is a good start. The tag does not, however, follow along with the lamp's bending.

- *Inertia* takes over when the lamp is not actively dragging the tag. At the top of the lamp's parabola, for instance, the tag changes from following the lamp's lead to following its own parabola. Because the CG of the tag is below its pivot point, the tag shows inertia by swinging up toward the direction it had been traveling.

- *Gravity* pulls the tag down whenever the lamp motion and the tag's inertia are not strong enough to resist it. At rest, gravity keeps the tag firmly resting at 13 degrees of bank, as noted earlier.

- *Air resistance* is a factor due to the low mass and relatively large surface area of the tag. As the tag moves under the influence of the three preceding factors, it should also appear to be pushed around by the resistance of the air it passes through. For example, if the tag is descending under the influence of gravity (rotating in the bank axis), the tag may wobble in the heading and/or pitch axes.

If you are eyeballing the angles, it's much easier to work in a perspective view with the tag centered and OpenGL or other realtime shading options turned on, as in Figure 14.50. Adjust the view settings to give you a clear view of the tag's edges and where they may be intersecting other models. Figure 14.51 shows one possible solution for the price tag's overlapping action.

6. Save the scene with a new name. Render and play back the animation. You should end up with an animation similar to Figure 14.52, or the Proj1421.avi animation located in the Chapter 14 directory on this book's CD-ROM.

7. Critique your animation. Does the tag move lightly enough in comparison to the lamp? Does the lamp seem heavy and the tag lighter? Does the tag flutter enough to give the impression of a loose joint, or does it seem to be rigidly hinged? If the answers aren't what you intended, go back and revise the angles and timings for the tag (and perhaps the lamp as well) until you are satisfied.

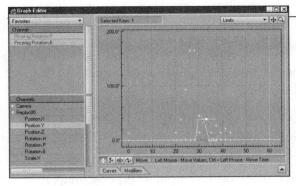

Figure 14.51
Rotation splines for the price tag's overlapping action.

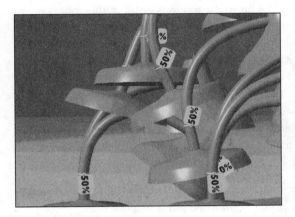

Figure 14.52
Overlapping action of a pivoting price tag.

Overlapping action can be set up and animated with just about every tool you learned in Chapter 11. Bones techniques are especially useful when parts of a seamless character model must overlap the main action.

Secondary Action

Overlapping action and secondary action are sometimes confused or even used interchangeably. They are not synonymous, and the difference between them is literally the difference between a dead character and a live one.

When a character has appendages that are not held rigidly to the main body but are still driven by their own volition, these appendages must demonstrate to the audience that they have mass, energy, and motivation of their own. A hound's tail, for example, will tend to drag behind after the dog begins to run, and after the dog stops, the tail will tend to flop forward under its own inertia. Unlike the ears, however, the tail has its own bone and muscle structure. Instead of simply following the dictates of gravity and inertia, the tail will wag, lift, or droop in addition to its inherited overlapping actions. The tail will never move on precisely the same frame as the dog's hips, so the tail's action *seconds* the hips' and the tail's aggregate motion is therefore a *secondary action*. Secondary action can precede the main action as well as follow it. Overlapping action can only follow the main action.

The usual guidelines for anticipation, snap, ease, stretch-and-squash, and follow-through apply to secondary action just as they apply to the main action because secondary action is also motivated by the character.

If you'd like a challenging project, try adding a very short power cord to the desk lamp. Animate it first as a limp appendage using overlapping action. Then animate it again, but make it move as if the lamp uses it as a sort of tentacle or monkey-tail that it can move of its own volition. Just for fun, you might consider giving the lamp the nervous habit of flicking its price tag with its plug.

A Nod Is as Good as a Wink: Eye and Head Motion

In this section, I'll show you how to apply some of the techniques you learned earlier in this chapter to mimic natural motions. A logical place to start is the character's eyes and head, the most expressive and closely watched parts of a character. Along the way, this section shows you how to partly automate natural eye motion using inverse kinematics (IK).

The first tool you can get rid of, at least for character animation, is your straight edge. It won't be of any use to you because nothing in the natural world moves in a straight line!

Throw 'Em a Curve

Now, you are probably thinking of movements that describe a straight line. Sorry, but you're mistaken. Straight-line movement is an illusion. Any simple projectile—whether bullet, spacecraft, or Olympic high-jumper—moves in an arc, defined by its velocity, mass, the force of gravity, and the resistance of the air. Over a short distance, the trajectory may appear flat, but it is actually a curve. Generally, the slower the movement, the more pronounced the curve. Billiard balls on a near-perfect table will still exhibit a little bit of table roll, and anything moving in three dimensions is even more prone to follow a curved path.

This is true for any unguided movement: Given the starting parameters, you can calculate the curve the object will follow and the impact point by using a class of mathematics called *ballistics*. You can also animate this kind of movement by using plug-ins that simulate physical laws, or *dynamics*.

If any part of an animation calls for accurate physical effects like these, use whatever tools are available to automate as much of the process as possible. It's like photography versus oil painting—if you want it accurate, use technology, but if you want it artistic, use human judgment. Animating dozens of billiard balls realistically bouncing downstairs is simply a matter of plugging in more numbers, using the right software. If you try to animate all that by hand, you won't impress anybody (animating it in a caricatured style is another matter entirely!).

Adding feedback to the equation, however, changes most movements from a simple parabolic arc to a more complex *slalom*. A slalom is the path followed by any system, natural or machine, that can correct its movement toward a goal. Guided missiles and torpedoes, a hawk swooping down on a field mouse, your feet as you walk toward a doorway, and your hand as you reach for the doorknob are each following a slalom path. Almost every action you take describes a slalom.

The basic components of a slalom are a starting point, a goal, and the limits that trigger feedback correction. Let's take walking toward a door as a simple two-dimensional example.

You start out across a large space, perhaps a plaza or parking lot. You identify the building you wish to enter and begin walking toward it. For the first step or two, you are following a nearly straight line. As you get closer, you notice the door you wish to enter by and turn toward it, bending your path slightly to the right. This adds a little bit of curve to your path, beginning the slalom. As you get even closer, you glance down to make sure you aren't going to stumble over an obstacle. When you look up again, you find that you have stepped a little too far to the right and correct your path to the left to line up with the door again. This process of making tiny corrections to your path continues until you actually pass through the doorway, at which point you are right on target—or you bruise a shoulder on the door frame if you aren't paying close enough attention!

The corrections when you are farthest away are mostly approximations, but your estimates are more accurate the closer you are to the target, and each following correction is that much smaller. In this case, you are basing most of your correction limits on visual cues. Your first goal is the building—as long as your planned path appears to intersect the building, that's good enough. Once you spot the door, the limits become much tighter, and you correct your planned path to intersect the door. As you approach even closer, you plan to walk through the middle of the doorway and correct your path accordingly. The result might look like Figure 14.53.

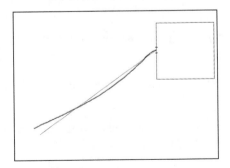

Figure 14.53
Walking toward a goal produces a simple two-dimensional slalom.

Slaloms are not just for movement through three-dimensional space, either. Any natural system that rotates around one or more axes will also describe a slalom. For example, the hawk I cited earlier describes a separate slalom with its head as it dives. It keeps its eyes on the mouse by making small, rapid corrections to the angle of its head and eyeballs. If you plotted these rotations on a graph, they would describe a slalom, with larger corrections at the beginning and very small corrections nearer to the goal.

What appear to be static poses can make use of slaloms, too. If you hold a heavy object at arm's length and try to keep it level with your shoulder, every joint in your arm and shoulder will be describing small slaloms. Every time a small twinge or weakness in one muscle causes a joint to vary from the target, another muscle will compensate. This is feedback, and feedback expressed mathematically describes a slalom.

"So what," you say? So you must animate your characters to follow slaloms or their actions will seem mechanical and dead and you will lose that illusion of life you've been working so hard to maintain. Traditional animators have known and practiced this for years, although they have used other terms, such as "arcs" or "natural paths," to describe these types of motion.

Fortunately, LightWave uses splines to define motion paths, so it is relatively easy to make objects follow slaloms. Let's try animating an object with a slalom motion.

Animating a Slalom Head Turn

To animate an object with a slalom motion, follow these steps:

1. Load scene file Proj1422 from the Chapter 14 directory of this book's CD-ROM. This is essentially the same as the setup you built in Chapter 11, but with the IK disconnected to allow manual keyframing of the face, eyes, and eyelids for the next three projects.

2. Go to frame 0. Turn the head 30 degrees to the left. Set a keyframe.

3. Go to frame 15. Turn the head 30 degrees to the right (60 degrees total). Set a keyframe.

4. Save the scene with a new name. Render and play back the 15-frame animation. Your results should look something like Figure 14.54.

   The head moves kind of like a tank turret, doesn't it? This is very mechanical, not lifelike at all. Let's find out why.

5. Take a look at the rotation spline for the animation. You should see something like Figure 14.55.

   Note that the spline is a straight line, not a slalom or curve. Now, you'll add some rotation in the pitch axis to turn the straight line of the rotation spline into a slalom.

6. At frame 7, add a keyframe to the pitch channel and set the value to -5.0 degrees, as in Figure 14.56.

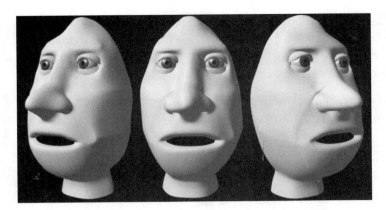

Figure 14.54
Frames 0, 7, and 15 of the head-turn animation.

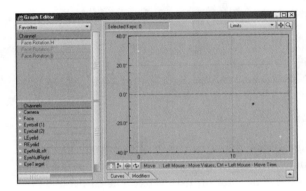

Figure 14.55
Heading Angle spline.

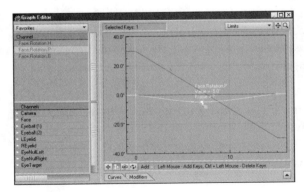

Figure 14.56
Pitch angle keyed to -5 degrees at frame 7.

LightWave automatically interpolates this spline as a smooth curve between the old end-points and the new midpoint you just created. With good spline control tools, it is possible to shape a curve using only endpoints and the spline controls. With poor spline controls, it is usually easier to add keyframes. Let's see how changing the pitch changed the animation.

7. Save the scene with a new name. Render and play back the 15-frame animation. Your results should look something like Figure 14.57.

Figure 14.57
Frames 0, 7, and 15 with pitch added to heading.

This looks a little more natural, doesn't it? Just adding a few degrees in another axis is enough to give a more natural appearance. Experiment with the pitch keyframe setting. How subtle can you get and still make the head rotation seem more natural? How extreme can you get to make the head rotation seem caricatured and overacted?

In head movements, the slalom rule generally expresses itself as a few curves leading from the starting position to the goal, with the swell of the largest curve pointing down. The only general exception to this rule is when the character is looking toward something well above the horizon line, as in Figure 14.58, in which case the largest curve will swell upward. The smaller curves are near the starting position and the goal and represent the anticipation before and the follow-through after the main action.

As in the project you just completed, the character's head will generally pitch down slightly as the head rotates side to side, then come up to the goal pitch angle at the end of the rotation. For simplicity's sake, the origin pitch and the goal pitch in this project were the same. If you like, repeat the project with different origin and goal pitch angles and see what effects you can create.

The Eyes Have It

Although it is possible to animate a character with no facial features at all, it's much easier to get your audience to identify with a character if it has eyes and eyelids and the range of

Figure 14.58
Frames 0, 7, and 15 with positive instead of negative pitch.

expression that they make possible. Reflexive eye movement is also fairly easy to mimic and can be a great asset to directing your audience's attention and selling a shot.

The following projects show you how to animate eyeballs and eyelids within a head model by using the parented hierarchy setup you created in Chapter 11 (Figure 14.59).

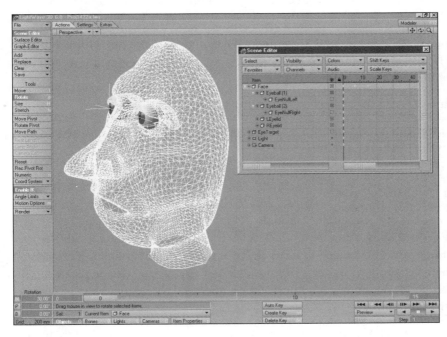

Figure 14.59
Scene with head and eye hierarchy set up.

Giving them eyes opens up a whole new range of acting capabilities for your characters. Aside from emotional expressions and other intentional communication (which we'll cover in Chapters 15 and 16), the eyes can convey an extraordinary amount of unintentional or unconscious information. Any parent, teacher, or police officer can tell you how a miscreant's eyes move when he is lying. A loud noise, bright light, or rapid motion also produces an involuntary or unconscious reaction, which is usually readable in eye movement.

If you animate your character to mimic these natural motions, you'll be taking a big step toward convincing your audience. You'll also be able to use those motions to tell the audience in a subtle and natural way what is going on and so advance your story. This technique is especially important with animals or creatures that have little facial expression and eye movement and body posture are about all you have to work with.

You've already animated the head to follow a slalom. Now let's do the same with the eyes.

 ## Eyeballing a Slalom

To animate eyeballs with slalom motions, follow these steps:

1. Use the scene you animated in Project 14.22. Select the left eyeball. Go to frame 0.

2. Change the eyeball's heading 30 degrees to the left, mimicking the heading of the face object.

3. Set two more keys for the left eyeball, changing the heading to its original setting at frame 7 and setting it 30 degrees to the right at frame 15. Again, each of these rotations mimics the rotation of the face object at the same frames.

4. Go back to frame 7. Pitch the eyeball downward by 5 degrees. Set a keyframe.

5. Repeat Steps 1 through 4 for the right eyeball, or copy and paste the pitch and heading from the left eyeball in the Graph Editor.

6. Save the scene with a new name. Render and play back the animation. You should end up with an animation like Figure 14.60.

You probably noticed that simultaneous rotation of the head and eyeballs is neither convincing nor realistic. The eyes can move much more rapidly than the entire head. Their purpose is to track rapid movement, to scout ahead of the slower movements of the head and body. When a creature with eyes is nervous or keyed up, the eyes tend to flicker all over the landscape. If you tried to do that with the entire head, you'd appear to be giving your character whiplash.

A more realistic approach is to animate the eyes' rotation in advance of the head's. If the character is to look up and to the right, the eyes should follow a slalom up and to the right just before the head begins to follow its own slalom. In other words, the eyes should always lead the head. Let's give it a try.

Figure 14.60
Keyframes 15, 7, and 0, with eyeballs rotated.

7. Select the face object and open the Graph Editor. By default, all the position, rotation, and scale channels for the selected object are loaded in the Curve Bin in the upper-left section of the Graph Editor. Select all the curves in the bin. This will display all the curves and their keyframes in the Curve Edit window at the upper-right section of the editor.

8. Choose Limits|Automatic Limits to resize the Curve Edit window. In the Curve Edit window, right-drag a selection bounding box to include all the keyframes for the face object.

9. Choose Move mode. Left-drag any keyframe from frame 0 to frame 5, as shown in Figure 14.61. This will shift all the keyframes for the face five frames to the right, making them occur slightly after the eye motions.

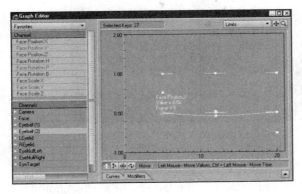

Figure 14.61
Face object keyframes dragged to create a five-frame delay.

10. Save the scene with a new name. Render and play back the animation.

The head should hold still for five frames, then perform the same slalom rotation you animated before. If it doesn't, see if you can figure out what's wrong (and fix it) by looking at the splines. The five-frame pause gives you enough time to animate the eyes turning before the head. The next step, reasonably enough, is to animate the eyes leading the head motion.

11. Select the left eyeball again. Go to frame 0. Restore the eyeball's original heading to match the heading of the face object.

12. Delete the keyframes at 7 and 15.

13. At frame 5, rotate the heading 40 degrees to the left, which is a fairly extreme rotation for normal eye movement. Make a keyframe.

14. Add a key at frame 20. Restore the original heading to bring the eye back into alignment with the head.

15. Go back to frame 5. Pitch the eyeball downward 5 degrees.

16. Repeat Steps 11 through 15 for the right eyeball, or copy and paste as in Step 5.

17. Save the scene again. Render and play back the animation. You should end up with an animation like Figure 14.62.

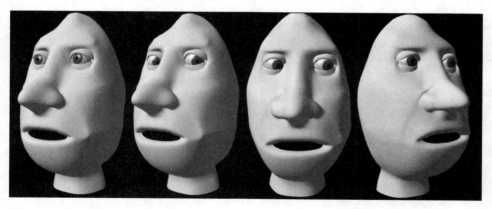

Figure 14.62
Keyframes 0, 5, 12, and 20 for eyes leading head motion along slalom.

This is a more natural motion for the eyes, but something is still missing. The eyelids should always frame the iris (the colored part of the eyeball surrounding the pupil) unless you are trying to show fright, rage, rolling of the eyes, or another extreme effect.

In most cases, you can get away with animating eyelids in just the pitch axis. This makes it very easy to pose the eyelids—just lock off the heading and bank axes and use the mouse. It's usually best to set the key positions for eyelids with the mouse rather than the numeric panel because you will generally be trying to match the edge of the eyelid to the edge of the iris.

The edge of the eyelid should just cover the upper curve of the iris (see Figure 14.63). You should not be able to see the white, or *sclera*, completely surrounding the iris unless you are animating a very surprised look. The eyelid should not cover more of the iris unless the character is squinting in pain, anger, or bright light. The pupil itself always remains visible between the upper and lower eyelids unless a blink or squint closes the eye almost completely.

Figure 14.63
Positions of the upper eyelid over the iris: No, Yes, No.

PROJECT 14.24 Keeping a Lid on It

To position the eyelids, follow these steps:

1. Select the left eyelid. Go to frame 0. Change the pitch rotation to align the bottom edge of the eyelid with the top of the iris, as in Figure 14.63. When you are satisfied with the result, create a keyframe.

2. Go to the next keyframe for the left eyeball.

3. Repeat Steps 1 and 2 until all the keyframes for the eyeball have a matching keyframe for the eyelid.

4. Repeat Steps 1 through 3 for the right eyelid. Because the face is not perfectly symmetric, copy-and-paste may not reproduce precise alignment of the eyelid to the iris.

5. Save the scene with a new file name. You will be using it for the next project. Render and play back the animation. You should end up with an animation like Figure 14.64.

That's a lot better, isn't it? Keep in mind that when the head or eye turns, the eyelid will often cover more of the upper part of the iris in a partial blink. The faster the turn, the more of the iris is covered until a snap turn produces a full blink.

By now, you are probably tired of repeatedly posing one eyeball, then matching the rotation for the other eye. Imagine trying to do this for a long shot, in which your character intently watches the erratic and convoluted flight of a mosquito!

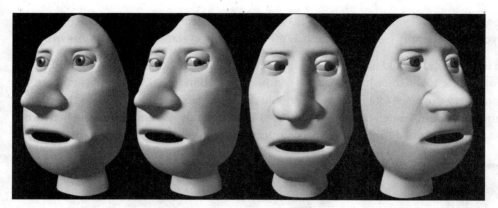

Figure 14.64
Keyframes 0, 5, 12, and 20 of eyelids matching eyeball rotation.

The sensitivity of your audience to *sight lines*, the apparent direction of the eyeball, makes your job harder. We learn almost from birth to deduce exactly what people are looking at by observing tiny variations in the angle of their eyes. Your smallest mistake in aligning the eyes can shatter your character's credibility.

Of course, there is a better way to align the eyes. LightWave supports a function called *inverse kinematics* (IK), which can make an object in a hierarchy point consistently and precisely at another object.

Animating with Inverse Kinematics and Goals

If you worked through all the setup projects in Chapter 11, you should have a setup of the head and eyeballs that has an IK goal named EyeTarget, a null or invisible object set up for the eyeballs to track automatically (see Figure 14.65).

You can animate the EyeTarget as you can any other object and the eyes will follow along. You can use the EyeTarget to rotate the eyes along slaloms more easily and quickly than by setting separate sets of keyframes.

It is also much easier to mimic realistic eye movement. Researchers have compiled a lot of data about how humans and animals move their eyes in different circumstances and environments. One branch of this research is *eye-gaze tracking*. Figure 14.66 is from one of the most often cited sources in this field, Alfred L. Yarbus's 1967 book, *Eye Movements and Vision*. You can find out more by looking it up on the Web or in your local library.

The eye-gaze track on the right represents three minutes of examination of the picture on the left. If you duplicated this eye-gaze track in a series of EyeTarget keyframes during a three-minute animation and positioned the test image at the appropriate distance in front of the face, you could accurately mimic the original subject's perusal of the image. Why you'd want to, I don't know, but the point is that you could.

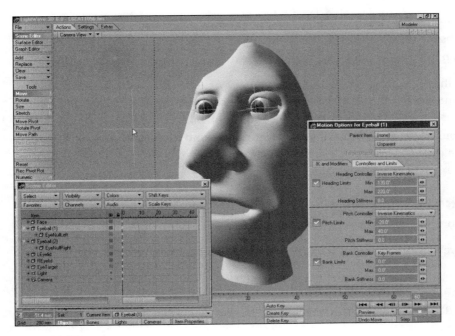

Figure 14.65
EyeTarget null positioned in front of nose.

Figure 14.66
Test image and resulting eye-gaze track.

From this and related research data, we can extract a few general guidelines that are useful in character animation.

When a person is confronting a new situation, such as entering an unfamiliar room, the eyes will case the area. This probably evolved as a survival trait—the first caveman to spot the bear tended to get out of the cave alive. What first attracts the eye is motion, especially a living creature. If nothing is moving, the eye tends to explore the lighter areas first, looking at television screens, windows, and lamps. After that, the eye examines the darker areas of the scene.

If the roving eye finds a living creature, the first reaction is to look at the creature's eyes. From there, the eye's path depends on the type of creature. If it is armed, the eye is drawn to the immediate threat, whether gun, knife, fang, claw, or tentacle. If the creature appears unarmed and has an expressive face, the eye tends to rove between the hands and face, cross-checking and corroborating information gathered from both areas.

Please note that these are gross generalizations and there are always exceptions and modifications depending on the situation. We all know people who would overlook a bus unless it hit them, and others who would ignore a roomful of purple baboons for the television set in the corner. Part of your job as a character animator is to expose and accentuate those differences to show your audience, via animated eye movement, what your character is thinking about and what the character's likes, dislikes, and habits are.

PROJECT 14.25 A Reading Test

To complete this project, follow these steps:

1. Use the IK eyeball scene you set up in Chapter 11 to animate the character reading an invisible page of text.

   At a reasonable reading distance for the character, the EyeTarget should move left to right along the width of a printed line, then zip right to left and down a little to the beginning of the next line.

2. If you'd like to add a little personality, insert keyframe pauses and back-and-forth stutters into the middle of lines, as if the character is having trouble reading an unfamiliar word.

   You can leave the head immobile, pitch it down slightly to follow the eyes down the page, or combine pitch and heading so the head follows along with each line. Moving the head more nearly matching the eyes will convey the laborious reading of a semiliterate character, and a minimal pitch and no heading changes at all can convey the actions of a speed-reader.

Blinkin' Good

Unless you are animating a zombie movie, your characters will need to blink. Blinks are one of the unconscious signals that can help convince your audience that a character is alive.

Blinks are especially important for LightWave character animation. One of the problems of this medium is that an absolute hold, where all movement stops, immediately destroys the illusion of life. This is not true for other animation media. In fact, limited animation and camera-motion animation can get by with almost no in-screen movement.

As mentioned earlier, if a character needs to pause for a moment, it must do so in a *moving hold* to remain believable. This is a hold as a human actor might perform it, with all the tiny motions of breathing, muscular twinges, nervous tics, shifting weight—and the occasional blink.

The mechanics of a blink are deceptively simple. The upper eyelid closes until it meets the lower lid, then rises again to its normal position. The pupil should also follow the lower edge of the lid as it closes and follow it up again as it opens.

Ah, but how fast? For how long? Timing—both its placement within the longer sequence and the speed of the blink itself—makes a great deal of difference in how a blink helps or hinders the credibility of the character.

Then, too, the blink must relate to the animation of the eyes, the face, and the rest of the character. A random blink in the middle of a staring match destroys the tension, and a quick blink at a sudden action can really sell the shot. Remember, your audience will watch your character's eyes more than any other part of the scene.

Your character should blink quickly when alert, slowly when sleepy or stupid, repeatedly when surprised, and partially or fully, depending on speed, when the head changes direction. Sections of Chapters 15 and 16 on facial animation include more examples.

Winkin', Blinkin', and Nod

If you completed all the projects so far, you should have learned to use the slalom path, linear and interpolated splines, parented eyes and eyelids, and IK goals. Now, you'll get a chance to put them all together.

Rather than a step-by-step set of instructions, this project is more like the assignments you'll get as a professional character animator. All you will get is a brief description of the action for a single shot, and it's up to you to interpret it:

- The character you've been working with is asleep, head nodding forward. He is startled and wakes suddenly. His eyes blink rapidly as his eyes roam, looking for the source of the disturbance.

- His eyes lock onto the source of the noise—a fly! (Don't worry. It's invisible—you don't have to animate it.) He stares at it intently, in a moving hold.

- The fly takes off, and the character tracks it with his eyes and, with less accuracy, his head. The fly swoops and circles erratically, getting closer to the character's face with each pass.

- Finally, the fly swoops in and lands—on the character's nose! He goes cross-eyed trying to see the fly and blinks repeatedly in disbelief.

- He shakes his head violently, apparently dislodging the fly.

Now, how would you end the sequence? Would he fall back to sleep? Just sit there blinking? Keep looking for the fly? You decide! Animate the whole shot, and keep the results in a safe place for future reference:

- How did you decide on the timing for the blinks? What effect would it have on the whole piece if you put the blink keyframes closer together or spaced them farther apart?

- Did you remember to move the head and eyes on slaloms? Did the eyes always lead the head? Did you keep the eyelids lined up with the iris of each eye?

- Was the action convincing? Did you believe in the character? Did he seem alive?

This is the kind of short project that you will want to revisit as your animation skills improve. With each new tool you learn, you will probably think of an embellishment or refinement you'd like to add. It's exactly this kind of practice that will hone your skills and help you become a better character animator.

Most of the preceding projects have included some initial timings or at least a hint or two about the appropriate range of timings. As a professional animator, you need to be able to write up actions on an exposure sheet without mocking them up in LightWave first. This is for your own development and discipline and so you can communicate effectively with other production team members.

X-Sheet Practice

X-sheet shorthand varies from studio to studio, and even from animator to animator, but there are a few general conventions. The start or stop of an action is usually marked with an X, especially if it must match a *hit* on the sound track. A hold is marked with a straight line between the Xs. An action is represented by a curve, and an anticipation before an action is a loop. A repeated action, such as a walk or run, is drawn as a series of curves connecting Xs located in each heel-strike frame.

PROJECT 14.27 Writing It Up

This project gives you some practice in writing up an x-sheet:

1. Make a lot of copies of the blank x-sheet from Chapter 4.

2. For each project in this chapter, write up x-sheets for the different timings you used. It is not necessary to mark each keyframe. The start, stop, anticipation, follow-through, and a brief written description of each action are adequate.

3. Critique your x-sheets. Could you re-create the animation from just the exposure sheets and a sketch of a keyframe in the sequence? That's pretty much what you're expected to do as an animator working from an x-sheet and a story sketch or two.

It's a good idea to keep practicing x-sheet markup as you work through the next two chapters. X-sheet shorthand should be second nature by the time you're done.

If you've completed the preceding projects, you now have a solid grounding in basic timing and in mimicking lifelike head and eye movement. Now that you've got the essentials of character movement under control, the next step is to apply it. One of the simplest tests of character movement is to animate the camera.

Characteristic Camera Movement

You can animate the camera as a character's POV. This makes the camera an actor, giving it the ability to help tell a story.

You can use point-to-point spline interpolation to animate a camera for a character's POV. This will give a very Steadicam-style movement. However, real people don't run around with a Steadicam for a neck, and neither should your LightWave camera.

Choosing an appropriate style of camera movement can add a great deal to your animations. For example, let's use a short involving two characters: one extremely active and zany (Speedy) and the other placid and lethargic (Sleepy).

When shooting from Speedy's point of view, you need to zip the camera around much more rapidly and in more directions than when shooting from Sleepy's point of view. Otherwise, audiences will not be as quick to identify whose viewpoint they are sharing at a particular moment, and your story will not get across as effectively. Handled properly, character-based camera styles can be a major storytelling tool.

Even for something as basic as an architectural walkthrough, there are human perceptual factors you can use to make a stronger impact. The idea is to make audiences feel as though they are in the scene. You won't do that if you run the camera straight down the centerline of every hallway, do perfect 90-degree pans around every corner, and keep a dead-level line of sight. Instead, you'll make audiences feel like they've been dumped on an amusement park ride with a hefty dose of Quaaludes.

So, how do you make the camera more human? As mentioned previously, the extensive body of work on the subject of eye-gaze tracking can be boiled down to a handful of general rules that are applicable to character animation. Just as these rules can be used to animate the rotation of a character's eyeballs, they can be applied to the animation of the camera. Keep in mind that these are generalizations and are not to be followed without judgment or exception.

If there is a person or creature in the scene, the character's first focus is the eyes, followed by the rest of the face. The hands are next, unless two or more people are facing each other. In that case, the scan typically goes back and forth between the faces, attempting to correlate their interaction before moving on to the rest of the scene.

After faces and hands, objects are examined in order of brightness and contrast. A bright object on a dark tabletop will attract the eye, as will an open window in a dim room. Television sets, brightly lit pictures on the walls, anything moving, and other details will attract attention for longer periods of time. Blank, unchanging areas will be dismissed with a quick glance. Lower-priority items with many details may be revisited later, after other elements of the scene have been examined.

Finally, the eye roves to clues needed for navigation. Occasional glances at the floor, followed by slight corrections in the direction of travel, mimic the way people actually walk. These corrections are the defining points for slaloms.

If the camera is going to go through a door, the camera needs to dip to locate the knob or handle, then quickly return to nearly eye level as the door opens.

Keep in mind that you shouldn't exactly mimic the rapid eye movement of a real person, unless you want a particularly frantic and disorienting effect. Real eye movements can be very rapid without disorienting the observer because the observer is in control of his own eyes and is expecting the rapid shifts. Your audience is not in control and needs more time to recognize the character's surroundings. Instead of mimicking the quick, angular rotations of a real eye-gaze track, you should animate your character POV tracks to be more gradual and rounded. You should also use a little ease-in and ease-out for all the major camera moves for a character POV, and don't forget to use slaloms.

PROJECT 14.28 Animating the Camera for Character POV

This project shows you how to animate the camera to mimic a character's point of view:

1. Load the STREET01 scene file from the Chapter 14 directory on this book's CD-ROM.

2. Position the camera at roughly eyeball height above the sidewalk at the left side of the storefront. Rotate the camera to look down the sidewalk, past the storefront. Create a keyframe for the camera at frame 0.

3. Go to frame 90. Move the camera down the sidewalk to the opposite side of the storefront. Set a keyframe.

4. Save the scene. Render and play back the animation.

   This makes the camera move smoothly down the sidewalk, at an appropriate height for an average human character. Now, you'll add a null object for the camera to look at as it moves. This makes it much easier to control the camera angle than it would be if you manually set three rotation axis values for each keyframe.

5. Add a null to the scene. Name the null CamTarget.

6. Move CamTarget to the surface of the sidewalk, just in front of the storefront doorway. Set a key for CamTarget at frame 0.

7. In the Motion Options panel, set the camera's Target Object to CamTarget. Save the scene.

   At this point, you have a scene where the camera travels at character eye level down the sidewalk, looking at a null object, CamTarget. In frame 0, the CamTarget is positioned to direct the camera toward the sidewalk just past the doorway (see Figure 14.67).

   Consider what details in this scene would attract the attention of the character during a 14-frame walk. Would he look at the ground? How about the lamppost? Perhaps the shop doorway?

8. Make a list of three to six points of interest for the character. Number them in the order the character would look at them.

Figure 14.67
Camera looking at null goal.

9. How long (for how many frames) would the character look at each point of interest? Write this number on the list next to each point of interest.

10. Using a copy of the blank exposure sheet from Chapter 4, write up the points of interest in order from first to last, spacing them according to the numbers you wrote in Step 9.

11. Select the CamTarget. Refer to the exposure sheet you just created. Each point of interest is going to be a keyframe. The first point of interest should be at frame 0.

12. Move the CamTarget to the point of interest. Make a keyframe for CamTarget at the current frame. Refer to the exposure sheet for the next point of interest.

13. Repeat Step 12 for each point of interest on your exposure sheet.

    You should end up with a 90-frame animation of the camera looking at several points of interest as it travels down the sidewalk.

14. Save the scene. Render and play back an animation.

LightWave will automatically create a slalom running through each of the keyframe null positions you set up so you won't jerk the camera around too sharply. You can use spline controls to change the shape of the slalom. You can make the slalom even smoother, or you can tighten it up to make the ride a little rougher.

This brings us to fine-tuning. Just how rough is too rough? If you are animating a sedate walk down a corporate corridor, you want the movement to be just a little rougher than Steadicam style. If you are animating a character running down a flight of stairs and want a real documentary feel to it, bang that camera around a lot!

PROJECT 14.29 It's a Dog's Life

To complete this project, follow these steps:

1. Repeat the preceding project, but this time start the camera at about 20 centimeters above the sidewalk. Make up another point-of-interest list, but this time for a small dog.

2. Try to remember everything you have ever observed about the behavior of dogs. In what are they most interested? How do they approach it? Do they follow a direct path or a more roundabout, wandering path? How close do they get to what interests them? How much time do they spend looking at (and sniffing) it? How do they move and how does their POV change while examining it?

3. Make up an exposure sheet that is at least three seconds (90 frames) long. This will give you a little more time to develop the character. Mark both the points of interest and the camera positions on the exposure sheet. Make an effort to convey the character and behavior of the dog by the way the camera and the CamTarget move.

4. Animate the camera and CamTarget according to the exposure sheet.

5. Render and play back an animation.

6. If you are not satisfied with the camera's characterization of the dog, go back to your exposure sheet and tweak it a little. Try using spline controls to make the camera or CamTarget slaloms smoother or rougher.

7. When you are satisfied with the timing, save the scene and render the animation. Play back the animation.

Does the animation seem to be a dog's-eye view? Does this seem like the behavior of a dog? Ask someone else, preferably a dog owner, to look at the animation. What is her reaction? If you get a laugh, consider your animation a success!

Don't Stop Now!

Practice, practice, practice! Try every project with variations in timing and note what works and what is communicated differently with each change.

I have heard several traditional artists quote this piece of advice: "Everyone has a hundred thousand bad drawings inside them. The sooner you get them out of your system, the better." I'd like to extend the spirit of that quote to LightWave character animation. I believe knocking out a hundred thousand keyframes (not just rendered frames!) should be enough experience to make you a really good character animator.

Moving On

At this point, you should have a solid understanding of the essentials of timing for character animation. You have practiced with some basic setups and found you can create a sense of life and character with a minimal level of complexity.

In the next chapter, you'll apply the tools you've learned to more complex character setups. From the handful of variables for animating the desk lamp, you'll be stepping up to animating dozens or more for a bipedal walk and other humanoid actions.

Chapter 15

Advanced Animation Using Constraints

The best setup in the world is useless unless you can make your characters act through posing and timing. This chapter shows you how to pose your characters for best effect, mimic weight and balance, create walks, runs, and other *motion cycles*, and use the *animation hierarchy* effectively. You'll also learn to analyze and caricature motion, including the classic cartoon repertoire of takes, sneaks, staggers, and zips.

The first part of this chapter explains how to compose your character within the frame so the action reads clearly and with the strongest dramatic effect. The next section shows you how to animate basic walks for bipedal characters of humanoid proportions. Later sections explore runs, other gaits, and nonhuman and caricatured motion cycles. This chapter also introduces the concept of the animation hierarchy, the division of the character into levels of a hierarchy for the creation of keyframes. Finally, this chapter provides a guide to materials that can help you develop skills for analyzing and reproducing motion and resources for animal and human motion studies. One of your goals in this chapter is to learn how to extrapolate your observations of natural motion to create caricatured animation. Along the way, projects will show you how to animate actions from the repertoire of classic cartoon animation, including takes, sneaks, staggers, and zips. You'll also learn the concept of *staging* for foreshadowing action.

Posing Characters within the Shot

You can set up an acceptable camera distance, angle, and movement yet still have a composition that is boring or hard to read. The success of the shot's composition depends as much on the character's pose as on the camera setup.

You should keep two concepts in mind when evaluating your character's poses: *line of action* and *twins*. Your key poses should always have a strong, clear line of action, and you should avoid twins like the plague.

Line of Action

Line of action is a pretty simple concept. The line of action should grow from the visual base of the character, up through its centerline, and out to the goal of the action. If this line is bent too sharply or in different directions, it is more difficult for your audience to read the pose, as you can see in Figure 15.1.

Figure 15.1
A line of action splitting toward two goals is harder to read.

Each part of a character's pose should add something to the main line of action. If part of the character is jutting out at an angle, that part breaks up the visual flow of the pose, as in Figure 15.2.

Figure 15.2
A jagged pose with parts of the character interfering with the line of action.

In 2D drawing, the line of action can be drawn first, and the character sketch built around the line. You can do the same for a storyboard sketch if the sketch represents a key pose. In 3D, it's generally more useful to add the line of action afterward, as an analysis and critique for making changes. Figure 15.3 is the result of an animator applying a line of action. Compare this to the two previous poses. The head and torso point toward the same goal as the outstretched arm. A much smoother arc can be drawn from the character's feet up through the body centerline and out through the arm.

Figure 15.3
A pose with a clearer line of action.

Twins

Twins is a label used to describe perfectly symmetric poses. Beginners often compose a character in a twins pose, lining up each joint as if the character were a soldier standing at attention (see Figure 15.4).

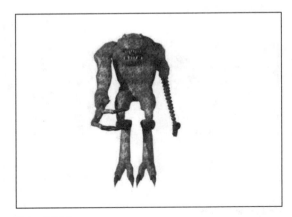

Figure 15.4
Twins. Yuck!

A perfectly symmetric pose is highly unnatural and will make your character look boring, mechanical, and dead.

The first step to preventing twins is to avoid head-on camera angles. Even if a character is posed symmetrically, an angled camera will show enough variation between left and right that the pose will hold the audience's interest (see Figure 15.5).

Figure 15.5
A stronger pose, but still a touch of the twins.

The second step is to make sure that the left and right sides of your character are never perfectly matched. Even if a pose seems to require symmetry, make it just a little off—slide one foot forward a few centimeters, or tilt the hips and shoulders in alternate directions. Do whatever is necessary, as long as the resulting pose looks imperfect enough to be natural (see Figure 15.6).

Figure 15.6
A much more dynamic pose, without a trace of the dreaded twins.

Testing Poses in Silhouette

As you probably noticed, poses of complex or heavily textured characters are often hard to analyze. Camouflage still works, I guess. What you need is a tool that masks all that extraneous stuff and leaves just the pose itself. One such tool is the *silhouette*, a simple black-and-white outline or negative image of the character, with no details internal to the outline.

It's important to test your key poses in silhouette. If the action does not read well as an outline, your audience is probably going to have to rely on much more subtle clues to understand what the character is trying to do or say. That takes more time, makes your audience work harder, and is generally poor animation practice. On the other hand, an action that reads well in silhouette will only get better and stronger when you add color, depth, and surface details.

Figures 15.7, 15.8, and 15.9 are examples of the same pose considered in different camera setups. The heavy texturing of the character makes the color images difficult to read, but the matching silhouettes are very easy to evaluate.

Figure 15.7
A very confusing pose. There's a lot of information inside this outline that you just can't see.

Figure 15.8
Better than the pose in Figure 15.7, but still a little cluttered and confusing.

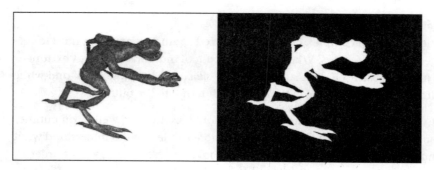

Figure 15.9
A much better pose than shown in Figures 15.7 or 15.8, very easy to read.

In traditional drawn animation, testing in silhouette requires making another drawing or tracing of the pose in question, blocking out or omitting the details inside the character's outline. LightWave enables you to do essentially the same thing automatically by rendering an alpha channel image. Another advantage to LightWave is that you can render an alpha channel animation to test an entire action in silhouette.

PROJECT 15.1 Easy Silhouette Checking with LightWave

To render an alpha channel animation, follow these steps:

1. Set the Render Options panel to save a sequence of alpha images.

2. Render frame 0, just to save a single alpha channel image.

3. In the Images panel, load the frame 0 alpha image as a sequence.

4. In the Options panel's Layout View layer, activate the Background Image feature.

5. In the Effects panel's Compositing layer, choose the alpha sequence as the background image.

Whenever you need to check a silhouette, simply render the frame you want, then get an unobstructed view of the alpha channel image by opening the Scene panel and choosing the Hide All Objects option.

Composing Shots for Multiple Characters

If you are animating a crowd scene or the interaction between two or more characters, you should apply these principles of composition to the individuals and to the group as a whole.

Evaluating the distance, angle, depth of field, and movement of the camera, the characters' and groups' lines of action, and especially avoiding twins and checking silhouettes, are just as important for groups as for individuals. Animating a solo character is generally a piece of cake compared to coordinating a group.

For every important action, you need to clear enough space around the character so that the action reads well in silhouette. The space between characters must be appropriate to the action, neither too far nor too close. If the characters take turns in leading the action, getting good poses can require a constant reshuffling of the composition. This is another instance where you will need to experiment a lot and develop your own judgment.

Composition for Direct Playback and Game Design

If you are animating for computer games, multimedia, or any other application that will play back through a computer, there are a few more factors you need to keep in mind.

At the current state of technology, most desktop computers can't play back full-frame video without skipping frames. The problem is that a computer can only push so much information through the system, and most video sequences contain much more information than a computer can handle at full speed.

There are several approaches to solving this problem. One is, of course, to get a faster computer. In time, this will be the solution for most people, and this text will be obsolete. For now, other options are within the reach of more people.

There are several techniques for compressing a video or audio/video stream for computer playback. Three of the more common are MPEG, AVI, and QuickTime. Each has its advantages and disadvantages, zealots and critics, but they all share a few important attributes.

The amount of information in an animation is not necessarily all the information about each pixel in each frame. That is what is called an *uncompressed stream*, which can run about 30 megabytes per second for a broadcast-quality image. Most compression techniques take advantage of the fact that most of the pixels in frame 1, for instance, will be identical to the corresponding pixels in frame 2. These duplicated pixels do not have to be recorded all over again, just their locations. The minority pixels, the ones that show a change, or *delta*, have to be recorded completely. Do you see the implications? If a video clip has very low deltas, it can be compressed a great deal. If the deltas are high, the clip may be near its original, uncompressed size.

So, how do you ensure low deltas? Simple—don't move the camera.

Ouch. No camera movement. No cuts or transitions, either. The whole screen is one big delta when you do that. This is why a lot of early computer animation was (and is) boring. The playback penalty simply ruled out any use of dramatic camera movement or cutting. This limitation just isn't acceptable any more. So, what else can you do?

You can lower the size of the animation file by limiting the number of colors. If you cut a 24-bit video clip down to 8-bit, you just trimmed two-thirds of the file. The downside is that you will see *banding*, an abrupt borderline between adjacent color areas, because there are not enough different colors to seamlessly shade the borders.

You could cut back the frame rate too. If you have to display only 15 frames per second (fps) instead of 30, you've cut the data stream in half again. The disadvantage is that motion starts to look choppy, and below about 10fps, you can do better with flipbooks.

You can also reduce the resolution. Using 640x480 pixels takes up a lot of screen real estate; 320x240 is one-quarter the data but still acceptable to most audiences. Even smaller resolutions are acceptable for animations designed to accompany text or occupy small screen windows in a computer game.

What it usually comes down to is a combination of all these techniques. If you need fast action, cut down the color depth and lock down the camera but keep the frame rate high. If you want a talking head with good color reproduction, lock down the camera, lock down the subject, use a compromise frame rate, and boost the color palette back to 24-bit. If you want to move your camera or do a lot of cuts and edits, you'll have to sacrifice something else. For more details on output formats, media, and compression, see Chapter 20.

Take a Walk

This section concentrates on the animation of basic walks for bipedal characters of humanoid proportions. It also introduces the concept of the *animation hierarchy*, the division of the character into levels of a hierarchy for the creation of keyframes.

Step by Step

A motion cycle is an action, such as walking, running, hammering a nail, or any other repetitive action, that you can repeat by connecting duplicates end to end. Cycles require special attention to the *hookup*, the matching of beginning and ending frames to eliminate jerks or strobing when you loop the action or play it repeatedly. You generally use cycles in what is referred to as *transportation animation*, walking or other means of moving the character around within the shot.

Walk and run cycles are not difficult to animate once you understand the basics, but they are a core requirement for character animation. A prospective employer may even ask you to animate a simple walk, just to ensure that you know what you're doing. It may be to your advantage to practice the following projects until you can do a simple walk by reflex and an emotional or characteristic walk with a minimum of thought.

> *"I think walks are terrific exercises. They are technical by nature, but are key to describing character and attitude."*
> —Chris Bailey

People do lurch and limp; what they don't do is repeat cyclic motion with the precision of a computer, at least not for very long. Even in Saturday morning television, you should limit yourself to two and a half repetitions of any cycle. Once you've noticed the cycle, your eye is drawn to the dissimilarities—any hitches in your gitalong, as it were.

The sparse occasions in feature animation when characters walk for any period of time are usually broken up with a lot of specific pieces of business. Rather than seeing only a simple walk, you should be seeing their characters revealed in the way they move.

As far as the problem of resolving undesirable lurches, you can go to some trouble to build your walk in such a manner that guarantees symmetry at first so you'll be able to introduce asymmetry only where you want it. Give yourself at least half the duration of the cycle lead-up both before and after your walk's frames. If it's a 24-frame walk, make sure that a keyframe in the middle appears at the appropriate distance before the first frame and after the last frame. You may be chasing down artifacts of curve shapes not matching because they started only on the first frame of the walk, thus missing the curve that the identical pose on frame 24 had leading up to it. Frame 24, of course, needs the curves after it that frame 1 had. Naturally, this affects the interpolated frames rather than the keyed ones. You also might work out a method to make sure motion from one side can be mirrored and offset to the other with a minimum of effort, either by copying and pasting in the Graph Editor or through the use of expressions.

Still, it's much easier to build a shot that has objectives for the character to accomplish, something for it to do. Without acting, your walk will be an exercise in which you'll quickly discover the degree of control you have (or don't have) over your character.

Animation Hierarchy

The *animation hierarchy* does not refer to the hierarchical organization of parts to form a boned or parented character. The animation hierarchy refers to the division of the character into levels of a hierarchy for the creation of keyframes.

This concept is unique to computer-generated character animation. In cel and puppet animation, the entire character is posed completely for every frame of film, then the pose is modified as a whole for the next frame. No matter how many layers of cels are used for different character parts or how many replacement parts are socketed into a puppet, the complete character has to be assembled in front of the camera for every frame of film exposed. At the most basic physical level, every frame is a keyframe for cel and puppet animation.

LightWave enables you to set a different sequence of keyframes for each channel of each item in a character setup. You can use as few as one or two keyframes to move the hierarchical root, the character's *center of gravity* (CG), along a shallow slalom. In the same shot, you can keyframe a part in the lowest level of the hierarchy (perhaps the character's toes) a dozen times, none of them on the same keyframe as the CG. This enables you to move, rotate, and scale each part of a character along its own slalom, creating smooth action with the absolute minimum of keyframes.

So, what's the big deal about a hierarchy? Think about this: Every part of a character is a dependent of the hierarchy, right back to the CG. If a part moves, every unconstrained part below it in the hierarchy moves along. If a part above it moves, it has to move along. Each part of the character also has to interact with the character's world. Feet must contact the ground properly, hands must grasp and move objects, and so on.

Now, what happens if you spend hours posing a character's hands just right, setting dozens of keyframes, and then discover you didn't pose the hips correctly and the whole figure must be reposed? Short of hiring another animator to do the shot over, you have to chuck out all your work on the hands and start from scratch. Discouraging. Not to mention costly, especially if you are on a tight deadline or budget.

On the other hand (pun intended), if you had animated according to the character's animation hierarchy, you would have found the error in the hips before you even started on the hands. Which leads to the next question: How do you use the animation hierarchy? Very simple: Start at the root, and animate each level of the hierarchy completely before going down to the next level.

For most characters, this means you start with the CG. You need to plan where you want the character to travel and then keyframe the CG to follow that *slalom*, the feedback curve that describes all natural, directed motion.

Walking has been described as a fall interrupted by the interposing of a limb. This observation has a special significance for LightWave animation. In Chapter 14 you learned how to animate a fall using a spline-based parabola. You can use the same parabola, slightly modified, to describe the repeated falls of a walking character's body.

The first step is to determine how high and low the character's CG will move and the distance between the ends of the parabola. To calculate these distances, you need to understand the key poses for a walking character.

Best Foot Forward

There are only three basic key poses in a walk: *heel strike*, *squash*, and *passing*. These poses are repeated in sequence for each side to give a total of six key poses for a complete bipedal walking cycle.

The heel strike, shown in Figure 15.10, is the primary pose for the walk. The leading leg is straight, the ankle joint holds the foot at nearly a right angle to the leg, the trailing foot is solidly planted and flat to the ground, and the character's CG is evenly balanced between the feet. The arms are also at the limit of their forward and backward slaloms, balancing the opposite legs. For a natural walk, the heel strike is the low point in the CG's parabola.

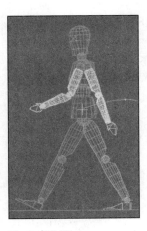

Figure 15.10
Heel strike pose.

The heel strike is kind of like a pole vault, converting the forward inertia of the body into an upward arc, with the straight leg defining the arc's radius.

The heel strike pose also determines the *stride length* for the character's walk, that is, the distance the character travels with each step. This is the distance between the ends of the CG's parabola. If you want the character to travel a specific distance in a certain number of frames, you must pay close attention to stride length when planning the animation.

The squash pose, shown in Figure 15.11, is just what it sounds like—the leading leg bends at the knee, squashing down slightly to absorb the impact of the heel strike. If you didn't include the squash pose and kept the leg straight from heel strike to passing, the character would walk very stiffly, like an extra from a bad monster movie.

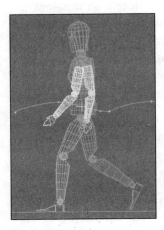

Figure 15.11
Squash pose.

In the squash pose, the trailing foot's toes barely touch the ground, with none of the character's weight on them, and the sole of the trailing foot is angled 70 degrees or more to the ground. This pose is the prime candidate for exaggeration in a caricatured walk, as detailed later in this chapter. Cartoon squash positions are often the CG's low point, giving the walk much more bounce between heel strike and passing poses.

Passing pose, shown in Figure 15.12, is where the leading leg straightens out again, boosting the CG to its highest position. The passing CG height is the peak of the CG's parabola.

Figure 15.12
Passing pose.

The trailing leg is bent at nearly its sharpest angle, raising the foot high enough that the toes clear the ground as the leg rotates forward.

Simply copying these basic poses onto a series of keyframes will not produce a natural-looking walk. The results will be stiff, artificial, and lifeless. Look at the 15WALK01.AVI animation file, located in the Chapter 15 directory on this book's CD-ROM. This animation has only six keyframes, one for each of the basic poses for left and right sides. This is obviously not enough detail for either a realistic or caricatured motion.

Compare 15WALK01.AVI to the 15WALK02.AVI animation, which has more keyframes but is still derived from the basic three poses. To produce these results, you need to set the timing and spline controls for each object in the character's hierarchy, using anticipation, ease-in, snap, ease-out, and follow-through.

The following projects lead to the goal of a more natural-looking humanoid walk cycle, as shown in the 15WALK02.AVI animation. Along the way, you'll learn how to apply the concepts introduced in Chapter 14 to a more complex action.

Steppin' Time

The following project is longer than previous ones because all the explanatory notes about walks in general are included with the project steps. Take your time, think about the explanations, and save your work every now and then.

To set each motion's timing appropriately, you need to understand the *dynamics* of a walk, the motions that connect each key pose. Different parts move at different rates, accelerating and decelerating in a complex balancing act that you must learn to mimic.

It's often useful to divide the motions of a character among as many different objects as possible. This enables you to animate the height of the Puppet above the ground by changing the CG's y-position, then animate the figure's travel along the ground by moving another control, typically the root of the hierarchy. Keeping the two motions separate gives you clearer control over where you put your keyframes and how you set the parameters for each spline.

For a simple walk, you can determine the position of the CG by the geometry of the legs and hips relative to the ground. Because the character geometry is fixed, it is possible to set the height of the Puppet's CG in advance, with a fair degree of accuracy, for the entire walk cycle.

In the heel strike pose, the legs form an equilateral triangle with the CG at the apex. This height is one keyframe for the Puppet's CG. According to my measurements for the heel strike pose in Figure 15.10, the vertical (y-axis) distance from the sole of the Puppet's foot to its CG is 0.867, and the stride length is approximately 0.75. Therefore, the distance traveled in a full two-step walk cycle is 1.5. Different setups or a deeper or shallower pose would give different numbers, but let's stick with this example for now. Measurement of the other poses gives 0.954 for the CG height at passing and 0.913 at squash.

PROJECT 15.2 Animating a Basic Walk

To animate a basic walk, follow these steps:

1. Open the default Puppet scene file you set up in Chapter 11.

2. Select the Puppet's root. Set the root's x position to 1.5 at frames 0 and 1 and 0.0 at frame 33. Set the interpolation to Linear at frame 33.

   These keyframes will make the Puppet's root travel 1.5 units over the 33 frames of the walk cycle. This is a very mechanical approximation of the motion for the finished walk, with no anticipation, ease, or follow-through. You'll refine it later.

   It is generally not an effective approach to try to pose the entire character in precise relation to the ground if you don't have foot constraints set up as in Chapter 12. With an unconstrained hierarchy, every little tweak, from the CG on down, changes the position of the feet relative to the ground. You'll find it much more productive to tweak the character's CG position at the end, after you have finalized all the other adjustments.

The three basic key poses for this walk cycle are each mirrored—used on both the right and left sides of the character—once, for a total of six key poses. The spacing for these poses is as follows:

- Heel Strike Left, frame 1

- Squash Left, frame 6

- Passing Left, frame 11

- Heel Strike Right, frame 17

- Squash Right, frame 22

- Passing Right, frame 27

Heel Strike Left, from frame 1, is duplicated in frame 33 to produce an accurate hookup.

Later in this chapter, we'll explore how you can vary the spacing of the key poses to change the character of the walk. The spacing used in this project produces an ordinary brisk walk when played back at 30fps.

3. Select the Puppet's CG. Set its y position to 0.867 in frames 0, 1, 17, and 33, the heel strike keyframes. Set it to 0.913 in the squash frames, 6 and 22. Set it to 0.954 in the passing frames, 11 and 27.

You may have to adjust the tension, especially at the peaks and valleys. I set the tension to 1.0 in frames 11 and 27 and -1.0 in frame 17. The scene should now resemble Figure 15.13. The white line represents the motion of the Puppet.

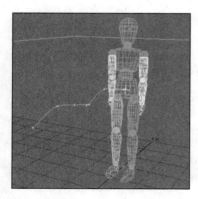

Figure 15.13
Puppet with keyframes set for Puppet's CG and root.

4. Save the scene with a new file name. Render and play back the animation.

    Look at the motion of the hips, chest, and head. Does the bouncing action seem appropriate for a walking character?

    It's a little distracting to have the figure's arms and legs dragging along before they are posed. Let's limit the view to just the parts you're actually working on.

5. Hide the entire Puppet hierarchy, then manually reselect the CG and root and the hips, chest, and head.

6. Render and play back the animation. You should get something like Figure 15.14.

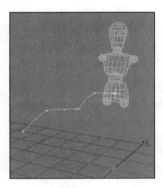

Figure 15.14
Frame 1 after hiding the lower levels of the animation hierarchy.

It's a lot easier to evaluate an action when just the pertinent parts are visible, isn't it? Keep this in mind, and hide or show objects as you need them.

You should animate each level of the hierarchy so it reads perfectly before you begin to animate the next lower level. If you don't remember this rule, you will waste a lot of time revising poses you shouldn't have been animating in the first place.

The second level in the animation hierarchy includes the hips and chest. Before you go any further, save the scene under a new name. You should develop the habit of saving the scene file every time you make significant changes to a motion.

The hips are the driving force behind walks and runs. Just try walking without using your hips. If you manage to stay on your feet, you'll look like an arthritic penguin.

The hips rotate around the CG. At the heel strike poses, the hips rotate on the axis of the Puppet's spine, effectively giving a little more length to the stride by pushing the leading leg forward and the trailing leg backward. At the passing poses, the hips bank to raise the trailing leg slightly, giving it more ground clearance as it swings forward. The hips can also rotate on the pitch axis to give a forward lean to the character, especially when it is moving quickly.

All these movements should be kept as subtle as possible. Each of these rotations acts from the center of the character and can, therefore, have a disproportionate effect on the extremities. A single degree of pitch in the hips, for example, can move the feet several centimeters.

7. Select the hips. Make keyframes at frames 6, 11, 17, 22, 27, and 33. Set the hips to bank at the passing poses, 3 degrees at frame 11 and -3 degrees at frame 27. Set the other frames to bank 0, and set Spline Controls to Linear for frames 22 and 6 to keep the bank flat for the other poses.

   The Linear settings are needed to flatten out the spline between frames 1 through 6 and frames 17 through 22 because that's where the feet are on the ground. The hip action is a smooth slalom during the passing pose, then—Boom!—the heel strike literally stops it flat.

8. Set the hips' heading to help lengthen the stride by rotating 10 degrees at the left heel strike frames 0, 1, and 33 and -10 degrees at right heel strike frame 17. Drag the intervening keyframes to make a smooth slalom.

9. Set the hips' pitch to 5 degrees for each keyframe. This tilts the figure forward, to lean into the walk. A slower walk could use a smaller angle, whereas a faster walk needs a larger one.

10. Render and play back the animation.

    How does the hip action look? Does it seem natural? Try a different view.

    You can try changing the peak bank values a degree or two in either direction. More bank tends to produce a more feminine walk, and less bank makes it more robotic. Reducing the heading values makes the character walk like a windup toy, and increasing them stretches the stride as if in preparation for a run.

    Hip action can be the toughest part of animating a character. It is usually very subtle, and attempts to analyze it from life seem prone to trigger all sorts of bizarre reactions from informal test subjects. Be discreet. (If you can't be discreet, have a good excuse handy.) Whenever possible, study your own actions, then try to find confirmation of your conclusions in film or video motion studies. Good hip action can be a matter of a fraction of a degree, so still photos or video sequences that you can rerun and study in detail are extremely valuable tools.

    Once the hips are animated to your satisfaction, the chest is relatively easy. You can animate the chest by using the hip settings as a guide to setting up a *dynamic balance*.

    During a walk, the upper and lower parts of the body are in dynamic balance—the combination of mass, inertia, and energy in the lower body is equaled by the mass, inertia, and energy in the upper body—so the body as a whole is in balance. This is different from static balance, in which opposing parts are in balance at rest. Dynamic balance means the parts are constantly changing and reacting to change to actively maintain the balance.

For this project, dynamic balance means that for every clockwise heading rotation of the hips, the chest heading must rotate counterclockwise. It's pretty simple, really. You need to keep in mind that the chest rotations are measured from the hips, the chest's parent, so you need to double the angle in reverse to get the same effect. That is, if the hips are at heading 10 degrees and you set the chest to heading -10 degrees, the chest will just be facing straight ahead again. Set the chest heading to -20, and the chest will rotate as far to one side as the hips do to the other.

11. Select the Chest object. Set each heading keyframe to twice the negative value of each corresponding hips' heading keyframe.

12. Set each chest bank keyframe to the exact negative value of each corresponding hips' bank keyframe. This keeps the shoulders level. Keep the pitch keyframes set to 0.

13. Render and play back the animation.

    Do the hips and chest rotate properly? Does the motion seem natural? Does the action look alive, or is it mechanical and dead? Are the upper and lower body in dynamic balance? If the animation is working, you should be able to visualize arms and legs following the motions of the hips and shoulders.

    Save the scene file again, if you haven't already. You've completed level 2 of the animation hierarchy for the Puppet. The next level includes the head, upper arms, and thighs.

    The head is already visible, so let's start there. The head is a hierarchical dead end because it isn't a parent to any other objects and it doesn't have to align or make contact with any other parts of the scene. For a simple walk, all the head has to do is look straight ahead until animated to do otherwise. Note that if you set up the Puppet with constraints as detailed in Chapter 12, this would be handled automatically.

14. Select the Head object. Set each heading keyframe for the head to the exact negative value of each corresponding chest heading keyframe. This keeps the head pointing in the direction of the Puppet's travel. You can set the head's pitch keyframes to the negative of the hips' pitch if you want the Puppet to walk with its head up. You can leave the head's bank keyframes set to 0.

15. Render and play back the animation. Does the head remain looking forward, counterbalancing the motions of the chest and hips?

    After this point, the x-position animation of the root is more trouble than it's worth. You will find it easier to compare poses and analyze motion if the Puppet remains centered in all the views. To do this, you will need to change the root's keyframes to a constant value.

16. Select the root. Change its x position to 0.0 at keyframes 0, 1, and 33.

    Whenever you render and play back the animation, the Puppet will now appear to be walking in place. Later, we'll restore and fine-tune the root's spline.

    Now for the fun part! Animating the thighs is nearly as hard as animating the hips, although it usually requires less judgment. Most of the thigh animation is dictated by the hips, another fraction is guided by the three key poses, and the rest depends on you to add anticipation, ease, snap, and follow-through.

17. Make the right thigh and left thigh visible again.

18. Set the heading and bank rotations of right thigh and left thigh to counter the heading and bank angles of the hips in each keyframe.

    You don't need to set the Linear option for any bank keyframes as you did for the hips because the thighs' motion should have more ease.

    This just gets you back to zero with the thighs. Entering inverse angles like this is probably the most noncreative part of character animation, but it beats mousing everything around by hand and eyeballing poses that would probably become glaring errors in the finished animation. When you can get away with animating "by the numbers," it's smart to take advantage of it.

    The thighs must be heading in the direction of travel or the character will appear to waddle. The combined bank angle of hips and thighs should be near 0 or the character may appear knock-kneed, bowlegged, or listing to one side. This would be good for caricature (again, see later portions of this chapter), but it's not so good for a normal, plain-vanilla walk.

19. Render and play back the animation. Do the thighs head and bank properly? If not, go back and compare the splines. Did you forget something?

    The next step in posing right thigh and left thigh is to set the pitch angles for the heel strike, squash, and passing poses. The poses are repeated exactly on the left and right sides, so you only have to create one side's poses and copy those settings to the other side's corresponding keyframes.

20. Adjust the right thigh's pitch in keyframe 17 to match the leading thigh's angle in Figure 15.10, the heel strike pose. I used an angle of about -26.5 degrees, but your results may vary. Set the left thigh to the negative of the right thigh's pitch. Both thighs should have the same amount of pitch in the heel strike poses. When you are satisfied with your results, copy the pitch values to the opposite thigh in keyframes 0, 1, and 33.

21. Adjust the right thigh's pitch in keyframe 11 to match the lifted thigh's angle in Figure 15.12, the passing pose. I used an angle of about -39 degrees. When you are satisfied with your results, copy the pitch value to keyframe 27 for the left thigh. The opposite thighs in both keyframes 11 and 27 are easy ones—set their pitch to 0.

22. Adjust the right thigh's pitch in keyframe 6 to match the leading thigh's angle shown in Figure 15.11, the squash pose. I used an angle of about 9.5 degrees. Adjust the left thigh's pitch in keyframe 6 to match the trailing thigh's angle. I used -24.8 degrees. When you are satisfied with your results, copy the pitch values to the opposite thighs in keyframe 22.

Note the shape of the right thigh spline. Frame 1 shows the thigh trailing as the opposite heel strikes. The right thigh eases in to frame 6, where it reaches maximum velocity. It passes through frame 11 as it begins to ease out, then follows through to the heel strike pose at frame 17. The sharper curves between frames 1 and 6 and frames 11 and 17, and the relatively straighter segment between frames 6 and 11, give the action a fair amount of snap. This gives the impression of a quick, energetic movement. The heavy muscles of the upper leg are only moving themselves and don't have to support the body's weight or accelerate its larger mass.

The spline for the rest of the cycle is the other side of the story. The thigh is now the prime mover for accelerating the whole body. It's hard work to move all that mass, so the thigh rotates in a smooth, efficient acceleration curve, close to a 45-degree angle, between frames 22 and 33.

The timing and control of each thigh pitch keyframe can make the difference between a stroll, strut, march, and many other types of walk.

You could also change the walk dramatically by leaving each key value right where it is but edit the tension, bias, and continuity of each keyframe to smooth out these curves. This approach would give you the typically overinterpolated, mushy, boring action that just screams, "The computer animated this!"

23. Render and play back the animation. Do the thighs pitch properly? Do they ease in and ease out at acceptable rates? Is there enough snap in the motion?

When you are satisfied with the motion of the thighs, it's time to move on to the last parts of the animation hierarchy's fourth level, the upper arms. Save the scene again before proceeding with the next step.

24. Make the right upper arm and left upper arm visible.

25. Set the heading rotations of the right upper arm and left upper arm to counter the heading angles of the chest in each keyframe.

This rotates the upper arms' headings back to zero, relative to the overall position of the Puppet. The upper arms should usually be heading in the direction of travel, but when you are animating an energetic walk, you may want them to head slightly inward for balance.

26. Render and play back the animation. Do the upper arms have appropriate headings?

27. Pitch the right upper arm and left upper arm according to the three key poses in Figures 15.10, 15.11, and 15.12.

    How would you set the ease-in, snap, ease-out, and follow-through of the upper arms? These limbs do not have to carry any weight other than their own, and they are much more like ideal pendulums swinging to counterweight the legs. Therefore, the right upper arm and the left upper arm should move in near-perfect slaloms.

    At this point, you have a torso with one level of stump for each limb, the head included.

28. Render and play back the animation.

    Look very closely at this animation. Render more animations, from each principal view and whatever perspective angles and zoom factors you find useful. You want to make absolutely sure that the action so far is to your liking. Changing your mind later is a good way to waste time and effort, not to mention your patience.

    When you are satisfied with the action, save the scene again and proceed to the fifth animation hierarchy level, the shins and lower arms.

29. Make the lower arms visible.

    The lower arm joint—the elbow—is a simple hinge, and it generally only rotates in the pitch axis. This level of the animation hierarchy is a piece of cake!

30. Pitch the lower arms according to the three key poses shown in Figures 15.10, 15.11, and 15.12. As with the upper arms, you can animate these objects in near-perfect slaloms.

31. Render and play back the animation.

    How does the full arm motion look? You have plenty of leeway with the timing of the arm swings. You can tweak the spline control tools a lot as long as the arm positions match the three key poses.

    This is a good place to introduce another phrase borrowed from traditional animation—*successive breaking of joints*. This technique is a little like overlapping action, but it applies specifically to the hierarchy of joints in a character. Basically, when a higher joint starts to rotate, there should be a slight lag before the lower joints start to rotate as part of the same action. In practical terms, this means the rotation of a child object should begin, peak, and end some time after the parent performs the same actions.

There is a very easy way to do this in LightWave, if you're using a forward kinematics (FK) setup. Simply pose the *successive joint*, the next child down the hierarchy, on the exact keyframes as its parent object. When you have completely animated the action, use the shift function of the Graph Editor to delay the child's rotation a frame or two behind the parent's. The rotations of each joint will break in succession, down through the animation hierarchy.

32. Shift all the keyframes for the right lower arm and left lower arm back (toward frame 33) by one frame. Render and play back the animation again.

    What difference did the successive breaking of joints make? Try shifting the lower arm keyframes back another frame or two. Increase and decrease the shift until you get a feel for timing this technique.

    When you have a timing you like, save the scene again and proceed to pose the shins.

33. Make the shins visible.

    The shin joint—the knee—normally moves as a simple hinge and can rotate only in the pitch axis. This action is relatively easy to animate, but you have to pay extra attention to the timing of the heel strike-to-squash transition. This is supposed to be a reaction to the mass of the Puppet striking the ground and the shin and thigh squash to cushion the impact. The squash should be a little faster than the rebound.

34. Pitch the right and left shins according to the three key poses shown in Figures 15.10, 15.11, and 15.12.

35. Render and play back the animation.

    How does the full arm motion look? Is there enough snap to the forward motion leading into the heel strike?

    You must hold the straight leg of the heel strike (the shin's zero-degree pitch angle) long enough for it to register visually with the audience or the adjoining poses (preheel strike and squash) will blur together and the step will appear mushy. It's a good idea to keep the leg straight for at least two or three frames.

    This is one of the critical parts of a walk—a mushy heel strike looks tired or lazy, whereas a very sharp snap can define a march or strut. The depth and snap of the squash also say a lot about the amount of muscle tone and tension in the leg and the character as a whole.

    When you are satisfied with the action, save the scene again and proceed to the sixth and last animation hierarchy level—the hands and feet.

36. Make the hands visible.

    The wrist is a *universal joint* and can rotate in both pitch and heading. For this project, you only need to use the pitch axis.

37. Pitch the right and left hands according to the three key poses shown in Figures 15.10, 15.11, and 15.12.

    As with the upper and lower arms, there are no critical alignments to the ground or other objects. Because this is the end of the hierarchy, there are no dependent actions to plan for either. You can animate these objects in near-perfect slaloms with very few keyframes and use successive breaking of joints, just as you did for the lower arms.

38. Shift the hand rotation keyframes down a frame or two, for successive breaking of joints.

39. Render and play back the animation.

    How does the timing look? Try shifting the keyframes back and forth a few frames and compare the effect of each shift on the overall action. This is a relatively loose and free-swinging action, so you do not need to add much snap to the hands' extremes.

40. When you are satisfied with the hand rotations, save the scene file again.

    You're almost done! Just the feet are left to pose, then you can make the final tweaks to polish off the action.

41. Make the feet visible.

    The ankle is also a universal joint and can rotate in both pitch and bank axes, but for this project, you only need to use the pitch axis.

42. Pitch the right and left feet according to the ground and the three key poses in Figures 15.10, 15.11, and 15.12.

    For keyframes where the foot is on the ground, it's more important to match the foot to the angle of the ground than to the precise angle of the pictured poses.

    Flatten the foot to the ground immediately after the heel strike pose so the joint appears flexible and lifelike. If the foot is held at an angle to the ground after the heel strike, the ankle joint appears stiff and unnatural. Just try walking that way once—you'll feel what I mean. The muscles that run up the front of your shin act as shock absorbers when you run or walk. Holding a bent ankle after a heel strike will quickly exhaust them, and the lack of shock absorption will pass a lot more heel-strike shock to the rest of your body.

43. Render and play back the animation.

    How does the timing look? Do you get a sense of the mass of the Puppet and the springiness of the leg muscles? You may want to go back and tweak the entire thighs, shins, and feet hierarchy to get better leg motion.

    If you haven't set up constraints, you'll probably have to add a number of keyframes to keep the feet level to the ground. Whenever the feet are lifted free of the ground, you can use fewer keyframes and create smoother slaloms, but matching feet to the ground tends to produce splines with lots of keyframes and a slightly jagged appearance.

44. When you are satisfied with the foot rotations, save the scene file again.

You've just finished the overall motion for the Puppet hierarchy. Congratulations!

No Skating Allowed

One of the major problems with unconstrained LightWave character animation is keeping the feet aligned with fixed points on the ground. If this is not done precisely, the figure can appear to *skate* (slip the foot forward) or *moonwalk* (slip the foot backward), while the character moves as if walking normally. Even the best animators occasionally make a mistake on foot slippage. There is even one example in *Toy Story*, where Bo Peep is walking away from Woody and her foot slides a bit. Nobody's perfect.

Without constraints, your best defense against foot slippage is a lot of keyframes. The combined hips-thighs-shins-feet hierarchy produces an undulating y-position sequence that is difficult to match with a simple spline. This complex movement for the Puppet CG's y-axis is loaded on top of the root's z- and x-axes, which makes it even harder to match the root's motions to a simple spline. The brute-force solution is a lot of keyframes; a better solution is to simply constrain the feet to the ground plane. If you did not set up constraints as described in Chapter 12, you will have to go back and tweak the position of the roots of the hierarchy to keep the Puppet lined up properly with its environment.

Looping the Loop

The last step in building a motion cycle is making it cyclical. LightWave has a set of options in the Graph Editor's spline controls that govern the end behavior of motions. You can set a motion to stop and hold at the last value of the spline, reset to the first value, or repeat the entire spline endlessly for the entire scene. In this case, you want each part of the Puppet to repeat its actions.

45. Set each spline's end behavior to repeat. Save the scene again.

    With every object in the Puppet hierarchy set to repeat, the Puppet will continue to execute the walk cycle for an animation of any length. Try it!

46. Render and play back an animation of frames 1 through 64.

You'll note that the lateral and vertical motions of the Puppet did not repeat. The rotations of the various objects were designed to be looped, but the x,y,z motions of the constraints were designed for just one linear motion. If you want to use them as well, try the Cut, Copy, and Paste functions in LightWave's Graph Editor to assemble longer, repeating versions of these motions.

You can use this scene as a stock action scene. Document it and file it away. Whenever you need a walk cycle, reload and edit it to suit.

It's good animation practice and a basic test of a new character to create and save a variety of walk cycles for every character you build.

Some Important Extras

If you're going to make a character walk, you'd better know how to make it start and stop, too. Unless, of course, you have an idea for an animated film that's nothing but walking. (Never mind, it's been done: Ryan Larkin's *Walking*, the definitive work on the subject.)

Starting a walk means accelerating all the Puppet's parts from a standstill to full walking speed. To start the forward movement, you must anticipate by leaning the Puppet back, then forward into the first fall, and bringing the leading leg forward as if from a passing pose. Accelerate the body forward into the first step by rotating the trailing arm forcefully to the rear, and continue into a normal heel strike position. You can proceed from there with a normal walk cycle.

 Starting Out

15.3 To start your character's walk, follow these steps:

1. Load your best walk cycle.

2. Add 20 frames onto the beginning of the cycle to give you time to move the Puppet from standing still into the walk.

   Because you shifted the original starting frame, you need to create a new start at frame 1.

3. Copy a key for all items from frame 0 to frame 1.

4. Go to frame 1. Set up the default standing pose for the Puppet at frame 1, as shown in Figure 15.15.

Figure 15.15
Before beginning walk.

5. Duplicate the Puppet keyframes from frame 1 through frame 14. Go to frame 14 and pose the Puppet in anticipation, as shown in Figure 15.16.

Figure 15.16
Just beginning walk.

Duplicating the nearest pose can save you effort in posing because some of the objects' rotations will stay the same from one keyframe to the next.

Frame 14 is the anticipation key pose that precedes the fall into the walk. The hips tilt back, shifting the Puppet's balance and enabling the leading leg to come up and slightly forward. The opposite arm also comes forward, preparing for the forward shift in balance of the next key pose. The same-side arm comes forward slightly less, preparing for an energetic backward swing.

6. Duplicate the Puppet keyframes from frame 14 through frame 18. Go to frame 18 and pose the Puppet falling forward, as shown in Figure 15.17.

Frame 18 is the falling key pose. The hips have come back to level, the leading leg and arm are more fully advanced toward the heel strike pose, and the trailing arm is strongly thrust back to add more forward acceleration.

7. Tweak the splines, and shift the keyframes lower in the hierarchy, to get the appropriate ease-in, snap, and ease-out for the motions leading into the first heel strike.

The trailing arm is especially important if the start is a rapid one. The backward swing of the arm helps push the upper body forward, accelerating it to a walking pace. You may want to shift the keyframes for the arm and pay special attention to the ease-in and -out in the spline.

Frame 21 is the heel strike, the transition to a normal walk cycle, which you can leave as is.

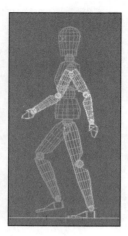

Figure 15.17
Leading to first heel strike position.

8. Edit the first squash pose, frame 26, to bend a little deeper. Change the leading foot, shin, and thigh pitch angles. You may have to adjust the trailing leg's shin, just to keep the trailing toes above the ground.

   This cushions the first heel strike impact and provides more visual bounce to the first full stride. A change of gait like this—from standing still to a walk—is visually jarring to your audience; make sure you anticipate, follow through, and generally make the action as easy to read as possible.

   If the timing seems a little off, try shifting the anticipation or falling keyframes. The procedures for tweaking keyframes to eliminate foot slippage are the same as in earlier projects.

9. Save the finished scene under a new name. You'll be using it for the next project.

Stopping a walk means decelerating all the Puppet's parts from full walking speed to a standstill. Stopping forward motion requires you to make the squash position deeper, using the thigh and shin as a spring to absorb most of the Puppet's forward inertia.

Because the Puppet is not continuing into another step, you should bring the trailing leg up only until it is level with the leading leg, not past it. You should also reduce the backward rotation of both arms and exaggerate their forward rotations.

Keep the upper body leaning backwards against the Puppet's forward inertia until the character is nearly at a full stop. Then, pitch it forward slightly in follow-through.

If the walk is an especially vigorous one or the stop very sudden, you might pose the Puppet to rise up its on toes before settling back into the *hold*, the standing pose. Keep the Puppet's CG behind its toes at all times, to maintain the appearance of balance.

PROJECT 15.4 Somebody Stop Me!

To stop your character's walk, follow these steps:

1. Reload the scene file you saved at the end of the preceding project. Go to frame 26.

   This is the squash pose for the leading left leg, which is close enough to the stopping squash pose that using a duplicate can save some posing.

2. Copy a keyframe for all items from frame 26 through frame 57.

   This adds a squash pose following the heel strike pose at frame 52.

3. Copy a keyframe for all items from frame 1 (the default standing pose for the Puppet) to frame 67.

   You now have a smooth default interpolation from the heel strike at frame 52 to the standing pose at frame 67, as shown in Figure 15.18. Your next task is to modify that interpolation to make a more realistic stop from a walk cycle.

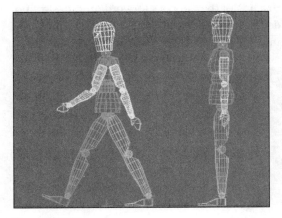

Figure 15.18
Left: heel strike, frame 52; right: standing, frame 67.

4. Go to frame 53. Tweak the left foot's pose so it is level with the ground.

   The foot still has to flatten to the ground immediately after the heel strike, but if you simply duplicated frame 27, it would introduce a lot of other keyframes that you don't need.

5. Go to frame 56. Pitch the hips back about 5 degrees, shifting the mass of the upper body backward to help the Puppet slow down. The hips don't need another keyframe until frame 67, although you should tweak the spline a bit to get a smooth deceleration. Pitch the right thigh so it continues to swing forward and the right shin so the right foot clears the ground, as shown in Figure 15.19.

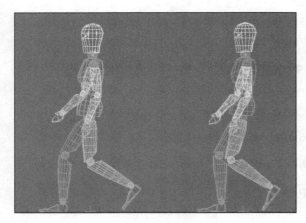

Figure 15.19
Frame 56 and 57 Puppet poses.

6. Go to frame 57. Pose the left shinbone so it reaches its maximum pitch, about 32 degrees. This makes the squash pose deeper to absorb some of the Puppet's forward inertia, slowing it down (see Figure 15.20). From about -25 degrees at this frame, the left femur should rotate almost linearly to 0 degrees at keyframe 65.

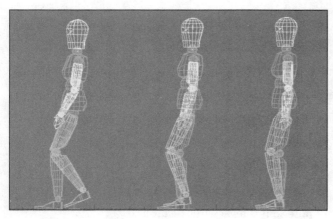

Figure 15.20
Frame 60, 63, and 65 Puppet poses.

7. Go to frame 60. The right femur should already nearly match the left, but you need to create a pitch keyframe for the right shinbone so the right foot still clears the ground. Pitch both arms so they are nearly aligned. They should be moving backward, as in Figure 15.20, to counterbalance the rise of the hips and upper body from the squash position of frame 57.

8. Go to frame 63. Create a pitch keyframe for the right shinbone so the right foot clears the ground. This is the peak pitch for the right shinbone. After this frame, you will be lowering the foot to flat contact with the ground.

9. Go to frame 65. Create pitch keyframes for the right femur, the right shinbone, and the right foot so the right foot is parallel to the ground and moving down toward flat contact with the ground.

10. Create follow-through and hold keyframes between frame 67 and 75, to soften the rigid "attention" pose of the Puppet.

11. Save the scene file under a new name. Render and play back the animation.

You will probably note some uneven decelerations between keyframes. Select each item in turn and take a look at its spline for pitch rotation. Use the spline controls to smooth out the graphs, but make sure you leave a little snap (a short, sharp curve near the last frames). It'll make the Puppet snap to attention. Snapping the character into a key pose generally makes the action look better.

If the timing seems a little off, try shifting the follow-through or deceleration keyframes for different objects, keeping in mind the guidelines for overlapping action and successive breaking of joints. The procedures for tweaking to eliminate foot slippage are the same as in the first walk cycle projects.

When you're done tweaking, you should have an animation something like PROJ1504.AVI, which you can find in the Chapter 15 directory on this book's CD-ROM.

By working through this section, you've mastered the basic principles of hierarchical animation, dynamic motion, motion cycle construction, and starting and stopping an action. Now, you're ready to apply the principles you used for walk cycles to animating run cycles and multilegged animal gaits.

Run for It

The two major differences between walks and runs are foot contact with the ground and strength of poses. Walkers, by definition, always have at least one foot on the ground. Runners may have both feet off the ground for the majority of the run cycle. This midair time, and the actions required to produce it, are the key poses of run cycles. Run poses are also much stronger visually than walk poses. Both cycles show the same actions, but almost every joint rotation is more extreme in a run.

The run cycle starts off just like the walk—with a fall forward. Instead of simply rotating one leg forward to stop the fall, a running character must also thrust upward by flexing the trailing leg and foot, as in Figure 15.21. Note the bends in the trailing leg and foot, which straighten to propel the runner forward faster than a simple fall would. This is the *thrust*, or push-off, pose of the run cycle.

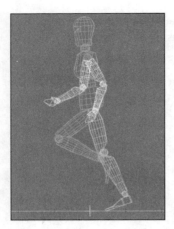

Figure 15.21
Thrust pose of a run cycle.

Instead of falling back to a more upright posture after the cycle is started, a running character must maintain a forward lean during the entire run cycle. A faster run requires the character to lean forward farther, pushing the upper body ahead of the CG. This continuous "fall" helps convert the thrust of the driving leg from vertical to horizontal movement. It's also the reason running is more hazardous than walking—if runners stop suddenly, they have to quickly get their feet under their CG or they fall down. A walker is stable at every heel strike position. There are no stable poses in a run cycle.

The result of the thrust pose is the midair pose, as shown in Figure 15.22. Both feet are well off the ground, and the character is ballistic. From the time the trailing foot leaves the ground until the leading foot makes contact, the running character is following a parabola.

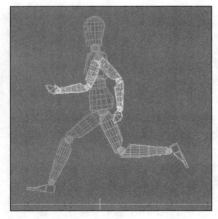

Figure 15.22
Midair pose of a run cycle.

The height and width of the parabola can say a lot about the character. A short, broad parabola is the mark of a serious runner or sprinter, who converts most of his energy into forward motion. A high, narrow parabola shows the character is very springy, spending more energy on moving up than on moving forward.

You can exaggerate this to create a very lively, bouncy character. The up-and-down motion of the walk cycle is limited by the arc of the character's pivoting legs. The only limit for a run cycle's vertical motion is the amount of energy you allocate your character. Just make sure that any extra energy you animate into a thrust pose is balanced by an extra-deep squash on the other end of the parabola. What goes up, must come down.

The midair pose makes your job of animating a running character a little harder because you can't rely on foot placement to keep the character properly positioned in the scene. For the midair part of the run cycle, you'll have to figure the trajectory of the character just as you did for the falling objects in Chapter 14. The pose itself is a simple extrapolation from the preceding thrust pose to the following squash pose. The trailing leg recoils from the full extension of the thrust and starts to bend forward again. The leading leg stretches out toward the ground, remaining slightly bent to absorb the anticipated impact.

The third pose is the squash (see Figure 15.23). Because everything happens faster in a run, several of the walk poses are compressed into one run pose. The important elements of the walk cycle's passing position, heel strike, and squash poses all happen at once in the run cycle squash pose. The leading foot makes ground contact and the leading leg bends to absorb the impact, and the trailing leg folds so the foot clears the ground as it kicks forward to pass the leading leg.

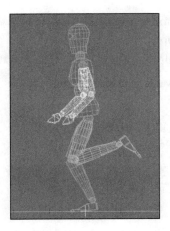

Figure 15.23
Squash pose of a run cycle.

The runner's foot can make contact either heel first, as in the walk, or on the ball of the foot. The faster the run, the more likely the character is to run on the balls of his feet. If the character heel-strikes, you should put a little extra deceleration in his forward motion. The jar of the heel strike slows a runner down perceptibly. When running characters brake to a stop, they literally dig in their heels. You might try to animate this, based on the stopping and starting projects in Chapter 14.

A running character's arms make pretty much the same motions as a walking character's. The difference is a matter of degree. The runner's extremes are a little farther out, and the speed of transition between extremes is faster. A runner does not move faster by throwing his arms out wider. Instead, a runner keeps his arms folded more closely, making them shorter and easier to move, and moves them more rapidly. A short arm can dynamically balance a longer, heavier leg by moving faster. When you animate a runner's arms, use all the snap you can and avoid ease-in and -out like poison, for it will surely kill your character.

Animating the Puppet Running

To animate a running puppet, follow these steps:

1. Open the Puppet scene file you set up in Chapter 11.

   This scene file should include the complete Puppet character, parented, lighted, and ready to animate, just as you used it earlier.

2. Follow the same procedures you learned earlier to pose the Puppet to match the key running poses shown in Figures 15.21, 15.22, and 15.23. Repeat the poses for the opposite side, making six keyframes in all.

   This is where you really start developing your judgment. How far apart should you place your key poses? Use pose copying and shifting procedures to move your key poses around. Experiment with different timings, and keep notes on what works best for you.

3. Look at the splines for each object. Look for patterns, especially for patterns that need a little help.

   You should be developing a sense of what a spline should look like for a sharp, snappy motion versus a gradual, smooth one. You should also be developing your judgment of when each type of motion is appropriate.

4. Calculate and set keyframes to define the parabola the Puppet travels during the midair part of the run cycle.

   Remember, the Puppet's CG should follow a parabola precisely, no matter what the rest of the character is doing.

5. Starting at the root of the animation hierarchy, tweak the motion of each object to make the run cycle more lifelike. Follow the usual procedure of rendering wireframe or preview animations to check your progress.

Look very closely at the hip and chest action before you jump to any conclusions. As I pointed out earlier, the hip and chest rotations are among the smallest in the whole character, but they affect everything else and are a real pain to revise. Keep to the animation hierarchy and most of your mistakes will be small.

One of the noticeable differences in timing between walks and runs is the kick forward of the trailing leg. In a run, this kick is very fast, with a lot of snap. You might try a straight linear interpolation over two or three frames just to see how extreme you can get before the Puppet starts moving like he sat on a high-voltage line. On the other hand, the thrust pose is accelerating the entire body weight up and forward, so there's a lot of effort to move a large mass. A more gradual acceleration for the trailing leg's extension, with more ease-in, is appropriate here. The same goes for the squash position. The idea is to absorb the impact gradually, using the leading leg as a spring to ease in to the flexed pose, then straighten again in an ease-out to the thrust position.

There are some considerations for the runner's attitude, as well. If the character's head is kept high, looking ahead rather than at his path, the usual perception is that the runner has plenty of energy and is nowhere near his limits. If the runner's head is low, he is more likely to be going all out or near exhaustion. Then again, maybe he's just watching for loose change on the sidewalk.

6. When you've got a run cycle you are happy with, save the scene under a new name. You'll probably find other uses for it.

If you're feeling adventurous, you can animate the Puppet through a running jump by exaggerating the leg compression of the thrust pose, stretching out the midair pose (make it follow a larger parabola), and exaggerating the compression of the squash pose at the landing. The same exaggeration principles apply to running hurdles and stairs, too.

Animating the Puppet Changing Gaits

In a preceding project, you animated the Puppet character to accelerate, walk, and stop. In this project, you'll animate the Puppet to change from a walking gait to a fast run:

1. Load one of the multiple-cycle walks you created in a preceding project.

2. Go to the heel strike position for the second step of the cycle. Modify it to have a deeper bend and forward lean, to match the squash position of Project 15.5.

3. Continue with the remaining key poses for a fast run, as in Project 15.5. If you want to animate a fast run, make sure that the Puppet runs on its toes, that the heel never makes contact with the ground, and that the hips are pitched at a more extreme angle.

You now have a better understanding of how to create walk and run cycles for bipedal humanoids. The following section tells where you can find information to help you mimic other natural actions, both for humanoids and other creatures.

Seeing Is Believing

A recurring question for character animators is, "How does a [creature to be animated] move?" The answer is sometimes found in a book or journal, often on file footage, recently even on CD-ROM, but always in nature. If you start building and animating a creature without studying it live, if you trust your assumptions and preconceptions, you will most assuredly end up scrapping most of your work. If you don't like wasting time and effort, do a little research before you start pushing pixels. And when you need the real data, go back to the source.

There are two broad categories for the information you need: *anatomy* and *kinesiology*, the studies of creatures' physical structures and the ways they move. You can get a lot of anatomical information from zoology and comparative anatomy textbooks, which any good library or bookstore should be able to find for you. I keep a few general zoological references around, but when I'm working on a new creature, I usually head to a library and research it from the most up-to-date sources.

The kinesiology information is a little harder to come by. Most of the research is done on humans or on "economically significant" animals:

- The best sources of information are films and videotapes of animals and humans performing a variety of actions against measurable backgrounds, called *motion studies*.

- Still images of the same subjects are second best, but when collected in books like Eadweard Muybridge's (see the Bibliography), they have the advantages of portability and independence from viewing equipment.

- A distant third in usability are the scholarly analyses, derivations, and explanations published in the scientific literature. Most of these studies ignore or omit at least some of the raw data necessary to the animator. Even if someone ran a study on the creature you're working on, there's no guarantee that she gathered or published the data you need.

The ideal study would include (at least) three-axis position data for each joint in a fully articulated skeleton, plus a complete analysis of muscle, fat, and ligament arrangements and their effect on surface appearances. In reality, what you're likely to find are very crude profile views of the creature, with the approximate locations of the major joints marked inconsistently between successive frames.

Until recently, access to most of this information was limited to people who could use film libraries or visit a zoo. The availability of consumer videotape players, and the production of nature videotapes by organizations like the National Geographic Society, have put the study of animal and human motion within reach of any aspiring animator. The development of the computer as a mass-market educational tool has also expanded the motion study resources you can acquire.

Motion Study Resources

My favorite motion study materials include the classic works by Eadweard Muybridge, a variety of National Geographic videotapes, several Discovery Channel videotapes, the other books on animal motion listed in the Bibliography, and an excellent CD-ROM, "How Animals Move," authored by R. McNeill Alexander and distributed by Maris Multimedia and The Discovery Channel.

I recommend that you invest in a laser disk player, one with a digital freeze frame. You can use this to repeatedly view motion studies (the Muybridge work is available on laser disk from Voyager), single-framing and looping segments without damaging either your player or a tape. A DVD player may also be a viable choice in the future, but as of this writing, there aren't enough pertinent titles available.

If you can't get a laser disk player, a video digitizer board for your computer can be the next best thing. Digitize clips of your favorite animation or nature videotapes and loop them to play back on your computer. As long as this is for private, educational use, it's within the fair use limits of copyright. Just don't do something like posting the clips on the Internet. It's illegal, and it's disrespectful to the people who produced the video in the first place.

If you get into digitizing reference material, sooner or later you are going to be tempted to try a process called *rotoscoping*. This is easy to do with LightWave. You just load the clip as an image sequence and assign it as a background layer. Set up a character that matches the one in the background, pose the character to match each frame of the background, and presto, you have a rotoscoped "animation"—only it isn't character animation, and it produces really crummy-looking action. Anybody who's watched a little animation can tell when something's been rotoscoped. Most professional animators hate it.

I mention rotoscoping only as a learning tool. One of the longer learning processes in LightWave character animation is the interpretation of splines. An experienced animator can read them like large print, having the experience to know when a spline isn't showing enough snap, ease, or whatever. If you are just starting out in LightWave animation, you need all the help you can get for learning to read and analyze splines. If you digitize some of your favorite animated or live-action clips, and rotoscope the Puppet or other characters over them, you can build yourself a set of splines to study and learn from.

If all these sources on motion studies don't help, you can always fall back on real-life simulation. When in doubt, act it out. You will find it easier to animate actions if you first act them out yourself. Get in the habit of walking through an action, testing the different approaches a character might take. If you feel silly at first, get over it. Professional animators at the major studios do this all the time. Jumping on and off desks and walking around with a board nailed to your sneakers seem to be normal, acceptable behavior for character animators. Wearing a tie to work, however, can get you blacklisted.

On All Fours

Aside from bipedal humanoids, the largest class of creatures you are likely to animate are the four-legged variety. They present some interesting problems for character animators—creating motions contrary to bipedal intuitions, visualizing actions you are unable to act out accurately, keeping twice as many legs locked to the ground, and animating a lot more gaits than you'd use for two-legged critters.

Basic anatomy accounts for the first two problems. Humans walk on the equivalent of the palms of their hands, on the metatarsal bones that form the arch of the foot. Many quadrupeds, in contrast, move on the equivalent of their toes. Cows, deer, and other hoofed animals actually walk around on tiptoe. Dogs and many other mammals walk on the balls of their feet, with the digits spread for balance. You can come close to emulating this without joining the ballet—just stand barefoot and lift both heels off the ground at once. This feels very awkward, but the change in tendon and muscle layout makes trotting and running more efficient for the animals.

When it comes to preventing moonwalking or skating, the solution for four legs is the same as for two: Use constraints.

The gait "problem" isn't really a problem. You just need to know what's available and what's reasonable in certain circumstances for certain creatures. There are six common four-legged gaits—walk, pace, trot, canter, transverse gallop, and rotary gallop:

- The *quadruped walk* is similar to the human walk. Each foot is grounded for more than half the cycle. The usual order of foot placement is left fore, right hind, right fore, left hind.

- The *pace* is an odd gait used naturally only by camels and some breeds of dog. It can also be taught to other animals. In the pace, the legs move together on each side; that is, both left feet would move forward together, then both right feet. This produces a unique rocking motion.

- The *trot, canter,* and *gallop* are similar to the human run, where each foot is grounded for less than half the cycle. The feet move in diagonal pairs in the trot, left fore with right hind and right fore with left hind. In the gallop, the fore and hind feet move separately; that is, if the forefeet are grounded, the hind feet are in motion, so the spine can bend and add longer reach and more muscle to the stride. The canter is like a slow gallop crossed with a trot, in which the grounding of the fore and hind pairs overlaps.

- The *rotary gallop* is the fast gait of cats and some other animals, in which the spine curls up and stretches out to lengthen the stride and increase the animal's speed.

The exact sequence and range of motion for each gait varies according to the animal. If you have to animate one of these gaits, your best bet is to observe or acquire photos of an animal similar to the one you are animating and work out the poses from the guidelines just listed and the creature's individual proportions.

There is also a rare gait called a *pronk*, in which all four legs extend simultaneously in a sort of four-legged pogo. In nature, certain antelope and deer are known to pronk. In animation, one of the most memorable examples is Chuck Jones's Pepe le Pew. This gait can be very amusing when used sparingly, but only when it's appropriate to the character. Otherwise, stick to the more common gaits.

PROJECT 15.7 Animating a Walking Cow

This project uses the cow object included on the LightWave CD-ROM. You can also try setting this up with any four-legged animal model you have handy, using the same techniques you learned in Chapter 12.

I've set up a very basic arrangement of the minimum bones necessary to animate a four-legged walk or other simple gait. The bone names are fairly self-explanatory. All the bones have been set up to animate only in the pitch axis. This is not perfectly anatomically correct, but it's good enough for this project. The bones have also been laid out in order—shoulder to hoof, then next leg—so navigating through the skeleton is as easy as possible.

To animate a walking cow, follow these steps:

1. In Layout, load scene file COW.LWS from the Chapter 15 directory on this book's CD-ROM. The scene file will look in the default Content directory and the OBJECTS\ANIMALS subdirectory for the cow object. If it is not there, you will have to specify the correct path and directory.

2. Set keyframes for the entire cow and all dependent items at frames 0, 1, 13, 17, and 21. The first two frames are a baseline reference; the last three are the minimum keyframes for the walk cycle.

3. Pose the cow in frame 13 to match Figure 15.24. This is the heel strike pose for the front feet.

4. Pose the cow in frame 17 to match Figure 15.25. This is the squash pose for the front feet.

   Most of the shock-absorbing squash is accomplished by rotating bones that are concealed in the shoulder of the cow. This makes pose details hard to see in the rendered animation, but they're there.

Figure 15.24
Heel strike pose for walking cow.

Figure 15.25
Squash pose for walking cow.

5. Pose the cow in frame 21 to match Figure 15.26. This is the passing pose for the front feet.

    Now for the fun part. This particular motion repeats on a 20-frame cycle; that is, the left front hoof's setting in frame 13 is identical to that of the right front hoof's setting in frame 33. Also, the entire animation is designed to loop after frame 40, so you can "wrap around" keyframes that go over 40.

6. Duplicate the settings of the left front leg in frame 13 for the right front leg in frame 33. Repeat this alternating duplication of settings for the rest of the animation. For frame 21, duplicate the settings to frame 1 (21+20=41, 41-40=1).

Figure 15.26
Passing pose for walking cow.

When you're finished, you should have a decent approximation of the original walk cycle. Unfortunately, there's no easy solution to this object's difficulty with coordinating rear and front pairs—that requires full spine, pelvic, and shoulder skeletons to mimic whole-body flexibility. This means the vertical and lateral movements of the cow object will not match the original's, so you can expect that the foot placement won't match the ground, either.

Don't be discouraged if the cow doesn't walk the way you want it to. Coordinating the fore and hind legs of an object like this is a difficult job, as the next project illustrates.

PROJECT 15.8 Trying to Tune Up a Rotoscoped Cow

This project presents you with a partially completed cow walk cycle, rotoscoped from one of the motion study sources mentioned earlier in the chapter. The front legs seem to be animating all right, as shown in the animation file Front.AVI, which you can locate in the Chapter 15 directory on this book's CD-ROM:

1. Load the Front.AVI file, and play it. It isn't the greatest—it could use some bone weight maps to smooth out the muscle action—but it works. More important, the feet lock to the ground and don't skate all over.

   The downside to this setup becomes obvious when you look at the rest of the cow.

2. Load the Whole.AVI file, and play it. Yuck! What is going on with the back legs?

Both the front and back leg bones were rotoscoped to motion-capture footage on four-frame key intervals and are fairly reliable. The difficulty seems to be that there is no provision for spine or pelvic movement, so the body of the object is just a rigid block. Even a seemingly rigid creature flexes its spine and pelvis when moving, especially if it is as heavy as a cow. If the pelvis and spine moved accurately, the rear legs might be correct as is.

There are a couple of possible approaches to repairing this animation:

- Add bones to emulate the pelvis and spine, then manipulate the rear legs of the object to coordinate with the front legs.

- Tweak the existing bones in the rear legs to match the front legs, and just forget about matching the rotoscope footage exactly.

If you'd like to give it a try, load COW2.LWS in Layout, and give it your best shot.

PROJECT 15.9 Animating a Cat's Rotary Gallop

Arguably, one of the toughest character animation jobs is to animate a feline. Most other animals have a fairly rigid bone structure, but cats are extraordinarily flexible. They have only a vestigial collarbone, and their forelegs simply attach to an overlapping nest of muscles. Their spines are only a little less flexible than a snake's, enabling their heads to face 180 degrees from the direction of their hind feet. They also have the most extreme of rotary gallops, with the spine alternating convex to concave on each stride. But, they're *so* much fun to watch!

If you'd like to try this project from scratch, here are a few guidelines:

- Research your subject. Start with the appropriate references in the Bibliography and see where they lead you.

- Narrowly define your goal. One complete stride of a domestic cat's legs is plenty. You don't even need to do the whole cat.

- Keep it simple. Use something like the Puppet to start with. After you have a clear idea of the skeletal measurements, you can model an object and use bones to animate it more smoothly.

One additional reference you may want to check is an article by John T. Manter in the *Journal of Experimental Biology*, volume 15, number 4 (1938), "The Dynamics of Quadruped Walking." This report includes x-y plane data for a domestic cat's legs during a walk, plus a lot of other information about force analysis. Unfortunately, it completely ignores lateral displacement, so it's only about half the data you need for a complete animation.

Big cats move just like little cats, only heavier and slower. You can get a good idea of how a tabby moves by watching documentary footage of lions and tigers. Cheetahs are a little harder to translate because of the difference in rear leg geometry. My personal favorites are the panther and mountain lion because their hides are more closely attached. Tigers, especially, have skin that slides all over, making it hard to analyze the underlying muscle motion.

If you can set up and animate even a rough approximation of a feline gallop, you will have a serious example of work to put on your demo reel. Cats are *hard*.

You should now have a decent grounding in mimicking natural motion. Your goal in the next section is to learn how to extrapolate your observations of natural motion to create caricatured animation. Along the way, projects will show you how to animate actions from the repertoire of classic cartoon animation, including takes, sneaks, staggers, and zips. You'll also learn the concept of *staging* for foreshadowing action.

An Art of Essences

The art of character animation is not the literal reproduction of realistic movement. Simple reproduction can be automated, and anything that can be automated is not an art. The basic art of character animation is the same, whether expressed in LightWave, clay, or cel. It is distilling the essence of movement, then creating it again in a new form that is obviously different and just as obviously true in essence.

The first step, then, is to observe. As explained earlier, you must observe in detail exactly how an action is performed in real life before you can understand it well enough to re-create it as an animation. You must understand the forces acting on each part of the character—the mass, inertia, and energy that are expressed in acceleration, deceleration, and deformation.

> *"The continuous detailed analysis of all kinds of motion is basic to any animator's ability to re-create it or, better still, to transform it for his or her own purposes."*
> —Steven S. Wilson, Puppets and People

Develop the habit of watching people and animals move. Anywhere you go, there are lessons to be learned about movement. Keep your eyes open, and when you notice an especially fine movement (incredible grace running for the bus, a particularly elegant gesture in conversation), try to figure out why it was so good. Make notes, and try to animate the Puppet to achieve the same effect.

This is part of training yourself to really see. Your brain is very good at categorizing information as it comes in, pigeonholing it into classifications like "dangerous," "familiar," "food," and so on. This enables you to walk through a crowded shopping mall without having a nervous breakdown—most of the flood of information is immediately classified as unimportant noise so you can ignore it all and carry on a conversation with your companion.

The downside to this sorting process is that you miss a lot of the details in everyday life. You need to retrain your brain to sort information about human and animal movement into a "pay attention and analyze this" pigeonhole. With practice, you can watch a person walk and be able to reproduce the exact amount of knee flex for the squash, the precise speed of the kick forward to the heel strike, even the extent of the counterbalancing shoulder action. This analysis is the essence of mimicry and the beginning of animation.

What Makes a Chicken a Chicken?

Once you can analyze and reproduce movement, you are halfway to caricaturing it. The idea of caricature is to make something more like itself. In caricaturing movement, this means exaggeration of not just the individual key poses but also the acceleration, deceleration, and deformation that connect the poses. If a character walks with a certain amount of knee bend in squash, a caricatured version will bend the knee even farther, making the squash deeper.

The real art to caricature is the judgment of what is essential and what is not. The heart of an action may not be the broadest movement, the largest change, or the most visible deformation. It may be the smallest nuance that defines that action. For example, let's take a look at a basic emotional transition, from a pose of neutrality—simply standing, relaxed but alert—to a pose of aggressive anger, almost a boxer's stance. Act this transition out yourself. Create your own interpretation and analyze the changes between the neutral and anger poses.

You probably raised your arms, brought your hands up in front of your body, and clenched your fists. You may have also taken a half step forward, shifted your balance into a stronger stance, and perhaps pitched your head forward so you could glare at your opponent from lowered brows. This would be a typical "looking for a fight" pose.

So, what's the most important part? Which of these changes is the essence of anger? The motion of the arms is certainly the largest angular change, over 90 degrees to bring the hands up to waist level. The change in stance would probably be second, because the smaller angular changes of both legs plus the resulting forward movement of the body add up to a large perceived motion. Possibly the smallest motions are the forward pitch of the head and the closing of the hands into fists.

Guess what? The hands and head are the essential, defining motions for anger. How to prove this? Drop back to the neutral pose and use just the head pitch and glare. Not quite anger, but maybe severe annoyance. Now, clench your fists, but keep them at your sides. Bingo! If you took this pose in a bar, either your friends would try to calm you down or the person you were facing would be getting ready to rumble. This is *repressed anger*, a version of anger that minimizes the grosser body movements but communicates almost the same information. Pure aggressive anger is ready to throw a punch; repressed anger is aggressive anger restrained—just barely—by better judgment, but still ready to explode at the next provocation.

But the grosser body pose still has something to say, doesn't it? Try this: Assume the aggressive anger pose, then open your hands so your open palms face your imaginary opponent, and pitch your head level or a little bit back so you are looking straight at your opponent. Same body pose, just the hands and head are different, but it's the difference between starting a fight and trying to stop one.

The point to this exercise is that you can't assume any part of a movement is the essence. You have to look at the gestalt of the movement first, then start picking apart the individual elements. Until you develop the judgment that comes with experience, you would do well to analyze every element of every pose you look at and compare them to similar elements of other poses as we just did with anger, neutrality, and placation.

Try varying one element, one variable, at a time (using the ol' scientific method again) and evaluating the change in expression. Like most forms of systematic research, this can be slow going, but when you eliminate all the wrong answers, you are left with the right ones. Also, when you are forced to work through every possible permutation, you often stumble across valuable information that you weren't even looking for. Keep your eyes and mind open.

> *"In the fields of observation, chance favors only the mind that is prepared."*
> —Louis Pasteur

Mountains from Molehills

After you have identified the essence of a movement, the remaining question is how to exaggerate it. This breaks down naturally into two parts: the key pose and the transition. The key pose can be caricatured as if it were a drawing, so you can apply the guidelines used by artists working in 2D media to create a stronger pose, a more expressive silhouette, a smoother line of action, and a clearer definition of character. The goal is to make a key pose look even more like itself.

The caricature of a transition is a matter of timing and emphasis. This is another area where the importance of experience, judgment, and inspiration define animation as an art, not a science. You can exaggerate each of the principles of movement you learned in earlier chapters to create a caricature movement. You can push anticipation farther away from the main action, deform squash and stretch even further, delay overlapping action keys farther from the main action, and shorten snap to fewer frames.

The only principle you shouldn't usually exaggerate is ease. Caricatures look best when they are very snappy, the antithesis of ease. Too much ease makes an animation floaty, as if the character is performing underwater.

Subtlety is for live action. If you want an action to read well as a caricature, exaggerate more than you think you should. You learn from your mistakes, if you're smart. This is a time when you can learn most rapidly by deliberately making mistakes. Push the exaggeration of an action to a really outrageous extreme, both in key pose and transition. Try to do it wrong, to exaggerate too much. Examine each element of the action and push it to the virtual limits of the character. If a part of the character is supposed to squash, mash it flat. If part is to stretch, draw it out to a needle shape. If a joint is to bend, fold it as far as it will go. If the joint is to extend, make it perfectly straight. Shorten each snap to a linear transition across a single frame.

When you're done exaggerating this action, it should be so extreme even Tex Avery would disown it. So what's the point? This is an investigation, a search for the right amount of exaggeration. The low end is perfectly natural movement, the kind you could rotoscope or motion-capture straight from life. You know you don't want to go any further in that direction. When you animate an action that is too exaggerated, you establish a high end. Together, the high and low ends define the limits of your search, which is the first step in the process of solving the problem.

You may find that it's not possible to exaggerate an action too much. That's the fun part of cartoon-style animation. Sometimes, the absolute virtual limit is the exact effect you want. Sometimes, the antagonist does end up as a perfectly flat grease spot on the wall, and sometimes, the protagonist does stretch clear across the screen in a zip exit.

This is another time a laser disk player can come in handy. Rent or buy laser disks of classic Warner Bros. cartoons, and single-frame through the most extreme actions. It's amazing what you can get away with in a cartoon.

A Caricature Walk

You can thoroughly caricature an action the same way you originally animated it, starting at the root of the animation hierarchy and proceeding through the layers, exaggerating as you go. If you've already worked through the projects earlier in this chapter, you should be comfortably familiar with the key poses and transitions of walks, runs, and other motion cycles. Let's look at how you might exaggerate a normal walk cycle to create a caricature walk.

The easiest key pose to exaggerate is the squash. The limits to this pose are defined by the structure of the character: No squash at all is just a character walking with straight legs (Thud! Thud! Thud!), and maximum squash doubles up the knee joint so the character's hips are nearly on its heels. The variations on squash are mostly in the timing: How fast and far is the snap to the ease-in? How slow is the ease-in to full squash? How fast is the snap out of full squash? Almost all the exaggeration in the squash is concentrated in the knee joint because the hips are nearly level and the foot is constrained to be flat on the ground.

The passing position uses banked hips to help increase ground clearance for the trailing foot, so the hip is eligible for exaggeration as well. You can exaggerate the normal passing position to elevate the character in a bounce. You can also exaggerate both knees to a deeply flexed position and coordinate the rotations of the knees, thighs, and hips to maintain a constant distance between the hips' pivot and the ground. This will remove any up-and-down motion from the character's CG, mimicking a waddling duck-walk.

The heel strike provides lots of opportunities for exaggeration but must also be handled more carefully to produce the right effect. The heel strike is the result of a fast forward rotation of the trailing upper leg, with the trailing lower leg folded at least high enough that the foot clears the ground during the upper leg's forward rotation. This enables you to exaggerate the speed and angle of the hip, the speed and angle of the upper leg, the speed and angle of the lower leg, and the speed and angle of the foot all in the same motion.

For example, you could rotate the upper leg very quickly up past the final heel strike angle, whip the lower leg out straight at the same time, and point the toe at the leg's maximum extension. Hold that pose for a frame or three while the rest of the body continues to lean forward. Then, rotate the upper leg down rapidly to slap the foot flat on the ground. That's basically a goose step. Ugly, inefficient, and stupid, but it makes a loud noise. Hmmm. Sounds like a metaphor for certain political systems.

PROJECT 15.10 Animating the Puppet Doing a Caricature March

To animate the Puppet doing a caricature march, follow these steps:

1. Load one of the Puppet walk cycles that you created earlier in this chapter.

2. Exaggerate the key poses and transitions to animate the Puppet doing a caricature march.

   Here are a few guidelines, which you should supplement by acting out a marching action yourself—or perhaps watching the Rose Bowl parade—and trying to analyze what's going on:

   - The trailing leg should move rapidly through the passing position and kick out straight before the heel strike.

   - The foot should form a right angle, or even pull the toes back toward the knee a bit, until the heel hits the ground. This exaggerates the slap of the foot flattening to the ground immediately following the heel strike.

   - Lean the hips and chest back a few degrees.

   - Keep the Puppet's head high or even pitched back a bit.

   - Pose the arms to keep the hands high, the elbows out, and the arms pumping vigorously, with plenty of snap to balance the motions of the legs.

You might put some John Phillips Sousa on the CD player while you work on this, just to put yourself in the mood.

PROJECT 15.11 Animating the Puppet Doing a Caricature Sad Walk

To animate the Puppet doing a caricature sad walk, follow these steps:

1. Reload the basic walk scene you used to start the preceding project.

2. Exaggerate the key poses and transitions to animate the Puppet doing a caricature sad walk:

   - Pitch the hips back a few degrees and the thorax or chest forward a few degrees, effectively curving the spine and making the Puppet slump.

   - Pitch the head forward and keep the eye-tracking null on the ground.

- Keep the arms limp and without volition. Animate them using overlapping action, as if they were a pair of scarves tacked to the shoulders.

- Lift the legs as little as possible and make the stride very slow and short. Either keep the feet nearly parallel to the ground and shuffle them or drag the toes along the ground through each passing position.

- The feet should be very close to the angle of the ground at the heel strike position so there is very little distance for the foot to slap down.

- Use longer, more gradual anticipations and ease-ins, but shorten the ease-outs as if the character is too exhausted to effectively absorb the impact of the action.

PROJECT 15.12 Syncing Caricature Action to a Sound Track

The goal of this project is to match a caricatured walk to sound effects and a piece of music composed and mixed especially for it. The music is the opening sequence of "Easy Come, Easy Go," the film used as an example throughout this book:

1. Following the procedures detailed in Chapter 4, analyze the sound clip 00-00-00.WAV on this book's CD-ROM and transcribe it to exposure sheets. Pay special attention to marking hits for the sound of footsteps.

2. Animate a sad, slow walk, as in the previous project, but match the frame after the heel strike position to the footstep hits in the exposure sheet.

   Refer to the script in Chapter 2 and the storyboards in Chapter 3 for guidelines on camera angles and shot composition.

3. When you are satisfied with the animation, render it.

4. Using the AV editor of your choice, dub the sound file over your animation.

Quick Audio for Animation Tests

If you are using Adobe Premiere or another AV editor that lets you save a project, you can set up a dub project in which the WAV file is in place and an image sequence prefixed "TEST_" is in the first video track. Just render your wireframes or other quick tests to overwrite the original TEST_ files and you can load and run the Premiere project file to automatically dub the test animation. This is a little slower than most software's preview or wireframe mode, but it produces more accurate sync, and you can save your work.

If you match the first footstep and your track analysis is accurate, all the other footsteps should match as well.

Sneaks

The sneak is a time-honored part of the repertoire of any classically trained animator. What fun would an animated story be if no character snuck up on another? The comic potential for consequences befalling the sneaker or the intended victim are so rich, a sneak practically guarantees your audiences' full attention.

There are two basic classes of sneak: fast and slow.

The Fast Sneak

The fast sneak is essentially a compressed, fast walk on tiptoes. The hips and chest are pitched toward each other, as in the sad pose described earlier, to curve the spine and compress the body. The sneaker is trying to look as small as possible. The head is angled forward, and the eyes should either fixate on the intended victim or rove the scene nervously with the head following the eyes' lead.

The legs are bent throughout the sneak. If the sneaker straightened her legs, she would be a larger target. The stride is very short, with the thighs and knees rotating as little as possible. The feet are pitched downward, so only the toes make contact with the ground, and are also picked up higher than a standard walk, as if to avoid tripping over something.

The short stride, bent posture, and quick movement contribute a greater amount of up-and-down movement to the fast sneak, so the sneaker often appears to bob rapidly. The arms are carried high and the elbows are held close to the body. The arms do not swing to balance leg movement but are instead held ready to pounce.

 Animating the Puppet Doing a Fast Sneak

The sneaks are different enough from normal or caricature walks that you are probably better off starting from scratch than trying to adapt one of the actions you animated earlier:

1. Load the basic Puppet scene file you set up in Chapter 11.

2. Create a fast sneak passing pose at frame 1.

   The lifted foot should be level with the opposite knee, and the character's CG should be directly above or slightly in front of the grounded toes. The lifted thigh can be horizontal, or slightly above CG, for a really exaggerated sneak.

3. Create a fast sneak heel strike pose at frame 7.

   The toe should be planted slowly, not just slapped down, and the sneaker should immediately lean forward to move the CG toward the leading foot.

4. Create a fast sneak squash pose at frame 15.

As the CG moves over the leading foot, the leading knee must bend more to absorb the weight without being forced to drop the heel. The trailing foot lifts off the floor, again easing slowly (to avoid creaking floorboards).

5. Save the scene with a new file name. Render and play back the animation. Ignore the default interpolation for now. How does the timing of the key poses look? Are the keys too close together or too far apart? Use LightWave's keyframe editing tools to adjust the key poses' intervals.

6. Add keyframes and adjust the splines to add snap, anticipation, overlapping action, and follow-through to the sneak, just as you did for the walks and runs earlier in this chapter.

7. When you are satisfied with the animation, save it under a new name.

The Slow Sneak

The slow sneak is an elongated, slower walk, only partially on tiptoes. The action is a more rolling, fluid gait, with the intent being to cover as much ground as possible, as smoothly and quietly as possible. The hips and chest are pitched toward each other, and the head is angled forward in the squash position to curve the spine and compress the body. In the heel strike position—actually a toe strike, but let's not quibble—the angles are reversed to make the entire body a convex arc from head to leading toe.

The eyes, again, should either fixate on the intended victim or rove the scene nervously with the head following the eyes' lead. The legs range from a compressed pose as the trailing leg squashes to a full extension as the lead toe stretches toward the next footstep. The stride is quite long, at least equal to the normal walking stride. The feet are picked up higher in passing position than a standard walk, to avoid tripping. The long stride and slower movement smooth out the action, but the deeper squash position still exaggerates vertical motion.

PROJECT 15.14 Animating the Puppet Doing a Slow Sneak

To animate the Puppet doing a slow sneak, follow these steps:

1. Reload the default Puppet scene file, just as you did for the preceding exercise.

2. Create a slow sneak passing pose at frame 1.

   The lifted foot should be level with the opposite knee, and the character's CG should be directly above or slightly in front of the grounded foot, which is flat on the ground. The lifted thigh is not quite horizontal. The body should be nearly vertical, making the transition from the forward to the backward lean.

3. Create a fast sneak heel strike pose at frame 15 and supporting keys immediately following.

   The toe should be planted slowly, as if testing the floor for creaks. The body is leaning backward at full extension, counterbalancing the extended leg. After contact, the foot should be rolled slowly ball–to heel to make full sole contact with the ground. As the leading heel touches the ground, the sneaker begins to lean forward to move the CG toward the leading foot.

4. Create a fast sneak squash pose at frame 30.

   As the sneaker leans fully forward and the CG moves over the leading foot, the leading knee must bend more to absorb the weight. The trailing foot lifts off the floor, again easing slowly (to avoid creaking floorboards).

5. Save the scene with a new file name. Render and play back the animation. How does the timing of the key poses look? Are the keys too close together or too far apart? Use LightWave's keyframe editing tools to adjust the key poses' intervals until you are satisfied with the timing.

6. Add keyframes and adjust the splines to add snap, anticipation, overlapping action, and follow-through to the sneak, just as you did for the walks and runs earlier in this chapter.

7. When you are satisfied with the animation, save it under a new name.

Staging

Staging is the posing of a small action to foreshadow the character's next major action, preparing the audience to read it. Examples of staging are looking intently at the object of the action; pointing the hands toward the object, as if targeting it; and aligning the body to face the direction of the action. In real life, people tend to unconsciously stage their actions. Good negotiators and salespeople know this. You put your hands in your pockets when you really want something, to hide their involuntary twitching toward the object of your desire.

In animation, you should make your characters look at or point toward the object of the foreshadowed action in the reverse of the usual animation hierarchy order: eyes, head, hands, limbs, torso. You should also vary the lead timing of the eyes, depending on the nature of the following action. The more violent the action, the faster (shorter) you should make the staging.

 ## Staging a Reach

To stage the Puppet leaning on a street lamp, follow these steps:

1. Load the default Puppet scene file (the one with more detailed head and movable eyes), which you set up in Chapter 11. Add model Street.lwo from the Chapter 15 directory on this book's CD-ROM. Your scene should now contain the Puppet character and a one-piece set including storefront, sidewalk, street, and street lamp.

2. Pose the Puppet beside the street lamp in easy arm's-length leaning distance.

3. Animate the eyes first, to glance toward the street lamp.

4. Follow the motion of the eyes with a slight head turn.

5. Animate the hand nearest the street lamp to lift from the wrist, pointing the fingertips toward the post.

6. Animate the nearer arm to lift and the Puppet's body to lean toward the street lamp. Maintain the angle of the hand until the palm is parallel to the street lamp's surface.

7. Continue the Puppet's lean until the palm makes contact with the street lamp. Complete the leaning action with an elbow bend for squash, follow through, and rebound to a moving hold.

8. Animate the eyes and head to face the camera again.

9. Experiment with the timing and transitions for each key pose until you are satisfied with the animation.

Do you see how staging an action can help sell a shot? How the audience will read it better if they are prepared by a character's foreshadowing of the next action?

If you want to try a more humorous treatment of this project, have the Puppet glance toward the post, then nonchalantly look back toward the camera. As it leans toward the post, animate the wrist and arm to just barely miss the post. The Puppet should not react at all until its hand is several inches past the post. Improvise a fall. You may want to read through the next section to pick up some tips on weight and balance so you can better pose the Puppet's off-balance fall. Have fun with this one!

Balance and Mass

These two factors, balance and mass, are closely related, but you must handle them in completely different ways. You must animate balance with realism. Mass requires some of the most extreme exaggeration. Your characters must always keep their visible supports under their CG or the audience will wonder why they don't fall over. When a character's CG shifts, as when it picks up a heavy object, you must pose the character to place its feet under the new center of gravity.

Mass, on the other hand, simply begs for exaggeration. If you want to animate a character struggling with a heavy load, you can use every trick in the book: bent posture, stretch-and-squash arms, exaggerated anticipation, very slow accelerations upward, and dangerously fast ones downward, just to name a few. The comic uses of differential application are fun to play with too. Cool characters can appear to lift anything effortlessly; uncool characters can get squashed flat trying to move those same items.

Animating the Puppet Picking Up Objects

To animate the Puppet picking up objects, follow these steps:

1. Reload the default Puppet scene file you set up in Chapter 11. Add a variety of primitive objects, of sizes suitable for the Puppet to handle one- or two-handed.

2. Animate the Puppet picking up objects and moving them to different parts of the scene.

Assign any mass you like to the different objects, but be consistent. A small object can be very heavy (plutonium is apparently easy to come by in cartoonland), but it must remain heavy for the entire animation.

Pay attention to staging, shifting CG, and appropriate posing of legs and arms to brace the masses and maintain balance. Don't forget to add anticipation, overlapping action, follow-through, and especially, stretch-and-squash.

Takes, Double Takes, and Extreme Takes

A *take* is a character's overreaction to a surprise. The nature of the surprise can determine the appropriate extent or type of take, and the shot composition will determine whether you need to animate a full-body take or just a head take.

There are three key poses for all takes: the normal pose, the squash, and the stretch. Some takes require special in-betweens, but they all use the same key poses:

- A standard take starts out with a *normal* pose.

- The character presumably sees something to induce surprise. This causes the *squash* pose. The character's eyes squeeze shut as if to block out the sight, and the head (and possibly the entire character) recoils from the source of the surprise. Depending on the animation style and the construction of the character, this can be a literal squash.

- The next pose is the *stretch*, the reaction to the squash position. The character stretches out, eyes wide—just the opposite of the squash—commonly with an extremely surprised expression.

- The last part of the take is a return to the *normal* pose. Unless, of course, the character gets smashed flat by whatever caused the take in the first place.

Anticipation is very important to a take. For every action in a take, there should be a very pronounced anticipation in the opposite direction.

Animating the Puppet Doing a Take

To animate the Puppet doing a take, follow these steps:

1. Reload the default Puppet scene file you set up in Chapter 11.

2. From frame 1, set a key for all items at frames 4, 8, and 13.

3. Leave frame 1 as the normal pose. In frame 4, squash the character for a full-body take or just the head for a head take. Close the eyelids tightly. Clench the arms and legs tightly to the body. Make a keyframe to save the changes.

4. In frame 8, invert all the changes you made to frame 4, doubled. Stretch out everything you squashed, and open the eyelids wide. Fling the arms and legs out wide. Save the changes.

5. Leave frame 13 alone as the return to the normal pose. Save the scene with a new file name. Render and play back the animation.

You should experiment with the timing of the key poses and the splines connecting them. Try different amounts of snap in the transitions. How briefly can you hold a pose before the audience can't read it? How long can you hold a key pose, and what's the minimum animation needed in a moving hold to keep the character from going dead? How far from the root's keyframes can you push keyframes for the overlap of the extremities?

A double take is a regular take with a head shake between the squash and the stretch, as if the character is trying to deny what it sees.

PROJECT 15.18 Animating the Puppet Doing a Double Take

To animate the Puppet doing a double take, follow these steps:

1. Reload the scene you saved in the preceding exercise. Shift all the keyframes from the stretch pose down about 15 frames to give you room to insert a head shake.

2. Insert a head shake between the squash pose and the stretch pose. Make the shake very abrupt and snappy, with very little ease.

If you'd like a little more of a challenge, you can try to animate the double take depicted in Shot 4 of the storyboard in Chapter 3.

PROJECT 15.19 Animating the Puppet Doing an Extreme Take

This should be fun! Just follow these steps:

1. Reload the default Puppet scene file you set up in Chapter 11.

2. Given the limits available in this character's setup, see how close you can come to duplicating the extreme stretch pose of the take depicted in Shot 15 of the storyboards. Just how much stretch can you use before the character comes apart?

3. Try to create a matching squash pose.

Staggers

In animation, a *stagger* is when a character or object oscillates rapidly between two extreme poses, often in alternating frames, to give the appearance of vibrating from a shock or other overwhelming force. If one part of the character is affected more strongly by the impact, the remaining parts can be animated in overlapping action to emphasize the stagger. Stagger techniques can be very effective and, like takes and sneaks, are borrowed from classic cartoon animation.

You have several ways to create staggers in LightWave. You could simply move the staggered object on alternating frames, using linear interpolation and gradually diminishing the distance the object is displaced as the stagger tapers off. This should work well as long as Motion Blur is turned off or its percentage is set low enough that the key poses are visible.

If you want more detailed differences between the staggered poses, you could create separate extreme key poses on two successive frames—one odd, the other even. Then, duplicate each pose to alternating frames, keeping one pose on odd frames and the other on evens. When all the stagger poses have been duplicated, you work down the keyframes, incrementally reducing the extreme poses toward the "normal" pose at the end of the stagger. This is probably the most tedious method, but it does give very precise control—you can even animate gestures and lip sync during the course of the stagger.

You could also create three morph target objects with the two extreme poses plus a normal pose. If you set the objects up in a morph sequence with the normal pose as the baseline, you could simply vary the morph to create any sort of stagger pattern you wanted. One drawback to this technique is that morphing requires straight-line transitions. Any difference in the poses that required a rotation or bend is going to look really bad in the in-betweens.

PROJECT 15.20 Animating the Puppet Staggering

To animate the Puppet staggering, follow these steps:

1. Refer to Shot 11 from the storyboards in Chapter 3, where Fred gets hit by a windblown $1,000 bill.

2. Reload the default Puppet scene file.

3. Choose one of the preceding methods for creating a stagger, and try to animate an action like that depicted in Shot 11 as applied to the Puppet character.

Zip Pans

A *zip pan* is exactly like a stagger, except the camera gets oscillated instead of the character. This is very effective for animating earthquakes or high-speed character impacts with immovable objects. To create one in LightWave, simply edit the spline for the camera to create a single-framed zigzag line in the axis of the camera's vibration.

PROJECT 15.21 Animating the Puppet Hitting a Wall

To animate the Puppet hitting a wall, follow these steps:

1. Load the default Puppet scene and add the Street.lws model, as you did for the earlier project.

2. Animate the Puppet hitting the storefront wall, from extreme squash and stretch and rebound to moving hold. Make sure you include the overlapping action of the arms and legs because they would rebound faster and flop around while the main body was still stuck to the wall.

3. Animate a zip pan of the camera, synchronized to the impact of the Puppet against the wall.

4. Experiment with the timing and duration of the zip pan to discover what works for you.

Sorting Out the Animation Hierarchy

The animation hierarchy is not always going to start with the hips, CG, or even the body of a character. Sometimes the center of a composition is one of the extremities. In cases like this, the center of the composition temporarily becomes the root of the character's hierarchy. Reasoning from earlier statements about animating from the root of the hierarchy outward, it seems logical to pose models in the current order of importance. The root of the animation hierarchy can change, even within a single shot. If the character's hand is the center of the composition, you should pose the hand first and make the rest of the figure follow naturally from the hand. This is where a good constraint setup can make the animator's job easy—or nearly impossible.

Get Unreal!

One of the most challenging fields in LightWave character animation is motion picture special effects. Creatures like *Dragonheart*'s Draco, *Dinosaur*'s eponymous characters, and *Alien Resurrection*'s swimming horrors represent the state of the art in fantastic creature creation and character animation. In each case, the goal was to make the audience believe that the creatures on the screen were alive. To achieve this, the character designers had to work out all the details of anatomy and kinesiology that would affect how the creatures looked and acted. In the case of *Dinosaur*, they were able to extrapolate from the work of generations of paleontologists. For the other two, sheer fantasy was to be brought to life.

If you want to do the same, you need to study anatomy, physiology, zoology, anthropometry, kinesiology, and a host of other disciplines. Not enough to get a degree, mind you; just enough to soak up the basic principles and learn where the really good references are. You can always look up the details of the *orbicularis oculi*, but at least you'll know what to ask for. Once you understand how the underlying structure—the muscles, tendons, and other tissues—all contribute to the way a creature looks and moves, devising a realistic-looking simulation of a completely fantastic character does not seem so impossible.

Getting Your Point Across: Acting by Proxy

This section shows you how to apply acting technique to character animation, covering posing, gesture, mannerisms, and emphasis. Animating for emotional communication requires at least as good a sense of timing as stage acting. In fact, acting classes are a pretty good idea for an animator—they break down inhibitions about performing and can acquaint you with a lot of references on physical expression that apply as well to animation as to live action.

There are many resources available on acting technique. These resources can help you define a mood or attitude with a pose. The essential truths of acting, whether on stage or through character animation, are based on natural, observed behavior. If you want to become a better animator, study candid photos and films of people who are not acting but reacting to real-world situations. I strongly encourage you to take movement classes of any kind, but acting or mime classes are generally best for animation purposes.

Show Some Character

A character is defined by its actions. To define a character, you will have to animate some sequence of actions that tells your audience who this character is.

> *"Get everything to read just in the acting, the pantomime, then when you stick the face on, it'll only plus that."*
> —Pete Docter, *The Making of Toy Story*

The basis of all action is posture, the broadest stroke of establishing mood. A change in posture, with all else remaining the same, can completely change the effect of a scene.

Posture can be defined as the line from the feet to the head, but I prefer to include the upper arms, and sometimes the entire body as well. The eyes always lead a change in posture, preparing the audience for the following action. If the character becomes sad, the eyes drop first; if the character becomes happy, the eyes open wider and sparkle.

As you learned in earlier chapters, you must work to create consistently strong poses. You can judge this by testing them in silhouette, as described earlier in this chapter. Make this testing a habitual part of your work flow so it becomes second nature.

You must time transitions so the audience has a chance to read them, but don't make them so long that the audience is bored and their attention wanders. Never start an action within the first quarter second of a shot—you must allow your audience at least that much time to adjust to the new camera angle and contents of the scene before they are ready to read an action. If you start an action too early in the shot, your audience may miss it entirely.

If the scene setup has been done well, your job as animator will be much simpler. You can use the standard scene views to relate the character to its environment and use the dedicated detail views (see Chapter 11 for details) to see the close-ups you'll need when you pose the face or hands of a complex character.

Don't forget to follow the animation hierarchy when animating changes in posture. The same rules apply for saving time, effort, and aggravation whether you're animating a simple walk cycle or a very complex dramatic performance.

PROJECT 15.22 What a Moody Guy!

The goal of this project is to create a series of strong, dramatic poses:

1. Reload the default Puppet scene file.

2. From frame 1, create a keyframe for all objects at frame 30.

   Let's suppose the character starts off in a normal pose, then is given some very sad news by an opponent we don't see. Suppose the opponent then threatens the character, frightening him. Next, the opponent ridicules the character, causing the character's fear to transition to anger. Finally, the character's anger causes the opponent to leave, and the character exults in his victory. That's four major emotional poses: sadness, fear, anger, and exultation.

3. Pose the character in frame 30 in an expression of sadness. Remember to pose the character in order, using the animation hierarchy. Set the hips first, then the chest, and so on.

   You have a number of options for figuring out what a sad posture looks like. You can find a full-length mirror and look at yourself while acting sad. You can find a movie or news video that shows a real person or a good actor acting sad. You can look for a sad pose from a traditional cartoon or comic strip. You can ask someone else to act sad for you. You can look up an example of a sad pose in one of the references cited earlier.

   If you can't find your own example of a sad posture, here are a few suggestions: Slump the chest forward and tilt the hips back. For this character, this is the closest pose to curving the spine and slumping the shoulders. Make the arms hang straight down, as if the character has neither the energy nor the inclination to do anything else with them. Pitch the head forward, and track the character's eyes to look at the ground in front of him. It's difficult to avoid a twins pose when mimicking sadness—the general lack of energy in the character seems to preclude any difference between the sides. To avoid the appearance of twins, rely on three-quarter camera angles for sad poses.

4. Make a key for the character at frame 30 to save the sad pose. Repeat Step 2 to create a "normal" key at frame 60.

5. In frame 60, pose the character to express fear.

   Again, try to extract the essence of a fearful pose from your own observations.

   A fearful pose is a natural progression, both emotionally and physically, from the posture of sadness. The concave slump of hips and chest is held a little deeper, and the knees bend to lower the body even further. The arms are posed with the elbows held close to the body and bent sharply to bring the hands, open and palm forward, in front of the chest as if to ward off an attack. A little jitter in the hands protecting the body will add to the expression.

The head is pitched back, looking up, and the eyes tracked to the object of the fear. In this case, pick a point where an opponent's face would be, a few steps in front of the character you are posing. To avoid a twins pose, tweak bank and heading to turn the head slightly away from the direction of the eyes, move one foot a little behind the other, and raise one hand slightly above the level of the other.

6. Make a key for the character at frame 60 to save the fearful pose. Repeat Step 2 to create a "normal" key at frame 90.

7. In frame 90, pose the character to express anger.

An angry pose is a very strong dramatic change—from a passive, weak pose that folds the character in on itself to a strong, aggressive pose that extends the character to full height and toward the object of the anger. Straighten the alignment of the hips and chest and pitch the hips forward so the entire character is leaning toward the imaginary character with a ramrod-straight spine.

Trail one foot farther back and advance the other as if in the first step of an attack on the opponent, keeping the character's CG between the feet for proper balance. Rotate the arms to bring the hands down to waist level and clench the hands into fists. Keep the eyes tracked on the opponent's face, but rotate the head to match the eyes' alignment, with a little extra pitch to make the jaw jut out aggressively.

8. Make a key for the character at frame 90 to save the angry pose. Repeat Step 2 to create a "normal" key at frame 120.

9. In frame 120, pose the character to express exultation.

You're on your own for this one. I'm sure you can come up with something.

10. Evaluate all four poses in silhouette. Look for strength, readability, and no twins. Tweak the poses as necessary.

11. When you are satisfied with the four dramatic poses, save the scene under a new name.

You've got a logical series of solid, dramatic poses. Now, let's see you connect them with appropriate in-betweens and timing.

PROJECT 15.23 Timing Transitions

To complete this project, follow these steps:

1. Render and play back the animation from the preceding project.

LightWave automatically creates smooth interpolations between the key poses you set. This action looks too smooth, more hydraulic than human or caricature. The changes all happen at the same time, too. There is no overlapping action, anticipation, or follow-through. You need to change that by setting more keyframes that add anticipation, snap, moving holds, overlapping action, and follow-through to the animation. These are the same procedures you learned earlier in this chapter and in Chapter 14.

2. Hide all of the hierarchy except the hips (or pelvis, depending on your naming preferences).

   You'll be using the animation hierarchy again, posing the root of the hierarchy throughout the animation before proceeding to the next level.

3. Add keyframes, and use the spline control tools to animate a sharper snap between key poses and to add a very slight motion around each key pose to produce a moving hold.

   The largest part of the transition from one pose to the next should occur over just a few frames, starting with an abrupt change at the end of the preceding pose's moving hold. An ease to a moving hold should occupy the rest of the interval. Remember, if your character holds perfectly still for even a few frames, it will lose the illusion of life and become dead.

   Consider how long the transition between two key poses should take. The transition between fear and anger, for example, should happen much faster than that between normal and sadness. How long does it take you to get angry when someone plays a nasty trick on you? Relocate the key poses to shorten or lengthen a transition.

   Keep in mind that the root of the hierarchy carries the load of moving the entire character. The pitch or heading of the hips has to give the impression of driving the mass of the whole character, so don't use quite as much snap for the root of the hierarchy as you would for the higher, less-massive levels.

4. Save the scene with a new file name. Render and play back the animation. Critique the animation of the hips and make revisions until you are satisfied with this level of the animation hierarchy.

5. Make the next level of the hierarchy visible.

6. Repeat Steps 3 and 4 for this level of the hierarchy.

   When you add keyframes, make sure they aren't all on the same frames as the keys for other parts of the character. Different parts of a character should reach their extreme poses at different times. If all the parts peak together, the animation loses continuity. Always keep some part of the character moving, especially during long moving holds.

   For each higher level of the animation hierarchy, make the snaps a little sharper, the eases a little shorter. Each level has less mass to move and can, therefore, speed up and slow down faster. The higher levels of the animation hierarchy can also vary more during a moving hold. A 5-degree twitch in a finger is not nearly as noticeable as a 5-degree twitch in the chest.

7. Repeat Step 5, then Steps 3 and 4 again, for each level of the hierarchy.

8. When you are satisfied with the entire animation's timing and all the additional keyframes, save the scene. Render and play back the animation.

You should end up with a series of dramatic transitions that have strong poses; read well; show appropriate anticipation, snap, overlapping action, and follow-through; and hold well without going dead. Don't be discouraged if your first try at this animation isn't as good as you hoped—timing emotional transitions well takes lots of practice. Make up other sequences of emotional transitions and animate them for practice. Pivotal scenes from plays or movies are excellent source material for animating emotional transitions.

Gestures and Mannerisms

Body language and hand gestures are an international language. Although some gestures have special meanings in certain countries or regions, there are many gestures that have almost universal meanings. Your characters will seem much more lively and self-motivated if they use gestures and body language to emphasize the message of their posture.

You can build up a repertoire of gestures by your own observation, but I recommend studying one or more of the available books on the subject. Desmond Morris's *Bodytalk* is one of the more accessible works on the subject and includes notes on regional usage.

Mannerisms are a personal version of gestural communication. A particular motion, gesture, or posture may have a special meaning when expressed by one character but not when used by another. Mannerisms are only effective in repetition. If one of your characters displays a mannerism, it will probably not be interpreted correctly by your audience the first time they see it. With repetition, the audience can associate the mannerism with the character and understand the intended message. Over time, a mannerism can become a character's identifying characteristic. One has only to think of the phrase, "What's up, Doc?" to realize how powerful a mannerism can become.

Both gestures and mannerisms should help to further define the character. Whenever you pose a character, ask yourself, "Could another character hold that pose to get that effect?" If the answer is "Yes," the pose doesn't help define the character—it's weak and should be changed. A gesture, mannerism, or other action should specifically and exclusively define the character performing the action.

The hands are a rich source of expression. Most gestures involve at least one hand, and many require both. The average character's hands have more joints than the rest of the body combined, even when using the classic three-fingered cartoon character gloves. The most important guideline for animating character hands is to avoid mittens, the tendency to clump all the fingers side by side in an undifferentiated lump. Even if an illustrated gesture shows the fingers aligned, it's a good idea to express some individuality by moving one of the fingers slightly out of line.

The hands are closely watched, ranking right behind the eyes and face in attracting your audience's attention. You should therefore practice animating hands and pay at least as much attention to fine-tuning them as you do to the rest of the character's body. Also, try to keep the hands above the waist unless you intend the character to look exhausted or sad.

 Get Over Here!

The goal of this project is to apply what you've learned about posture, gesture, and mannerisms to animate a unique performance for the character:

1. Reload the default Puppet scene file again.

2. For the first keyframe, pose the character to show an imperious, pompous attitude. Use your imagination. I'm sure you can think of a suitable model.

3. Make additional keyframes at appropriate distances. Pose the character to summon another (unseen) character; use hand gestures and posture to communicate the action and define the character.

   Typical poses might include a forceful pointing movement with a fully extended arm in the direction of the unseen character, a withdrawal of the extended arm, and a second forceful pointing movement down toward the pointing character's feet, as if to say, "You! Get over here!" as one would summon a dog.

   Pay special attention to the nuances of the hand pose. Don't forget to stage the action by pointing the hand first.

4. Animate the character waiting impatiently for the summoned character to respond.

   Animate whatever waiting twitches you prefer. Toe-tapping, clenched fists on hips, or crossed arms are all good indicators of impatience.

5. Animate the character directing the summoned character.

   Lots of pointing fingertip jabs should communicate the idea adequately.

6. Animate the character dismissing the summoned character.

   This is comparatively easy; you can use a backhanded flipping hand motion as dismissal, while the rest of the character is animated to be looking elsewhere, bored. Remember to keep an upright, imperious posture throughout the animation.

7. Save the scene with a new file name. Render and play back the animation. Tweak the moving holds, timing, and other settings as necessary. When you are satisfied with the animation, save the scene.

PROJECT 15.25 Come Here, Please

To complete this project, follow these steps:

1. Repeat Project 15.23, but this time create a more persuasive character.

   This is a variation on a theme: Animate the character to summon, direct, and dismiss an unseen subject in a cajoling way. Spend more time on the directing part, using lots of encouraging and even imploring hand gestures.

2. Save the scene with a new file name. Render and play back the animation. Tweak the moving holds, timing, and other settings as necessary. When you are satisfied with the animation, save the scene.

PROJECT 15.26 Would You Care to Step This Way?

To complete this project, follow these steps:

1. Repeat Project 15.23 again, but this time create an extremely diplomatic and polite character.

   The character should spend a good amount of time bowing and making other polite, considerate gestures. The key pose groups might be described as invitation, ingratiation, negotiation, and farewell.

2. Save the scene with a new file name. Render and play back the animation. Tweak the moving holds, timing, and other settings as necessary. When you are satisfied with the animation, save the scene.

Timing Is Still Everything

Timing actions to emphasize lip sync dialogue is the best way to sell a shot. If the action is timed well, even poor lip sync looks acceptable. If the action is not timed to emphasize the dialogue properly, even excellent lip sync will not look very good.

When you are working with a lip sync exposure sheet, one approach to accents is to listen to the track and mark each syllable that the voice talent emphasized. You can animate physical gestures like head nods to emphasize the dialogue. These forms of emphasis always precede the actual syllable.

Try it yourself. Read a particularly dramatic bit of prose or poetry while watching yourself in the mirror and you will see that you nod or lift your head well before the sound you are accenting.

You will probably need to experiment at first, but a good starting offset is three to six frames. In the Action column of the exposure sheet, simply write the emphasis (*nod* or *lift*) for the desired number of frames in advance of the lip sync frames.

PROJECT 15.27 A Dramatic Reading, Sans Mouth

To complete this project, follow these steps:

1. Play back the Finest Hour WAV clip on this book's CD-ROM. Note the emphasized syllables and mark them on the exposure sheet from Chapter 4.

2. Transpose all the emphasis marks from three to six frames to allow for physical emphasis to precede the sound.

3. Load the default Puppet scene file again.

4. Animate the character according to your modified exposure sheet.

   Because the character does not yet have a mouth, you will need to convey the desired emphasis by head and body motions alone.

5. Using the editing software of your choice, dub the provided sound track over the rendered animation to check the sync.

6. When you are satisfied with the quality of the finished piece, save the file under a new name.

Moving On

If you have learned (and continue to practice) the principles of character animation described in this and the preceding chapter, you should have a solid repertoire of performances. Don't neglect these basics, even after you've moved on to the complexities and challenges of animation power tools, as shown in the next chapter.

Chapter 16

Power Tool Animation

Power tools and procedural setups, like any animation tools, are only as good as the animator applying them. You need to know when a power tool will save you work without reducing the quality of the final animation and when the power tool will drag down the quality of your work. Power tools are seductive, and you need to have a well-developed suspicion of inflated claims or inappropriate applications.

The preceding chapters show you the essential tools, processes, and skills you need to create good character animation using computers. Chapter 13 introduces a class of optional tools, power tools that you can use to create animation with less effort (sometimes) by giving more animation control to the computer. Sometimes, the trade-off in control isn't worth it, but sometimes, the right power tool can make a difficult or impossible shot feasible.

As an animator, you need to strike a balance somewhere between posing individual vertices frame-by-frame and winding up behavioral actors. Most animators will agree that hand-animating every particle in your character's universe is too much control. Most animators will also agree that directing a behavioral actor to go through a sequence of preset motions is not truly character animation. There is a vast gray area between these two extremes, and you will have to choose your own boundaries.

How much should you automate? Computers are like fire—powerful tools but terrible masters. In LightWave character animation, as in many computer-dominated fields, there is a strong tendency to rely too heavily on the computer. It's the old hammer-and-nail dilemma again. As long as the computer is relieving you of the mindless drudgery associated with traditional animation production, well and good. If the computer begins to cramp or fight part of your creative style, it's time to back up and take another look at who's *really* running things. Computers are simply complex tools—don't ever let them dictate your creative options.

Some of the most useful character animation power tools have applications for lip sync, facial animation, cloth simulation, physical simulation, and hair. This chapter shows you how to animate these phenomena effectively, building on the power tool setups detailed in Chapter 13 to improve the quality of your animation.

Lip Sync

Lip sync is generally the finishing touch, the last tweak that makes a big difference. The pantomime and composition may get your main point across, but it's the subtlety of the facial animation that really sells the shot to your audience. It's amazing what you can convey by using a well-arched eyebrow instead of a whole-body shrug or gesture.

It seems that everybody who learns character animation is initially excited about doing lip sync. OK, we'll work through lip sync first (animators have to know how to do it), then move on to more important things.

"Why this attitude," you ask? Good question! Lip sync is arguably the least creative of character animation tasks. You are slavishly following the frame-by-frame timing of the voice talent, and you have little leeway in which to be creative with the timing. Your audience is sensitive to glitches in lip sync and will often criticize an otherwise fine animation job based on a few mismatched frames.

Furthermore, because the process is so closely coupled to the sound track, a lot of R&D work has been done on completely automating it. For example, the proprietary software used by Mainframe Entertainment to animate *Reboot* and *Beast Wars* uses a component called *GRIN* that automates lip sync. Other animation houses probably have similar software in use or development. LightWave plug-in developers have typically added new functions to desktop software within a few years of their high-end proprietary development. My advice, therefore, is not to spend a lot of time mastering lip sync; it most likely will be automated by a plug-in very soon.

This is not to say you shouldn't work through the projects in this chapter. At the least, you'll understand what the old hands are talking about when they complain about doing lip sync the old-fashioned way.

Lip sync starts, as does everything else in animation, with a lot of foresight and planning. If your goal is the best quality lip sync, you don't even need to think about animating for lip sync until the script and storyboards are finalized, the voice talent has recorded all her tracks, and the director and editor have pieced together the takes they want for the final sound track. Once the sound track is locked (at least as far as the dialogue is concerned), the track can be analyzed and the exposure sheets (x-sheets) written up (see Chapter 4 for details).

What you will be given on the x-sheets is a frame-by-frame phonetic breakdown of the vocal track, along with all the other information about action, camera directions, and so on. For this set of projects, you can ignore everything but the phonetic breakdown.

Lip sync is one of the skills that transfer directly from traditional stop-motion or cel animation to LightWave. There is a 70-year body of work on synchronizing sound to animation, most of it already available to the animator in book or video form. There is little call for cut-and-try experimenting when it comes to lip sync.

Timing for Lip Sync

Timing good lip sync isn't just a matter of sticking an *A* map in the frame where the x-sheet is marked "a." Different phonemes are held for different lengths of time and transition to and from other phonemes in different ways. Here are a few rules to keep in mind:

- *Snap open, close slow*—The mouth should snap open quickly in a single frame, two at the most, to full extension for vowels. It should close much more slowly to hold the vowel.

- *Hold for emphasis*—Hold important or emphasized vowels longer, just as you hold an important pose.

- *Shut up with in-betweens*—Use transition or in-between maps when closing the mouth slowly from a held phoneme.

- *Explosive plosives*—The "T," "D," "B," and "P" cannot be held. Snap them out in a frame or two or your character will look mush-mouthed.

- *Speed kills*—Don't try to keep up with a very fast speaker or your audience won't catch it. If the mouth actions become too frenetic, use in-betweens rather than full poses for alternating mouth actions.

- *Watch yourself*—Just as discussed in the preceding chapter, you are your own best model. Keep a mirror handy. Most professional animators keep a nice-sized mirror propped right next to their monitors when doing facial animation. When in doubt about a mouth action, pronounce it yourself and observe what your face does.

Mapped Lip Sync

Just about every book on cel or cartoon animation has a section on lip sync, usually including a model sheet of basic drawings for the mouth. These drawings can be adapted directly as image maps for the following projects. The image maps reproduced in Figure 9.29 are provided with the Magpie Pro track analysis software.

If your technical director (TD) has not already made up a phonetic map library, or if you are doing everything yourself, you can either use the map library provided on this book's CD-ROM or create your own maps. If you choose to roll your own, refer to Chapter 13 for details on their construction and application.

Animating with image sequences generally provides the lowest level of realism in animation. Stylistically, this method lends itself to a number of approaches. The burden of realism or style is lifted from the TD or sculptor building the objects and transferred to the artist drawing the maps. The map artist can therefore employ almost any drawing style, ranging from the harshest minimalist abstractions to the softest, most realistic textures possible. With the right image processing software and a good deal of patience, it is possible for a talented graphic artist to turn a primitive egg shape into a photorealistic human face and head.

That goal is beyond the purpose of the projects in this chapter. We'll concentrate on a very simple approach—the standard cartoon mouth shapes applied to the face object you animated in Chapter 14.

You can use a color image sequence to change the surface colors of the object, painting on the mouth shapes. If the background of the color maps is not the exact shade of the object, you may need to apply matching alpha maps to make the background of the color maps transparent.

These image sequences can be used alone if it suits the style of the animation. This is the simplest approach, but it will not change the profile or give any impression of a third dimension to the mouth. Also, any specularity or diffusion spot will continue to reflect from the open mouth, spoiling the effect, as in Figure 16.1.

Figure 16.1
Head with color and alpha mouth image maps applied.

The next step in complexity—a precisely matched bump or displacement image sequence—gives the lips the appearance of some depth. A bump map permits the use of a simpler object, but it will not alter the profile of the object and is less realistic. If you use a displacement image sequence, it will alter the profile of the object. The trade-off is that the object must have a finely divided geometry in the area to be mapped or the mouth will appear to have unsightly jags. With the combination of color, alpha, and either bump or displacement image sequences, any specularity or diffusion spot will still reflect from the open mouth, as in Figure 16.2.

Figure 16.2
Head with color, alpha, and bump mouth image maps applied.

The last level of image sequence mapping is the addition of a matched clip image sequence. The clip map cuts away the surface of the object where the mouth is open to reveal the teeth, tongue, and inner mouth surfaces, as shown in Figure 16.3.

Obviously, the border between the inner edge of the lips and the opening of the mouth must be carefully drawn or the lips will appear jagged or uneven. Although it is possible to dither and otherwise cheat the resolution of both color and bump images, the clip images should be the highest resolution consistent with memory resources.

With the clip image sequence, the highest level of mapped realism is possible. If the bump or displacement map is drawn correctly, the clip should occur exactly where the surface is distorted to a 90-degree angle, and the clipping will take effect exactly where the surface would disappear if it were modeled in three dimensions. The only giveaways will be at this abrupt edge of the lips. If the camera is positioned at an angle approximately tangent to the lips, the inner surface of the object's face may be visible. You should avoid these camera angles if you use clip mapping.

"You pays your money and you takes your chances;" every cheat and trick used in animation has its downside. Your challenge as an animator or TD is to make those choices depending on the demands of the job at hand.

Figure 16.3
Head with color, alpha, bump, and clip mouth image maps applied.

Track Analysis

Track analysis is not really difficult, just painstaking. There are a relatively small number of *phonemes*, or unique sounds, used by all spoken human languages. Track analysis is the art of transcribing exactly when each phoneme occurs in a voice track.

I highly recommend keeping a good dictionary handy while analyzing vocal tracks; it can save you a lot of time while you are developing your track-reading skills. Any good dictionary will have a pronunciation guide. This will list all the phonemes for the dictionary's language and explain the letters and diacritical marks used in phonetic spelling. I recommend that you use the following cheat until you can rely on your own skills: Make up a copy of the script for the vocal track, double- or even triple-spaced so you can write legibly under or over each word. Look up each word in the dictionary. Copy the phonetic spelling of each word under the normal spelling in the script. Now you know exactly what phonemes you need and in what order.

Project 16.1 shows you the basics of track analysis using Magpie Pro. Magpie Pro is a track analysis program written by Miguel Grinberg. The Magpie directory on this book's CD-ROM contains a demo version of the program. Magpie Pro is copyrighted shareware, and you may evaluate it for a period of no more than 30 days. After this time, you must either register and pay for it or remove it from your system. Failure to comply with this condition is a violation of international copyright law—not to mention being very rude to Mr. Grinberg, who graciously makes this software available to animators worldwide. If you use it, please pay for it. For details on registering and free updates, please refer to the information files in the Magpie directory on this book's CD-ROM.

To run Magpie Pro, you need a PC-compatible computer running Windows NT/95/98, 16MB RAM, about 5MB free hard disk space, a true color graphics display, and an MCI device capable of playing 8- or 16-bit WAV audio files. Magpie Pro has many improvements and additional features over Magpie 1, including a live-action reference video window, multiple simultaneous expression sets, whole-word libraries, and speech recognition to automate first-pass lip sync (Figure 16.4). Magpie Pro also supports both Morph Gizmo for LightWave 5.5 and EndoMorphs for LightWave [6]. To take full advantage of these export formats, Magpie Pro now includes a spline editor you can use to tweak transitions between expressions. These new features put Magpie Pro solidly in the professional animator's must-have toolkit.

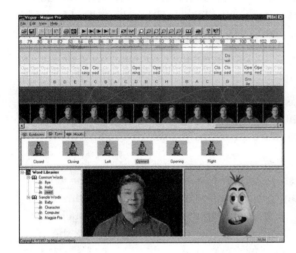

Figure 16.4
The Magpie Pro interface with a demo file loaded.

Track Analysis Using Magpie Pro

PROJECT 16.1   We'll be using a digitized sample from a speech by Sir Winston Churchill, THISHOUR.WAV, which you can find on this book's CD-ROM. The phrase is "This...was their finest hour." You can complete the following project more easily if you transcribe this phrase in phonetic spelling before you begin:

1. Follow the instructions for installing Magpie Pro, which you can find in the Magpie directory on this book's CD-ROM. You should immediately add the character expression set you created in Chapter 13 so you have phoneme expressions to work with. When installation is complete, start Magpie Pro.

   The Waveform pane displays the sound file you will be analyzing. Magpie Pro opens up by default with no sound file loaded.

2. Open the THISHOUR.WAV audio file from the Chapter 16 directory on this book's CD-ROM. Opening up a new WAV file automatically loads a clean session for you to work on.

3. Click on the Play button to hear the WAV file.

4. Each pair of vertical lines in the Waveform pane brackets a single frame. Select the second frame from the left by clicking on it once. The frame turns red. Double-click on the frame to hear it play. You can tell from your phonetic transcript (and from listening carefully) that the sound at this frame is a soft "TH" sound, the first phoneme of the word "this."

5. The Magpie Pro interface refers to phoneme images as expressions. Double-click on the expression labeled TH. Magpie Pro copies the expression labeled TH to the second frame of the Exposure Sheet pane. The TH image appears in the Preview pane.

6. Repeat Steps 4 and 5 for all the other frames, listening carefully and matching the sounds to your phonetic transcript.

At any time during this process, you can use the different Play buttons to play the entire sound, only the selected frames, or everything up to or following the selected frames. As the sound plays back, the images matching the expressions you selected will also play back in the Preview window.

What you will be doing is looking—and listening—for characteristic shapes in the waveform that correspond to phonemes. Human speech is made up mostly of clicks, buzzes, and hisses. For example, a sharp spike—a click—can represent a plosive sound such as "P" and "B." The word "baby" would therefore have two spikes, and you would mark the frames next to those spikes with the letter "B." Buzzing phonemes like "M" or "N" show up as relatively even zigzags with very similar individual waveforms sustained over a number of frames. A hissing "S" or "C" looks a lot like static, just a little louder.

Rather than go into a rambling theoretical discussion of all the different phonemes and how they are produced, I'm going to encourage you to experiment and develop your own rules. This all goes back to the principles discussed in Chapter 15—you can take someone else's word for it, or you can observe and draw your own conclusions. Observing speech is a wonderful way to lose your preconceptions about how people communicate.

If you are working with a large audio file, you may need to use the Zoom In and Zoom Out tools to see frames more clearly.

Find the plosives and clicks in the audio file. Look for peaks or other sharp changes within the word. Select and play them back until you can identify their start at a particular frame.

You can select more than one frame in the Waveform pane by dragging the mouse. All the selected frames will turn red. Double-clicking on a phoneme in the Mouth pane will assign that Mouth to all the selected frames.

Find the buzzes and hisses. These will appear as relatively even areas, drawn out over several frames. Select all the affected frames and assign the appropriate Mouth shape.

The remaining phonemes will probably be mostly vowels. They tend to fill in everywhere but the clicks, buzzes, and hisses. They are also the most visible mouth shapes to animate because they are held longer and generally require more facial distortion.

7. When you are satisfied with your results, save the file.

   Magpie Pro saves the session, including expression settings and the path to the original audio file, in a Magpie Pro format with the extension .mgp.

8. Choose the File|Export|Animation File menu option. In the Video For Windows Export panel, set the options to output an uncompressed AVI.

   As you can see, Magpie Pro's combination of visual and audible feedback is a great help to track analysis. The features added since the original Magpie—voice recognition, spline controls, shape weighting output, and so on—make this program even more valuable to the character animator. To contact Miguel Grinberg—preferably to tell him how much you like Magpie Pro, but also for technical support—you can send him email at **miguelg@teleport.com**.

9. In LightWave, load and apply the Magpie AVI to the character's face surface.

10. Test render a few frames at a high enough resolution that you can check for map misalignments. Compare the maps in the rendered frames to the x-sheet callouts to make sure they match.

11. If all the spot checks are OK, test render the entire shot in 1/4 screen resolution as an AVI. Be careful to use the same frame rate as the x-sheet. This is for the next step in checking, before you commit the time to rendering at full resolution and antialiasing.

12. In an editing program such as Premiere, dub the lip sync WAV file over the rendered AVI. Render the results to a new AVI file.

13. Play back the dubbed file to see if the lip sync reads accurately. Make sure the playback is locked to the frame rate at which you animated it.

If you have to slip the entire shot, use LightWave's offset function or slip the sound track in Adobe Premiere. In LightWave, using a positive Frame Offset value is like slipping the image sequence ahead. Add an Offset of 5 and the sequence image for frame 15 will be used in frame 10 of the animation. Conversely, using a negative Offset value is like retarding the image sequence. A value of -5 means frame 15 of the sequence will be used for frame 20 of the animation.

Usually, you will want to push the image sequence ahead so the screen has a chance to show the lip image before the audience hears the phoneme. Some animation houses slip the images ahead of the audio track three or four frames as a matter of standard procedure. Nobody seems to know why, but it works for the audience.

You should now have a solid grasp of the principles of lip sync. Play around with this setup a little more, making it say anything you like. Follow the procedures in Project 4.9 to break out your own x-sheets from digitized sound samples, and in Chapters 9 and 13 to create additional mouth maps for caricatured mouth actions.

As with most skills in character animation, you can learn the basics of lip sync very quickly, but honing and polishing your timing and caricature skills is a lifetime pursuit.

Lip sync for either replacement or displacement animation uses the same principles. Each has the advantage of providing its own in-betweens, which means you only have to model or pose the actual keyframes. If you really like doing lip sync, you can repeat Project 16.1 using these techniques.

Dialogue with Weighted Shapes

In Chapter 13, you learned that LightWave's EndoMorph or weighted shape setups are especially versatile for facial animation. You can create many lip shapes, including those necessary for lip sync, with only a few weight maps. When a neutral is modified by just three targets—open, raised smile and pursed lips—you can get a lot more workmanlike dialogue lip synced than you'd think. Note that it will take some experimentation with this approach to pull the most from it as an animator. The shapes you want as an animator more often come from combinations of simpler targets.

Try something simple at first, like drawing out the word "meow." The mouth closes, A, with either a closed mouth target or a negative value of the open for the consonant, B, then reveals teeth as the mouth broadens into a raised smile, C. Keeping the raised smile target, you may want to introduce a slight negative value of the pursed lips target, D, to widen the smile.

While opening the mouth for the "ow" (Figure 16.5, left), use the negative value of the smile to move the mouth down while it opens (right). Then fade out the open mouth in favor of the pursed lips (Figure 16.6, left), but keep bringing that raised smile from the negative back up, and keep it there while fading out the pursed lips (right). When you act it out in front of a mirror, you can see it and feel which targets to use.

If you feel compelled to hit every imaginable phoneme, you might spend some time animating to some old Lenny Bruce routines. If you can read the lips of your cute cuddly corporate icon mouthing the seven words George Carlin can't say on the air, you're ready for anything, maybe even a guest spot on *South Park*.

The temptation is to go overboard at first, nailing every phoneme. Get it out of your system, a little goes a long way. Use weighted shapes for the broad strokes, refining if you have to. In general, dialogue is the last thing to think about, after you've acted everything out with your

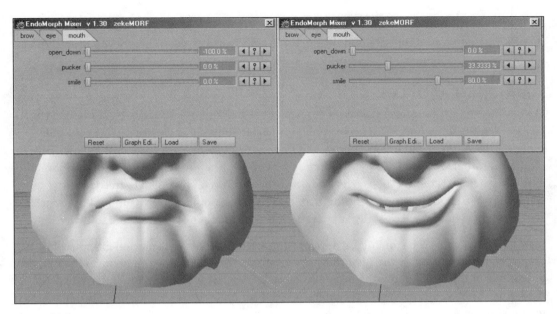

Figure 16.5
First syllable of "meow."

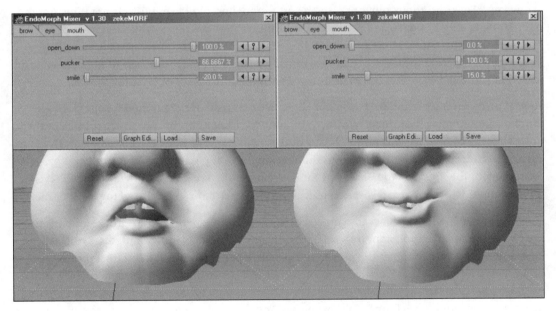

Figure 16.6
Second syllable of "meow."

body and the attitude of the head. You can use a few extra targets just to exaggerate the mouth moving around the face and hitting some emotive expressions before you even think about synchronizing just a few carefully selected phonemes.

Animating with LipService

LipService is a fairly successful attempt to reconcile the dichotomy that is part of the lip sync process. On the one hand, lip sync key poses are dictated by the voice track, with very little room for the animator to interpret how long or how strongly to emphasize a phoneme. This requires a rather technical, analytical approach. On the other hand, the facial animation to express emotions is highly subjective, and the animator has a great deal of freedom (and responsibility) to create a strong performance. This requires a fluid, improvisational approach. The problem is how to successfully support both these approaches in the same software.

Joe Alter's LipService is a standalone application plus a LightWave displacement map plug-in. There is a demo version in the Alter directory on this book's CD-ROM. You perform the lip sync operations in the application, then import objects and deformation files into LightWave for rendering. Once you have a set of phoneme objects set up in LipService, as described in Chapter 13, you can load a WAV file and start setting keyframes.

You can drag the frame slider with the mouse or step frame-by-frame using the left and right arrow keys. For continuous playback, the reverse, stop, and play icon buttons are nonstandard but relatively easy to figure out. The keyboard shortcuts for them are, respectively, A, S, and D. This keeps the most-used shortcuts under three fingers of your left hand, so once you get used to it, you can operate these functions very quickly. The audio playback is disabled in reverse or with the frame slider; it only works in forward with the arrow keys or the play button.

You set a key on the current frame by left-clicking on the cell of the phoneme object. For example, I clicked on cell 43, labeled MM, to add the MM key to frame 1 of the first track of the animation, as shown in Figure 16.7. If you make a mistake, the backspace key deletes the current keyframe. You continue setting, shifting, and deleting phoneme keys until you are satisfied with the lip sync. You can get a more accurate playback with the View|Make Preview menu option, which creates a smaller animation (Figure 16.8) synchronized to the WAV file.

Once you have the lip sync locked, you can select track 2, the performance track, and animate the rest of the facial expression. Instead of requiring you to select individual poses and set keyframes, LipService enables the user to record a live performance, making this part of the process very much like puppeteering. You select one of the performance groups, each of which includes four cells. These four cells should contain complementary poses; for example, up and down positions for both left and right eyebrows. You then simply move the mouse cursor over the work area to set the weighting of each cell from the group. For example, moving the mouse to the upper-left corner of the work area sets the upper-left object of the selected cell to 100% weighting; returning the mouse to the center of the work area reduces the weighting to 0%. So

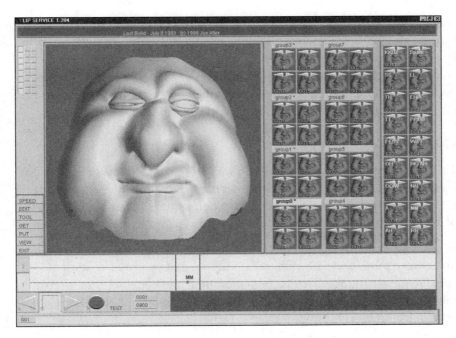

Figure 16.7
LipService interface.

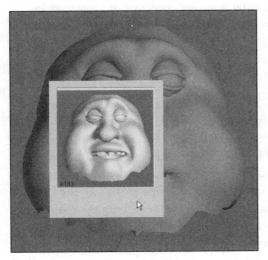

Figure 16.8
LipService preview animation.

that you can get used to this technique, LipService has a Test mode that allows you to play with the selected group's weighting without recording the performance. Once you are ready to record, you simply press X to start recording, move the mouse to create the performance, and press Esc to stop recording. If you don't like the results, you can press C or choose Edit|Clear Performances to erase the performance track. Once you get the hang of it, this is the slickest way I know of to layer a performance over lip sync.

Facial Animation

Animating facial expressions makes lip sync look like a walk in the park. Conveying emotions, especially complex transitions and slow, subtle changes, is a much tougher proposition. As I stated in Chapter 15, animating for emotional communication requires at least as much judgment and sense of timing as acting on the stage.

Although you can animate emotions using layers of image sequences, this requires such a large number of in-between maps and such care in their timing that you will lose most of mapping's usual production advantage. Because both morphing and bones techniques create in-betweens automatically and with finer control, they give you a significant advantage when you animate emotional transitions.

The human face is made up of many layers of muscle and other tissues, overlapping in different directions and bridging attachment points from the shoulders to the top of the skull. The goal of character facial animation is not to realistically simulate every one of these muscles, but to mimic the surface appearance produced by their combined actions well enough to tell the story. Refer to Chapters 6 and 7 if you want more detail on how to model an expressive face. For the purposes of this chapter, I'm just going to summarize the functions a LightWave face has to emulate.

Most of a human face attaches closely to the underlying bone structure. The cheeks and lips have a great deal of freedom because they are only attached to bones at their outer edges and their muscles and skin are flexible and elastic. Other areas of the face can't move as freely because they are on a shorter leash, so to speak. The jaw and the skull proper are the two major divisions for animating the human face. The face from the upper lip upward is mostly attached to the skull. From the lower lip downward and back to the angle of the jaw, the face is attached to the jawbone. This is a good start for defining the animation hierarchy for the face. The skull is the root, the jawbone is the second layer, and all other animation controls will be attached to either the skull directly or through the jawbone.

The visible function of most facial muscles is pushing skin around, changing the shape of the face in small increments. The jaw and eyeball muscles are notable exceptions because they rotate through comparatively large angles. To animate skin deformation, you can either use a lot of overlapping bones to deform the object or model the changes in a series of objects and use morphing techniques to animate them.

The human face has an enormous dramatic range, with nearly infinite gradations of expression. To attempt even a brief summary of facial expression in this space would be futile. Instead, I recommend that you consult one of the facial expression works listed in the Bibliography. And, as I've noted before, one of your most useful study guides is a mirror beside your monitor. When you want to create an expression, act it out and observe yourself.

Even though the full range of human facial expression is too large to catalog, there are a relatively small number of types or classes of emotional expression. Sadness, anger, joy, fear, disgust, and surprise are the basics. You may find it useful to create one facial pose of each type, then experiment with variations between the poses to create a library with more dramatic range.

Keep in mind that a library of standard emotional poses is only the starting point for developing a character's expressions. You shouldn't use the same expression on any two characters. Each character should have idiosyncrasies, minor variations on the common pattern, that make each expression uniquely suited to the character.

 ## It's That Moody Guy Again

This project is an extension of the projects in Chapter 15, but it's designed for the face rather than the entire body:

1. Load the most expressive face scene you set up in Chapter 13, or use LipService or Magpie Pro's default setups for this project.

   To review from Chapter 15, let's suppose the character starts off in a normal pose, then is given some very saddening news by an opponent we don't see. Suppose the opponent then threatens the character, frightening him. Next, the opponent ridicules the character, causing the character's fear to transition to anger. Finally, the character's anger causes the opponent to leave, and the character exults in his victory. That's four major emotional poses—sadness, fear, anger, and exultation.

2. Using the appropriate controls for your chosen setup, animate the character from normal through sadness, fear, a quick burst into anger, and finally a victorious exultation.

3. Experiment with the timing and spline controls for each transition and observe the overall effect. Which transitions do you have to stretch out? Which work better when shortened? If you're using EndoMorph Mixer, experiment with transitioning the eyes and mouth at different times.

4. When you're satisfied with the timing of each transition, save the scene file under a new name.

Timing is still everything. When you set the timing for an emotional transition, you must hold each stage in the transition just long enough for the audience to read it and no longer. The best acting job in the world is useless if it flashes by so quickly the audience can't see it or drags on so long that the audience is bored and their attention wanders. The timing of a transition alone can make a big difference in how your audience perceives a character. Imagine a character taking several seconds for a transition from confusion to comprehension. You might think this character is a little slow. On the other hand, compress this same transition to a half-dozen frames and the character appears to be very bright, even inspired. Timing emotional transitions is another skill that takes time and practice to develop. Experiment, practice, and experiment some more. You can never have too much experience in timing character animation.

Avoid twins in posing the face, just as you would for the character's body. A perfectly symmetric face is rarely found in nature, and few human expressions are balanced. The smirk, sneer, lopsided grin, and wink are just a few of the stronger examples of one-sided facial expressions. Even blinks can be slightly offset to good effect, as you might observe in the early parts of *Toy Story*.

The principle of overlapping action applies to emotional transitions, too. You should offset the keyframes of each facial feature. If the eyes, mouth, and other features all peak at the same frame, the transition will look artificial. The action of the eyes generally leads the transition, just as it leads other actions, with the mouth following last. The mouth is controlled less by reflex and instinct than by volition. So, although the eyes immediately react to a situation, it takes a conscious decision by the character to move the mouth. This is why a surprised person's mouth may hang open—they simply don't think about doing something with it. Therefore, keep the eyes under tight control. The eyes should be the first part of the face to animate, and even in extreme situations, the eyes are the last part of the face to lose control—eyes rolling up in the head as the character loses consciousness, for example. The mouth lags behind and represents conscious decisions rather than reflexes. The mouth can lie more easily, but it's often betrayed by the more truthful actions of the eyes.

A facial pose should precede the sound or phoneme the action is supposed to emphasize. In lip sync, for example, the lower lip should curl under the upper teeth several frames before the "F" sound occurs. The lead time for emotional transitions is even longer. If a head movement or facial expression is intended to emphasize a word, the entire action should end just when the word begins.

For example, look at the x-sheets at the end of Chapter 4 while listening to the FINESTHR.WAV sound clip. The word "this" has a strong vocal emphasis. You might choose to emphasize this word with a strong facial expression, as well, and perhaps a nod of the head. This visual emphasis should completely precede the sound. The nod and the facial transition to a strong key pose should end just at the first frame of the "TH" phoneme, at which time the lip sync poses should dominate. If you lap the action over the sound, the action will look stilted and poorly rehearsed. If you run the action and sound at the same time, it will look out of sync. If you run the action after the sound, it will look like a first reading by a very poor actor. When you are animating for lip sync or emotional transitions synced to a sound track, a good rule of thumb is, "Deeds before words."

Be selective in what you emphasize. If you bob the character's head at every lip synced syllable, the character will look spastic. When you first look at a lip sync x-sheet, look for the emotional or dramatic high and low points of the passage and start off with just those for emphasis. If you need emphasis, you can add poses to support the major points. But, it's better to start off with too few emphases in the action than too many.

If they are appropriate for your character, bump maps to add wrinkles can be a nice finishing touch to smiles and other expressions that crinkle up parts of the face. You are generally better off adding the wrinkle maps at the very end, after the action has been finalized. At that time, you can add wrinkle notes to the x-sheet, specifying the depth of the wrinkles at particular frames. With these notes, you can create a batch file to duplicate bump maps of different wrinkle depths. This is just like lip sync—maybe we should call it *crinkle sync*.

Animating with Physical Simulation

As stated in Chapter 13, physical simulation is one of the most tempting classes of power tools for LightWave character animation. Unfortunately, physical simulation is also one of the best ways to kill the illusion of life. You must be careful, as an animator, not to let setup people restrict your ability to animate by chaining too much control to simulation engines.

This is not to say you should never use simulation software. If you need a half ton of tribbles to pour out of a storage bay, bouncing all over the place, only a lunatic would suggest hand-keyframing every furry tumble. At the same time, only a way-gone propeller-head would suggest unadulterated physical simulation for a character like Wile E. Coyote. You need to make intelligent, informed, appropriate choices. Toward that end, if you have not already read through the section "Physical Simulation" in Chapter 13, you should do so now. I also suggest you first work through the exercises in the MotionDesigner online documentation. Once you've completed those, you'll be ready for the challenge of Project 16.3.

 Fred Goes Splat!

To complete this project, follow these steps:

1. Refer to the story sketches in Chapter 3's storyboard that show Fred being ejected from the restaurant and slamming face first into a street lamp.

2. Using the humanoid character of your choice and the street scene models provided, set keyframes to animate your character to match the storyboard's actions.

3. If you like, you can add animation controls to the street lamp to make it shudder slightly under the character's impact. You might also consider adding a stagger to the camera, as detailed in Chapter 15. Play back the pertinent section of the sound track for timing clues and inspiration.

4. When you're satisfied with the keyframe animation of the character and set, modify the setup to make the character squash and wrap around the street lamp. There are several possible approaches to this shot:

- Define surfaces and parameters for the character and deform it using physical simulation in MotionDesigner.

- Save a transformed version of the whole character and deform it manually in Modeler to create the extreme poses.

- Apply LazyPoints to distort the character.

5. Experiment with different settings for elasticity, compressibility, damping, and resilience. At the most extreme, the character's limbs should stretch clear out of the frame, and the head and torso should spread around the street lamp like a water balloon. At stiffer settings, you can minimize the distortion so the character appears as solid as wood. Find an appropriate medium between these two extremes.

6. When you are satisfied with the results, render the animation. Synchronize the appropriate clip from the sound track with your animation.

Cloth Simulation

Cloth simulation setups using MotionDesigner are best applied after you have finalized the keyframe animation of your characters and scenes. The calculations necessary to animate the cloth's mesh take a relatively long time compared to the rapid feedback of simple keyframe animation. You should also be aware of any cloth control handles available to you so you can tweak the movement of the cloth to suit the composition of the shot rather than passively hoping for a good-looking result. Again, the best place to learn how to create good-looking cloth simulations is the MotionDesigner documentation included with LightWave. Work through the exercises, particularly the T-shirt and skirt, and you should be able to adequately clothe your own characters.

Moving On

If you have worked through all the chapters and projects up to this point, you've learned enough about character animation to model, set up, and animate your own characters in your own film. The next chapters show you how to wrap up that work by creating a complete film or demo reel.

Part VI

Post-Animation Production

Chapter 17

Lighting and Rendering

A ll your test renderings are no more than dress rehearsals. Your final lighting and rendering are opening night: Here are the results you will place before your audience. If you staged actions, avoided twins, balanced your compositions, and posed for strong lines of action, it's all worthless if the lighting and rendering doesn't reinforce the point of your animation. You need to set up lighting just as carefully as you pose and time your characters.

You need to render your animation as carefully as you modeled, textured, and set up your characters. What you produce at this stage is going to be seen by your audience, so attention to detail is paramount. You also need to render as efficiently as possible, because you won't get paid for a beautiful rendering that misses the delivery deadline.

Lighting Design

Lighting design is a whole profession in itself, and much has been written elsewhere on creating good lighting designs with LightWave. Therefore, this chapter concentrates on lighting tips specifically for character animation. Appropriate lighting can help tell your story, whereas poorly designed or inappropriate lighting can obscure or ruin it.

Before you go further in this chapter, you should have worked through the first tutorial, "Front Projection Image Map," in the *LightWave [6] Introduction and Tutorials* manual and at least skimmed through Chapter 12, "Shadow and Light," in the *LightWave [6] Motion* manual. These readings will acquaint you with the basics of LightWave lighting features.

You can save time and effort if you set up lighting last, after all camera and character animation has been finalized and approved. You will be modifying the lighting to support the animation, so if there are revisions to the action, you will have to revise the lighting as well. There's no sense doing a job over if you don't have to.

A useful way to light the shot before turning it over to the animators is to add one light above and to one side of the camera, with intensity from 50 through 100 percent, and set ambient light values to around 50 percent. This makes the whole scene clear enough for the animators to see what they're doing, reduces the setup's complexity, and keeps shaded-mode redraws and test-rendering times to a minimum. After the animation is final, you can set up a more aesthetically pleasing and dramatically useful lighting design.

Basic Three-Point

The standard three-point lighting setup of key light, fill light, and rim (or back) light works just fine as a starting point for character lighting:

- *Key light*—Illuminates the strongest part of the character's face or action and casts the strongest shadows

- *Fill light*—Softens the shadows to bring out the remaining areas

- *Rim light*—Outlines the character's profile

The usual photographer's three-point setup is a key light high and to one side of the camera and a fill light low and to the other side, both pointing toward the subject, and a rim light high in back of the subject and on the same side as the fill, pointing toward the camera.

PROJECT 17.1 Three-Point Lighting for the Imp

In this project, you won't have to animate the Imp; it is just for lighting tests. The Imp was modeled by Ken Cope, and I added the surfaces and the eyeballs. The scene contains the standard default light, a bright green gradient backdrop (for contrast), the Imp model, two copies of the imp_eye.lwo model, and the three image maps for the eye.

The project shows you how to set up the basic three-point lighting for a humanoid character:

1. In Layout, load the Imp.lws scene from the Chapter 17 directory on this book's CD-ROM. Your scene should look like Figure 17.1.

2. Open the Light Properties panel and click on the Global Illumination button. Set Ambient Intensity to 0. Close the Global Illumination window.

3. In the Light Properties panel, change the default light to a 100-percent white spotlight and name it Key. Close the Light Properties panel.

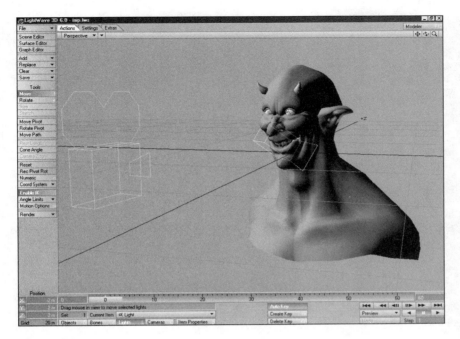

Figure 17.1
Imp scene with single default light.

4. Move the Key light above and to the left of the Camera and point it at the Imp. Set a keyframe for the Key light.

5. Add another spotlight. In the Light Properties panel, set this spotlight to diffuse only, with no specular highlights, 50-percent intensity, color blue, and named Fill.

6. Move the Fill light below and to the right of the Camera and point it at the Imp. Set a keyframe for the Fill light.

7. Repeat Step 5, but make the new light a 200-percent white spotlight named Rim. In the Light Properties panel, set this spotlight for full specular highlights with no diffuse lighting.

8. Move the Rim light above and behind the Imp and point it at the crown of the Imp's head. Set a keyframe for the Rim light. Your scene should look like Figure 17.2.

9. Render an image. You should end up with something like Figure 17.3.

10. When you are satisfied with your results, save the scene as Imp2.lws. You'll need it for the next project.

If you want to adjust the positions of the lights, you should always turn off the supplemental lights and adjust the Key light first. Once you have the Key nailed down, adjust the Fill. Finally,

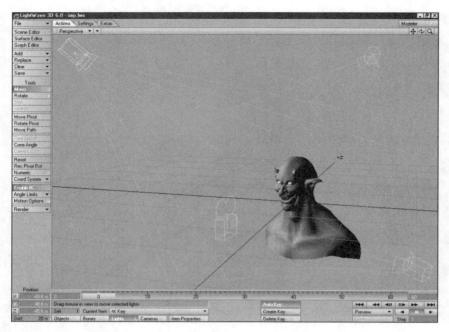

Figure 17.2
Imp scene with three-point lighting.

Figure 17.3
Imp illuminated with a standard three-point setup.

adjust the Rim light to get the halo or edge specular reflection you want. If you try to adjust the lights all at once, or out of order, it can be difficult to see the results of your adjustments.

Setting the Mood, Telling the Story

The three-point setup is adequate for illuminating the character, but it doesn't do much for telling the story. Lighting can set the mood of a shot, highlight an action, and even foreshadow a character's behavior.

Light for the story, light for the character, but never light to show off. Your audience will rarely care that you can light every form of lens flare known to cinematography or that you can simulate light refracting through a lava lamp. The audience wants you to tell them a story. No one should notice your lighting. It should be completely taken for granted. If the lighting stands out enough to be noticed by a nonprofessional audience, you've been soloing when you should have been harmonizing.

You can help establish the mood of a shot by carefully selecting and balancing the lighting colors. Generally, warm lights (daylight and firelight; warm whites to reds) as keys make for a positive mood, accented by cooler fill and rim lights. Cooler lights (night and moonlight; cool whites to blues) as keys, especially in an overall darker shot, can create a sense of foreboding unless they are strongly balanced by warmer fill and rim lights.

You also need to consider the effect of colored lights on the character's textures. Complementary colors in light and surfaces can go black or otherwise produce unintended effects. You should always begin your lighting setups with white lights and only change the lights' colors after you have the intensities nailed down.

Shadow is at least as effective as light in setting a shot's mood. What you do not light is often more important than what you do light. Your audience's eye is drawn to the bright areas of the frame. Keep the character in the light while shading the rest of the scene, and the audience will keep their eyes on your character. Go easy on the shadows, not only to minimize rendering time but for simplicity in the shot composition. I usually prefer to leave all but one light's shadows off. Only one light in a scene is the best one to create a shadow that helps tell the story or define the character—find that light and turn its shadow on. Whenever possible, use shadow mapping instead of raytracing. Shadow mapping generally gives you better control and shorter rendering times, although it does consume more RAM. Also, if you use only one light's shadow mapping, that shadow will be colored by the other lights, producing an elegantly realistic effect.

I'm Ready for My Close-Up, Mr. DeMille

If you can, start off with lighting the character. In a minimalist stage production, it's just the actor and the lights, right? It's the same principle here. You can create a good story with just the character shot against a plain background, but the lighting still has to show that character to the audience. A completely dark stage doesn't have a lot of dramatic range. There will be times you have to start with the lighting of the set, but try to put the character first whenever you can.

You shouldn't plan to set up a character's lighting just once for an entire sequence. To get the right effect, cinematographers and gaffers usually relight the subject for each change in camera angle and shot composition. This is especially important when lighting a character's face. A perfectly good lighting setup for one camera angle may give a completely wrong effect from another angle. You will also want to set up lighting for any other character action. Bringing up the intensity of a supplemental key light on a hand, just before the hand gestures, can be as strong a precursor for the audience as the traditional staging motion.

Lighting Stereotypes That Work

Good people are lit from heaven, bad people are lit from hell. Key lighting a character's face from a low angle is a common technique in horror and mystery films when a sinister effect is desired. Keep the key light high for more sympathetic characters and nearly overhead for that angelic, haloed effect.

The eyes are the windows to the soul. If the audience can't see your character's eyes, the animator will have a harder time communicating emotional transitions and the character's mental processes. The character's eyes should show a bright specular spot unless they are unhappy or otherwise emotionally down.

Lights used in cinematography specifically to bring out that spot are called *eyelights*. You can set up good eyelights by parenting a pair of tightly focused spotlights to the camera (with enough offset to get a good reflection angle) and targeting them at the eyeballs. LightWave enables you to turn off the diffuse component of the eyelights while retaining their specular component. This can make lighting the rest of the face much easier because you don't have to worry about the eyelights overwhelming the rest of the lights.

 Eyelights for the Imp

This project shows you how to add eyelights to the three-point lighting you set up in Project 17.1:

1. In Layout, reload the Imp2.lws scene you saved from the preceding project.

2. Add another spotlight and name it Eyelight1.

3. With Eyelight1 selected, press "m" to open the Motion Options panel. Set Parent Item to the Camera and set Target Object to the first eye object, as shown in Figure 17.4.

4. In the Light Properties panel, set Eyelight1 to Affect Specular only, and set Shadow Type to off. Set Spotlight Cone Angle and Spotlight Soft Edge Angle to 0.5, as shown in Figure 17.4.

5. With Eyelight1 still selected, choose Add|Clone Current Item to duplicate the eyelight. Name the clone Eyelight2.

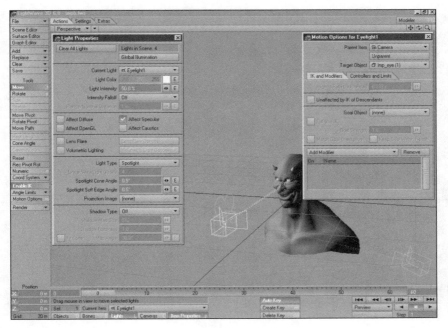

Figure 17.4
Imp scene with first eyelight added.

6. With Eyelight2 selected, press "m" to open the Motion Options panel. Set Target Object to the second eye object.

7. Render an image. You should end up with something like Figure 17.5.

The eyelights should be tight enough to illuminate only the eyeballs. Locating the eyelights directly on the camera puts the highlight on the center of the corneal bulge. If you want the highlight to appear off-center, you can offset the eyelights from the Camera without changing the parenting or targeting.

You should also create an Envelope for Light Intensity so you can dim the eyelights when necessary, such as during a blink or when the character transitions to a "down" emotional expression. Literally, the light should go out of its eyes. It doesn't take much light to get that sparkle in the character's eyes. Start off with a very low intensity and work your way up to the lowest value that gives you an acceptable specular highlight.

Matching Real-World Lighting

One of the most challenging forms of LightWave character animation is the *compositing* of a character into live-action footage. Over and above the character animation itself, this requires a seamless match of LightWave lighting and rendering. The additional work can make the

Figure 17.5
Imp's eyes highlighted with eyelights (compare this to Figure 17.3).

process time-consuming, but the results can fool even the most jaded professionals. If the lighting is off, even an untrained eye can see that something is wrong.

Documenting the Set

Before you shoot the live action, you need to thoroughly document the set. After the shoot, you will need to re-create those parts of the set that LightWave elements will touch, shadow, or be shadowed by. Trying to do this after the fact, when all you can measure are images from the live-action footage, is much harder. Take a few notes, measurements, and photos now, and you'll save yourself many headaches later.

The first priority is reference points. You need to choose or create several visual references that will be easy to pick out in each frame of the footage. You will use these reference points to stabilize and match camera motion and may also have to use them to create models of shadowed or shadowing surfaces. A good reference point contrasts strongly with its surroundings and shows a consistent profile throughout camera moves. In the sample footage shown in Figure 17.6, the sidewalk, steps, and door provided a number of excellent reference points.

If you can't find a good set of reference points, you may have to make your own. Ping-Pong balls painted Day-Glo green work well, and you can tack them temporarily to the set or props with putty. A solid, nonnatural color from the Day-Glo palette makes it easy for you to mask the reference marks out of the footage during compositing. Spherical reference marks provide a

Figure 17.6
A frame from the sample footage.

more consistent appearance through most camera moves, making tracking and motion stabilizing much easier. An excellent example of this technique is shown on the *Making of Jurassic Park* videotape or laserdisk, in the Gallimimus stampede sequence (see the Bibliography).

Your second priority is to measure the set, including the reference points and any surfaces that LightWave or other composited elements will touch, shadow, or be shadowed by. You will need to model these reference points and surfaces and add them to your LightWave scenes so you can set up and animate the scene to match. I've found the most reliable way to keep track of set measurements is to take a series of photos or digitized video prints of the set and then write my notes and measurements directly on the prints. If you can't mark up the photos, try grease pencil on a transparent overlay. Figure 17.7 shows my notes for the porch steps in the sample footage.

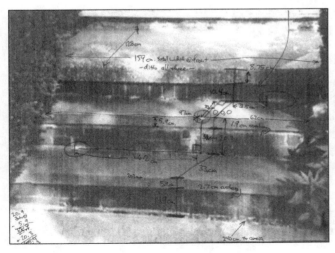

Figure 17.7
Measurements and notes on reference photo.

You should also measure the position of any local (other than sunlight) light sources and (very important!) the starting position and attitude of the camera's focal plane. Get the lens settings too. If you are working with a commercial film crew, you can get some of these measurements from the focus puller or 1st Assistant Camera. It's a good idea to cross-check your measurements. It's much easier to remeasure on the set than to locate and correct measurement errors during post-production.

Clean Plate

After you've got the data you need for modeling, you can start collecting what you'll need to match the lighting, shadows, and colors. The first step is a clean plate, an image of the empty set with lighting just as it will appear in the final footage. This is the visual reference you will consult on questions of shadow and highlight density, falloff (the shadows' soft edges), and color, as shown in Figure 17.8. You may also use a series of clean plates, taken in different directions, to build environment reflection maps.

Figure 17.8
Clean plate.

The second step is to repeat the clean-plate shoot with reference lighting objects in the frame. I like to use a set of plastic foam objects that are light, rigid, and easy to move around on the set. You can make your own easily with inexpensive materials from any craft shop. The only criteria are that you be able to extract shadow and highlight colors and deduce the angle of light sources from the reference shots. My own rig is a plastic foam block topped by a 1 cm grid, with a wooden dowel gnomon at one corner and a white plastic foam lighting ball (see Figure 17.9).

Just place the reference lighting objects in the frame, preferably as close as possible to the character's anticipated position, and take another clean plate (see Figure 17.10).

Figure 17.9
Close-up of a lighting reference object with gnomon and white ball.

Figure 17.10
Lighting reference object with gnomon and white ball.

The goal of all this is to be able to produce an exact match between LightWave elements and the clean plate, as in Figure 17.11. Note the exact match of shadow angle and density between the reference image and the final composite.

Once you've taken all the measurements and reference photos, you can use them to build shadow surfaces and lighting setups in LightWave. If you've taken thorough and accurate measurements, you can do this by the numbers and very quickly.

Shadow Surfaces

In order to perfectly composite LightWave elements to live footage, you must make sure shadows and reflections of the LightWave elements appear to fall on the appropriate live-action surfaces. One way to accomplish this is to model shadow-catcher or reflecting surfaces and position them accurately in a LightWave scene. Doing this correctly can really help sell the shot; doing it badly makes the LightWave element stick out like a sore thumb.

Figure 17.11
LightWave lighting reference objects and character composited into a clean plate.

PROJECT 17.3 Duplicating Porch Shadow Surfaces

The goal of this project is to make a duplicate model in LightWave of every surface on which the character will cast a shadow. This is necessary for LightWave to render the object's shadow so it will accurately match the footage.

To duplicate the porch shadow surfaces, follow these steps:

1. Refer to the measurements in Figure 17.7 to build a 1:1 scale model of the porch steps in LightWave. In case you can't read my scrivenings, here are the important measurements for building the model:

   - The top slab is 128cm deep, 8.75cm thick, and 159cm wide. All remaining elements are also 159cm wide.

   - The top riser is inset 5cm and is 10.4cm high.

   - The middle slab is 33cm deep and 5.9 cm thick.

   - The middle riser is inset 1.9cm, and the top of the middle slab is 20.9cm above the top of the bottom slab.

   - The bottom slab is 33cm deep and 5.9cm thick.

   - The bottom riser is inset 2.7cm and is 14.4cm high.

   If you don't want to build the model, you can use the PORCH.LWO object I've provided on this book's CD-ROM. I have also provided models of some of the lighting reference objects (LITEREF, LITEGRID) that appear in this chapter's figures. You'll need to add a matte white sphere to complete the next project, but then you wouldn't want me to do it all for you, would you?

2. In Layout, load file PORCH.IFF as the backdrop image.

3. Lay out the models according to the measurements and the background image of the clean plate. Add markers for the reference points noted in Figure 17.7.

Pay especially close attention to the position of the LITEREF object. The corner with the gnomon should be precisely 97 cm from the left corner of the middle slab, and the front edge of LITEREF should be flush with the front edge of the slab. I aligned the reference object with a chip in the concrete, which I measured as a reference mark and wrote up on Figure 17.7.

You can also load file PORCH.LWS from this book's CD-ROM to see an example of how I set up the matching scene.

If you have to match only natural daylight, it is possible to set up a default sunlight scene in LightWave that will simulate most of daylight's effects. Tweaking the last few percentage points for a perfect match is much easier than starting from scratch.

PROJECT 17.4 Matching LightWave Lighting for Porch

The goal of this project is to match the angle, intensity, color, and falloff of the light sources in the footage. It's relatively easy in this case because the only direct light source is the sun, the shadows are distinct, and the ambient light is consistent throughout the character's area of movement.

To match the lighting for the porch, follow these steps:

1. In the scene you set up in Project 17.3, add a single spotlight at a long distance from the porch model. Position the camera to look down at the LITEREF/LITEGRID grid, as in Figure 17.12.

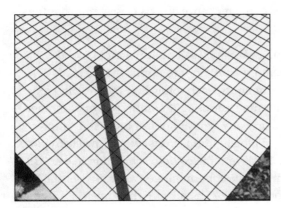

Figure 17.12
LITEREF/LITEGRID as rendered by the LightWave camera.

2. Look at Figure 17.9 for reference. Move the light source around and rerender the camera view until the end of the rendered shadow appears at exactly the same grid coordinates as the shadow end in Figure 17.9.

3. Change the light falloff to mimic the falloff of the gnomon's shadow in Figure 17.9.

   The next step is to match the color of the light. This isn't just matching the color of sunlight—you have to match the color distortions produced by the video camera and the digitizing process too. The most reliable way to do this is to sample the final rendering and compare it to the same areas of the footage.

   You'll need to keep Photoshop or other image-processing software open while you render and rerender the scene. If you don't have enough system memory to do this, the process will get tedious very quickly.

4. Set the light to pure white. Render a frame. Open the frame in Photoshop.

5. Use the Photoshop eyedropper to sample the image at the highlight of the white sphere. Make a note of the RGB values. Take another sample at the center of the darkest part of the shadow behind the sphere but still on the LITEREF object's surface. These two samples give you the brightest and darkest color values for the light.

6. Repeat Step 5 on reference image LITETEST.TGA, which you'll find in the Chapter 17 directory of this book's CD-ROM. I found the highlight sample of this image colored 239,232,238 and the shadow behind the sphere colored 14,16,16. Your results may vary.

7. Change the light's color values to match the sample you took from LITETEST.TGA. Rerender the image and check the identical sample areas. Readjust the light and rerender until you are satisfied that the rendered color of the reference objects closely matches the original colors.

   One way to make more-realistic sunlight in LightWave by setting Ambient to 0 and parenting a starburst of Distant lights to the main (Sun) light to mimic the effect of radiosity. For example, a rosette of eight Distant lights, each rotated on the Heading axis 45 degrees from its neighbors, with one additional Distant light pointing up and another down, gives you enough controls to mimic nearly any type of natural light. You simply modify each light's color and intensity to match the lighting effects seen in the clean plate. For starters, you can probably set the Sun to 100% and the color to something like R=235, G=245, B=255 to match the slightly bluish tint of sunlight on film or video. Try setting the 45-degree lights to 20% and the up/down light pair to 75%, all with the same color as the Sun light. To prevent confusing shadows and specular highlights, turn on the No Specular button and set Shadow Type to Off for every light but the Sun. Your results should look something like Figure 17.13.

Figure 17.13
Sunlight setup rendered in LightWave.

8. When you have completed the lighting match, remove the light reference objects and add an animated character.

   The animated character doesn't have to be complicated, just something that casts a moving shadow over the steps and upper surface of the Porch object. If you like, use Load From Scene to add objects and motions from the LampHop.lws scene file on the CD-ROM. This is a desk lamp object that I animated to hop up the porch steps. After you use Load From Scene, you will need to parent the desk lamp object to the porch object.

9. Position the animated character to rest on the upper surface of the porch at the end of the animation.

You can leave the porch surface and background image as is if you want to render the character over the background in one pass. Your results should look something like Figure 17.14.

However, you will retain more control over the shadow density and color if you render an alpha channel (Figure 17.15) and use that to composite the LightWave objects over the clean plate.

If you prefer to composite an additive merge, you can drop the image maps from both the porch surface and the backdrop, resulting in a completely black frame except for the desk lamp. You can then load the rendered image as a foreground, the alpha channel as foreground alpha, and the clean plate as the background image, as shown in Figure 17.16.

To tweak the appearance of the LightWave elements to match the footage more closely, you may want to add a blur, noise, or grain filter or a combination of them (see Figure 17.17). Almost anything that will take the too-clean, perfectly rendered polish off the LightWave elements is a good idea. One of your goals is to match the visual textures of elements from different sources so the final composite is internally consistent. A good composite should look like it was simply photographed, that every element was actually there at the same time.

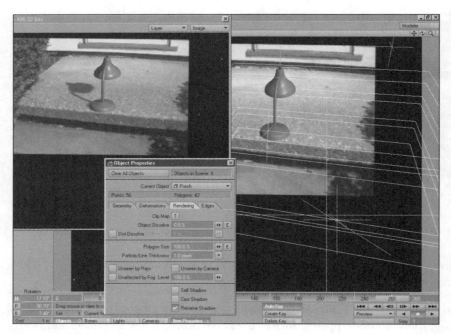

Figure 17.14
Desk lamp and shadow rendered over the image-mapped porch object and backdrop.

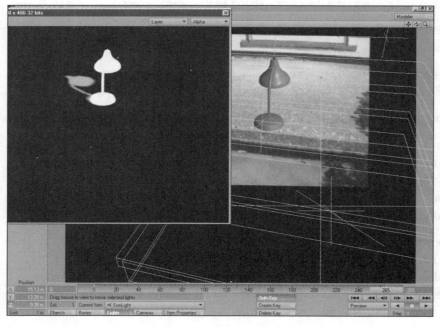

Figure 17.15
Alpha channel from Figure 17.14.

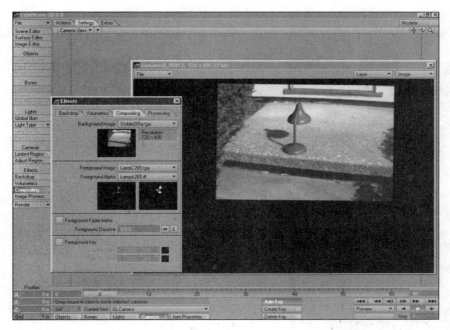

Figure 17.16
Rendered foreground and alpha channel rendered over clean plate background to create a composite.

Figure 17.17
Slight blur and grain filters added to LightWave elements to match blur and noise in the original footage.

Matching Set Lighting

If it's a clear day and you have a good record of the sun angle, matching daylight can be relatively easy. Matching live-action lighting gets a little more challenging when you have an internal set with a number of light sources. Figure 17.18 shows a set and lighting rigged by Chris Nibley (**www.nibley.com**) for a motion control shot that produced Figure 17.19. Note the position of the two lights and the bounce card.

Figure 17.18
Props and lights set up for a motion control shot.

Figure 17.19
A frame from the motion control shot, ChesP276.iff, showing reflections, highlights, and shadows on the chessboard.

If you have to match studio lighting, you should have gathered complete information about light placement, colors, and intensity while on the set. A clean plate with lighting reference objects is the next best thing. If all else fails, you will have to make a series of educated guesses based on the footage you are given.

PROJECT 17.5 Matching LightWave Lighting and Reflections for Chessboard

The goals of this project are to make a LightWave model of the chessboard surface visible in the motion control footage and to mimic the multiple lights and the reflective chessboard surface in a LightWave scene. In addition to catching the shadow of any LightWave elements, the chessboard must also create matching reflections. Each effect in itself is minor, but the overall effect makes the difference between a seamless composite and one that does not ring true.

To match the LightWave lighting and reflections for the chessboard, follow these steps:

1. The chessboard is composed of 2-inch squares. In Modeler, it's easiest to create a square 16 inches on a side, with eight divisions in both length and width. If you choose not to build your own model, you can use object file BOARD.LWO from the CD-ROM.

2. Open a new scene. Load the chessboard image ChesP276.iff as the background.

3. Position the chessboard object in the scene to match the position and rotation of the chessboard in the background image. You should end up with something like Figure 17.20.

Figure 17.20
The LightWave chess scene showing the chessboard object matched to the background image.

4. Examine the photo of the set (Figure 17.18) to estimate the approximate position and color of each light source.

5. Add a light to the scene in the appropriate position for the strongest shadow-casting light.

6. Place a null at the peak of one chess piece and another null at the peak of that piece's shadow, as shown in Figure 17.21.

Figure 17.21
Nulls placed to mark the peak of the chess piece and shadow.

7. Target the new light at the null marking the peak of the chess piece's shadow.

8. Change to Light View. Choose the new light. Move the light until the null marking the peak of the chess piece aligns with the null marking the peak of its shadow, as shown in Figure 17.22. The selected light will now cast accurate directional shadows for any LightWave objects placed on the chessboard object.

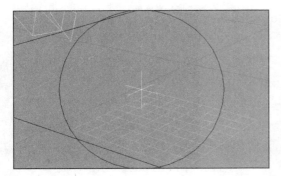

Figure 17.22
Light View aligned with nulls.

9. Place any object on the chessboard object. Refer again to Figure 17.18 and modify the light's shadow settings to match shadow falloff and density.

10. Repeat the preceding steps for the other light sources.

11. Set surface reflection attributes for the chessboard object. For example, I used 80% Luminosity, 20% Diffuse, 20% Reflectivity. The surface color is white, with the image applied as a Front Projection Image Map.

You should now be able to add other LightWave elements that will composite seamlessly with the background. Figure 17.23 shows one example of the effects you can create.

Figure 17.23
The Walker robot crossing a chessboard, with matching shadows and reflection.

Projecting Shadows

If you need to match real-world lighting, you may sometimes have to match shadows cast across the character by lights and shadowing objects outside the frame. This can be challenging, but if you do it successfully, it is one of the most effective techniques for making your LightWave creations blend seamlessly with reality.

LightWave enables you to project a map with a light. In cinematography, a cutout or filter used this way is called a *cucaloris*, or cookie. Two common examples of this are a horizontal pattern of light and dark stripes to mimic window blinds and a vertical pattern to mimic prison bars. Figure 17.24 shows another example of cookie lighting. Compare the effect of the image on the left, with no cookie, to that on the right, which uses a cookie to mimic the dappled pattern of leaves casting shadows on the iguana.

Iguana images courtesy of Kim Oravecz.

Figure 17.24
Iguana with basic lighting (left) and a cookie to mimic shadows of leaves (right).

If you need to match shadows in live-action footage, you'll need an accurate (or at least plausible) cookie map to project. If possible, you should try to capture important shadow profiles on the live-action set. One way to do this is to position your still camera in line between the primary shadow and the light source, pointed at the shadowed surfaces. Your camera will see precisely the shadow outline that you need to project, so you can edit the digitized photo into a cookie map. If possible, keep your camera entirely within the shadows cast by other objects. If you can't do this, you may have to take several photos, with your camera's shadow occluding different parts of each shot, so you can assemble a cookie map from the clear parts.

The cookie map will be projected across the scene and may appear at several times its original size, so you should use the highest-resolution PhotoCD format available. If you are projecting color, such as sunlight filtered through green leaves, you will need to maintain the full 24-bit color depth. If you are simply projecting solid shadows, you can save most of the file size by converting the map to 8-bit grayscale, but you shouldn't cut it down to a 1-bit black-and-white mask unless you want all the shadows to be razor-sharp. Grayscale edges in the cookie map will automatically give you the soft-shadow edges you need to match real-world lighting.

Miscellaneous Tips

Here are a few more lighting ideas you may find useful:

- When you're ready to start lighting the finished animation, turn down the ambient light to 5 percent or less. Ambient light may be good for sunny outdoor scenes, but too much will wash out a shot and leave it looking flat. You can create a more natural look by using soft lights for area lighting. For a nice soft fill light, use a Distant light with 100% diffuse but no specular component.

- When in doubt, keep lights low to start. You can always add more.

- Turn off Affect Diffuse if you want to crank up a light for highlights, such as a Rim or Backlight.

- Turn off Affect Specular to keep fill lights from creating unwanted highlights.

- Turn off Affect OpenGL for all lights except the ones you need to compose the shot, such as the main Key and Fill lights.

- Don't use lens flares in character animation. Most cinematographers are very careful to prevent lens flare, so why should you deliberately add it? It has also been overdone so much that lens flares on a demo reel are usually interpreted as an amateur's touch.

- If you have a lighting setup that you use often, set up a scene with just those lights, parented to a null object at the origin. LightWave enables you to merge elements from other scenes, so you can easily load the null and its parented lights into your current project. Also, it helps to name your lights in case you want to tweak them later. WarmKeyLight is a lot easier to understand than Light003.

- If you have particular light settings that you use repeatedly, you can build a library of lights by using the Save Light function. This is especially useful if you need to match real-world light sources. With a little effort, you can build a library of lights to match the most common gaffer's rigs.

- Experiment with lighting every chance you get. Lighting often takes as much time as staging the scene. A lot of that time goes to the numerous test renders needed to get things lit exactly right. If you've practiced lighting, you'll be able to get closer to the final setup on your first rough, and you won't have to waste time on test renders when your deadlines are tight.

With these tips firmly in mind, you should be able to light any character's action to good effect. In the next section, I will show you how to get the best images possible, considering your computer, budget, and schedule.

Rendering

The goal of this section is to point out some of the tips and tricks you can use to minimize rendering time. This is especially important in a production environment, but even hobbyists like to see their animations as quickly as possible. Sometimes you have to choose between rendering time and image quality, but many of the following techniques can be used without reducing quality. If you can reliably get good images out of a system faster than anyone else, you'll never be unemployed for long.

If you want to get the most out of your LightWave renders, you should read through Chapter 9, "Rendering Options," in the LightWave *Motion* manual.

Your Computer

The first thing you should do to shorten rendering time is get a bigger, faster machine. Just kidding! Although you can never have too much RAM, hard disk space, or processing speed, most of us have to work in the real world. Fantasies about the ideal rendering monster system won't improve your work. On the other hand, if you can produce really outstanding work on a rinky-dink machine, your problem-solving skills and can-do mind-set will be valuable assets even when you're wrangling a 20-teraFLOP network.

LightWave follows the same steps every time it renders an image. It loads the objects, maps, and other files required for the current frame into RAM, calculates the image, and saves the image to storage. You can add optional steps (post-processing plug-ins, image file compression, and so on) to this process, but most of them slow it down. Each step in the rendering process is a potential bottleneck. Learn the bottlenecks of your particular system's RAM, storage drives, and CPU and how to work around them.

If you are thinking about upgrading or purchasing a machine, pay as much attention to the bus speed as to the CPU speed. The bus speed determines how fast LightWave can push data around your system, from hard disk to RAM to CPU and back again. If the bus speed is significantly lower than the CPU speed, you may not be getting all the performance you should. The CPU may render images fast enough, then sit there wasting cycles waiting for the next batch of data from the bus.

If you have plenty of hard disk space but little RAM, you can split up scenes into more manageable layers, render each layer as an image sequence, and composite the layers together (see Chapter 18 for details). This enables you to render complex scenes that would otherwise overload your machine. If you don't have enough RAM and you try to render the scene anyway, LightWave will treat part of your hard disk as if it were RAM (a swap file) and move bits of the scene to and from your hard disk as necessary. This repeated disk accessing is sometimes referred to as *thrashing*. As you may imagine, it really slows down the rendering process and doesn't do your hard disk any good, either.

If you have plenty of RAM but loading files from the hard disk seems to take up a lot of time, you might try allocating a RAM disk. (The exact procedure will depend on the hardware platform you are running.) If you load some or all of the scene's files to the RAM disk, LightWave can load them for rendering much faster.

PROJECT 17.6 Setting Up a WinNT RAM Drive

You can set up a RAM disk in Windows NT 4 by using a Microsoft software-only device driver that is included on this book's CD-ROM. This is old code (1994), and although it works for me, you should think hard about whether the benefits are worth the risks to your own system. If you are not comfortable using RegEdit (or don't know what this term means), you should not try this.

To set up a Windows NT 4 RAM drive, follow these steps:

1. Copy the self-extracting archive NTRamdsk.exe from the CD-ROM to your default TEMP directory. For most systems, this will be C:\TEMP.

2. Run NTRamdsk.exe by double-clicking on it. It will self-extract into four files: RAMDISK.SYS, RAMDISK.INI, REGINI.EXE, and README.TXT.

3. Read the README.TXT file before you go further. If you have any doubts about what the next steps may do to your system, stop now and delete the extracted files from your TEMP directory.

4. Copy RAMDISK.SYS to your system's 32-bit driver directory, most commonly C:\WINNT\SYSTEM32\DRIVERS.

5. From the Start menu, choose Run. In the Run dialog box, type the path to your TEMP directory, followed by "\REGINI.EXE RAMDISK.INI", as shown in Figure 17.25. Click on OK.

Figure 17.25
The Run dialog box ready to execute REGINI to configure a RAM disk.

The REGINI program will make entries and changes to your system's Registry, based on the values in the RAMDISK.INI file. These include the drive letter V for the RAM disk and an allocation of 2MB.

6. Reboot your system. When it comes back up, you should see a new V: drive with a file size a little less than 2MB.

If you need to change the size of the RAM disk or the drive letter assignment, you can use RegEdit directly. Keep in mind that you can severely cripple your operating system by making a mistake in the Registry. If you are not confident of your ability to edit the Registry, don't try this.

7. From the Start menu, choose Run. Type "REGEDIT" and click on OK. The Registry Editor will appear.

8. Press Ctrl+F, or choose the Edit|Find menu option. In the Find dialog box, type "DiskSize", then click on the Find Next button. When the first (and only) instance of DiskSize is found, the Registry Editor should look like Figure 17.26.

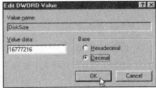

Figure 17.26
The Registry Editor (RegEdit) ready to edit the DiskSize parameter for the RAM disk. The Value data is set to 16MB in decimal notation.

9. Right-click on the DiskSize parameter and choose Modify from the pop-up menu. A dialog box entitled Edit DWORD Value will appear.

10. In the Value data field, type the desired RAM allocation for the RAM disk, then click on OK.

11. If you would like to change the drive letter, right-click on the DriveLetter parameter, choose Modify, and in the Edit String dialog box, type the new drive letter. Be sure you are choosing a drive letter that will not conflict with either drive ordering or an existing drive letter. If you have any doubts, leave the parameter as is.

12. Close the Registry Editor. Reboot your system.

If all went well, your system should now have a RAM disk with the size and drive letter you set, as in Figure 17.27. This can be a handy location for files that require very fast access, such as animations, video clips, and large sound files. However, you should remember that a RAM disk keeps the rest of your operating system from using that block of chip memory. Unless you have far more RAM than you ever need, you should keep the RAM disk as small as possible. Remember also that the RAM disk is volatile memory; if the system hangs or reboots, the contents are gone. For this reason, you should never use a RAM disk as an output location, and you should always retain a backup copy of any file you place in a RAM disk.

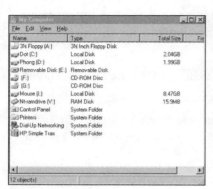

Figure 17.27
The appearance and properties of the 16MB RAM disk.

Buying the Farm

If you've got a lot of rendering to do on a regular basis, you may want to consider building a small render farm. The advantage to this lies in rendering on inexpensive stripped-down systems while keeping your more expensive animation workstation free for your creative use. A render farm node might consist of a moderately fast motherboard and CPU, sufficient RAM for rendering your largest scene without thrashing, a minimal video card, a floppy disk drive, a network card, and a hard drive just large enough to hold the bare-bones operating system plus LightWave and the current scene files. As of this writing, you should be able to put together a rendering node like this for less than half the price of a full system. You can even adapt old, semi-obsolete computers as nodes. Who cares if they're slow, if they're cranking out images nonstop? Many hands make light work!

If you have a lot of rendering to do, and a very short deadline, it may be cost effective for you to buy time on a commercial render farm. There are several companies currently offering rendering services for LightWave, including R3D (**www.ren3d.com**), Alternate Perspective Online (**www.ap3d.com/core/render_farm.htm**), 3-id (**www.3-id.com**), and others. I'm only citing these companies as examples, not recommending them from personal experience. Companies go in and out of this business rapidly; you should do your own research when you are planning your production schedule.

For details on the variety of distributed rendering options available in LightWave, you should read Chapter 10, "Distributed Rendering," in the *LightWave [6] Motion* manual.

Files

LightWave can render much faster if the object and image files for a scene are designed to load and render efficiently. Here are a few simple guidelines that can speed up your rendering.

For images, keep it simple. If an image is going to occupy a quarter of the screen at the camera's closest distance and your output resolution is 640x480, any resolution higher than 320x240 will be wasted. Design your color, bump, and other maps to suit the resolution at which you will actually render them. The same goes for color depth. It's just wasting RAM and disk space to use a 24-bit color image for a bump map when only 8 bits worth of luminance information is used. Make a habit of asking yourself, "How much detail is the audience able to see?" Whenever possible, use image maps instead of procedural shaders because maps render much faster. One approach is to apply a shader to an object, render an image of it, and apply the rendered image as a map to the original object.

For objects, again, keep it simple. If an object is going to appear small or in the background of a shot, replace it with a simplified version. Save the full zillion-polygon versions for extreme close shots in which all the detail will show. If you will be using a character in a number of different shots, you may be able to save a lot of rendering time by creating different versions of the object for different Camera distances. Even if an object is seen only in close shots, if it is very complex, you may find it worthwhile to model alternate versions with back surface polygons deleted. If a shot only shows the character's face, loading the polygons that form the back of his head is a waste of time.

Shadows

After you've finished laying out a scene and have done a test render, take a good look at where the shadows are falling. Note which models have to cast shadows, receive shadows, or shadow themselves. For each model, turn off the shadow options that aren't needed.

Just as for models, turn off shadow options for lights that don't need them. Use only the minimum lights necessary to the scene. More lights always cause a longer render but do not always produce better-looking results. If you must set up a complex lighting scheme, try lighting layers of a scene separately to save rendering time (a rendered layer applied as a background image needs no lights).

Use shadow maps rather than raytraced shadows whenever possible. They render faster and generally look better because of their soft edges. You can fake shadows, too. If you are really pressed for rendering time, you can model shadow objects. For example, if a table has a shadow below it, make a dark transparent polygon shadow and place it beneath the table.

Render Modes

One of the options that beginners tend to waste a lot of time on is raytracing. This rendering algorithm generates images by calculating the path between each screen pixel and each light source in the scene. Although raytracing produces images that are more realistic than those produced by some faster algorithms, raytracing is a real brute-force overkill solution for most images. Other than the gee-whiz factor of creating complex scenes, do you really need photorealistic glass, chrome, or other raytraced surfaces? You should keep in mind that potential employers will have seen a lot more CGI than you have and are thoroughly sick of raytraced reflection studies. They will be more interested in a good application of shadow, reflection, and projection maps to achieve a realistic effect with more finesse. If you have a lot of obviously raytraced stuff on your demo reel, it won't say much about your ability as a technical director (TD) to fake a "look" without resorting to brute-force rendering. It's better to dazzle them with your skills, not your tools.

You should always try to keep enough RAM available to render the scene in one segment. Split the rendering into foreground and background layers, if necessary, and you'll still save time overall. Select an appropriate anti-aliasing level. Overdoing it for a particular resolution just wastes time. Motion blur can be increased to cover a number of problems, but it can also increase rendering times. If you plan to use a lot of motion blur, you may want to split the scene into layers again. You can generally render a background layer without motion blur (unless the camera is moving), but the foreground characters should have as much motion blur as they can handle.

If you are rendering an animation to put on a demo reel or otherwise impress someone, you might try rendering it in wide-screen. You will actually be rendering a smaller-size image, but it will look like a letterboxed film, so people tend to think of it as higher-quality work.

Output File Formats

If you will be compositing any layers of animation and have plenty of hard disk space, you should save the rendering as a numbered sequence of image files. Your renderer won't have to assemble an AVI or QuickTime animation after rendering, and the rendered images will look a lot nicer than the compressed animation frames. You will also find it easier to rerender a few missing frames than to rerender the whole animation if something interrupts the rendering. Choose an image format that your compositing software can load in numbered sequence.

If you have the file space to spare, I recommend rendering AVI or other animation files with zero compression at first. You can always use an editing program or video utility to compress the finished file. If you render to a compressed file and something goes wrong, you will have to rerender the entire sequence. If the file is uncompressed, you can edit it or insert rerendered sequences without losing image quality to repeated compressions.

One of the most powerful tools you can use to fine-tune your imagery, especially if you use LightWave or another program for compositing, is the LW_SpecialBuffers image filter plug-in. You access this feature from the Processing tab of the Effects panel, as shown in Figure 17.28. It enables you to save the contents of 15 different render buffers to separate files or to the RGB or alpha channels of the rendered image. You can load the output from these buffers into LightWave or a compositing program to fine-tune a variety of fussy parameters—including specular highlights, shadows, and reflections—without having to rerender a time-consuming scene.

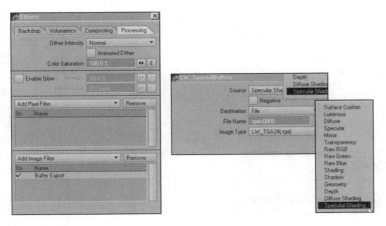

Figure 17.28
LW_SpecialBuffers plug-in options.

Watching the Kettle Boil

LightWave gives you the option of watching the rendering in progress. This is a bad thing, generally. It encourages you to waste time watching the screen, and it costs time for every pixel rendered. Instead of simply saving the data to the image file, LightWave has to translate it into a form it can present in the display window, then update the display. This can be a significant fraction of the actual rendering time. You should only use this option when you are experimenting with lighting and rendering options. When you are ready to render the completed animation, turn this option off.

NTSC Rendering

If you followed my earlier advice on timing, you've been animating all your characters to 24 fps. LightWave makes it very easy for you to convert those animations to the 30 fps, 60 fields per second required for NTSC video. When you are ready to render, open the Render Options panel and choose the Output Files tab. Next to Save Animation, choose FilmExpand from the Type pull-down menu. The FilmExpand window will appear; choose the image format and the field dominance you want for your NTSC video animation, as shown in Figure 17.29.

Further Study

If you are interested in the technical theory behind rendering, you can find out more by reading some of the computer graphics textbooks cited in the Bibliography. The ACM SIGGRAPH publications mentioned in Chapter 21 are also good resources once you have a basic grounding in CGI theory.

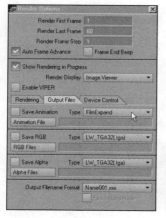
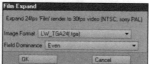

Figure 17.29
FilmExpand window.

Moving On

In this chapter, we've covered the basics of lighting your characters and a number of simple tricks to render your animations faster or more efficiently. The next chapter shows you how to use compositing software to add dissolves and special effects and to composite your LightWave characters over background footage.

Chapter 18

Compositing Effects

Compositing is a means to add your LightWave creations to live-action footage or to combine effects you couldn't render in one pass. Add compositing to your animation toolkit, and you'll more than double the utility and effectiveness of all your other tools.

Digital compositing is the digitally manipulated integration of at least two source images to produce a new image.

The operative words in that definition are "digitally," "integration," and "images." *Digitally* means we are not working directly with film or other analog media; we are using computers to manipulate digital information. *Images* means we are working with more than one image at a time; if we were working with only one image, we would simply be painting or retouching. *Integration* is the heart of compositing: The new image must appear real (completely and seamlessly integrated), as if it were actually photographed by a single camera at one instant, or the illusion of compositing has failed. Digital compositing is the art of the invisible effect.

Film and video work uses compositing for several functions. You can composite parts of a duplicate background, or clean plate, to cover unwanted parts of the image to salvage footage that might otherwise have to be reshot. This is often used to conceal safety lines and other equipment in live action. You can also composite shot transitions, such as dissolves, wipes, and special effects. If you have to split LightWave scenes into layers to speed up rendering or stay within your computer's capacity, you can reassemble the scene with compositing. Although these other applications are useful, the most important use of compositing in the context of this book is adding an animated character to digitized backgrounds or live-action footage.

Compositing software has nearly as many bells and whistles as 3D animation software. As with LightWave, you don't need to understand or use every feature in order to produce decent results. Therefore, this chapter provides a brief overview of the most necessary and often-used compositing processes.

Before you go further in this chapter, you should have worked through the first tutorial, "Front Projection Image Map," in the *LightWave [6] Introduction and Tutorials* manual. This tutorial explains how to use one of the basic LightWave techniques for compositing rendered elements into live-action footage.

You should also review pages 8.4 through 8.7 of the *Motion: Animate & Render* manual for information about the Foreground Image, Background Image, and Alpha Image features found in the Compositing tab of the Effects panel. These features enable you to perform many compositing operations within LightWave without using specialized compositing software. However, you should generally avoid using the Foreground Fader Alpha and Foreground Key features. Both these features can be useful with certain types of footage or rendered effects, but when used to comp rendered elements over ordinary backdrop images, they create nasty edge artifacts.

Compositing with an Alpha Channel

One of the most common compositing operations is to comp a foreground image over a background image using a matte or alpha channel. This process uses a grayscale image to control the transparency of the foreground, allowing the background to show through the black areas, the foreground to cover the white areas, and a proportional mixture of the foreground and background in gray areas.

Mattes or alpha channels can be created in many ways. Alpha channels are generally easiest to use when they are rendered by LightWave at the same time the RGB color channels are rendered. The edges and gradients of a LightWave rendering are precisely controlled, and because the images are digital from the beginning, there are no film scanning or video digitizing artifacts. Just to make this first project an easy one, I've provided a LightWave-rendered element and alpha channel.

The Walker is a stock character setup included with LightWave, which I used to render the WALKR000.JPG sequence shown in Figure 18.1 and the matching alpha channel sequence shown in Figure 18.2. The chessboard footage used throughout this chapter (see Figure 18.3) was set up, lit, photographed, and digitized by Chris Nibley (**www.nibley.com**) using one of his motion control camera rigs. Later in this chapter, I'll explain how you can use this footage to animate your own LightWave characters to match the camera move.

Figure 18.1
Frame 276 of the LightWave-rendered Walker RGB image sequence.

Figure 18.2
Frame 276 of the LightWave-rendered Walker alpha channel image sequence.

PROJECT 18.1 Compositing with an Alpha Image

The goal of this project is to composite a rendered LightWave character, the Walker, over digitized video of a chessboard and table. You'll learn how to merge background and foreground elements in LightWave by using an alpha image:

1. Open LightWave Layout.

2. Open the Effects panel and choose the Compositing tab.

Figure 18.3
Frame 276 from the chessboard footage.

3. From the Background Image pull-down list, load the last image, ChesN276.jpg, in the sequence from the ChessN directory on this book's CD-ROM.

4. From the Foreground Image pull-down list, load image file Walkr276.jpg from the Chapter 18 directory of the CD-ROM. To conserve space on the CD, I've included only the last frame of this sequence. Later in this chapter, I'll show you how to render your own complete sequence from a LightWave scene.

5. From the Foreground Alpha pull-down list, load image file WalkM276.jpg from the Chapter 18 directory of the CD-ROM. This is the alpha channel image rendered with the RGB image you loaded in Step 4. Your screen should look like Figure 18.4. Close the Effects panel.

6. Set the Camera to D1 NTSC to match the 720x480 resolution and pixel aspect ratio of the loaded images.

7. In Render Options, turn on Image Viewer for the Render Display. Press F9 to render the current frame. Your results should look like Figure 18.5.

8. From the Image Viewer, you can choose to view the RGB image or the alpha channel. If you save the image in one of the 32-bit formats, the alpha channel will be included with the color image. Sometimes it's a good idea to preserve an alpha channel through a composition, just in case you need to fine-tune the comp later.

   If you have an RGBA image or sequence, which includes an alpha channel, you need to make a slight modification to this process.

9. In the Image Editor, load the RGBA file. Make sure the Alpha Channel setting is enabled.

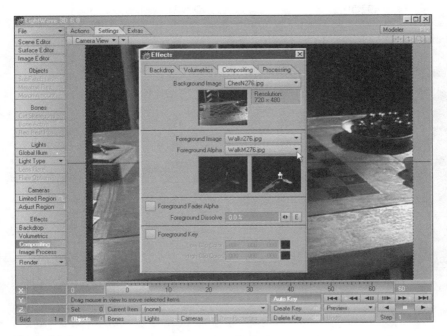

Figure 18.4
RGB, alpha, and background images loaded in Effects panel.

Figure 18.5
RGB image comped over background using alpha image.

10. Clone the RGBA file. The clone's file name will appear with a (1) suffix, and its file type will change to Reference. Using a clone is more efficient than simply loading a second copy of the file because LightWave only has to load the file once. This may not seem like much for a single file, but over the course of a long image sequence, the time savings can be significant.

11. Select the cloned file. Change the Alpha Channel setting to Alpha Only. Your screen should look something like Figure 18.6.

Figure 18.6
RGBA image cloned to provide an alpha image for compositing.

12. Repeat Steps 4 and 5, loading the original RGBA file into Foreground Image and loading the cloned file into Foreground Alpha. Repeat Steps 6, 7, and 8.

This project has shown you how to use separate matte or alpha images to composite color images, and how to composite RGBA images with integral alpha channels. These procedures can be used for the majority of CGI-over-footage comps, and they can also be used to comp bluescreen or difference-keyed live-action footage that has had an alpha channel added to it.

Dealing with Live Action

Compositing your LightWave character animation onto live-action footage usually requires some processing prior to the final alpha channel comp. If the extra processing is done carefully and well, the results can make the LightWave elements indistinguishable from the live action. I find this to be one of the most fun and rewarding forms of character animation—bringing LightWave creatures into the real world.

One of the most common compositing tasks you'll face is cleaning up live-action footage by removing a piece of rigging, a low-hanging microphone, or a crew member who inadvertently ended up inside the frame. This cleanup process is called *rig removal*.

Rig Removal with a Clean Plate

If you have a clean plate (as described in Chapter 17), you can apply it as a front projection image map to a simple object, then position that object in front of any element you want to remove from the backdrop image. This is the simplest, fastest kind of rig removal and is yet another compelling reason to shoot a clean plate whenever possible.

The ChessP sequence was shot with chess pieces arranged on the table (Figure 18.7), and the ChessN sequence was shot as a clean background plate without the chess pieces (Figure 18.3). This enables you to use the ChessN sequence as a clean plate for a rig removal of excess chess pieces.

Figure 18.7
Frame 276 from ChessP motion control footage, showing chess pieces.

Rig Removal with a Masking Object
PROJECT 18.2   The goal of this project is to remove a single foreground element by using a clean plate and a masking object. These are the most basic tasks in rig removal and are used every day by professional digital compositors.

To remove a foreground element, follow these steps:

1. In Modeler, build a disk that is one meter in diameter with zero depth. Apply a white surface named mask. Save the object as mask.lwo.

2. In Layout, open a new scene. In the Image Editor, load the image sequences from the ChessN and ChessP directories on this book's CD-ROM.

3. Open the Effects panel. In the Compositing tab, load the ChessP sequence as the background image.

4. Load the mask object. Rotate it to face the Camera and set a keyframe. Your scene should look like Figure 18.8.

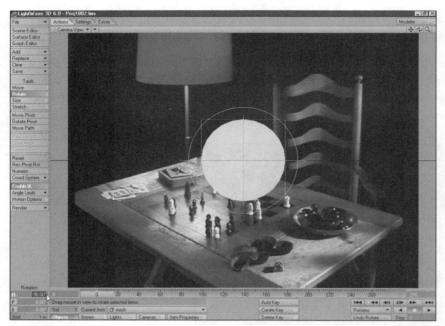

Figure 18.8
Mask object loaded and rotated, and ChessP image sequence loaded as background image.

5. In the Surface Editor, increase the mask surface Luminosity setting to 100 and reduce the Diffuse setting to 0. This will override any shadowing of the mask object, making the rendered surface exactly as bright as the original foreground image.

6. Click on the T button next to the Color setting to open the Texture Editor. Add the ChessN image sequence as a front projection image map, with settings as shown in Figure 18.9. Click on Use Texture and close the Surface Editor.

7. Open the Object Properties panel. With the mask object selected, turn off all three shadow options in the Rendering tab. Close the panel and save the object to preserve the new texture and rendering settings.

   Press F9 to render an image. Your results should look like Figure 18.10, with the chess pieces removed by the mask object in the middle of the image.

8. Move the mask object to center it over the white rook in the right-hand corner of the chessboard. Stretch the mask object along its y- and z-axes to closely match the size of the rook, including its reflection in the chess table. Set a keyframe. Your screen should look like Figure 18.11.

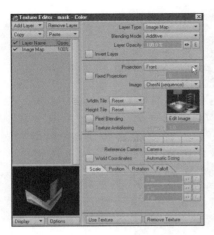

Figure 18.9
Texture Editor settings for the mask surface.

Figure 18.10
Background ChessP image partially masked by ChessN-textured object.

For a variety of reasons, sometimes a clean plate isn't an exact match to the rest of the footage. If you can get the plate to align within a pixel or two, you can often conceal the problem by softening the edges of the masking object. This won't completely fix the discrepancy, but it will make the mismatch harder to spot. If the shot is short or the subject and background are moving fast, it's often good enough.

9. Using a paint program such as Photoshop, create an image that shades from white in the center to black at the edges, like Figure 18.12.

Figure 18.11
The white rook and its reflection are covered by the mask object.

Figure 18.12
Alpha image for softening the edges of the mask object.

10. In the Surface Editor, set the mask object surface transparency to 100 and click on the T button to open the Texture Editor. In the Texture Editor, load the alpha image you created in Step 9, with settings as shown in Figure 18.13. Close the Texture Editor and the Surface Editor and save the mask object again.

11. Render the frame again. You should see a much softer transition from the ChessN to the ChesP footage around the edges of the mask object. If this were a lock-down shot, you'd be done. However, the point of using motion control footage is that the camera moves. That

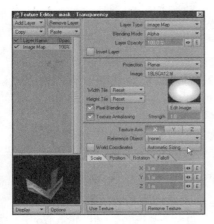

Figure 18.13
Alpha image applied as a texture map to the mask object.

means the masking object has to move, too, in order to continue to cover the white rook without covering any other chess pieces.

12. There is already a keyframe on frame 0 for the mask object. Go to frame 276. Move and stretch the object to cover the white rook again (as shown in Figure 18.14) and set a new keyframe.

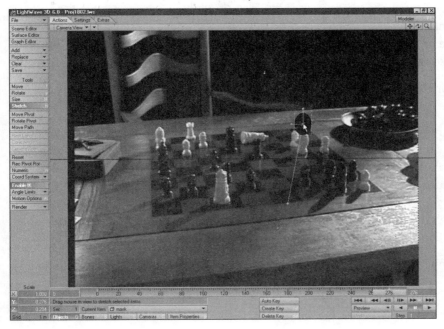

Figure 18.14
The white rook is covered by the mask object at frame 276.

13. Go back to frame 0 to make sure that none of your changes to the mask object have affected the rook's removal at frame 0. Reposition or stretch the mask object if necessary.

14. Go to frame 138, halfway between 0 and 276. You should be able to see that the interpolation between the keyframed positions at frames 0 and 276 does not accurately describe the motion of the white rook around the screen. The motion control camera was moving in an orbit, an elliptical pattern roughly centered around the table. The rook's perceived motion is roughly an inverse of that orbit. In any case, a two-keyframe line won't work, so you need to add more keyframes.

15. While still on frame 138, adjust the mask object to remove the white rook again.

16. Go to frame 69, halfway between 0 and 138. Adjust the mask object to remove the white rook again. Do you see the pattern here? This is what is called *bracketing* a solution. You add each new keyframe halfway between the existing ones. Every time you split a segment of the motion graph in half, you also split the size of any potential errors in half. Pretty quickly, you find that the errors have grown so small that you don't need to add any more keyframes. This is a good approach for most examples of keyframe animation. Even if the final solution ends up having a key on every frame, this bracketing approach reduces the amount of correction you have to apply to each frame.

17. Keep adding keyframes and making corrections until the white rook is removed from every frame. Note that some keyframes are closer together and others are farther apart. If you have to work around tight areas, as when the rook is directly above and behind the other pieces, you will need to set more keyframes. In other parts of the shot, the rook has plenty of open space around it, so the effect mask doesn't have to be placed so precisely. In this example, I used 16 keyframes; you may need more or less.

18. Render the animation. The white rook should be completely invisible, including its shadow and reflection.

Unless you are very good at this, you will probably see a little *chatter* (rapid back-and-forth movement of the masking object) where the rook's base passes closely behind the white knight and pawns near the end of the sequence. You may also notice that the shadow of the rook passes across the corner of the adjoining square and that the mask object doesn't really address the shadow's removal for most of this shot. You can fix the chatter by being more careful in setting your keyframes. You can remove the shadow (and any similar problems) by using a second mask object or by creating a mask object with an animatable outline.

You have just completed a simple rig removal. In this project, you have learned how to do several things:

• Apply a mask object to remove a foreground object

• Use an image map to blend a removal seamlessly into the footage

- Animate a mask object to match the movement of a removal subject

- Bracket keyframes to simplify and speed up hand-keyed animation

Rig removal is one of the most basic, necessary, and often-used digital compositing tasks. In larger shops, the most junior compositors may comp rig removals exclusively until they've paid their dues and can move on to more creative work. Being able to comp rig removals quickly and well can keep you employed and grease your track to more challenging assignments. Most compositing software includes tools that make rig removal easier or more powerful, but it's handy to know how to do it within LightWave too.

Motion Control Cameras

If the shot calls for a camera move coordinated with a composited element, you can avoid the uncertainties and expense of match-moving by using a motion control camera. This is a powered and computer-controlled rig that can repeat precisely the same move time after time. Figure 18.15 shows one type of motion control camera rig.

Figure 18.15
Chris Nibley of Nibley Studio and one of his motion control camera rigs.

A rig like the one pictured enables you to shoot several takes that will register perfectly for compositing. For example, Figure 18.16 shows a set and lighting rigged by Chris Nibley for a motion control shot. One end of the motion control rig is visible at the bottom right in the photo.

As shown in Figures 18.3 and 18.7, one pass was made with an empty chessboard and the other with a full chessboard. With these two shots, you could easily make a controlled dissolve

Figure 18.16
Props and lights set up for a motion control shot.

sequence in which one chess piece at a time materializes onto the chessboard, all while the camera moves.

Besides the two-dimensional information contained in the footage, motion control rigs provide data on the third and fourth dimensions. The motion control data that determines the camera movement can also be ported to LightWave as a time sequence of position and rotation keyframes. This means that you can precisely match the movement of your LightWave camera to that of the real camera. The catch is that the Kuper software that runs the camera rig uses a different keyframe scheme and unit of measure than most CGI software, so you have to do a little translation.

You can load the Kuper data (see Listing 18.1) in a text editor to see the raw data. The first three columns record the camera's movement along the vertical, east-west, and north-south axes, in inches. The second three columns are the axes of the camera's rotation, in degrees.

Listing 18.1   Kuper data for frames 0, 1, 2, 275, 276, and 277 of chess shot.

Vtrack	VEW	VNS	VPan	VTilt	Vroll
-22.1349	44.0368	31.7283	-42.9325	-17.9018	0.0000
-22.1352	44.0350	31.7279	-42.9314	-17.9036	0.0000
-22.1360	44.0309	31.7268	-42.9288	-17.9079	0.0000
<snip>	<snip>	<snip>	<snip>	<snip>	<snip>
-29.1937	-8.1112	19.5570	14.0579	-21.5415	0.0000
-29.1947	-8.1145	19.5550	14.0690	-21.5401	0.0000
-29.1951	-8.1157	19.5543	14.0733	-21.5396	0.0000

For this example, the original data was converted to a LightWave motion (MOT) file with a conversion utility. This produced a literal translation, but that still leaves one problem: LightWave uses metric units, and the MOT file is scaled in inches. This is relatively easy to fix in LightWave. Simply load the MOT file, open the Graph Editor, and scale the x-, y-, and z-axes by .0254 to convert inches to meters. The rotation data does not have to be converted because degrees are not dependent on units of linear measure. The final tweak to this data is to shift all the keyframes up one, because the footage is numbered from frame 1 but the motion file starts at frame 0. After all these changes, the LightWave motion file should look like Listing 18.2.

Listing 18.2   LightWave motion file data for frames 0, 1, 2, 275, 276, and 277 of chess shot.

```
LWMO
1
9
278
1.118535 0.8058988 0.5622264 -42.9325 17.9018 0 1 1 1
0 0 0 0 0
1.118489 0.8058887 0.5622341 -42.9314 17.9036 0 1 1 1
1 0 0 0 0
1.118385 0.8058608 0.5622544 -42.9288 17.9079 0 1 1 1
2 0 0 0 0
<snip>
275 0 0 0 0
-0.2061083 0.496697 0.7415454 14.069 21.5401 0 1 1 1
276 0 0 0 0
-0.2061388 0.4966792 0.7415556 14.0733 21.5396 0 1 1 1
277 0 0 0 0
```

This data enables the LightWave animator to integrate rendered LightWave elements with background plates with a minimum of effort and a great deal more confidence. The advantages of motion control cameras include built-in measurements, no need to match-move manually, and the ability to shoot multiple passes both for effects and for the director's choice of takes. The disadvantages include higher shooting costs ($3,000 per day and up for the rig, camera, and support services), possible loss of or inability to use the data, and the fact that mechanical margins of error can sometimes exceed the optical tolerances for an effect. If the machine is not tuned up properly, camera slop becomes visible in the final composite.

PROJECT 18.3   Using Camera Motion Data

The goal of this project is to make a duplicate model, in the computer, of the chessboard surface visible in the motion control footage. In addition to catching the shadow of any LightWave element, the chessboard must also create matching reflections.

To create a duplicate model, follow these steps:

1. Open a new scene. Load the chessboard object you created in Chapter 17. Load one of the chessboard image sequences as the background.

2. Apply the motion control file to the camera. The motion graph should look like Figure 18.17.

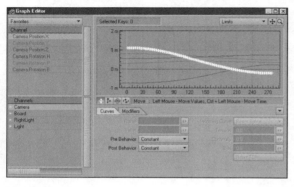

Figure 18.17
The camera motion graph, based on the Kuper motion control data.

3. Using the bracketing approach described in Project 18.2, set keyframes to position the chessboard object in the scene so that it matches the position and rotation of the chessboard in the background image. You should end up with something like Figure 18.18.

You may have to create several keyframes to correct for minor mechanical errors in the motion control rig. For example, Figure 18.19 shows the motion path I created to more accurately match the chessboard object to the background image sequence. The variation was very small, only a few centimeters overall.

Once you have the chessboard object accurately matched to the background image, you can parent an animated character to the chessboard object. Any action the character performs will automatically be matched to the background image sequence. This is how I created the Walker footage used earlier in this chapter.

Remember that motion control data is only slightly less valuable than the footage itself. If you lose the data (and it seems to have happened to everyone at least once), you will be facing a manual move match process and will probably blow your schedule and budget. If possible, get a diskette of the raw data before you leave the set. The motion control data is digital, it does not lose anything in duplication, and it is usually small enough to fit on a single diskette. Always be sure to make backups and keep tabs on your motion data!

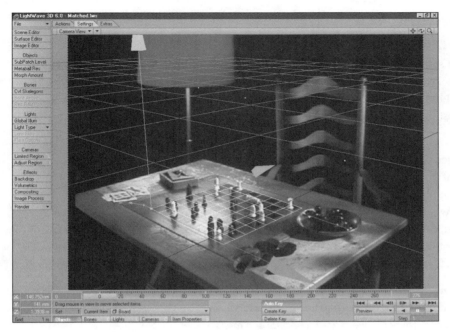

Figure 18.18
The LightWave chess scene showing the chessboard object matched to the background image.

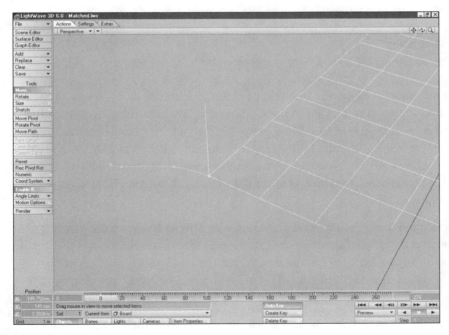

Figure 18.19
LightWave chess scene close-up showing the chessboard object motion path.

Match-Moving

In this book, you have learned how to measure the set, construct LightWave models for shadow-catching surfaces, match lighting direction and color, and animate a character to a single still image. These are all parts of a complex puzzle, the match-move, and now you're ready to put it all together. Being able to do a match-move is a valuable job skill. This is a job that even the most advanced software tools can only partly perform. Human artists are still necessary to put the final polish on a match-move, even at top-end effects houses like ILM.

If you've completed the preceding project, you've got a pretty good handle on the process of compositing LightWave elements onto still background images. This was pretty much the state of the compositing art until *Jurassic Park*. All LightWave compositing was done with footage from a locked-down, immobile camera because it was simply too difficult and expensive to match elements to a moving camera. When Steven Spielberg challenged the JP effects team to allow him to shoot from a handheld camera, they came through with the basic techniques used in most effects houses today.

> *"Our job was to create a computer camera move that matched what the cameraman did on the set. If there were reference points such as tennis balls or glow sticks, we'd match-move to them. Otherwise, we'd use blueprints and measurements from the actual set or location to build rough 3D models to represent people and props in the plate. The idea is to move the computer camera around until it locks into the actual cameraman's view of the set. When we had an accurate match-move program, we'd deliver that information to the animator, who would use it as a guide to lock the choreography of the creatures to the live-action plate."*
> —Charlie Clavadetscher, ILM 3D match-move team member

The next step is to animate the LightWave camera to precisely mimic the movements of the footage camera. This requires you to stabilize the footage in translation, rotation, and scaling and extract camera motion from a tracked reference point. The primary hassle of match-moving is tweaking rough footage. A handheld camera, even on a Steadicam, changes location and attitude on every frame. This means that without other assistance, the match-mover has to hand-animate the camera in all three axes of rotation and all three coordinate axes, for each frame of footage. Ouch!

But of course, there's good news. (You knew it all along, didn't you?) Necessity drove clever innovators to develop a technique called motion stabilizing, which removes most of the frame-by-frame camera motion and smooths out the remainder. The end result is like having the world's best camera dolly but without having to set up, tear down, or have extra grips—all the freedom of a handheld camera with the ease of use of a dolly or Steadicam.

The example footage of my front sidewalk and porch was shot on Hi8, then digitized through an ATI All-In-Wonder video card at 30 fps. I then saved it out as an image sequence and ran it

Figure 18.20
The first frame, Stable001.jpg, from the stabilized image sequence.

through several stabilizing processes using Eyeon Software's Digital Fusion. This produced the image sequence you will find in the Stable directory on this book's CD-ROM (see Figure 18.20).

The wide black border was added to allow room for the image to rotate and scale during the stabilization process without any part of the image being lost. After the match-move and render, a corresponding destabilization process (also in Digital Fusion) will remove the border and restore the camera movement. The following project shows you how to perform the middle part of the match-move process, the manual camera animation in LightWave to match the movement of the real camera in all six axes of position and rotation.

PROJECT 18.4 Match-Moving the Porch Model

The goal of this project is to animate a shadow-catcher object in LightWave to precisely match the tracked pattern in the background footage. You will use a motion file and stabilized footage from the CD and the shadow surfaces and lighting you created in Chapter 17. If you didn't build the models and lighting scenes, you can use the files provided on this book's CD-ROM.

1. Open LightWave and clear the scene. Set the Last Frame field to 265.

2. Set the Camera to 0 on all axes of rotation and translation, and set a key on frame 0. Switch to Camera View.

3. Open the Camera Properties panel. The camcorder I used to record this footage has a 1.6 to 3.6 focal length zoom lens. I shot this at approximately 1.0 zoom factor, so set Lens Focal Length to 2.4mm as a first approximation. Set Aperture Height to 1/2" CCD. Set Width to 2160 and Height to 1458 to match the resolution of the stabilized footage. Close the Camera panel.

4. Open the Image Editor. Click on Load Sequence and choose the image sequence located in the Stable directory on this book's CD-ROM. Close the Image Editor.

5. Open the Effects panel. In the Compositing tab, select the image sequence as the background image. Close the Effects panel.

6. Open the Display Options panel. Turn on Background Image for Camera View Background. Close the panel. Your scene should look like Figure 18.21.

Figure 18.21
Stabilized footage loaded as background image in LightWave.

7. Add a null and name it OriginNull. (First person to make a pun gets 30 whacks with a wet noodle.) Parent the Camera to this null.

8. Load object 1_meter.lwo, located on the CD-ROM. This is your reference frame, a simple 1-meter square. Parent this object to the OriginNull. Move 1_meter to 2.0 meters on the z-axis, and set a key on frame 0. This 2.0 meter offset is not completely arbitrary; it's a rough estimate of the distance-from-camera-to-tracker pattern in frame 154.

9. The 1_meter object is used strictly for reference during the match-move and should not appear in the final rendering. Open the Objects panel, and in the Appearance Options tab, turn on Unseen By Rays and Unseen By Camera and turn off all three shadow options. This will make the object invisible to the Camera during rendering. Close the Objects panel.

10. You only need to see the reference frame as a wireframe object. Open the Scene Editor and change 1_meter to wireframe display. Close the Scene Editor.

11. Add a null. Name it TrackerNull and parent it to 1_meter. This is the object that will move to follow the tracker pattern.

12. With TrackerNull still active, open the Graph Editor. Click on Load Motion. Choose the TrackerNull.mot file from the Motions directory of the CD-ROM. Now click on Use Motion. Your scene should look like Figure 18.22.

Figure 18.22
Tracker motion file applied to TrackerNull, which is parented to the 1_meter reference frame. Note the motion path trailing below null.

You will notice that TrackerNull is not positioned anywhere near the second-step chip that was the tracking pattern. Tracking is based on x,y plane movement of the tracker pattern. The motion file's x-,y-coordinates are expressed as fractions of the image dimensions; that is, a pattern in the center of the screen would have the coordinates 0.5, 0.5. No value can be lower than 0.0, 0.0, and no value can be higher than 1.0, 1.0, because those coordinates are off the screen where the tracker could not follow the pattern. These coordinates are precise to six decimal places. The catch is that they are intended to match an image with the same proportions as the tracked footage. That means you need to resize the reference frame, the 1_meter object, to fit the boundaries of the background image as it appears in LightWave's Camera View. This is easy to tweak with the Numeric input.

13. Select 1_meter and change the size until its edges precisely match the boundaries of the background image in the Camera View, as shown in Figure 18.23. Use the Numeric panel to tweak the size in x- and y-axes to at least three decimal places. Set the z value equal to the x value. Take your time and get it right; this will affect every other step in the match-move. When you are satisfied with the size, set a key at frame 0. If you step through the frames now, the TrackerNull should precisely match the chip in the second step.

Figure 18.23
Resizing the reference frame, which is barely visible as a narrow border around the background image, scales the motion of TrackerNull to match the tracker pattern's position.

14. Add another null, name it PorchPivotNull, and parent it to TrackerNull.

15. Load the Porch.lwo object from the CD-ROM. Parent it to the PorchPivotNull. In the Scene Editor, set the Porch to full wireframe display. The nulls and reference frame can be bounding box wireframes, but you'll need to see all the Porch's edges in this project.

16. With the Porch object selected, open the Surfaces panel. Select the PorchSurface surface, set its color to black, and click on the T button next to Surface Color to open the Color Texture subpanel. For Texture Type, select the stabilized footage as a front projection image map. Set Texture Opacity to 100% and close the subpanel to return to the Surfaces panel. This will make the Porch render as nearly invisible except for shadowing effects.

17. In the Advanced Options tab, set Alpha Channel to Shadow Density. This will make the Porch surface a shadow-catcher for any other objects you animate over it. Close the Surfaces panel.

18. With the Porch object still selected, open the Objects panel. Turn off Self Shadow and Cast Shadow. In the Appearance Options tab, turn on the Polygon Edges checkbox and set Edge Color to bright blue. Close the Objects panel.

This will make the wireframe outline of the Porch visible in your test renderings, making it much easier for you to evaluate the matching of edges to the background image. The critical details of the background image can be very small and difficult to see in some frames, and the wireframes in Layout can obscure those details. The rendered polygon edges are a very good visual aid. Just remember to turn off Polygon Edges before you start the final rendering!

Child objects inherit the scaling of their parent objects. We don't want the Porch object to be scaled to match the background image's aspect ratio, so we need to resize the PorchPivotNull to counteract the scaling of the 1_meter object.

19. Resize the PorchPivotNull to the inverse of 1_meter's scaling. Figure 18.24 shows 1_meter object's scaling to be 6.345, 4.260, 6.345. Dividing 1 by each of these numbers gives a scaling correction of 0.1576, 0.2347, 0.1576. Apply these scaling corrections to PorchPivotNull.

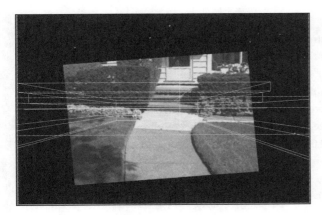

Figure 18.24
Porch object and PorchPivotNull scaled by TrackerNull's scaling, 6.345 x, 4.260 y, and 6.345 z.

Your results should look like Figure 18.25. You can check the scaling correction, if you like, by loading another copy of the Porch object and positioning it to match the first one. You'll have to give it the vector sum XYZ translations and HPB rotations of all the parent objects to get a precise alignment for your comparisons. When you're done with the check, delete the duplicate Porch object.

The Porch object is constructed according to the reference sketch used in Chapter 17, with its pivot point set at the location of the chip in the edge of the second step, which was used as a tracking pattern. This means that applying the x,y motion of the tracker to this model will automatically make it match the x,y motion of the real object in the background footage with no offsets.

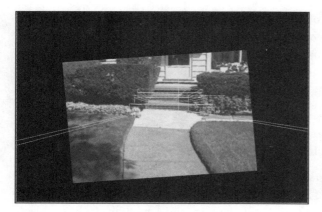

Figure 18.25
PorchPivotNull scaled to correct for the TrackerNull's scaling, 0.3748 X, 0.5 Y, and 0.3748 Z. The Porch object remains at 1.0 scaling on all axes.

The stabilization of the footage, combined with the tracker-derived x,y animation of the model, takes the place of two-thirds of the animation of the LightWave Camera. The only positional variable left to animate is the z-axis distance between the camera and the model. In order to animate the Camera, you would have to animate the 1_meter reference object's scaling to keep it exactly matched to the edges of the background image in the Camera View. You would also have to animate the counter-scaling of the PorchPivotNull to keep the tracker motion accurate. That's the reason for all the nulls and parenting; you can simply scale the OriginNull to adjust the distance between Camera and target, and the 1_meter reference object automatically scales to match. You still have to counter-scale the PorchPivotNull, but because everything is proportional, you can do that with a single click and drag.

In the example footage, the camera moves in a complex path, partially orbiting the porch steps. This is fairly difficult to animate. However, the camera-and-porch relative motion can also be described as a comparatively simple set of rotations of the porch around the pivot located at the tracker pattern. That's why the Porch object is built with the pivot point in that location.

The camera's focal length determines the amount of parallax at any given distance. With the model located at the appropriate distance from the LightWave camera and positioned over the background image, you can adjust the LightWave camera's focal length to match the parallax of the model to that of the original object. If you have an accurate measure of either the camera-to-target distance or the camera's focal length, finding the missing measurement is not difficult. However, if you have neither the focal length nor the camera-to-target distance, you have to twiddle and tweak until you find a usable setting. This is why it is so important to record this information when you are on set, and why you should be especially nice to the focus puller. Fortunately, for the purposes of this project, the initial setting of 2.4mm is usable.

With this setup, you need to animate only a few, low-frequency variables to complete the match-move:

- Size of the OriginNull to approximately match the distance from Camera to target, substituting for Camera z-axis motion

- Size of the PorchPivotNull in all three axes to control the height, width, and depth of the Porch

- Rotation of the Porch in all three axes

As I mentioned previously, a useful strategy is to animate the lowest-frequency variable first. That means animating the OriginNull scaling first; you may need only a handful of keyframes because you can be pretty sloppy with this variable and it doesn't change very quickly. The interaction of the PorchPivotNull scaling and the rotation of the Porch object means that you will have to animate these variables pretty much simultaneously.

20. Go to frame 154. Because this was the reference frame for stabilizing the footage, there should be no position, rotation, or scaling distortions in this frame. The distance from the tracker pattern (the chip in the second step) to the camera in this frame is roughly 2 meters, so you don't need to scale the OriginNull. With no scaling of the OriginNull, you shouldn't have to make major scaling corrections with the PorchPivotNull.

21. Rotate the Porch object so the line representing the upper front edge of the second step, which passes through the pivot point, is aligned with the upper front edge of the second step in the background image. Modify the Heading, Pitch, and Bank values so as many as possible of the horizontal lines in the model align with horizontal references in the background image. Your results should look something like Figure 18.26. Set a key for the Porch at frame 154.

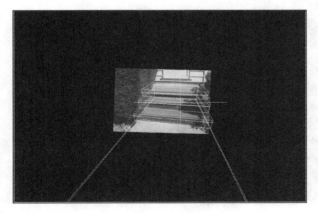

Figure 18.26
The Porch object aligned with the horizontal background lines in frame 154.

The Porch still appears a little too large. Tweak the PorchPivotNull size. Try all three axes at once first, then tweak individual axes to adjust width, height, and length. You may find that you need to go back and tweak the Porch rotations to get a more precise alignment with the background. When you think you have matched the background's scale and rotations as closely as possible, set keyframes for the Porch, PorchPivotNull, and OriginNull. Your results should look like Figure 18.27.

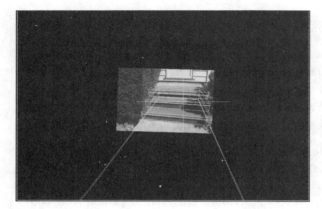

Figure 18.27
The Porch aligned and PorchPivotNull and OriginNull scaled to match the background in frame 154.

You can check your work by rendering the frame with the same settings you will use for your final renders. With Polygon Edges still turned on for the Porch object, your results should look something like Figure 18.28.

Figure 18.28
Rendered test of frame 154. Note how blue polygon edges make evaluating the match much easier.

Repeat the preceding steps for the other keyframes in a bracketing pattern as described earlier in this chapter. I suggest frames 1, 75, 180, 211, and so on.

- First, size the OriginNull. Examine the background image and make your best estimate of the distance from the chip pattern to the camera. Divide that estimate by 2 (remember, 1.0 for the OriginNull is 2 meters' distance) and enter the result as the size of OriginNull.

- Second, rotate the Porch to align its horizontal lines with the corresponding horizontal edges in the background image.

- Third, size PorchPivotNull to bring the width, depth, and height of the Porch into alignment with the background image.

- Finally, go back and tweak Porch rotations and PorchPivotNull size to correct any remaining errors. Set keys for all three elements and go on to the next frame.

The fewer the keyframes, the smoother the motion and the less likely you will make errors that produce chattering. With every keyframe you set, the discrepancies to be corrected in the adjoining keyframes become smaller. It's up to you when to stop the tweaking; on a short deadline, "good enough" may be only the six initial keyframes. With a longer production schedule, you may have time to tweak a couple dozen keyframes.

For frames 212 through 265, you have a slightly harder job. Because the chip on the edge of the second step is no longer visible in the background image, you don't have tracker data in the imported motion file. That means you don't know where the Porch is supposed to be located in the x,y plane. That adds those two variables to the list you have already animated, and compensating for the interdependencies between all these variables can be a very demanding juggling act. This is where you practice your interpolation skills. Your first step is to eyeball what variable settings you can simply by looking at the background image for frames 212 through 265. The most obvious candidate is the OriginNull scaling.

22. Go to frame 212. In the Scene Editor, choose Hide All Objects. This gets the wireframes out of your way so you can see the background better.

23. Scrub through frames 212 to 265, looking only at the distance between the camera and the porch. At what frames does the camera stop moving toward or away from the porch? Ignore side-to-side, pitch, bank, or heading changes; concentrate on that z-axis motion. By my estimate, the camera stopped moving closer to the porch on frame 231.

24a. Go to frame 231, or whichever frame you think is correct. Estimate the distance from the camera to the estimated position of the tracker pattern. You'll have to extrapolate the leading edge of the second step. Divide that estimate by 2 (remember, 1.0 for the OriginNull is 2 meters' distance) and enter the result as the size of OriginNull. Set the same value for a key on frames 232 and 265. That nails down the z-axis motion for the rest of the match-move.

24b. Another approach is to select the OriginNull and open the Graph Editor. Choose the X Scale graph and look at the curve. You should be able to see a definite shape to the curve and estimate pretty closely the value that will extend the curve to frame 231. Click on Use Motion to close the Graph Editor.

25. The scaling of the OriginNull directly affects the scaling corrections for the PorchPivotNull. Set keys at OriginNull's keyframes for the scaling of PorchPivotNull. As a first approximation, keep the same PorchPivotNull scaling as in frame 211.

26. The next lowest-frequency variable is the Porch object's Bank rotation. In the Scene Editor, make the Porch object visible as a full wireframe. On frames 231 and 265, adjust the Porch object's Bank rotation to align the horizontal edges of the Porch object with the nearest horizontal edges in the background image.

27. On frame 231, move the TrackerNull on its x- and y-axes to match up the rear edge of the second porch step with the corresponding line in the background image. Cross-check this with the alignment of the front edge of the object's step and the estimated front edge of the step in the background image. If you can't get the two alignments to reconcile, you may need to change the PorchPivotNull scaling and try again.

From this point on, you will need to simultaneously tweak the PorchPivotNull scaling on all three axes, the TrackerNull x and y position, and the Porch rotation on all three axes. An error on one variable affects the other seven. That may seem like a lot of variables to juggle at once, but remember that any remaining changes should be very small. By this time, any remaining errors in alignment, scaling, or position should only be the width of a pixel or two on your screen.

28. When you have frame 231 matched to your satisfaction, do the same for frame 265.

Because frame 231 marks the end of the camera's movement in several axes, I recommend that you copy the settings for Porch rotation, PorchPivotNull scaling, and TrackerNull position to frame 265. This will accomplish over 95 percent of the necessary tweaks for you; the remaining tweaks are relatively easy. Your final results should look like Figure 18.29.

29. Now you need to step through the entire animation, looking for the frames where discrepancies peak. Wherever the match is off enough that it will show in the final rendering, create a set of keyframes to correct the problem.

Some variables will require more keyframes than others. OriginNull and PorchPivotNull scaling should require the fewest (and identical number of) keyframes. Porch rotation will require slightly more keyframes. TrackerNull may require a key for every frame after frame 211, when the tracked motion file runs out. The x,y plane movement of TrackerNull is the highest-frequency variable in this match-move and therefore the one that you will spend the most time and effort tweaking. Your manual keyframing between frames 212 and 265

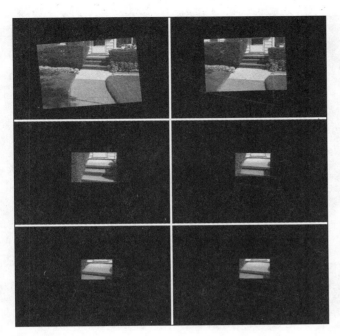

Figure 18.29
Test renderings of frames 1, 75, 180, 211, 231, and 265.

should look very much like the tracker motion of frames 1 through 211, with tiny changes on most frames and the occasional larger jump.

30. When you have completed the match-move, add an animated character or other moving LightWave element, and parent it to the Porch object.

    This doesn't have to be complicated, just something that casts a moving shadow over the steps and upper surface of the Porch object to show how well you've match-moved the shadow-catching surfaces. If you like, use Load From Scene to add objects, motions, and lights from the LampHop.lws scene file on the CD-ROM. This is a desk lamp object that I animated to hop up the porch steps. After you Load From Scene, you will need to delete the original scene's default Light, leaving the SunLight imported from the LampHop scene. You will also need to parent both the desk lamp object and the SunLight to the Porch object so they inherit the match-move, as shown in Figure 18.30.

31. You may want to leave Polygon Edges on to check the first set of renderings with the character added; after that, turn off Polygon Edges so you can accurately judge the lay of the character's shadow over the edges of the Porch object.

32. When you are satisfied with the test render results, render the entire image sequence. If you plan to comp a subtractive merge, you can leave the PorchSurface and background

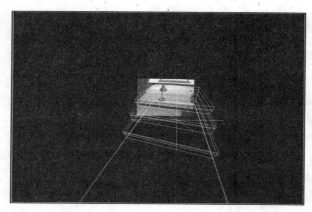

Figure 18.30
Match-move scene with desk lamp added.

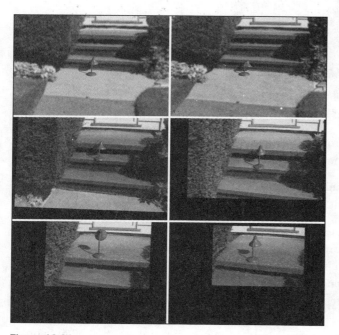

Figure 18.31
Final renderings of frames 1, 75, 180, 154, 211, and 265 with animated desk lamp and sunlight added. Images are cropped to 720x486 to show detail; the full images are still 2160x1458.

image as is. Your results should look something like Figure 18.31. If you prefer to comp an additive merge, you should drop the image maps from both PorchSurface and the background, resulting in a completely black frame except for the desk lamp.

By finishing this project, you have learned how to do the following:

- Apply a tracker motion file to position an object relative to the background image

- Match camera distance and focal length

- Divide the position, rotation, and scaling variables between several objects to enable the use of fewer keyframes

- Choose and keyframe the lowest-frequency variables first

- Set keyframes in a bracketing pattern to minimize the total number of keyframes

- Coordinate the interrelating variables of rotation, scaling, and position

- Extrapolate a new value from the slope of the existing motion graph

- Check your alignments in a test render by using Polygon Edges

Completing a match-move takes a lot of effort and attention to detail, but with practice, you will accumulate techniques and shortcuts that make it faster and easier. Once you have a match-move locked down, you can use it to render separate shadow, ambient, specular, and Z-buffer passes. This can greatly increase your options for compositing effects and can make comping the LightWave elements seamlessly into the live footage much easier.

Match-Move Power Tools

Worley Laboratories' Taft Collection is a set of seven specialized utility plug-ins, designed to perform such useful tasks as gluing image maps to matched objects, stringing flexible hoses, and creating automatic gunfire and projectiles. These solve real-world production problems or at least automate the stupid and boring parts of existing solutions. This collection packs a lot of fun into a small, affordable package.

The documentation is what we've come to expect from Worley: functional, well organized, complete, and written with an offbeat sense of humor that makes the 68-page manual an entertaining read. You never know what obscure fact or outrageous fiction will come next. Even the blank page at the end, usually reserved for the user's notes, is retitled to a more ambitious purpose. (I won't give away the joke; buy the product, if you must know.) 39 demo scenes, 46 objects, and 13 images are included on a second "Taft Extras" disk. The demos are a nice complement to the manual and enable users to get up to speed quickly. In addition to the publisher's direct support, you can subscribe to the worleylabs listserv on eGroups to share experiences, tips, and tricks with other Worley Laboratories' customers. To sign up, go to **www.egroups.com/group/worleylabs**.

Like other Worley Laboratories products, the seven Taft plug-ins share several useful interface features. If you already use the Polk plug-ins, you'll be familiar with the Load, Save, and Disable buttons, the Item Picker, and the general look and feel of the plug-in interfaces. To Worley's credit, all the controls do exactly what you'd expect them to (unlike some LightWave plug-ins).

Camera Match

The preceding projects in this chapter have demonstrated that even a single-frame camera match is difficult and time-consuming, and a full six-axis match-move can be nearly impossible. By using the Camera Match plug-in, you can significantly reduce the workload for both still matching and match-moving.

Worley is very clear on the purpose of this plug-in: "A caveat: Camera Match is designed for use only with photographs, not animations. Animated camera tracking is significantly different and far more specialized." However, he also provides a concise half-page description of how to apply Camera Match to execute a successful match-move. It's still not fun, but it's about 80 percent less work than a fully manual match-move.

Camera Match requires a fair amount of up-front setup. If you didn't take measurements at the set, and you no longer have access to the objects or fixed features that were photographed, don't bother trying to make a match. Your results depend on accurate measurements; no numbers, no results. Guesstimates? You're better off eyeballing a manual match.

Once you have your measurements, you need to define feature points by placing nulls at the measured locations. As a test, I used the same front porch object as in the preceding projects. I had already built the model, and had pretty accurate measurements of the visible artifacts I had used for tracking and stabilization. In Layout, I added nulls to each feature location. I opened the first image in Photoshop and used the Info panel to get the x,y coordinates of each feature. Finally, I opened the Camera Match plug-in and typed in the data, as shown in Figure 18.32.

The first pass produced a pretty good match, as shown in Figure 18.33. Not bad for about 15 minutes' work; it also identified where my measurements were off, so I was able to make corrections for an even better match on other frames. In my opinion, Camera Match is a tool you should not do without, if your work ever requires you to match LightWave elements with real-world images or footage.

Sticky Front Projection

LightWave's Front Projection Image Map is very useful when you're trying to composite LightWave elements over a photo or live-action footage. You simply model a few rough shadow-catching surfaces, apply the photo as a Front Projection, and render. However, moving the camera or the object requires you to perform an exact match-move, a very expensive process.

The StickyFP plug-in enables you to stick the image map to the surface, so when you move the object or the camera, the image map is still applied accurately. With this tool, you can add depth to make a 3D animation from a single image, hide problems in a less-than-perfect match-move, or create photorealistic maps for an object to be used in another animation.

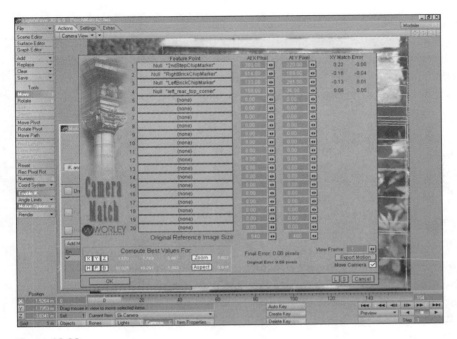

Figure 18.32
Camera Match plug-in interface, showing x,y position data entered for four of the feature points in the first porch image.

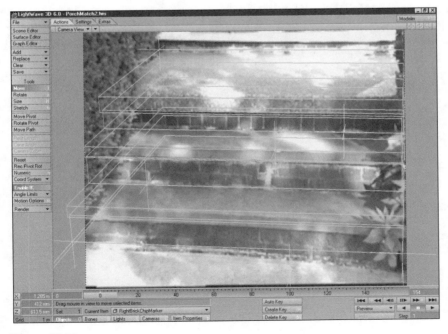

Figure 18.33
First pass of Camera Match, the result of about 15 minutes' work.

StickyFP is especially powerful when used with Camera Match. Apply Camera Match to nail down an accurate camera position, apply StickyFP to stick down the image map to the object's surface, and you have as accurately mapped an object as possible. If your work requires matching live-action objects, StickyFP and Camera Match will be your new best friends. My only complaint is that I didn't have these plug-ins a year ago!

Worley Laboratories
405 El Camino Real #121
Menlo Park, CA 94025
Tel: (650) 322-7532
www.worley.com

Moving On

If you have completed all the exercises in this chapter, you should now be able to composite your characters over other LightWave layers, backgrounds, and live footage. This gives you an enormous creative range for your own films. Even if you work in an environment where someone else does the compositing work, your mastery of the jargon and technology will make it easier for you to understand their job and, therefore, make you a more productive and valuable member of the team.

Chapter 19

Title Design and Finishing Touches

There are a few finishing touches you should consider for your completed character animation. Depending on your audience, you may want to add titles, end credits, bars and tone, and perhaps even some post-process effects like film grain. None of these are crucial to your character animation per se, but when done well, they do add a final polish. Good title design and readable credits add to the professional appearance of your animations. Take the time to do them right, especially for your demo reel or an independent short.

If this is just for your demo reel, minimal contact information and technical credits are enough. If you plan to distribute your work through any public channels, you should create main titles and credits at the very least. If you are considering broadcast or animation festival submissions, you should do the whole nine yards.

Title Design

Even a great animation won't look quite as good without titles, and a bad animation looks a little more professional with good titles. Titles are cheap, quick to create, and easy to animate (compared to characters, anyway), but you still have to put some thought into them. They should at least conform to basic principles of typographic design, because your audience has to read them. These rules are few, simple, and easy to follow.

Keep each title card on screen long enough for your audience to read it, at least one second for every five words. Don't dally, though. If you leave a title card in place for too long, you can lose your audience's attention, not to mention subtract from the time you are allotted to actually tell your story. If you are titling for a demo reel, you should keep your titles down to the minimum time—the reviewer will probably fast-forward through them if they last longer than

10 seconds. If you've got a lot to say, put it in the credits. If the reviewer gets that far, he will take the trouble to read it.

Don't move your titles around too much. Zooming titles that fly all over the screen are the hallmark of an amateur. There are some "professional" title designers out there who should be ashamed of the titles they've done for feature film and television. Flash, glitz, and a virtuoso animation performance are just annoyances if they don't help you get your message across. A prime example of this is the horrendous title and credit work for *Spawn*, in which even the expected and well-known names in the credits are almost impossible to read because of the rapidly oscillating text and poorly contrasting colors. It looks like the optical printer's gate had been left unlocked and the film just went through any which way. If it was designed to be disturbing, it succeeded, but if the titles were meant to be read, the design failed. Hold still, and let the words in the titles speak for themselves!

Don't get fancy with shaders and textures for titles. Brushed metal and polished chrome are very much passé and the mark of an amateur. The only circumstances under which you should texture a title are when the texture ties the titles directly to the story, the texture is not obtrusive or distracting, and the text will remain easily legible. A very nice example of this is the ribbon texture for the word "Beauty" in the title sequence of Disney's animated remake of *Beauty and the Beast*. The final effect is subtle, attractive to the eye, unobtrusive to the text, and it links to the story thematically by its similarity to Belle's hair ribbons.

If you're absolutely positive that you want to animate your titles, at least make them animate legibly in the direction the audience will be reading them. If you bring letters on screen from right to left like a television streamer, the audience can read them as they appear. This enables you to minimize the title's on-screen time and doesn't annoy your audience. If you bring the letters on screen in reverse order, the audience can't read them until the last (first) letter appears. Unless there's a thematic reason for doing things backwards, this is just an annoying affectation.

Many fonts are unsuitable for modeling and animation or for reliable reproduction in video or film. The first disqualification is the minimum width of a stroke. Many typefaces that are designed for print have fine serifs, the thin strokes that cross the ends of the major strokes in a letter (see Figure 19.1). By comparison, sans serif typefaces have no minor strokes and tend to reproduce much more evenly for both film and television.

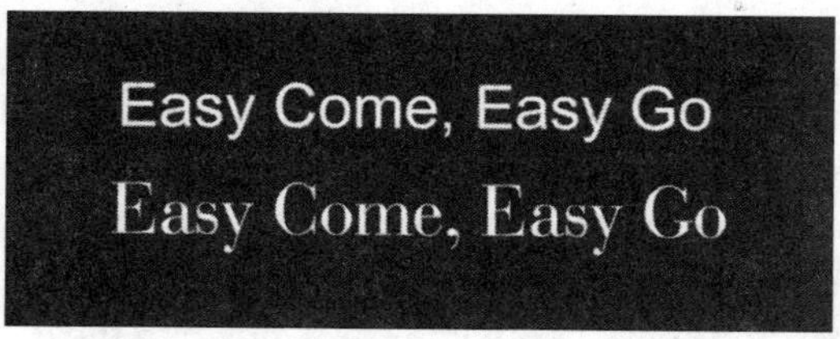

Figure 19.1
Sans serif and serif fonts.

Keep your delivery medium in mind when you choose a title font. When reproduced on film, fine serifs are very sensitive to the timing of film development and can close up or bleed out. They are also sensitive to the projection environment, when low projector light can cause serifs to disappear into the background. In video, a serif that is too fine may disappear entirely or break up into a multicolored fringe effect. This is caused by the video monitor's attempt to reproduce a single line of contrasting pixels—computer monitors are built for this, but the typical consumer television isn't anywhere near that precise. Any misalignment of the video monitor's three color guns will give the contrasting pixels a border of red, blue, and green. If the text moves at all, this multihued border will also appear to crawl, the illusion of secondary movement produced as pixels are handed off unevenly from one row of screen phosphors to the next.

Keep your letters open. This is closely related to the problem of serifs. Some fonts have such small letter openings that they can close up completely when reproduced on film or video. Letters like "b," "d," and "o" have less frequent problems with occluded openings, but letters like "e," "a," and "g" have smaller openings and can run into problems more easily. Letter openings are important visual cues for your audience, so choose title fonts that have letter openings that are easy to see (see Figure 19.2).

Figure 19.2
Open and closed fonts.

Make sure the title letters differ enough for the audience to read them easily. Some fonts are so heavily stylized that the letters appear almost identical, forcing the reader to search for more subtle clues to identify them. Figure 19.3 shows examples of good and inadequate differentiation.

Figure 19.3
Good and bad differentiation.

Keep your ascenders and descenders as reading cues for your audience. Ascenders and descenders are the strokes that go above the midline or below the bottom of some letters. Lowercase "b," "d," "h," "k," and "l" have ascenders, and "g," "j," "p," "q," and "y" have descenders. These are strong visual cues that make it easier for your audience to read your titles quickly and easily. Some stylized fonts compress the ascenders and descenders into the midline space, distorting the shape of the letter. These fonts are harder for your audience to read (see Figure 19.4), so you should avoid them. The same is true of font cases. If upper- and lowercase characters are difficult to tell apart, or if you run titles in all caps, small caps, or all lowercase, your audience will have a harder time reading your titles. Keep your text simple and legible, and leave the storytelling and showing off to your characters.

Figure 19.4
Normal ascenders and descenders compared to vertically compressed fonts.

Use italic fonts with caution and moderation. A typeface that leans in odd directions is difficult to read. Choose an italic angle (if any) less than 30 degrees and preferably less than 15. Inclining the angle of a letter's major strokes changes its appearance enough to make it harder to identify. If you choose to use an italic font, at least keep the angle consistent. Once the audience identifies the italic angle, it's a little easier to read until the angle changes again. If a stylized font changes the inclination of each letter, it's confusing and difficult to read. See Figure 19.5 for examples.

Figure 19.5
Normal and italic fonts.

Keep your titles consistent. Once you have selected a good font, use it for all your titles. Changing fonts in the middle of a title sequence requires your audience to readjust, in effect reducing readability and wasting screen time. Stick to one font throughout your titles.

Finally, keep in mind that your audience presumably is interested in your animation, not the number of oddball fonts (Figure 19.6) you keep on your computer. Don't select a strange font just because it caught your eye. You don't want your audience to be so distracted with your titles that they miss the beginning of your animation. Choose title fonts carefully!

Figure 19.6
Good and bad font choices for titles and credits.

Choose your title colors carefully. Sometimes appropriate colors can be a nice touch, but more often any colors other than black and white are a bad idea. Your primary goal is to ensure that your audience can read the titles, and poor color choices can reduce the visual contrast to the point where the letters blend into the background. At the other extreme, clashing color choices can create a disturbing effect that is not only illegible but causes a majority of the audience to look away from the screen. In NTSC video, using high-saturation adjacent colors that are of opposite hue (i.e., red-green or yellow-blue) produces chroma crawl, dots that seem to crawl along the contrasting edges. This is actually the subcarrier, visible when the dot interlace is defeated by the 180-degree hue phase shift. You can minimize this effect by choosing less contrasting hues and less saturated colors. In general, plain white letters on a black background are the best title colors you can use.

If you are superimposing titles over a background image, try to select a light primary color that contrasts pleasantly with the dominant hues of the background. If the background image changes markedly, which is common with live footage or strong camera movements, you may have problems getting consistent visual contrast between titles and background. In these situations, it's generally a good idea to use drop shadows or a darker outline to completely separate the superimposed titles from the background. The main title sequence from *Silence Of The Lambs* is an excellent example of simple, strongly contrasting superimposed titles. Throughout a long sequence of camera moves and widely varying backgrounds, the titles never lose contrast.

Be careful where you put your titles in the frame. For best results in all media, titles must be limited to the video text-safe area. Most televisions cut off the outer edge of the picture with a bezel over the tube's edges or rounded corners in the tube itself. Even if you are working in film, it's smart to title with eventual television broadcast in mind. Keep your titles in the safe area or the work will have to be retitled for broadcast—and you won't necessarily have control of the new titles!

LightWave provides built-in video text-safe guidelines. Press "d" to bring up the Display Options panel, then click on Show Safe Areas. The Camera view will show two concentric rectangles with rounded corners (see Figure 19.7). The outer one is the action-safe area, and the inner one is the text-safe area.

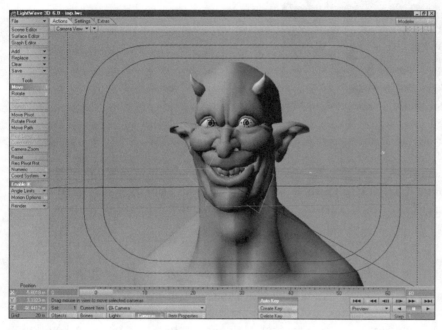

Figure 19.7
Action-safe area (outer) and text-safe area (inner).

When you are designing credits, start by laying out the credit with the widest single line. Will it fit within the text-safe area? Your maximum font size (and therefore the legibility of your titles) will be limited by the longest line you can fit inside the text-safe area. If you simply can't reconcile these two factors, you may have to edit your longest line(s) to shorten them so you can use a larger font size.

 Rendered Main Titles

This project gives you a few guidelines for creating your main title sequence, but because titles can vary so much, the creative details are left up to you.

To render a main title sequence, follow these steps:

1. In Modeler, build and surface text objects for your main titles. If you want to animate each title as a unit, model it as a single object. If you want to animate the letters individually, model them as separate objects. If you haven't modeled text objects in LightWave before, you should work through the Text Tool section on pages 3.7 through 3.10 of the *Shape* manual. Remember your typography, and don't make the text hard to read.

2. Animate the text objects for your main title sequence. If you want a real challenge, why not animate a character putting the title together or otherwise interacting with the letters?

Lens Flare Geeks Need Not Apply

As you lay out the animation, be creative, but don't move the camera around, don't use chrome textures on the text objects, and don't use lens flares or any other techniques that scream "Beginner!" This is not some cheap cable television flying logo. This is supposed to be the introduction to your best work. Trust me, a cheesy title practically guarantees your demo reel will be ejected immediately. This is the consensus of a number of professional animators who have to review demo reels on a regular basis.

Are all your titles legible at the resolution your audience will be viewing them? Do they detract from the value of your animation or add to it? When in doubt, keep it simple—your character animation should be able to speak for itself.

PROJECT 19.2 Image Sequence End Credits

This project shows you how to lay out your technical end credits. There are two common ways to handle end credits: the roll and the dissolve. I prefer the dissolve, just because the text holds still and is therefore easier to read.

To lay out your end credits, follow these steps:

1. Use whatever graphics software you prefer to create a series of black-and-white images, one for each credit. Make them the same size as the final resolution of your demo reel, and use anti-aliased text if you can. Make a solid black image to use at the beginning and end of the credits.

   I used Adobe Photoshop to create the credits images for "Easy Come, Easy Go" located in the Chapter 19 directory on this book's CD-ROM. They look like Figure 19.8.

   If you use any of the provided sample materials to create your own demo reel, please include the appropriate credit images (or your own versions, with the same phrasing) in your demo reel's end credits.

   The remaining steps show how LightWave's Foreground Dissolve and Image Sequence functions make dissolving credits very easy to create and modify.

Figure 19.8
Director's credit card from "Easy Come, Easy Go."

2. Figure out the beginning frame for each credit. Remember to leave at least 30 frames (1 second) for each 5 words. You can use more, but try not to let your credits drag out longer than your animation.

3. Rename each credit image with its starting frame number, TITL0000.IFF, TITL0050.IFF, and so on.

4. Open Layout. Open the Image Editor and load TITL0000.IFF. Change Image Type to Sequence. Set Sequence Start to 0 and End to 700, as shown in Figure 19.9. Close the Image Editor.

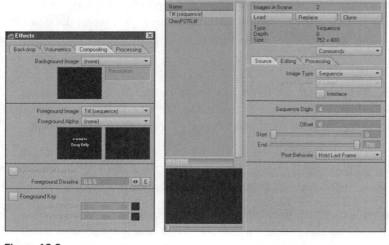

Figure 19.9
Title image sequence loaded in Image Editor and selected as Foreground Image in Effects panel Compositing tab.

5. Open the Effects panel, and select the Compositing tab. Choose Titl(sequence) as the Foreground Image (see Figure 19.9).

6. You can also set black-and-white titles to matte themselves over a background image by loading the title sequence again as Foreground Alpha, as shown in Figure 19.10.

Figure 19.10
Title sequence loaded as Foreground Alpha to matte the Foreground Image over the Background Image.

7. Click on the E (for Envelope) button next to Foreground Dissolve to open the Foreground Image Dissolve Envelope panel. Create an envelope like Figure 19.11 for the Global.FGImageDissolve channel. The foreground image sequence should normally be 0 percent dissolved but transition to 100 percent for a few frames during the credit images' changeover. You can do this most efficiently by setting keyframes for the first cycle, then setting Post Behavior to Repeat.

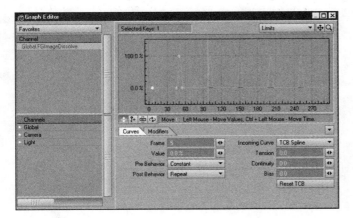

Figure 19.11
Foreground Image Dissolve Envelope.

8. Set the Render and Camera options to render the credits in the same aspect ratio as the title and background image sequences. Render the complete animation. Your results should look something like Figure 19.12.

Figure 19.12
Title matted over background.

9. Save the scene for use in the next project.

This is a low-memory method of creating titles or credits because only one image map has to be loaded in RAM at a time.

PROJECT 19.3   Elegant Text

Here is a quick way to create the kind of elegant type seen in many television commercials. Instead of simply compositing the type using its own alpha channel, do something with a little more depth:

1. Reload the scene you saved from the preceding project. In the Effects panel, go to the Processing tab and add the LW_Bloom Image filter.

2. In the LW_Bloom window, set Threshold to 95%, Strength to 40%, and Size to 20, as shown in Figure 19.13.

3. Make a few test renders and modify the LW_Bloom settings to get the effect you want. The render should show a subtle edge glow, similar to the soft light bleed you can see in some old black-and-white films (see Figure 19.14).

4. When you are satisfied with the test renders, render the entire title sequence.

This is a beautiful and subtle effect that adds a nice touch to almost any text work. This effect works equally well over more complex footage or a simple black background. You can fine-tune this effect by adding just a hint of color to the text, as if the film stock has discolored with age.

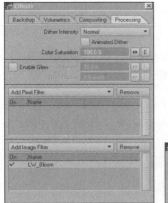

Figure 19.13
LW_Bloom image filter settings.

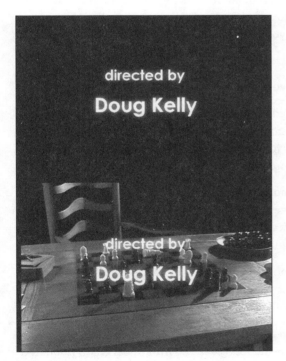

Figure 19.14
Bloomed text comped over black (above) and footage (below).

Rolling Credits

The cast and crew listings that are shown at the end of most feature films, television programs, and videos usually roll from bottom to top. These *rolling credits* (also called *scrolling credits*) are more efficient for giving a large number of people the maximum screen time; a series of dissolves would take forever.

Timing the roll speed is very important, especially if your production is going to be shown on video. Certain roll speeds on video will inevitably look smoother than others due to a possible mismatch between the scanning frequency and the speed of the roll. The roll will be smoother if the text moves up one scan line (or a multiple thereof) every 30th of a second. Other odd speeds will cause more or less of a crawling effect on the leading and following edges of the type. Anti-aliasing, subpixel rendering, and motion blurring are all devices that can minimize this effect, but sometimes just picking the right roll speed can do a lot to clean up the look of a roll.

PROJECT 19.4 Animating a Credit Roll

The goal of this project is to create a classic credit roll. This is a relatively simple job that needs to be done for nearly every production. At the least, you should be able to do good-looking credit rolls for your own productions or demo reel. LightWave makes it easy; with a little practice, you should be able to set up and animate a credit roll with about as much thought and effort as you need to brush your teeth.

To create a credit roll, follow these steps:

1. Make a copy of the credit image sequence you used in Project 19.2.

   Using multiple credit images in an animated sequence gives you more flexibility to make changes through timing, changing individual images, and shuffling their order. Creating a single huge image is also a valid approach, but it eats up much more RAM and forces you to make more changes in the paint program rather than in LightWave.

   For the densest credits, you can pack the image with text from top to bottom. Because the image will roll up the screen, you don't have to worry about LightWave's Safe Area restrictions at the top and bottom, only at the sides. This enables you to pack more credit lines into a given amount of screen time and explains the popularity of rolling titles.

2. Divide the credit images into two alternating series, A and B, by inserting the appropriate letter into the root file name. At the same time, renumber the images in 60-frame increments. You should end up with a sequence like titlA000.iff, titlB060.iff, titlA120.iff, titlB180.iff, and so on.

   Alternating 60 frames between two image sequences gives 120 frames per credit image. At 30 fps for NTSC video, this gives four seconds of screen time for each image, but nearly a second of that is lost outside the text-safe area. Three seconds of screen time is reasonable for a rolling credit, and you can fine-tune the timing later.

3. Open Modeler. Build a rectangle in the same proportions as your finished animation—for example, 720×486—and centered around the origin, as shown in Figure 19.15.

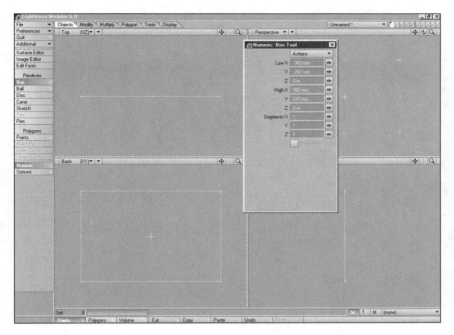

Figure 19.15
Title card modeled.

4. Add a surface named Title1 to the object. Apply the first image in the titlA sequence as a color map and orient and autosize it so the image will precisely cover the object, as shown in Figure 19.16.

5. In the Surface Editor's Advanced tab, set Additive Transparency to 100%. This will make the black areas of the credit image transparent, giving the effect of an additive composite of the white letters over the background footage.

6. Save the object as Title1.lwo.

7. Rename the surface Title1 as Title2 and change the color map to the first image in the titlB sequence.

8. Save the modified object as Title2.lwo. Exit Modeler.

You should now have two credit objects, one mapped with the A image sequence and the other mapped with the B image sequence.

9. In Layout, set the scene to begin at frame 0 and end at frame 780. Set the Camera to D1 (NTSC). In the Display Options panel, turn on Show Safe Areas so you can make sure your titles are legible for the right length of time.

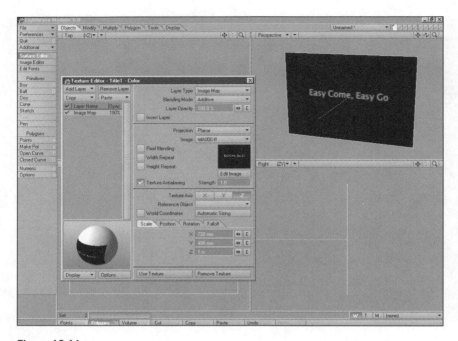

Figure 19.16
Title card surfaced.

10. Load Title1.lwo and Title2.lwo. Parent both rectangles to the Camera.

11. In frame 0, position Title1.lwo to precisely fill the Camera view (see Figure 19.17). You may have to scale the object to match the pixel aspect ratio (in this case, 0.9) to get a precise match with the Camera view. Lock off the x- and z-axes when you get a close match; you will only be animating the object along the y-axis.

12. At frame 0, move Title1.lwo down on the y-axis so the top of the object just touches the bottom edge of the Camera view. Set a keyframe. Make a note of the position and scale settings.

13. At frame 60, apply the identical position and scale settings from Title1.lwo to Title2.lwo. Set a keyframe.

14. At frame 120, move Title1.lwo up on the y-axis so the bottom of the object just touches the top edge of the Camera view.

15. At frame 180, move Title2.lwo up on the y-axis so the bottom of the object just touches the top edge of the Camera view.

16. In the Graph editor, set the y-axis Post Behavior for both Title1.lwo and Title2.lwo to repeat, as shown in Figure 19.18.

Figure 19.17
Title1 object positioned to exactly fill the Camera view at frame 0. Note that all four edges of the object match the dashed lines of the Camera view guides.

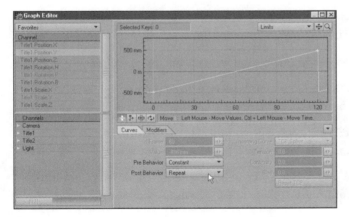

Figure 19.18
Y-axis motion graph for Title1.lwo, showing Post Behavior set to Repeat.

This should make the first object rise smoothly across the Camera view followed by the second object (Figure 19.19), and both objects return to their starting position after passing the upper edge of the Camera view. As long as the image sequence changeovers occur when the respective objects are out of sight, the appearance will be that of a seamless roll rather than multiple separate objects.

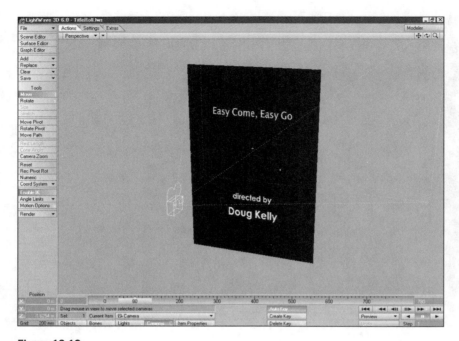

Figure 19.19
Perspective view showing Title1.lwo followed by Title2.lwo rising in front of the Camera to create the illusion of rolling credits.

17. Open the Surface Editor. Select the Title1 surface of the Title1 object and click on the Color Texture button to open the Texture Editor.

18. In the Texture Editor, click on the Edit Image button to open the Image Editor.

19. In the Image Editor, select titlA000.iff. Change Image Type to Sequence and set Start to 0 and End to 720. Set Post Behavior to Hold Last Frame, as shown in Figure 19.20.

20. Select titlB060.iff. Change Image Type to Sequence and set Start to 60 and End to 720. Set Post Behavior to Hold Last Frame. Close the Image Editor, Texture Editor, and Surface Editor.

21. Make a few test renders to check your work. You can experiment with different backdrop colors, gradients, or images to confirm that the white text will composite correctly over the background.

As you can see, a simple credit roll is relatively simple to set up in LightWave once you've done it a few times. You can easily reuse a credit roll scene simply by changing the image map sequence and modifying the timing. Practice making your own credit roll, or download a credit list from the Internet Movie Database (**www.imdb.com**) and re-create the credits of one of your favorite movies. Just for fun, you can even cast yourself in a starring role.

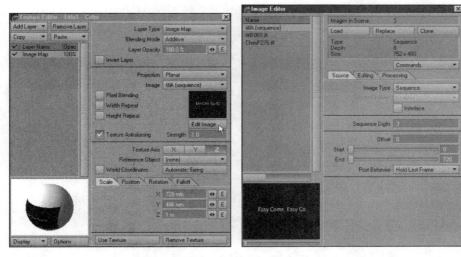

Figure 19.20
Changing image map for Title1 surface from a single image to an image sequence.

PROJECT 19.5 Fade to Black

Credits sometimes roll after a fade to black, but often they begin over the tail end of the fade or run mostly over footage with a fade to black at the very end. Let's add a background and a fade to black to run under the credit roll created in Project 19.4:

1. In the Compositing tab of the Effects panel, load whatever background footage you have handy and set it as the Background Image.

   Make a note of the length of your footage; you'll want the fade to be complete before the footage ends, unless you want the credits to roll over a freeze-frame. For this project, I'll use a still image, MountainHighway.iff, from the LightWave Content directory.

2. In the Surface Editor, select surface Title1. In the Advanced tab, click on E-for-Envelope next to Additive Transparency. Set the envelope to 100% at frame 0, 100% at frame 720, and 0% at frame 780, with all sections set to Linear interpolation, as shown in Figure 19.21.

3. Copy and paste the Additive Transparency envelope from surface Title1 to surface Title2.

   These two Additive Transparency envelopes will keep the black areas of the credits transparent, superimposing the white letters over the background image for most of the animation. The last 60 frames fade the image from transparent to solid; because the last credit image is all black, this will emulate a fade to black. Figure 19.22 shows a few frames from the rendered credit roll.

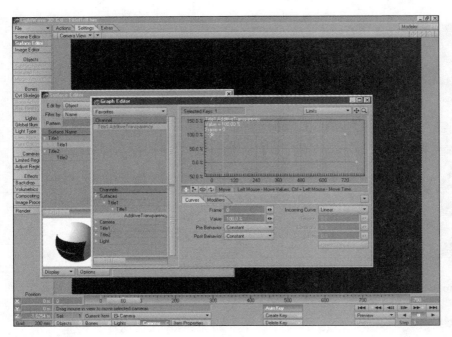

Figure 19.21
Additive Transparency envelope for fade to black in frames 720 to 780.

4. You can check the playback speed with a reduced-size rendering, but to check the legibility of the text, you'll need to look at 100% resolution. When you're satisfied with all the settings, render your credit roll.

Finishing Touches

Here are a few last-minute additions you may want to consider before you transfer your finished work to film or video.

Bars and Tone

If you have put a lot of effort into sound synchronizing, color composition, and lighting for your character animation, you will want that effort shown to best advantage in the final product. If you are transferring your animation to videotape, you should consider adding a few seconds of SMPTE color bars and a standard 1kHz tone to the beginning of your tape. This standard reference enables the video engineer to optimize for color, image quality, and sound level at the time of broadcast or projection. You can use the SMPTE.iff image file in the Chapter 19 directory on this book's CD-ROM or the BarsSmall.tga file in the VideoFX subdirectory of the LightWave Content. For the audio tone, you can download one of the shareware test tone generators or use the 1K_10sec.wav file, also on this book's CD-ROM.

Figure 19.22
Rendered images from credit roll, showing the text composited over the background image and the fade to
black at the end.

Film Clutter

If the content of your animation would benefit from it, you might consider a number of post-process effects that reproduce artifacts of the film projection process. This can be useful for matching perfectly clean LightWave animation to naturally grungy real-world footage. You can also use it to give your animations the appearance of a silent film, an old home movie, or a historic newsreel.

Film grain adds the visual artifacts typical of the chemical film process. This is the most subtle of the effects and the most basic film-simulation effect. If you are compositing your LightWave elements into live footage, you will need to add film grain to make the rendered element look as if it belongs in the shot. If you are creating a completely rendered world for your characters, adding film grain will make it more believable to the audience.

Dirt and scratches can be overdone very easily—use them sparingly and only when they'll help you tell your story or increase your work's verisimilitude to the original effect you're trying to mimic.

Antique or stylized leaders can help prepare your audience for a "period" reproduction or parody. If your animation fits one of these categories, by all means, use the appropriate leader. If you want to maintain the illusion, you should also use a matching trailer, even if it's just the words "The End" in graceful script.

Reference footage or predigitized video clips for these and other effects are available from a number of vendors, including Artbeats, the publishers of some very good texture collections. You can request a sample Artbeats CD-ROM to evaluate its video clip collections from its Web site at **www.artbeats.com**, or you can call them at (541) 863-4429. I've purchased a number of Artbeats products and always found them to be a good value.

Adding Timecode

Besides titles and credits, character generators are often handy for adding technical information to your compositions. For example, in Chapter 20 I advise that you put SMPTE timecode on approval footage and only hand over the clean footage after the client pays you for it. LightWave makes adding timecode easy:

1. Open the Render Options panel.

2. In the Rendering tab, select SMPTE Time Code from the Data Overlay drop-down menu. Add whatever short text you like to the Label field, as in Figure 19.23.

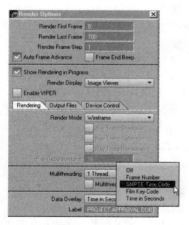

Figure 19.23
Data Overlay and Label settings for SMPTE timecode.

That's all there is to creating very cheap and effective payment insurance. The rendering now includes time code that can be useful for editing and a text label that can identify the shot, project, or artist (see Figure 19.24). Together, these overlays make it a little more difficult for an unscrupulous person to use your work without your permission.

Figure 19.24
Rendered footage with label and time code superimposed.

Moving On

Once you've worked through this chapter, you should have the completed titles, credits, and post-process effects you need for the next chapter. Chapter 20 will show you how to put all the pieces of your animation together and transfer them to videotape, film, or other publishing medium.

Chapter 20

Final Output

E ven the best character animation is worthless if an audience can't see it. After your animations are rendered, you need a way to deliver them to your client or audience, to record them for future viewing or reuse, and to make reference copies for your demo reel or personal archive. How you record, distribute, and play back your animations will depend on your resources and your target audience. This chapter will show you the basics of transferring your finished animation to the most common delivery media, including videotape and film, and how to finish off your demo reel.

If you are working in a large studio and doing animations exclusively, your responsibility for the shot probably ends when you render the final animation to the network server. Someone else handles the technical details of editing your work into the final production, dumping it to tape, and delivering it. However, knowing something about the final transfer and delivery process can make a difference to your work. You'll kick yourself if you spend days tweaking an animation that ends up so reduced and compressed that you can't see the results of your extra work. On the other hand, animation shortcuts you could get away with for streaming video will look like the dog's breakfast on broadcast television. You should also understand the transfer process if you ever hope to be a supervisor or to start your own studio. You need to understand the options available so you can make the right choices for media, hardware, and work flow.

Playing back video, whether it is on a computer, the Internet, or analog or digital television systems, requires a pipe that is big enough to shove all that data through without clogging up. That pipe is called *bandwidth*, and it is the single most important limit to delivering your finished production. The first factor in bandwidth is the resolution and frame rate of the end-use media. This can range from postage-stamp-size 15fps video clips for Internet distribution at slow modem speeds all the way up to 2K 24fps film or e-cinema files for theatrical display. This chapter will cover low-end multimedia, standard-definition television (SDTV), high-definition television (HDTV), film, and e-cinema.

The number one criterion for reproducing your animations is frame rate. As you have learned in earlier chapters, the essence of an animation performance is in the timing. A difference of a single frame can make or break the believability of an action. Therefore, you should choose a medium that enables you to set a consistent frame rate so you can animate specifically for that rate with the assurance that what you animate is what your audience will see.

For film or video, the frame rate is fixed by the standards of the technology. Feature films are projected at 24fps, NTSC video at 29.97fps, and PAL video at 25fps. You don't have to worry about the distribution side of those formats; a perfectly accurate frame rate is automatic.

FilmExpand

If you have been animating to 24fps as I recommend and want to output your animations to 30fps NTSC video, all you have to do is choose the FilmExpand option. In the Render Options panel, choose the Output Files tab. From the Save Animation Type drop-down menu, choose FilmExpand. The FilmExpand panel will appear. Choose the image format and field dominance you prefer, then close the panel. FilmExpand works best with field rendering (in the Camera panel) enabled.

For other reproduction methods, you will have to do a little more work. Some computer animation formats, for example, allow you to specify a frame rate for playback. These rates can be modified by the end user and are limited by the speed and transfer rate of the user's system, but these formats generally play animations the way you intended them. Other computer animation formats and the purely mechanical animation formats do not allow you to specify a frame rate. All you can do in these circumstances is animate for an average range of frame rates and hope that most of your audience will fit within that range.

Mechanical Playback: Flipbooks

Flipbooks are the second most basic form of animation players (the flipping disk is the first) and have been used for so long that we don't really know when the first one was made. They're simple to use, portable, and don't require any other equipment to view. At least one professional animator uses flipbooks as business cards, and Disney recently revived the practice of publishing flipbook excerpts from its animated films. They're also fun to give away or trade with other animators, and it's often handy to have one to help explain your work to nonanimators.

The disadvantage to flipbooks for character animation is that you can't control the playback frame rate—it's entirely up to the skill and preference of your audience. Depending on how you produce them, flipbooks can also be somewhat more difficult and expensive to produce than videotapes, disks, or CDs.

The cheapest way to create a flipbook from your animations is to set up a table in a spreadsheet or word processor. The following project shows you how to create your own flipbook template in Microsoft Word.

PROJECT 20.1 Making Your Own Flipbook

To create a flipbook, follow these steps:

1. Create a new folder and render at least 40 frames of an animation into it in BMP format. For this example, I created the folder C:\CAPTURE3 and rendered images MATCH001.BMP through MATCH040.BMP into it.

2. In Word, open a new document. Set the page margins to the maximum printing area for the printer you will be using. Choose Select All and set the font to something like Courier 10 point. This will be the label font for the individual frames of the flipbook, so you will want to keep it small.

3. Choose the Table|Insert Table menu option. Set the table to 4 columns and 10 rows. This will give you space in each cell for an image about the size of a postage stamp.

4. Set the alignment of the entire document to Align Right. This will keep the images at the right margin of each cell, leaving the extra space at the left edge for the staples or other means of holding the flipbook together.

5. Click in the top-left cell to select it. Choose the Insert|Picture menu option and choose the first rendered image in the directory you created. In the Insert Picture dialog box, turn on the Link To File checkbox at the lower right. Directly underneath it, turn off the Save Picture In Document checkbox. Click on OK.

   This sets up a link between the cell in the Word table and the image file in the new directory. The image itself will not be included in the Word file, just the path and file name information, so the document remains small even when you link it to very large images. This also means that every time you open, print, or even scroll around the table, the images will be reloaded from the directory. You can even leave Word open while you render new images, and as they're completed, they'll replace the old images in the table.

6. Click in the same cell, in the empty space to the left of the image you've just linked. Type in the last three digits of the image file name. Save the document.

7. Repeat Steps 5 and 6 for the remaining 39 cells in the table. You should end up with something like Figure 20.1.

8. When you've finished all 40 cells, print off the page on some heavy card stock. Cut the frames out along the lines, stack them up in order, and staple or clip them together. That's all there is to it!

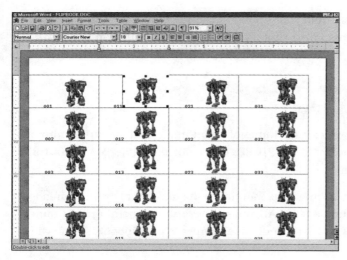

Figure 20.1
Word table with images linked to cells.

Now that you've got the flipbook template set up, it's very fast and easy to make a flipbook of your current animation. Just set the rendering to the path and file name root you linked to the Word table cells, and you can print off a flipbook sheet faster than you can render a single frame. If you're feeling ambitious or have a use for larger flipbooks, you can try increasing the size of the cells or making multipage tables that contain more than 40 cells. As a general rule, flipbooks get awkward to use after about 200 sheets, so don't go overboard without testing first.

Flipbook Software

If you run a Macintosh or Power Mac, you can take advantage of a software product named Flipbook (how original!), specifically designed to print flipbooks. Flipbook is published by S. H. Pierce & Company and is available directly from the company's own Web site and through several mail-order software distributors. This is a handy little utility that converts QuickTime movies into a printed layout on preperforated flipbook paper.

S. H. Pierce & Co.
One Kendall Square
Building 600 PMB 323
Cambridge, MA 02139 USA
Tel: (617) 338-2222
Fax: (617) 338-2223
www.moxie.com

Advanced Flipbook: The Mutoscope

If you get hooked on flipbooks, you might be interested in a nineteenth-century super-flipbook called a Mutoscope. The heart of this device is a cylinder with a large series of flipbook cards mounted around its circumference. It's as if the card deck is so large that it can wrap around with its last card next to the first. Figure 20.2 shows a picture of one type of Mutoscope, an opened view of a slightly different model, and a cylinder or *card reel* removed from the player.

Figure 20.2
Mutoscopes and a card reel.

The viewer looks through the eyepiece and turns a crank. The crank turns the cylinder, which rotates the edges of the cards against a stop. The stop holds the cards in view, just as your thumb does with a flipbook, until the crank is turned enough to flip the card over and reveal the next one. It's a mechanically simple device, and if you're handy with tools, you can probably build one yourself.

Mutoscopes can be large enough to hold thousands of cards, so you can get many seconds of animation onto a single cylinder. The original machines are now collector's items that fetch thousands of dollars at auction, and the card reels are bought and sold like vintage baseball cards. If you are interested in seeing a working Mutoscope, there are several in the Main Street Arcade in Disneyland and in some of the older amusement parks, like Cedar Point in Sandusky, Ohio.

Computer Playback

There are a variety of reasons to deliver animations through a computer. In many cases, the quality of video playback on a new desktop computer can be better than VHS videotape. Direct playback on the computer depends on the system's bus speed, CD-ROM drive speed, available RAM, video display card, and sometimes hard drive space. As far back as 1995, the MPC III specifications included 4X CD-ROM, 44kHz stereo sound, Pentium 75 MHz or better, and

MPEG-1 playback support. That was just about good enough to mimic second- or third-generation VHS tape quality. New machines in 2000 typically have bus speeds of 100 MHz or higher, 40X CD-ROMs, DVD/MPEG-2 playback support, and video display cards optimized for the high refresh rates of video games. The "bottleneck" in the pipeline for playing back video from a CD-ROM is usually at least 1.5MB per second, enabling standard television resolutions at full frame rate with a moderately efficient codec. The catch is, how do you produce animations that can take advantage of all this technology?

The first step is choosing delivery media. The most cost-effective delivery media for shorter video formats is CD-ROM. You can pack a few minutes of full-screen, high-quality animation onto a single CD-ROM, or more than an hour of lower-quality half-resolution animation. You can make one-off or short-run CDs for less than a dollar each with a CD-R drive that costs less than $300. If you need higher volume, you can find CD-ROM duplicators that will turn out hundreds or thousands of copies of the master CD-R for under 50 cents a pop. If you have so much footage that a half dozen or so CD-ROMs aren't enough to hold it, you may want to consider the expense of having a DVD mastered and duplicated. As of this writing, DVD mastering is not yet cost effective for the hobbyist or freelance artist. Other possible delivery media include removable media such as Zip or Jaz disks, but their blank-media costs are generally too high for anything but in-house distribution.

File Formats

The second step is to choose a file format. There are a number of video compression formats and *codecs* (compressor/decompressor) in common use. Each of them has advantages and disadvantages. At the moment, there is no clearly superior codec or file format for all-purpose animations. Your decision should take into account the platforms and operating systems of your audience. Do you care whether Windows, Mac, Unix, BeOS, or Amiga users can view your animations? If you do, you need to either use a file format that everyone can view or provide duplicate files in enough formats to cover all the possibilities.

The GIF89a format can be displayed by Web browsers as an inline animation that takes up very little space and downloads quickly. This is the format commonly used for animated headers, buttons, and other decorations on Web pages. The format's main disadvantage for character animation is that you cannot control the frame rate at all, so the playback over the Web depends entirely on the connection speed. The GIF89a format is appropriate mostly for short loops of a dozen frames or less. There are a variety of commercial, freeware, or shareware utilities that can assemble a LightWave-rendered image sequence into an animated GIF. Adobe Photoshop 5.5 includes one such utility as a plug-in.

QuickTime (QT) is an audiovisual compression format initially pushed by Apple and still a part of the Mac OS, but it is now also available on a variety of platforms. QuickTime players and Internet browser plug-ins are bundled with many software packages or available for free download. Choosing this format to distribute your animations is a fairly safe decision. There are several codecs available for QT.

AVI, which stands for Audio Video Interleaved, is the official video format for the Microsoft Windows platform. It's not supported on as many platforms as QT, but the larger installed base of Windows machines makes AVI a viable video-distribution format. I suggest you experiment with every codec available to you and draw your own conclusions based on tests with your own animations.

MPEG is a family of formats originally designed to compress live-action video. With this goal in mind, MPEG excels at irregular, near-chaotic images like human faces in motion and performs less competently with abstract, linear patterns like amateurish CGI. The good news is that the closer your animations get to the complexity of the real world, the better MPEG is at reproducing them. A significant advantage of the MPEG format is that it is public domain, so there are a variety of hardware and software solutions from competing vendors, and the prices range from free to quite reasonable. Later in this chapter, we'll run through Project 20.2 using the MPEG format to transfer character animations to videotape.

Codecs

Once you've settled on a file format, the next step in creating computer-playable video is choosing a compression codec. Even with bandwidth in excess of 1.5MBps, you'll need to compress the video stream quite a bit before you can get it to play back without dropped frames.

The sample footage used for comparisons in the rest of this chapter was originally a 158-frame sequence of images at 720x486 resolution and 24-bit color depth, with a total file size of 159MB in uncompressed TGA format. I selected this footage because it has a mix of locked-down and moving camera, varying light levels, motion of both human skin tones and organic textures, complex inorganic background objects, a patch of nearly saturated red, and a fixed corner graphic with both fine and thick lines. This presents some tough problems for compression and is a pretty fair test for all the codecs. Figure 20.3 shows frame 53 from this sequence at 2X magnification so you can compare it to artifact patterns from other figures in this chapter.

A number of viable video codecs are available that can do an adequate job of compression, but each has trade-offs. As a basis for comparison, the uncompressed AVI of the example footage weighs in at 159MB. The image quality is essentially identical to the original stills, but the video plays back at 9.56fps.

One of the most popular (and deservedly so, in my opinion) codecs is Cinepak. You can get impressive file compression with high-quality settings with Cinepak. Set for 95-percent quality, the reference AVI file squashed down to 9.88MB, a 16:1 compression. On a PII 400 MHz equipped with the ATI All-In-Wonder Pro card, both the ATI Player NT 5 and Microsoft Media Player can play back this video clip at 28.92fps, just shy of recordable. The Cinepak codec for Windows shows compression artifacts in the form of *banding*, but not as prominently as the Cinepak codec for QuickTime.

Sample footage courtesy Eyeon Software.

Figure 20.3
Frame 53 from sample footage at 2X magnification.

The Microsoft Video 1 codec is neither as robust nor as efficient as Cinepak. The same level of quality only compressed the sample footage to 58.6MB, a compression ratio of 2.7:1. This clip also consistently crashed Media Player, but it played back on the ATI Player at approximately 17fps.

I used Brad Beyerly's bbMPEG encoder (discussed in detail later in this chapter) to create a video-only MPEG-1 clip based on the uncompressed AVI. With data stream settings of 150Kbps, this yielded a file size of 916K, for a compression ratio of 173:1. This file played back on both ATI Player NT 5 and Microsoft Media Player at 29.83fps, close enough to dump to tape for short pieces. File size savings from basing the MPEG-1 compression on Cinepak or other AVI codecs were not significant enough (plus or minus 1 percent) to justify the double compression. As Figure 20.4 shows, the compression artifacts of MPEG-1 bring the D-1 quality images down to approximately a second- or third-generation VHS tape. However, repeating the encoding with the stream set for 500Kbps produced a file size of 2.3MB and a playback speed of only 25fps. The image quality difference (see Figure 20.5) shows how much you can gain by tweaking a setting or two. If you choose to deliver MPEG video, you should encode at the delivery system's best sustainable playback bandwidth.

MPEG-2 can be encoded via the same bbMPEG software utility, but most professional MPEG-2 production relies on hardware compression. If you plan to distribute your animations via MPEG-2 or DVD, you should thoroughly research the available options before investing in hardware or software. This is a very fast-moving sector of the video industry, and what was hot six months ago is a dog today.

The QuickTime file format has at least one codec in common with AVI, plus several others. The QuickTime Cinepak codec set for 95-percent quality compressed the sample footage down

Figure 20.4
Frame 53 of 150Kbps MPEG-1 based on uncompressed AVI, at 2X magnification.

Figure 20.5
Frame 53 of MPEG-1 compressed for delivery at 500Kbps.

to 7.93MB, for a 20:1 ratio. This file plays back in the QuickTime MoviePlayer at 28.28fps but shows more prominent banding than the same codec applied to the AVI clip.

Repeating the QuickTime compression with the Sorenson codec yielded a 12.4MB file, for a lower compression ratio of only 13:1. This clip also plays back more slowly, at approximately 16fps. The advantage of the Sorenson codec is that banding is much less prominent, so the image quality is significantly improved. Depending on your delivery system's parameters, you might get better image quality with higher Sorenson compression than with lower Cinepak compression.

Whatever combination of delivery media, file format, and codec you use, make sure you keep a backup of your uncompressed footage. It's very likely that you will want to distribute it at some future date in a format and codec that doesn't even exist yet. You will get the worst-possible results if you try to convert from one encoded video to another codec; the difference between the old and new sampling patterns will create really ugly moiré patterns and other artifacts.

Output Issues

Your animation's final output is the only evidence your client or supervisor will have that you did anything worth your pay. Treat your output with the same care and planning that you would devote to a pile of cash equivalent to your pay for the time you spent working on the animation. I have found more than one software manual that recommends rendering to RAM to save time. Personally, I'd rather juggle razor blades blindfolded; at least half the time, I wouldn't get hurt. In my experience, those odds are better than for the reliability of RAM storage of your final work. If you value your animations at all, render your final output to a safe, reliable HDD as an uncompressed image sequence. Adding compression is one more time-consuming step that can go wrong. When you render to AVI, QuickTime, or other video clip format, you risk losing the whole render if the last frame goes bad. Rendering to RAM is asking for trouble. If your final delivery medium requires compression or a video clip format, you can easily and quickly compile that from the uncompressed image sequence, secure in the knowledge that your rendered images are safely available for revisions and tweaks during the compression process. Keep in mind that some of today's most popular distribution media, including DVD and streaming video, look best when derived from clean image sequences.

Streaming Internet Video

Streaming video is a compressed video signal transmitted through the Internet and played back in realtime. The smallest video bandwidth in common use is a 28.8Kbps modem connection. This tiny pipe requires very high compression and the smallest resolution your production can get away with. Streaming compression ratios range from a minimum of 200:1 up to 500:1. 320×240 or even 160×120 resolutions are not uncommon, especially if the production is a "talking head," a spokesperson who doesn't move much in a head-shot close-up. Your biggest problem is going to be making titles and text legible at these low resolutions. In addition, the compression codecs used for streaming video usually introduce a lot of artifacts, which can make text even harder to read. You should discuss these issues with the director or producer as early as possible. You will probably not be able to use streamers or subtitles; you will have to rely on larger text that intermittently covers most of the screen.

Streaming video is, like most video technology, changing rapidly. As of this writing, the market leader in streaming video is RealNetworks (**www.real.com**), publishers of RealSystem G2 software including RealPlayer, RealProducer G2, and RealSystem G2 Basic Server. The player, encoder, and basic server are free for downloading from the company's Web site. By encouraging free downloads, RealNetworks has put over 65 million RealPlayer copies on users' desktops. Multiple-stream servers and more-advanced creation and distribution tools cost a few hundred dollars, a reasonable outlay for small companies or educational institutions. The software is a minor part of the budget for setting up streaming video servers. If you own Adobe Premiere, you already have a version of the player (shown in Figure 20.6), which is located in the Real directory of Premiere's installation CD-ROM. Real products can produce compression ratios as high as 500:1, resulting in a 20Kbps data stream. This is well within the limits of a 28.8Kbps modem connection.

Figure 20.6
RealPlayer—showing 320x216 Cinepak-compressed AVI, compressed at a ratio of 154:1 for LAN bandwidth of 150Kbps—plays at 17.4 fps. Although fine details are still lost to compression artifacts, this is an acceptable video quality and frame rate for most Internet viewing.

Some of the other streaming video software currently on the market include Microsoft's ActiveMovie, Netshow, and Media Player (**www.microsoft.com**); Apple's QuickTime 4 (**www.apple.com**); Macromedia's Shockwave (**www.shockwave.com**); and GEO Interactive's Emblaze (**www.emblaze.com**). For the latest information, I recommend that you conduct some research on the Internet and test all the available demos and freeware before you choose any commercial streaming video software. This market is too volatile to pick a winner even a few months in advance. Also, with Microsoft in the market, you never know who's going to be bought out.

Downloadable Internet Video

An easier alternative to streaming video is to simply load video clips on a Web site so people can download them to view later. This bypasses the need for special streaming Web servers. Web distribution requires videos to be assembled in MPEG, AVI, QuickTime, or some other common video format. Image sequences are not an acceptable way to distribute video on the

Internet. Some browsers can start playing back a video clip while still downloading the rest of it, emulating streaming video, but that function depends on which browser is being used and what plug-ins have been installed. It's best not to assume anything if you want your videos to be viewable by as many people as possible. Most video-heavy Web sites include links to sites where you can download the necessary video plug-ins or players.

As with streaming video, file size is very important in downloadable video because your audience may be using anything from a 28.8 modem to a fiber-optic backbone. Your most flexible options are to have several sizes of each clip, use the most common codecs, and label everything clearly so your audience can choose for themselves. The most common size for Internet video is half-resolution. If you are downsampling the entire frame, use an even divisor (720 goes evenly into 360, 240, or 180) for your horizontal resolution and keep the vertical resolution proportional. This reduces round-off errors in the downsampling operation and minimizes artifacts while preserving (as much as possible) fine details in the reduced video.

The framing you use for SDTV is not necessarily the best framing for downloadable video. For one thing, you don't have to worry about text-safe or action-safe areas; the entire frame is always visible. You can put image and text right out in the corners and it won't get lost. Second, you are not bound by the 4:3 or 16:9 aspect ratios of a hardware-based video system. If your source video never uses the outer two-thirds of the frame, you can crop it to a 1:1.5 portrait aspect ratio. This is an especially useful approach for talking heads. Third, an "artistic" framing in which the majority of the screen is occupied by irrelevant background is inappropriate for the Internet. When every pixel has to be folded, bent, spindled, and mutilated to fit through a narrow pipeline, you can't afford to waste any. Save your wide-screen framing for stills or other delivery media and keep your Internet frames full of foreground content. Fourth, camera motion is anathema to efficient Internet video. If possible, you should lock down your LightWave camera. If the conversion from a wide-screen framing to a narrower one requires pan-and-scan, try to do it with cuts rather than pans. These techniques will greatly reduce the frame-to-frame deltas that bloat even the most thoroughly compressed video.

The popularity of various codecs for Internet video changes over time, but more slowly than the cutting edge of this technology. There are a lot of old video clips out there, and many people are slow to add the latest codec to their browser. For the widest distribution of your videos, I recommend compressing with a common codec that has been in popular use for a while. The Cinepak codec is effective for both AVI and QuickTime formats, and I highly recommend it. The test footage, downsampled from 720×486 to 360×243, was compressed using Cinepak at 50-percent image quality from 169MB to 1.38MB for AVI and to 1.68MB for QuickTime.

Web-Page Issues

Many Internet users pay for their access by the minute or have slow connections that make downloading large video clips time-consuming. To be polite, you should give your audience as much information as possible before they start downloading so they can choose when or whether to download your clips. You should never embed a video clip in your home page. You should instead use a thumbnail image of a representative frame from the video as a link to the page containing the video. In addition, you should use the **<ALT>** tag to include the file size. For example, this line defines a graphical link to download an MPEG clip:

```
<A HREF="MortyB.mpg"><IMG SRC="MortyB.gif" ALT="370K MPEG of Morty"></A>
```

When readers pass the mouse cursor over the image link, the ALT message informs them of the file size, type, and subject before they start downloading. This can save your readers a lot of wasted time and bother and can spare you a lot of complaints.

If you are publishing AVI, MPEG, or QuickTime files on a Web site, one of the simplest ways of adding video clips to a Web page is with the **<EMBED>** tag. For example, the following lines produce a complete HTML page that loads an AVI file from the current directory with a resolution of 360x243, padded to 289 with 46 extra pixel rows to allow space for the Internet Explorer control bar. This is a simple, reliable way of displaying your video clips in both Internet Explorer and Navigator. Figure 20.7 shows this HTML page loaded into both browsers.

```
<HTML>
<HEAD>
<TITLE>Close-Up Explosion</TITLE>
</HEAD>
<BODY>
<CENTER>
<EMBED SRC="CINEPAKB.AVI" HEIGHT=289 WIDTH=360>
</CENTER>
</BODY>
</HTML>
```

Embedding video clips in HTML pages is also a handy way of keeping track of archive footage. For example, you could keep about five and a half minutes of high-quality clips of your best work on a CD-ROM, with a thumbnail index page linked to separate pages for each clip. This is a convenient place to record important details such as who worked on the project, the client's name and contact information, who owns the intellectual property rights to the elements and the finished animation, and any technical information that might be useful later. This is also a good way of having a complete but compact form of your personal or studio demo reel.

Video

You have several options for recording and showing your finished demo reel on videotape. There are three levels for standard video production: consumer, industrial, and broadcast. For most individual purposes, including demo reels, consumer grade will do fine. The most commonly accepted format in the United States and United Kingdom is VHS. Character animation

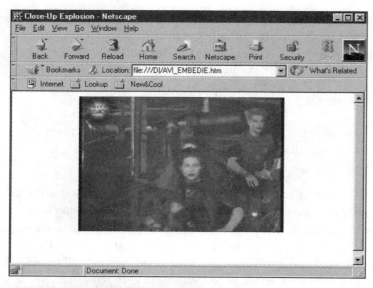

Figure 20.7
Screenshots of a half-size AVI clip as it appears in the Microsoft Internet Explorer and Netscape
Navigator browsers.

studios usually have a selection of machines capable of playing back just about any format,
but if you're looking for work, you don't want to put your potential employer to any extra
bother. If you have access to industrial or broadcast equipment, make your master reel on the
best format you can handle, but make VHS dubs to mail out with your résumé.

Transferring animation to video is relatively inexpensive, but cutting corners with cheap compression boards can really hurt the final appearance. The most cost-effective solution at present for industrial or broadcast standards is to use a special hard-drive recording device, then dump the finished piece to broadcast-quality videotape. Many of these hardware solutions also work with your choice of editing and post-processing software. The market is constantly changing, and new products with lower price tags and more features are coming out all the time. At the moment, you're still looking at several thousand dollars to get true broadcast-quality video, so you may be better off finding a service bureau or fellow animator who has equipment you can borrow or lease.

If your system's output resolution justifies it, rent a broadcast-quality recording deck for a day to make your master tape. You can usually get a broadcast-quality deck for under $200 a day in most major cities. Do all your prep work before you pick up the deck—you don't want to have to pay for another day because you couldn't find a cable or a blank tape.

Short Tapes Save Reels

Buy short, 5- or 10-minute videotapes in bulk for your demo reels. This keeps studio staff from taping reruns of *Gilligan's Island* over your demo reel. It can mean the difference between getting a job and getting lost in the shuffle. If your reel stays on a shelf because no one bothers to tape over it, yours may be the only tape sitting there the next time they need to hire someone.

Buying lots of tapes is important, too. You have to look at demo reels as résumés. Make lots, send out lots. You're going after some pretty high-paying jobs, either as a technical director (TD) or animator. Would you worry about the price of each sheet of paper if you were getting your résumé duplicated? What fraction of your first year's income are you willing to spend on a résumé that gets you the job? You'll be sending out quite a few demo reels before you get that first job, so resign yourself to spending the money or working a barter. Nothing ventured, nothing gained.

If you can't afford film or professional video, you may be able to record a low-budget demo reel using direct computer playback. This is limited by trade-offs in resolution, speed, and color depth, but it's cheap. You use a relatively inexpensive device called a *scan converter* to convert your computer's video signals to something acceptable to your consumer-grade VCR. Generally, the cheaper the converter, the lousier the videotaped images. Don't despair if this is all you can afford. Several studios have assured me that they look for the quality of the animation, not the professional polish on the tape production. Make sure the playback is at the same rate as you animated it, the images are relatively clear, and the tape tracking doesn't wander all over the place, and you should be all right.

Cheap Demo Reels: Inexpensive Video Transfer

If disk recorders, single-frame VTRs, or scan converters are too expensive for your budget, I have some good news for you. With a little effort and a very small amount of money, you can put all your animations onto videotape from your own PC. The results of this process aren't broadcast quality, but they're good enough to display your character animation skills.

As with the previous methods of distribution, dumping your finished animations to videotape requires a system with enough bandwidth to push out the video signal without clogging up. The less compression in that signal, the wider the bandwidth you'll need, and (generally) the more expensive your system will become. In addition, you need the right output circuitry and connectors to suit the VTR or other recording devices you want to use.

ATI All-In-Wonder

The least-expensive option for tape-recording video from your computer is an NTSC video output card such as ATI's All-In-Wonder 128, shown in Figure 20.8. This card has breakout cables that provide composite and S-Video connectors. Unfortunately, the ATI Player software does not support NTSC input or output under WinNT. However, under Win98, the software enables you to tweak the NTSC output to correct the image's color, geometry, and centering. This card also has hardware acceleration for MPEG playback. Based on my tests, it doesn't do too badly on AVI playback either. The video playback rate depends on your system's bus, RAM, and hard drive speeds. For output to tape, you need to compress an AVI or MPEG stream until it can play back consistently at 29.97fps. This system does not enable precise locking of frame rate, so it's a hit-or-miss proposition. (Hey, what do you expect from a card that costs less than $120?) The output looks comparable to VHS. This may be good enough for personal projects or a student demo reel, making the ATI card a good choice for students and hobbyists who simply need an affordable way to output short animations to VHS.

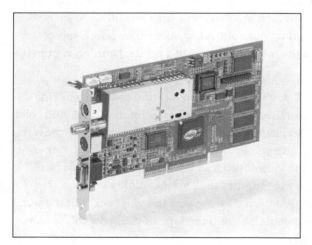

Figure 20.8
ATI All-In-Wonder 128 video display card with NTSC S-Video output.

I've written the following project for PC-compatibles running Windows 98 or NT. Similar solutions do exist for other platforms and operating systems, so you can use this project as a guide to finding a solution that fits your system. I have deliberately limited this project to free or shareware programs, with the exception of the drivers and utilities bundled with ATI video boards. My experience has been with the ATI All-In-Wonder, but other ATI video cards with MPEG acceleration should be able to give you similar playback rates. I haven't tested boards from other manufacturers, but any board that accelerates MPEG playback and provides NTSC video output may give you acceptable results. The ATI boards aren't limited to television output, either. This series is a pretty nice video board overall, and I recommend them if the specs suit your needs. For details, check out **www.atitech.com**.

PROJECT 20.2 Transferring Your Animation to Videotape

The basic process is to render your LightWave animation as an uncompressed AVI, edit the AVI to add a synchronized soundtrack, encode the AVI into a multiplexed MPEG audio/video stream, and play the finished MPEG movie through the ATI board to produce 30fps NTSC video to your VHS VCR:

1. Render an uncompressed AVI to D1 (720×486) resolution, 24-bit color depth, at 30fps for the best NTSC video recording through the ATI output.

   Make sure you have plenty of room! D1-resolution animations get very large very quickly. Alternatively, you can render to 360×243. This may seem like low resolution, but it's not actually much lower than a typical consumer VHS deck can reproduce, and it's adequate for showing your timing and poses.

   It's a good idea to append at least 30 frames of SMPTE color bars (with a test tone), then another 30 frames of black (with silence) at the beginning of the first video sequence. You can either append these during editing or render them at the beginning of the image sequence. If you plan to append other sequences on videotape, you should also end each rendered sequence with 30 frames of black. This "handle" will give you a little more slack in matching your assemble edits, especially if you are using a consumer-grade VCR that doesn't make clean edits.

   Because some pixel-size detail is lost in the MPEG compression, it's a waste of rendering time to use too much anti-aliasing. Motion blur or a post-process soft filter is a good idea because either one may help smooth over the occasional dropped frame. It's also a good idea to apply LightWave's NTSC_Legalize image filter in the Processing tab of the Effects panel. Without these color limits, rendered colors may oversaturate the video output and create glaring artifacts on your videotape.

2. Edit and assemble the AVI and sound track. If you rendered the AVI just as you want it on videotape, you can skip ahead to Step 6. Otherwise, load the AVI clip(s) and WAV files into a new project in your editing software. Adobe Premiere is used in this project, but you can do most of this with shareware programs, too.

3. Edit the source files together to get the final effect you want on the videotape. Make a thumbnail AVI Preview to check the sound sync, video f/x, and transitions. 160x120, one of Premiere's presets, is usually adequate and will give 30fps playback on any MPC2-compatible computer.

4. If the project has a sound track, make sure the bitrate, mode, and sampling rate are compatible with your machine's playback capabilities. To test your machine's playback rates, you can try loading sample MPEGs and watching (and listening) carefully for dropped frames or slow playback. Windows's Media Player or the ATI Player will both give you information about an MPEG's audio and video streams, including the actual playback rate.

5. When the project is edited to your satisfaction, save it with a new file name. Output the video as a 24-bit, full-resolution, uncompressed AVI with the sound track specs your machine can play back at full speed.

6. Your next step is to use one or more utilities to encode the AVI into an MPEG-1 file. The bbMPEG subdirectory on this book's CD-ROM contains several useful examples. bbMPEG and AVI2MPG2 are freeware Windows programs, created by Brad Beyeler, that encode AVI files to MPEG-1 or MPEG-2. The file bbMPEG.dll is also a compiler/export plug-in for Adobe Premiere 5.x. The file AVI2MPG2.exe is a graphic user interface (GUI) for bbMPEG.dll, so you can use bbMPEG without Adobe Premiere. For more details, read the bbmpeg.html file in the bbMPEG subdirectory.

   bbMPEG is a huge improvement over the previous generation of freeware MPEG encoders. This utility does not require you to understand or edit a parameters file; you simply choose your options either from within Premiere or in the AVI2MPEG2 interface, shown in Figure 20.9.

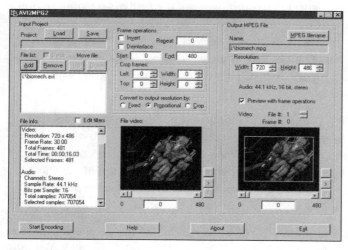

Figure 20.9
AVI2MPEG2 interface.

The encoding usually takes less than a second per image, but long sequences add up. On a PII-400, it can take nearly 30 minutes to convert the 1,800 frames necessary for one minute of NTSC video. It's like an extension of the rendering process. Be patient, and make sure you have plenty of disk space.

7. When the encoding is complete, move the original AVI to another drive for storage or back it up and delete it. If the next step goes wrong, you may need it again, but if you're making a series of long MPEGs, you will probably need the storage space the AVI files are occupying.

8. To test the new MPEG file's playback, you'll need to hook up your VCR to your ATI board's video output. Hook up a television or monitor to the VCR's output so you can preview what will be going onto the tape. Use the ATI Desktop controls to adjust the video output position and size to completely fill your television monitor. It's OK if the television bezel cuts off a little bit of the image's margin on each side, but you don't want a distracting black border around your animation.

9. Launch and set up Media Player (with the ATI MPEG driver) or the ATI Player for full-screen playback to videotape. If you use the ATI Player, press F2 to hide the Player controls during full-frame playback. If you use Media Player, press Alt+Enter to view the playback full-screen.

10. If the MPEG file works, rename it and make a backup copy so you won't accidentally overwrite it with your next MPEG.

11. If your MPEG files won't play back at 30fps, try reencoding them with a lower bit rate setting in the AVI2MPEG2 interface. The lower the bit rate, the lower the image quality, but you have to work within your system's limits.

With the MPEG acceleration of the ATI board, I've been able to get some pretty good-looking videotape. You can't expect a client to pay you for the VHS-quality playback you'll get from this process, but it's good enough to build your animation demo reel. The most important factor is getting an accurate, consistent frame rate so the reviewer can assess your timing. The slightly smeared edges and color artifacts of MPEG-1 compression aren't going to harm your work, at least as far as most animation studios are concerned.

Faster Playback from RAM

If the video clip you are dumping is small enough, you may get faster playback by creating a RAM disk (as detailed in Project 17.6) and playing back the clip from RAM. This takes the hard drive out of the loop but still requires a fast system bus and video card. A RAM disk is a section of your computer's chip memory that is set aside and handled as if it were a disk drive. Loading files from a RAM disk is usually much faster than loading them from a hard drive. However, if anything goes wrong and your system shuts down or reboots, any data on the RAM disk will be lost.

Video Toaster NT

NewTek's Video Toaster NT (VTNT, shown in Figure 20.10) is designed to output uncompressed ITU-R-601 video, but it requires a drive or striped array that can sustain at least 22MBps transfer rate. If the drive hesitates, no frames are dropped, but the playback slows. As long as the drive keeps up, the output rate is a solid 29.97fps. The Toaster does not monopolize the video HDDs, which enables you to use them for other purposes when they're not full of video clips. The VTNT doesn't even dictate what type of drive you can use—SCSI, IDE, whatever, as long as it has a sustained data transfer rate of at least 22MBps. The most cost-effective way to achieve this data rate is to use Windows NT's striping utility to make the computer see several smaller, slower HDDs as one large, fast HDD. For example, if you have four HDDs that can each sustain 6MBps, you can stripe them into one virtual HDD that can sustain 24MBps. This enables you to use slower, less-expensive HDDs. Setting up the striped HDD array is easy too. If you haven't done it before, the VTNT manual includes a step-by-step guide that had my system dumping animations to tape less than an hour after I opened the box.

Figure 20.10
NewTek Video Toaster NT card.

The image quality from this system is also excellent because there are no compression artifacts. One minor quibble is that the Toaster's connectors are all BNC cable-ends rather than a nice, neat breakout box, so changing connections is a matter of chasing big black snakes around the floor. NewTek is working on an affordable 16-input switcher, and I recommend that you add it to your shopping list if you're considering a Toaster. I/O options are also available for SDI and DV. The Video Toaster NT bundle includes an optimized version of in:sync's Speed Razor editing software, so you can edit your animations, assemble them with other footage, sync the audio, and output a complete production. Taking into account the $2,995 price, plus the bundled Aura and LightWave software, the Toaster is an excellent end-to-end choice for the small studio or individual artist who wants to output animation to broadcast-quality videotape.

Video Recording Options

Your choice of recording media can either preserve the work you put into your animations or toss it all in the trash. You should choose the best format you can get your hands on. Don't go cheap on the media either. For both analog and digital tape formats, the wider the tape and the faster the tape speed, the better. The wider the track and the more tape you run past the recording heads per second, the more robust the recorded signal will be and the lower your chances of losing data to dropouts. The trade-off is that using more tape is more expensive and reduces the time you can fit on a single cassette. However, character animation is such a time-consuming, labor-intensive process that tape costs are usually negligible in proportion to the rest of the costs for a shot.

Analog Recording Options

A good rule of thumb for analog formats is to record your master tape at least one step higher in quality than your distribution medium. Any analog medium incurs *generational losses*—that is, a copy of a copy of a copy doesn't look nearly as good as the original. If your master tape is at least one step higher in recording quality than your distribution format, it will go a long way toward counteracting that generational loss. For example, if you plan to distribute a production on VHS tape, your master should be at least S-Video quality or higher. On the other hand, if a production will be distributed only on VHS, it's overkill and a waste of money to master it on Digital HD. One way to choose an analog format for mastering tape is to contact your duplication service. If you tell them what format you want it duplicated to, they can tell you what master format they prefer for it. These are the people with the most experience, and they'll have to work with your choice in the end, so you should be able to rely on their advice.

If you are making a one-off tape for personal use, you can simply run a composite output to a consumer VHS deck. However, this will give you muddy colors, a maximum of about 350 lines of resolution, and a high rate of dropouts and other tape-induced artifacts. It will look lousy on anything better than a medium-grade 13-inch television. The tape will also wear out faster, because most consumer-grade VHS tape is the cheapest media the manufacturers produce. This level of output is definitely not suitable for further duplication. This is not a good level of quality to show off your animations; even good animations look bad. However, if you're a starving student and this is the only way to dump your demo reel to tape, you can make it work. Just make sure your interviewer is aware of the restrictions on your tape output and doesn't blame your lack of animation skills for the bad color control and crawly edges.

You can dramatically improve the quality of your VHS recording by using S-VHS. S-VHS decks will also record standard VHS tapes, and they are very affordable. Think of the price difference between the VHS and S-VHS deck as an upgrade to your computer's video output capabilities. The colors in your animations will remain more nearly true to what you saw on your workstation, the grayscales will be sharper, and you'll get between 25 and 50 additional lines of resolution. You can even use an S-VHS master to have VHS copies duplicated, although I don't recommend it. Whichever VHS or S-VHS option you choose, select the best-quality tape for your master. If you are making demo reels to send out, they should also be on the best-quality VHS tape, but make sure they are just long enough to hold your demo reel. If you send a tape that's over half an hour long, odds are good that someone will use it to record their favorite television shows. You can buy standard short-length (5-, 10-, 15-minute) VHS tapes in bulk from a number of vendors (**neemannmedia.com**, **vhsduplication.com**, **camaudio.com**, et al.). If you are serious about getting into the character animation business, you should consider a case of short VHS tapes as an investment in your career, just like a box of résumé paper.

You will get marginally better results if you record your S-Video master to Hi8, a common camcorder format. I've been very happy with the transfers to VHS I've made from my Hi8 camcorder through an S-VHS deck. Again, this is fine for personal use and for cost-limited student demo reels, but I don't believe it's good enough for the paying customers. Also, the narrow and relatively low-speed Hi8 format is more prone to dropouts than more robust formats. I don't recommend Hi8 for archive tapes or for masters that will be used for bulk duplication.

For professional work or archival tapes, you should record a master tape on an uncompressed component medium whenever possible. Compression will almost always introduce some loss, and combining video signal components into either S-Video or composite signals will muddy the colors and blur the grayscales irretrievably. Even if you can't afford to own the necessary D-1 or D-5 recording deck, you can rent them to record your master tape, then create dubs to compressed or composite formats from the uncompressed masters. If your workstation can be lugged down to the rental shop, you can even bypass the deposit and insurance charges by making the transfer right there.

If you can't find a suitable VTR for rent in your area, talk to the folks at the nearest studio that uses one and find out what they'd charge you to make a transfer from your workstation. If you are starting up a small studio, they may be willing to make regular arrangements that benefit you both. You get the best-quality output for your animations, and they make a little more money to help pay off their expensive gear. If your work looks good, they may also throw the occasional job your way or subcontract you for the occasional animation they don't have the time or expertise to do in-house. Remember, every contact you have with a vendor is a chance to generate more business.

Digital Recording Options

Choosing to record digital S-Video or composite would be less than smart because your animations are rendered in either RGB or YUV digital color space. Squashing that perfectly clean color signal into S-Video or composite is a complete waste. If you are going to the expense of recording digitally, you should only consider digital component video. For the same reasons, you should try to record with the best sampling pattern; 4:2:2 is the minimum you should accept. Formats such as DVCPRO that drop to 4:1:1 may be acceptable for some so-called "professional" uses, but your animations should demand a higher quality of sampling.

If possible, you should choose a larger tape format, wide enough and fast enough to give you a robust signal. Despite all the advances in technology, tape is not perfect: Digital dropouts do happen. If you consider that a video frame is typically held on a space about the width of a human hair and that the read/write heads are spinning at about 9,000 RPM, you can see that dust or tape flaws can easily cause dropouts. Given the choice between the 1/4-inch DVCPRO50, the 1/2-inch Panasonic D-5, and the 3/4-inch Sony D-1, which tape would you trust with your best work?

Digital tape formats have an additional layer of protection that analog machines don't. The error correction circuitry in digital machines can detect a dropout and substitute data from adjacent blocks to fill the gap. If the dropout is small, you won't even see it. If the dropout is larger, you may see a correction as large as an entire freeze-frame that lasts until the uncorrupted signal resumes.

If you are recording to digital tape for professional use, the lowest you should go is DVCPRO50 (not just DVCPRO!). This format offers 4:2:2 signal processing and a 3.3:1 compression ratio. This is relatively low compression, and differences from the original uncompressed images are barely visible. If you can't afford D-1 or D-5, DVCPRO50 is not a bad compromise. DVCPRO50 decks, such as the Panasonic AJ-D950A, are expensive for a small studio or individual artist, but they're not out of the ballpark for a medium-sized studio or a rental shop. This deck lists for $25,000 and records at 67 millimeters per second of 1/4-inch metal particle tape.

A better choice is the D-5 format. This is uncompressed component video, so you don't have to worry about any image quality loss other than tape dropouts. Because this format records to 1/2-inch tape at 167 millimeters per second, the recording should be robust enough that you don't have to worry much about dropouts either. You can fit up to two hours on a tape, and the high bandwidth means you can convert some D-5 decks to HDTV. You'll pay high for the peace of mind: The Panasonic AJ-D580H deck originally listed for $75,000, and even at overstock and used sales, the best price I've found is $28,000.

The D-1 format is the undisputed top of the heap in standard-definition video recording. It was the first digital videotape standard and is used primarily in specialized post-production applications where the image quality has to be perfect. It should come as no surprise that recording equipment for this format is also some of the most expensive available. Even when they are available used, D-1 equipment like the Sony DVR2100 can run $64,000 or more. For your money, you'll get uncompressed component video sampled at 4:2:2 and recorded at 286 millimeters per second onto 3/4-inch tape. If you're fortunate enough to find a studio that has one, expect to pay $200 or so per hour for the use of it.

HDTV, Film, and E-cinema

This is the final step on the animation path to the big time, the big bucks, the big screen. If you can make it here, you can make it anywhere. Your animations have to look good on screens so large that every pixel is several inches square, in front of audiences with trained eyes and high expectations. If you want to succeed on the big screen, you have to understand how that screen works. HDTV, film, and e-cinema media pose special problems that have a major effect on the appearance of your animations. You need to understand the idiosyncrasies of these media so that you can create the best possible animations. If you don't know the limits and demands of these media, you may choose tools or techniques that work for standard video but look like junk on the big screen.

Until recently, film was the undeniable top end of special effects work by a huge margin. That margin has narrowed significantly with the ongoing conversion of broadcast television to high-definition television. The difference between the best HDTV and the worst 35mm feature film is now less than the difference between the best and worst film projection standards. Sloppy film projection can sabotage the brightness, contrast, and resolution advantages of that medium, and exemplary digital projection can maximize the video equipment's performance. In other words, HDTV done right can look better than feature film done wrong. In addition, a number of technologies have come together in the last few years to make transfers from film to HDTV, or vice versa, much cheaper and to produce better results. The divide between video and film is narrowing and may soon be erased completely. The latest developments in electronic cinema, or *e-cinema*, are the precursors of the completely digital, film-quality processes that will soon become the new theatrical cinema standards.

Part of your responsibility as a LightWave character animator is to create art that can be transferred to whatever new media become available. Knowing which production process to use can make the difference between losing your shirt and running your production into a dead end or making money and distributing to every format that develops. If you choose a production process or recording format that makes transfers difficult, expensive, or lossy, you risk painting yourself into a very expensive corner. If you choose processes and formats with maximum compatibility, you will be able to adapt your production to any new format inexpensively and with the best quality.

High-Definition Television

At the time of this writing, HDTV has not yet settled into a single format for use in the United States. The networks and major content producers have largely chosen up sides, but there is no clear winner (or losers) as yet. By the time you read this, the dust may have settled. Despite this uncertainty, I believe there are choices you can make that will guarantee your animations' success in any HDTV format.

The first choice you need to make is when. You should know your clients. Do they really need HDTV? Can you generate a reasonable return on investment (ROI) from HDTV equipment purchases? Unless you can make a very solid business case for an immediate purchase, you should practice with rental equipment to get your feet wet and to buy time for prices to drop. As of this writing, HD equipment prices are as high as they are ever going to be. If you can temporarily record HD animations with rental equipment, that puts off the day you have to commit to purchasing that equipment. By that time, prices will be lower, you'll have more choices, and you'll have the experience from the rental equipment to help you make well-informed purchase decisions. You may even be able to pick up bargains from early adopters who overspent and went under.

Before you see your first frame of HDTV footage, you should be aware of production changes necessary to this format. The higher level of detail means that all your production values need to be higher. Those "minor" flaws will become glaringly obvious in HDTV. Everybody connected with a production needs to be aware of the differences between SDTV and HDTV or gremlins will take a bite out of the budget and schedule when you can least afford it. To play it safe, you should budget production costs as if for film on your first few HDTV projects and adjust the budgets downward if necessary. That's a lot safer than budgeting for SDTV and having to adjust upward!

Experienced SDTV animators who are new to HDTV will need to practice composing shots for both 16:9 and for possible conversion to the standard 4:3 box. There are two other new limits on the camera: no swish pans and no extreme close-ups. Early adopters have found that HDTV's higher-quality images encourage people to sit closer to the screen, creating a more immersive environment for your audience. Extreme close-ups are overwhelming, and swish pans can make viewers motion sick. The larger frame makes the director's storytelling job a little different. The 4:3 box enabled the director to restrict the audience's view, to tell a story with more control. The larger 16:9 frame allows the audience to decide what to watch. The director has to make allowances for that or viewers may miss important story elements. Editing needs to make allowances too; whenever you cut in HDTV, the viewer needs an extra beat to scan the screen and make sense of the new point of view. Editing that is too fast will disorient the viewer.

Animation for HDTV has to balance a paradox. The center of the shot will be visible in SDTV's 4:3 ratio, and the edges of the screen will be visible only in 16:9 HDTV and film transfers. However, the wider formats are the ones that will most clearly show any flaws in the animations or other effects. The director can frame "4:3-safe" shots that keep the 16:9 edges unimportant to the story line, but you have no such shortcuts: Every HDTV animation has to be perfect across the entire frame. Welcome to the next level.

HDTV Hardware Selection

The quality of high-definition television recording is controlled by the same factors that control standard definition: bandwidth, compression, sampling, and media. You need to check the same specifications on compression ratios, tape widths and speeds, and sampling frequency, pattern, and depth to judge the quality of the recording medium and hardware. The most significant difference is that all the numbers relating to bandwidth are much higher, mostly on the order of a factor of 4. If the animation needs to be shown in HDTV, don't go cheap and try to produce in anything lower, then try to up-res the footage in post. It just won't look as good, no matter what equipment or software you use. If you need HDTV playback, you should render and output in full HDTV.

At this time, there is a push to standardize HDTV on 1920×1080×24p. This is one of the standard HDTV resolutions, so that part is no surprise. The most significant change from NTSC SDTV is from 29.97 to 24fps. The ATSC digital television standard covers multiple frame rates, including 24fps, so this choice fits within the available standards. The particular advantage of 24p is that it bypasses the necessity for 3:2 pull-down from film sources and the reverse 2:3 pull-up to go back to film. Therefore, 1920×1080×24p can be output to film or down-converted to most other HDTV and SDTV formats easily, including 480i@24, 480p@60, 720p@60, and 1080i@30. Telecine for this format would be done at the highest resolution and lower-quality formats downconverted from that master. Because 24p is progressive rather than interlaced, it can also be compressed more efficiently using MPEG-2. In short, if you render your animations in 1920×1080×24p, you maintain simple and inexpensive compatibility with nearly every common film or video format. You can then shift all the conversion issues downstream and perform all your animation in full-frame 24fps, enabling you to use the same tools for film, HDTV, and SDTV. That can make an enormous difference to your work flow and your investment in your toolbox.

Sony and other manufacturers have been shipping a number of new HDTV cameras, VTRs, and other production equipment, including 24p digital cinematography gear. At this time, you have relatively few choices among top-end machines suitable for recording your HDTV animations.

The Sony HDWF500 VTR records 1920×1080 (16:9) 10-bit digital component data stream through HD-SDI inputs with a bit rate of 1.5Gbps at 24, 25, or 30 progressive frames, or 50, 59.94, or 60 interlaced fields per second. It can also record frame-by-frame for recording animation from systems that can't sustain realtime playback. Visit **http://bpgprod.sel.sony.com** for details. Note that the color sampling depth for the HDWF500 is component and 10 bits per channel rather than 8. This isn't quite as good as some film scanners, but it's a significant step up from SDTV, and it will make a difference in the color quality of your animations. There is also an option for a down-converter to produce SDTV output. Currently, this deck is available for rental in major markets for upward of $750 per day. The purchase price? If you have to ask, you can't afford it.

The Panasonic AJ-HD2700 VTR records a 10-bit digital component serial data stream sampled 4:2:2 at 74.25 MHz. Using JPEG intrafield compression at a 5:1 ratio, this deck fits the HD digital video onto standard 1/2-inch D-5 tape running at 167 millimeters per second. You can record up to 124 minutes onto a single large cassette and select 1035i, 1080i, or 720p mode. This deck has already become a studio standard and was used to feed Texas Instruments' DLP Cinema presentation of Disney's *Tarzan*.

Film

If you are an independent filmmaker, you should stick with video formats until you can find financial backing for film transfer. If you carefully archive all your animation scenes, objects, and related files, you can always go back and rerender to higher resolution for film. Film output is expensive, but it definitely gives the best-looking results. Unless you can afford your own film recorder, you will be sending your rendered images to a service bureau to be transferred to film. I recommend against trying to save money by transferring to 16mm. Go with 35mm. The price difference in film is relatively small compared to the transfer charges for the recorder. Also, if you are trying to get into film festivals or sell your animation, 35mm prints have a wider potential audience.

If you need to do a film transfer, I strongly recommend that you spend some time talking with the professionals at reputable service bureaus before you make any binding decisions. They're the ones with the expertise, and they can save you a great deal of time, money, and aggravation.

Film Recorders

Even after e-cinema systems have proven themselves, there is going to be a long period when many 35mm film projectors are still in use. And if you listen to Kodak and other film industry technologists, there's plenty of room for improvement in film stocks. If the order-of-magnitude improvements in color, resolution, and contrast that they predict ever materialize, they will go a long way toward prolonging a side-by-side existence for both electronic and film cinema. With that in mind, an animator working today needs to be familiar with the existing needs of film recording technology. It's going to be around for a while.

Film has high resolution, random grain, wide contrast, and a continuous, nearly infinite color space. It has a fixed frame rate of 24fps that is in use worldwide, as are the handful of common apertures or aspect ratios. What this means for character animators is that for film work, you need to output your animations in the highest resolution and color depth that your workstation can handle, but you don't have to worry about interlace. If you have to match other film footage, you'll need to add grain to any live-action elements that were smoothed out during compositing or any LightWave elements that never had grain to begin with.

One big advantage to film output is that recorders don't need the data in realtime, so your workstation does not have to have huge bandwidth or expensive output hardware. As long as you can dump the images to Exabyte, Jaz, CD-R, removable HDD, or whatever digital media your service bureau prefers, you can take hours to record each frame. Oddly, this makes the slowest workstation nearly equal to the fastest, at least for final data transfer to film. Rendering at film resolution—that's another story. Measuring by file size alone, you're talking about the difference between rendering a 1MB SDTV frame and a 12MB 2K Cineon frame.

Kinescope

The simplest and oldest way of transferring digital images to film is the kinescope. Basically, you point a single-frame-capable film camera at a high-resolution monitor, defocus the monitor slightly to hide the pixel grid, and film the frames as they are displayed one-by-one on screen. When the kinescope is home-built, this low-budget approach is even more reasonable today for student and independent projects. You can find bargains on old 16mm or 35mm animation cameras, and the latest monitors have flatter, higher-resolution displays. It's up to the operator to keep track of lens and monitor settings for brightness, color balance, focus, and exposure, which need to be consistent or the film will show obvious fluctuations. Because of these quality-control problems, for any distribution more serious than minor film festivals, you need to make the transfer with a film recorder.

CRT Film Recorders

Cathode-ray tube (CRT) film recorders are essentially a fine-tuned version of pointing a camera at a monitor. The CRT itself has at least 2K resolution, and the camera is a precisely registered film transport and exposure system that guarantees that each frame will be placed and exposed exactly like the frames before and after it. The most popular recorder design uses a monochromatic (black-and-white) high-resolution CRT. This makes it easier to get higher resolution because you only have one set of phosphors in the tube rather than three. To expose colors, a color wheel containing filters for red, green, and blue rotates between the camera lens and CRT. The camera takes three exposures for each frame, one for each color filter. The exposure process is time-consuming, as much as 40 seconds per frame on some of the older film recorders. The camera is often an adapted animation stand camera. The industry-standard Oxberry pin-registered animation camera is popular.

CRT film recorders are more affordable than other types due to their relative simplicity. However, the precision engineering that goes into fine-tuning even simple technologies runs their prices into the hundreds of thousands of dollars. Only the largest studios with constant film output needs can make a good business case for buying a film recorder plus hiring a skilled operator. Most studios and independent producers use service bureaus for film recording. If turnaround time is not critical, the slower CRT film recorders will usually bring bargain rates of under $2 per recorded frame. Most major metropolitan areas will have at least one service bureau with a CRT film recorder.

Laser Film Recorders

Laser film recorders can be more precise than CRT-based film recorders because lasers can expose smaller spots on the film, producing less-grainy, sharper images. Lasers are also brighter, enabling the use of less-sensitive, lower-grain intermediate film stocks rather than grainier camera stocks. However, laser film recorders are more expensive than CRT film recorders.

The largest effects houses and film studios develop their own technology in-house. For example, Pixar Animation Studios cofounder and Director of Photo Sciences David DiFrancesco received his second Academy of Motion Pictures Arts and Sciences Scientific and Technical Academy Award in 1999 for work that led up to the new PixarVision Laser Film Recorder. DiFrancesco has been working on the use of solid-state lasers to record on motion picture materials since 1986. The PixarVision recorder exposes the film to all three colors simultaneously rather than sequentially, resulting in a speed of 8 seconds per frame. PixarVision also uses solid-state lasers, eliminating the cross-talk problems of the gas lasers used in other laser film scanners.

> *"This means that when you expose in the red channel, you don't get any blue exposure, and likewise, when you expose in blue, you don't get any green. That's very important for densities under one, so you don't get muddy-looking shadows. You get higher-quality color reproduction."*
> *—David DiFrancesco, Pixar Animation Studios*

Solid-state lasers are also easier to use and maintain because they don't require special power supplies or cooling systems and can simply be unplugged and replaced. The PixarVision scanner can print to virtually any film stock, including print stock. The scanner was used to print Pixar's 1998 film, *A Bug's Life*, and to print 1999's *Toy Story 2*. The film recorder was developed for internal use, and at this time, Pixar has no plans to make it available for sale. There are several other laser film recorders currently on the market. These are high-end, expensive machines in a very competitive market, so specifications and features change rapidly.

The laser film recording process starts with loading the film into the supply magazine of the recorder. Three solid-state lasers—one each for red, green, and blue—are behind a heat wall in the optics module to shield the rest of the scanner from their waste heat. Temperature control is important for film scanners, as for most precision equipment, so most facilities keep them in a climate-controlled room. The three laser beams are adjusted for intensity by the attenuators, which are neutral-density filters that compensate for differences in film stock sensitivity or drifts in beam strength. Each beam then passes through an acousto-optical modulator (AOM). The AOMs modulate the intensity of the beams according to the data stream, controlling how strongly each color will be recorded onto the film. From the AOMs, the beams are combined by a set of dichroic mirrors and finally reflected up to the scanner module.

The scanner module guides the tricolor laser beam to the film. Lenses focus the beam, and a motorized prism deflects the beam to scan lines across the film. The deflected tricolor laser beam and the film shuttle's motion combine to expose the entire film frame. The scanning beam moves vertically at a very high speed, recording each line of the image. The film shuttle moves more slowly and horizontally, so that each pass of the vertical beam is precisely aligned to a new line of unexposed film. In only a few seconds, the combined motion of the shuttle and beam can record an entire full-aperture frame at 4K resolution.

The film shuttle is only one part of the film transport. First, the frame is positioned with two registration pins, mounted on the film gate, that precisely locate the film to prevent any unwanted frame-to-frame motion. When the film is locked in place, the film shuttle moves four perforations (one frame) to the right at a precisely controlled rate, synchronized with the laser beam scanning. In the second phase, after the frame is completely exposed, the film shuttle stops and the film stage moves away from the gate, removing the film from the registration pins and transferring it to the stationary transport pins. This keeps the film stationary during the third phase, when the film shuttle returns to its starting position at the left. From this position, the film shuttle moves toward the film gate in the fourth phase, picking the film off the transport pins and moving it onto the registration pins. Once the film is registered, a new exposure phase can begin.

Although advances in laser film recording have speeded up the process considerably, it still takes a relatively long time to transfer long-format productions to film. It's also expensive: Even the lowest-quality film recording is going to cost you a few dollars per frame, and top-end recording can be over $5 per frame. You will also have to search a little harder to find service bureaus that use the highest-quality machines, but if you're in either the Los Angeles or New York metro areas, you can take your pick.

Electron Beam Recorder

A relatively new and potentially more cost-effective way of getting your digital files to film is the electron beam recorder, or EBR. This device uses electrons rather than photons to record an image, so no optics are necessary. The difference is similar to the inherent difference between the sharpness of an electron microscope image and the fuzziness of a light microscope image. Electrons don't scatter in the film emulsion, and the result is that the image on film is unlimited by either optics or its own halation.

Because electrons have no color, black-and-white film is used. Sony Pictures High Definition Center (SPHDC) is one of the few shops that use this process, but its results have been very promising. Because very fine resolution is possible with an electron beam, the image quality is exceptionally good on 35mm fine-grain positive stock (Sony uses Fuji 71337). To get color, you output color separations for the red, green, and blue channels, and each channel is printed to a separate black-and-white film. The three films are step-printed on an optical printer to an MOS color negative (Kodak 5245). The color negative is hard-matted to 1.77:1. The negative is developed, with quality very close to an original camera negative, and an MOS one light print is struck. If you need them, you can have many apparently original print negatives struck, each with identical high quality. This gives EBR film a visible advantage in projection because most theater prints are two generations farther from the original. As of this writing, SPHDC was charging $1.30 per frame for transfers from digital files. If you are coming from HDTV video, SPHDC will handle the conversion to film resolution and frame rates. For details, visit the SPHDC Web site at **www.spe.sony.com/Pictures/Hidef/sphweb.htm**.

E-cinema

E-cinema is a system of projecting cinema-quality images directly from digital data without the use of film. E-cinema poses special problems for LightWave character animators. Several attributes of conventional 35mm film projection work together to hide small details. Grain masks imperfections; e-cinema has no grain. Projected film can weave and jitter, which combines with the lower refresh rate and (possibly) incorrectly set optics to degrade its effective resolution; e-cinema is rock steady. Film collects damage and dirt, and over time, it fades; e-cinema is digitally identical from first to last show. Acceptable film print resolution for feature film is 2K, or 2,048 lines of resolution. This is partly the result of theater prints being several generations removed from the original footage. One of the advantages of digital cinematography is that it has no generational losses, so it can preserve every bit of its lower resolution and end up looking just as good as fourth-generation film on the big screen. Also, electronic projectors can run at higher refresh rates, effectively increasing brightness while reducing visible flicker.

Whenever a medium has imperfections, the audience comes to expect them and allows the artist more leeway. The more perfect the medium, the more perfect the work the artist has to produce. Even at the current stage of e-cinema development, the audience response has been clear. As with HDTV, the difference between film and e-cinema is noticeable, even for nonprofessionals. One group of viewers of the e-cinema presentation of *Star Wars: The Phantom Menace* remarked that the CGI shots looked "like a video game." Comments on the e-cinema quality of *Shakespeare in Love* also pointed out flaws in makeup, sets, or props that had gone unnoticed in the film presentation. In order to make audiences buy into a shot shown in e-cinema, the animation is going to have to be absolutely perfect.

The technical challenges of e-cinema are significant. From 5,000 to 10,000 lumens are required from the e-cinema projector to provide the same brightness of image a conventional 35mm film projector provides. The image contrast ratio needs to be higher, too, which means luminance sampling depth needs to be at least 10 bits and preferably 12. At least 1,500 vertical lines of resolution are necessary to make a digital image difficult to distinguish from a film image. As of this writing, only two manufacturers have systems that meet theatrical film standards.

The Hughes-JVC (**www.hjt.com**) projector (see Figure 20.11) puts out 10,000 lumens, projecting images at up to 2000×1280 resolution, with contrast greater than 1500:1. It can accept RGBHV, digital serial 4:2:2, RGB analog, composite, Y/C, and component inputs in NTSC, PAL, and SECAM. Its heart is a light modulator composed of three proprietary image light amplifiers (ILAs), 100-percent solid-state liquid crystal light valves. The ILA processes and amplifies the image from a CRT and adjusts color, contrast, and brightness to match the look, tone, and texture of film footage. The current CRT is limited to 2K resolution, but the ILA itself is capable of 4K resolution, so this system has a clear upgrade path. The projector's light source is a standard 7,000-watt xenon arc lamp. The list price on this projector is $250,000. Hughes-JVC has partnered with QUALCOMM to form CineComm Digital Cinema, L.L.C., chartered to "provide a full turn-key system for movie delivery and exhibition." CineComm provided half the projectors for e-cinema showings of *Star Wars: The Phantom Menace* in 1999.

Figure 20.11
Hughes-JVC projector.

The other projectors for the *Star Wars* e-cinema presentations used Texas Instruments' (**www.ti.com/dlp**) Digital Light Processing (DLP) imaging technology. The core of this technology is the Digital Micromirror Device (DMD). This technology is limited to the actual pixel resolution of the device, so higher-resolution images depend on the development of higher-resolution DMDs. TI has already produced a 16:9 ratio DMD with 1920×1080 resolution on a trial basis, so we can expect to see 1600×1200 or even 2000×1500 DMDs in the not-too-distant future. The DMD is a matrix of microscopic mirrors that rapidly switch on or off more than 5,000 times per second, creating an image in the light beam that reflects off the DMD's surface.

DLP-based projectors can use up to three DMDs in one system. A three-chip system utilizes a prism to split and recombine color. Filters deposited on the surface of the prism split the light into red, green, and blue components. Each of the primary colors is assigned to its own DMD, which reflects monochromatic light back into the prism, where it is recombined and projected onto a screen.

E-cinema technology is already being accepted at the highest levels of the special-effects industry. At ShoWest in Las Vegas on March 11, 1999, George Lucas announced his plans to shoot *Star Wars* prequels 2 and 3 with digital cameras, edit and post digitally, and screen them digitally. In April, at NAB '99, Sony and Panavision announced an agreement to develop filmless, digital cameras for Lucasfilm. The first production-ready prototype camcorders have been delivered to Lucasfilm for testing with Panavision lenses prior to shooting *Star Wars: Episode II.*

Multiplex cinema owners are not likely to start ripping out their film projectors immediately, but the demonstrations of e-cinema to date have been impressive. The remaining technical questions are only of time. The financial questions are a matter of allocating the changeover costs between the cinema owners who need the expensive new projectors and the film distributors who stand to save large amounts of money on distribution costs. This changeover affects your future as a LightWave character animator, but fortunately, the outlook seems positive. Your work will come under closer scrutiny, and that's an opportunity to hone your craft and show what you can do.

Moving On

This chapter has provided you with the information you need to make the right choices for recording equipment and media to preserve your animations at their best quality for multimedia, video, HDTV, film, and e-cinema. If you've worked through the entire book, you should now have a solid understanding of character animation and a pretty good demo reel. Congratulations! That's the last of the technical information you will need to master to be a successful character animator.

However, there's more to being a success than mastering your art; business skills are important too. The next chapter contains information you can use to manage your career, whether you are trying to break into the business, stay employed, or start your own studio.

Chapter 21

Starting Out

When you're trying to break into the business, you need to know what employers are
looking for and where to find animation industry information. This chapter is intended to
provide information you can use to start or continue your career in LightWave character animation. This information is as accurate as I could make it, but this industry is moving fast and the
details change all the time. I encourage you to check my Web site's online updates before taking
any irrevocable actions—like mailing your last copy of your demo reel to an out-of-date address!

> *"Happiness lies in being privileged to work hard for long hours in doing whatever you
> think is worth doing."*
> —Robert A. Heinlein

Animation is not a career choice you should make lightly or on the spur of the moment. Most
successful animators I have interviewed have always had an interest in animation, and many
wanted to be animators from early childhood. If you have been attracted to LightWave character
animation by recent publicity on high salaries and many job opportunities, think again—this is a
job you do because you love it, not because you get paid a lot to do it. The "high" salaries are not
enough to compensate you for long hours and grueling work if you don't sincerely love what
you're doing.

Self-Education

Trying to teach yourself character animation with LightWave is a long, slow road, fraught with
peril and liberally pitted with potholes. The only signposts along the way are the contacts you
make and the feedback you receive from your fellow students and colleagues. It's not a choice
for the weak or fainthearted.

"Yes, we are all students in the School of Life
Pain and toil are our teachers
Love and joy are our holidays
Character animation our evil Headmaster"
—Jim Studt

Fortunately, there are more resources for the self-taught LightWave animator today than at any previous time. This book and other LightWave-specific titles are good places to start. Books on traditional animation (see the Bibliography) are excellent sources of information if you don't mind translating their techniques into LightWave. For more timely information, there are magazines and professional journals in a variety of related fields. Here are the journals I use myself—long on information, short on fluff, and generally reliable to get the story straight.

Keyframe is the best collection of tutorials and case studies for artists using LightWave. Of course, I'm biased, because I'm the editor. Our focus is on what is being used in the television and film industry, the tutorials are generally written by artists actually using LightWave for a living, and the product reviews concentrate on utility rather than gee-whiz. In addition to my regular "Character Shop" column, there is usually at least one other article pertinent to character animation.

Keyframe Magazine
2756 N. Green Valley Pkwy. #261
Henderson, NV 89014
www.keyframemag.com

3D Artist is a good source of tutorials and hands-on information for artists using popular desktop 3D software. The focus is on what works, the tutorials are good, and the product reviews are honest. There is usually at least one article on one of the desktop character animation packages, and tutorials for any software are often written to be applicable elsewhere.

Columbine Inc.
P.O. Box 4787
Santa Fe, NM 87502
ISSN: 1058-9503
www.3dartist.com

ACM Transactions on Graphics is a quarterly academic research journal dealing with the algorithms and other theoretical arcana behind graphics programming. Techniques first published here sometimes take years to show up in commercial desktop software. Smart technical directors (TDs) read this journal and work out their own implementations to stay ahead of the commercial pack.

ISSN: 0730-0301
www.acm.org/pubs/tog

Computer Graphics is a sister publication to *Transactions*. The contents are more about implementations and tutorials, and the annual SIGGRAPH Conference Proceedings are always a worthwhile collection of eye candy and solid information.

Association for Computing Machinery
11 West 42nd Street
New York, NY 10036
ISSN: 0097-8930
www.siggraph.org

Animation Magazine is a trade journal covering traditional and CGI animation. Industry news, help wanted, bios, retrospectives, and business-related articles are a big help to novices and old pros alike. This one's definitely worth a subscription.

Animation Magazine
30101 Agoura Court, Suite 110
Agoura Hills, CA 91301
ISSN: 1041-617X
www.animag.com

Cinefex is the trade journal of the feature film special effects community. Slick and heavily illustrated, this quarterly publishes long, in-depth, nuts-and-bolts articles on f/x techniques. Stopmo, miniatures, CGI, you name it—if it ends up on the big screen, *Cinefex* shows how it's done. Even the issues that don't include CGI articles have lots of useful information for character animation, and the advertiser's index reads like a who's who of houses you'd like to work for.

Cinefex
P.O. Box 20027
Riverside, CA 92516
ISSN: 0198-1056
Tel: (800) 434-3339
www.cinefex.com

Computer Graphics World prints news coverage of pretty much what the title says. You'll find articles here about hardware, software, and other technical issues, and the industry news leans more toward hardware and software vendors than animation houses.

CGW
10 Tara Blvd., 5th Floor
Nashua, NH 03062-2801
ISSN: 0271-4159
www.cgw.com

Game Developer is often short on animation-specific articles but long on contact info and industry buzz for the game community. If you're looking for a way to break into the character animation business, game developers are often less picky than feature animation houses are about your demo reel. If you're not already a gamer, read the back issues so you understand the problems and can talk about them intelligently at your job interview.

Miller Freeman Inc.
600 Harrison Street
San Francisco, CA 94107
ISSN: 1073-922X
www.gdmag.com

Post is a post-production trade journal useful primarily for news on who's doing what. You should at least scan the promotional and help-wanted ads scattered throughout the magazine for production houses that may want to hire you.

Advanstar Communications
Post Magazine
One Park Avenue
New York, NY 10016-5802
Tel: (212) 951-6600
Fax: (212) 951-6717
www.postmagazine.com

Just the FAQs, Ma'am

A FAQ (Frequently Asked Questions) is a document containing questions and answers that are often asked of a discussion group or help desk. Just about every major newsgroup, mailing list, or Web site has a FAQ. Smart vendors compile their own FAQs for technical support and make them freely available via the Internet.

Reading FAQs has got to be the easiest, cheapest way in the history of the world to fake being an expert. Contrariwise, jumping into a newsgroup or mailing list and asking the Number One Question from that group's FAQ instantly labels you as a dweeb too dumb to pour sand out of a boot.

In addition to FAQs, there are an increasing number of Web sites that organize a growing amount of quickly changing information that you may find useful. Lists and ratings of animation schools, job openings, industry rumors about forthcoming productions, and behind-the-scenes news on the latest LightWave tools and tips are all available somewhere, and they change much too quickly for print publications to cover. Here are the URLs of a few of the best sites to investigate.

www.flay.com

Flay.com is maintained by Christopher Stewart and is one of the best sources for timely and lasting information about LightWave. The plug-in database alone makes this site worthwhile; add to that the jobs postings, industry rumors, and eye candy links and you've got an invaluable resource.

www.eGroups.com/list/lw3d

As of late 1999, this is the new home of the LightWave Mailing List, the somewhat-moderated (and therefore less noisy) alternative to comp.graphics.apps.lightwave. Anything affecting the LightWave community usually gets posted here, although the rumors and flames can fly thick and fast too. When in doubt, wait for someone with personal knowledge to weigh in with the facts. One of the nice things about the eGroups hosting is that the old messages are searchable online, so you can come late to the party without missing anything.

Deja.com

Although this is not a LightWave-specific site, it does enable you to search the Usenet newsgroup comp.graphics.apps.lightwave (and others), enabling you to glean the gems while bypassing the dross that seems to accumulate in any public venue.

www.NewTek.com

Although this site can be woefully behind schedule, it is the home Web site of the publisher of LightWave and therefore the only really authoritative source. If the information is sometimes out-of-date, at least the updates, patches, and other goodies are available for downloading.

www.lightsource-3d.com

Lightsource is a nice grab bag of tutorials, news, download links, and general-interest good stuff for LightWavers.

www.wpcusrgrp.org/~scameron/lightwavetutorials.htm

This page is an excellent compendium of links to LightWave-related tutorial files all over the Internet. (Last time I checked, I think my name came up twice.)

Schools

Choosing to attend a school to learn character animation is a big decision. You'll be dedicating several years (depending on the program) and anywhere from a few thousand to tens of thousands of dollars. Make sure you'll be getting your time and money's worth!

The most important factor in choosing a school is the faculty. You are better off with great teachers and lousy equipment than with lousy teachers and state-of-the-art computers. Any computer store can sell you the hardware and software. Experienced animators who can also teach are much more difficult to find. If possible, use your network contacts to find teachers with solid reputations, then get into whatever program they're teaching. If you take this approach to its logical extreme, you might consider tracking down a really good animator and negotiating private lessons. Your best resource in making this decision is the school placement office. Animation schools like to brag about the studios that have hired their students, so ask for the names and contact information of well-placed graduates. Most animators will be happy to discuss their educational adventures, such as which teachers to seek out, which ones to avoid, and pitfalls in the curriculum that you should sidestep.

To help with your research, I suggest you consult the online resources listed previously and search specifically for school information. This information becomes out-of-date quickly, so make sure you're getting the latest scoop from people who know what they're talking about.

Practice

Practice, practice, practice! An animator animates! Whether you are in school or studying on your own, you should try to animate something every day, for as many hours as you can afford. Keep a default character scene handy so you can just fire up LightWave and start animating whenever you have the time. If you don't have an original action in mind, go back and reanimate any of the projects from Part V. The more practice you have on the basics, the more easily you'll be able to animate the hard stuff. Set a goal for yourself to animate so many seconds per week. Over time, you'll get faster. Raise the goal, and keep challenging yourself. Resist the temptation to animate schlock just to make your goal. You should insist on every shot being the best you can do at that time. Don't throw away any of your finished practice efforts—these animations are a record of your progress as an animator. Append everything to your archive reel so you can show it to mentors, fellow students, and potential employers.

Harold Harris, creative director at TOPIX, told me he was dismayed at the low quantity of animation shown by animation school graduates. Some of them had as little as two or three minutes to show for their entire school career. He said good animators should practice enough to have 10 minutes of quality animation on their archive reel. If you animate something every day, completing as little as 10 seconds a week will enable you to assemble a 10-minute archive reel in just over a year. If you've got three times as much animation to show as the other candidates for a job, you'll definitely have an advantage. Get to work on it!

Best Foot Forward: Your Demo Reel

Completing the step-by-step projects in this book will not get you a job. You need to go beyond this, to put together a presentation that tells potential employers that you can breathe life into any model they hand you. This presentation will be your demo reel.

You should be keeping all your material, including textbook exercises, on an archive reel. You can take this to an interview, where you may have the opportunity to discuss your learning experiences and techniques. All those bits and pieces of work in progress will help convince a potential employer that you actually did the work on your demo reel.

For your demo reel, select at least three minutes of your best work from your archive reel. You can get by with less than three minutes if your work is very good, but you should have a reasonable explanation ready if you're under two minutes. Don't go over five minutes. Reviewers will have decided in the first few minutes whether they want to talk to you—they will probably not look at anything over five minutes.

Put your absolute best 10 to 30 seconds of character animation at the beginning of your reel. At least one supervisor told me he'll hit the fast-forward button if he doesn't see something interesting in the first 10 seconds. Remember, these people sometimes have several hundred reels to go through, so don't waste their time or test their patience!

If you have a lot of material you want to show, resist the urge to do an MTV-style montage of fast cuts. Some reviewers won't mind this, but it annoys others, and you won't want to risk that. If at all possible, arrange your pieces in some logical order to minimize the jarring effect of cuts.

Put your name and contact information at the beginning and end of your reel. Keep your titles simple and legible and, if possible, incorporate some character animation into them. Perhaps you can animate a character pushing the titles on screen or otherwise interacting with the letters. Don't put a date on your reel, and don't tell them you used LightWave in your animations, either. Some houses will automatically turn you down if you don't use their favorite software. On the other hand, if you apply to a LightWave house, it is pretty easy to put an explanatory printed insert in the cassette case. Your philosophy should be to let your work speak for itself, and don't give reviewers any irrelevant information they could use to weed you out. One exception to this is credit for others' work—make sure everybody who contributed to the work on your reel is credited on the insert, with details of who did what on which pieces. It's a lot better to volunteer this information up front than to be answering awkward questions at an interview.

Depending on how good your material is and how paranoid you are, you may want to rig your demo reel so nothing can be lifted from it by unscrupulous persons. One simple technique is to run an animated streamer through the middle of each scene, traveling behind your main characters but in front of the sets and background. The streamer can say something like "Doug Kelly's Demo Reel—Not for Commercial Use." If you use color cycling in the streamer or vary its transparency values, it's very difficult to remove. If you choose to do this, make sure the "protection" you employ doesn't protect you from becoming employed! Keep it as subtle and unobtrusive as you can.

Animation houses are going to be looking for some very specific elements in your reel. They want to see that you can do the work you are applying for, not just that you have the potential to be able to do it someday. If your demo reel doesn't show what they are looking for, you can expect a polite letter to the effect that, "We have no requirement for your services at this time."

So, what do you need to show? That all depends on what job you are applying for.

Character Animation Demo Reel

If you want to be a character animator, then show character animation in your demo reel. The animators who review your reel are going to be looking for a clear understanding of stretch-and-squash, anticipation, secondary motion, timing, and the other animation concepts you worked through in Part V. Beyond that, they will be looking at the whole effect of your work. Do your characters seem motivated? Do they act convincingly? Do they appear to be thinking? Can the viewer understand what the character is expressing?

You don't necessarily have to show off texturing, lighting, and other rendering details. If you are looking for character animation work, you can show your ability just as well with simple wireframe skeletons. A 30-second wireframe of excellent character animation beats 3 minutes of mediocre raytraced walk cycles any day.

Make sure the playback speed on your videotape is high enough; 30 fps is best, but you can get by with 24 or even 12. Any speed lower than that and the reviewer really can't get a fair idea of your timing. This shouldn't be a problem. Today, even most low-end video cards can play back animation at 24 fps or better. If you're looking for work in the United States, use standard VHS videotapes. You can buy inexpensive 10- or 15-minute videotapes in bulk at very reasonable prices. (The short length keeps people from taping soap operas over your reel.) That's what everybody in the industry uses, and if you're the only one in the stack with a DVD-RAM, CD-ROM, Zip, or floppy disk, reviewers are unlikely to make the extra effort to look at your work. Even if they do, they are going to expect more from you than from the tapes that made their job a little easier.

A good rule of thumb is to pretend that the reviewer is busy, irresponsible, disorganized, and forgetful. Make your reel fast and easy to view, hard to lose, and easy to remember and to locate on a crowded shelf or in a box of other tapes. Rewind the tape before you send it, and pop out the no-erase tabs. Unique or colorful labels with your name and contact information on the spine, face, and ends of the cassette will help. If your tape has a label and the rest of the shelf is just blank black plastic, you've improved your chances. Remember, it can take months before a busy studio gets to your reel, or they may be keeping you in mind for an upcoming job. Make sure they can find your reel when they remember you!

You can also jog the reviewer's memory by putting a thumbnail image on your demo reel labels. A strong pose of a character from the reel is best, but a personal logo or other simple graphic will work too. You are sending your reel to people with good visual memories and perhaps only so-so verbal skills. Make it easy for them to remember and identify your reel!

Technical Director Demo Reel

If you are looking for work as a technical director, your reel should focus on character construction and rendering. You need to be familiar with modeling, texturing, and animation tools from the technical side. You'll also need strong problem-solving skills and usually some programming knowledge and experience. Unlike animators, you will want to put examples of work in progress in your demo reel and portfolio. Include shots of your best models rendered in wireframe and close-ups of the especially tricky parts. You may want to include prints of some of your best images because you can get better quality than videotape and the reviewer can examine them at leisure.

It's a good idea to have duplicates of models, setups, and other electronic files to show at an interview. If you've written any custom shaders, modeling plug-ins or utilities, or any other examples of useful code, bring them along too. Just don't leave any files on the demo machine or leave the disk—most interviewing companies will be scrupulously honest, but there are always a few bad apples who will try to use your work without paying for it.

Your lighting samples should show a solid understanding of the basic principles. Subtlety is usually better than an overwhelming light show. It's better to show that you can work well with a few lights to establish mood, appeal, and direct the viewer's eye than to overwhelm the scene with a technically challenging but poorly designed profusion of lights. Any effects shots should go well beyond any tutorial you may have read. As a TD, you will be expected to solve new problems, not just use others' solutions. Show that you understand your tools well enough to push their limits.

Quality, Not Quantity

What you leave off your demo reel is at least as important as what you put on. You are only as good as the worst piece on your reel. If you want to be employed as a character animator, leave the flying logos, bouncing checkered balls, zooming spacecraft, architectural walkthroughs, tunnel flythroughs, and game rides on your archive reel (unless you're applying to a house that produces that kind of work). And even if it looks like good character animation, leave off the dinosaurs. Everybody has seen dinosaur animations by now, and they are definitely old hat. The same goes for monster animations; most game monsters show very little in the way of acting (I see you! I kill you!), and unless they show very good posing and timing, you're better off without them.

What They Don't See Won't Hurt You
You are only as good as the worst piece on your reel.

If you're shooting for one of the top studios, you can leave off the "transportation" animation as well. The bar has been raised in the past few years. Previously, a good walk cycle could get you a job. Now, you should only include a walk or run cycle if it is technically proficient and shows character. Otherwise, cycles tell very little about your abilities as a character animator.

Don't ever put the results of an exercise or tutorial on your demo reel. That includes the projects in this book! Supervisors or directors at animation studios have seen every demo, exercise, and tutorial a zillion times by the time they get to your tape, and you can guarantee an instant ejection and trashing if you put an over-used demo from the LightWave Bonus CD on your reel. Keep your reel original!

It should go without saying that "original" means your own work, but some people still haven't gotten the message. Character animation is a very small professional community, and everybody sees the good demo reels sooner or later. I've heard similar stories from just about every reviewer about really stupid plagiarists who assemble "their" demo reels from other people's. It's especially stupid when reviewers find their own work, or a friend's, with the plagiarist's name on it. Of course, the reviewers immediately tell all their industry friends about it, and the plagiarist can't get work anywhere. Plagiarism is an excellent way to cut your career off at the knees. Don't do it!

As I stated in Chapter 1, one of the most liberating things about desktop animation software is that you really can do it all yourself. There are software tools that can assist you in doing screenwriting, storyboard and layout art, modeling, texturing, audio digitizing, track breakdown, animation, rendering, record keeping, financial and scheduling project management, music composition and recording, audio and video mixing and editing, title design, and film or video recording.

The question is, do you want to handle it all?

It may be to your advantage to work with a complementary partner or group to produce a joint demo reel. If your talents are in the area of technical director, working with an animator can build a reel that is more coherent and entertaining and that demonstrates that you work well as part of a team. On the other hand, as an animator, you will find that working with a good technical director gives your reel an extra polish that puts it above the competition.

Whatever your approach, if you follow this book's guidelines in putting together a coherent, story-telling demo reel, you will have a good chance at landing a job interview.

So, how can you improve your chances? Sending in a demo reel "cold" is a common approach, but this has some drawbacks because the most popular studios receive hundreds of reels. At some studios, a nonanimator, often a secretary, filters out the absolute trash before any of the creative or supervisory staff get to see it. This can occasionally result in a reel being trashed for reasons having nothing to do with the talent of the animator—the "filters" simply don't know what they are doing.

If you are sending a demo reel, it is a good idea to get the email address, fax number, or phone number of a senior animator or director at the studio and send him a polite message that you would like to send in your reel. If he agrees, tell him exactly when you are sending it, and if he gives you permission, add his name to the Attention line. This way, the reel is more likely to be put aside for someone who knows what he is looking at, and the person you contacted may even ask to see the reel before the filter gets to it.

Remember that your contact person is doing you a favor. Be polite. Don't call him at home. Don't nag. Send a follow-up thank-you note. And never broadcast whatever personal contact information he gives you!

Résumé, Portfolio, and Cover Letter

Do include a résumé and cover letter with your demo reel. Keep it businesslike, neat, and correct. If you submit a résumé with typos, it does not speak well for your attention to detail. Run a spellchecker—that's what word processors are for. Creative layouts are OK, but make sure both the letter and résumé are easy to read. Some supervisors are getting along in years, and their eyes aren't what they used to be. Tiny or confusing typography is counterproductive.

Stress your schooling and/or industry experience. Include your outside interests, especially physical pursuits like martial arts, dance, or acting that contribute to your talents as an animator. The better studios have gotten past the sweatshop mentality and are looking for people with balanced lives. The burnout rate on workaholics is too high to support in the long run.

In your cover letter, stress the position you are applying for and why you want it. Show that you understand what the job entails and why you want to work for this particular studio.

If you have other artwork, sending in a duplicate portfolio is acceptable to many studios. Call or write ahead to make sure it's OK, and if possible, put as much of it on your video demo reel as possible. The simplest approach is to borrow a camcorder and do a pan-and-scan coverage of your 2D art or sculptures with close-ups of the fine details. If you do send a portfolio, make sure it's a duplicate. Color photocopies are perfectly acceptable, and most studios can't guarantee that they will return materials. Don't ever send your only copy of anything!

Interviews

You got the call to come in for an interview. Great! Now calm down. That's the first rule in surviving an interview. Yes, it's a stressful part of life, but nobody has ever been executed for a poor interview in the animation business. You'll live through it.

Right now, you are in a very good position for doing well in an interview. The demand for competent, talented character animators is still high, and most production studios are doing anything they can to lure new hires. That puts more control in your hands (just don't abuse it), so relax and just be yourself. The interviewer has every reason to try to hire you—she will be looking for reasons to hire you, not to turn you away.

If the interview requires air travel, the company should arrange and pay for your travel and lodging. Never fly to an interview on your own nickel; if the company won't pick up the tab, it's not serious. If it's just a short drive or a crosstown trip, you'll be expected to handle it on your own.

Don't "Dress for Success"

Most animation houses are very casual places, and the few that aren't are nasty places to work. Typical attire is jeans and T-shirts. If you show up for an interview in a suit or other business attire, that's two-and-a-half strikes against you. I know several people who were hired after interviewing in ripped jeans and grungy T-shirts, but that's pushing it a little. Casual but clean is your best bet.

You probably were asked to come in for an interview because of your demo reel. If your reel was an accurate representation of your talents, the interview is going to be relatively easy for you. The interviewer will probably ask some technical questions about your work and may ask to see some rough work-in-progress examples from your archive or story reel. This is just a check to make sure you actually did the work on your reel.

Your interview portfolio should include examples of every step in the process for your demo reel: story, script, story sketches, character designs, exposure sheets, model documentation, test renders, and so on. You don't have to bring the complete set of everything, just representative samples. Don't just whip the samples out first thing—that's a little pushy, and there's always the chance that you'll show the interviewer something she doesn't like. Just keep your portfolio case in plain sight and wait for the interviewer to ask to see it. If she asks a technical question about something on your reel that is best explained by one of the samples, go ahead and show it.

Aside from the technical interview, the interviewer will be trying to assess whether you will fit in with other employees. I've heard stories from several studios about very good technical hires that just didn't work out. The persons in question could do the work, and were in fact very talented, it's just that they couldn't work well with the other members of the team or in that particular studio's culture.

The interview is also a chance for you to ask questions about the working environment. In most shops, the interview includes a tour of the facilities and introductions to many of the other team members. Use this time to ask questions about the work environment. How much creative input do people have in the position for which you're interviewing? Who will you be reporting to? How long does a typical project last? What's your potential career path within the studio? What's a typical day like? How long do people work, and at what hours? Is the daily routine regimented or free-form? Is there a lot of informal cross-pollination of ideas, or do people pretty much stay in their cubicles? Where do people go for lunch? Is the local takeout any good, or do a lot of people pack lunches? This isn't as trivial as it sounds—you'll be spending an hour a day (at least) with these people at one or more meals, and if the gang's favorite takeout is something you're violently allergic to, you'll be miserable.

Read the cartoons on the walls, especially the work areas of people who'll be working closely with you. If there's nothing on the walls and the interviewer tells you "Dilbert" has been banned, I'd look elsewhere. On the other hand, if it looks like the interior was inspired by the Marquis de Sade, you may be happier somewhere else. One popular litmus test in the animation industry is *The Spirit of Christmas* or its spin-off series, *South Park*. If you haven't seen this short animation, try to find a copy. Are you offended by it, or do you think it's the funniest thing you've ever seen? If you feel strongly about it, ask (at an appropriate time on your tour) if they have a copy lying around. If they get all stiff and say that sort of material is inappropriate, you'll get an idea of their tolerance for off-color humor. If they enthusiastically pull up a copy on the nearest workstation and tell you the animation has its own directory on the main fileserver, again, you have a better picture of their comedic standards. Either way, you can tell if you'll fit in.

Getting Hired

So you get a phone call, or the interviewer asks when you can start. Congratulations! But don't quit your current job just yet. Think about the offer at least overnight. The interviewer shouldn't get upset if you tell her you need to sleep on it. Also, you should ask for a letter or fax, on company letterhead, spelling out the terms of the offer. I learned this one the hard way: I accepted a verbal offer of employment from a fairly large company, relocated across the continent, then was informed that the position had been eliminated in a reorganization. Nothing was in writing, so I didn't have a leg to stand on legally. Don't let that happen to you—get the offer in writing!

Are they offering enough compensation, both pay and benefits? Will you be able to cover your living expenses plus savings, IRAs, and other financial needs? There's nothing wrong with making a counteroffer if their offer is too low. Benefits like vacation time, overtime, and comp time are negotiable too. Unless the studio is very large and has ironclad labor contracts, everything is on the table. If your annual two-week trip to Yosemite is more important than an extra $3,000 in salary, negotiate for the extra time off.

Before you sign an employment contract, read it carefully and run it past a good entertainment lawyer. Not the family lawyer; you need an entertainment specialist. There are some serious land mines in entertainment law that can make your life miserable if you're not aware of them. For instance, some studios insist on a noncompete clause, which means that, if you quit, you can't work anywhere else in the industry for a number of years. There's some question as to whether this practice is even legal, but the threat of a lawsuit can definitely dampen your chances of being hired elsewhere. Even if you decide to go ahead and sign a restrictive contract, you should at least know what you're in for. If you have questions, I suggest you contact MPSC Local 839 (listed in "Unions" later in this chapter) for advice.

Not Getting Hired

So you don't get a phone call. Don't just sit there—send out some more demo reels! The best way to wait for that one perfect job is to go out searching for others. The worst way is to sit by the phone, waiting for the call that never comes. At the end of each interview, ask when you can expect to hear from them again. Wait until that time passes before you call, but then you should definitely call them back. Remember that the people who looked at your demo reel and who interviewed you are also the ones doing the work, and they do get swamped. Dealing with clients takes precedence over hiring new staff, but that doesn't mean they don't want you. Jogging their memory can make a big difference in how long it takes to hire you, or at least let you know that you should be looking elsewhere. You may also be just the right person for a job opening they'll have in six months, so stay in touch.

> *"Press on—nothing can take the place of persistence. Talent will not; nothing is more common than unsuccessful men with talent. Genius will not; unrewarded genius is almost a proverb. Education will not; the world is full of educated derelicts. Perseverance and determination alone are omnipotent."*
> —Calvin Coolidge

If you get a definite turndown, don't take it personally, and don't give up. Use this opportunity to ask the interviewer (politely, of course) for a critique of your demo reel and/or interview. If the decision was based on the quality of your work, ask what you need to improve and for advice about additional training or practice. If the decision was based on personal compatibility, ask if he can recommend any shops that might be more suitable. The animation community is a very small one, and most of the players know one another. It never hurts to ask for a referral.

Networking

Speaking of referrals, you should try to build up your list of contacts in the business. Keep track of everybody who's seen your demo reel, interviewed you, or spoken with you at SIGGRAPH, ASIFA (Association Internationale Du Film d'Animation), or other animators' gatherings. If possible, collect their email and other contact information, and keep it up-to-date. Get on the Internet, if you aren't already. The minimum service packages available from most Internet service providers are reasonable and a worthwhile investment. Watch the industry press and the appropriate mailing lists and Usenet newsgroups for announcements or gossip about upcoming projects, and use that contact information to let them know you are available. Whenever you update your demo reel, send out notices to the appropriate people asking if they'd like to see it.

This is very important: Do *not* simply add all these people to a personal mailing list and send them a lot of trivial form-letter emails. When you have new information to distribute, send an individual email to each person. If you reuse most of the text, at least make enough changes to make the message personal and not an obvious form letter. Unless you are already on a first-name basis with the recipient, you should make your emails as formal and structured as a cover letter for a résumé. Keep the message brief, make your points clearly and succinctly, and be polite. Each message you send to a potential employer is the same as showing up on her doorstep unannounced—you'd better have a good reason for doing so, and it had better be in the employer's best interests to hear what you have to say. Being an inconsiderate nag can get you on everybody's filter list, meaning they'll never listen to you again. Use your best judgment.

If you want to survive in this business, stay in touch with your colleagues. The animation business is still project based; only the largest studios (and not all of those) keep animators on staff when there is no paying work for them. Many animators follow the work, staying at a studio through a project, then moving on to another project at another studio. Others may stay at a studio for years, working on whatever comes by and hanging on through the dry spells. For either approach, it's a good idea for you to stay informed about who's working where, on what project, and for how long. Even a large studio may have to suddenly cancel a project and lay off the animation team for business reasons having nothing to do with the merits of the project. The July 1997 closing of Warner Digital is a case in point. If you're well-connected and up-to-date, you'll be able to find another job immediately, but if you've been out of the loop for a while, you'll have a harder time of it.

CG-CHAR

One of the best places to start networking is the Computer Generated Character Animation listserv. This is a closed mailing list, maintained by and for character animators working in the CGI medium. It has been around since early 1996 and at last count had over 1,000 subscribers. The tone of the list has varied over time, from a hard-core group of experienced professionals to a more student-and-novice tone as of this writing. It's not a moderated list, but if you misbehave, you'll be unsubscribed. It's a lot like a medieval guild hall, where novices, journeymen, and masters all meet informally to share information and socialize.

The CG-CHAR home page is a collection of resources by and for subscribers of the CG-CHAR listserv. Galleries of art, works in progress, book reviews, shareware, and job postings are there now, and plans for the future include complete listserv archives and interactive chats.

To quote the founder of the listserv, Rick May: "The CG (computer generated) Character Animation List was created for artists and TDs to share information and ideas on creating computer-assisted character animation. We are hoping to discuss not only software and (a little) hardware, but techniques and ideas. Although we are applying our artistry through the computer, we welcome postings from people with cel or stopmo experience. A lot of people creating CG character work nowadays have cel or stopmo backgrounds anyway—techniques learned from these disciplines are always helpful. Traditional animators could also benefit from our list, perhaps learning how to use the computer in their animation work."

For more information, email Rick at **rick@cg-char.com** or visit the Web site **www.cg-char.com**.

ASIFA

ASIFA, Association Internationale Du Film d'Animation, is "devoted to the encouragement and dissemination of film animation as an art and communication form." This is another great place to network, but because it includes all forms of animation, you may find it less focused on your needs than CG-CHAR. It has over 1,100 members in 55 countries. The United States has the most members, 280, and Canada is a close second with 250.

ASIFA produces a newsletter, annual calendar, and animation school list. It also maintains an employment database and a film archive. The ASIFA Workshop Group runs animation workshops for children in over 30 countries. ASIFA membership is open to all individuals interested in animation. For more information, contact ASIFA International at **www.swcp.com/~asifa/asifaint.htm** or ASIFA Hollywood at the following address:

ASIFA Hollywood
725 South Victory Boulevard
Burbank, California 91502
Tel: (818) 842-8330
Fax: (818) 842-5654
www.asifa-hollywood.org

Computer Game Artists (CGA)

"The CGA exists to form a community of computer game artists that interact with (share, learn, teach, influence) each other and their industry." This is a fledgling organization of and for game artists. It's an excellent place to build up your network if you are interested in character animation for games. Currently it has a Web site and a listserv, and IRC chats occur now and then. For more information, visit **www.vectorg.com/cga/basics.htm**.

Mentoring

Whether you're a student, self-taught, amateur, or professional, you can use a good mentor. Mentoring can include occasional career advice, a fresh pair of eyes to critique your work, frequent tutoring, and even collaboration. It all depends on what you need and what your mentor can provide. There are lots of ways a more experienced person can assist your growth as an animator.

Finding a mentor will take some effort on your part. If you are working in an animation studio, you may have coworkers willing to act as mentors. If you're a student, one of your teachers may be able to give you the extra time outside of class. If you're on your own, try meeting senior animators or technical directors through the networking resources listed in this chapter. If you hit it off with one of them, ask if he would be willing to mentor you.

Women In Animation

If you happen to be female, this organization is specifically chartered to address the special concerns of women in this business. To quote from its Web site: "Women In Animation is a professional, nonprofit organization established in 1994 to foster the dignity, concerns, and advancement of women in any and all aspects of the art of animation. Women In Animation was formed by a number of prominent women in all areas of animation, from producers to academics to the former publisher of *Animation Magazine*. Every major studio in Hollywood is represented, as well as most independent studios and New York-based members of the animation industry."

The Web site has a lot of useful information about meetings and workshops on a variety of animation-related topics. I highly recommend it.

Women In Animation
PO Box 17706
Encino, CA 91416
Tel: (818) 759-9596
www.women.in.animation.org

Kellie-Bea Cooper has assembled a useful site (**www.animation.org/women**) showcasing Women In Animation with interviews and photos, a mentoring match-up system, lots of related links, and a questionnaire for those who would like to contribute. This is definitely worth visiting for anyone who'd like a candid look inside the industry.

SIGGRAPH

SIGGRAPH is the special-interest group of the ACM that deals with computer graphics, from scientific visualization to entertainment. The annual SIGGRAPH conference is the major CGI event of the year, with several LightWave-related activities. If you're at all interested in computer graphics as a profession (or even a serious hobby), don't miss it. This is where NewTek and other software and hardware vendors and the larger LightWave-using studios pull out the stops. SIGGRAPH is held in Southern California every other year, and the alternate years rotates from city to city. You can find the venue at the SIGGRAPH Web site. Don't miss this conference!

Association for Computing Machinery
11 West 42nd Street
New York, NY 10036
www.siggraph.org

Unions

The following is a quote from the Motion Picture Screen Cartoonists (MPSC) Local 839 Web site:

"What is Local 839? Simply put, we are a union of artists, writers and technicians making animated films. We've been around since 1952 helping animation employees get decent wages, better working conditions...and a little respect.

"Animators are among our members. Writers of television cartoons hold MPSC union cards. Digital painters, computer animators and modelers are part of the MPSC. We negotiate contracts, create resumes, provide legal and negotiating advice to artists and technicians working for the largest and most profitable animation companies in the world."

For more details, use the following contact information:

MPSC Local 839 IATSE
4729 Lankershim Boulevard
North Hollywood, CA 91602-1864
Tel: (818) 766-7151
Fax: (818) 506-4805
Email: **mpsc839@netcom.com**
www.primenet.com/~mpsc839

Potential Employers

Following is a list of major animation and special-effects houses, in addition to those mentioned previously, that have advertised recently for TDs or animators. As always, contact information is subject to change without notice. Sending a reel is the best approach, but it has some drawbacks because, as mentioned earlier, the most popular studios receive hundreds of reels.

Digital Domain is easily one of the most popular "dream jobs" in the industry. They did effects for *True Lies* and *Titanic*.

Digital Domain
300 Rose Avenue
Venice, CA 90291
Tel: (310) 314-2934
Email: **digital_hiring@d2.com**
www.d2.com

ORIGIN Systems is a major game developer, with too many credits to list. They use LightWave 3D, among other software.

ORIGIN Systems, Inc.
Attn.: Human Resources
5918 W. Courtyard Dr.
Austin, TX 78730
Email: **jobs@origin.ea.com**
www.origin.ea.com

Sony Pictures Imageworks does digital visual effects. One major project was *Stuart Little*. It accepts reels, résumés, and portfolios.

Sony Pictures Imageworks
9050 West Washington Boulevard
Culver City, CA 90232
Fax: (310) 840-8888
Email: **resumes@spimageworks.com**
www.spiw.com

Windlight Studios did the animated Gymnast Barbie ads. Windlight specializes in long-format computer character animation and uses motion capture for some of its work.

Windlight Studios
Attn.: Human Resources
702 North First Street
Minneapolis, MN 55401
Email: **hr@windlight.com**

Being an Employee

Once you've landed a job in animation, you'll have to work to keep it. You'll also need to look after yourself if you want to avoid being underpaid, exploited, obsolete, or disabled.

If you've landed your first animation job, congratulations! You're on your way in a career with lots of opportunities for personal growth, increasing public recognition, and artistic satisfaction, not to mention that at least some of your work will be just plain fun. Seeing your work in public for the first time, whether in a video game, on television, or on the silver screen, will be a rush you won't forget. Most senior animators I've talked to still get opening-night jitters when they attend premieres—it's a thrill that won't fade, as long as you care about your work.

Now What Do I Do?

So, what is your job? No matter what your job title or description reads, your number one job is getting the work done. That means doing your own assigned work plus working well with others, taking direction, and understanding how the rest of the studio works. You're not a cog in a machine—you're a voice in the chorus, a creative artist who collaborates with professional colleagues to produce great character animation. The better you understand others' work, the better you can do your own.

Whenever possible, find out how you can make your coworkers' jobs easier. If other people are depending on your work, ask what they need from you. If some small additional task on your part makes their part much easier, do it. Conversely, you should tactfully let coworkers know how to make your job easier. One way to do this is to show polite interest in the jobs of people who provide models, setups, and other materials for your job. If the studio has been running successfully for a while, you'll probably find out that they're way ahead of you on labor-saving tricks. However, once in a while, you'll find they're spending a lot of effort on something that isn't crucial. Handle this diplomatically. Don't say, "You've been wasting your time tweaking that model for six weeks. It'll all have to be done over anyway." Try something like, "Wow, that looks great. Why don't you let me run some animation tests on the model right now? We may be able to use it as is." This way, you've prevented further wasted effort, and the "bad news" will be in the animation tests rather than your personal observations. As a general rule, make positive reports and compliments in a personal way, but try to put negative reports and critiques in as objective a form as possible. It's just human nature—nobody enjoys criticism, even when it's constructive.

It's important to your career and your current project that you understand exactly where the studio priorities are. It's not unreasonable that two weeks of your time may very well be less expensive than two days (or even two hours) of someone else's. I ran into this a few years ago when I was coordinating materials from about 60 individuals for a corporate project. I was presented with more than 20 different file formats, which meant I'd have to spend a lot of time translating them to a single common format. I tried to impose some file format standards. The project director took me aside and very reasonably explained that it was more time and cost effective for one person (me) to be stuck doing a week's worth of translating than to retrain 60 other employees who all had more technically demanding work to do. Sometimes doing tedious, apparently stupid work is the most effective use of your time on a project. It's nothing personal, so don't take it that way. Remember your position. You will be starting off on a very low rung and should not try to act like you're a director. Entry-level positions, even well-paid ones, are for people who are there to learn.

One of the best things about the character animation business is that, once you're on the job, nobody cares whether you graduated from a premier school or that you taught yourself by hand-drawing flipbooks. The majority of animation production studios are well-run businesses where hard work and talent are rewarded. It's a complete meritocracy. It's only your work they notice. Make sure your work says the right things about you: good, solid, on time, and with no unpleasant strings attached. If you do magnificent work but are a prima donna, every time the director sees one of your shots, he's going to remember the temper tantrum you threw while working on it. On the other hand, if you put in a lot of extra effort to make an excellent shot, every time the director sees it, she'll remember you in the best possible way. Give your employer good value for value received. Work for the hours you are paid, and give the best efforts that your talents, skills, and full attention can produce. Make them glad they hired you.

Make Your Boss Look Good

One of the smartest things you can do on your first job is to make your boss look good. If there is a problem on the project, resist the urge to blurt out the solution to all and sundry. Instead, see your supervisor privately and float your idea as a possible solution. If it's not viable for some reason, you haven't embarrassed yourself. If it's a good idea, your supervisor can help you develop it and can share in the credit. This is good for both of you—your boss gets a solution, and you get your boss's good will. If your boss chooses to take full credit for your idea, I suggest that you let it slide as long as this is your first job. Think of it as part of paying your dues. As I mentioned earlier, the animation community is a very small one. A good recommendation from an experienced supervisor is worth a lot. You'll have lots of good ideas throughout your career, so one idea is a small price to pay to start your career on the right foot.

Most of the supervisors and managers you'll work for will be reasonable people, great to work for, and helpful to your career. A small percentage of supervisors can be more difficult. If you're working for one of them, you'll have to show more self-control and be more solidly centered. Don't be a prima donna, but don't be a doormat either. Getting a paycheck doesn't mean they own you, just as being an artist doesn't mean you should abuse or rip off your employer. Be honest, reasonable, and fair, as long as your employer does the same.

It's to your advantage to build a reputation of reliability. The first rule is, Don't promise what you can't deliver. You're not making a sales pitch to a client, you're telling your boss what you can and can't do. It's not good for anyone if you bite off more than you can chew. Of course, we all make mistakes sometimes. If you can't deliver on a promise, go to your supervisor as soon as you've identified the problem. Work with your supervisor to find a solution. Don't just throw it in his lap and run away. And don't wait until two seconds before the deadline to ask for help.

"Och, laddie, ye've got a lot to learn about being a miracle worker."
—Capt. Montgomery Scott, UFP, Ret.

When you're being asked to do a job that you're unsure of, be willing to say, "I don't know." Be just as willing to say, "I can try to find out." If you've really got a bad feeling about a job, or you can see major problems, don't just say "No." Instead, say, "We can do it that way, but it will cost X dollars and Y days extra." It's the supervisor's, director's, or producer's job to make the call. It's your job to provide them with your best professional assessment, then carry out their decision.

Most large studios have a cadre of "suits," the business-school graduates, attorneys, and financiers that make the business decisions. If you're lucky (or simply did your research), the suits at your studio have also had a background or at least a solid personal liking for motion pictures and storytelling. The best situation is where former animators have built their own studio, so the top executives once had your job and understand both the creative and business side of animation. If you're stuck in a studio managed by suits who don't understand filmmaking, animation, or art in any form, you are probably not going to have a long and happy career there. A case in point is the July 1997 closing of Warner Digital. The creative part of Warner Digital was topnotch, some of the best people in the business, and their work was outstanding. Unfortunately, the suits made a series of this-quarter, bottom-line calls and decided to fold the studio.

Despite incidents like this, it's important to your career survival that you be able to cooperate with suits. Don't bite the hand that feeds you. The suits in your studio are the people who make your paycheck show up on time. If they weren't out there meeting with clients and hustling for projects to keep you and your buddies busy, you'd be out looking for another job. The bottom line is that suits who may know little or nothing about the creative process can nevertheless green-light or kill projects. It's a classic example of the Golden Rule: He who has the gold makes the rules. If you antagonize the wrong suit, you can find yourself unemployed (the project was killed) or doing scut work (the project was bastardized), with a bunch of your coworkers alongside you. This doesn't mean you should grovel, just that you have to make your observations, criticisms, and suggestions in polite form, through proper channels, and in language suits can understand.

Most suits are not inherently bad people. They don't enjoy producing schlock any more than you do. Many of them have years of training and experience in the financial and business side of animation, and their expertise is a valid contribution to the production. To get where they are, odds are that they either put in a lot of time, are very talented or very lucky, or have serious connections. Any one of these cases is sufficient reason for you to treat them with a modicum of respect. If they are making decisions that make your job harder, you should discuss this fact, privately, with your supervisor. If you point out that a change they've asked for will require weeks of expensive overtime and a missed delivery date, they will most likely see reason. If you rant and rave and call them names, you'll do yourself more harm than good, and they're not likely to listen to you in the future. Be professional, be reasonable, and if the suits won't reciprocate, keep your demo reel and résumé updated—you'll probably need them sooner rather than later.

Maintaining Your Space—and Yourself

If you are a typical animator, you will spend more time at work than away from it. With that in mind, make sure you are going to be comfortable. Windows? What windows? Get used to the idea of not seeing the sun very much. Sunlight glaring off your monitor's screen and the cost of commercial office space mean you will usually be working in a windowless cubicle or sharing a room with other animators or TDs.

You'll probably spend more time decorating your cubicle than you spend furnishing your home. Animators are famous for cluttering their workspace with toys. It may be a good idea to arm yourself—there have been hair-raising reports of Nerf wars in some shops. Try to keep a sense of humor. When deadlines are tight and nerves are thrumming, the catharsis of a good Nerf battle can save your production team's sanity.

Make sure you take care of yourself physically. LightWave animators, like other computer workers, are prone to repetitive stress injury (RSI), including carpal tunnel syndrome, DeQuervaine's, and related maladies. Set up your workstation to provide proper support, and if you have already injured yourself, follow the directions of your therapist. A lot of animators use wrist braces and ergonomic supports. Get yourself a good chair with proper back support. After searching unsuccessfully for decent workstation furniture, I finally designed and built my own. It's a standing-height work surface for my keyboard and tablet, with my monitor at eye level, and a matching draftsman's stool. I alternate standing and sitting on about a 20-minute cycle to keep from stiffening up over the course of a 16-hour workday.

> *"Animation can be a bit of an endurance sport, physically and mentally, and you have to make sure you're up to it."*
> —Phil South, animator

Take especially good care of your eyes. Staring at a monitor for hours can exhaust the focusing muscles of your eyes, getting them in a rut that can affect your ability to change focus rapidly. Try to have a brightly colored object within view at least 20 feet away, and periodically (every 15 minutes or so) look up and focus your eyes on it. Looking out a window is best, but if your work area is too enclosed, set up a mirror on the far wall to double your line of sight. If you ever have any doubts about the effect your job is having on your vision, talk to your optometrist or ophthalmologist.

Even if you love your job, you need to keep a balanced perspective. Set aside some time, on a regular basis, to keep up your personal life.

Collecting Your Due

The intangible rewards of a job you love are wonderful, but you've got to pay the bills, too. Don't ever work for free. Negotiate comp time, overtime pay, a percentage of the project, or even stock options, but don't agree to work uncompensated overtime. If there's a real crunch on to finish an important job, management should at least agree to give you an equivalent amount of time off (with pay!) after the crunch is over.

Mandatory unpaid overtime happens to be against the law. The Fair Labor Standards Act (FLSA), passed in 1938 and enforced by the U.S. Department of Labor, requires premium pay for work in excess of 40 hours per week. If management attempts to end-run this law by telling you you're salaried and therefore exempt, here are some of the other criteria the Department of Labor will apply: setting work schedules, requiring employees to keep time sheets, docking pay for partial days worked, paying overtime for "extra" hours worked, reporting pay on an hourly basis, and using the same disciplinary system for exempt and nonexempt employees. Essentially, if the studio wants you to work and be paid like management, you must be treated like management. Penalties are serious, including back pay and punitive damages. Usually, employers who try to require unpaid overtime are simply new to running a business and don't understand the situation. Once in a great while, you'll have an employer who knowingly and systematically breaks this law. I suggest you find work elsewhere and perhaps send a letter to the Department of Labor after you're safely employed again.

Benefits

Take advantage of company benefits that improve your quality of life. When you're hired, the HR (Human Resources) department should provide you with a list of official benefits. At least one shop has an on-site masseur, which is great for muscle cramps and RSI, the character animators' occupational hazards. If you wear corrective lenses and have optical health insurance, you should consider getting the new prescription glasses designed especially for computer work. Some studios also have discount purchase programs for everything from movie tickets to groceries to computers. Take advantage of what you can, and if you think of a good benefit for you and your coworkers, suggest it. Good benefits are cost-effective ways for your employer to stay competitive, and they'll usually appreciate your suggestions.

Even if this is your first job as an animator, you should start planning for your retirement. There are entirely too many horror stories of traditional animators having to work into their 80s or dying broke because they didn't plan for retirement. Don't let that happen to you. The nature of the business is that you will probably move around a lot, being a "project gypsy" or being head-hunted from one studio to the next as your skills and reputation improve. There is also the fact that LightWave character animation is a very young industry, and even the oldest shops have not been around very long. Shops tend to open, have a more or less successful run, then close, just like any other small business. If your career is going to last 25 to 40 years, you can't count on retiring from the first studio you work for.

The ephemeral nature of the industry means you need a retirement plan that you can take with you. Plans administered through a union are one option. IRAs and other savings plans that you run for yourself are another. Social Security will probably be broke or completely overhauled by the time you can collect from it, so don't count on that. If you have no idea how to invest money over the long term, I suggest you consult a personal financial planner. Your banker or insurance agent may be able to help, but they'll have an understandable bias toward the products they'll try to sell you. My personal recommendation is investment in income properties like real estate or intellectual property. If you build up a portfolio of marketable assets, you can practically guarantee a steady cash flow from leasing or licensing without having to work very hard after your retirement. This is the strategy followed by some of the wealthiest people in the entertainment business. For details, I recommend *Fortune* magazine.

Screen Credit

There is one benefit you will probably not be able to negotiate for your first job, but you should get it as soon as you can and then never let it go. It's screen credit. This isn't just about vanity, it's about money. If you have a string of screen credits on your résumé and the people who watch credits (most of the industry, plus the fans) recognize your name, that's worth serious cash when you negotiate your next contract. It's also the way your name gets attached to the industry's awards—they go to the people named in the credits, not necessarily the people who did the work. If you're ever going to cash in on your professional reputation, make the lecture circuit, try to get an independent project green-lighted, or publish your memoirs or even a technical book, your screen credits are even more important than your demo reel. You should start collecting screen credits as soon as you have the leverage to demand them—you don't need to wait until your current contract is up.

Renegotiation Is Not a Bad Thing

After you've been working for a while, and especially if you are doing exemplary work, it's a good idea to think about changes you'd like to make. More money is always nice, but think about additional vacation time, company sponsorship of private projects, or more creative input/control. Everything is subject to renegotiation, but you've got to be willing to leave for greener pastures if management won't give you what you need. Don't even think about trying to bluff; they'll call you on it, every time.

Professional Development

LightWave character animation is an art that you'll never completely master. It's a lifelong pursuit, a process of honing your skills toward a perfection you can reach for but never grasp. There's always something new to learn, some new method or fine-tuning of an older method that will get you closer to your goal. You should always be developing your skills and professional knowledge. Never rest on your laurels. Always be learning, always be curious about what's around the bend, technically and cinematically.

The resources listed earlier in this chapter will continue to serve you well throughout your animation career. Learn from others' work at every opportunity. See every film or television program that includes character animation, and collect laser disks or DVDs of the best examples. Try to keep up on the literature, keep an eye on the most useful listservs and newsgroups, and don't miss SIGGRAPH if you can possibly avoid it. If you're working in games, the Computer Games Development Conference is another must-see. You can find details online at **www.cgdc.com**.

If traditional art training will help you hone your skills, you should investigate the opportunities available in your community. Most art schools have open life-drawing classes where you can practice for a small fee. Classes in related disciplines such as sculpture, photography, film-making, or industrial design may be available, too. Opportunities tend to be more plentiful in larger cities, but you can find an art teacher willing to tutor in even the smallest town. If you're a union member, the local chapter may offer classes or referrals to other members who can be of assistance. Keep an eye out for special seminars, too. According to the animators I've talked to, Richard Williams' master classes are more than worth the fee, lodging, and airfare. Classes in martial or theater arts or sports that require discipline in movement are excellent training for character animators—and they get you away from the monitor and keyboard for a while.

Speaking of which, you should habitually pull out all the stops on your tools. Learn to do absolutely everything you can do with the software and hardware you have access to. Go beyond the manuals, books like this one, and the conventional solutions others rely on. Find new solutions to problems that haven't even been recognized yet. When you have the time and budget to make your own projects, that intimate familiarity with your tools will pay you back manyfold.

The path you follow to develop yourself depends entirely on the type of work you like to do. If you enjoy being a generalist, you may want to stay with smaller studios. Conversely, if you are working for a larger studio, you may find it difficult to get assignments outside your narrow job description.

> *"Being responsible for it all is the norm in the small startups, with the luxury of specialization arriving only as the shop scales up over time. Specialization is more to the studio's advantage than to the individual's. Production roles become apprenticeship rungs on a ladder that's hard to climb inside just one studio. A three-year contract is to keep your slot occupied, NOT to assure you a chance to find the place in production where your strengths can best be utilized."*
> *—Ken Cope*

You may choose to stick with one studio through many projects or follow the most interesting work from studio to studio. You may decide to remain an animator, or with experience, you may find that you prefer to direct or even produce. If you can't find personal satisfaction at any studio, you may even choose to branch out on your own.

Side Projects

Odds are good that you became interested in animation because you want to tell stories, to make characters come to life. At some time in your career, you are going to want to take on a side project, a personal film to scratch the storytelling itch you can't indulge at your regular job. Some studios are very supportive of side projects, providing facilities, budgets, and personnel to assist you. Others don't support side projects, but they don't forbid them, either. Some studios actively discourage side projects with a myriad of sanctions, legal and otherwise.

Despite what your employer or the company's lawyers may say, what you do on your own time is yours, unless your contract states something to the contrary. If you develop valuable ideas—character designs, scripts, any kind of intellectual property—you should be very careful not to use any company resources. If you so much as borrow a company pencil, the company may have a legal claim on the properties you develop. If you do it on your own time, in your own place, on your own equipment, it belongs to you. Just make sure you can prove all this in a court of law.

This is why it's important to own your own equipment and software. With appropriate tools at home, you can pursue side projects without official support or sanctions. You can choose to use the same software tools you use in your regular job or branch out and experiment with other solutions. In either case, the skills you hone at home will make you a better animator at work too. Reasonable companies understand this and encourage it. If your company doesn't, you might want to reexamine your reasons for continuing to work there.

> *"One of the more difficult-to-learn animation skills is learning when it's time to move on."*
> —Ken Cope

Even if you're deliriously happy with your current position, you should keep your demo reel and résumé up-to-date. Every time you finish a nice shot, especially when you wrap up a major project, add those bits to your archive reel. If the new material justifies it, update the editing of your demo reel. You never know when an opportunity is going to knock, and a prepared demo reel can make the difference between grabbing the brass ring and missing it clean.

Moving On

I hope this chapter has provided you with some sound advice and that it will make your first animation job a little easier and save you the painful lessons others have learned the hard way. I also hope you will find encouragement here, and go out and build your own character animation career. Good luck!

Case Study 21.1
Getting a Job: An Interview with Jeff Scheetz

I recently had the opportunity to sit down with Jeff Scheetz, Project Lead of Foundation

Jeff Scheetz.

Imaging's teams for *Starship Troopers*. Jeff is responsible for (among other things) reviewing demo reels and conducting interviews. If you want to work at Foundation, you'll need to see Jeff. He provided some valuable (and sometimes surprising) advice to, and comments on, the current LightWave talent pool.

DK: Are you seeing an improvement in the quality of demo reels that you review?

JS: No; in fact I'm seeing a sharp decline.

DK: Really? Would you assign any reasons to that?

JS: I think that all the really good people are working. The reels I'm getting don't make my eyes bleed or anything, but you caught me in the middle of my big disappointment festival. [*Foundation Imaging had been recruiting heavily, and on the day we interviewed Jeff, he was doing open walk-in interviews in conjunction with SIGGRAPH '99.—DK*] We're just not getting as many good submissions as we once were. In the early days of LightWave, there were all these people who learned at home and didn't know how good they were. They kept getting better and better while taking lesser jobs and honing their craft. One day they would hit Hollywood with this really stellar reel that got them their first job. Recently, the demand has gotten so great that those types of people were being pulled out and given jobs at a much earlier level in their development. Right now there are too many people who bought the software last week and are trying to get out there and sell themselves.

DK: Are you seeing the LightWave tutorials or demos on these people's reels?

JS: Sometimes, but not very often. Occasionally I get a person whose reel looks like they just rendered whatever was on the LightWave CD-ROM. I've had people send me the little space fighter animation, which is especially funny here, since Ron [Thornton, founder of Foundation Imaging] did it.

DK: That's the classic plagiarist's blunder, handing the piece to the person who actually did it.

JS: Yeah, that happens to other people here too. Some of our people work freelance or have come from other projects, and I'll see a piece they did show up on an applicant's demo reel. And I'll ask our people about it, and they'll tell me the real story. Once we had somebody send us essentially a whole other company's demo reel and try to pass it off as their own work. I guess he thought that, just because this other company was in Texas, I'd never figure this out. It turns out that the owner of this other company is a good friend of mine, and (laughing) it came back to haunt this person in about an hour. I have also shared this story with many of my friends at other companies.

DK: I warn people at every opportunity that CGI animation is a very small community. I was at the CG-CHAR meeting earlier this week, and there were fewer than 600 people in the room, and someone said that this was probably most of the character animation talent on the planet. It only takes one person standing up in a group like that and saying, "So-and-so is trying to pass my work off as their own," to kill your career.

JS: That'll kill you.

DK: What advice do you have for someone who has LightWave, thinks they're hot stuff, and wants to apply here? What do you want to see, what do you not want to see on their demo reel?

JS: It's not what I don't want to see as much as what I do want to see. Even if it's stuff that people do a lot of (spaceships are a good example), you should do what you really want to do and have the guts to just do that. A lot of people will try to show that they can use so many different parts of the program, or handle so many animation genres, that they haven't really taken the time to master any one of them. If there's a part that they really enjoy, they should really focus on that, learn it well, and then they'll have something to offer the community.

When we hired for *Troopers*, no matter what your specialty was, I could probably give you a job doing something very similar. We found so many people who had tons of very different stuff, but none of it was really good, and I couldn't hire them. If they're a jack-of-all trades and master of none, then I don't know what to do with them the first week, and that makes it really really hard to get them into the flow and have a starting point of usefulness.

DK: So should people put their best work, what they really want to do, on their demo reel first...

JS: Yeah.

DK: ...or only?

JS: Well, I like to see some examples of something that has been completed, something that's not just another animation test. That's because finishing things is a big part of what we do as well.

DK: You're not working to your own creative impulses, you're working to the client's.

JS: Yeah. And it's never as good when I'll get a tape with just a head, talking, and the applicant will say, "I just wanted to show you that I could do lip sync." And another shot is a faceless character moving, and they say, "I wanted to show you I could do a walk cycle." And instead of a cool set, these tests are done against the default gradients. Well, if you have a head saying something cool and put that on top of a body that's doing a good walk cycle, in an interesting environment, then you have something! This one shot can be three times more powerful than it was because you were just trying to show me one thing.

DK: So you want at least one finished piece, pulling it all together?

JS: Yeah. I would hire someone based on a whole bunch of interesting tests if I needed the kinds of individual skills they had proven. But by creating great shots, the whole is definitely greater than the sum of its parts.

DK: So if you want to show lighting, still lifes are OK, if you want to show character animation, the wireframe skeletons are OK to show the timing and sense of weight, but you want to see at least one finished piece where it's all put together.

JS: I just think it's a waste if you do a bunch of independent pieces that together would have been better. When we go through the *Trooper* process, we do a lot of mocap but still a lot of it is hand-keyed. Then we go through and do the face. Then we go through and do the eyes. Then we put it in an environment. Then we do lighting on it. And these are all individual skill sets that are pretty much required.

DK: Does one of your animators do all that through an entire shot? It's not like, one just does lighting and all the shots come through on the production pipeline?

JS: It varies a little bit, but everyone can do these things. And more often than not, they wind up taking a shot all the way through it. And they do this in a day! I mean, if someone needs to spend three weeks building something, I totally get that. But when they actually have all their production elements lined up, they should be able to create shots in a day or two, because that's really all the time they get here.

During interviews, beginning animators will say, "I think I spent about a month on this." That really means about two hours on a Sunday, two half hours in the course of a weeknight, and then an entire weekend finishing it up, all over the course of a month. But if you can train yourself to sit in your chair and actually finish your shots, and know when they're done, it's much more advantageous than this nebulous "I've been tweaking this walk cycle for five months" claim.

DK: You feel pretty strongly about this.

JS: I'm the project supervisor for *Troopers*, but I still hire *all our shows*. I had to put together 70 people to come work on this show. And this week, I'm trying to find 10 more. And it's *really* hard.

DK: Can you hire people from Canada?

JS: If they can work in the United States under the North American Free Trade Agreement, it's not really a problem. NAFTA requires a related university degree. Most other types of visa can be tough. When *Troopers* started four months ago, I hired Dave Jarrard, and yesterday they called me up to say that he can come into the U.S. It's worth it, because he's good, but it's not practical by any stretch of the imagination to wait that long while you are in production. It would have been more practical to find an American woman to marry him. (Laughs) Not that I would ever do that!

DK: Let's get back to the demo reels for a moment. How soon do you get poisoned when you watch a reel?

JS: I'll fast-forward before I'll stop watching. I always fast-forward to the end.

DK: Are they there with you when you watch the reels?

JS: Today they are; most of the time they're not.

DK: Do you fast-forward with them here?

JS: No, I'll sit through the whole thing. I always try to turn this around, to tell them what we're looking for. The most common problem new animators have is that they fall in love with their own work without comparing it to anything. I know it's really tough in a vacuum, because everyone you know is going to say, "Damn, that's really good! That's better than Babylon 5!" because they know you did it. But it's important to have the objectiveness to look at it fairly.

I suggest to people that they download a picture of *Voyager* and paste in their spaceship like it's in the same shot, then ask yourself if this picture makes sense. And I can't see where they'd actually say, "Yeah, it's just as good," even though it's three boxes with procedural noise on them.

DK: Do you actually get that?

JS: Yeah.

DK: Oh, ow.

JS: But everybody that applies to me gets my full, undivided attention, even at fast-forward. Every day, mail comes when I'm at lunch, and the first thing I do when I get back is look at demo reels. Even if I've got a lot of other things to do, I do it first, because the most important thing I can do is to have a really good crew. And we do have a really good crew here. But we have a team on this show that from day one has run at least one man down. And then I've been able to replace that person, except then I'll need to create a specialty team and pull from different teams, you know, beg, borrow from so-and-so, whatever. So I have not been able to have a perfectly full crew *yet*.

DK: You're dealing with company commander problems, you've always got attrition, and every time you've got the special teams out, that's pulling your best troopers from their individual platoons.

JS: But with all the unemployed animators, I'm still running with holes in the teams because I'm having trouble finding people who are good enough. And I'm not *that* big a snob.

DK: They have to be able to pull a performance. That's what it comes down to. And that takes practice, practice, practice.

JS: Uh-huh. And the thing about it is, you should know. Because I remember staring at my work, before I had a job, and I was going, "What's not right?" And then I'd read Mojo's VTU articles. He had a really good "Here's how to do Babylon 5 shots in 10 easy steps" article. I did everything it said and it came out really good. I also tried to do other shots using the theory and spirit of what he was talking about.

DK: Not just follow the recipe.

JS: Not just follow the recipe, but definitely respecting the recipe, and not second-guessing it. He hired me. I watched him watch my reel, and it was like, "Mm-hm, mm-hm, mm-hm, *hired*, mm-hm, mm-hm, mm-hm, *hired*, mm-hm, mm-hm, mm-hm, *hired*" it was like that. Looking back, I guess he was thinking, "He did what I said, and his job is to do what I say, so he's hired." That was pretty cool.

DK: I'm active on the CG-CHAR list, and I know there have been some online classes and things like that. What do you think of the Internet as a critique and mutual support tool for animators out in the boonies? Is this a good thing?

JS: It's good, but nobody likes to get rude.

DK: Do you read the CG-CHAR list? I mean, they're not rude, but they're merciless.

JS: Are they?

DK: Oh yeah. They'll say things like, "There was no sense of weight, it just floated all over, your f-curves must be crap, you must have like 3 keyframes in 30 seconds," and they'll *say* that.

JS: Then that's a *great* thing. Wow. What we're looking at, though, is increasing this company to double again, probably in the next year. What we're pretty much acknowledging is that's going to mean a sizable chunk of our buildup is going to be a school. We're still working out how we're going to do it.

DK: You're going to have to ramp up teaching staff.

JS: Yeah. There are teachers teaching LightWave, making money teaching LightWave, that I won't hire because they're not very good. So how good are their students going to be?

DK: Did you know that the enrollments in just about every LightWave school have dropped off drastically? I don't know if it's because people have decided they're not getting enough out of it or what.

JS: They're not. The schools come to us and ask us what we want, and we tell them, and they don't listen. I could totally write you a curriculum, tell you exactly what skills they need to work here. If they could do that, it would be a no-brainer to hire their students.

I totally believe that large-scale CGI action-adventure shows aimed at eight-year-old boys is a big part of the future of LightWave. Because after *Troopers* comes out, kids are really not going to want to watch *Godzilla: The Animated Series* done in 2D. And if we can get enough people who will be content to do this kind of work, there will be enough work for everybody. And dare I say, we'll keep these jobs in America instead of seeing them go overseas. It's an excellent field to get into if you can find the right training or you can train yourself intelligently. Maybe what we need is a curriculum on how to teach yourself LightWave. Do I know how to do the following things? Check this off before sending a reel to Hollywood.

DK: Do you know how to do certain things? Do you know how to evaluate and explore the use of a new tool?

JS: Mm-hm. And do you know how to tape *Voyager* and watch animation shots 16 times until you see what's really happening? Do you know how to keep this from getting too difficult? Do you know how to do something that you can actually finish in one day that's demo-reel quality? If you left me, or anyone at Foundation, alone with a computer, a PVR card, and a copy of LightWave, in a week (minus rendering time), I could totally do a demo reel that would get me a job where I need to be, because I know this stuff. And I think a lot of new animators think, "Well, I did my first walk cycle, so I'm ready to send out my demo reel." I hear that, "This is my first giz file, and this is my first explosion," and I think, show me your tenth one and maybe it'll be in better shape.

DK: Yeah. I get email from people who buy my book and ask, "Where does the 3D stuff start? I'm bogged down in the storyboard stuff and don't get it."

JS: Yeah, that's the other thing, just having the patience to sit down and practice. Practice! Dare we say practice!? They just think, "I just have to get the software to prove I can do it."

One thing that's kind of interesting about this is that age really has nothing to do with it. There's a guy here, Brandon MacDougall, who started with us a couple years ago; he's nearly 40, he's a model builder, and he's really, really good. And his son Tom, who was, like, 19, was playing with LightWave and really getting into building characters. And his dad told him, "Hey, they're going to need this Cyclops creature for *Mystic Knights*." And a week later he shows up with it. And he's out of high school, so we hired him. Now he's head of the *Starship Troopers* character development team. And the funny thing is, he's got a 14-year-old brother who I would hire like that [snaps fingers] if it weren't for child labor laws. Right now he's just building pod racers and stuff like that for fun. But talent-wise, he's awesome.

DK: This whole industry is very much a meritocracy, except where you've got the politics at the higher levels of the bigger studios. Do you care at all about what someone has on paper, or is it just what you see on the demo reels?

JS: Just the demo reel. Because for so many people here, this is their first job in the entertainment industry, let alone the animation industry. So I don't really care about the paper. In fact, it would take an amazing résumé to get me to call without seeing a tape. People will write on résumés, "Call for a demo reel." I think, "What are you saving it for? If you want to work in Hollywood for television or movies, there are only about seven places to apply!"

DK: I warn people, this is like sending out a résumé. You don't grudge a stamp or the paper or the envelope. You make a lot of 10-minute dubs and you mail them out to everybody and his kid brother, and then you follow up. But you have to do a stack of them. But they say, "It's a lot of money!"

How many post-hires, how many people either crack or don't work up to the level of their demo reel, they don't work well in teams?

JS: Almost none. A while back we had one guy who didn't really know LightWave when he started, which would have been OK, but he spent most of his time trying to convince everyone else we were using the wrong software. If you take on a job that requires using new software, you should be ready to embrace it.

DK: Have you had any hires that just didn't fit into the corporate culture?

JS: There's not really much of a corporate culture. Foundation Imaging is full of very fun and sometimes *very* strange people, but as long as they keep doing great work and don't prevent others from working, I don't care how odd they are. That's also why my interviews are a breeze and I often hire over the phone. If you want to work here, I like your work, and I have an opening, you will probably get the job! Why do we even need to meet?

You also need to be a team player. But here, it wouldn't even occur to you to not be a team player, because there's so much of that around you. Everyone's swimming downstream; you don't think, "Hey, I'm going to turn around and swim upstream." A prima donna attitude would not last a minute here. No one dares even try it because no one else is getting away with it. Outside work, it can be a little different. You catch a Foundation artist at a party full of wannabes, and he can be quite a prima donna. You get a Foundation artist in a room full of other Foundation artists, and no one cares; it's just our job.

Send your demo reels (if you dare) to Jeff at the following address:

Jeff Scheetz
Foundation Imaging
24933 West Avenue Stanford
Valencia, CA 91355

Case Study 21.2
How I Got Here

by Michael B. Comet

Mike Comet.

I have always been interested in both computers and art. I started programming and drawing even before middle school. The old Warner Bros. (WB) cartoons and Disney films started my interest in animation. I really like Chuck Jones' work, in particular the stories he did with Mike Maltese. Chances are if it's a WB cartoon directed by Chuck Jones and written by Mike Maltese, it's one of my favorites. I also saw a number of old CGI pieces—from Pixar shorts to NASA space simulations, as well as stop-motion like *Closed Mondays*—that really made me want to be an animator. The CGI stuff in particular excited me because I was into computers and programming and I liked the look. Whether it was the ILM effects in *Young Sherlock Holmes*, spacecraft in *Babylon 5*, submarines in *SeaQuest DSV*, or even commercials, I knew it was what I wanted to do.

In seventh grade I got a Super 8mm animation camera and started doing claymation, cutout animation, cel animation, and things like that. I used to sit in high school biology class and draw flipbooks. I also started programming little graphics apps like little video games and paint programs. I had always wanted to do computer graphics work but never really looked into it. In 1991, I saw a demo of a 3D animation on an Amiga. I had wanted to do 3D stuff before but never knew it was possible on a PC. Upon realizing I could actually raytrace on a home computer, I was hooked. I ended up getting an Amiga 3000 and Imagine 1, which was brand-new at the time. I started making animations and working on basic 3D skills. I did some graphics for my high school talent show as well as a logo here and there, but for the most part, I just did it for fun. A few years later, Imagine 3 came out for the PC, so I picked up the PC version and switched to that platform. During this time, I had also been programming on the PC doing things like VGA paint programs and games and starting my own 3D modeler and renderer for Windows.

Finally, I was off to college. I met this person on campus, TJ, who was doing a sci-fi magazine on CD-ROM and ended up doing some graphics and animations for them with Imagine 3 PC. The CD-ROM never got published (TJ landed a full-time job doing CD-ROM work in Florida), but I got some experience. In addition to all my computer classes, I enrolled in drawing and painting. I also bought a DPS Personal Animation Recorder (PAR) board so I could output to tape. By that point, I had graduated and had started working at the university as a network software engineer.

I started looking around for graphics jobs around this time. I found that I could get a job as a technical director (TD) because I had good experience in both graphics and programming. However, I wasn't sure if it was what I really wanted to do. So I decided to hold off and try to work on more animation work and character work.

When LightWave 3D 4 standalone came out for the PC, I switched to that. At the same time, I met this guy on the Internet who was working on a PC video game, Vicious Circle. He was looking for 3D animators to do some character animation stuff for the game. I decided to work on it in hopes that I would get good royalties and good experience. I ended up designing and animating this mutant person and cyborg character for the game (which still hasn't been published as far as I know). During the same time, I also did some logo designs and freelanced for people I knew.

When I was using Imagine, I wrote the Imagine FAQ for the mailing list. One of the guys on the list, Doug Kelly, had visited way back then, and we got together and exchanged some models and things. After I switched to LightWave (and wrote the FAQ for that), I found out he had moved back to Cleveland and actually now worked at the same university I graduated from (and now worked at myself). So we got together and talked about graphics and things. It ended up that he was writing a book about character animation and LightWave 3D. He asked if I was interested in helping out with the book as well as this short film he wanted to make. I said sure and ended up helping him with LightWave techniques for the book and modeling a character for his film.

Part of my compensation was a "crew trip" to SIGGRAPH '96. I looked for some jobs there and found that, while I had now started to do more character work, I was still mostly qualified as a TD and not an animator. So I decided to work more on animation and joined the CG-CHAR list. I got a bit better and kept a lookout for other job openings. I used my PAR to lay off my best work to VHS tape, and mailed out quite a few demo reels before I started getting interviews.

A little while later, I found some video game companies that were hiring for a jack-of-all-trades-type person who would specifically be good at the cinematic cutscenes. This is exactly what I was looking for because I could utilize my TD skills as well as work on character animation and things like that. I ended up getting a job at Parallax Software, now called Volition Inc. My primary focus was character animation and setup for cinematics and realtime.

Technically, I started working seriously with CGI around 1989, however, I didn't focus specifically on character animation until years later. Even with my background in other forms of computer-generated animation, it took about a year and a half for me to land my first character animation job. However, that was with a lot of luck and good timing. The quality of my reel then wouldn't be accepted today as good enough for character animation. The requirements have gone up.

In 1999, I was hired as Animation Supervisor at Creative Digital Images to work on a direct-to-video 3D animated children's cartoon.

In 2000, I was hired as an animator at Big Idea, the creators of *Veggie Tales*, where I am working on a new cartoon series called *3-2-1 Penguins!*

One of my favorite quotes is:

> *"Animation means to invoke life, not to imitate it."*
> — *Chuck Jones*

Since I began working full-time, I continue to do some freelance as well as help with other books. For example, I have some sections in Doug Kelly's book *Character Animation In Depth* (that's my frog image on the spine), and I've also written a chapter on Magpie in Bill Fleming's book *Animating Facial Features & Expressions*. I also now maintain the FAQ for the CG-CHAR mailing list.

I try to work on personal projects when I have time. Typically I find myself drawn to whatever aspect I'm not involved with at work. For example, if I'm mostly animating, I might work more on modeling in my personal time. Staying in practice is kind of like riding a bike—you can always get back on. There is definitely a mode you can get into after a while of animating, however, where you kind of pick up a better pace because of consistent work.

My advice to beginning character animators is to study traditional animation principles. Work on the basics like weights and walk cycles until you can get stuff to move correctly. Then start working on acting, emotions, and life. It's no longer enough to just be able to move something around, you have to make it act. Read the CG-CHAR FAQ document. And above all, practice, practice, practice!

*You can email Mike Comet's at **comet@comet-cartoons.com** or visit his Web site, **www.comet-cartoons.com.***

Case Study 21.3
Changing Tracks

by Dave Bailey

Although I was formally trained as a commercial artist, I am completely self-taught when it comes to computers and animation. That is why I like to challenge myself with new things whenever I do a personal project.

I graduated from the Art Institute of Philadelphia in 1978. I worked as Newspaper Staff Illustrator for The News-Journal Company in Wilmington, Delaware, for a year, then went freelance. Over the next 18 years, I created illustrations, designs, and animation for industrial videos and computer-based interactive multimedia, technical literature, book covers, and advertising in both digital formats and the traditional mediums of oils, acrylics, pencil, ink, and airbrush. Some of my work includes educational game kiosks for the Smithsonian Postal Museum, the Smithsonian National Museum of American Indians, and the Delaware History Museum. I was also an Instructor of illustration techniques in the University of Delaware Continuing Education program.

In 1997, after being inspired by a lecture given by Doug Kelly, I picked up a copy of the first edition of this book, *LightWave 3D 5 Character Animation F/X*.

The next year, I attended Richard Williams' Animation Masterclass in New York.

While continuing my freelance work, I assembled a demo reel centered around my Mudpuppy character animation, which is described in detail in case studies elsewhere in this book.

In early 1999, I was hired by Sony Development in Burbank, California, as a team leader and Lead Character Animator for the ride film, *The Yellow Submarine Adventure*. I was responsible for animating all of the main characters in the 3,000-frame finale. I also modeled and set up the Beatles and Captain Fred characters and modeled seven minor characters.

When the *Yellow Submarine* project wrapped up, I moved over to Station X Studios in Santa Monica to work on the feature film, *Dungeons and Dragons*, for which I animated a flying dragon.

I am currently at WB, working on the feature film *Osmosis Jones*.

Along the way, I have accumulated experience with a variety of software, including Maya, LightWave, Messiah, Photoshop, Premier, Magpie, Sound Forge, Director, Illustrator, Freehand, Painter, Detailer, and Elastic Reality. I have also programmed in Lingo, Visual Basic, Arexx, and C.

I find inspiration for my work in life, the incredible work done by the artists at Pixar, Bluesky, PDI, ILM, WB, and Disney, and great stories and acting in films.

Since the early 80s I had been fascinated with computer graphics. When I saw the light cycles in the movie *Tron*, I thought "Wow, how can I do that?" At the time the only computers capable of that kind of work cost way more than my first house, so I had to be satisfied with my eight-color still images on my Apple II.

I first started "animating" in 1986 when I sold my first "moving" video graphic using color cycling and moving type in Aegis Animator on my Amiga 1000. Looking back, my stuff was horrid. I had no knowledge of the principles of animation. Over the next 11 years, animation was a very small part of the services I provided, although I always wanted to do more of it. It wasn't until I read Doug's book and practiced my character animation every day for over a year that I did what I consider to be my first animation—a character that gave the illusion of life!

Once I made the decision that I was going to really learn the needed skills and make character animation my career, it took me about 18 months before I really started to produce characters that could give the illusion of life. I was working anywhere between 4 and 24 hours a day on my animation, pretty much 7 days a week, depending on my workload and sleep requirements. "I'm a man on a mission," I would say to my wife as I would head back to my studio after dinner or whenever she would tell me I was crazy, usually as I was crawling into bed while she was getting up to go to work.

I had an interview at SIGGRAPH '98 with Tippet Studios that was very insightful. My demo reel had an early version of my Mudpuppy character on it, plus a few other pieces. The interviewer told me that I should do a dozen more studies of that character and send him a new reel in six months. He also told me that I should never show any of the other animation on my reel because they were not good. I took his advice, but only managed to get three animations done, because I spent several months reworking the model and character setup.

I had a few cattle call interviews at SIGGRAPH '98 that went nowhere. Six months later, with a new demo reel and a move to California, I had two offers from two interviews.

Being a "project gypsy" is an unfortunate reality of the business. It would be wonderful if I could land a job at a studio where there were enough projects, all timed perfectly so that there were no down times for any of the departments from story development to final editing, but I know of no such place.

I do work on personal projects outside my job. Keeping in practice is the most important thing. My advice to beginning character animators is to read everything you can get on the subject, join the CG-CHAR mailing list (**www.cg-char.com**), practice, practice, practice, and never give up on your dreams. It's not about making the perfect walk cycle, it's about acting.

Dave Bailey
3540 S. Centinela Avenue #9
Los Angeles, California 90066
Tel: (310) 398-7333
*Email: **dbailey@pixinc.com***

Bibliography

Inside LightWave [6] **by Dan Ablan.**
Indianapolis, IN: New Riders Press, 2000. ISBN 073570919X.

Good general coverage of LightWave's features, with excellent tutorials and several sections pertinent to character modeling and setup. If you own the software, you should definitely own this book, especially because the official manuals have fewer tutorials than previous versions.

Grammar of the Film Language **by Daniel Arijon.**
Hollywood, CA: Silman-James Press, 1991. ISBN 187950507X.

An exhaustive guide to the visual narrative techniques that form the "language" of filmmaking regarding the positioning and movement of players and cameras, as well as the sequence and pacing of images. Heavily illustrated with line drawings. In print for nearly 20 years in several languages. Highly recommended.

No Strings Attached: The Inside Story of Jim Henson's Creature Shop **by Matt Bacon.**
Indianapolis, IN: Macmillan, 1997. ISBN 0028620089.

History, techniques, problem-solving, and lots of illustrations from the best puppeteers in the business. Includes behind-the-scenes from *Dark Crystal*, *Labyrinth*, *Pinocchio*, and other projects. Animators have a lot to learn from puppeteers, and this is an excellent place to start.

A Dictionary of Theatre Anthropology: The Secret Art of the Performer
by Eugenio Barba and Nicola Savarese.
New York, NY: Routledge, 1991. ISBN 0415053080.

An academic approach, heavy on theory and a little long-winded, but an incomparable resource of photographs and analysis to worldwide physical expression, dance, and acting. Not a substitute for acting classes, but close.

Cartoon Animation by Preston Blair.
Wilton, CT: Walter Foster, 1994. ISBN 1560100842.

Best collection of caricature motion studies in a form easily adapted to 3D computer animation. Especially useful for character design of head and hands.

The Elements of Screenwriting by Irwin R. Blacker.
New York, NY: Collier Books, 1986. ISBN 0020002203.

One of the best, and certainly the most compact, source about writing for film or video. This book is the absolute minimum necessary for the amateur to understand the mechanics of writing usable scripts. Not a bad reminder for the experienced screenwriter either!

"Animation Tricks." by Jim Blinn, Mark Henne, John Lasseter, Ken Perlin, and Chris Wedge, *ACM SIGGRAPH Course Notes* 1 (1994).
P.O. Box 12114, New York, NY 10257. Annual.

A collection of short lectures from some of the top working professionals. These tips and tricks are the hard-won lessons of experience. Required reading.

The Making of Toy Story by Jonathan Bogner, prod., and Mike Bonifer, dir.
Burbank, CA: Walt Disney Co., 1995. Videocassette.

A little light on the animation side and proportionally heavier on the celebrity voice talent, but some good quotes and a little behind-the-scenes at Pixar. Originally shown on The Disney Channel around *Toy Story*'s opening.

Film Art: An Introduction, Fourth Edition by David Bordwell and Kristin Thompson.
New York, NY: McGraw-Hill, 1993. ISBN 0070064466.

A more historical and theoretical, although shallower, approach to Arijon's subject, with stills and sequences from Hollywood and foreign films. Also covers sound and film criticism.

Constructive Anatomy by George B. Bridgman.
New York, NY: Dover, 1973. ISBN 0486211045.

One of the most often-cited resources for drawing from life, written and illustrated in a way that is especially useful for 3D modeling and character setup.

The Art and Science of Digital Compositing by Ron Brinkmann.
New York, NY: Morgan Kaufmann, 1999. ISBN 0121339602.

This is an excellent introduction to the theory and general practice of digital compositing at the feature-film level. Brinkmann has impeccable credentials and an impressive credits list, and he has been teaching digital compositing worldwide for years. He is also involved in the ongoing development of the Shake line of software at Nothing Real, so he speaks with experience from all sides of the business. This book is deliberately software-free, but the author does include a very useful appendix on comparing features to select your own digital compositing software.

Dog Locomotion & Gait Analysis by Curtis M. Brown, Bonnie Dalzell, and Robert W. Cole. Wheat Ridge, Colorado: Hoflin Pub Ltd., 1986. ISBN 9997847326.

A detailed and thorough breakdown of canine movement, including structure and physiology. Very useful for studying all kinds of animal motion; once you learn the details for dogs, you can apply the same principles to most mammals and many other species as well.

A History of Narrative Film, Third Edition by David A. Cook. New York, NY: W. W. Norton, 1996. ISBN 0393968197.

Good basic history of film, especially cinematic technique and influences.

Digital Cinematography by Ben De Leeuw. New York, NY: AP Professional, 1997. ISBN 0122088751.

Excellent coverage of lighting and camera work for CGI, tied to the real-world equivalents. Profusely illustrated.

The Art of Dramatic Writing by Lajos Egri. New York, NY: Simon & Schuster, 1960. ISBN 0671213326.

The best source on how to write an interesting, dramatic story. Lots of guidelines for developing convincing characters.

The Artist's Complete Guide to Facial Expression by Gary Faigin. New York, NY: Watson-Guptill Publications, 1990. ISBN 0823016285.

Useful for modeling and animating facial expressions, especially the more realistic. For the exaggerated or caricatured, refer to Blair.

Cyclopedia Anatomicae by Gyorgy Feher. Illustrated by Andras Szunyoghy. New York, NY: Black Dog & Leventhal Publishers, Inc., 1996. ISBN 1884822878.

A monster of a book, probably more information than you'll need to design your characters. Always a fascinating browse, you'll continue to stumble over interesting bits for years.

Clay Animation: American Highlights 1908 to Present by Michael Frierson. Twayne's Filmmakers Series. New York, NY: Twayne Publishers, 1994. ISBN 0805793283.

Mostly a history, but some useful tips that can be applied to CGI. An excellent companion to Wilson's *Puppets and People*.

The Contemporary Animator by John Halas. Boston, MA: Focal Press, 1990. ISBN 0240512804.

Excellent survey of the art up to 1990. Dated in areas pertaining to computer graphics, but a wealth of information on the various styles and techniques of animation. Worth tracking down for the glossary alone.

Growing a Business by Paul Hawken.
New York, NY: Fireside, 1988. ISBN 0671671642.

The best single source on how to start and grow a small business. Learn from other people's mistakes, and save yourself a lot of pain, money, and time.

Scriptwriting for Animation by Stan Hayward.
Boston, MA: Focal Press, 1978. ISBN 0240509676.

Animation here means 2D cel work, but there are some useful tips that still apply. Out of print; check your local library.

Animation: A Reference Guide by Thomas W. Hoffer.
Westport, CT: Greenwood Press, 1981. ISBN 0313210950.

Exhaustive reference and critical bibliography on the genre. Probably more information than you'd normally want, but if it's about animation and it existed prior to 1979, it's in here.

The Elements of Color by Johannes Itten.
New York, NY: Van Nostrand Reinhold Company. ISBN 0442240384.

Standard reference for art classes. If you need help on composing colors for sets, characters, or lighting, this chunk of theory may be what you need. If you won't use it very often, try the library; the hardcover edition is expensive.

Chuck Amuck: The Life and Times of an Animated Cartoonist, First Edition by Chuck Jones.
New York, NY: Farrar Straus Giroux, 1989. ISBN 0240508718.

This and *Chuck Reducks* comprise the autobiography (to date) of one of the best-loved classic cartoon directors. Bugs, Elmer, Daffy, and the rest of the Warner Bros. gang acquire a little more life when you read this book. It's also a valuable peek inside the workings of the Hollywood system. Don't think the bozos aren't still in charge.

Small Time Operator: How to Start Your Own Small Business, Keep Your Books, Pay Your Taxes, and Stay Out of Trouble! Sixth Edition by Bernard B. Kamoroff.
Willits, CA: Bell Springs Publishing, 1999. ISBN 0917510151.

Precisely what the title says. 'Nuff said.

Serious Business: The Art and Commerce of Animation in America from Betty Boop to Toy Story by Stefan Kanfer.
New York, NY: Simon & Schuster, 1997. ISBN 0684800799. Illustrated, color and b/w, hardbound.

This is more about the business than the art and is a sweeping chronicle that actually turns out to be a fairly fast and enjoyable read. Well researched and comprehensive, if a bit too encyclopedic; it's hard to trace that many strains of cartoon DNA through so many studios. This is a good overview of the history of the business that you had to be nuts to want to get into until fairly recently. You really ought to know this stuff, and if you don't, this is a good source for it.

Film Directing: Shot by Shot by Steven D. Katz.
Studio City, CA: Michael Wiese Productions, 1991. ISBN 0941188108.

Excellent resource on the creation and use of storyboards for directing a film.

Film Directing—Cinematic Motion: A Workshop for Staging Scenes.
Studio City, CA: Michael Wiese Productions, 1992. ISBN 0941188140.

Less important (for effects work, anyway) resource on the actual composition and framing techniques used in directing a film. Discussions on staging, choreography, blocking, and so on are included, along with meaty interviews with professionals such as John Sayles and Ralph Singleton. A good complement to Arijon's book, with a different perspective.

Digital Compositing In Depth by Doug Kelly.
Scottsdale, AZ: The Coriolis Group, 2000. ISBN 1576104311.

If you need to combine two or more images seamlessly, insert your LightWave characters into live-action footage, or simply clean up production mistakes such as in-frame microphones, this book shows you how. All projects can be completed with the software and footage on the two CD-ROMs, including 2K Cineon film images.

7 Minutes: The Life and Death of the American Animated Cartoon by Norman M. Klein.
New York, NY: Scribner, 1993. ISBN 0860913961. Illustrated b/w softbound.

This is a dense book. Klein taught at Cal Arts and the book is a lot more scholarly than the Kanfer tome, but it's of far more interest to anybody who wants to know what made the shorts work. There is plenty of theory and film nerd de-construction, yet because of its subject, it informs more than abstracts. I expect that familiarity with the ideas the author explores in this book will help anybody make better short animated films. There is a lot of insightful and comprehensive comparison, context, and chronology. A lot of basic cartoon structures are illuminated as they go from fresh to formula. Highly recommended.

Advanced Layout and Design Workbook by Brian Lemay.
Oakville, Ontario: 1997. ISBN 09969941927.

Designing Cartoon Characters for Animation.
Oakville, Ontario: ISBN 0969941919.

Layout and Design Made Amazingly Simple.
Oakville, Ontario: 1993.

Lemay, an instructor at Sheridan, has done an incredible job in these three volumes. These detailed, exhaustive books make Blair's pale in comparison. Unfortunately, these are at present only available directly from the author, but they are well worth the extra effort. Send queries to Brian Lemay, Suite 1422, 1011 Upper Middle Rd., Oakville, Ontario, Canada, L6H 5Z9 or email to **blemay@pathcom.com**.

"Principles of Traditional Animation Applied to 3D Computer Animation." by John Lasseter, *Computer Graphics* **21, 4 (1987): 35-44.**
Association for Computing Machinery, 1515 Broadway, 17th Floor, New York, NY 10036. ISSN 1069529X.

Lasseter translates the principles of animation taught at Disney (see Thomas and Johnston) to 3D computer animation and also introduces the concept of layering or "hierarchical" animation. Solid gold; if you skip everything else in this list, get a copy of this paper.

Toy Story: The Art and Making of the Animated Film **by John Lasseter and Steve Daly. New York, NY: Hyperion Press, 1995. ISBN 0786861800.**

A wonderful collection of production art and interviews with the principal creators, both at Pixar and Disney. A must-have for 3D CGI enthusiasts and professionals.

The Animation Book **by Kit Laybourne. New York, NY: Crown, 1979. ISBN 0517529467.**

Beginner's guide to most of the film-based techniques, from drawing on film to sand and clay stop-motion.

How to Draw Comics the Marvel Way **by Stan Lee and John Buscema. New York, NY: Simon & Schuster, 1984. ISBN 0671530771.**

Useful as a study guide for constructing humanoid characters, strong poses, and dramatic scene composition. 2D drawing exercises translate well to 3D modeling.

Handbook of Animation Techniques **by Eli Levitan. New York, NY: Van Nostrand Reinhold, 1979. ISBN 0442261152.**

Focused on production for television advertising, this is a very nuts-and-bolts volume. Although technically dated, it contains solid production advice that should be taken seriously by anyone trying to do business in animation. Direct and written in plain English, with a minimum of philosophizing.

"Storyboarding." by Verin G. Lewis, *3D Artist* **18 (1995): 32-33.**
P.O. Box 4787, Santa Fe, NM 87502. Irregular. ISSN 10589503.

Concise argument for the necessity of storyboarding commercial 3D animation and a brief overview of storyboard production.

LightWave 3D Book: Tips, Techniques, and Ready-to-Use Objects.
San Francisco, CA: Miller Freeman Books, 1997. ISBN 0879304553.

A collection of 100 tutorials from *LightWavePro* magazine. Worth acquiring, even though there isn't much on versions later than 5. It includes a CD-ROM of objects, scenes, and other goodies.

Photography, Fifth Edition by Barbara London and John Upton.
New York, NY: Harper Collins, 1994. ISBN 0673522237.

Useful for chapters on lighting, composition, color, lenses, and film vocabulary, all of which are readily adapted to 3D computer animation.

Getting Ready for a Career as a Computer Animator by Bill Lund.
Mankato, MN: Capstone Press, 1997. ISBN 1560655496.

One more in a series of vocational guidance books from this author. Some good advice, but be aware that he's not an industry insider. Better than nothing, but do your own research before you blow serious money on an animation school.

Film Lighting: Talks with Hollywood's Cinematographers and Gaffers by Kris Malkiewicz.
New York, NY: Prentice Hall Press, 1986. ISBN 0671622714.

This is the working expertise of an impressive collection of lighting professionals. Not exactly an easy read, but lots of information. Derived almost entirely from live-action production, a lot of the hardware specifics won't apply to LightWave work, but the principles are the same.

"Storyboard Design for Computer Generated Animation." by Stephen Michael Martino.
Master's thesis. Columbus, OH: Ohio State University, 1989.

Well written and adequately illustrated, this is one thesis that won't put you to sleep. The author had previously worked as a designer and animator at Cranston/Csuri in Columbus and as a director at Metrolight Studios in Los Angeles. Storyboard examples include Dow "Scrubbing Bubbles," and KTLA, NBA, and HBO logos, among others. Solid practical advice on dealing with clients too.

Bodytalk: The Meaning of Human Gestures by Desmond Morris.
New York, NY: Crown Publishers, 1994. ISBN 0517883554.

A readable popular version of somewhat scholarly research on informal gestural communication. Excellent resource for animators, either for practice or to build up a library of reusable motions.

In the Blink of An Eye by Walter Murch.
Los Angeles, CA: Silman-James Press, 1995. ISBN 1879505231.

An excellent book on editing. If you are a freelance artist, work in a small studio, or simply want to understand why the director and editor chopped up your shots or asked you to stretch them, you will learn a lot from this book.

The Human Figure in Motion by Eadweard Muybridge.
New York, NY: Dover Press, 1989. ISBN 0486202046.

Animals in Motion.
New York, NY: Dover Publications, 1957. ISBN 0486202038.

Muybridge took carefully measured sequences of photos of animal and human movement in the late 1800s. These sequences are a great help for anyone trying to make something move realistically or to derive the essentials of an action for caricature.

Computer Facial Animation by Frederick I. Parke and Keith Waters.
Natick, MA: A K Peters Ltd., 1996. ISBN 1568810148.

Exhaustive, very scholarly compilation of research and applications of facial animation. A difficult read, but even the figures and captions will give you a lot of information that isn't available anywhere else. If you make a living with lip sync or facial expressions, you need to have this book on your reference shelf.

Atlas of Facial Expression: An Account of Facial Expression for Artists, Actors, and Writers by Stephen Rogers Peck.
New York, NY: Oxford University Press, 1987. ISBN 019504049X.

Excellent technical reference on the facial structure and the uses of muscles in emotional and vocal communication.

Disney Animation: The Illusion of Life by Frank Thomas and Ollie Johnston.
New York, NY: Abbeville Press, 1981; reprint, Hyperion Press, 1995. ISBN 0786860707.

Referred to as "the animation bible" due to its size and the value of its contents. The Disney "rules of animation" and many other useful rules of thumb are included. Recently reprinted, with some loss of color and image quality since the 1981 edition, but still well worth the price.

Tim Burton's Nightmare Before Christmas: The Film, the Art, the Vision: With the Complete Lyrics From the Film, First Edition by Frank T. Thompson.
New York, NY: Hyperion, 1993. ISBN 156282774X.

A really good behind-the-scenes book about one of the most technically challenging puppet animation films ever. This is an excellent idea-generator for replacement modeling and armature construction that applies to CGI as well as traditional methods.

Industrial Light + Magic: Into the Digital Realm by Mark Cotta Vaz and Patricia Rose Duignan.
New York, NY: Ballantine Books/Del Rey, 1996. ISBN 0345381521.

In the decade covered by this book, ILM invented or developed nearly every digital special effect process used today. This book does not describe the intricate details of the work, but it adequately covers the history of ILM's transition from optical to digital special effects. The photos and narrative text are great, but the most valuable content of this book is the spirit of problem-solving communicated by the many interviews with ILM staff.

3D Computer Animation by John Vince.
Reading, MA: Addison-Wesley, 1992. ISBN 0201627566.

Introductory technical animation theory for programming. Recommended for technical directors (TDs).

Advanced Animation and Rendering Techniques by Alan Watt and Mark Watt.
Reading, MA: Addison-Wesley, 1992. ISBN 0201544121.

An excellent technical text, covering important implementation theory and details. Recommended for TDs.

"Tricks of the Trade: Computer Graphics Production." by Jerry Weil, Neil Eskuri, Andy Kopra, John McLaughlin, and Kathy White. *ACM SIGGRAPH Course Notes 5* (1995). P.O. Box 12114, New York, NY 10257. Annual.

A gold mine of production rules of thumb, collected from technical directors at different production houses. Recommended for TDs, animation supervisors, and others who need to produce CGI animation on time and within budget.

Timing for Animation, First Edition by Harold Whitaker and John Halas.
New York, NY: Focal Press, 1981. ISBN 024051310X.

An absolute treasure trove of information on timing. Difficult to find, but well worth it.

Puppets and People by Steven S. Wilson.
London: Tantivy Press, 1980. ISBN 0498023125.

A history, a filmography, and a smattering of basic nuts-and-bolts for the motion picture techniques of compositing live-action with stop-motion puppets. Examines the work of Willis O'Brien, Ray Harryhausen, Phil Tippett, and others. Lots of photos, and because the physical models tend to decay or be salvaged for parts, a collection of information hard to find elsewhere. Worth looking for, if only to use the extensive bibliography pointing to primary sources in the industry press.

The Making of Jurassic Park by Zaloom Mayfield Productions, prod.
MCA Universal Home Video, Universal City, CA: 1995. ISBN 0783208898. Laser disk.

A good collection of behind-the-scenes information and interviews, featuring Steven Spielberg, Stan Winston, Phil Tippett, Dennis Muren, Michael Lantieri, Mark Dippe, Steve Williams, and others. Includes a sequence on the techniques used for move-matching CGI elements to live-action footage from a moving camera. Originally broadcast on NBC. The laser disk edition has even more production stills, plus home movies of preproduction meetings. Spielberg at work, with the top VFX supervisors in the business, is a glimpse of Hollywood reality that is worth tracking down.

Glossary

16mm—A smaller film size for educational and film festival use.

3:2 pulldown—A process to convert 24fps film footage to 30fps for NTSC television.

35mm—The standard film size for motion pictures in wide release.

Academy field ratio—A standardized ratio for the film frame. Created in 1930, it began at 1:1.33 (height versus width) and currently stands at 1:1.85.

Academy leader—A length of film appended at the beginning of a reel to assist the projectionist in framing and focusing.

acceleration—Increase in velocity.

action—Any visible change in a scene; movement, rotation, size, or deformation of an object.

action axis—See *line of action*.

algorithm—A procedure or set of rules for solving a problem. An algorithm is implemented by a programmer to create software.

aliasing—The stair-step pattern seen along the edge of a curve or diagonal border when presented in a raster display, as on a computer monitor or in print. See also *antialiasing*.

alpha—In software, the first draft of a computer program, before the faults have been corrected.

alpha channel—A grayscale or black-and-white rendering of a scene, used as a *matte* in compositing.

altitude—Rotation on the x-axis, or left-to-right horizontal axis. In LightWave, the pitch rotation.

animation—Any technique that makes inanimate objects move on the screen.

animation channel—A parameter that can be animated, including an item's position, rotation, or scale; a light's intensity; or any other setting that can be made to vary over time. See also *motion channel*.

animation cycle—See *motion cycle*.

animation hierarchy—The sequence of levels, from root to outer extremities, followed to efficiently animate a complex character. See Chapters 12 and 15 for examples.

animator—The person who sets the frame-by-frame timing and posing of the objects in a scene.

antialiasing—A technique for blending color values near an aliased border to visually smooth it out for raster display. In LightWave, this requires rendering multiple passes and blending aliased areas.

anticipation—A brief action in the opposite direction, preceding and foreshadowing the main action.

aperture (lens aperture)—In cinematography, the size of the lens opening divided by the focal length, expressed as an f-stop—for example, f/8, f/11.

arc—See *slalom*.

armature—An internal skeleton designed to support and hold the pose of the outer material of a stop-motion puppet.

aspect ratio—The ratio of the width to the height of a film frame. In computer-generated imagery (CGI), it also refers to the ratio of the resolution or of the individual pixels.

attributes—In LightWave, the set of parameters, including color, specularity, transparency, and so on, that can be used to control the rendered appearance of the surface of an object.

AVI—Audio Video Interleaved. A playback compression format designed for the Microsoft Windows operating systems.

axis—One of the three coordinates used to define an item's position, rotation, or scale in 3D space. The three axes are usually labeled x, y, and z.

azimuth—Rotation on the vertical or z-axis. In LightWave, the heading rotation.

back light—See *rim light*.

back projection—In cinematography, projecting footage onto a screen placed behind the action as a means of compositing in the camera.

background—An image or sequence rendered behind all the objects in a scene.

backplane—An object sized and positioned to act as a background.

ball-and-socket joint—A rotational joint having three degrees of freedom. The human hip is a ball-and-socket joint with limited range of movement.

ballistics—The branch of mathematics that describes the behavior of falling bodies.

banding—Borders between areas of similar color or brightness, visible because the image does not contain enough colors to shade the border more smoothly. Dithering can make banding less noticeable.

bank—Rotation on the front-to-back horizontal or z-axis.

bar sheet—Diagrams similar to sheet music, used to set the broad timing for long sequences of animation.

beta (software)—The next generation of software after alpha, ideally with fewer faults but not yet ready for public release.

beta tester—An optimist who believes he can do production work with faulty software. One who tests beta software.

Bezier spline—A versatile type of spline developed by Pierre Bezier, originally to assist in the design of automobile body panels. See also *spline*.

Betacam—A family of VTR formats developed by Sony.

BG—In cinematography, abbreviation for background.

bit—The smallest unit of information processed by a digital computer, a 1 or 0. Bits are grouped into *bytes*.

blocking—In stage or cinema direction, setting marks or positions for actors in a scene.

bluescreen—The process of shooting live action against a saturated blue background so the background can be replaced in a post-production composite process. See also *chroma key*.

Bone—In LightWave, a type of deformation control inserted into an object in a scene. A collection of bones makes a skeleton that can be animated to change the shape of the object.

bouncing ball—Basic animation exercise demonstrating timing, squash, and stretch.

bounding box—A simple six-sided rectangular box drawn as a wireframe to stand in for a more complex object to improve screen refresh and system response rates.

breakdown drawings—The stage of drawings between key and *in-between*, developing the timing of the action in more detail. See also *in-betweens*.

bug—An error in computer software that produces an unintended result; a.k.a. *fault*.

byte—A group or word of bits, a unit of digital data. Computer file sizes are usually measured in thousands (KB) or millions (MB) of bytes.

CAD—Computer Aided Design. The use of computers and graphics software to design products, partially automating traditional drafting and engineering tasks.

camera—A machine designed to expose photosensitive film or a sensing element to a focused image for a controlled period of time to create an image on the film or other recording media. In cinematography, a camera is a machine to perform this operation repeatedly for successive frames to create a motion picture. In LightWave, the camera is the point from which the scene is rendered, emulating a physical camera.

camera animation—Animation performed exclusively with the camera—as pans, dollys, zooms, or other changes—while photographing a scene or image with no other action.

camera body—The main part of the camera between the back and the lens, containing the shutter and film transport. Film recorder and stop-motion camera bodies have very accurate pin registration for the film sprocket holes to ensure that each image is recorded in precisely the same position.

camera shake—See *pan, zip.*

cameraless animation—Animation that is drawn or etched directly on film stock.

caricature—Exaggeration of the peculiarities or unique attributes of a person or thing. In character animation, caricature is the exaggeration of the essentials of a motion to create unrealistic but truthful action.

cel—Acetate sheets used in cel animation.

cel animation—Animation drawn or painted on transparent acetate sheets and layered with foreground and background cels or images. Named after the celluloid sheets used in the early development of the technique.

center of gravity—Abbreviated CG, the center of an object's balance.

CG—See *center of gravity.*

CGI—Computer Generated Imagery. Any graphic image created with the assistance of a computer.

channel—See *animation channel.*

character—In CGI, an object that displays volition and personality in a scene.

character animation—In CGI, the process of timing and posing a character object to create the illusion of life.

character model—In CGI, an object or collection of objects to be animated as a character.

charts—In traditional animation, graphic notes or diagrams to show the timing for *inbetweens* or camera motion. In LightWave, charts are splines, envelopes, or motion graphs.

cheating—Repositioning objects between shots to improve a composition without tipping off the audience that the scene has been changed.

child—In LightWave, a dependent item in a hierarchy. In a normal skeleton, the knee is a child of the hip. See also *parenting.*

chroma key—Keying a composite layer by color, typically blue or green. See also *bluescreen.*

clay animation—Stop-motion cinematography of clay or other plastic material that is manually deformed by the animators for each pose. Clay can be used alone or supported by an armature.

clean plate—A live-action shot with no actors in it, to be used in compositing effects.

cleanup—Adding changes to a storyboard that has gone through its first round of revisions.

climax—In drama, the most important *crisis* in the story.

close-up—Literally, a shot of the subject face alone. Generally, any close shot.

code—Part of a program as written by a programmer. "Fixing that fault only took a few lines of code."

collision detection—An algorithm used in some LightWave plug-ins to detect when one object intersects another. Can be used to automate animation tasks such as bouncing balls.

color depth—The number of bits used to store color information for each pixel in an image: 1-bit is black and white; 8-bit can be color or grayscale having 256 different values; 24-bit has 8-bit values for red, green, and blue, approximating the color depth of a television screen.

color key—See *chroma key.*

commercial—A brief advertisement, generally intended for television. Typically 15, 30, or 60 seconds in length. Also known as a spot or ad.

compression—Removing redundant information from a data file to make it smaller; often used for storing or playing back images and animations. Different algorithms and software have different definitions of "redundant."

computer—A machine capable of running a program to produce the intended result. A machine that can't run a program correctly is sometimes referred to as a boat anchor— for example, "Your 286 is a boat anchor as far as LightWave is concerned."

computer animation—Animation timed and posed by a human and rendered by a computer. If a nonanimator is ignorant enough to say something like, "The computer does all the work," the nearest animator is entitled to whup them upside the head with a blunt instrument.

computer graphics—See *CGI.*

conflict—In drama, the collision between character and circumstance that drives the story.

constraint—An object or null in a setup that controls or influences the movement or position of another object or null.

control mesh—In LightWave, an object constructed of a lower number of points and used to automatically create a more complex object using subdivision surfaces.

coordinates—In geometry and CGI, a set of numbers that describes a location from the origin of the local system. In LightWave, x-, y-,z-coordinates are used to describe the location of an object in world coordinates and the location of each point in an object's local coordinates.

coverage—Additional camera angles and setups rendered to give the editor more leeway in assembling the final cut. Almost never used in traditional animation, and rarely used in CGI animation.

crane—Vertical movement of the camera; a.k.a. boom.

crawl—Very slow camera move intended to build tension; a.k.a. creep.

creeping titles—A.k.a. scrolling titles. Titles that move across the screen, typically from bottom to top, making it easier for the audience to read credits that are displayed briefly.

crisis—In drama, a decision point where a character's actions determine the direction of the story.

crossing the line—Shifting the camera to the opposite side of the line of action, which can confuse the audience if not handled carefully.

CRT—Acronym for cathode ray tube, a common type of computer or video display.

CU—In cinematography, close-up.

cut—The act of moving from one shot to another through the editing process.

cutting height—In cinematography, the height where the bottom of the frame intersects the actor(s).

cutting on the action—Changing from one camera position to the next during the character's action. This relieves the *visual jar*, because the audience focuses its attention on the action, not the shot composition.

cycle—See *motion cycle*.

default scene—A LightWave default scene contains a single character with all its associated textures, bones, hierarchies, constraints, plug-ins, and lights set up and ready to animate.

delta—A change in value from one frame of an animation to the next. Large deltas in rendered image sequences make animations more difficult to compress for direct computer playback. Large deltas in envelopes can make the animated parameter seem to jump or strobe.

depth of field—The area in which objects are in focus. See Chapter 14 for exercises demonstrating depth of field.

dialogue—Any sound track, script, or storyboard incorporating an actor's vocal performance.

digitizer—A device, often a computer peripheral, for converting analog signals to digital data. In CGI, typical source materials are 3D models, film or video footage, or still images.

direct to video—A growing market segment for videotape sales and rentals of films that have never been theatrically released. A potential opportunity for independent animators.

director—The person who oversees the big picture of the production and who generally has final creative control over the look, story, timing, and editing of an animated film.

displacement—A class of animation techniques based on posing or deformation of a single object. Contrast with *replacement*.

display buffer—A section of RAM that contains the current image.

dissolve—A special effect shot transition where the first shot gradually fades out and is replaced by the second shot fading in. See also *wipe*.

dither—Scattering pixels of one value over the border of and into an area of a different value to visually blend the two areas together. See also *banding*.

dolly—Camera move as if on a *dolly*, truck, or other horizontally mobile platform; a.k.a. track. See also *pan, truck*.

dope sheet—See *exposure sheet*.

drawn-on-film—See *cameraless animation*.

dubbing—The process of correcting mistakes in dialogue or sound track by rerecording. In animation, the process of adding sound to the silent animation.

dynamic balance—Constantly changing but balanced equilibrium between mass, inertia, and energy in a character. If the combination of mass, inertia, and energy in the lower body is equal to the mass, inertia, and energy in the upper body, the body as a whole is in dynamic balance.

dynamics—The motions that connect each key pose. Different parts move at different rates, accelerating and decelerating in a complex balancing act.

ease-in—Gradual acceleration from the preceding hold or beginning of an action to the snap, the fastest part.

ease-out—Gradual deceleration from the snap to the end of the action.

e-cinema—Electronic cinema, the use of digital projection systems with high brightness and contrast to replace film-based theatrical projection systems.

ECU—In cinematography, extreme close-up.

edge—A line connecting two points; the boundary between one polygon and the next.

editor, film editor—The person who assembles shots in sequence and synchronizes the sound track(s) according to the director's instructions.

effects—See *special effects animation*.

effects animation—Animation created to mimic phenomena such as fire, smoke, clouds, rain, or anything else that moves but is not a character or prop.

effects track—A sound track containing sound effects rather than music or dialogue.

elevation—A side or front view of a set design.

ELS—In cinematography, extreme long shot.

EndoMorph—A LightWave object that contains one or more morph maps.

envelope—A collection of values used to animate a parameter over time.

ergonomics—Design of objects to fit the user's shape and actions to prevent injury and increase comfort and efficiency.

establishing shot—Shows the audience the general environment in which the action will take place.

exposition—In drama, necessary background information communicated to the audience—usually by dialogue, sometimes by a title sequence or insert shot—that would be difficult or impossible to convey by a character's actions.

exposure sheet—A form filled out by the animator with frame-by-frame information for character action, lip sync, backgrounds, and camera.

expression—Short for "mathematical expression." Using one object or control to manipulate another object or control by way of an algorithm or set of rules.

extreme take—A gross distortion of a character to show surprise.

eye movements—Animation of the eyes and eyelids; used to define the character and foreshadow actions.

eyelights—In cinematography, lights set up specifically to bring out a highlight spot in an actor's eyes.

fade—A *dissolve* to or from a solid color, usually black or white.

fade in—The process where an image gradually appears from a blackened screen by lightening up to scene.

fade out—The opposite of *fade in*.

fair use—A doctrine of copyright, prevalent in the United States, that a free duplicate of a portion of a copyrighted work may be made for personal educational use.

fairings—See *ease-in, ease-out*.

fault—An error in a computer program that produces unwanted or unintentional results. Less scrupulous developers may document the behavior of a fault and call it a feature.

fcurve—Short for *function curve* or *spline*.

FG—In cinematography, foreground.

fill light—A light used to soften shadows and make hidden details visible without washing out the key light.

film grain—Tiny imperfections in an image produced by the crystals in film emulsion.

film recorder—A system that uses a camera to record digital images from a high-resolution CRT or laser. For motion picture film, the camera must have a pin-register film transport.

flicker fusion—The visual phenomenon that blends a rapid series of still images into the illusion of continuous motion. The frame rate at which flicker fusion occurs varies widely, from as low as 15fps to over 100fps. See also *Showscan*.

focal length—The length of a camera lens assembly, measured from the rear nodal point to the focal plane. After all, it's not the size of the lens, it's how you use it.

focal plane—A.k.a. film plane. The plane behind the camera lens where the image is in sharpest focus.

focus—The sharpness and clarity of an image.

focus pull—Animating the depth of field to match the area of sharp focus to an object's movement.

foley—Sound effects recording by professional noisemakers.

follow-through—Animation to mimic inertia during deceleration. A character coming to a rapid stop must overshoot the target slightly to show follow-through.

foot slippage—Unless the grounded foot is the root of the animation hierarchy, changes to a character's pose can cause the foot to slip forward or back inconsistently with the character's overall motion. A forward slip is called skating; a backward slip is called moonwalking.

footage—In cinematography, exposed film from a camera, measured in feet.

fps—Acronym for frames per second, the rate at which images are projected to create the illusion of motion in film, video, or other media. See also *frame rate*.

frame—In cinematography, the boundaries of the projected image. In projection and CGI, one image in a sequence.

frame rate—The speed at which separate images are viewed in a motion picture or other device for creating the illusion of motion. See also *sound speed, silent speed, flicker fusion, fps*.

frame-accurate—A VTR with a tape transport that can accurately record a single frame or field at a time. Used until recently to record animation to tape; now largely replaced by digital recorders.

fricative—A class of *phonemes* including "F" and "V."

front projection—Projecting an image into a scene from the front; used to composite in the camera. Contrast with *rear projection*.

full animation—Animating a complete character on ones or twos; the highest quality of *cel animation.* See *limited animation.*

function curve—Long form of *fcurve.* A spline used to animate a function.

gag—A visual joke or humorous situation.

geometry—In LightWave, the collection of points, edges, and polygons that defines the shape of an object.

going ballistic—An uncontrolled emotional outburst. In animation, when a character leaves the ground in a ballistic trajectory or parabola.

good take—A live action shot or sound track recording good enough to be used.

graphics—See *computer graphics.*

hardware—Computer equipment that you can see and touch, in contrast to software, which is intangible.

heading—See *azimuth.*

heel strike position—A character's pose in a walk cycle where the leading heel first contacts the ground. One of three key poses for a standard walk cycle. See also *squash position, passing position, motion cycle.*

held cel, hold cel—In cel animation, an image duplicated for a number of frames.

Hi-8—A consumer video format developed by Sony and popular for camcorders; provides higher image quality than 8mm or VHS.

hidden line removal—An algorithm that removes lines not visible to the camera from a wireframe rendering, producing a cleaner image.

hinge—The simplest rotational joint, having only one degree of freedom.

hit—A musical beat or sound effect used to synchronize the action.

hold—A pose or shot repeated over a number of frames.

hold, moving—A pose held by a character for a number of frames, animated to vary slightly to keep the character visually alive.

hookup—Matching the beginning and ending poses in a motion cycle so the cycle can be looped. See also *loop, motion cycle.*

hot spot—Specular highlight on an object's surface where a light source reflects directly into the camera's lens.

in-betweener—In traditional 2D animation, the junior or assistant animator who draws the *in-betweens.*

in-betweens—Frames between key or breakdown poses that show the smallest incremental changes.

index of refraction—A number representing how much a material bends or refracts the light passing through it.

inertia—The tendency of objects to keep doing what they've been doing.

ink and paint—The transferring of original drawings to ink on acetate sheets, and filling the outlined areas with the correct colors.

inking—The first step in *ink and paint.*

input—Communicating information to a computer.

input devices—Peripherals designed to make it easier to communicate information to a computer. Common examples include the mouse, keyboard, *pen and tablet*, scanner, and *digitizer.*

insert shot—A shot filmed or rendered separately from the master shot—usually a close-up for exposition or from a character's POV—and edited into the main shot.

inter-cut—Shots edited together in a sequence.

inverse kinematics—Usually abbreviated IK. A class of algorithms for determining the posing of a hierarchical chain by the positioning of the end links. Drag a finger, the arm follows along.

iris—The colored portion of the eye surrounding the pupil.

iris out—In cinematography, a transition in which a circular *matte* shrinks until the entire frame is obscured. Iris in is the reverse.

item—In LightWave, an object, bone, light, or camera.

joystick—An input device usually relegated to games, but occasionally useful in CGI.

key animator—A.k.a. lead animator. The senior animator trusted with creating the *key poses.*

key drawings—In cel animation, drawings of the *key poses.*

key light—The primary light in a scene, providing most of the illumination. See also *fill light, rim light.*

key pose—One of the extreme positions of a character that defines an action.

key sounds—Points in the sound track used to match the animation—for example, footsteps.

keyframe animation—Setting key poses and interpolating between the keys to create animation. Contrast with *procedural animation.*

lateral—A sideways camera move.

Leica reel—See *story reel.*

level—Status in an animated character's hierarchy; determines when in the animation process a part is posed. Generally, the root of the hierarchy is posed first, and the extremities last.

limited animation—Animating on fours or more, or holding the majority of an image while animating a small part of it. A lot of television animation is limited.

line of action—In reference to posing characters, an imaginary line drawn through the character's center and any limbs protruding beyond the body's silhouette. Ideally, there should only be one line possible for a key pose, and the line should have a pronounced curve that directs the audience's eye to follow the action. In cinematography, the main line (or slalom) of the action. The camera should stay on one side of the line of action during a sequence to avoid confusing the audience.

line test—See *pencil test.*

lip sync—Coordinating a character's facial animation to a sound track to create the illusion that the character is speaking.

live action—Footage shot in the real world (OK, maybe sometimes in Hollywood, too).

local coordinates—In LightWave, x,y,z values for some purposes are calculated from the pivot of an object rather than the origin of the entire virtual world.

lockdown—In puppet animation, a fastener inserted into a puppet's foot to keep it in place on the set. In cinematography, securing the camera so it does not move during a shot. In LightWave, setting several identical values with linear interpolation in adjacent frames of a motion graph to prevent any undesired movement.

long shot—A shot in which the entire figure, as well as a good deal of the background, is visible.

loop—Repeat a motion cycle within a shot. See also *hookup, motion cycle*.

LS—In cinematography, long shot.

luma key—Similar to *chroma key*, but composites images based on luminance or brightness rather than color.

master shot—A shot that establishes the entire environment of a sequence, laying out a visual map for the audience. A camera setup wide enough to encompass an entire scene, designed to be intercut with closer shots.

match—See *move matching, dissolve*.

match dissolve—A dissolve from one image to a similar image, to show the passage of time or other gradual change or to smooth the transition.

match-lines—Rows or columns of pixels within an image that have similar patterns on both sides and are used for creating seamless tileable maps.

matte—A mask used to block part of an image for compositing.

MCU—In cinematography, medium close-up.

metamorphosis—See *morph*.

mittens—The tendency to pose all of a character's fingers side by side in an undifferentiated lump. Closely related to *twins*.

mocap—Abbreviation of *motion capture*.

model interpolation—Technically correct but generally unused name for *morph*.

model sheet—In cel animation, a collection of drawings showing the character in a variety of poses. In CGI animation, screenshots or test renders of the character from several angles and in a variety of poses, with notes from the technical director on animation controls, constraints, and limits for the character.

modeling—In LightWave, creating objects by manipulating points, edges, and faces.

modulus of elasticity—A number representing the ability of a material to return to its original shape after being deformed.

moonwalk—see *foot slippage*.

morph—A process that changes one model for another gradually by interpolating the position of each vertex or control point in the original model to match those of the target model.

morph map—In LightWave, a set of shape deformation changes, or *deltas*, that are stored within the object as an EndoMorph. See also *shape weighting*.

motion blur—Motion occurring while the camera shutter is open produces a blurred image; LightWave can reproduce this effect by rendering and compositing images of a moving object's position between frames.

motion capture—A.k.a. *mocap*. Recording of motion information from a live subject with the intent of applying it to a CGI character. See also *Satan's Rotoscope*.

motion channel—In LightWave, the subset of animation channels that controls position, rotation, and scaling, but not other parameters, such as light intensity.

motion cycle—An action that you can repeat by connecting duplicates end to end; for example, walking, running, hammering a nail, or any other repetitive action. See also *loop, hookup*.

motion study—Detailed, sustained analysis of the movement of a subject; motion study is necessary to realistic or caricature animation.

mouse—Input device, common but not well suited to character animation. See also *pen and tablet*.

mouth action—See *phoneme*.

move matching—Matching the LightWave camera movements and settings to live action footage in order to render LightWave elements that will merge seamlessly with the live action.

moving hold—A pose that a character must maintain for at least several frames, with slight changes to avoid losing the illusion of life.

MPEG—A lossy compression format popular for direct computer playback of animation and live action.

MS—In cinematography, medium shot.

natural path—See *slalom*.

noodle—Tweaking settings back and forth and repeatedly creating previews long past the point of diminishing returns.

normal—An imaginary line perpendicular to the surface of a polygon. Surface normals are used in many animation and rendering calculations.

NTSC—National Television Standards Committee. The standard for television signals used in the United States.

null object—An object that has no points, edges, or polygons and that will be invisible in the final rendering. Nulls in LightWave are displayed as three short intersecting lines corresponding to the x-,y-,z-axes and are used as placeholders and hierarchical items.

NURBS—Non-Uniform Rational B-Splines.

object—A collection of points, edges, and polygons that defines one or more shapes.

object animation—Traditional stop-motion animation of objects instead of puppets or clay.

omniscient observer—In cinematography, a camera directed as if it were an invisible, all-seeing actor in a scene.

on-axis cut—Abrupt change in camera setup on the long axis of the lens, either closer to or farther from the subject.

ones, twos, or fours—The number of frames exposed for a single composition. The fewer the frames, the smoother and more expensive the animation.

one-shot—One subject fills the frame; a.k.a. single.

optical printer—A machine that produced a film print by combining two or more prints; used for transitions and other compositing effects.

opticals—Effects produced by an optical printer.

origin—The center of the coordinate system, where x, y, and z all equal 0.

orthogonal—A projection system that represents only two dimensions, removing all effects of perspective and parallax. Construction blueprints and LightWave's Front, Side, and Top views are examples of orthogonal projections.

OTS—In cinematography, Over The Shoulder.

out of sync—Sound track running behind or ahead of the animation.

out take—A shot that is not included in the final print of the film.

overlapping action—Animating a passive part of a character to show flexibility, mass, and inertia effects that result from the character's main action. Contrast with *secondary action*.

PAL—A standard for television signals used in Europe.

palette—The range of colors available to a display device. A 24-bit palette can reproduce as many shades of color as the average person can see.

pan—Abbreviation of panorama. Horizontal camera rotation around a fixed point; a y-axis rotation.

pan, truck—A pan executed by moving the camera sideways rather than rotating it.

pan, zip—A caricatured camera motion representing a fast stop, as if the entire camera is vibrating rapidly.

parabola—A mathematical curve describing the path of a projectile in a gravity field.

parenting—In LightWave, arranging items into a hierarchy.

passing position—One of the three main poses for a walk or run, in which the trailing leg is rotated past the supporting leg. See also *walk cycle*.

PAVLOV—Parameterized Animatable Values Linking Objects and Variables. A collection of all animatable parameters for a LightWave scene.

pen and tablet—A more artist-friendly substitute for the standard computer mouse; simulates the behavior of a pen on paper; a.k.a. *stylus*.

pencil test—A preliminary rendering of an animation used to test an action, often created without color, maps, or background objects. Originally sketched with pencil, shot on film, and viewed as a negative image. See also *preview*.

pencil test reel—See *story reel*.

performance capture—See *motion capture*.

peripherals—Additional equipment for a computer—for example, external hard drives, *pen and tablet*, *film recorder*, or *digitizer*.

persistence of vision—See *flicker fusion*.

personality—The collateral effect of animated actions, creating the illusion that a character has unique motivations, volition, and thought processes.

phoneme—A.k.a. mouth action or phonic shape. The shape of the mouth when pronouncing a particular sound.

pin registration—Securing the film precisely in an animation camera or *film recorder* with a set of pins to ensure that each frame is registered exactly like all the others.

pitch—In LightWave, the left-to-right rotational axis. A character's head nods on the pitch axis. Also, the presentation of a storyboard, related to a salesperson's presentation.

pixel—Contraction of picture element. The smallest individual dot visible on a computer monitor. Rows and columns of pixels together make an image.

pixilation—Stop-motion animation created by posing living actors frame by frame.

plan—A top or overhead view of a set design.

plane—A surface with points in only two dimensions.

plug-in—An additional program that works within the core program to add features.

point—One set of x-,y-,z-coordinates that defines the end or intersection of an edge; a.k.a. vertex.

point of view—See *POV*.

polygon—A surface defined by three or more edges and three or more points; a.k.a. face, surface.

pose—In LightWave, the total of all bone and object translations, deformations, and transforms for a character in a particular keyframe.

pose-to-pose—Animating by setting all the key poses first, then going back over the animation and tweaking the *in-betweens*.

POV—Abbreviation of point of view. A camera directed to show the scene as it would appear to one of the characters.

premise—A very brief summary of the point of a story, generally a sentence or two at the most; for example, "easy come, easy go."

preview—A rapidly rendered part of an animation; created as a test.

procedural animation—Movement or other animation that is controlled by an algorithm; for example, Dynamic Realities' Impact plug-in. Contrast with *keyframe animation*.

propeller head—A term applied to CGI artists who come from a more technical, especially computer science, background. Can be comradely or pejorative, depending on usage.

pull-back—See *zoom*.

puppet animation—Stop-motion animation techniques using jointed or flexible puppets.

puppet—A jointed or flexible figure designed either to be animated or to be manipulated by a puppeteer in a realtime performance.

push-in—See *zoom*.

rack focus—Directing the audience's attention by animating the depth of field to change the area of sharp focus.

RAM—Random Access Memory, the type of memory used to hold program information for fast access. Equivalent to having information on your desk rather than filed in a drawer. CGI requires a lot of RAM.

range of movement—The limits to which a character can be posed before it distorts unacceptably. Part of the information that the TD should write on the character's model sheet.

raster—Data generated or displayed one row of points at a time, adding rows to create a matrix or image. In CGI, the data is usually an image or scanner dataset.

raytracing—A class of CGI rendering algorithms that calculate the value of each pixel by mathematically tracing the path of a ray from the pixel through all the reflections and refractions it would encounter in a scene.

realtime—"Live," or in a 1:1 temporal ratio, in contrast to animation or computer time.

rear projection—Projecting images or sequences on a screen behind the actors in a scene to composite the image and live action in the camera.

render—Calculating the color of each pixel and assembling the pixels into an image.

repeat—See *loop*.

replacement—A class of animation techniques in which objects or parts of objects are sequentially replaced to create the illusion of changing shape or pose. Contrast with *displacement*.

resolution—The number of pixels in an image, usually expressed as the width by the height—for example, 640x480.

rev. (revision)—In software, a new or improved edition of a program, presumably superior to, or at least not as flawed as, the preceding revision.

reveal—Moving the camera to gradually expose more of a scene.

reverse angle—Cutting from one camera angle to another nearly 180 degrees from the first.

rim light—A light used to highlight the edges or rim of the subject.

room tone—The ambient or background sound and acoustic nature of a space where recording is done. Room tone is recorded for dubbing into blank spaces in the track because completely blank spots in the sound track would be noticed by the audience.

Rotoscope—A technique originally patented by the Fleischer studio, in which live action footage was traced over to create cel animation. See also *Satan's Rotoscope*.

rough cut—The first complete edit of the film. Still needs to be fine tuned.

RSI, RMI, CPS—Repetitive Stress Injury, Repetitive Motion Injury, Carpal Tunnel Syndrome. Occupational hazards of animation workers; can permanently disable the victim's hands. Prevention is the best cure.

rubber hose construction—A style of character design in which the limb has no fixed joint; it simply bends in an arc to connect the torso to the hand or foot.

run cycle—action of a running character that has hookup frames suitable for looping.

Satan's Rotoscope—A.k.a. motion capture. Term coined by Ken Cope, Jeff Hayes, and Steph Greenberg.

scene—In LightWave, a file containing all the settings from Layout necessary to create a series of images. In cinematography, a collection of shots in the same set and in a close temporal series.

sclera—The visible white portion of the human eyeball, surrounding the iris.

script—The written plan for a film, including dialogue and some stage direction. The precursor to the storyboard.

scrub—Dragging a temporal control (such as a Frame Position slider) back and forth to check the timing of an action or the sync of a sound track.

secondary action—A motivated, volitional action by a character that is of less importance than that character's main action. Blinking, breathing, and other moving hold actions are secondary to the pose and timing of a dramatic gesture or an emotional transition main action. Contrast with *overlapping action*.

sentence measurement—Transcribing the timing of each take in a vocal recording session, to be used in selecting takes for track analysis.

sequence—A number of shots, in order, that tell part of the story.

set—The place where a scene is shot.

setup—In cinematography, the positions of actors and camera. In CGI, the links, constraints, and expressions created to make animation of a character easier.

shape weighting—Blending or weighting two or more sets of deformation changes into a base object to create a new shape. In LightWave, shapes are called *morph maps* and shape weighting is performed in the EndoMorph Mixer.

short—Film with running time between 2 and 20 minutes. Classic cartoon shorts usually ran between 6 and 7 minutes.

shot—The basic unit of film. A continuously exposed unedited piece of film. In CGI, an uncut sequence of frames.

shot on twos—In traditional animation, exposing two frames of film for each change in the animation, so a 24fps projection speed will only show 12 new images per second.

shot volume—The space contained in the pyramid formed by the lens (the apex) and the four corners of the frame. The apparent volume of the shot ends at the central object or character.

Showscan—A projection system combining 65fps frame rate and a wide-screen format to enhance perceived realism.

sibilant—A class of phonemes including the consonants "S" and "Z."

SIGGRAPH—The Association for Computing Machinery's Special Interest Group on Computer Graphics.

sight lines—An actor or character's line of vision, from the center of the eyeball through the pupil to the point being observed.

silent speed—16fps, the minimum required to prevent *strobing*.

silhouette—The filled outline of a character in strong contrast to the rest of the scene, usually black and white. Useful for evaluating poses. In LightWave, created by rendering an alpha channel image.

skate—See *foot slippage*.

skeleton—The arrangement and hierarchy of bones in a LightWave character setup that enables the animator to pose it. See also *armature*.

slalom—The path followed by any system, natural or machine, that can correct its movement toward a goal.

slip—Moving the sound track forward or back in relation to key sounds, deliberately modifying the sync so the action reads better.

slow-in, slow-out—See *ease-in, ease-out*.

snap—Rapid, energetic changes within an action; the opposite of ease.

sneak—A caricatured action of attempting to move quietly on tiptoe.

software—The set of instructions, or programs, used to control a computer.

sound effects—See *foley*.

sound speed—24fps.

sound track—The dialogue, music, and sound effects from a film.

special effects animation—Smoke, water, or other noncharacter visual effects, generally animated in LightWave by a specially designed plug-in.

speed lines—In traditional animation, drybrush lines drawn to show the path of a quickly moving object or character. Superseded in LightWave by *motion blur*.

spline—A method of efficiently defining a curved line by specifying the coordinates of one or more control points and the tension, continuity, bias, or other parameters of the portion of the curve affected by the control point. TCB, Bezier, and Hermite are three of the spline types supported by LightWave.

spline cage—An object defined by splines rather than polygons.

spline patching—Transforming a spline cage into a polygonal object.

sprocket hole—An evenly space series of holes matching the sprocket that pulls film through a camera or projector.

squash and stretch—Exaggerated distortion of an animated object; intended to emphasize compression (squash) in deceleration or collision and elongation (stretch) in acceleration.

squash pose—In a take, the key pose in which a character or the character's face is most compressed in recoil.

squash position—In a walk cycle, the key pose in which the body is at its lowest and the supporting leg is bent to absorb the impact of the *heel strike position*.

stagger—A caricatured rapid oscillation of a character, especially after the character strikes or is struck.

staging—Animating a character to foreshadow the main action, making it easier for the audience to read.

static balance—Balance achieved with no ongoing adjustments or changes in mass, inertia, or energy. See also *dynamic balance*.

still shot—A.k.a. lockdown; a shot in which the camera does not move.

stop motion—Action created by stopping the camera, making changes to the scene or camera settings, and starting the camera again. Originally used to create dissolves and other optical effects in addition to animation; now generally used to describe clay or puppet animation. See also *pixilation*.

story reel—An animation composed of story sketches synchronized to the sound track. Usually, each sketch is replaced with finished sequences as production proceeds.

storyboard—A sequence of story sketches depicting the major actions and layout for each shot. Often pinned to a large board or wall for group review and critique. See Chapter 3 for an example.

straight ahead action—In 2D animation, drawing each pose as you come to it, working out timing and posing on the fly. Contrast with *pose-to-pose*.

stretch—Deforming all or part of a character to show acceleration. Contrast with *squash*.

stretch pose—In a take, the key pose immediately following the squash, in which the character's recovery from the squash is exaggerated beyond the original pose.

stride length—The distance a character travels with each step.

strobing—Changes between frames that are too extreme, catch the audience's attention, and destroy the illusion of smooth movement.

stroboscopic photography—Capturing a series of images on a single film frame by leaving the shutter open and firing a sequence of flashes or strobes; often used to capture a complex or rapid motion.

studio animation—Animation produced by specialists within a larger organization, so the product is more of a team effort than an individual creative achievement.

stylus—See *pen and tablet*.

subdivision—An algorithmic process for creating a smoothly rounded surface by progressively breaking large polygons into smaller ones.

SubPatch—In LightWave, a modeling mode in which the points of a polygonal model are converted to a control node for a NURBS object.

successive breaking of joints—When a higher joint starts to rotate, there should be a slight lag before the lower joints start to rotate as part of the same action. This means that the rotation of a child object should begin, peak, and end some time after the Parent performs the same actions.

surface—A set of parameters or *attributes* that define the rendered appearance of a polygon. LightWave objects can have many surfaces.

sweatbox—In an animation studio, projection room used to review and critique animation. Term originated at Disney studios due to lack of air conditioning and was retained and used elsewhere due to the animator's stress levels during critiques.

sync—Short for synchronization, the matching of sound to action on film or videotape.

synchronization—See *sync*.

synopsis—A brief summary of a script.

tablet—See *pen and tablet*.

take—A character's recoil of fear or surprise. See also *stretch pose, squash pose*.

telephoto lens—A camera lens assembly constructed so its focal length is significantly longer than its physical length.

television animation—Animation designed for the limitations of the television cutoff and safe-titling areas and (sometimes) for the higher frame rate.

television cutoff—The outside border of the television image that is visible on studio monitors but is not displayed by many home televisions.

television safe-titling—The area within the television image that is safe for titles and other written communication.

test—See *pencil test*.

texture—A set of maps or procedural shaders that modify the base attributes of a surface to affect the rendered appearance of an object.

three-shot—Three subjects fill the frame.

thumbnail—A smaller version of an image, used for convenience or, in CGI, to save memory.

tie-down—In traditional 3D animation, usually a threaded rod with a keyed head that locks into the bottom of a character's foot. The animator passes the rod through a hole in the stage and tightens it down with a wing nut, securing the puppet in place.

tilt—Vertical equivalent of pan. See *pan*.

time encoding—Adding time code to a videotape to enable accurate measurement and reference down to the frame and field. Generally using the SMPTE standard HH:MM:SS:FF.

time sheet—See *exposure sheet*.

track analysis—The transcription of a vocal track to a series of phonemes in an exposure sheet. A.k.a. track breakdown.

track breakdown—See *track analysis*.

track reader—The specialist who performs *track analysis*.

transfer—In cinematography, a moving object carries the audience's attention across the frame. A.k.a. hand-off. In editing, duplicating images or sound from one media format to another.

transform—In CGI, a change in shape, size, or attributes. Contrast with *translate*.

transition—In drama, a visible change from one dominant emotional state to another. In editing or cinematography, the effect or cut used between shots.

translate—In CGI, to change position. In general computer usage, changing data to a different file format, as when importing an LWO or DXF file and saving it in another model format.

transport— In a VTR, the mechanism used to move the tape past the recording and playback heads. A very accurate and expensive transport can reliably position the tape to within one frame, enabling single-frame recording for animation.

transportation animation—Walking or other means of moving the character around within the shot.

traveling shot—A camera move that follows a character or other action.

treatment—A short form of a script, used by some studios when considering a production.

trucking, truck pan—See *dolly*.

tweak—To make fine adjustments or changes to settings. See also *noodle*.

tween—Abbreviation of *in-between*. In LightWave, the calculation of interpolated parameter values between keyframes.

twins—Posing a character to appear symmetric in the frame. To be avoided because it makes the character look stiff and lifeless.

two-shot—Two subjects fill the frame; a.k.a. double.

twos—See shot on twos.

U-matic—An industrial videotape format, rarely used in consumer or entertainment venues.

union shop—A studio or production house that has signed an agreement with a union to hire only members of that union. Non-union workers can (sometimes) still get a job there, but they may have to join the union to keep it.

universal joint—Rotational joint having two degrees of freedom.

user friendly—A matter of opinion regarding the utility of computer software, because people have different cognitive and working styles. Hostile for some is friendly for others.

vector graphics—Images drawn on a screen by lines connecting points. Good for outlines and wireframes; not good for color images of solid objects.

vertex—In LightWave, a point.

V maps—Vertex maps. In LightWave, optional information that is stored in the object file and is associated with the object's vertices, such as morph maps (EndoMorphs) and UV maps.

VGA-to-NTSC converter—An adapter that converts the VGA output of a computer to the NTSC standard video signal used by most video equipment. Inexpensive ones have inferior video signals; you should test them before buying or renting.

VHS—A consumer-grade videotape format that uses half-inch tape in a cassette and has a maximum resolution of approximately 400 lines.

visual jar—A sudden change in shot volume or camera orientation; momentarily disorients the audience.

voice track—The part of the sound track that contains dialogue.

voice-over—An off-screen voice that is dubbed over footage and does not need to be lip synced. A fast and cheap way to make changes after animation is completed.

VTR—A Video Tape Recorder of any format. Frame-accurate VTRs can be used to record animations as they are rendered, one frame at a time, under computer control.

walk cycle—A walk action that has hookup frames suitable for looping.

WAV—A file format for digitized sound, commonly used with the Microsoft Windows operating systems.

weights—The proportions for a set of morph maps required to create a particular shape from the base object. For example, a negative weight for a raised smile morph map can make the base object frown. See also shape weighting and EndoMorph.

wide angle lens—A lens having a focal length shorter than the diagonal measure of the image at the focal plane.

wide-screen—A film format designed for a higher aspect ratio, producing panoramic images.

wild wall—In a set, a wall or other object that can be deleted or moved when not in camera range to make room for lighting or camera movement.

wipe—A special effect shot transition where the first shot is gradually replaced by the second shot with a relatively sharp dividing line. A wipe can go from any direction but typically moves top to bottom or left to right. See *dissolve*.

wipe the frame—Passing a foreground object in front of the camera at the moment of a cut, usually used to smooth a transition.

wireframe—An abbreviated representation of an object, showing just the edges defining the object's polygons. Computers can draw wireframes very fast, so they are widely used for previews and tests.

workstation—Marketing term for a more powerful personal computer system.

world coordinates—A coordinate system of measuring translation from a single origin for all items.

WS—In cinematography, wide shot.

x-sheet—See *exposure sheet*.

x,y,z—Coordinate axes of three-dimensional space; in LightWave, the y-axis is up and down, the z-axis is front to back, and the x-axis is side to side.

zip pan—See *pan, zip*.

zoom—Using a lens capable of various focal lengths in order to change a shot.

Index

If you like this book, you'll love these...

LOOKING GOOD ON THE WEB

Daniel Gray
ISBN: 1-57610-508-3
224 pages • $29.99 U.S. • $43.99 CANADA

Speaking from the user's perspective, this book provides a comprehensive, non-technical introduction to Web design. You'll learn how to design and create friendly, easily navigable, award-winning Web sites that please clients and visitors alike.

CANOMA™ VISUAL INSIGHT

Richard Schrand
ISBN: 1-57610-626-8
256 pages • $24.99 U.S. • $37.99 CANADA

Takes you on a guided tour of this powerful program, showing you the key features that will make your 2D work stand out in 3D. After you learn Canoma basics and tricks of the trade, you'll apply your skills to real-world projects like creating an interactive city complete with storefronts, houses, and people.

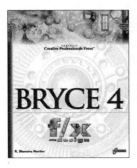

BRYCE® 4 F/X AND DESIGN

R. Shamms Mortier
ISBN: 1-57610-482-6
340 pages with CD-ROM • $49.99 U.S. • $73.99 CANADA

Bryce® is the software for developing photo-realistic environments, and *Bryce 4 f/x and Design* shows you the program's tricks. Learn from the masters as a dozen computer graphics and animation professionals share their secrets for creating spectacular effects and stunning scenes in Bryce.

3D STUDIO MAX® R3 IN DEPTH

Rob Polevoi
ISBN: 1-57610-432-X
700 pages with CD-ROM • $49.99 U.S. • $73.99 CANADA

Build your special effect skills while becoming familiar with the many features of 3D Studio MAX®. By following along with the book's visual examples, you will receive quick answers to common MAX questions in an easy-to-use and easy-to-understand manner.

What's on the CD-ROM

The *Character Animation with LightWave [6]* companion CD-ROM contains an HTML version (INDEX.HTM) of this text that you can open with any Web browser. Because this book's digital files are distributed among many folders, you must be aware of which files are in which folder. Most files are located in the folder for the chapter in which they are first needed. If you can't find a file for a particular project, search the other folders. If you have any questions or problems, or if you want to chat, email me at **dakelly@earthlink.net**.

- *Alter directory*—contains demo versions of Joe Alter's LipService and Shave And A Haircut plug-ins for LightWave, plus documentation.

- *bbMPEG directory*—contains a zip archive of the software and documentation to convert AVI animations to MPEG-1 and MPEG-2 format for inexpensive video recording from your computer. A brief overview and links and a FAQ are included in HTML format.

- *Ch02, 03, and 04 directories*—contain files for "Easy Come, Easy Go". Ch02 contains the script plus links to screenwriting resources and tools. Ch03 contains blank and completed storyboard panels and story sketches assembled into AVI and QuickTime format story reels. Ch04 contains audio files, including the complete sound track, sound effects, and excerpts from a speech by Sir Winston Churchill, plus blank and filled-in exposure sheets for lip sync projects and the shareware programs ToonTimer (for timing animation) and GoldWave (for processing sound files).

- *Ch05 directory*—contains two 360-degree views of the Fred maquette under construction, one of the skull and one of the fleshed-out maquette, in AVI format.

- *Ch06 directory*—contains a set of digitized and registered photographs of the Fred maquette used in the photogrammetry projects, plus a half-model that was created with this technique.

- *Ch07 directory*—contains the assembled Cyberscans of the Fred maquette at high, medium, and low resolution, in native PLY format and translated to LightWave LWO format. Four subdirectories, a, b, c and d, contain raw scan data. The PLY viewer located in the Cyberware directory displays these files.

- *Ch08 directory*—contains a single example animation, 08_05.avi.

- *Ch09 directory*—contains digitized images of a variety of fabrics, several views of the author's eyeball, and a Cyberscan color map of the author's head, used to create texture maps.

- *Ch11, 12, 14, and 15 directories*—contains the objects, images, and scenes required to complete the chapters' projects and rendered animations of those projects' results.

- *Ch16 directory*—contains a library of lip sync face maps and audio clips for lip sync projects.

- *Ch17 directory*—contains objects, images, scenes, and executable programs for use in the chapter's projects.

- *Ch18 directory*—contains object, image, motion and scene files used in the compositing projects in Chapter 18.

- *Ch19 directory*—contains the IFF images and LightWave objects used in the main title sequence project, plus test patterns and sound calibration signals.

- *ChessN and ChessP directories*—contain the chessboard motion control footage. The ChessN directory contains footage shot with a motion-controlled camera rig. The ChessP directory contains matching footage for the ChessN sequence with the chess pieces on the board.

- *Cyberware directory*—contains contact information, sample male and female full-body scan models, and a free object viewer from Cyberware.

- *Magpie directory*—contains demo versions of Miguel Grinberg's Magpie Pro lip sync software, with additional information in HTML format and a basic tutorial in PDF format.

- *Motions directory*—contains the motion control camera data files, in ASCII and LightWave MOT formats, in original and metric conversions. It also contains the TrackerNull.mot file used in the match-move project in Chapter 18.

- *Stable directory*—contains 265 frames of four-point stabilized footage for use in the match-move project in Chapter 18.